SOURCE OF WISDOM:
OLD ENGLISH AND EARLY MEDIEVAL LATIN STUDIES
IN HONOUR OF THOMAS D. HILL

Thomas D. Hill
The Fons

EDITED BY CHARLES D. WRIGHT,
FREDERICK M. BIGGS,
AND THOMAS N. HALL

Source of Wisdom:
Old English and Early
Medieval Latin Studies in
Honour of Thomas D. Hill

UNIVERSITY OF TORONTO PRESS
Toronto Buffalo London

© University of Toronto Press Incorporated 2007
Toronto Buffalo London
Printed in Canada

ISBN 978-0-8020-9367-7

Printed on acid-free paper

Library and Archives Canada Cataloguing in Publication

Source of wisdom : Old English and early medieval Latin studies in honour of Thomas D. Hill / edited by Charles D. Wright, Frederick M. Biggs, and Thomas N. Hall.

(Toronto Old English series)
Includes bibliographical references and index.
ISBN 978-0-8020-9367-7

1. English literature – Old English, ca. 450–1100 – History and criticism.   2. Latin literature, Medieval and modern – England – History and criticism.   I. Hill, Thomas D., 1940–   II. Wright, Charles D. III. Biggs, Frederick M.   IV. Hall, Thomas N.   V. Series.

PR260.S65 2007   829.09   C2007-904835-8

Frontispiece photo of Thomas Hill courtesy Cornell University Photography

University of Toronto Press gratefully acknowledges the financial assistance of the Centre for Medieval Studies, University of Toronto, in the publication of this book.

University of Toronto Press acknowledges the financial assistance to its publishing program of the Canada Council for the Arts and the Ontario Arts Council.

University of Toronto Press acknowledges the financial support for its publishing activities of the Government of Canada through the Book Publishing Industry Development Program (BPIDP).

Contents

Preface ix
Abbreviations xxi
Note on Quotations xxiv

Part I: *Beowulf*

Beasts of Battle, South and North   3
JOSEPH HARRIS

The Fates of Men in *Beowulf*   26
JAMES H. MOREY

Folio 179 of the *Beowulf* Manuscript   52
FREDERICK M. BIGGS

Part II: Old English Religious and Sapiential Poetry

Trinitarian Language: Augustine, *The Dream of the Rood*, and Ælfric   63
JAMES W. EARL

The Leaps of Christ and *The Dream of the Rood*   80
JAMES W. MARCHAND

'Ðu eart se weallstan': Architectural Metaphor and Christological Imagery in the Old English *Christ I* and the Book of Kells   90
JOHANNA KRAMER

Remembering in Circles: *The Wife's Lament*, *Conversatio*, and the Community of Memory   113
SACHI SHIMOMURA

A Word to the Wise: Thinking, Knowledge, and Wisdom in
The Wanderer 130
ALICE SHEPPARD

Part III: Old English Prose

Alfred's Nero 147
PAUL E. SZARMACH

The 'Remigian' Glosses on Boethius's *Consolatio Philosophiae* in Context 168
JOSEPH WITTIG

Why Ditch the *Dialogues*? Reclaiming an Invisible Text 201
DAVID F. JOHNSON

Hagiography and Violence: Military Men in Ælfric's *Lives of Saints* 217
E. GORDON WHATLEY

A New Latin Source for Two Old English Homilies (Fadda I and Blickling I): Pseudo-Augustine, *Sermo* App. 125, and the Ideology of Chastity in the Anglo-Saxon Benedictine Reform 239
CHARLES D. WRIGHT

Christ's Birth through Mary's Right Breast: An Echo of Carolingian Heresy in the Old English *Adrian and Ritheus* 266
THOMAS N. HALL

Part IV: Old English beyond the Conquest

The Peterborough Chronicle and the Invention of 'Holding Court' in Twelfth-Century England 293
ANDREW GALLOWAY

Echoes of Old English Alliterative Collocations in Middle English Alliterative Proverbs 311
SUSAN E. DESKIS

Part V: Early Medieval Latin

Bede's Style: A Neglected Historiographical Model for the Style of the *Historia Ecclesiastica*? 329
DANUTA SHANZER

Crux-busting on the Danube: *uel Coniectanea in* Cosmographiam Aethici, *ut dicitur*, Istri   353
MICHAEL W. HERREN

The *Revelationes* of Pseudo-Methodius and Scriptural Study at Salisbury in the Eleventh Century   370
MICHAEL W. TWOMEY

Appendix 1. Publications of Thomas D. Hill   387

Appendix 2. Dissertations Directed by Thomas D. Hill   399

Contributors   401

Index   403

Preface

Source of Wisdom: Thomas D. Hill has been one for all of us, as a scholar, as a teacher and mentor, and as a friend and colleague. Our title, however, is a bibliographical descriptor as well as an honorific. Tom's OE scholarship has always been about sources, especially the Christian-Latin sources of OE religious poetry and prose, and much of it has focused on what Tom, in his 1967 Cornell dissertation, termed the 'Sapiential Tradition.'[1] A student of R.E. Kaske's (first at the University of Illinois at Urbana-Champaign, then at Cornell), Tom was trained in the methods of primary-source research in medieval literary scholarship by the man who was to write the book on the subject, or at least one major aspect of it.[2] Back in the day when locating a given idea or motif and tracing its development in the ocean of *printed* patristic and medieval Christian-Latin literature was both a fine art and honest work, no one was more adept than Tom. If it was in the *Patrologia*, he could find it. And no one was more thrilled by the advent of searchable electronic databases, or quicker to exploit them. Since Tom acquired a personal copy of the *CETEDOC Library of Christian-Latin Texts*, no crux of the sacral variety in OE poetry or *Piers Plowman* has had a safe place to hide. He gave us fair warning and a chance to compete with his 1992 essay 'CETEDOC and the Transformation of Anglo-Saxon Studies' (no. 122; references are to the bibliography of Tom's publications in appendix 1 at the end of this volume), but it takes more than databases, user's manuals, and a head full of cruces that need busting. Tom solves cruces that nobody even realized *were* cruces, and that is where the art lies now.

Tom is the undisputed master of the scholarly note in Old and Middle English studies. In the late 1960s and 1970s he practically owned *Notes and Queries*, publishing more than twenty concise explications in that journal (and as many again in other outlets) of motifs ranging from 'Punishment According to the Joints of the Body in the Old English "Soul and Body II"' (no. 7, and 'Again' in no. 15) to 'The Hypocritical Bee in the Old English "Homiletic Fragment I"' (no. 5). But it would give a false impression of the range and depth of Tom's work to characterize it merely as crux-busting and source-hunting. Even his notes usually consist of more than local explication of discrete passages. Typically they conclude by drawing out the literary implications of a source-discovery in ways that illuminate the structure, imagery, or ethos of an entire poem. A case in point is the modestly titled 'Notes on the Imagery and Structure of the Old English "Christ I"' (no. 29). After explicating and suggesting possible sources for several individual passages, Tom takes up the broader question of the poem's diffuse structure and allusive imagery, proposing brilliantly that it reflects the medieval technique of *ruminatio*, best known to Anglo-Saxonists through Bede's story of Cædmon. Tom was even able to cite a passage from a liturgical commentary by Amalarius of Metz declaring that the 'Great O' antiphons (the major source for the poem, cf. no. 48) were particularly suited for meditative *ruminatio*. To characterize the poetic mode of *Christ I* as 'ruminative' has since become a critical commonplace, though few who invoke the term seem to be aware that Tom was the first to have done so.

Even if all the brief notes were removed from Tom's bibliography, what remained would suffice to make him one of the most prolific and influential scholars of OE poetry. Early in his career he sparked a revolution in OE literary studies with his 'figural' readings of *Andreas* (no. 13) and *Elene* (no. 25; cf. no. 65), both inspired by Erich Auerbach's seminal essay 'Figura.'[3] Typological interpretation was in the air at the time, in part due to the influence of D.W. Robertson, but a very different kind of 'exegetical' school had emerged at Cornell under Kaske, one that was fundamentally opposed to the reductive Robertsonian method of reading all medieval literature in terms of *caritas* and *cupiditas*, sharing only the conviction that medieval biblical interpretation (and Christian-Latin imagery generally) could be an important and valuable resource for understanding medieval literary works.[4] A more kindred spirit and true antecedent than Robertson was J.E. Cross, a frequent visitor to Cornell who became a close friend of Tom's, and who had paved the way with a number of articles on Christian-Latin sources of OE poems such as *Exodus* and *The Wanderer*.[5] Another was the great American Dantist John Freccero, whose learned essays on the *Divine Comedy* brought to bear a remarkable range of medieval Christian-Latin sources, and who

Preface xi

was also at Cornell when Tom was a graduate student there.[6] At about the same time, fellow Cornellians James W. Earl (whose dissertation was among the first that Tom directed) and Joseph Wittig were publishing influential figural readings of *Exodus* and *Juliana*.[7] If the heyday of the typological approach is now past, it is not because it was misguided or even because it was overtaken by new theoretical approaches, but rather because the most compelling cases to be made (at least for OE poetry) had mostly been made (and mostly by Tom) by about the mid-1980s.[8] Tom's early figural readings of *Andreas* and *Elene*, as well as his later typological explications of poems such as *Guthlac B* (nos 41, 70; see also nos 12, 38, 45, 67, and 68) have stood the test of time, and even critics of very different persuasions who prefer to stress other dimensions of these poems generally acknowledge the validity of the typological patterns that Tom first discerned.

Typology is only one dimension of the Christian-Latin tradition, of course, and Tom's work has focused on a wide variety of medieval literary imagery derived from the Bible and its interpretation (e.g., nos 3, 4, 5, 6, 8, 11, 18, 20, 24, 26, 29, 34, 37, 42, 47, 52, 53, 54, 55, 72, 74, 82, 92, 95, 124, 129, 147, 149, 157, 161, 162, 174). He has also drawn on his encyclopedic knowledge of patristic and medieval theology (nos 12, 22, 32, 119, 130), eschatology (nos 7, 14, 15, 23, 28, 64), demonology and angelology (nos 9, 17, 24, 30, 36, 38, 43, 47, 60, 85, 128), etymology and onomastics (nos 44, 63, 83, 87, 102, 152, 158, 166, 174), historiography (nos 69, 81, 97, 107, 142), hagiography (nos 96, 133, 134, 137), numerology (nos 16, 21, 41, 108), apocrypha (nos 10, 27, 93, 123), and liturgy and paraliturgical literature (nos 31, 39, 48, 71, 77, 84, 88, 111, 126, 128), often in order to clarify the literal significance of motifs and imagery in OE and other medieval religious poetry and prose. In addition to tracing the history of religious motifs, he has devoted considerable attention to legal (nos 113, 145, 156, 175), genealogical (nos 101, 108, 131), proverbial (nos 59, 100, 127, 135, 155, 159, 167, 168), and folkloristic (nos 46, 105, 114, 118, 149) analogues for medieval texts. Tom's familiarity with the remotest byways of medieval learning, as well as his abiding interest in riddles and dialogues as forms of sapiential literature (cf. nos 106, 153, 160, 173), is perhaps best displayed in the monumental commentary accompanying his edition with Jimmy Cross of the *Prose Solomon and Saturn* and *Adrian and Ritheus* dialogues (no. 76). Here we discover the curious history of such medieval notions as the eight pounds from which Adam was created, the name of Cham's wife, where the sun goes after it sets, and why stones do not bear fruit.

Another kind of collaboration with Jimmy Cross was the idea for a 'new Ogilvy,' a vision which they, together with Fred Biggs and Paul Szarmach, made into the federally funded reality *Sources of Anglo-Saxon Literary Culture* (SASLC), intended to survey the evidence for knowledge of individual authors and texts in Anglo-Saxon England.[9] Everyone involved in this massive collaborative project underestimated its scope and difficulty, but the *Trial Version* published in 1990 and the A-volume (part 1!) published in 2002 have vindicated the project's ambitions, even if its original deadlines are receding as fast as its directors' hairlines. Tom's introduction to these volumes (nos 115 and 151) is a masterful survey of the methodology of source-scholarship, placing SASLC on a secure footing both for authors of individual entries and for editors of subsequent volumes. For many years Tom also organized the sessions on literary sources of the annual SASLC Symposium at Kalamazoo.

If I had to single out one critical essay that best exemplifies the breadth of Tom's conception of source-studies, it would be 'Literary History and Old English Poetry: The Case of *Christ I, II*, and *III*' (no. 93). In this paper Tom shows how a careful analysis of sources can compensate in some measure for our lack of an absolute or even a firm relative chronology of OE poetry. Once believed to be the work of a single poet, Cynewulf, these three poems are still often read as a thematically unified codicological triptych. Tom shows how fundamentally unalike the three poems really are, not only in their choice of very different *kinds* of sources, but also in their methods of adapting them. *Christ I* handles its liturgical source very freely and allusively – or more specifically, ruminatively – presupposing an audience (presumably monastic) well versed in exegetical imagery drawn from standard patristic authorities. In *Christ II*, however, Cynewulf follows rather closely one major patristic source, Gregory's Ascension homily, explaining carefully the meaning of images such as the 'Leaps of Christ' (cf. no. 95) or the bird of Job, as if composing for a less learned audience for whom they might not be familiar (but who would be at home with the kind of traditional Germanic poetic imagery that the *Christ I* poet avoids). Finally, *Christ III* draws on a more nebulous and dubiously orthodox tradition of apocryphal eschatology (often most closely paralleled in Irish sources, cf. nos 14, 16, 23, 28) that emphasized literal and often lurid miracles and signs such as bleeding trees and the burning of the sea. By defining the stark differences among these three poems in terms of their choice and use of sources, the essay sketches 'the beginnings of a typology' (in the modern sense!) of OE poetry in default of a more conventional literary history based on a corpus of dated and localized texts.

Tom's contributions to OE literary scholarship have also included several major studies of heroic poetry, notably of *The Battle of Maldon* and *Beowulf*. An early paper on 'History and Heroic Ethic in *Maldon*' (no. 19) is still often cited as a sensitive and balanced view of Byrhtnoth's *ofermod* and the tension between heroic rhetoric and the exigencies of real combat (on this problem cf. also no. 155). More recently Tom has reexamined the poem from the perspective of the alternative account of the battle in the *Liber Eliensis* (no. 142), noting a striking parallel for the *Maldon* poet's term *ofermod* in the Latin account's characterization of Byrhtnoth's *nimia animositas*.

Beowulf has occupied Tom's attention throughout his career, both as a critic and as a teacher (in addition to his frequent *Beowulf* seminars at Cornell, he and Joe Harris twice taught an NEH Summer Seminar on *Beowulf* and the reception of Germanic antiquity).[10] His splendid essay for Bob Kaske's Festschrift, 'Scyld Scefing and the *stirps regia*' (no. 98) was an incisive structuralist analysis of the myth of Scyld as an exemplary 'charter of kingship.' Another *Beowulf* paper (no. 156) relating to the ideology of kingship in Germanic tradition identified a 'lordship formula' in Hrothgar's lament for Æschere. 'Beowulf's Confession and the Structure of *Vǫlsunga Saga*' (no. 75) highlights the value of Norse comparanda by reading the dying Beowulf's gratification at not having been treacherous or killed his own kinsmen against the brutality and kinship-violation that characterized the lives of the Volsung heroes. Two other *Beowulf* papers have advanced a compelling and historically rigorous approach to what Klaeber famously termed the poem's 'peculiar spiritual atmosphere.' In 'The Christian Language and Theme of *Beowulf*,' recently reprinted in a Norton Critical Edition (no. 130), Tom introduced the term 'Noachite' to *Beowulf* studies as a biblically grounded historiographical context for the poem's non-Christian yet virtuous and monotheistic heroes. Less well known is a paper (no. 107) that identified the 'variegated obit' as a distinctive stylistic feature of Christian (especially Anglo-Latin) historiography, concluding boldly that the virtuous 'pagans' whose deaths the *Beowulf* poet favoured with such circumlocutious obits are to be understood unambiguously as numbered among the saved.[11]

I have not even touched upon Tom's many contributions to the study of ME literature, especially *Piers Plowman* (nos 31, 37, 39, 42, 52, 88, 102, 119, 124, 147, 150, 152, 158, 162, 167, 177) and ME lyrics (nos 40, 53, 54,

82, 92, 95, 100, 149, 166, 171, 175), or to Old Norse and other Germanic literatures (nos 11, 21, 64, 69, 81, 96, 97, 111, 123, 127, 133, 134, 145, 172, 180), or again to medieval Romance literatures (nos 1, 2, 4, 35, 59, 74, 99, 118, 131). The range is simply too big to do justice to in one Festschrift, and so we have chosen to focus on his primary specialization in Anglo-Saxon studies. No volume, in any case, could keep pace with Tom's ever-expanding bibliography or his diverse interests (which lately include *Buffy the Vampire Slayer* and the graphic novels of Neil Gaiman). Any extended conversation with Tom will yield news of some recent source discovery, some remarkable connection gleaned from readings far afield, or some insight into a historical process or cultural phenomenon that he has been pondering ('You know, I have a theory about that ...'). This preface to *Source of Wisdom* has, however, been a welcome occasion to take stock of the sources, and the wisdom, that Tom has shared with us to date.

Several of the papers in this volume were presented in two Kalamazoo sessions on the occasion of Tom's sixty-third birthday in May 2003,[12] and many of them reflect Tom's specific interests in *Beowulf*, OE sapiential and religious literature, Christian-Latin traditions, and source-studies. In the first of three papers dealing with *Beowulf* (Part I), Joseph Harris ('Beasts of Battle, South and North') revisits the well-known theme of the 'Beasts of Battle,' finding that analogues in Middle High German as well as Norse texts bespeak a common Germanic tradition (as Tom had suggested in no. 67), but also that the *Beowulf* poet's use of the theme transcends both tradition and criticism. James H. Morey ('The Fates of Men in *Beowulf*') performs a kind of actuarial analysis of throne-worthy persons in *Beowulf*, observing that Geats and Swedes tend to meet violent ends, while many Danish royals or potential claimants die in mysterious or 'unexplicit' circumstances. The unambiguous circumstances of the deaths of Beowulf's immediate predecessors facilitate Beowulf's succession to the Geatish throne without taint of treachery, but Morey suspects that Hrothgar's path to the Danish throne was cleared by fratricidal violence. Frederick M. Biggs ('Folio 179 of the *Beowulf* Manuscript') autopsies the manuscript instead of the characters, intervening in the controversy precipitated by Kevin Kiernan's claim that folio 179 is a palimpsest. Biggs finds no evidence for deliberate revision or retouching, concluding on the basis of his own examination of the folio – as well as a careful consideration of the habits of scribe B when correcting his own work – that most of the damage was accidental, and that the text on the folio is not a revision in progress but an imperfect scribal record of the poet's intentions.

Much of Tom's scholarship has centred on the Christian-Latin background of OE religious and sapiential poetry, the subject of five contributions to *Source of Wisdom*, all by former Cornellians (Part II). James W. Earl's 'Trinitarian Language: Augustine, *The Dream of the Rood*, and Ælfric' focuses on the striking image of a talking cross and the theological implications of prosopopoeia. Augustine's theory of language and his trinitarian analogies for the operations of the human mind, Earl suggests, help to explain how things can 'talk' to us: because language (*verbum*, the Logos) mediates between thought and the world. In 'The Leaps of Christ and *The Dream of the Rood*,' James W. Marchand focuses on a motif that has exercised a particular fascination for Cornell medievalists (running a close second to *sapientia et fortitudo*; see no. 157), with publications by Bob Kaske, Tom (no. 95), and Mike Twomey. Marchand argues that, in addition to the well-known enumeration of the 'leaps' in *Christ II*, *The Dream of the Rood* also alludes to the motif in its use of the verb *(on) gestigan* to describe Christ's action at the Crucifixion (the third 'leap' in Cynewulf's enumeration). Johanna Kramer ('"Ðu eart se weallstan": Architectural Metaphor and Christological Imagery in the Old English *Christ I* and the Book of Kells') discusses the biblical and exegetical sources of the *Christ I* poet's rumination on architectural imagery in the first (surviving) lyric of *Christ I*, which she illustrates (literally) through a comparative analysis of the representation of the temple in the Temptation of Christ page from the Book of Kells.

In his dissertation Tom defined the sapiential tradition as 'that body of traditional wisdom concerning what is to be chosen or avoided in our doings.' His recent encyclopedia entry 'Wisdom (Sapiential) Literature' (no. 146) focused on OE texts that are most similar to the biblical sapiential books, including the 'gnomic' poems *Maxims I* and *II* (cf. no. 20) and *Solomon and Saturn II* (cf. nos 18, 26, 106, 176), but also noted that much sapiential material is incorporated in 'elegiac' poems such as *The Wanderer* (cf. no. 168) and *The Seafarer*. Sachi Shimomura's and Alice Sheppard's contributions to *Source of Wisdom* are also concerned with problems of narrative form in OE sapiential poems. Shimomura ('Remembering in Circles: *The Wife's Lament*, *Conversatio*, and the Community of Memory') argues that the narrator of *The Wife's Lament* has to escape a repetitive immersion in her own past and memory to arrive at a more generalized, gnomic (and therefore communal) understanding; in doing so the Wife, despite her continuing isolation, undergoes a socializing 'conversion.' The poem, Shimomura argues, reflects a social conception of time that she illustrates by analysing the use of the word *conversatio* and its OE equivalents *drohtnoþ/drohtung* in Bede and *Beowulf*. Sheppard's paper ('A Word to the Wise: Thinking, Knowledge, and Wisdom in *The Wanderer*') focuses on OE *gyd* as a sapiential form, distinguishing between the *gyd* as an inert embodiment of conventional wisdom (often a literally prescriptive gnome or maxim) and the *gyd* as an enigmatic mode (whether gnome, riddle, or narrative) that represents the acquisition of wisdom as a dynamic interpretive process. In moving from *anhaga* to *snottor on mode*, the Wanderer must disengage himself from grief and memory by learning to 'think through' (*geondþencan*) the meaning of proverbial wisdom about transience.

The six contributions on OE prose in Part III include three relating to the translations written or commissioned by King Alfred of 'those books most necessary for men to know.' Paul E. Szarmach and Joseph Wittig both deal with Boethius's *Consolatio Philosophiae* and its Latin glossing tradition. In 'Alfred's Nero,' Szarmach finds that Alfred often allows different perspectives to emerge in his prose and poetic adaptations of the Boethian portrait of Nero, and that the king develops the portrait (with hints from the commentary tradition) into a sustained meditation on the limitations of royal power. Wittig, who published a major study of the 'Remigian' glosses on Boethius in 1983, returns to the subject (and to his projected edition of the glosses on III.m.9 and m.12) in 'The "Remigian" Glosses on Boethius's *Consolatio Philosophiae* in Context.' Wittig offers samples of the texts as part of a broader reconsideration of their manuscript transmission and textual status, and includes a full listing of the manuscripts in an appendix. If for modern critics the OE *Boethius* is the favourite son of the Alfredian translation program, the poor stepchild is surely Wærferth's rendering of Gregory's *Dialogues*. David F. Johnson ('Why Ditch the *Dialogues*? Reclaiming an Invisible Text') surveys the reasons for the scholarly neglect of the work (ranging from unfair and unfavourable comparison with other texts in the Alfredian canon to inadequate scholarly editions), urging that it be read as a form of hagiography and by the standards of medieval exemplary and figural narrative.

Later OE prose writers are discussed by E. Gordon Whatley, Charles D. Wright, and Thomas N. Hall. Whatley ('Hagiography and Violence: Military Men in Ælfric's *Lives of Saints*') compares Ælfric's lives of military saints (The Maccabees, the Forty Soldiers, the Theban Legion, Martin, Oswald, and Edmund, among others) with their Latin sources as a way to assess Ælfric's attitude towards violence in defence of self and country. While Ælfric does glorify the passive martyrdom of Edmund, elsewhere he explicitly endorses the patristic view of just warfare and the legitimate role of soldiers (*bellatores*) fighting for righteous causes. Ælfric was not a pacifist, Whatley concludes, and his Edmund was no exception, for the martyred king did not give up his life to the Danes until after their victory had been assured and only his personal safety was at stake. In 'A New Latin Source for Two Old English Homilies (Fadda I and Blickling I): Pseudo-Augustine, *Sermo* App. 125, and the Ideology of Chastity in the Anglo-Saxon Benedictine Reform,' Wright shows that an anonymous OE homily for Lent, as well as Blickling Homily I, drew upon a pseudo-Augustinian Nativity sermon in explaining why Christ chose to be born of a virgin. The two OE homilies diverge sharply, however, in their understanding of Christ's exemplary *castitas* (OE *clænness*): Fadda I, in accordance with the Benedictine reformers' emphasis on clerical celibacy, understands it as sexual purity, while Blickling I expands its reference to include virtues accessible to the laity such as mercy and faith. Hall's essay ('Christ's Birth through Mary's Right Breast: An Echo of Carolingian Heresy in the Old English *Adrian and Ritheus*') is devoted to a motif in the OE *Adrian and Ritheus* dialogue that all but baffled Tom Hill and Jimmy Cross in their edition. Picking up on a hint from their editorial commentary, however, Hall traces persistent (albeit unorthodox) efforts, particularly during the Carolingian period, to rationalize Mary's post-partum virginity by asserting that Christ was born not through her womb but through her side or some other part of the body. However crude – and they were generally denounced and ridiculed by the writers who alluded to them – these efforts were motivated by a desire to assert the miraculous quality of Christ's physical birth while avoiding docetism.

Few, if any, post-war scholars have published as extensively as Tom has in both OE and ME. Two contributions to *Source of Wisdom* (Part IV) bridge this historical and disciplinary divide through a focus on the OE roots of ME collocations. Andrew Galloway ('The Peterborough Chronicle and the Invention of "Holding Court" in Twelfth-Century England') traces the earliest attestations of the formulation 'to hold court' to the First and Second Continuators of the Peterborough Chronicle, who use the expressions *hired healdan* and *healdan curt* respectively of William the Conqueror and Henry II. Equivalent expressions in Anglo-Norman (*tenir curt*) and Latin (*curiam tenere*) subsequently become widespread, and Galloway argues that the Second Continuator's formulation *healdan curt* is not merely precocious, but is the source of the Anglo-Norman and Latin expressions via Anglo-Norman historians (such as William of Malmesbury) who used the Peterborough Chronicle. In her contribution, Susan E. Deskis discusses 'Echoes of Old English Alliterative Collocations in Middle English Alliterative Proverbs.' Since relatively few OE proverbs survive, it can be difficult to determine whether an ME alliterative proverb had a pre-Conquest source, but Deskis examines several methodologically instructive examples of well-attested OE collocations (such as *hatan/healdan, bealu/bot*, and *hord/heort*) that occur in ME proverbs and appear to have been formulaic templates that generated alliterative proverbs, whether in the Anglo-Saxon period or later.

Though Tom's extensive bibliography includes relatively few items (nos 9, 43, 81, 83, 96, 153, 157, 178) dealing with medieval Latin texts as their primary object of investigation, many of his essays and notes situate motifs and images in OE texts in the context of medieval Latin literary traditions. *Source of Wisdom* concludes with a group of essays on medieval Latin authors and texts (Part V), one Anglo-Latin (Bede) and two (Aethicus Ister and Pseudo-Methodius) that were influential in Anglo-Saxon England. Danuta Shanzer ('Bede's Style: A Neglected Historiographical Model for the Style of the *Historia Ecclesiastica*?') takes up the mechanics and sources of Bede's prose style, particularly his fondness for complex yet tightly controlled periods. How did he learn to compose them? Shanzer suggests that his model may well have been Rufinus's Latin translation of Eusebius's *Ecclesiastical History*. (While canvassing other influences on Bede's prose style, Shanzer also proposes a biblical source for Bede's famous sparrow simile.) In 'Cruxbusting on the Danube: *uel Coniectanea* in Cosmographiam Aethici, *ut dicitur*, Istri,' Michael W. Herren contributes a textual study of the *Cosmographia* of Aethicus Ister, an enigmatic work that was apparently popular in Anglo-Saxon England.[13] The text is often corrupt, but Herren believes that an editor can and should restore sense wherever possible through conjectural emendation based on sound principles, and he demonstrates the results that can be achieved with a series of concrete examples from his edition and translation in progress. Finally, Michael W. Twomey ('The *Revelationes* of Pseudo-Methodius and Scriptural Study at Salisbury in the Eleventh Century') discusses the English transmission of the *Revelationes* of Pseudo-Methodius (a source for vernacular annotations in the OE *Hexateuch*). Focusing particularly on manuscripts at Salisbury in the eleventh century, Twomey finds that of the two major recensions of the *Revelationes*, the one favoured on the Continent as an anti-Islamic apocalypse was neglected in England, where the other recension served as a resource for biblical studies, especially for information on Old Testament genealogies.

Source of Wisdom concludes with two appendices: a bibliography of Tom's publications and a list of the dissertations he has directed. The seven contributors (including myself) whose dissertations Tom directed can attest, but cannot convey, how much we owe to his encouragement as a mentor, to his inspiration as a teacher, and to his example as a scholar.

Tom, your friends offer these essays as a tribute to your scholarship and as a token of our gratitude for your unfailing generosity, warmth, and good humour.[14]

CHARLES D. WRIGHT

NOTES

1 Hill, 'Old English Poetry and the Sapiential Tradition.' Tom received his BA from Harvard University (where an ancestor and namesake Thomas Hill had been president from 1862 to 1868) in 1961, and his MA from the University of Illinois at Urbana-Champaign in 1963.
2 Kaske, *Medieval Christian Literary Imagery: A Guide to Interpretation*, in collaboration with Arthur Groos and Michael W. Twomey, Toronto Medieval Bibliographies 11 (Toronto: University of Toronto Press, 1988). For Tom's review of the reviews of Kaske's book, see no. 139 in the bibliography of Tom's publications in the appendix at the end of this volume.
3 Auerbach, 'Figura,' in *Scenes from the Drama of European Literature*, trans. Ralph Mannheim (New York: Meridian Books, 1959), 11–76. Also fundamental were Jean Daniélou, *From Shadows to Reality: Studies in the Biblical Typology of the Fathers*, trans. W. Hibberd (Westminster, MD, 1960), and A.C. Charity, *Events and Their Afterlife: The Dialectics of Christian Typology in the Bible and Dante* (Cambridge: Cambridge University Press, 1966).
4 Kaske and Robertson have often been crudely lumped together in field historiographies, but Kaske outlined his differences with Robertson in a review essay of *A Preface to Chaucer: Studies in Medieval Perspectives* (Princeton: Princeton University Press, 1962) entitled 'Chaucer and Medieval Allegory' (*ELH* 30 [1963]: 175–92) and in his essay 'Patristic Exegesis in the Criticism of Medieval Literature: The Defense,' in *Critical Approaches to*

Medieval Literature: Selected Papers from the English Institute, 1958–1959, ed. Dorothy Bethurum (New York: Columbia University Press, 1960), 27–60, 158–9. For Tom's strictures against Robertsonianism, see his review of Robertson's collected essays (no. 86). For his very un-Robertsonian readings of the *Romance of the Rose* (nos 2, 35) Tom was named (together with his English Department colleague Pete Wetherbee) as a founder of 'the Ithaca heresy' by Robertson's disciple John V. Fleming (see Tom's review of Fleming's *Reason and the Lover*, no. 89).

5 For obituaries of Cross by Tom, see nos 138 and 144.
6 Freccero's major papers have been collected in *Dante: The Poetics of Conversion*, ed. Rachel Jacoff (Cambridge, MA: Harvard University Press, 1986).
7 Earl, 'Christian Traditions in the Old English *Exodus*,' NM 71 (1970): 541–70; Wittig, 'Figural Narrative in Cynewulf's *Juliana*,' ASE 4 (1975): 37–55, repr. in *The Cynewulf Reader*, ed. Robert Bjork, Basic Readings in Anglo-Saxon England (New York: Routledge, 2001), 147–70. For a pseudo-OE ditty alluding to Cornell Anglo-Saxon studies during this era (with reference to 'Hill hilderinc'), see Penn Szittya, 'Geomorgidd Larsmiðes. An Elegy: Composed upon the B.U. Bridge upon the Occasion of Teaching a First Old English Course: Or *Vox Clamantis in Deserto*,' OEN 7.1 (1973): 1–2. A list of the dissertations Tom has directed to date is given in appendix 2, pp. 399–400.
8 Successful and original typological readings of OE poetry do continue to appear, albeit infrequently.
9 For a history and bibliography of the project, see Paul E. Szarmach's foreword to *Sources of Anglo-Saxon Literary Culture I: Abbo of Fleury, Abbo of Saint-Germain-des-Prés, and Acta Sanctorum*, ed. Frederick M. Biggs, Thomas D. Hill, Paul E. Szarmach, and E. Gordon Whatley (Kalamazoo: Medieval Institute Publications, 2001), vii–xiv.
10 When Fred Biggs and I were taking Tom's *Beowulf* seminar he even had a dog named Beowulf.
11 Tom has elsewhere (no. 119) traced the history of the idea of universal salvation in patristic and medieval sources. On Beowulf's funeral obsequies see now no. 179.
12 The contributions to *Source of Wisdom* were submitted to the editors in 2004.
13 See Helmut Gneuss, *Handlist of Anglo-Saxon Manuscripts: A List of Manuscripts and Manuscript Fragments Written or Owned in England up to 1100*, MRTS 241 (Tempe, AZ: Arizona Center for Medieval and Renaissance Studies, 2001), nos 386, 439, 839.
14 I thank my co-editors, Fred Biggs and Tom Hall, for their advice and assistance at every stage of the preparation of this volume.

Abbreviations

ANQ	[formerly] *American Notes and Queries*
AASS	*Acta Sanctorum*, ed. Socii Bollandiani, 1st ed., 71 vols (1643–1931; repr. in 65 vols Brussels, 1965–70)
ASE	*Anglo-Saxon England*
ASPR	The Anglo-Saxon Poetic Records, ed. G.P. Krapp and E.V.K. Dobbie, 6 vols (New York: Columbia University Press, 1931–42)
BaP	Bibliothek der angelsächsischen Prosa, ed. Christian W.M. Grein, Richard P. Wülker, and Hans Hecht, 13 vols (Kassel [etc.]: G.H. Wigand [etc.], 1872–1933)
BHL	*Bibliotheca Hagiographica Latina*, 2 vols, Subsidia hagiographica (Brussels: Société des Bollandistes, 1898–1901); with a *Novum Supplementum* by H. Fros, Subsidia hagiographica 70 (Brussels: Société des Bollandistes, 1986)
BT, BTS	Joseph Bosworth and T. Northcote Toller, *An Anglo-Saxon Dictionary Based on the Manuscript Collections of the Late Joseph Bosworth* (Oxford: Oxford University Press, 1882–98); T. Northcote Toller, *An Anglo-Saxon Dictionary: Supplement* (Oxford: Oxford University Press, 1908–21); Alistair Campbell, *Enlarged Addenda and Corrigenda to the Supplement by T. Northcote Toller to An Anglo-Saxon Dictionary ...* (Oxford: Oxford University Press, 1972)
CCCM	Corpus Christianorum, Continuatio Mediaevalis
CCSL	Corpus Christianorum, Series Latina
CSASE	Cambridge Studies in Anglo-Saxon England
CSCO	Corpus Scriptorum Christianorum Orientalium

CSEL	Corpus Scriptorum Ecclesiasticorum Latinorum
CUL	Cambridge, University Library
DA	*Deutsches Archiv für Erforschung des Mittelalters*
DOE	*Dictionary of Old English*, ed. Antonette diPaolo Healey et al. (Toronto: University of Toronto Press, 1986–); also in CD-ROM: *Dictionary of Old English: Fascicle F and Fascicles A–E (with Revisions)*, CD-ROM version 1.0 (Toronto: University of Toronto Press, 2003)
DOE Corpus	*Dictionary of Old English*, Corpus of Old English (2000 Release), http://ets.umdl.umich.edu/o/oec/
EEMF	Early English Manuscripts in Facsimile, 29 vols (Copenhagen: Rosenkilde and Bagger, 1951–2002)
EETS	Early English Text Society
o.s.	Original Series
s.s.	Supplementary Series
ELH	*English Literary History*
ELN	*English Language Notes*
ES	*English Studies*
HE	*Historia Ecclesiastica* (Bede)
JEGP	*Journal of English and Germanic Philology*
JML	*Journal of Medieval Latin*
MÆ	*Medium Ævum*
ME	Middle English
MGH	Monumenta Germaniae Historica
AA	Auctores Antiquissimi
SRM	Scriptores rerum Merovingicarum
MHG	Middle High German
MLN	*Modern Language Notes*
MP	*Modern Philology*
MRTS	Medieval and Renaissance Texts and Studies
MS	*Mediaeval Studies*
NM	*Neuphilologische Mitteilungen*
NQ	*Notes and Queries*
OE	Old English
OEN	*Old English Newsletter*
OLD	*Oxford Latin Dictionary*, ed. P.G.W. Glare (Oxford: Oxford University Press, 1982)
ON	Old Norse
PG	*Patrologia Graeca*, ed. J.-P. Migne, 161 vols (Paris, 1857–66)

PL	*Patrologia Latina*, ed. J.-P. Migne, 221 vols (Paris, 1844–64)
PMLA	*Publications of the Modern Language Association*
PQ	*Philological Quarterly*
RES	*Review of English Studies*
SN	*Studia Neophilologica*
SP	*Studies in Philology*
YLS	*Yearbook of Langland Studies*

Note on Quotations

Quotations from *Beowulf* are from Fr. Klaeber, *Beowulf and the Fight at Finnsburg*, 3rd ed. with First and Second Supplements (Boston: D.C. Heath, 1950), by line numbers (Klaeber's diacritics have been omitted).

Quotations from other OE poems are from the ASPR (by line numbers), unless a different edition is specified.

Quotations from the Vulgate are from *Biblia Sacra iuxta Vulgatam versionem*, editio minor, ed. Robert Weber, 3rd ed. by B. Fischer (Stuttgart: Deutsche Bibelgesellschaft, 1984), with punctuation added; translations, unless specified otherwise, are from the Douay Version, *The Holy Bible, containing the Old and New Testaments, translated from the Latin Vulgate* (Baltimore: John Murphy, 1911).

Quotations from Bede, *Historia ecclesiastica gentis Anglorum* [*HE*] are from *Bede's Ecclesiastical History of the English People*, ed. and trans. Bertram Colgrave and R.A.B. Mynors (Oxford: Clarendon Press, 1969), unless otherwise noted.

PART I
Beowulf

Beasts of Battle, South and North

JOSEPH HARRIS

[Witnesses] described scenes of chaos and fear ... Grey smoke billowed as grenades exploded ... A few minutes after the shootout ended, ambulances raced ... [O]ffice workers came out on the roof ... to watch the action *as broad-winged black birds circled on currents of air high above* [emphasis added].

Celia W. Dugger

The association of certain 'beasts' – the wolf, the eagle, and, in this paper, especially the raven – with battle sticks fast in the imagination, even in the modern world. How do you explain a detail like that in the report by Celia W. Dugger of the suicide raid on the Indian Parliament (*New York Times*, 14 December 2001)? Does it, for example, reflect the homology of a real incident with a 'cultural memory' arising out of an ancient layer of the unconscious? Direct answers could only be mystical or jesting (lingering influence of a college OE course? oral-formulaic theme survival?) while indirect answers will remain largely implicit in the treatment of old texts.

Old English Formalism

The admirable tradition of scholarship on the beasts of battle in OE has been little concerned with any *mysterium tremendum* that dark wings might suggest. Instead it has been predominantly formalistic, dealing mostly with some fourteen familiar passages in eight poems considered chiefly as a compositional unit – topos, motif, theme, or type-scene. The recognition of these passages, their number and limits, has evolved somewhat over the years, eventuating in the following current canon:

Beowulf 3024b–7; *Battle of Brunanburh* 60–5a; *Elene* 27b–30a, 52b–3a, 110b–13a; *Exodus* 162–8; *The Fight at Finnsburg* 5b–6a, 34b–5a; *Genesis A* 1983b–5a; 2087b–9a, 2159b–61; *Judith* 205b–12a, 295–6a; and *Battle of Maldon* 106b–7a. In length the passages vary from two half-lines to about fourteen and contain varying combinations of a total of ten repeated constituent motifs.[1] The topos was quite familiar to the older scholars, and since Jacob Grimm hardly any general account of OE poetry has lacked an allusion to them. The most conspicuous thread in modern scholarship, however, has been the oral-formulaic one introduced by Francis Peabody Magoun in 1955, where form was treated as a key to composition in the poetic language mastered by an Anglo-Saxon 'singer'; after Magoun's seminal article some studies related the topos more to artistic individuality or generally to aesthetics, but few or none were completely uninfluenced by the Oral Theory's brand of formalism.[2] So closely associated with Magoun is the topos that the phrase 'beasts of battle' would itself now probably be felt as an allusion to the Oral Theory by most OE scholars.

Some post-Magoun studies used form to throw light not on the core topos, but on marginal passages that seem not so much to deploy the topos itself as – in some cases debatably – to play off its familiarity, passages such as *Beowulf* 2448a, 2941a; *Wanderer* 80b–3a; *Fortunes of Men* 10–14, 33–42; *Maxims II* 18b–19a; *Riddle 24* 4–5a; and *Riddle 93* 28–9.[3] Post-Magoun scholars recognized metaphorical extension of the topos to lines relatively remote from the canonical core when Viking warriors are called 'wælwulfas' in *Maldon* 96a or Elamite soldiers 'herewulfas' and 'hildewulfas' in *Genesis A* 2015b and 2051a, tropes that seem to stand in for the wolves missing from the realization of the topos at *Maldon* 106b–7a and from all three instances in *Genesis A*. M.S. Griffith convincingly embeds this 'substitution,' on the one hand, in a well-developed pattern of interchange between beast and hero and, on the other, in further techniques of variation in composition.[4] In this vein I was about to propose of some lines from the storm scene in *Andreas* – 'ond se græga mæw / wælgifre wand' [371b–2a: and the gray seagull, greedy for carrion, circled] – that they presented an example of the *Andreas* poet's malapropian handling of a formula from the topos comparable to his relation to poetic tradition elsewhere. But working further, I found that Gustav Neckel had said more or less the same thing in 1915.[5] *Nihil sub sole novum?*

The three most recent studies of the OE beasts of battle I have seen all bring something new, even while their contributions reflect one or more of the types already mentioned. John Miles Foley treats the issue of originality within the context of oral-formulism; his main emphasis, however, is on the semantic effect of the topos, which, for its audiences, will have carried associations from the tradition as a whole and which, therefore, had a metonymic force more important than individual formal factors. Thomas Honegger analyses and arranges OE realizations of the topos into 'naturalistic-approach' and 'poetic-approach' groups, and the latter into 'mechanistic applications' and 'creative applications' – a literary taxonomy calculated to raise disagreement, especially with readers who regard tradition as a powerful and subtle force in early poetry.[6]

The most valuable recent contribution is that of Griffith. The point of view here is neo-Oral Theory, and the article makes original refinements to the theory of oral-formulaic composition itself and to the beasts-of-battle unit, but its careful analysis of the core passages chiefly presents well-supported formal facts; for example, 'no proper battle takes place without the obligatory beasts.'[7] The remarkably limited vocabulary of the scene is thoroughly explored, and going beyond form, the sonic 'trigger' for the topos is related to the suggestive beast-human interchange.[8] The 'originality' of the article's title is related convincingly to objectively describable techniques and individual emphases (*Exodus*'s darkness, *Elene*'s sonics), though like most critics Griffith defaults to poetic effect when faced with *Beowulf*; following Bonjour's wonderment over *Beowulf*'s 'largely original' 'indirect use of a conventional theme,' Griffith writes: 'Formalist analysis of conventions cannot, perhaps, adequately prepare us for this kind of free treatment. The intensity and the elegiac power of the end of *Beowulf* is rooted in the traditional, but this underlying structure has been radically transformed and the result is both poignant and extraordinary.'[9] The limitations of formalism seem to call for a broader and looser approach.

The Beasts in the North

The northern sister literature in ON is thickly populated by eagles, wolves, and ravens, even if no intrepid philologist-naturalist has attempted to chart them in all their manifestations through the widely disparate sources, saga prose, learned prose, skaldic poetry, and finally eddic poetry. Ravens, like the two that appear out of nowhere to accompany Skarpheðinn and Hǫgni on their mission of revenge in *Njáls saga* (ch. 79), make appearances even in the realistic saga genres, while

Snorri's *Prose Edda* offers famous mythological instantiations of each of the three animals, chiefly drawn from his poetic sources. Skaldic poetry is replete with kennings such as 'Muninn's mouthful' ('Munins tugga') for carrion or 'the reddener of Huginn's claws' ('fetrjóðr Hugins') for a warrior.[10] Meissner, who catalogued kennings by referent but also sub-catalogued the base words and determiners, had, for many decades, probably the most elaborate discussion of the beasts of battle in skaldic verse.[11] (The skaldic kennings show, by the way, that Óðinn's ravens, despite the allegorical sound of their names Huginn [thought] and Muninn [mind] are not learned borrowings – the point of departure of A.H. Krappe's essays on the raven and raven god.)[12] Meissner attended strictly to kennings, so that if a poet said plainly, 'The warrior fed the wolves,' or the like, he would not have registered the fact, but Meissner did pause on 'Formeln' that put two or three of the beasts together: 'Die Dichter lieben es, die Tiere der Schlacht zusammen vorzuführen, besonders Rabe und Wolf zu gesellen. Hierfür Beispiele zu geben, dürfte überflüssig sein ...'[13] Very recently, Judith Jesch has surveyed the motif in skaldic verse, also placing it in wider contexts, chiefly runic monuments and OE and Welsh poetry; she notes, however, that 'no rigorous and systematic analysis' of the beasts in ON has been done and that none is undertaken in her studies.[14] Jesch is chiefly concerned to examine the use of the motif in the context of the skaldic encomium as evidence of Viking Age values, but despite this auspicious beginning, skaldic poetry still lacks any comprehensive consideration comparable to that lavished on the well-cultivated canon of the OE topos.

Among Norse sources, it is only eddic poetry, and in fact only the *Poetic Edda* proper, whose beasts of battle have been systematically studied. And even here the brief *Forschungsbericht* almost begins and ends with Heinrich Beck's admirable 'Tiere der Jagd und Walstatt in den eddischen Liedern.'[15] Beck's interest in semiotically laden animals goes back to his earliest work on the boar symbol, but this study of the beasts of battle is also clearly influenced by the OE formalistic tradition. Beck cites about seventy-four passages from the *Poetic Edda*, some very brief, others extending over several stanzas and including different types of allusions to animals; one is struck, however, not so much by the larger number of allusions in the *Edda* by comparison to OE, as by the relative variety of ideas connected with what still seems chiefly a set of related images. Beck does not take a position on the Oral Theory; instead his brand of formalism establishes a grid of the types of representation: directly presented naturalistic *Abbilder* or more or less obliquely conveyed symbolic *Sinnbilder*, an arrangement anticipating Honegger's. This point of view may be related to passing remarks about inspiration from nature vs stylization in the more copious OE scholarship. I find such distinctions difficult to grasp; for me *all* these images are cultural and therefore 'poetic' *Sinnbilder*, even when not in defiance of nature. In any case, Beck was equally interested in the language and structure of particular passages, in the ultimately religious connections he alludes to, and in the Common Germanic poetics the animals bear witness to: 'Die Dreiheit *hræfn – earn – wulf* findet sich in gleicher Beziehung zur Walstatt auch in der altenglischen Dichtung und sichert dieser sprachlichen Figur innerhalb der germanischen Dichtersprache ein beträchtliches Alter.'[16]

Before Beck I have been able to discover only a handful of treatments of our theme in Norse. One well worth mentioning is by Gustav Neckel, whose casual – not exhaustive, and not formally organized – list of raven, eagle, and wolf passages in both languages contributes to his presentation of a Common Germanic poetic culture rooted in the warlike organization of the Migration Period.[17] Even so, Neckel's ultimate point in his treatment of the beasts of battle is what we might call a culture-critical one based on contrast of the Anglo-Saxon and Norse uses of the common material, a contrast emphasized also by Jesch.[18]

Back in the OE arena, it is only Roberta Frank who has made somewhat similar use of the formally described passages for literary-historical purposes – but what a difference from Neckel! She harnesses the shared materials to the suggestion of skaldic influence on OE narrative poetry, especially in *Exodus* and *Beowulf*. Taking exception to Thomas D. Hill's belief that the *Exodus* poet 'revels' in 'traditional Germanic diction' *generally*, Frank argues that his revels are instead distinctly *skaldic*.[19] In refuting Jacob Grimm on the Common Germanic ancestry of the beasts of battle, Frank seems to imply their complete absence from continental Germanic literature, making Grimm's reconstructive bent a romantic fantasy: '[Grimm] could have mentioned that these three camp-followers never show their faces in continental Germanic literature.'[20] This disagreement, though narrowly focused on one topos, is of far-reaching importance and worth pausing on.

'Germanic' Substrate?

Frank's scepticism, if I have interpreted her correctly, is misplaced, for a number of continental instances of the topos do exist.[21] The earliest I have encountered is from the early MHG *Annolied*, composed after 1075 and describing a civil war so disastrous 'daz dî gidouftin lîchamin / vmbigravin ciworfin lâgin / ci âse den bellindin, / den grâwin walt-hundin' [40, 17–20: that the bodies of Christians were lying strewn around unburied as carrion for the howling ones, the gray forest-hounds]. I suggest, developing a discussion by Gottfried Schramm, that *walt-hund* is the descendant of one of the earliest kenninglike noa names (euphemisms for tabooed names) for the wolf, the man's name *widuhu(n)daR* on a Danish brooch of about 200 (the Himlingøje II brooch), and that *bellen* is a later replacement for a verb cognate with Icelandic *geyja* and found in the Gothic hero name *Vidigoia* 'he who howls in the woods.'[22] This oldest German instance of the topos gives us only the wolf, but in formulas that could reflect an old tradition.

The other MHG occurrences of the topos that I know of are chiefly those discussed by Jacob Grimm in his 1840 edition of the OE *Elene*. After a brilliant listing and discussion of the most salient passages in OE and ON, he introduces his German *Belege* in this way: 'Hätte die ahd. echte dichtung sich gerettet, es würde nicht an lauter bestätigenden wendungen mangeln, selbst die mhd. des 12. 13 jh wahrt noch einige nachklänge.'[23] Though he missed the *Annolied*, Grimm reported five instances of the topos from both translated and original epics: *Wiener Exodus* 157–64; *Willehalm* IX: 462, 20–3; *Rabenschlacht* st. 527; *Dietrichs Flucht* 6437–40 and 8459–61. (I supply more modern titles and locations for Grimm's quaint nomenclature.) From references in one of Grimm's essays and various annotations of MHG editors we can assemble at least three or four more instances from MHG epic.[24] Of these nine putative instances of the topos, one mentions only 'birds,' one only 'birds and animals,' one 'black birds' and 'wolves,' two 'ravens and vultures,' three 'wolves and ravens,' and only one text links more than two beasts of battle, but that text, the early MHG *Wiener Exodus* of ca. 1120–30, offers a quartet of wolf, raven, vulture, and a type of hunting dog, *hessehund(e)*. Perhaps due to the growth of its positive political significance,[25] the eagle does not appear as a carrion beast in these MHG texts, replaced, apparently, by the vulture. Thus triads of wolf, raven, and eagle do not occur in precisely the OE form, Frank's 'companionable triads.' But the full triad is limited to only four of the fourteen canonical OE passages and seems to be relatively rare in skaldic poetry.[26] Generally, the contrasts between the OE topos and its skaldic cognate suggest to me (as to Neckel and apparently to Jesch) different developments from a common point of departure; in any case, the triad itself cannot be historically definitive of the topos and instead appears to be artistic hypertrophy. The poetic continuity entailed in identifying the MHG passages as instances of the old topos is, of course, not unquestionable, and each of these passages deserves an individual discussion in the comparative context. For now, however, I conclude only that scholars like Neckel, who wrote that the beasts of battle occurred 'in nordischen, angelsächsischen, und *seltener* in deutschen Versen' (my italics), were not inaccurate;[27] the tradition, in the narrower, toposlike interpretation, did after all leave distinct traces on the Continent, and collectively the traces constitute a considerable, though intensely localized, argument in favour of conventional views of Common Germanic poetic tradition.

Frank's more specific case for skaldic influence in the *Exodus* beasts-of-battle passage is based less on the distribution of the topos than on four problematic terms there that evoke for her Nordic, chiefly skaldic, memories.[28] But counterarguments could be launched in each case. The diction of *Exodus* is famously complex and difficult, and so is skaldic poetry. But the smoking gun of specifically skaldic influence on our passage seems lacking, and one is on firmer ground with Hill's more comprehensive term 'Germanic.' Frank begins her conclusion: 'In discussions of the beasts of battle, Anglo-Saxonists have tended to treat as "German" an image of dissolution that has a much wider currency (as in the Psalms) and have called "Teutonic" a decorative triad whose mutual assistance pact has a much narrower currency, limited as it is to ON verse and eight OE poems.'[29] I agree that our comparative net should be cast more widely, but 'German' in this sentence would seem to refer to a mere slip of the pen in the Hill article ('German poetic idiom' for 'Germanic').[30] The tendency she refers to here did exist in various ways in the history of the field, whether or not the immediate factual basis is in error; but that this tendency is any more a baseless 'bias' (as Frank terms it) than its countertendency remains for me doubtful.

Moreover, Neckel's broad cultural comparison does bring out one feature that argues rather impressively against skaldic influence on the OE topos in general, namely the fact that most of the OE passages occur before or during battle as instances of foreshadowing while the skaldic image is basically of the beasts actually feeding or having been fed.[31] Neckel drew far-reaching consequences from this contrast, which, he said, agreed with the literary, monastic, elegiac, romantic nature of OE poetry compared with the harsh, unblinking rendition of battle experience in the skalds. The topos in its skaldic form is for Neckel the direct continuation of what he imagines as the early Common Germanic poetry of the comitatus during the late Migration Period, and he rounds out his large culture-critical speculations here by suggesting that the OE topos be understood as a cultivated byway. I am sceptical of a number of interpretative details in Neckel's picture, and I am even reluctant to rely blindly on his summary of the facts of skaldic deployment of the beasts of battle. Jesch's work, however, does support Neckel on this point, even though she has not parsed her skaldic corpus strictly in terms of 'before' and 'after.' It looks, then, as if general influence from the north on OE use of this topos is unlikely.

The main OE exception to this contrast with skaldic art is constituted by *Brunanburh*, a clearly Viking-Age poem in which direct skaldic influences have already been argued by John D. Niles and by me.[32] Niles compares the image of feeding beasts here with the 'hard, cold tone' of skaldic verse, contrasting the more 'evenhanded' anticipatory deployment of the topos generally characteristic of OE.[33] When the beasts appear after the battle, they are evidence, as here in *Brunanburh*, of terrible slaughter, the harshness of the victors; and the skaldic variant in which a prince is described as a feeder of the beasts encapsulates the post-battle appearance as a characteristic of the man. Whether or not this skaldic variation is based solely on observation of nature, the majority OE usage contrasts as a herald, a sign, a prognostication.

Natural and Supernatural

Neckel's conviction that the harsh naturalistic topos of skaldic (and, we might add, MHG) verse was the original form is presumably coloured by the trope of the 'hard' *alten Germanen*,[34] but as good a claim can be made for roots in religion. Tacitus sceptics may be disinclined to accord much authority to his notice of avian omens among the Germanic tribes: 'et illud quidem etiam hic notum, avium voces volatusque interrogare'[35] [and indeed even here (in Germania) is known the interrogation of the voices and flights of birds]. The prophetic direction of bird flight looks at first glance more Roman than Germanic, but rather than compass direction, direction relative to the protagonist might be at issue.[36] Óðinn's advice in *Reginsmál* [*Rm*] 20 offers a good luck sign of this type: 'dyggia fylgio hygg ec ins døcqva vera / at hrottameiði hrafns' [I think that having a dark raven in his following is helpful to a warrior].[37] The raven banners mentioned in several early texts clearly attempted to insure the lucky presence of a raven flying in one's company, in agreement with the well-known bird-accompanied rider from the helmet in Vendel grave I.[38] The Tacitean reference is, of course, very general but agrees, as far as it goes, with the religious tinge of many of the Nordic items noticed by Beck. Though scholarship frequently mentions a basis in nature for the images of the carrion beasts, they will have become prophetic by a reversal of stimulus and response, a cultural rather than a natural move. Carrion-eaters learn to hear Pavlov's dinner bell whenever they see certain signs, including warriors heading out; but it is the bell-ringers, the wearers of the rustling byrnies, who turn the beasts into predictors.[39] A number of studies, including Krappe's rich collection, emphasize the prophetic nature of the raven in antiquity and in folklore, a religious image naturalized.[40]

The OE beasts of battle, for all their ornamental stylization, are still undeniably in touch with fate, the future, and death, however the relationship between natural (generally skaldic and MHG) and supernatural (generally OE) is to be imagined. The attribution of voice and even of language to the beasts in many of the OE passages is a less-noticed factor here. Griffith counted fourteen instances of the motif 'give voice to' in six of the eight canonical OE poems.[41] A few of the terms used in OE, while still applicable to humans, can extend to sublinguistic cries (*hreopon, gylleð*); most imply language, some also a speech genre and quasi-human communication. Beyond the canonical OE passages, the wolf is imagined (though the idea is negated) as a funeral lamenter (*Maxims I* 146–51); a somewhat similar eddic passage (cast as a curse) contrasts natural with cultural behaviour but does not allude explicitly to language.[42] Eddic verse also offers analogues to the cultural reception of natural sounds and to the actual language of the beasts, including prophecies possibly suggestive of the constellation of ideas lying behind the ornamental topos in OE. Again, there are natural bases for this cultural construction; ravens, in particular, are supposed to be able to mimic human sounds.[43] Obviously, however, the poets, both south and north, went far beyond nature, but as a young Klaeber commented on the gift of speech in Norse ravens and eagles: 'This may or may not be of significance.'[44]

Beowulf's Beasts of Battle

Expanding the field of reference can, on occasion, increase our understanding of individual texts, as Beck showed in a discussion of OE *wælrun* compared contextually to its Norse cognate.[45] A similar case would be the reference to the blithe-hearted raven of *Beowulf* 1799–803a: 'Reste hine þa rumheort; reced hliuade / geap ond goldfah; gæst inne swæf, / oþ þæt hrefn blaca heofones wynne / bliðheort bodode. Ða com beorht scacan, / [scima ofer sceadwa] ...' [the great-hearted one (Beowulf) rested; the hall towered wide-gabled and gold-adorned; the guest slept within until the black raven, blithe-hearted, announced the joy of heaven. Then, bright, came hastening (the shiner over the shadow)]. Here the raven we moderns expect to encounter melancholy upon a midnight dreary or else red in tooth and claw instead rejoices at the light of dawn. The passage has been accorded two especially fruitful studies. The first, by Kathryn Hume in 1969, mentioned appropriate parallels ranging from Audubon to ON, weighing the possibility of 'an extrinsic tradition';[46] but by foregrounding a justification based on close reading, however elegant, she seems to shift the balance against an historical explanation. A few years later Martin Puhvel searched more explicitly for a tradition for the passage but went to the opposite extreme in attempting to trace the morning-raven all the way back to Indo-European as an attribute of sun worship. He performed a good service, however, in bringing forward one ON passage (already slumbering in Klaeber's notes to the passage) that perfectly unites the carrion-happy raven image with this bird's equal joy at daybreak.[47]

In this passage the valkyrie heroine enters a funeral mound to meet her beloved, returned from the dead: 'Nú em ec svá fegin fundi ocrom / sem átfrekir Óðins haucar, / er val vito, varmar bráðir, / eða dǫgglitir dags brún siá' [*Helgaqviða Hundingsbana ǫnnor* (*HHII*) 43: 'Now I am as fain of our meeting as Óðinn's hungry hawks (ravens) when they learn of slaughter, warm flesh, or, dewy-feathered,[48] they see the brow of day']. Sigrún's joy ('fegin') is equated with that of ravens; in *Beowulf* only the raven is 'bliðheort,' but the balanced structure of a scene where everything is in its proper place makes the adjectival link to the 'rumheort' human irresistible. Two other parallel concepts – the colour or appearance of the ravens ('dǫgglitir': 'blaca')[49] and the kenninglike, lightly personified dawn ('dags brún': 'heofenes wynne') – speak for themselves. The feature conspicuously missing in the OE, the raven's connection with carrion as a product of battle, is present in the ON, opening the possibility that the *Beowulf* passage, which has always seemed in need of some explanation, may be a variation on a rare, but genuine poetic tradition.[50]

This argument is strengthened by a second passage not cited by Puhvel. The first Helgi poem begins with the hero's birth, and his future is predicted in a conversation among ravens: 'hrafn qvað at hrafni – sat á hám meiði, / andvanr áto – : "Ec veit noccoð. // Stendr í brynio burr Sigmundar, / dœgrs eins gamall, nú er dagr kominn; / hvessir augo sem hildingar; / sá er varga vinr, við scolom teitir"' [*Helgaqviða Hundingsbana in fyrri* (*HH*) 5–6: one raven spoke to another – he sat in a high tree, famished for food – : 'There's something I know: The son of Sigmundr, one day old, is standing in his byrnie; now day has come; his eyes flash like those of warriors; he will be a friend of wolves; we shall be joyous']. Both reasons for joy mentioned in *HHII* 43 are also here, daybreak and future feed, but only one is linked to the ravens' pleasure; the hunger of the ravens ('átfrekir'; 'andvanr áto') is expressed in formulas obviously reminiscent of the OE beasts-of-battle topos, but lacking in *Beowulf* 1799–803a.[51] By a forceful reading this collection of motifs might be taken to associate the 'emergence' of each hero with sunrise – his birth (*HH* 5–6), his egress from the funeral mound and this world (*HHII* 49),[52] and just possibly his coming forth by day (*Beowulf*).[53] More conservatively we could summarize: *HHII* shows the two sources of a raven's joy (food, implicitly a product of battle, and daybreak) while *HH* associates the hero with day and lets the raven rejoice over the food he will provide as a warrior; perhaps wishing to avoid the ungentle implication that his hero will sate ravens, the OE poet associates his hero only loosely with heaven's joy and the raven's. *Beowulf*'s morning raven seems deeply, though not mechanically, traditional, but the ultimate significance of 'daybreak' – simply the time when battle begins?[54] – remains hovering between sign and symbol.

Beowulf's full realization of the beasts-of-battle topos (3021b–7), with its animal voices in a miniature drama, stands out from its OE colleagues like the leek above the grasses. It does have a significant connection back to the morning raven, however, for the imagined scene is morning, with the spear 'morgenceald' in hand. Warriors will be wakened, not by the harp,[55] that symbol of ease, but implicitly by the chatter of the dark raven – no sunrise and no hero here. The rhetorical trick of casting narrative elements into the future where they act as a 'hypothetical' resembles Beowulf's account of the Heathobard feud (2032–69a), even to including as its crux an imagined speech within the framing speech. If the morning-raven passage is an example of the poet's variation of a tradition by elision, these passages reveal complementary elaboration.

For the beasts-of-battle passage itself, the beast drama, the richest parallels are offered by the marginally skaldic, 'eddic praise-poem' *Haraldskvæði*, where a bright-haired valkyrie conducts an interview in 'bird-language' ('fuglsrǫdd,' 2⁴) with the dark-feathered oath-brother of the eagle, who bears all the marks of having recently dined; this raven's report casts his carrion-feasting in the immediate past, a product of the deeds of Haraldr fairhair. The dialogue engages two types of 'chooser of the slain,' valkyrie and 'wælceasega' (*Exodus* 164a) raven, light and dark sides of the same religious coin;[56] the effect is almost as if two beasts-of-battle were conversing about a meal of carrion. A similar but weaker effect is produced by the valkyrie Sigrún's comparing herself to a raven in *HHII* 43 (quoted above, p. 12).

For the predictive aspect of the beasts' dialogue, eddic poetry offers *HH* 5–6 (quoted above) and a prophecy of ruin in *Brot af Sigurðarkviðu* [*Brot*] (5; 13); the first of these passages seems to me aesthetically worthy of the comparison to *Beowulf*. Though the human listeners, awaking ('wigend weccean,' 3024a), would inevitably interpret the birds' chatter about a past meal as predictive, *Beowulf*'s beasts foreshadow, but do not directly predict battle or human death. Of course, the human listeners are imaginary, part of the hypothetical; the really ominous factor in all these elements of the scene is a product of their deployment by the messenger. Thus the inter-beast discourse in *Beowulf* contrives to be at once *post factum* and predictive and leaves all the comparanda behind for complexity and imagination. Griffith and Bonjour were right about the bankruptcy of formalism in the face of this passage.

The literary-historical possibilities do not seem much stronger; except in the uncontested skaldic influence on *Brunanburh* and in Frank's arguments about *Exodus*, the OE passages do not seem to offer a developmental pattern (like those found in art) or individual toeholds for dating. True, Frank also interprets the Norse affiliations of the *Beowulf* passage as skaldic influence, but the best analogues belong either to the typologically older eddic style or else (in *Haraldskvæði*) to the skaldic subgenre (eddic praise-poem) that comes closest to demonstrating how skaldic verse evolved out of the simpler type. Nor does the *Beowulf* passage solve the problem of a unified evolutionary model for the topos, from naturalistic to predictive or the reverse. It does, however, unite in a single scene the two strands of the topos, considered in all genres, south and north, and so perhaps hints at a unity of original conception.

By Way of a Conclusion

The Anglo-Saxon topos and the beasts in most of their other OE contexts are 'part fact and part symbol,'[57] but a grasp of the full scope of the symbolism must lead beyond formal contexts. In my opinion only ultimately religious roots can account for the persistent supernatural features, connections with the future and death, and the survival into later folklore.[58] These roots establish the most meaningful way of relating the Germanic materials to the overrich Celtic analogues, most conspicuously among them the avian-form war goddesses.[59] These subjects themselves have found excellent exponents; only the nexus to the secularized and decorative OE topos itself is somewhat neglected.[60] And no wonder: it remains a challenge to learn how to read the OE material beyond formalism and in its widest context. Grimm approached that goal by locating the aesthetic value of OE Christian poetry such as *Elene* in the native freedom of its style;[61] surprisingly, he thought the OE expressions of native style in the beasts of battle surpassed the Norse 'an frische der ausführung.'[62] His characterization of the topos in OE as 'durch und durch heidnisch,' breathing 'die älteste poesie unsrer vorzeit' can, sympathetically, be understood as a generous – and, yes, 'romantic' – evocation of the cultural depths out of which these merely stylistic figures arise. Such an approach cannot be the last word, but it serves well as a first.

NOTES

1 See the content analysis in M.S. Griffith, 'Convention and Originality in the Old English "Beasts of Battle" Typescene,' *ASE* 22 (1993): 179–99 at 184–6.
2 Francis P. Magoun, 'The Theme of the Beasts of Battle in Anglo-Saxon Poetry,' *NM* 56 (1955): 81–90. Post-Magoun examples: Adrien Bonjour, '*Beowulf* and the Beasts of Battle,' *PMLA* 72 (1957): 563–73; repr. with additional comments in his *Twelve 'Beowulf' Papers: 1940–1960* (Neuchâtel: Faculté des lettres, 1962), 135–49; Robert E. Diamond, 'Theme as Ornament in Anglo-Saxon Poetry,' *PMLA* 76 (1961): 461–8; Allan A. Metcalf, 'Ten Natural Animals in *Beowulf*,' *NM* 64 (1963): 378–89; Metcalf, 'Ornamentale Tiermotive in der altenglischen Versdichtung,' in *Das Tier in der Dichtung*, ed. Ute Schwab and Fritz Harkort (Heidelberg: C. Winter, 1970), 74–90, 268–71;

Alain Renoir, 'Christ Ihesu's Beasts of Battle: A Note on Oral-Formulaic Theme Survival,' *Neophilologus* 60 (1976): 455–9; Renoir, 'Oral-Formulaic Rhetoric: An Approach to Image and Message in Medieval Poetry,' in *Medieval Texts and Contemporary Readers*, ed. Laurie A. Finke and Martin B. Shichtman (Ithaca, NY: Cornell University Press, 1987), 234–53; Renoir, *A Key to Old Poems: The Oral-Formulaic Approach to the Interpretation of West-Germanic Verse* (University Park, PA: Pennsylvania State University Press, 1988), 162–4, 207.

3 One example of such an approach is George Hardin Brown, 'An Iconographic Explanation of "The Wanderer," Lines 81b–82a,' *Viator* 9 (1978): 31–8. Another is Marijane Osborne, 'The Finnsburg Raven and *guðrinc astah*,' *Folklore* 81 (1970): 185–94 at n. 17; but the 'swearta href(e)n' in *Soul and Body II* 54b and *Soul and Body I* 51b is something abhorrent to man (though less abhorrent than the dead body); thus the syntax does not appear to agree with Osborne's analysis.

4 Griffith, 'Convention,' 190–2. Thomas Honegger, 'Form and Function: The Beasts of Battle Revisited,' *ES* 79 (1998): 289–98 at 297–8, treats the metaphor of *wælwulfas* in *Maldon* as a displacement from the topos (but does not comment on the parallels in *Genesis*). Griffith's 'substitution,' too, seems to involve displacement in those two texts, but there are aspects of the concept's exposition that I do not fully understand.

5 Gustav Neckel, 'Die kriegerische Kultur der heidnischen Germanen,' *Germanisch-Romanische Monatsschrift* 7 (1915 [1915–19]): 17–44 at 28, n.; repr. in his *Vom Germanentum: Ausgewählte Aufsätze und Vorträge* (Leipzig: O. Harrassowitz, 1944), 240–68.

6 John Miles Foley, *Immanent Art: From Structure to Meaning in Traditional Oral Epic* (Bloomington: Indiana University Press, 1991), 224–31; Honegger, 'Form and Function.' Jonathan Watson, 'The Minim-istic Imagination: Scribal Invention and the Word in Early English Alliterative Tradition,' *Oral Tradition* 17 (2002): 290–309, subsumes our topos under a broader conception of traditional diction in order to trace the decline and evolution of oral poetic language. I thank Thomas N. Hall and a reader for alerting me to this and other titles, mostly contemporaneous with or later than my work on this article (mid-2002).

7 Griffith, 'Convention,' 183.

8 Griffith, 'Convention,' 189–91. Cf. Gottfried Schramm, *Namenschatz und Dichtersprache: Studien zu den zweigliedrigen Personennamen der Germanen*, Ergänzungshefte zur Zeitschrift für vergleichende Sprachforschung auf dem Gebiet der Indogermanischen Sprachen 15 (Göttingen: Vandenhoeck & Ruprecht, 1957), 77–83 (a section entitled 'Der Mann als Tier') and a

somewhat similar interchange in Welsh heroic poetry, involving 'warrior similes, in which the beast is used either as a simile or a metaphor for the war-like and praiseworthy characteristics of the hero' (David N. Klausner, 'The Topos of the Beasts of Battle in Early Welsh Poetry,' in *The Centre and Its Compass: Studies in Medieval Literature in Honor of Professor John Leyerle*, ed. Robert A. Taylor et al., Studies in Medieval Culture 33 [Kalamazoo: Western Michigan University Press, 1993], 247–63 at 253); see also the 'Discussion' section of Judith Jesch, 'Eagles, Ravens, and Wolves: Beasts of Battle, Symbols of Victory and Death,' in *The Scandinavians from the Vendel Period to the Tenth Century: An Ethnographic Perspective*, ed. Jesch, Studies in Historical Archaeoethnology 5 (Woodbridge, Suffolk: Boydell and the Center for Interdisciplinary Research on Social Stress, San Marino, CA, 2002), 251–71 [with conference discussion at 271–80] in which D.H. Green adduces theriophoric personal names (in the vein of Schramm) as evidence of high antiquity (271–2, 275).

9 Bonjour, '*Beowulf* and the Beasts,' 569; Griffith, 'Convention,' 196.
10 Finnur Jónsson, *Lexicon poeticum antiquæ linguæ septentrionalis: Ordbog over det norsk-islandske skjaldesprog*, 2nd ed. (Copenhagen: Møller, 1931), s.v.
11 Rudolf Meissner, *Die Kenningar der Skalden: Ein Beitrag zur skaldischen Poetik* (Bonn: Schroeder, 1921), 116–26, 202–8. See also Bjarne Fidjestøl, *Det norrøne fyrstediktet*, Universitetet i Bergen, Nordisk institutts skriftserie 11 (Øvre Ervik: Alvheim & Eide, 1982), 200–3 ('Ramn, ørn og ulv').
12 Alexander Haggerty Krappe, 'Tyr et le Loup' and 'Les Corbeaux d'Odin,' in his *Études de mythologie et de folklore germaniques* (Paris: Ernest Leroux, 1928), 11–44.
13 Meissner, *Kenningar*, 118.
14 Jesch, 'Eagles, Ravens,' 254; Jesch, *Ships and Men in the Late Viking Age: The Vocabulary of Runic Inscriptions and Skaldic Verse* (Woodbridge, Suffolk: Boydell, 2001), 247–54 at 248.
15 Heinrich Beck, 'Die Tiere der Jagd und Walstatt in den eddischen Liedern,' in *Das Tier in der Dichtung*, ed. Schwab and Harkort, 55–73, 259–67. Nils von Hofsten, *Eddadikternas djur och växter*, Skrifter utgivna av Kungl. Gustav Adolfs akademien 30 (Uppsala: Lundequist, 1957) is a study of eddic fauna and flora with a view to localization in time and place, rather than in oral–literary history; Jesch, 'Eagles, Ravens,' 261–5, surveys 'other Norse poetry' in order to delineate 'the specifically Scandinavian symbolic uses of this motif and to demonstrate what these reveal about the ideologies of early Scandinavian society' (251).
16 Beck, 'Tiere,' 56.
17 Neckel, 'Die kriegerische Kultur.'

18	Joseph Harris

18 Jesch, 'Eagles, Ravens,' 254, 258, 260, 263, 266; *Ships and Men*, 250.
19 Hill, 'The *Virga* of Moses and the Old English *Exodus*,' in *Old English Literature in Context: Ten Essays*, ed. John D. Niles (Cambridge: D.S. Brewer, 1980), 57–65, 165–7 at 64; Roberta Frank, 'Did Anglo-Saxon Audiences Have a Skaldic Tooth?' *Scandinavian Studies* 59 (1987): 338–55 at 348 and more generally 347–52.
20 Frank, 'Skaldic Tooth,' 348.
21 Jesch also disagrees with Frank on the point of a common Germanic origin (explicitly, 'Eagles, Ravens,' 272; implicitly, 266 and elsewhere, though without mentioning the MHG passages) and on the case for skaldic influence.
22 *Das Annolied: Mittelhochdeutsch und Neuhochdeutsch*, ed. and trans. Eberhard Nellmann (Stuttgart: Reclam, 1975). Schramm, *Namenschatz*, 81–3, with a note (83, n. 6) from Wolfgang Mohr, citing the *Annolied* passage.
23 Grimm, *Andreas und Elene* (Cassel: T. Fischer, 1840), xxvii and generally xxv–xxviii. If Frank ('Skaldic Tooth,' 348) overlooked Grimm's MHG passages, she may have been misled by E.G. Stanley (*The Search for Anglo-Saxon Paganism* [Cambridge: D.S. Brewer, 1975]; repr. in his *Imagining the Anglo-Saxon Past: The Search for Anglo-Saxon Paganism and Anglo-Saxon Trial by Jury* [Cambridge: D.S. Brewer, 2000], 3–110 at 16), whose translation from Grimm she quotes; Stanley correctly cites the page (xxvii) on which Grimm's discussion of MHG analogues begins, but does not mention them.
24 *Wiener Exodus*, ed. Edgar Papp, *Die altdeutsche Exodus: Untersuchungen und kritischer Text* (Munich: W. Fink, 1968); Wolfram von Eschenbach, *Willehalm: Text der 6. Ausgabe von Karl Lachmann*, trans. and ed. Dieter Kartschoke (Berlin: Walter de Gruyter, 1968); *Rabenschlacht*, ed. Ernst Martin, in *Deutsches Heldenbuch*, 5 vols, Reihe Texte des Mittelalters (1866–70; repr. Dublin: Weidmann, 1963–68), 2:219–326; *Dietrichs Flucht*, ed. Martin, in *Deutsches Heldenbuch*, 2:57–215. To Grimm's examples add *Biterolf und Dietleib* 3776–9, ed. Oskar Jänicke in *Deutsches Heldenbuch*, 1:1–197; *Kudrun* 911, 1–3, ed. Ernst Martin (Halle: Waisenhaus, 1872); *Kaiserchronik* 4293–300, ed. Edward Schröder, *Die Kaiserchronik eines Regensburger Geistlichen*, in *Deutsche Chroniken und andere Geschichtsbücher des Mittelalters*, 6 vols, MGH, Scriptorum qui vernacula lingua usi sunt (1892; repr. Dublin: Weidmann, 1969), 1.1:1–392; and *Dietrichs Flucht*, 9891–2. Grimm, 'Über das verbrennen der leichen,' in his *Kleinere Schriften*, vol. 2: *Abhandlungen zur Mythologie und Sittenkunde* (1849; repr. Hildesheim: G. Olms, 1991), 211–313 at 212, n. 1, gives two more MHG references, in addition to others from Homer, the New Testament, Scandinavian ballads, ON, and chansons de geste; the other significant

annotations are notes to the cited editions of *Kudrun*, *Biterolf*, and *Exodus*. Professor Hill has pointed out to me (personal communication) a fine instance of all three beasts of battle together in Italian epic (Ariosto, *Orlando furioso*, canto 14, st. 1); Frank, 'Skaldic Tooth,' and J.R. Hall, '*Exodus* 166b, *cwyldrof*; 162–67, The Beasts of Battle,' *Neophilologus* 74 (1990): 112–21, cite numerous similar allusions from the Bible and Carolingian literature.

25 Some support for this speculation may be found in V.I. Kulakov and M.Yu. Markovets, 'Birds as Companions of Germanic Gods and Heroes,' *Acta Archaeologica* 75 (2004): 179–88, esp. 180–1, and their references.

26 Frank, 'Skaldic Tooth,' 349, gives two instances, Jesch, 'Eagles, Ravens,' 255, two more (not counting a repetition of one of Frank's examples), and Meissner, *Die Kenningar*, 118, one more (not counting a repetition, 119). All this is, of course, premature without a complete interrogation of the corpus and consideration of the differing styles at play. Klausner, 'Beasts of Battle,' 255, comments that 'the three-animal grouping' is absent in Welsh; but when, citing Frank, he states that the beasts 'do not appear in their traditional grouping in continental Germanic literatures' (248), is he defining the topos by the triad?

27 Neckel, 'Die kriegerische Kultur,' 26, and 29, n. 2, citing Grimm, *Andreas und Elene*, and the *Kudrun* passage with its annotation.

28 J.R.R. Tolkien, ed., *The Old English 'Exodus': Text, Translation, and Commentary*, ed. Joan Turville-Petre (Oxford: Clarendon, 1981), 49–50, took three of the four as echoes of dark pagan words, implicitly English; I would largely subscribe to Tolkien's treatment of *wælceasega* and *cwyldrof*, but to the overall textual interpretation of lines 161–9 in Peter J. Lucas, *Exodus*, rev. ed., Exeter Medieval English Texts and Studies (Exeter: University of Exeter Press, 1994). See Hall, '*Exodus* 166b' for a thorough discussion from a different angle.

29 Frank, 'Skaldic Tooth,' 350.

30 Hill, 'The *Virga*,' 64. On this troubled equation see now Heinrich Beck et al., eds, *Zur Geschichte der Gleichung 'germanisch-deutsch': Sprache und Namen, Geschichte und Institutionen*, Ergänzungsbände zum Reallexikon der Germanischen Altertumskunde 34 (Berlin: Walter de Gruyter, 2004). Frank's criticism of Hill is focused on his example of *Exodus*'s Germanic poetic idiom ('The *Virga*,' 64): 'ecg grymetode' (408). Frank counters that '[t]he half line occurs nowhere else in Old English; it is unknown in Frisian, Old Saxon, Old Low Franconian, Old High German, and Gothic; but there are exact parallels in the verse of the skalds' ('Skaldic Tooth,' 348). The negative evidence would be more impressive if there were more traditional verse preserved in Gothic and the rest, but the skaldic parallels are also less than

satisfying. The half-line does not occur there either; *grenja,* the verb we are referred to, is etymologically unconnected with *grymet(t)an*; Jónsson, *Lexicon poeticum,* gives only five examples of *grenja* with a sword (never with *egg*), one from the late tenth century, the rest composed long after the Junius manuscript. There is at least one parallel in *Beowulf* that seems as good as those of the skalds (if a singing weapon is as good as a growling one), 'þæt hire on hafelan hringmæl agol / grædig guðleoð' (1521–2a), and it is strongly supported as traditional by an eddic passage that equally imagines a sword singing on someone's head: 'Bítia þér þat sverð, er þú bregðir, / nema siálfom þér syngvi um hǫfði' (*HHII* 33) and weakly by another that mentions simply the song of weapons (*Atlakviða* 32, 7). (Oddly, Beowulf's singing sword also 'bitan nolde' [1523] as in *HHII* 33.) Grimm's essay 'Vom singen der schwerter und pfannen,' in his *Kleinere Schriften,* vol. 5: *Rezensionen und vermischte Aufsätze,* Part 2 (1846; repr. Hildesheim: G. Olms, 1991), 362–5, collects a variety of singing weapons and armour, including *Beowulf* 322b–3a (see also Hugo Gering, *Kommentar zu den Liedern der Edda,* vol. 2: *Heldenlieder,* ed. Barend Sijmons, Germanistische Bibliothek 7, Die Lieder der Edda 3 [Halle: Waisenhaus, 1931], 2:124 [my source for the Grimm reference], 357; and Jónsson, *Lexicon poeticum,* s.v. *syngva*). In fact, singing may *not* be as significant as growling in this context, and I obviously do not mean to suggest that in the large skaldic corpus there are not many noisy weapons, but only to recall that skaldic poetry too is a development of the general Germanic poetic tradition.

31 Neckel, 'Die kriegerische Kultur,' 27–9. Clearly placed before battle and anticipatory in mood are the three passages from *Elene* (listed on p. 4), *Genesis A* 1983b–5a, *Finnsburg* 5–7, *Judith* 205–12, and the *Exodus* passage (though here no real battle develops). *Maldon* 106–7 also stands anticipatorily on the cusp of the main battle, although some action has taken place before; the similarly worded *Finnsburg* 34–6 is likewise an omen of the general engagement to come even though some individuals have already fallen. *Judith* 295–6a is slightly more problematic: a stage of the battle has finished, and the dead lie at the pleasure (*willa*) of wolves and to the joy (*frofor*) of carrion-greedy birds; but they are not shown at work, and the battle continues. The passage seems both anticipatory and retrospective. Omitting *Beowulf,* which is to be discussed separately, three of the thirteen OE passages qualify as epilogues to battle: *Brunanburh* 60–5a and *Genesis A* 2087b–9a and 2159b–61 (the latter in a speech that reports the incident of lines 2087b–9a, in effect doubling it). Griffith, who is not concerned with the idea I am pursuing, summarizes the OE topos as anticipatory of battle in about half its occurrences ('Convention,' 187); I would modify that percentage to at least two thirds.

32 John D. Niles, 'Skaldic Technique in *Brunanburh*,' *Scandinavian Studies* 59 (1987): 356–66; Joseph Harris, '*Brunanburh* 12b–13a and Some Skaldic Passages,' in *Magister Regis: Studies in Honor of Robert Earl Kaske*, ed. Arthur Groos, with Emerson Brown, Jr, Thomas D. Hill, Giuseppe Mazzotta, and Joseph S. Wittig (New York: Fordham University Press, 1986), 61–8. Cf. Jesch, 'Eagles, Ravens,' 258: 'The *Battle of Brunanburh* can be seen as a kind of Old English praise poem which has occasionally (and rather superficially) been likened to skaldic verse'; and Joseph Harris, 'Die altenglische Heldendichtung,' in *Neues Handbuch der Literaturwissenschaft*, vol. 6: *Europäisches Frühmittelalter*, ed. Klaus von See (Wiesbaden: AULA-Verlag, 1985), 237–76 at 248–54 ('Preislied und Zeitgedicht: *Brunanburh* und *Maldon*').

33 Niles, 'Skaldic Technique,' 358.

34 Joseph Harris, 'Hadubrand's Lament: On the Origin and Age of Elegy in Germanic,' in *Heldensage und Heldendichtung im Germanischen*, ed. Heinrich Beck, Ergänzungsbände zum Reallexikon der Germanischen Altertumskunde 2 (Berlin: Walter de Gruyter, 1988), 81–114 at 82 and passim; Daniel Sävborg, *Sorg och elegi i Eddans hjältediktning*, Acta Universitatis Stockholmiensis, Stockholm Studies in History of Literature 36 (Stockholm: Almqvist & Wiksell, 1997), 5 and passim.

35 Tacitus, *Germania* 10.9, ed. Rudolf Much, in *Die Germania des Tacitus*, 3rd. ed. rev. by Herbert Jankuhn and Wolfgang Lange (Heidelberg: Winter, 1967), 189, with commentary at 194.

36 Much's note (*Die Germania*, 194–5) constructs an interesting nativistic schema of compass direction.

37 All quotations from the *Poetic Edda* are from *Edda: Die Lieder des Codex Regius nebst verwandten Denkmälern*, vol. 1: *Text*, ed. Gustav Neckel, 4th ed. rev. by Hans Kuhn, Germanische Bibliothek, Reihe 4: Texte (Heidelberg: Carl Winter, 1962). A related sign of luck there [*Rm* 22] pertains to the wolf's voice: 'Þat er iþ þriðia, ef þú þióta heyrir / úlf und asclimom' [this is the third (sign) if you hear a wolf howl under the boughs of the ash].

38 For a thorough study of the complex raven-banner material, see Nils Lukman, 'The Raven Banner and the Changing Raven: A Viking Miracle from Carolingian Court Poetry to Saga and Arthurian Romance,' *Classica et Mediaevalia* 19 (1958): 133–51; for a briefer one, Jesch, *Ships and Men*, 252–4. The Vendel helmet-plate is widely reproduced in a schematic drawing that shows two presumably Odinic ravens, but the photograph in Jan de Vries, *Altgermanische Religionsgeschichte*, 2nd ed., 2 vols, Grundriss der Germanischen Philologie 12 (1956; repr. Berlin: Walter de Gruyter, 1970), Tafel XIII and page 43, leaves room for doubt. An incident in the Anglo-Latin *Vita Gregorii*, ed. and trans. Bertram Colgrave, *The Earliest Life of Gregory the*

Great by an Anonymous Monk of Whitby (1968; repr. Cambridge: Cambridge University Press, 1985), cites as an ill omen a raven's call and the direction it comes from (*ad plagam peiorem*); but the raven would seem to be on a tree rather than flying ('from an unpropitious quarter of the sky') since it is shot dead with an arrow (96–9; see also Colgrave's note referring to Tacitus). Cf. the eddic *Brot* 5 and 13.

39 Cf. Derek Ratcliffe, *The Raven: A Natural History in Britain and Ireland* (London: Poyser, 1997), 14.
40 See the authoritative collections in *Handwörterbuch des deutschen Aberglaubens*, ed. Hanns Bächtold-Stäubli and Eduard Hoffmann-Krayer, 10 vols (1927–42; repr. Berlin and Leipzig: Walter de Gruyter, 1987), s.v. 'Rabe,' 'Krähe,' 'Adler,' and 'Wolf'; and in *Reallexikon der Germanischen Altertumskunde*, ed. Heinrich Beck et al., 2nd rev. ed. (Berlin: Walter de Gruyter, 1967–), s.v. 'Adler' and 'Adlerssymbolik.' Among many relevant collections of popular lore, see, for example, Ernst Gattiker and Luise Gattiker, *Die Vögel im Volksglauben: Eine volkskundliche Sammlung aus verschiedenen europäischen Ländern von der Antike bis heute* (Wiesbaden: AULA-Verlag, 1989); Ludwig Hopf, *Thierorakel und Orakelthiere in alter und neuer Zeit: Eine ethnologisch-zoologische Studie* (Stuttgart: Kohlhammer, 1888); R. Bosworth Smith, *Bird Life and Bird Lore* (London: John Murray, 1905); and Ratcliffe, *The Raven*, esp. ch. 1.
41 Griffith, 'Convention,' 185.
42 Unless very indirectly as *gaman*: *HHII* 33.
43 Bernd Heinrich, *The Mind of the Raven: Investigations and Adventures with Wolf-Birds* (New York: HarperCollins, 1999), esp. ch. 16; Ratcliffe, *The Raven*, esp. ch. 14; Smith, *Bird Life*, chs. 2–4 passim.
44 Frederick Klaeber, 'A Few Béowulf Notes,' *MLN* 16 (1901): cols 28–35 at 36.
45 Beck, 'Tiere,' 70–2.
46 Hume, 'The Function of the *hrefn blaca*: *Beowulf* 1801,' *MP* 67 (1969): 60–3 at 62. Andy Orchard, *A Critical Companion to 'Beowulf'* (Cambridge: D.S. Brewer, 2003), 77–8, lists some other studies of this passage in connection with his own reading, based on internal parallelism and audience expectations; but most general interpretations of the poem will have treated this conspicuous passage.
47 Puhvel, 'The Blithe-Hearted Morning Raven in *Beowulf*,' *ELN* 10 (1973): 243–7 at 247. The name *Dæghrefn* may belong to this strand of tradition.
48 More literally 'dew-coloured' (see Jónsson, *Lexicon poeticum*, s.v.); *litr* alone had a special usage connected with daybreak (Richard Cleasby and Gudbrand Vigfusson, *An Icelandic-English Dictionary*, 2nd ed. rev. by William A. Craigie [Oxford: Clarendon, 1957], s.v.; Jónsson, *Lexicon poeticum*, s.v.).

49 The reading 'hrefn blaca' is of course unobjectionable in view of nature and the regular application of the colour words *sweart, salwigpada, sealobrun,* and *wonn* (but apparently not *blæc*) to ravens elsewhere in verse, including *Beowulf* 3024b; but *dǫgglitr* does tempt one to think of the less obvious *blāc* 'shining.' Hume, '*Beowulf* 1801,' 63, anticipates this speculation (without the comparative material) but seems to think (as I do not) that the manuscript form is intended to capture both meanings in a pun. E.G. Stanley, 'Old English Poetic Diction and the Interpretation of *The Wanderer, The Seafarer* and *The Penitent's Prayer*,' *Anglia* 73 (1956): 413–66 at 443, relates the raven in this passage to quite different contexts. John Edward Damon, 'The Raven in Beowulf 1801: Bird of a Different Color,' *Work in Progress: Working Papers by Graduate Students of the English Dept. at the University of Arizona* (Tucson, AZ) 1 (1990): 60–70, also anticipates my suggestion here, constructing a good case with the Norse sources; however, I cannot follow him further to the meaning 'white' with all that would entail (65–9). I thank librarians at Harvard and the University of Arizona for procuring this bibliographical rarity for me at the eleventh hour.

50 An interesting analogue, attributed to an Icelander of about 955, is preserved in two stanzas of *Hrómundar þáttr halta*, ed. Einar Ól. Sveinsson, Íslenzk Fornrit 8 (Reykjavík: Hið íslenzka fornritafélag, 1939), 303–15. (Hume, '*Beowulf* 1801,' 61, who was the first to cite this passage, quotes the first stanza from the *Landnámabók* version, where the passage is condensed from this *þáttr*.) In the introductory prose the hero awakens to the call of a raven sitting on his house, then speaks two verses (translated with resolved kennings marked *): [1:] 'I hear a black-feathered *raven call as morning comes; [expectation of or need of] food wakens the cautious-minded one; so sang the *raven of old when (*) heroes were doomed, when *ravens spoke their prophecies.' [2:] 'Sprayed with hail, the *raven calls when it comes to *blood; tired [from its flight?], it craves its morning meal; so sang in times of yore the *raven from the ancient oath-tree when *ravens wanted *blood.' The scene in both the story and the poem is early morning though 'sun' is lacking; the ravens' state of mind contrasts with *Beowulf* and the eddic passages, but the poet (or poets, for there are controversies here I cannot go into) shows awareness of the antiquity of the conventions he is using.

51 Cf. 'ætes on wenan' (*Exodus* 165b) and similar expressions (*Genesis A* 1985a; *Judith* 210a; *Maldon* 107a); *HH* and *HHII* (but not *Beowulf*) are further linked by the expression of the beasts' knowledge with *vita* (cf. *Judith* 207b; *Haraldskvæði* 3, 8, in *Skjaldevers*, ed. Jón Helgason, 3rd ed. [Copenhagen: Munksgaard, 1968], 10–21).

52 But this is simply the widespread belief that the dead come by night and vacate the world at or before daybreak (as also in *HHII* 50–1); the light effects associated with the opening of funeral mounds in *The Waking of Angantýr* are infernal rather than diurnal.

53 Could the bright one who hastens (1802b) to the hastening colleagues (1803b) be Beowulf ([*scealc*] perhaps?) instead of the sun? In *Beowulf, beorht* is applied twice to the Danes, but not to an individual man.

54 Cf. Klaeber's note to line 3022 and *Haraldskvæði* 3, ed. Helgason, which puts the ravens' feast at daybreak ('at degi ǫndverðum').

55 The (seemingly unrealistic) idea of warriors being awakened to the harp resonates with the famous performance of the *Bjarkamál* or *Húskarlahvǫt* on the morning of the battle of Stiklastaðir and with the controversy over the authenticity of that passage (Joseph Harris, 'Eddic Poetry,' in *Old Norse-Icelandic Literature: A Critical Guide*, ed. Carol J. Clover and John Lindow, Islandica 45 [Ithaca, NY: Cornell University Press, 1985], 68–156 at 118–19). The familiar waking topos itself implies a (final) catastrophic battle; cf. esp. the warriors of *Finnsburg Fragment* (5b–7a, 10), who are wakened against a background of the sounds of war-gear and the vocalizing beasts. Cf. Foley, *Immanent Art*, 230–1, on the harp here.

56 On the affiliation of valkyries with ravens, see Gustav Neckel, *Walhall: Studien über germanischen Jenseitsglauben* (Dortmund: F.W. Ruhfus, 1913), 79, 130; Charles Donahue, 'The Valkyries and the Irish War-Goddesses,' *PMLA* 56 (1941): 1–12 at 3–4 and passim; Angelique Gulermovich Epstein, 'The Morrígan and the Valkyries,' in *Studies in Honor of Jaan Puhvel*, ed. John Greppin and Edgar C. Polomé, 2 vols, Journal of Indo-European Studies Monograph 20–1 (Washington, DC: Institute for the Study of Man, 1997), 2:119–50.

57 Stanley, 'Old English Poetic Diction,' 443.

58 The wonderful ballad analogue 'The Twa Corbies/Three Ravens' (*The English and Scottish Popular Ballads*, ed. Francis James Child, 5 vols [1882–98; repr. New York: Dover, 1965], no. 26) is noted by Klaeber; and Grimm compared folktales: 'so führen noch in heutigen kindermärchen die raben und krähen ihr gespräch' (*Andreas und Elene*, xxviii). The grotesque American derivatives of Child 26 may be related to the buzzards' eerie funeral for Matt Bronner's mule in Zora Neale Hurston's *Their Eyes Were Watching God* (Philadelphia: J.B. Lippincott, 1937), but the hypothesis of continuity implied by 'survival' poses classic questions.

59 For a sampling of the huge literature on the relevant Celtic themes, see the following: Donahue, 'Valkyries'; Epstein, 'The Morrígan'; and Anne Ross,

Pagan Celtic Britain: Studies in Iconography and Tradition (1967; repr. Chicago: Academy Chicago, 1996), esp. ch. 6.
60 For two examples of efforts to make the connection, see Osborn, 'Finnsburg Raven' (with emphasis on mediation); J.S. Ryan, 'Othin in England: Evidence from the Poetry for a Cult of Woden in Anglo-Saxon England,' *Folklore* 74 (1963): 460–80 (with emphasis on a cult of Woden). Klausner, 'Beasts of Battle,' writes within the formalist tradition, taking OE as the starting point of his survey and ending elegantly with the two eagle poems from the Heledd group, where the topos has become 'the core of the poems': 'These two poems provide an extraordinary glimpse of the effects a fine poet could produce by utilizing a traditional topos in an unusual manner' (263). Jesch's excursus into early Welsh is concerned with secular functions rather than religious roots ('Eagles, Ravens,' 259–60), and her general comments on this subject are cautious (267, 275).
61 Grimm, *Andreas und Elene*, xxv.
62 Grimm, *Andreas und Elene*, xxviii; the quotation following is from page xxvii. Grimm's remarks are based on eddic poetry; in 1840 he knew very little about skaldic poetry (Neckel, 'Die kriegerische Kultur,' 30; Jesch, 'Eagles, Ravens,' 254, n. 3; 266, n. 32).

The Fates of Men in *Beowulf*

JAMES H. MOREY

For many readers of the Bible or *Beowulf*, genealogies are some of the most daunting and least interesting features. All teachers of *Beowulf* struggle to disentangle for their students the various members of the Danish, Geatish, and Swedish royal houses and to these ends every edition or translation of *Beowulf* provides the obligatory outline of the relevant dynastic stemma. This essay is no different, but in order to clarify my argument the genealogies here note how each of the kings and princes met his demise. In analysing the mode of death for each of the successors to the various thrones I hope to explain how Beowulf qualifies for kingship and to suggest why Grendel has been visited upon the Danish house. At the risk of oversimplification, one can say that Geats and Swedes meet violent ends, and Danes meet non-violent, or at least unexplicit, ones (figure 1). I also suggest that the various modes of death, and the oxymoronic idea of an 'unexplicit end,' are themselves meaningful. Nothing is more central to the poem than the connection between the *cyning* and the *cyn*, and like the old Heathobard warrior who incites his younger kinsman to behold the spoils of his ancestors and to avenge them (2041ff.), listeners to and readers of the poem – especially aristocratic ones with personal and family dynastic ambitions – would be keenly interested in the identity, claim to the throne, and fate of each of these princes and kings.

The poem itself provides a great deal of information concerning the fates of the royal figures, such that the role played by death in the succession to the Danish, Geatish, and Swedish thrones is a recurrent and almost obsessive theme. The poem could indeed be called a series of 'sad stories of the death of kings' (*Richard II*, III.ii.156). At points, other literary and historical texts – for example, *The Saga of King Hrolf Kraki*,

The Fates of Men in *Beowulf* 27

Figure 1. The Fates of Men in *Beowulf*

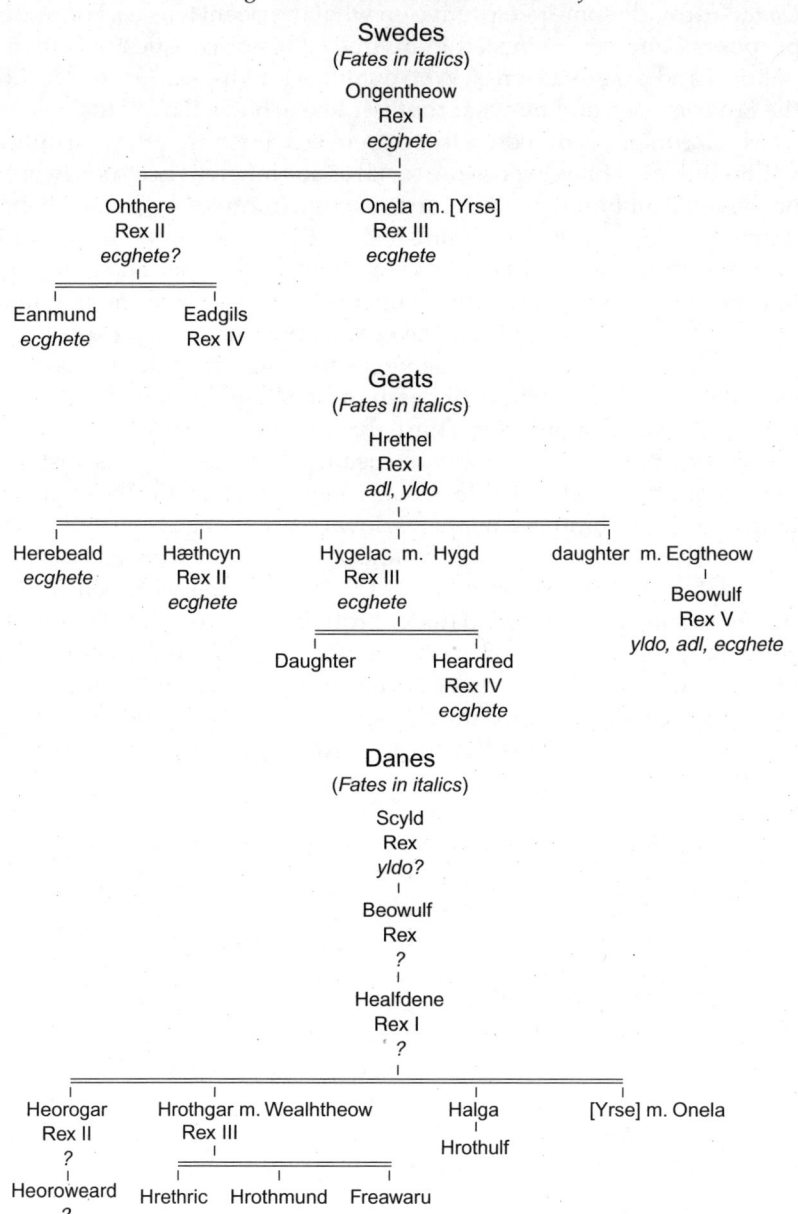

Swedes
(*Fates in italics*)

Ongentheow
Rex I
ecghete

- Ohthere — Rex II — *ecghete?*
  - Eanmund — *ecghete*
  - Eadgils — Rex IV
- Onela m. [Yrse] — Rex III — *ecghete*

Geats
(*Fates in italics*)

Hrethel
Rex I
adl, yldo

- Herebeald — *ecghete*
- Hæthcyn — Rex II — *ecghete*
- Hygelac m. Hygd — Rex III — *ecghete*
  - Daughter
  - Heardred — Rex IV — *ecghete*
- daughter m. Ecgtheow
  - Beowulf — Rex V — *yldo, adl, ecghete*

Danes
(*Fates in italics*)

Scyld
Rex
yldo?

Beowulf
Rex
?

Healfdene
Rex I
?

- Heorogar — Rex II — *?*
  - Heoroweard — *?*
- Hrothgar m. Wealhtheow — Rex III
  - Hrethric
  - Hrothmund
  - Freawaru
- Halga
  - Hrothulf
- [Yrse] m. Onela

Snorri Sturluson's *Ynglingasaga*, and Saxo Grammaticus's *History of the Danes* – provide some perspective on what the poem tells us. For present purposes I am less interested in mythic or historical questions than in political and pragmatic ones. Who qualifies for kingship in the world of the *Beowulf* poet, and by what route did he achieve that status?[1]

My argument is based on three premises. First, that the disruptions within the royal lines expose the social chaos inherent in a society based on personal ambition, feuding, and revenge (motives for human behaviour which have not yet diminished in their potency).[2] Second, that sons and brothers would either know how their father and close male kinsmen died, or would dedicate themselves to discovering that information. The issue is cognitive: the *Beowulf* poet knew, and expected his audience to seek to know, the same information. Even the omission or elision of the circumstances of death can be, like the dog that does not bark in the night, significant. Third, that primogeniture was in theory, if not in practice, the conventional means of succession. As historical studies of the period make clear, many men are theoretically eligible for kingship – sons, brothers, nephews, loyal thanes, or anyone with an ego and a sword – and one can find almost any permutation among these candidates in the historical record.[3] The tension between vertical (father to son) and horizontal (older brother to younger brother or other close male relative) models is ever present; the case of Alfred is a spectacular example of horizontal succession, as personal aptitude and political necessity trumped the claims of the sons of four elder brothers, three of whom had ruled Wessex in turn. It still remains the case that the usual mode of succession – as we see in *Beowulf* itself – is by the first-born son of the first-born son. The opening genealogy from Scyld to Healfdene endorses the practice, as do lines 910–11: 'þæt ðeodnes bearn geþeon scolde / fæderæþelum onfon, folc gehealdan' [(it was hoped that) that prince's son would prosper, receive his father's rank, rule his people].[4] *Ceteris paribus*, the son should succeed the father, as in fact happened after Alfred's death. Strict primogeniture may be a fiction, but it is an appealing fiction; it may be an anachronistic projection of later practice on earlier Germanic custom, but it provides the kind of political clarity and stability that the *Beowulf* poet seeks.

Chapter 7 of Tacitus's *Germania* is usually cited as one of the few hard pieces of evidence concerning the Germanic mode of succession to the throne: 'Kings they choose for their birth, generals for their valour.'[5] What Fritz Kern calls 'throne-worthiness' is surely a combination of hereditary right, merit, and approval by the ruling elite if not by the people at large.[6] Various combinations of succession by first-born male, succession by oldest relative, and succession through some kind of election have been adduced, inconclusively, to ascertain some kind of rule for succession. The *Beowulf* poet assumes the normative force of primogeniture, but highlights the exceptions to that norm as the stuff of poetry. The most obvious threat to an orderly succession is intra-generational, from younger brothers and cousins who seek the throne. As Kemp Malone demonstrates in his *Literary History of Hamlet*,[7] stories of family treachery are of ancient Nordic vintage.

Hrothgar, in lines 1736–8 of his 'sermon,' specifies the three causes of death for humankind: *adl* [illness], *yldo* [age], and *ecghete* [violence]. The narrator of *The Seafarer* specifies the same three alliterating alternatives (70), and these 'fates of men' are treated at length in the Exeter Book poem of that title. In examining the fates of kings and princes in *Beowulf*, close attention to the language used, and sometimes simply to the amount of language used, to describe the deaths reveals that the poet was careful either to make explicit, or deliberately to obscure, who killed whom by what means. The poet's reasons are strategic and political. In this regard, I follow the model Thomas D. Hill provides in his essay 'The Variegated Obit,' where he demonstrates that the language used in the obituaries for various kings by Christian historians and by the *Beowulf* poet reveals 'metaphysical claims [concerning the salvation or damnation of individuals] whose truth they cannot really claim to know, in order to affirm the validity of specific institutions – in the first instance the English church, in the second Germanic kingship.'[8] Leaving aside metaphysics, and making no claims with regard to actual fact, I hope to impose some order on the dynastic confusion by examining how the poet chooses to convey the information surrounding the deaths of princes and kings.

Brothers, uncles, and nephews feud in the Swedish royal family, creating a dark microcosm of events impinging on the Danish and Geatish thrones. The patriarch Ongentheow dies at Ravenswood in a battle described twice in the poem, first briefly where the King 'hreas heoroblac' [2488: staggered, corpse-pale] and later in a dramatic last stand, full of counter-strokes and reversals, when two young Geats, Eofor and Wulf, bring him down.[9] The language in the second episode is almost operatic in its pathos, covering Ongentheow in glory even as he falls: 'ða gebeah cyning / folces hyrde, wæs in feorh dropen' [2980–1: then the king stumbled, shepherd of his people, mortally stricken]. The number of lines – over twenty – devoted to his death indicates his importance, and though the expression *folces hyrde* does not guarantee his salvation, it carries a Christian overtone (see, for example Ps. 77:52, Matt. 9:36, John 10:11ff.). After the death of King Ongentheow, Onela disrupts the succession by seizing the throne from his older brother Ohthere (presumably violently, though the poem gives no indication of whether or how he dies), and by driving Ohthere's sons Eanmund and Eadgils into exile at King Heardred's court (2379–84).[10] Weohstan, father of Wiglaf, kills Prince Eanmund on behalf of King Onela: 'Þam æt sæcce wearð / wræccan wineleasum Weohstan bana' [2612–13: that friendless exile was slain in battle with the edge of a sword by Weohstan]. Thus, presumably, Eadgils will seek vengeance on Wiglaf, as he fears in lines 2999–3001, and we know that Onela dies violently at the hand of Eadgils: 'he gewræc syððan / cealdum cearsiðum, cyning ealdre bineat' [2395–6: He wreaked his revenge with cold sad journeys, and took the king's life]. All of the deaths result from *ecghete*. In the Swedish house we thus see a three-generation pattern that the other houses seem to follow: a lionized and long-reigning patriarch who represents an older, more stable order receives a complimentary obit, a younger son supplants his elder brother in ambiguous circumstances, and the grandson/nephew becomes king.

The house of Hrethel clearly emulates this pattern; I wish to argue that the Danish house does so as well, with only the implication of the struggle into the third generation. The Danish and Geatish royal houses share a significant genealogical parallel in that the action of the poem centres, in both instances, on the descendants of the two patriarchs, Healfdene and Hrethel, both of whom have a daughter, three sons, and various grandchildren. In the house of Hrethel, Beowulf must overcome two significant obstacles, in formal terms of the succession, to become king of the Geats. First, his claim runs through a female, not a male; second, no fewer than five men representing three generations have to die: Hrethel, Herebeald, Hæthcyn, Hygelac, and Heardred.

The deaths of all five are related in a dramatic passage of 130 lines late in the poem (2354–483). The narrator describes the most recent deaths of Kings Hygelac and Heardred, and Beowulf himself relates the more distant deaths of the other three in an extended analepsis before the attack on the dragon, when his own death is 'ungemete neah' [2420: immeasurably near]. Dead men tell no tales, but dying ones often do. The first to die (according to chronology, but again not in the order the poem presents) is Prince Herebeald, the eldest son of King Hrethel. Beowulf is speaking:

Wæs þam yldestan   ungedefelice
mæges dædum   morþorbed stred,
syððan hyne Hæðcyn   of hornbogan,
his freawine   flane geswencte,
miste mercelses   ond his mæg ofscet,
broðor oðerne   blodigan gare.
Þæt wæs feohleas gefeoht,   fyrenum gesyngad,
hreðre hygemeðe;   sceolde hwæðre swa þeah
æðeling unwrecen   ealdres linnan. (2435–43)

[For the eldest, undeservedly, a death-bed was made by the deeds of a kinsman, after Hæthcyn with his horn bow struck down his own dear lord with an arrow – he missed his mark and murdered a kinsman, one brother to the other with a bloody shaft. That was a fight beyond settling, a sinful crime, shattering the heart; yet it had to be that a nobleman lost his life unavenged.]

The death is clearly violent, and the passage qualifies as an elaborately variegated obit. Hill points out that a variegated obit is a sign of approbation (122); as the wronged party, deserving of sympathy, Herebeald receives one. To call him the 'freawine' recognizes his claim on the throne and is a further endorsement of primogeniture. The circumlocution of 'preparing a murder-bed' implies something more than an accident, and the phrase 'fyrenum gesyngad' conveys the moral import of the crime. Even so, the reference to the fight being 'feohleas' and the prince 'unwrecen' places the death in an unambiguously Germanic, not Christian, context. There are important parallels from Snorri's *Prose Edda* of Hæthcyn with Höð and Herebeald with Baldr, but I am more interested here in the practical implications of the death than the mythic ones.[11]

Hrethel's death follows almost immediately:

He ða mid þære sorhge,   þe him to sar belamp,
gumdream ofgeaf,   Godes leoht geceas;
eaferum læfde,   swa deð eadig mon,
lond ond leodbyrig,   ða he of life gewat. (2468–71)

[Then with the sorrow which befell him too sorely, he gave up man's joys, chose God's light; he left to his children his land and his stronghold – as a blessed man does – when he departed this life.]

For an older man, death by grief over the loss of a son is an ambiguous combination of *yldo* and *adl*, though more of the latter, it seems. Even *ecghete* functions as an ambiguous catalyst. Hill characterizes the death as 'obviously and unequivocally Christian in its ideological implications' given the references to choosing 'God's light' and being 'blessed.'[12]

It is sometimes overlooked that, despite the unhappy circumstances, primogeniture applies and Hæthcyn becomes the king.[13] Nevertheless, he is dead within a dozen lines, while fighting Ongentheow and his sons in back-to-back battles one day prior to the Swedish king's death. Beowulf is still speaking:

> ... Ongenðeowes eaferan wæran
> frome fyrdhwate, freode ne woldon
> ofer heafo healdan, ac ymb Hreosnabeorh
> eatolne inwitscear oft gefremedon.
> Þæt mægwine mine gewræcan,
> fæhðe ond fyrene, swa hyt gefræge wæs,
> ðeah ðe oðer his ealdre gebohte,
> heardan ceape; Hæðcynne wearð,
> Geata dryhtne guð onsæge. (2475–83)

[... the sons of Ongentheow were bold and warlike, wanted no peace over the sea, but around the Hill of Sorrows they carried out a devious and terrible campaign. My friends and kinsmen got revenge (at Ravenswood) for those feuds and evils – as it is said – although one of them paid for it with his own life, a hard bargain; that battle was fatal for Hæthcyn, King of the Geats.]

Later the anonymous messenger from Wiglaf to the Geats recalls how 'Sona him [Hæthcyn] se froda fæder Ohtheres / eald ond egesfull ondslyht ageaf, / abreot brimwisan' [2928–30: Immediately the ancient father of Ohthere, old and terrifying, returned the attack – the old warrior cut down the sea-captain]. Presumably because he is a fratricide, guilty and undeserving of sympathy, Hæthcyn's death is violent and unelaborated. Hygelac arrives the next morning to the relief of the besieged Danes but too late to help Hæthcyn (2941–5). In this sequence, no one can fail to notice that the older the brother, the sooner he dies.

King Hygelac's obit is the most difficult to locate, simply because the circumstances of his death are woven throughout the poem, in classic interlace style, at three different points. The death is violent at the hand of Dæghrefn, in the ill-advised Frisian raid (the narrator is speaking in the first two passages):

> ... hyne wyrd fornam,
> syþðan he for wlenco   wean ahsode,
> fæhðe to Frysum. (1205b–7a)

[... Fate struck him down when in his pride he went looking for woe, a feud with the Frisians.]

> No þæt læsest wæs
> hondgemot[a],   þær mon Hygelac sloh,
> syððan Geata cyning   guðe ræsum,
> freawine folca   Freslondum on,
> Hreðles eafora   hiorodryncum swealt,
> bille gebeaten. (2354b–9a)

[It was not the least of hand-to-hand combats when Hygelac was slain, when the King of the Geats, in the chaos of battle, the lord of his people, in the land of the Frisians, the son of Hrethel, died sword drunk, beaten by blades.]

(The anonymous messenger from Wiglaf to the Geats is speaking):

> Wæs sio wroht scepen
> heard wið Hugas,   syððan Higelac cwom
> faran flotherge   on Fresna land,
> þær hyne Hetware   hilde genægdon,
> elne geeodon   mid ofermægene,
> þæt se byrnwiga   bugan sceolde,
> feoll on feðan; ... (2913b–19a)

[The strife was begun hard with the Hugas, after Hygelac came travelling with his ships to the shores of Frisia, where the Hetware attacked him in war, advanced with valor and a vaster force, so that the warrior in his byrnie had to bow down, and fell amid the infantry.]

The poet first encapsulates the death in a classic Germanic formula – 'hyne wyrd fornam' – then gruesomely elaborates it one thousand lines later. In the person of the messenger the death is considerably softened as Hygelac 'bows downs' and 'falls.' Nonetheless the death is violent, with no hint of salvation. Beowulf escapes alive from that battle, though he does kill Dæghrefn (2501–2).

King Heardred's death is next chronologically, and it is related twice, casually and incidentally, first when 'part two' of the poem begins, with yet another brief reference to Hygelac's death. The narrator is speaking:

Eft þæt geiode ufaran dogrum
hildehlæmmum, syððan Hygelac læg,
ond Hear[dr]ede hildemeceas
under bordhreoðan to bonan wurdon,
ða hyne gesohtan on sigeþeode
hearde hildfrecan, Heaðo-Scilfingas,
niða genægdan nefan Hererices –
syððan Beowulfe brade rice
on hand gehwearf. (2200–8a)

[Then it came to pass amid the crash of battle in later days, after Hygelac lay dead, and for Heardred the swords of battle held deadly slaughter under the shield wall, when the Battle-Scylfings sought him out, those hardy soldiers, and savagely struck down the nephew of Hereric in his victorious nation – then came the broad kingdom into Beowulf's hands.]

The second account follows Hygd's surprising offer of the throne to Beowulf, apparently because she does not trust her son Heardred ['bearne ne truwode,' 2370a]. Bruce Mitchell takes the offer to note that 'direct succession from father to son was not automatic; indeed, Hrothgar himself succeeded his brother Heorogar at the expense of the latter's son Heoroweard.'[14] But what Mitchell cites as a normal occurrence is in fact another exception. That we find Hrothgar where we would expect to find Heoroweard, and that Hygd attempts to sabotage her son's succession, are the disruptions of and threats to usual practice that generate the drama of the poem. By refusing Hygd's offer, Beowulf honours his lord and the convention of primogeniture. In any event, Hygd's offer becomes immaterial as Heardred, an almost forgotten detail, is dead within ten lines (at the hand of Onela, for having sheltered Eanmund and Eadgils). The narrator is speaking:

Him þæt to mearce wearð;
he þær [f]or feorme   feorhwunde hleat,
sweordes swengum,   sunu Hygelaces;
ond him eft gewat   Ongenðioes bearn
hames niosan,   syððan Heardred læg,
let ðone bregostol   Biowulf healdan,
Geatum wealdan;   þæt wæs god cyning. (2384b–90)

[That cost him his life: for his hospitality he took a mortal hurt with the stroke of a sword, that son of Hygelac; and the son of Ongentheow afterwards went to seek out his home, once Heardred lay dead, and let Beowulf hold the high throne and rule the Geats. That was a good king.]

The king is dead; long live the king. The way is finally clear, and Beowulf is 'crowned' with a half-line unmistakably reminiscent of the fabled patriarch Scyld (cf. 11b). For the moment I am less concerned with the convolutions of the succession, and with whatever motives we may assign or infer, than with the modes of death. Of the five men who must die before Beowulf can be king, four die violently, in secular, pagan circumstances. Only Hrethel the patriarch dies from some other cause, with a significantly varied obit that implies salvation. The reflex of the Cain and Abel story generates the legacy of violence, and Beowulf is the final beneficiary, the 'I Claudius' whom, in his youth, no one suspected of royal potential: '(wen)don, ðæt he sleac wære / æðeling unfrom' [2187–8a: they thought that he was slothful, a cowardly nobleman]. Hrethel is also the only figure for whom multiple causes of death could be said to apply. In this respect he foreshadows Beowulf, whose death is an ambiguous mix of *adl*, *ecghete*, and *yldo*.

The Danish line beginning with Healfdene is no less complicated, and it is structurally parallel to the Geatish succession with regard to the number and relationship of the heirs to the throne. There is, however, a significant difference in that none of their fates is specified, and none except Scyld, the arch-patriarch, receives what could be called an obit. Given how meticulously the poet details – sometimes more than once – the deaths of the Swedes and of the Geats (all by *ecghete*) it is very odd that the poet should be reticent about the fate of the Danish royals. A variety of Icelandic and Latin sources sometimes supply this information, and despite their later date and often inconsistent treatment I think it reasonable that the *Beowulf* poet could have supplied this kind of information had he chosen to do so. In the remainder of this essay I shall try to account for this strange contrast. Either the poet was wilfully ignorant and obscure, or he knew that his audience was in command of, or at least curious about, dynastic relationships and the fates of the Danish princes and kings.[15]

For Hrothgar to be king, of course, the patriarchs Scyld, Beowulf Scylding and Healfdene must die, all apparently from *yldo* or *adl*, in unspecified circumstances. Thomas D. Hill finds Scyld's obit in lines 26–7 to be 'unequivocally Christian': 'him ða Scyld gewat to gescæphwile / felahror feran on Frean wære' [Scyld passed away at his appointed hour, the mighty lord went into the Lord's keeping]. Likewise, Hill finds lines 1179–80, though not an obit for Hrothgar, to have 'Biblical and Christian resonances' as Wealtheow anticipates the time when Hrothgar 'forð scyle / metodsceaft seon' [must go forth to face the Maker's decree].[16] Hill also demonstrates Scyld's distinction in that his kingship is divinely sanctioned.[17] The almost messianic Beowulf Scylding, like Enoch or Elijah, lives on, at least insofar as the poem informs us. Scyld and his son live in mythic space, implying some exemption from the sordid contingencies of political life. The events of their reigns are elided into brief commentaries on their characters and a description of Scyld's burial. In like fashion, Beowulf's own fifty-year reign is compressed into two and one half lines (2207–9) followed by an even more elaborate burial scene.

The poet, and presumably the audience, is much more interested in the post-Healfdene dynastic struggle – notably the fitt numbering begins with the advent of Healfdene – but he is ostentatiously vague and even mystical when it comes to telling us how any of the Danes got there, or how they died. Scyld comes and goes from the great deep to the great deep, Beowulf Scylding is born ('cenned,' 12b), reigns gloriously, but then vanishes, and Healfdene 'awakens' ('onwoc,' 56b) with no mention of how he died.[18] His children also 'awake':

Ðæm feower bearn   forðgerimed
in woruld wocun,   weoroda ræswa[n],
Heorogar ond Hroðgar   ond Halga til,
hyrde ic þæt [... wæs On]elan cwen. (59–62)

[Four children, all counted up, were born to that bold leader of hosts: Heorogar, Hrothgar, and Halga the Good, I heard that ... was Onela's queen.]

Line 62, concerning the daughter, has a textual problem; one emendation supplies the name 'Yrse.'[19] Since Hrothgar calls Heorogar his 'yldra mæg' (468) we may assume that Hrothgar is the middle brother. BT define the verb *geriman* as 'to number, reckon,' and they translate 'to him four children, numbered forth, were born into the world.' The primary meaning of the verb *riman* is also 'to count, number,' though it can also mean 'to enumerate, recount, describe in succession' (sense II). Even though the words *forð* and *gerimed* are clearly spaced, Klaeber combines them and glosses the construction 'counted up, all told.' Klaeber's note to line 61 suggests that the order conforms to an 'ancient idiom' of presenting three coordinate proper names with an epithet attached to the last of the three, increasing the 'weight' and importance of that figure, and according to *The Saga of King Hrolf Kraki* Helgi is younger, but more prominent: 'Hroar [Hrothgar] was then twelve years old, but Helgi who was only ten was the bigger and more courageous of the two.'[20] It is worth noting that we have no evidence for the place in the birth order of either daughter (Healfdene's or Hrethel's).

Of the three sons, Halga (Norse Helgi) is best documented, along with his son Hrothulf (Norse Hrolf Kraki) who succeeds his father as king in Denmark.[21] The order Heorogar – Hrothgar – Halga creates another instance of symmetry between the Geatish and Danish lines; a brother (Hæthcyn/Heorogar), now dead, ruled between the current king (Hygelac/Hrothgar) and the patriarch (Hrethel/Healfdene). Heorogar turns out to be the most mysterious figure, in that he is not documented outside of *Beowulf*.[22]

As we have seen, the poet has been careful to specify, often on more than one occasion, the mode of death for all of the Geatish Hrethlings and each Swede except Ohthere. The question remains why we are not told how any of the Danish royals die. When Hrothgar is king, brother Heorogar is definitely dead. We know nothing about the fate of brother Halga and nephew Heoroweard who, by primogeniture, should be king.[23] Hrothgar, recalling the time when Ecgtheow sought his protection, offers only the following cryptic comments:

> Þanon he gesohte   Suð-Dena folc
> ofer yða gewealc,   Ar-Scyldinga;
> ða ic furþum weold   folce Deniga
> ond on geogoðe heold   ginne rice,
> hordburh hæleþa;   ða wæs Heregar dead,

min yldra mæg   unlifigende,
bearn Healfdenes;   se wæs betera ðonne ic! (463–9)

[Thence he (Ecgtheow) sought the South-Dane people over the billowing seas, the Honor-Scyldings; then I first ruled the Danish folk and held in my youth this grand kingdom, city of treasures and heroes – then Heorogar was dead, my older brother unliving, Healfdene's firstborn – he was better than I!]

The account progresses from an unequivocal 'dead,' to a euphemistic 'unliving,' and finally to a wistful half-line eulogy, suggestive but very obscure.[24] Much later Beowulf tells Hygelac that King Heorogar declined to give his son the corselet, which Hrothgar gives to Beowulf and Beowulf gives to Hygelac (2155ff.), even though Heoroweard was loyal to his father ('þeah he him hold wære,' 2161b). Heorogar owned the corselet as king for a 'long while' (2159b) when for some mysterious reason he does not give a dynastic treasure to a loyal son. Because no reason is given for the snub, and because the death of King Heorogar is not specified, creating a vacuum which Hrothgar fills, one suspects that the poet or even Beowulf himself fails to supply these pieces of the puzzle not out of ignorance but because of some tactful politics known to an audience contemporary with the poem but unknown to us.[25] Beowulf is in a position to know the circumstances surrounding the gifts and the succession because he was present in Denmark as a boy (372), presumably when Ecgtheow fled to Denmark shortly after Hrothgar 'first ruled the Danes' (465). Whatever happened to Heorogar (and Heoroweard?), it had happened not long before Ecgtheow arrived with the young Beowulf in tow. Like a taciturn junior executive who knows the company secrets but still plays by the rules and waits his turn, Beowulf is politic enough to leave some things unsaid. In another uncomfortable moment, Hrothgar poses the hypothesis that if Hygelac were to succumb to *adl* or *iren* (1848) Beowulf would be a suitable successor, thus ignoring the claim of Heardred. Even more than a compliment for Beowulf, Hrothgar's suggestion may be a nervous post hoc rationalization of the position in which he finds himself. Beowulf maintains his silence, but as we have seen, he rejects this possibility when it is in fact presented by Queen Hygd (2369). Thus Beowulf honours primogeniture. The poem supplies nothing but a positive reading of Hrothgar who, like Scyld and Beowulf, receives the same half-line endorsement: 'ðæt wæs god cyning' (863). Nevertheless the silence over the fates of his elder brother and nephew raises questions that deserve answers.

Hrothgar is *god*; Halga is *til*, and Heorogar is *betera*. Apart from these adjectives modifying Halga and Heorogar, we know virtually nothing about them insofar as the *Beowulf* poet tells us. There are clues, however, to reconstruct what may have happened. When male kinsmen die, one recalls the litany of kin-slaying among the Swedes and Geats and indeed a story hovering over the entire poem: Cain and Abel. In this context another character is worth investigating: Hunferth, the cryptic *þyle* (1165b, 1456b) at the Danish court. We actually know a good bit about him: he holds an honoured position at Heorot, he possesses a sword of note (Hrunting, 1458), he dislikes being bested by anyone (501–5), and he is accused by Beowulf of fratricide and kin-slaying:

> þeah ðu þinum broðrum   to banan wurde,
> heafodmægum;   þæs þu in helle scealt
> werhðo dreogan,   þeah þin wit duge. (587–9)

[though you became your brothers' killer, your next of kin; for that you needs must suffer punishment in hell, no matter how clever you are.]

The charge is confirmed by the narrator:

>   Swylce þær *Un*ferþ þyle
> æt fotum sæt frean Scyldinga;   gehwylc hiora his ferhþe treowde,
> þæt he hæfde mod micel,   þeah þe he his magum nære
> arfæst æt ecga gelacum. (1165b–8a)

[Likewise Unferth, spokesman, sat at the foot of the Scylding lord; everyone trusted his spirit, that he had great courage, though to his kinsmen he had not been merciful in sword-play.]

As Carol Clover demonstrates, 'Kinship crimes ... form a major theme in the genre [of Norse flytings], and it is a rare flyting that does not exhibit at least one such accusation. It may furthermore be concluded by extrapolation from documentable examples that such insults tend as a group to be true – true at least with respect to the received tradition. The duplicate charge in *HHI* [*Helgakviða Hundingsbana in fyrri*] ... is verified elsewhere.'[26] Hunferth is much more than a clownish jester, the straw-man foil to the wise and strong Beowulf.[27] Whom, in short, did Hunferth kill, and why? We have a murder mystery in reverse in that we start not with the bodies, but with a known perpetrator and unknown victims. It would be a dull audience – medieval or modern – that would not be curious about which 'brothers' and 'kinsmen' Hunferth slew.

The words used to describe the victims progress from *broðor* to *heafodmæg* to the most general term, *mæg*, all in dative plural. The terms *broðrum* and *heafodmægum* may refer to the same two or more people, or they may differentiate between kin categories, much as Hildeburh laments the loss of 'bearnum ond broðrum' (1074) at Finnsburg. Since Hildeburh has actually lost only a son and a brother, we have a generic plural, where plural forms are used with singular reference. Depending on how one parses the lines, Hunferth killed as many as four (or more) kin, and at least two.

Because we know nothing about any of Hunferth's brothers, we may try to determine more precisely the meaning of *heafodmæg*. BT define *heafodmæg* as a 'near relation, a relation in the first degree.' The term appears once in *Andreas*, twice in *Genesis*, and again in *Beowulf*, when Beowulf refers to his uncle Hygelac (2151).[28] Consanguinity is clearly relevant, but if the sense of *heafod* resembles the use of the word adjectivally in words such as *heafodmann, heafodrice, heafodsynn*, and so on, we may infer that Hunferth's victims were in a privileged category. I would add a further refinement. The *Genesis* passages are concerned with succession and rulership, and both Enoch and Japeth are presented in their roles as kings: Enoch is the 'hyrde heafodmaga' after the death of Jared (Gen. 5:20) and Japheth fosters and rules the 'heorðwerod heafodmaga, sunu and dohtra' after the death of Noah (Gen. 9:29). Similarly Beowulf uses the term as he does fealty to his 'beorncyning' (2148) Hygelac: 'ic lyt hafo / heafodmaga nefne, Hygelac, ðec' [2150–1; I have few close kinsmen, my Hygelac, except for you]. These usages connote that *heafodmagas* refers to the close kin of the ruler – the Old English equivalent to a 'first family.' In other words, those closely related to the ruler have *heafodmagas* whereas others have *magas*.[29] The use of the *heafod* element elsewhere in *Beowulf* supports the association with royalty. In line 2909 Wiglaf holds 'heafodwearde' over Beowulf's dead body. BT define the word as 'the guarding of the [lord's] head, attendance as a guard upon the king,' but here too I would maintain that *heafod* should be construed in the sense of 'chief,' not in the literal sense of 'head' (as in, for example, 'heafodbeorg' [1030], a helmet). Wiglaf may well be standing over Beowulf's head, but more to the point he keeps what Kemble calls 'vigilia' over his king.[30] Similarly, the laws list *heafodwearde* as one of the duties owed by a thane to a king.[31]

The more serious objection, of course, is that Hunferth is not named as a relative of any member of the Danish royal house. In response, I offer two pieces of admittedly circumstantial evidence. The scribe – intentionally, I think, and not in error – writes his name consistently four times (the first time as a five-line initial) beginning with 'h.'[32] The 'h' could indicate a connection to the Danish house given that the names of all the other male members begin with that letter. The spelling of the name is usually emended because it requires vocalic alliteration, but Beowulf himself alliterates on the 'h' when he begins his rebuttal: 'Hwæt, þu worn fela, wine min Hunferð' (530). Compare Beowulf's address to Hrothgar, where the alliteration also crosses from 'h' to another consonant and then back: 'Hwæt, we þe þas sælac, sunu Healfdenes ...' (1652). This alliteration pattern is supplementary and ornamental, but it clearly exists. Rather than change what the scribe wrote, it is easier to allow variations in pronunciation based on metrical requirements and dramatic context. In the case of line 530, Beowulf accents the 'h' to signal something about Hunferth's status in Heorot.

The other link between Hunferth and the Danish royal family comes in a much discussed passage which is also the only other mention of Hunferth outside of the flyting:

Þa cwom Wealhþeo forð
gan under gyldnum beage   þær þa goden twegen
sæton suhtergefæderan;   þa gyt wæs hiera sib ætgædere,
æghwylc oðrum trywe.   Swylce þær Unferþ þyle
æt fotum sæt frean Scyldinga;   gehwylc hiora his ferhþe treowde,
þæt he hæfde mod micel,   þeah þe he his magum nære
arfæst æt ecgum gelacum. (1162b–8a)

[Wealhtheow came forth in her golden crown to where the good two sat, nephew and uncle; their peace was still whole then, each true to the other. Likewise Unferth, spokesman, sat at the foot of the Scylding lord; everyone trusted his spirit, that he had great courage, though to his kinsmen he had not been merciful in sword-play.]

Many read this ominous mise en scène to foreshadow future conflict between Hrothgar and Hrothulf, and that the word *swylce* correlates Hrothulf's future conduct with the otherwise otiose recollection of

Hunferth and his crime to indicate his complicity in that conflict.[33] Whether Hunferth continued in his nefarious ways or not, it is at least as likely that the comparison here is Janus-faced. In order to determine how a member of the royal family will behave in the future, note how one has acted in the past.

Because he still holds an honoured position at Hrothgar's court, it is untenable that the killings were outright murder. Another 'intentional accident' to facilitate self-advancement, as in the case of Herebeald and Hæthcyn, is possible, especially since the narrator tells us that 'he his magum nære / arfæst at ecga gelacum' [1167b–8a; to his kinsman he had not been merciful in sword play]. The ambiguous 'play of blades' is sufficiently exculpatory if we imagine a friendly competition gone wrong, though whatever personal advancement Hunferth envisaged it is hard to see him as royal material. I quibble with Liuzza's translation of *arfæst* as 'merciful,' since I would emphasize another sense of *ar*, which is 'honour.' Whatever the circumstances, it was a breach of honour more than a failure to show mercy. Nevertheless, Hunferth cannot be convicted by coincidence. One can only note the ubiquity of kin-killing, the presence of a kin-killer, the association of *heafodmagas* with the ruling family, and the otherwise unexplained death of King Heorogar.

Wealhtheow knows how the world works and therefore recognizes the potential threat posed to her sons from Hrothulf, even as she publicly commends his goodwill (1180ff.). Her entire speech follows the Finnsburg episode, a story in which another woman – Hildeburh – is caught in yet another murderous family feud. The significance of the juxtapositions and the irony in Wealhtheow's commendation are clear as she seeks the defence of last resort, and really the only defence available to a woman, by trying publicly to shame Hrothulf into abandoning his designs against her sons.[34]

John M. Hill argues for another motive for Wealhtheow's commendation of Hrothulf: that she has 'an intense desire to forestall Hrothgar's moves toward Beowulf. In doing so, she offers Hrothulf as an acceptable guardian should Hrothgar die soon.'[35] I disagree, and would point out that she has good reason to be suspicious of Hrothulf *and* Beowulf, whom Hrothgar has adopted in word ('me for sunu wylle / freogan on ferhþe' [947b–8a: I will cherish you ... like a son in my heart']) and deed (the giving of important dynastic treasures [1020ff.]). Beowulf has, in fact, almost literally inserted himself in the Danish line as he sits next to the two brothers in Heorot: 'þær se goda sæt, /

Beowulf Geata be þæm gebroðrum twæm' [1190b–1: the good man, Beowulf the Geat, sat between the brothers (cf. 2013)]. While giving Beowulf the neck-ring (1216), she uses the same strategy of public commendation to oblige Beowulf to be 'lara liðe' [1220a: mild in counsel] to her sons.

There is no suggestion that Hrothgar is complicit in Heorogar's death. Hrothgar, like Hrethel after the death of Herebeald, is another aged king trapped by circumstance, with no legal remedy or obvious course of action. If kin-killing is more than just a simmering possibility in the Danish house, kin-killing underlies the successions to the Swedish, Geatish, and Danish thrones and is the reason why Grendel, kin of Cain (107), has been visited upon Heorot, hall of Hrothgar.[36] In considering the role of Grendel, the monster in the hall is indeed the elephant in the room: what can account for Grendel's twelve-year long depredations upon what seems to be an honourable, well-ruled kingdom? The answer, I propose, is that Hrothgar owes his kingship to the kin-slayer who sits at his feet. Beowulf himself observes that fighting Grendel is really Hunferth's problem and responsibility (590–4). The severity of the supernatural intervention corresponds to the magnitude of the crime.

It is almost easy to suspect Beowulf of the same treacherous motives that operate among the brothers and cousins, and to believe that he engineered his own succession. Onela's apparent complicity in letting Beowulf hold the throne (2389) after the death of Beowulf's lord Heardred does not inspire confidence. The narrator seems to anticipate speculation in this direction when he assures us that Beowulf never wove 'inwitnet' [2167a: nets of evil] for his kin (a claim that Beowulf himself makes at lines 2741–2a: 'me witan ne ðearf Waldend fira / morðorbealo maga' [the Ruler of men need not reproach me with the murder of kinsmen]. He avenges his lord Hygelac ('ic ... Dæghrefne wearð / to handbonan' [2501–2a: I ... slew Dæghrefn ... with my bare hands] and the poet notes that Hygelac's own claim to the throne is only slightly stronger than Beowulf's: 'Him wæs bam samod / on ðam leodscipe lond gecynde, / eard eðelriht, oðrum swiðor / side rice þam ðær selra wæs' [2196b–9: Both of them held inherited land in that nation, a home and native rights, but the wider rule was reserved to the one who was higher in rank]. Beowulf establishes a fifty-year golden age among the Geats the likes of which had not been seen in Scandinavia since the reign of Scyld. The poet takes pains to absolve Beowulf of any treacherous motives lest someone attempt a subversive reading. Beowulf ends, or at least stabilizes for fifty years, the cycle of violence and treachery by refusing to act as so many of the other male figures in the poem do. Fate dictates that Beowulf has no sons of his own (2730–2) who would presumably commit or provoke future violence, so at least Beowulf enjoys a long reign if not a sure succession.[37] Beowulf is the only figure in the poem to avenge himself ('he hyne sylfne gewræc' [2875b]) and his own death – like Hrethel's – could be called a combination of *yldo*, *ecghete*, and *adl*. He must be close to if not over seventy years old, he is wounded in the neck by the dragon, and he describes himself as 'feorhbennum seoc' [2740a: sick with mortal wounds] from the dragon's poison. As the *summum bonum* of Germanic kingship, it takes all three fates to bring Beowulf down.

In a discussion of these lines, Beowulf's dying words (2732–3), Thomas D. Hill demonstrates how the poet foregrounds Beowulf's respect for kinship ties 'implicitly [to] contrast this hero with the heroes of the most famous cycle of heroic legend of the Germanic world, the Volsungs. The *Beowulf* poet does not say that his hero was stronger, or braver, or wiser than the heroes of old; but he does imply that he was better.'[38] Hrothgar says as much in a curiously open-ended comparison:

Þæt, la mæg secgan   se þe soð ond riht
fremeð on folce,   feor eal gemon,
eald eþelweard,   þæt ðes eorl wære
geboren betera! (1700–3)

[One may, indeed, say, if he acts in truth and right for the people, remembers all, old guardian of his homeland, that this earl was born a better man!]

Beowulf's claim to the Geatish throne must not fall under a shadow. Thus the poet carefully documents, however violent and dark the details, the deaths of every one of the five men who precede him. Every candidate who qualifies through primogeniture must die before the obvious choice becomes king. The facts may well be as violent and murderous in Denmark as in Geatland, but the poet submerges them in order to demonstrate the larger lesson that murder will out. Kin-slaying, however well hidden, is the dark family secret that must not be spoken, but haunts Hrothgar and the Danes in the form of Grendel.

NOTES

1 The following have been particularly helpful: Thomas D. Hill, 'Scyld Scefing and the *stirps regia*: Pagan Myth and Christian Kingship in *Beowulf*,' in *Magister Regis: Studies in Honor of Robert Earl Kaske*, ed. Arthur Groos et al. (New York: Fordham University Press, 1986), 37–47; Sam Newton, *The Origins of 'Beowulf' and the Pre-Viking Kingdom of East Anglia* (Cambridge: D.S. Brewer, 1993); Alexander Bruce, *Scyld and Scef: Expanding the Analogues* (New York: Routledge, 2002); M.G. Clarke, *Sidelights on Teutonic History during the Migration Period: Being Studies from Beowulf and Other Old English Poems*, Girton College Studies 3 (Cambridge: Cambridge University Press, 1911). Raymond P. Tripp, Jr, 'Fathers and Sons: Dynastic Decay in *Beowulf*,' *In Geardagum* 16 (1995): 49–60, addresses a related set of issues, in particular how the sons are not up to the job: 'heroes apparently do not beget heroes' (52). Where Tripp sees a pattern of decline, I see a pattern of repetition.

2 John M. Hill disagrees, especially in chapter 1 of *The Cultural World in 'Beowulf,'* Anthropological Horizons (Toronto: University of Toronto Press, 1995): 'Acts of revenge can be good and jurally definitive' (29).

3 See, for example, David N. Dumville, 'The Ætheling: A Study in Anglo-Saxon Constitutional History,' *ASE* 8 (1979): 1–33; Frederick M. Biggs, '*Beowulf* and Some Fictions of the Geatish Succession,' *ASE* 32 (2003): 55–77; and H.R. Loyn, *The Governance of Anglo-Saxon England: 500–1087* (Stanford: Stanford University Press, 1984), 14–19, 92, who accepts that primogeniture is 'the most natural step of all in theory' (16) while noting the inevitable disruptions in practice. Christopher Brooke, *The Saxon and Norman Kings*, 3rd ed., Blackwell Classic Histories of England (Oxford: Blackwell, 2001), notes that 'throughout the history of monarchy in England local custom has been adapted to political circumstance' (8) and that 'the succession to the thrones of the Anglo-Saxon kingdoms and the English kingdom was hedged round with a series of conventions, customs, and assumptions; and out of the dialectic between these conventions each succession was settled – sometimes peacefully, sometimes by violence' (23). Nevertheless 'in the large majority of cases a king was in fact succeeded by his eldest son or nearest male relative' (24).

4 Quotations are from Klaeber with translations from Roy M. Liuzza, *Beowulf: A New Verse Translation* (Orchard Park, NY: Broadview, 2000).

5 Tacitus, *Germania*, ed. J.B. Rives, Clarendon Ancient History Series (Oxford: Clarendon, 1999), 80. See pages 144–9 for a discussion of the difficulty in using classical sources to determine northern European practice.

6 Fritz Kern, *Kingship and Law in the Middle Ages*, trans. S.B. Chrimes, Studies in Mediaeval History 4 (1939; repr. New York: Harper & Row, 1970), 12. Francis B. Gummere, 'The Sister's Son,' in *An English Miscellany Presented to Dr. Furnivall in Honour of His Seventy-Fifth Birthday*, ed. W.P. Ker, A.S. Napier, and W.W. Skeat (1901; repr. New York: AMS, 1973), 133–49, argues for the special rights of the sister's son. Saxo Grammaticus, *The History of the Danes*, ed. Hilda Ellis Davidson, trans. Peter Fisher, 2 vols (Cambridge: D.S. Brewer, 1979–80), describes a 'new method' of voting whereby the electors stand on stones in the ground though the individual so elected – Humbli, son of Dan, eponymous founder of the Danes – resigns 'under the malice of his later fortune,' i.e., fraternal treachery, leading Humbli to conclude 'that a palace may contain more magnificence, but in a cottage there is more safety' (14). See also Bruce, *Scyld and Scef*, 134–8.

7 Kemp Malone, *The Literary History of Hamlet* (1923; repr. New York: Haskell House, 1964).

8 Hill, 'The "Variegated Obit" as an Historiographical Motif in Old English Poetry and Anglo-Latin Historical Literature,' *Traditio* 44 (1988): 101–24 at 123.

9 The literary effect of presenting the material non-chronologically and in the order the poet chooses – via 'interlace' – necessitates a curious and attentive audience. John Leyerle explains how the interlace design 'reveals the meaning of coincidence, the recurrence of human behavior, and the circularity of time ... It allows for the intersection of narrative events without regard for their distance in chronological time ... The significance of the connections is left for the audience to work out for itself' ('The Interlace Structure of *Beowulf*,' *University of Toronto Quarterly* 37 [1967]: 1–17 at 8; repr. in *Interpretations of 'Beowulf': A Critical Anthology*, ed. R.D. Fulk [Bloomington: Indiana University Press, 1991], 146–67).

10 See Kemp Malone, 'A Note on *Beowulf* 2928 and 2932,' *PQ* 8 (1929): 406–7, for evidence that Ohthere is the elder son, though the poem never makes the birth order explicit. I would note in addition that his priority legitimizes the grievance of Eanmund and Eadgils against Onela. It would be hard to imagine Beowulf going to such lengths to support the nephews' claim if they were not the rightful heirs (2391–5).

11 See John D. Niles, 'Myth and History,' in *A Beowulf Handbook*, ed. Robert E. Bjork and John D. Niles (Lincoln: University of Nebraska Press, 1997), 213–32 at 220.

12 Hill, 'Variegated Obit,' 120.

13 Both Klaeber and Liuzza identify Hæthcyn only as a 'Geatish prince' in their glossaries of proper names, and Andy Orchard, in his very complete

genealogies, does not place over Hæthcyn's name the crown that marks the other kings (*A Critical Companion to 'Beowulf'* [Cambridge: D.S. Brewer, 2003], xv).

14 Bruce Mitchell, 'Literary Lapses: Six Notes on *Beowulf* and Its Critics,' *RES* n.s. 43 (1992): 1–17 at 13.

15 Newton comments on a 'familiarity with matters Danish ... in contrast to Geatish and Swedish matters, references to which seem to require more information' (*Origins*, 55).

16 Hill, 'Variegated Obit,' 118–19.

17 The 'social significance of this myth is that it provides a charter ... for kingship as the inheritance of the *stirps regia* of the Scyldings' (Hill, 'Scyld Scefing,' 42). The 'miracle' of Scyld's arrival 'was granted by the God of the Christians' (44).

18 Chapter 25 of *Ynglingasaga* reports that 'King Hálfdan died in Uppsala of a sickness and was buried in a mound' (Snorri Sturluson, *Ynglingasaga*, in *Heimskringla: History of the Kings of Norway*, trans. Lee M. Hollander [1964; repr. Austin: University of Texas Press, 1995], 6–50 at 28). *The Saga of King Hrolf Kraki* describes how Hálfdan is killed by his brother Frodi, and in the Latin epitome of *Skjöldungasaga* Hálfdan is killed by Ingialldus (Old English Ingeld), Frodi's son. See *The Saga of King Hrolf Kraki*, trans. Jesse L. Byock (Harmondsworth: Penguin, 1998), 1 and notes.

19 See Kemp Malone, 'The Daughter of Healfdene,' in *Studies in English Philology: A Miscellany in Honor of Frederick Klaeber*, ed. Kemp Malone and Martin B. Ruud (Minneapolis: University of Minnesota Press, 1929); repr. in *Studies in Heroic Legend and in Current Speech*, ed. Stefán Einarrson and Norman E. Eliason (Copenhagen: Rosenkilde and Bagger, 1959), 135–58 at 124–41; Clarke, *Sidelights on Teutonic History*, 89, and Klaeber's note (including the note in his first supplement). Norman E. Eliason, 'Healfdene's Daughter,' in *Anglo-Saxon Poetry: Essays in Appreciation for John C. McGalliard*, ed. Lewis E. Nicholson and Dolores Warwick Frese (Notre Dame: University of Notre Dame Press, 1975), 3–13, expresses reservations about the name, or whether the daughter was named at all.

20 *The Saga of King Hrolf Kraki*, trans. Byock, 4.

21 Bruce, *Scyld and Scef*, provides copies of the relevant genealogies, all of which show Helgi succeeding Hálfdan. See his excerpts from the *Incerti Auctoris Genealogia Regum Danie* (thirteenth century), 113–14; *Langfeðgatal* (twelfth-century), 116–19; *Reges Danorum* (late fifteenth/early sixteenth century), 129–30; *Series ac Brevior Historia Regum Daniae* (thirteenth century), 140; Sven Aggesen's *Short History of the Kings of Denmark* (twelfth century), 150–2. See also ch. 29 of *Ynglingasaga*. Aggesen reports how 'he [Skiold, the

48 James H. Morey

Scyld of *Beowulf*] left heirs to the kingdom called Frothi and Halfdan. These brothers fought each other for the kingdom, and eventually Halfdan killed his brother and obtained the sole kingly authority. He begot a son called Helghi to inherit the kingdom ... His successor as king was his son, Rolf Kraki' (152). In *The Saga of King Hrolf Kraki* Hrothgar (Norse Hroar, Roe) has his own kingdom in Northumbria and is killed by his nephew Hrok. The analogues invite any number of suppositions, as Malone demonstrates in *Literary History* (see especially chapter 10, 'Helgi'). At the very least, the Norse traditions document a younger brother killing an elder brother, thus dispossessing a nephew/son, in almost every generational iteration.

22 Newton, *Origins of Beowulf*, discusses other Norse analogues and the Anglo-Saxon royal pedigrees on pages 24–5 and 54–76. He accepts the order Heorogar – Hrothgar – Halga, remarking that 'the variously stated relationships between Scylding family-members throughout the poem are nowhere contradictory' (55). The sequence of Geatish names in line 2434, which is highly reminiscent of line 62, also indicates that the names are presented in birth order.

23 *Ynglingasaga* (ch. 29) reports that 'Helgi' son of 'Hálfdan' dies in battle (33). In *The Saga of King Hrolf Kraki* King Adils of Sweden (OE Eadgils) kills Helgi in an ambush, and in Saxo Grammaticus (*History of the Danes*, page 52) he dies either from grief or from suicide because he married his daughter, Yrse. See Clarke, *Sidelights*, 82. The *History of the Danes* (56) and *The Saga of King Hrolf Kraki* (chs 33–4) tell of Hiarvarth (Hjorvard, whose name corresponds to Heoroweard) who is responsible for the death of Rolf (OE Hrothulf) and who in turn is slain by one of Rolf's thanes. In the Norse sources Hiarvarth is not related by blood but by marriage to a figure not in *Beowulf*, and there are numerous other differences. See R.W. Chambers, *Beowulf: An Introduction to the Study of the Poem with a Discussion of the Stories of Offa and Finn*, 3rd ed. with a Supplement by C.L. Wrenn (Cambridge: Cambridge University Press, 1959), 29–31 and 426–9.

24 The word *betera* appears only one other time in *Beowulf* (but cf. *selra*), again spoken by Hrothgar in an unspecified comparison praising Beowulf: 'ðes eorl wære / geboren betera!' (1702–3).

25 Chambers suggests that Heoroweard may have been too young to accept the rulership that such gifts would connote, and then that Hrothgar (the regent who becomes the king) gives them to Beowulf lest by returning them to Heoroweard he dispossess Hrethric (*Beowulf: An Introduction*, 428).

26 Carol J. Clover, 'The Germanic Context of the Unferþ Episode,' *Speculum* 55 (1980): 444–68 at 463; repr. in *The Beowulf Reader*, ed. Peter S. Baker (New York: Garland, 2004), 127–54.

27 See Michael J. Enright, 'The Warband Context of the Unferth Episode,' *Speculum* 73 (1998): 297–337, who argues that the poet presents Unferth negatively, as a pagan advocate, but nonetheless as 'an institutional figure who acts in an official manner blessed by the king' (309).
28 In *Andreas* God instructs Andrew to save Matthew his *broðor* and *heafodmæg* from the Meremedonians, though there is presumably no blood relation (939–42). *Genesis A* describes how Enoch 'nalles feallan let / dom and drihtscipe / þenden he hyrde wæs heafodmaga' [1198–1200: did not allow justice and lordship to fail while he was the guardian of the chief-kin] and how Japheth 'geogoð afeded, / hyhtlic heorðwerod heafodmaga, / sunu and dohtra. He wæs selfa til, / heold a rice, eðeldreamas' [1604–7: nurtured the youth, the pleasant hearth-troop of chief-kin, sons and daughters. He was himself good, always held the kingdom and the domestic joys].
29 The cognate term in Icelandic heroic poetry, *höfuð-niðjar*, refers to 'head-kinsmen,' whereas the term *höfuðbarmsmenn* is the term for 'agnates' in legal texts (see Richard Cleasby and Gudbrand Vigfusson, *An Icelandic-English Dictionary*, 2nd ed. rev. by William A. Craigie [Oxford: Clarendon, 1957], s.v.).
30 'Another right which the king claimed was that of having proper watch set over him when he came into a district. This, called Vigilia and Custodia in the Latin authorities, is the Heáfodweard, or *Headward* of the Saxons' (John Mitchell Kemble, *The Saxons in England: A History of the English Commonwealth till the Period of the Norman Conquest*, rev. by Walter de Gray Birch, 2 vols [London: 1876], 2:63).
31 See the *Rectitudines Singularum Personarum*, article 1.1: 'Eac of manegum landum mare landriht arist to cyniges gebanne, swilce is deorhege to cyniges hame & scorp to friðscipe & sæweard & heafodweard & fyrdweard, ælmesfeoh & cyricsceat & mænige oðere mistlice ðingc' [Also, in many realms more land-rights originate from the king's pasture and equipment for defence-ships and coast-guard and king-guard and camp-guard, alms and church-tax, and many other various things]; *Die Gesetze der Angelsachsen*, ed. Felix Liebermann, 3 vols (1903–16; repr. Aalen: Scientia, 1960), 1:444. Article 2 also notes how a thane must 'heafodwearde healdan'; the corresponding clause in the *Quadripartitus* reads 'heafodwardam custodire' (Liebermann, *Die Gesetze*, 1:445).
32 The spelling of Hunferth's name and his role at Heorot has inspired much criticism, usefully summarized by Orchard, *Critical Companion*, 247. R.D. Fulk argues against any allegorical reading and demonstrates that the name – spelled with initial 'h' – is a historically verifiable Germanic, though not English, name: '*hunferth* is the one Germanic name in the Old English

poetic corpus that begins with *h* – and yet takes vocalic alliteration' ('Unferth and His Name,' *MP* 85 [1987]: 113–27 at 120). See also D.G. Scragg, 'Initial *H* in Old English,' *Anglia* 88 (1970): 165–96, who documents many instances of the omission and inclusion of 'h,' and who posits a 'confusion of elements' to account for the 'h' in 'Hunferth' (178). Scragg also notes that the name 'Hunferd' appears in the *Liber Vitae Dunelmensis* and, in the *Anglo-Saxon Chronicle*, the name 'Hunferð' appears in 'annal 754, all versions, and annal 744, all versions except E which has *Unferth*' (179, n. 48). It would be easier to argue for a confused scribe in *Beowulf* if he had not been so consistent in his spelling of the name and if the name 'Hunferð' was not attested elsewhere.

33 See Orchard, *Critical Companion*, 245–6. Fulk agrees with other scholars that 'these lines can only allude to an important role in the affair [Hrothulf's future treachery] played by Unferth' ('Unferth and His Name,' 126). In discussing these lines Newton notes that 'a consideration of the ON *þulr* suggests that the OE *þyle* may have been both the custodian and teacher of the knowledge required by claimants to the throne. If so, we would have further reasons to suspect the involvement of Unferth the *þyle* in any question over the Scylding succession' (*Origins of Beowulf*, 92–3).

34 Here I agree with Fred C. Robinson, 'History, Religion, Culture,' in *Approaches to Teaching 'Beowulf'*, ed. Jess B. Bessinger, Jr, and Robert F. Yeager (New York: MLA, 1984), 107–22; repr. in his *The Tomb of Beowulf and Other Essays* (Oxford: Oxford University Press, 1993), 36–51: 'Anyone who does not hear anxiety in Wealhtheow's speech about how Hrothulf will act toward her offspring must think that Mark Antony genuinely believes Caesar's murderers to be honorable men' (109). Bruce Mitchell does not accept this as a 'fair comparison' ('Literary Lapses,' 14).

35 John M. Hill, 'Beowulf and the Danish Succession: Gift-Giving as the Occasion for Complex Gesture,' *Medievalia et Humanistica* n.s. 11 (1982): 177–97. Hill repeats and extends this argument in *Cultural World*, 100–3. Mitchell also advances the possibility that 'Wealhtheow's remarks were a statement of accepted fact and an endorsement of Hrothulf's position' ('Literary Lapses,' 13).

36 Biggs, '*Beowulf* and Some Fictions,' notes how 'As "Cain's kin" (l. 107a), Grendel and his mother are linked to the different problems, fratricide and kin-vengeance, that threaten the Danes when Hrothgar dies' (75–6). I agree, and would add that the failure to honour kinsmen significantly predates Hrothgar's death and that the poet is as much obsessed with the past as with the future.

37 Biggs, '*Beowulf* and Some Fictions,' discusses the problem of the succession:

'It is in the character of Wiglaf that the poet relates the issue of Beowulf's lack of a son to the theme of succession in the poem as a whole by establishing him as the only candidate to be the next king, but failing to depict him as assuming the office' (71).

38 Thomas D. Hill, 'The Confession of Beowulf and the Structure of *Vǫlsunga Saga*,' in *The Vikings*, ed. R.T. Farrell (London: Phillimore, 1982), 165–79 at 177.

Folio 179 of the *Beowulf* Manuscript

FREDERICK M. BIGGS

Folio 179 of London, British Library, MS Cotton Vitellius A.xv presents readers of *Beowulf* with some difficulties not only because of its losses of text but also because of the theories that have been advanced to explain these omissions.[1] According to Kevin Kiernan's controversial argument, folio 179 is a palimpsest executed by the second scribe, perhaps some twenty years after he had first completed the manuscript, in order to record a smoother transition between what had been before his efforts two independent poems about the hero.[2] Carl T. Berkhout has made the provocative suggestion that the folio was erased by Scribe B, or one of his associates, when he discovered that he 'had accidentally omitted a full clause after *syððan* [2207a; fol. 178v/20], amounting to two or three poetic lines'; it was then 'freshened up,' he suggests, some five and a half centuries later, probably by Laurence Nowell.[3] Indeed, by questioning Kiernan's use of the term 'palimpsest,'[4] Berkhout points to what I would consider the major weakness in Kiernan's argument: in considering putative changes such as *wintra* to *wintru* (2209a; fol. 179r/2) as significant,[5] Kiernan undercuts his position since it seems very unlikely that a new text would ever coincide so closely with the old. Yet, after adding another argument to challenge Kiernan's proposal,[6] I would like to suggest that Berkhout's own theory is open to question, and not only on the grounds that those who support a systematic 'freshening up' of these pages have pointed out little evidence for it.[7] Having now seen the manuscript, I maintain that much of the damage to this folio was indeed accidental.

My objection to Kiernan's argument centres on the significance of *syððan*, the last word on folio 178v. Somewhat surprisingly, he and one of his main critics, Leonard Boyle, agree on a striking interpretation of the second scribe's activity: that he probably wrote the two quires beginning with folio 179 and continuing to the end of the poem before he took over the first scribe's work (1939b; fol. 172v/4), since his decision to add four extra lines on folios 174v–6r indicates that he wished to join his two efforts neatly.[8] This insight does not challenge the position Boyle articulates: in his account, the two scribes divided their work before beginning and so the point at which the second scribe began copying the poem was dictated by his exemplar; he picked up from the top of the folio he was handed.[9] It is more troubling, however, for Kiernan's view since it means that the text at the bottom of folio 178v (2200–7a) must have been perceived by the second scribe as an appropriate link to what he had already written.[10] These lines could not have been added into a blank space at the later date, perhaps when folio 179 was erased and rewritten, since they are necessary to explain the four added lines on the preceding folios. By ending in mid-sentence, Scribe B must have been joining them to a text beginning in mid-sentence, an impossible opening for an independent story about Beowulf.[11] Kiernan's theory, then, cannot be correct unless, of course, folio 178v is also a palimpsest.

Discussion of folio 178v has focused on the letters lost at its top and along its left side due to the fire of 1731 and the placing of the folios in paper frames in 1845.[12] Kemp Malone does note, however, that 'the *r* of *frecan* [line] 19 is a bit damaged by abrasion,'[13] which may also have affected the following *e* and indeed the letters above these, *eso* in *gesohtan*. Indeed the manuscript confirms the impression conveyed by the facsimiles that elsewhere some letters are lighter than others. For example, the first seven, *læmmū sy* (2201), of line 15 are noticeably less dark than the following ones, *ðð an hygelac læg . 7*. Yet this difference appears characteristic of the rest of the page (for example, the first three letters of *æðeling* (2188a) in line 2 are lighter than the last four) and indeed of other folios (181r–v, 182v, 185r–v, 186r–v, 188v, etc.) in this part of the manuscript. I see nothing, then, that would support the view that all or part of folio 178v is a palimpsest.

Berkhout's theory, while less dramatic than Kiernan's because it conjures up only a few missing lines of text rather than an independent work about Beowulf with a radically different beginning, retains the first part of the earlier explanation for folio 179.[14] Scribe B or his colleague did not erase just the sections still visible as gaps in the manuscript; instead his effort extended to the entire folio (as well as the first three lines of fol. 180v), since Berkhout asserts that 'the readable text on

179 is nothing more than a moderately impressive though ultimately clumsy effort at restoration by the antiquary Laurence Nowell.'[15] In other words, the omissions that remain are primarily the places where Nowell did not trace over the Anglo-Saxon scribe's work.[16] In what he has published so far on the problem,[17] Berkhout focuses on the syntax of the sentence that spans folios 178v and 179r, arguing that the impersonal construction, 'eft þæt geiode' (2200a), with which it begins, would require a clause introduced by þæt or þætte to be complete.[18] It seems unlikely, however, that, even if he overlooked the simple solution of replacing syððan (2207a; fol. 178v/20) with þæt,[19] the scribe would have undertaken such an extensive program of erasure,[20] and indeed, the evidence of his excisions and additions elsewhere in the manuscript suggests that he might have been unwilling to do so.[21]

There is a gap on folio 173r/2 between heold and eðel (1959b–60a),[22] which Zupitza explains as due to 'the parchment being very thin, so thin, indeed that even in the FS. the letters of the back page show through it (hold).'[23] Malone, however, points out that if 'it was too thin to take writing on both sides one would expect the scribe to write on it recto and leave it blank verso'; he concludes that it is more likely 'due to erasure.'[24] Erasing, then, may have led to the parchment becoming unsuitable for writing on both sides. More revealing, if Malone's analysis is correct, is the erasure following wolde (2090b; fol. 176r/6); he suggests that 'the scribe first skipped manigra (the word to be copied next after wolde) and started copying sumne, but with the n went back to manigra, the rest of which he copied; when he saw what he had done he erased the whole.'[25] Because it is not a simple dittography,[26] this erasure can be more firmly assigned to the scribe himself and not some later reader. It is significant, then, that he chose not to write over it. A third erasure, although after folio 179, is almost certainly by the scribe: Zupitza comments that eowrum cynn (2885b; fol. 192v/2) is written 'in the same hand' over an erasure, 'to judge by the traces,' of the same words.[27] Again, the scribe did not write directly over his earlier work. These three examples, then, suggest that the scribe might have thought twice before beginning to efface not just one but both sides of a folio in order to include a relatively small amount of forgotten text.

Finally, the insertion of sceal (2659b; fol. 197r/4; official foliation 192r) may remind us that the scribe would have had a way to direct a reader even if he were forced to include text out of its proper sequence. The word stands in the left margin, preceded, according to Zupitza, by a ð, which corresponds to a ð above the line showing where the missing text belongs.[28] Although already ruled for twenty-one lines, there appears to be ample room at the bottom of folio 179r to include a small passage of forgotten text.

The initial conclusions to be drawn from these remarks are negative: since there is no reason to believe that 178v is a palimpsest, it is unlikely that 179r ever contained the beginning of a free-standing account of Beowulf's death; and given Scribe B's erasures elsewhere in the manuscript, it is doubtful that he would undertake to efface an entire folio in order to include a brief, mistakenly omitted passage. Yet they may lead us to question the theory that folio 179 was deliberately erased. There may be ways to preserve Kiernan's argument: in response to Berkhout's views he has proposed that this folio was written by a third scribe, contemporary with the other two, a suggestion that might allow us to imagine him rewriting this text as the second scribe completed the work of the first.[29] Even if, however, there was a third scribe – and the evidence is far from compelling – Kiernan would still need to explain why the letters of his new text line up directly over the old. Instead what appears to have happened is that this folio suffered accidental damage – Boyle suggests that the quires it began 'were for some time on a window sill or some other exposed area'[30] – that has been compounded by the touching up of individual words or letters and by attempts to recover faded readings through the use of chemical reagents. This explanation of the state of folio 179 does not make the recovery of damaged or changed readings any less urgent, an area where new technologies and the renewed efforts of editors may yield significant result.[31] Yet it allows us greater confidence in viewing the text of this transitional moment as our only record of the poet's intention.

NOTES

1 I would like to thank Carl T. Berkhout, Michelle Brown, and J.R. Hall for discussing the problem of folio 179 with me. Jim also gave me much practical advice for studying the *Beowulf* manuscript. I follow the old foliation with one exception (fols 197r/192r) where I provide both to avoid confusion; see *The Nowell Codex. British Museum Cotton Vitellius A.xv. Second Manuscript*, ed. Kemp Malone, EEMF 12 (Copenhagen: Rosenkilde and Bagger, 1963), 12–14. Malone uses the official foliation of 1884, which designates folio 179 as 182. I have also consulted the notes and facsimiles in

56 Frederick M. Biggs

'*Beowulf*': *Reproduced in Facsimile from the Unique Manuscript, British Museum Ms. Cotton Vitellius A.xv.*, ed. Julius Zupitza, 2nd ed., with an introductory note by Norman Davis, EETS o.s. 245 (London: Oxford University Press, 1959), and Kevin Kiernan, with Andrew Prescott et al., *Electronic Beowulf*, CD-ROM (London: British Library and University of Michigan Press, 1999).

2 Kevin Kiernan, '*Beowulf*' *and the* '*Beowulf*' *Manuscript*, rev. ed. (Ann Arbor: University of Michigan Press, 1996), 3 and 171. He summarized his argument in 'The Eleventh-Century Origin of *Beowulf* and the *Beowulf* Manuscript,' in *The Dating of Beowulf*, ed. Colin Chase, Toronto Old English Series 6 (Toronto: University of Toronto Press, 1981), 9–21.

3 Carl T. Berkhout, '*Beowulf* 2200–08: Mind the Gap,' *ANQ* 15.2 (Spring 2002): 51–8 at 54 and 56.

4 Berkhout, '*Beowulf* 2200–08,' 56.

5 Kiernan, *Beowulf*, 234.

6 In addition to the articles by Leonard Boyle and Johan Gerritsen discussed later, see Gerritsen's review of Kiernan's revised edition, '*Beowulf* Revisited,' *ES* 79 (1998): 82–6; David N. Dumville, 'Beowulf Come Lately: Some Notes on the Paleography of the Nowell Codex,' *Archiv für das Studium der neueren Sprachen und Literaturen* 225 (1988): 49–63; Dumville, 'The *Beowulf*-Manuscript and How Not to Date It,' *Medieval English Studies Newsletter* 39 (1998): 21–7; Michael Lapidge, 'The Archetype of *Beowulf*,' *ASE* 29 (2000): 5–41; and, with further bibliography, Andy Orchard, *A Critical Companion to* '*Beowulf*' (Cambridge: D.S. Brewer, 2003), 20. Kiernan's lexical evidence has been challenged by Phillip Pulsiano and Joseph McGowan, '*Fyrd*, *here* and the Dating of *Beowulf*,' *Studia Anglica Posnaniensia* 23 (1990): 3–13.

7 An example occurs in folio 179r/4 (2210a): Zupitza asserts '*o* in *ón* written by the later hand instead of an original *a*, which is still pretty distinct' (*Beowulf*, 102). Malone comments, 'the *ó* ... is an alteration of *á*' (*Nowell*, 84). Kiernan writes, 'There is no trace of an original *a* beneath the *o*' (*Beowulf*, 234). The only evidence I could see that would support an original *a* would be the slightly more angular form of the letter (compare, for example, the *o* and *a* in the following word, *ongan*); more conclusive, of course, would be the remains of a stroke in the lower right corner, and I saw no sign of this. There are two other occasions when Zupitza asserts that an original *a* can still be distinguished beneath an *o*: of *weoldū* (2221a; fol. 179r/14) Malone comments, 'I can see nothing to indicate that the *eo* ... is an alteration of *ea*'; and of *innon* (2244a; fol. 179v/14), 'the *o* ... is a bit pointed at the top (though not more so than that of *ofer* (fol. 185r/6) but I see no indication that it was an *a* to start with' (*Nowell*, 85–6). See also Kiernan, who agrees with Malone in the first case, but disagrees in the second (*Beowulf*, 237–8 and 241). There

are only three other places where Zupitza states he may find evidence still surviving of the lower script (*fæs* [2230b; fol. 179v/2], *si* [2237b; fol. 179v/8], and *mæstan* [2247b; fol. 179v/17]), but in each case Malone and Kiernan disagree. Johan Gerritsen offers eight more examples of 'lack of coincidence' in individual strokes: *heold* (2208b; fol. 179r/2), *weard* (2210a; fol. 179r/3), *þæs* (2239b; fol. 179v/10), *gestreona* (2240b; fol. 179v/11), *wunode* (2242a; fol. 179v/12), *gearo* (2241b; fol. 179v/12), *þær* (2244a; fol. 179v/14) and *of* (2251b; fol. 179v/21); 'Have with You to Lexington! The *Beowulf* Manuscript and *Beowulf*,' in *In Other Words: Transcultural Studies in Philology, Translation, and Lexicology Presented to Hans Heinrich Meier on the Occasion of His Sixty-Fifth Birthday*, ed. J. Lachlan Mackenzie and Richard Todd (Dordrecht: Foris, 1989), 15–34 at 29.

8 Kiernan, *Beowulf*, 258–62; and Leonard Boyle, 'The Nowell Codex and the Poem of *Beowulf*,' in *Dating of Beowulf*, ed. Chase, 23–32 at 25. It should be noted, however, that folios 179r–98v also contain 21 lines.

9 According to Boyle, the second scribe copied *Judith* first, beginning mistakenly on a new folio, which then led him to use two quires of ten folios ruled for 21 lines of text for his portion of *Beowulf* ('Nowell,' 27–8). Unlike this argument, which, while possible, seems inconclusive, Boyle's evidence about the rulings of lines 19 and 20 for folios 126–33 proves that the text of *Beowulf* now preserved in the Cotton manuscript did not circulate as a separate booklet as Kiernan suggests ('Nowell,' 23–4).

10 Although Kiernan claims that 'a case can be made for starting the dragon episode at line 2207, with the palimpsest' and that 'the last few lines of the eleventh gathering (lines 2200–2207a) do not lead inexorably to the kingship of Beowulf' (*Beowulf*, 257, n. 74), the text at the bottom of folio 178v does show the story turning away from Beowulf's adventure among the Danes to the later history of the Geats.

11 There is, moreover, no indication that there ever was an enlarged initial at the top of folio 179r, much less a line of capitals as one might expect at the beginning of a new work.

12 See Kiernan, *Beowulf*, 68–9.

13 *Nowell*, ed. Malone, 83.

14 Berkhout argues against Boyle's view that the losses to the text on folio 179 are primarily accidental; he also states that 'in a casual conversation,' Boyle 'essentially abandoned this suggestion' ('*Beowulf* 2200–08,' 57, n. 2).

15 The adverbs 'moderately' and 'clumsy' are perhaps used to explain the present uneven state of the folio, and if so recall Kiernan's explanation that Scribe B began rewriting while the parchment was still wet from the liquid he had used to remove the old ink, which led to the new ink not adhering

properly (*Beowulf*, 227–30). In both cases, it would appear more plausible to assume later damage, perhaps due to the fire of 1731. In any case, the script on folio 179, if not by Scribe B, is virtually identical to his own, a fact that Berkhout explains by noting Nowell's reputation as a scribe; see Carl T. Berkhout, 'Laurence Nowell (1530–ca. 1570),' in *Medieval Scholarship: Biographical Studies on the Formation of a Discipline*, vol. 2, *Literature and Philology*, ed. Helen Damico with Donald Fennema and Karmen Lenz (New York: Garland, 1998), 3–17. Gerritsen elaborates on this point, arguing that the effect would not be difficult to achieve by someone knowledgeable of and tracing over a formal hand ('Have with You,' 28–9). For comparison, see two other examples of Nowell's use of Anglo-Saxon script: lines 8 and 9 of folio 9r of the Exeter Book, where he touches up *pan þæt ðu* and *we þære wyrde*, and British Library, Henry Davis Collection MS 59 (M 30), an edition and translation of laws by Alfred; on the identity of these hands, see Berkhout, 'Laurence Nowell.' The former, to judge from the facsimile, is particularly relevant to the present discussion not only because it is much more limited in scope than what Berkhout proposes for folio 179, but also because several of the letters appear not to conform to the scribe's normal practice: note, for example, the exaggerated crossing of *ð* and the lack of serifs for the *u* in *ðu*, and the irregularly shaped *y* in *wyrde*. In contrast, again judging only from photostats made available to me at the British Library, the edition of Alfred's laws is extensive, and shows a remarkable command of Anglo-Saxon script.

16 Folio 179r/5 presents a difficulty for Berkhout's argument. Zupitza comments, 'very little of *hlæme* freshened up' (*Beowulf*, 102). Malone reads 'hofe' (*Nowell*, 84). Only the ascender of the 'h' is clear; it seems unlikely a later hand would rewrite only part of this letter, and indeed, Kiernan considers this to be 'the first line in which part of the new text was rubbed off afterward' (*Beowulf*, 235).

17 See a summary of Berkhout's 1986 Medieval Academy conference paper, 'Anglo-Saxon Studies in the Age of Shakespeare' (*OEN* 19.2 [1986]: A-28). He also discussed this topic in his paper 'In Search of Laurence Nowell' delivered at the 1987 meeting of the International Society of Anglo-Saxonists (abstract in *OEN* 20.2 [1987]: A-31-2).

18 Berkhout, '*Beowulf* 2200–08,' 52. Mary E. Blockley discussed the syntax of the sentence in 'Once More into the Breach,' presented in a session in Berkhout's honour at the Thirty-Seventh International Congress of Medieval Studies, Kalamazoo, 3 May 2002. See also my 'The Politics of Succession in *Beowulf* and Anglo-Saxon England,' *Speculum* 80 (2005): 709–41 at 735–6.

19 Berkhout offers some suggestions about the possible missing text, but unless we return to Kiernan's position that Scribe B is, in a sense, the author of *Beowulf*, it is difficult to imagine that he would have considered any information so crucial that it would justify the labour.
20 The scribe writes the text as prose, and so manuscript lines do not correspond to poetic lines. A glance, however, at Zupitza's facsimile, which includes line numbers for the poem alongside the transcription, reveals that, when Scribe B takes over from Scribe A, the manuscript and poetic lines on each page are roughly the same. It is also relevant that Scribe B writes more compactly near the end of the poem, fitting, for example, more than twenty-eight poetic lines into twenty-one manuscript lines on folio 196v. Moreover, he could have picked up about two-thirds of a line simply by moving or omitting the fitt number on folio 179r/13.
21 Berkhout himself suggests that the scribe abandoned his effort since 'it was impossible to erase 179 clearly enough to accommodate a recopied text without damaging the parchment' ('*Beowulf* 2200–08,' 56).
22 There is no gap in the poem (lines 1959–60).
23 *Beowulf*, ed. Zupitza, 90.
24 *Nowell*, ed. Malone, 76.
25 *Nowell*, ed. Malone, 80.
26 Examples would include *brond* (2126a; fol. 176v/19) and *hyrde* (3133b; fol. 198r/9).
27 *Beowulf*, ed. Zupitza, 133. He explains the decision as motivated by his first effort 'having been even more indistinct' than several other blurred words in the following lines.
28 *Beowulf*, ed. Zupitza, 124.
29 Kevin Kiernan, 'The *nathwylc* Scribe and the *Beowulf* Palimpsest,' electronic pre-print (http://www.uky.edu/~kiernan/Nathwylc/nathwylc-restore.htm) of an article forthcoming in *Poetry, Place and Gender: Studies in Medieval Culture in Honor of Helen Damico*, ed. Catherine E. Karkov (Kalamazoo: Medieval Institute Publications).
30 Boyle, 'Nowell,' 31.
31 See most recently Fulk, 'Some Contested Readings in the *Beowulf* Manuscript,' *RES* n.s. 56 (2005): 192–223 at 208–23.

PART II
Old English Religious and Sapiential Poetry

Trinitarian Language: Augustine, *The Dream of the Rood*, and Ælfric

JAMES W. EARL

A talking cross: it still remains a surprise. In her 1940 essay, '*The Dream of the Rood* as Prosopopoeia,' Margaret Schlauch did what she could to mitigate it by identifying the rhetorical trope of talking objects – prosopopoeia – and laying out the rather slim tradition of Latin literary texts that exhibit it; but she did not really lessen our wonder.[1]

One of my students decided to write a paper on the topic, and so I told her to read Schlauch. She returned upset, because Schlauch had said it all. So I gave her some other examples: King Alfred's 'talking poems' (which I had written about),[2] the talking objects in the Riddles ('Saga hwæt ic hatte'), swords that say 'So-and-so made me' (Alfred's *æstel* too), not to mention the Ruthwell Cross, which says 'Rod waes ic aræred.' The poet of *The Dream of the Rood*, I suggested, seems to have been *swimming* in OE prosopopoeia.

She did some more reading, but stalled again. Now Schlauch and I had said it all! I suggested there was still more to be said, because *our* culture is also swimming in prosopopoeia: think of all the cartoons and commercials with talking trees, toasters, and toilet bowls. What does it mean – rhetorically, philosophically, psychologically, cognitively – to imagine such things talking to us? How do we begin to think about it critically? We are so accustomed to the trope, frankly I am surprised it surprises us any more.

And, I said, even if you do not see the relevance of talking toilet bowls, a medieval monk would have bumped into prosopopoeia every day in the Bible, in his *lectio divina* and the liturgy. I pulled my Bible off the shelf, and quickly stumbled upon Psalm 19 [Vulgate 18]:

> The heavens are telling the glory of God
> and the firmament proclaims his handwork.

> Day to day pours forth speech,
> and night to night declares knowledge.³

Maybe this is not strictly prosopopoeia: the firmament's speech is reported rather than quoted, and might just be a metonymy for people praising God. Still, the trope is just beneath the surface – as it is in the *Dream of the Rood* when Creation is said to behold the Cross (11–12) and to lament Christ's death ('Weop eal gesceaft,' 55).⁴ More on the mark, though – and I am surprised Schlauch never mentioned them – are the talking trees in Psalms 96 [95] and 148:

> Then shall all the trees of the forest sing for joy
> before the Lord, for He is coming.⁵

> Praise the Lord ... mountains and all hills,
> Fruit trees and all cedars!⁶

There is an an especially nice case of a talking tree in Isaiah 14:

> The cypresses exult over you,
> the cedars of Lebanon, saying,
> 'Since you have slept,
> No one comes to cut us down.'⁷

Taking all the OE, biblical, and modern examples into account, then, perhaps prosopopoeia is more than just an uncommon rhetorical device in the classical tradition; maybe it is common enough to be a mode of expression, a mode of thought, or a mode of experience, like animism or mythology. What would an anthropologist say? What does it mean when objects are represented as alive and speaking to us? How universal is the phenomenon? In a psychological register, perhaps it is a form of projection or displacement; perhaps prosopopoeia is really a rhetorical term for the mental phenomenon we call 'hearing voices.' Freud might interpret it as paranoia, or guilt – which would fit our poem nicely, actually, since the Cross's speech is cathartic for the abject, guilt-ridden dreamer.

There is a philosophical side to the question too: in what sense *do* things actually 'speak'? When we say that a certain painting 'speaks' to us, what do we mean by 'speak'? What does it mean when an experiment 'tells' us something, or that history 'teaches us a lesson'? Are these metaphors, or does our notion of language extend in practice to non-linguistic signs like paintings, experiments, and events? For Augustine, everything was a sign; I wonder if *he* heard things talking to him. That is a rhetorical question, for we read in the *Confessions*:

> What is my God? I put my question to the earth. It answered, 'I am not God,' and all things on earth declared the same. I asked the sea and the chasms of the deep and the living things that creep in them, but they answered, 'We are not your god. Seek what is above us' ... I asked the sky, the sun, the moon, and the stars, but they told me, 'Neither are we the God whom you seek.' I spoke to all the things that are about me, all that can be admitted by the door of the senses, and I said, 'Since you are not my God, tell me about him. Tell me something of my God.' Clear and loud they answered, 'God is he who made us.' I asked these questions simply by gazing at these things, and their beauty was all the answer they gave. (10.6)[8]

He then asks why all people do not hear this message, and answers that indeed the world does speak to everyone; but it is heard only by those who interrogate it, and understood only by those who compare the message given to their senses with the truth in themselves, that is, reason.

By this point my student was quite overwhelmed. A few days later she told me that what had caught her attention in the first place, really, was that we are never told *how* the Cross speaks; does it have a face, and a little mouth, or does the dreamer hear it like a movie voice-over? The question had never occurred to me. She soon abandoned the project and chose another topic – but now I cannot stop thinking about that little mouth!

At Cornell I learned, mostly from Tom Hill, that medieval exegesis, with its fourfold typologies of sacred history, is more than a method for interpreting the Bible, more even than a theory of history; it is a way of understanding time itself – linear, cyclical, spiralled, thickly layered – and a world view one can inhabit completely. I arrived at Cornell as A.C. Charity's book on Dante, *Events and Their Afterlife*, appeared, and so we were always talking about Charity's 'applied typology' of the moral sense. Tom used to say, 'There's nothing that can't be interpreted typologically: if I walk through that door, there's a fourfold meaning!' Our actions are embedded in, are directed and organized by, are literalizations of, a coherent world of Christian meanings. When you internalize this system it becomes a comprehensive *mentalité*, or *lebenswelt*. Thus it became a parlour game for us to interpret the lyrics of Bob Dylan, Neil Young, and The Who the way Augustine might have: in the sixties at Cornell, scripture lay all about us.

Since those days I have come to think that in the Middle Ages the Trinity too was more than a theological abstraction. It too was an encompassing truth, an omnipresent reality – not just a theory of everything, but a structure – an experienced structure – of everything. For Augustine or Ælfric, the Trinity was comprehensive in the way that today we think of ourselves as living in a world of matter, energy, and time ($e=mc^2$, a physicist's trinity), or nature, culture, and language (a humanist's trinity), or race, class, and gender (a post-humanist's trinity).

Here I am going to focus on the existential aspect of the Trinity, that is, its nature as a global *mentalité* or *lebenswelt*. As a reader of literature I am especially interested in the role that language plays in it. The Son, the Second Person, the Saviour, is *Logos, Verbum*. Ipso facto, language is central to trinitarian mentality. The Word incarnate: we are familiar with the idea, but what relation does it have – does *He* have – to the language, the words, that we actually speak, read and write?

My first thought is that the Second Person of the Trinity (the Word) mediates between the Father's transcendence and the Spirit's immanence, as language mediates between the world of ideas and the world of experience. Seen this way, language would be not just a tool for communication, but an active principle of reality, and a particularly creative principle at that. God's Word, to which human language is at least analogous, creates the world. Literature written in a language so conceived and experienced should have some interesting features as a consequence; and among those many consequences – perhaps a trivial one, but it is where we started – would be the phenomenon of prosopopoeia, that things speak. In a world where language mediates between ideas and things, ideas and things can be experienced as speaking to each other.

De trinitate

The theology of the Word, and the Word's role in the Trinity and in various mental trinities, are laid out in Augustine's *De trinitate* 9.7–11 and 15.10–16. In Augustine's view the Word is emphatically not to be understood as identical with spoken language; however, spoken language is enough of a sign and an image of the Word that it serves as a way of understanding the Trinity. Words and the Word are both defined as knowledge animated by love – which gives us some idea of Augustine's form of analysis. Subject/object, mind/world, soul/body: each of these dualisms is joined in a sort of holy matrimony by a third element, language. Mind > word > world, or world > word > mind. The mind gives birth to words that give shape to the world; contrarily, the world seems to offer itself up in words which give shape to our minds. The formula 'thought, word, and deed' is not a static trinity, but a dynamic one. The meanings of words are not arbitrary, even if their sounds are. Today we may associate these ideas with Kant or Heidegger, but taken together they constitute one of Augustine's mental trinities. Only through such three-fold, dynamic, and contradictory structures of our mentality, Augustine claims, can we come to understand the three-fold, dynamic, and contradictory structure of the Trinity.

Because the world of ideas and the world of things meet in language, each is revealed to the other as the Word, or words, in more than just a rhetorical or metaphorical sense. Language is the interface. In fact it is the only interface, the one intermediary, the single connection between the inner and outer worlds. Language is the pattern that forms on the interface between the truth of the soul and our experience of the world – though that way of saying it does not quite capture its mediating activity and creativity.

This may seem a fairly extended notion of language and speech to us, but it was so fully internalized in the Middle Ages, at least in the monastic Middle Ages, that it could be taken utterly for granted by someone like Ælfric. To us, 'word' may seem to have a wide range of meanings, from the aural/linguistic to the spiritual/theological, but these meanings were once unified; each seemed a natural metaphor for the other. Today we say that the 'literal' meaning of 'word' is the linguistic one, which adheres to its extended symbolic meanings; but it is not so obvious that Plato experienced *logos* as two distinct concepts (word and idea); and Ælfric too may not have sensed a gap between word and Word, as if one were literal and the other metaphorical. Both were literal, and it would have been self-evident to him why a single word, *verbum*, was used to represent both. For Augustine too, although he analyses these distinctions, and in certain works he stresses the arbitrariness of words, in *De trinitate* words are the natural manifestations of ideas, born in the heart from the Truth, the Word of God.

For Augustine the truth that underlies these mental-linguistic-perceptual structures is the Trinity.

> With the eye of the mind, therefore, we perceive in that eternal truth, from which all temporal things have been made, the form according to which we are ... The true knowledge of things, thence conceived, we bear with us as a word, and beget by speaking from within; nor does it depart from us by being born ... No one willingly does anything which he has not spoken previously in his heart. This word is conceived in love ... Love, therefore, as a means, joins our word with the mind from which it is born; and as a third it binds itself with them in an incorporeal embrace, without any confusion. (9.7–8)[9]

The second person of this particular mental trinity (for there are many such trinities) is the language we beget in speaking; in its incorporeal embrace it conjoins *amor* on the one hand and *mens* on the other. Corporeal things, that is, are known to the mind in the form of words, by means of love, which motivates perception; from the other direction, the incorporeal truth in the mind gives birth to words through love: the Word, through love, gives endless birth to words, though never being diminished by their being spoken. Words pour forth from the commingling influences of the mind's truth on the one hand, and our love of the world on the other.

There are of course two kinds of love, the love of outer things (cupidity) and the love of inner truth (charity). In this context the love of worldly things is not bad, as long as they are held up to the truth within – as when Augustine understands the things of the world to say, 'God is he who made us.' When our *cupiditas* or *appetitus* for the world is redirected to the truth of the mind, it is transformed into *amor* or *caritas*, producing a trinity in us of such stunning co-equality that it is an even closer analogy to the upper-case Trinity we are trying to understand than the perceptual one we have been considering.

> The word, therefore ... is knowledge with love. Hence, when the mind knows and loves itself, its word is joined to it by love. And because the mind loves its knowledge and knows its love, then the word is in the love and the love in the word, and both are in him who loves and who speaks. (9.10, trans. McKenna, 37)[10]

We can almost hear 'amen' at the end. This is not the theory of language we are accustomed to thinking about in Augustine, explored by Eugene Vance in *Mervelous Signals*, words as arbitrary signifiers, which seems so curiously postmodern.[11] Here we are in the presence not of a theory but a theology of language, written not in the analytical style of *De magistro* or *De doctrina christiana*, but rather in lush metaphors of conception and birth – that is, incarnation.

Love, the third person of this mental trinity, is not begotten, as the second person is, but instead proceeds from the first and second persons together; to be a useful analogy, the mental trinity must resemble the divine Trinity in such ways as this. The lower form of love (*appetitus*) first seeks out the world; then, when it turns to present the world to the mind in the form of words, in order to compare it to the truth already known within, in turning to the mind it becomes a higher form of love (*amor*); this love, and the mind, and the word they produce between them, are all perfectly coequal. The resulting tableau is a sort of Holy Family of the mind:

> This same desire by which one yearns for the knowing of the thing becomes love of the thing when known, while it holds and embraces the beloved offspring, that is, knowledge, and unites it to its begetter. And so there is a certain image of the Trinity: the mind itself, its knowledge, which is its offspring, and love as a third. (9.12, trans. McKenna, 40)[12]

It is a sort of nativity scene, in which the mother presents the Son to God the Father, and they all embrace, and are all one.

Few religious ideas have as luxurious a linguistic history as the Word, first in the Hebrew Bible, then the Greek New Testament, then the Vulgate and the Latin Fathers. In Hebrew the word for 'word' is *dabar*, which happens also to mean 'thing' or 'event'; in Hebrew, that is, 'word,' 'thing,' and 'event' are not clearly distinct categories.[13] In Greek, on the other hand, *logos* means 'word,' but also 'idea' and 'reason.' There are theological, philosophical, and literary consequences of these conceptions and of the difference between them – that is, whether you think words are things or ideas, whether they manifest history or reason. Augustine, however, is not writing in Hebrew or Greek, but in Latin, where *verbum* just means 'word' – in Latin, as in English, words are distinct from the things and the ideas that they signify. On the other hand, he is interpreting sacred texts originally written in Hebrew and Greek with strikingly different notions of language; in fact he is working hard to restore for his readers the meanings of the Greek *logos* that have been lost in Latin. 'In the beginning was the word' needs some explanation if it is going to make sense in Latin. Here in *De trinitate* the two meanings of *logos* are restored to each other, now conjoined by love, in a fecund, interactive trinity.

So much for book 9; but in book 15 Augustine returns to the theology of the Word, the theology of language, raising it to new conceptual heights. He begins where he did before, with the fact that all actions are rooted in words. Words do not have to be spoken aloud; they can also be spoken inwardly by the heart. The heart, he says, has its own mouth:

> Some thoughts, then, are speeches of the heart, and that a mouth is also there is shown by the Lord ... In one sentence He has included the two different mouths of man, the one of the body and the other of the heart. (15.10, trans. McKenna, 185–6)[14]

Could this be that little mouth? Augustine does not go into detail about it, but rushes on to develop another equally unexpected synaesthetic idea, one that also brings us back to prosopopoeia. Inwardly, he says, seeing and hearing are the same thing:

> Yet because we speak of thoughts as speeches of the heart, we do not therefore mean that they are not at the same time acts of sight, which arise from the sights of knowledge, when they are true. When these take place outwardly through the body, then speech is one thing and sight is another thing; but when we think inwardly, then both are one. (15.10, trans. McKenna, 186)[15]

Thoughts, he explains, the words of the heart, are images formed in the mind; they are not in Latin or Greek or any other language, although we may choose words in those languages as signs for them. The sounds we hear outwardly are only audible signs of these words of the heart, which are images, not audible but visible within. When we speak, however, the word of the heart becomes uttered by the mouth of the flesh, 'as the Word of God was made flesh.'

> Whoever, then, can understand the word, not only before it sounds, but even before the images of its sound are contemplated in thought ... can already see through this mirror and in this enigma some likeness of that Word of whom it was said, 'In the beginning was the Word.' (15.11, trans. McKenna, 186)[16]

There are many ways in which the production of speech is like the Incarnation; but at this final stage of the argument it becomes more important to show that even the highest mental trinity is *unlike* the divine one. To understand that Trinity, we have to pass beyond speech and image to higher and higher meanings of *verbum*, and finally to what Augustine calls 'the word of man':

> This word cannot be uttered in sound nor thought in the likeness of sound, such as must be done with the word of any language; it precedes all the signs by which it is signified, and is begotten by the knowledge which remains in the mind when this same knowledge is spoken inwardly, just as it is. (15.11, trans. McKenna, 188)[17]

Even as he itemizes all the likenesses of language to the Word, he is at greater pains to stress its unlikenesses, the gap between our words and Christ, lest we mistake ourselves for God.

> But that word of ours, which has neither sound nor thought of sound, is the word of that thing which we inwardly speak by seeing it, and therefore, it belongs to no language; hence, in this enigma there is a likeness, be it what it may, to that Word of God who is also God, since it is also so born from our knowledge as that Word was also born from the knowledge of the Father. Such, then, is our word in which we indeed find a likeness, be it what it may, to that Word, but, insofar as we are able, we shall point out how great an unlikeness there also is, and let us not be sluggish in perceiving this. (15.14, trans. McKenna, 196)[18]

Having reached the ineffable word, we cannot argue further. So, since we began with the image of a talking cross, and must return to it, perhaps we should turn back here.

The Dream of the Rood

Whatever truth the *Dream of the Rood* poet sees, he sees in language – not a language of utilitarian denotativeness, however, but the language of the heart, a language of vision, produced by love's inward, not outward motion. Inwardly, vision comes as speech, and speech as vision; in the language of the heart, images are words, words images, both signifiers of an invisible and ineffable truth within us.

The Dream of the Rood is not about a man who sees a talking cross. There is no question of outward, sensory perception, no question of a physical cross talking; we are in a visionary mode, where love is turned inward and words are coequal with the love and knowledge that give them birth. Might prosopopoeia be a special feature of this inner world, a feature of dreams and visions primarily? On the one hand, yes, in the Middle Ages we find lots of talking things in dreams and visions, like Book and Kind in *Piers Plowman*, not to mention mental faculties like Wit and Imaginatif. On the other hand, in the biblical examples we started with, the technique seems less abstract: the heavens tell the glory of God, the firmament announces the works of his hand, trees say thank you for not being cut down. Augustine too, when he speaks to the world in the *Confessions* and it speaks back to him, seems to apply the trope to perception, not just intellection. And then there are the OE Riddles, with their talking onions and salt-cellars. The literary traditions are mixed on what prosopopoeia means, because there are many notions of language governing the trope.

A Christian visionary poem like *The Dream of the Rood*, however, is written in Christian language, language that understands itself as incarnating the Word. This is a power-language, a power-theory of language, no matter what language the Word is being incarnated into, Greek, Latin or OE. Augustine's is hardly the only such theory. Sacred languages typically have cosmic power: in Sanskrit, the Vedas bring the universe into existence when recited; in Hebrew, as Isaac Rabinowitz argues, the thingness of the word (*dabar*) gives rise to all the self-actualizing, self-fulfilling varieties of biblical speech, like blessings, curses, prophecies, prayers, and the idea of scripture as a ground of being. In Greek too, it is a heady experience to read John's opening hymn to the Word, in words: the Gospel itself, the book, the page, becomes, like Christ, an incarnation of the Word. Consider the Book of Kells' portrait of John the Evangelist, on a page that has its own hands and feet, the page itself, like Christ, an incarnation of the Word.[19]

The Dream of the Rood takes language seriously in the same way — and not just because the Cross happens to speak. Twice in the poem human beings are designated *reordberend*, speech-bearers — even in their sleep. The poem begins by saying 'I had a wonderful dream in the middle of the night, *syðþan reordberend reste wunedon*' [3: when speech-bearers dwelt in bed]. They are not talking, but 'bear language.' If the poem is as monastic as Fleming says, *reordberend* has a special irony in a Benedictine community where speech is largely prohibited.[20] I am reminded of Heidegger's remark:

> It is held that man, in distinction from plant and animal, is the living being capable of speech. This statement does not mean only that, along with other faculties, man also possesses the faculty of speech. It means to say that only speech enables man to be the living being he is as man.[21]

Heidegger's theory that language reveals Being is not unlike Augustine's 'word of man.'[22]

Man may be the speech-bearing animal, but in the poem it is the Cross that speaks and creation that weeps, while Christ never says a word. How do we think about that contradiction? *De trinitate* clears a path to an answer: it is precisely because man has language that the world speaks to him. Still, it remains to ask why the dreamer tells his story, and the Cross tells its story, but Christ's story unfolds at the heart of the poem like a pantomime or a silent film. There is not even a passing reference to his last words, so important in the Gospel narratives. Why is the Word himself utterly silent? Is he perhaps the Word that Augustine presented at the end of his long argument, 'that word of ours, which has neither sound nor thought of sound, [but] precedes all the signs by which it is signified'?

Rosemary Woolf brilliantly analysed the relationship between Christ and the Cross in her 1958 article, 'Doctrinal Influences on "The Dream of the Rood"': the poet succeeds in portraying the dual nature of Christ by apportioning his humanity to the figure of the suffering Cross, and his divinity to the heroic figure who strides forward and mounts it humbly with great zeal.[23] The idea was new when I learned it from Tom Hill, and Tom went on to develop it further.[24] The thought I have been developing here fits hand-in-glove into that one: Christ's dual nature is also reflected in the distinction between words and the Word: the Word is incarnated in words, just as Christ is in the flesh; whereas outward speech is heard but not seen, inward speech is seen but not heard. The silence of Christ's divinity, then, is perhaps an aspect of his ineffable transcendence. The closest we can come to his divine being is in *seeing* it, although we hear the words that flow in speech from his incarnated form, from the mouth of his flesh, represented in the poem by the Rood.

Christ may be silent in the poem, but he is explicitly acknowledged as the Word toward the end, in the Judgment Day scene:

74   James W. Earl

> Ne mæg þær ænig unforht wesan
> for þam worde þe se Wealdend cwyð. (110–11)

This does not merely mean, 'No one can be unafraid because of the word that the Lord will say'; it means, more precisely, 'No one can be unafraid before the Word which the Lord speaks.' The Word the Lord speaks is Christ, the Word, who has himself come to judge.

I have called attention to several features of *The Dream of the Rood*: that the Cross talks, that Creation beholds and weeps, that men are called *reordberend*, that Christ does not talk, although he is depicted as the Word that the Lord speaks. All of these features make more sense to me after reading *De trinitate* and grappling with the theology of language that Augustine developed there as part of his trinitarian mentality.

Ælfric and the Trinity

I conclude with an interesting puzzle. If my reading of *The Dream of the Rood* is plausible, we should be able to find traces of Augustine's theology of language in other Anglo-Saxon texts too. The most obvious place to look would be Ælfric's sermons, several of which are straightforward digests of Christian doctrine drawn from patristic sources, including *De trinitate*. There is a surprise, however, in Ælfric's discussions of the Trinity: although he often uses *De trinitate*, not once does he borrow from the sections of it that we have been examining; he never uses Augustine's metaphor of speech for the Incarnation, or expounds upon the relation of words to the Word. He seems actually to avoid the theme. Why is that? And does this avoidance weaken our reading of *The Dream of the Rood*?

Ælfric discusses the Trinity in several sermons, but most fully in six: *De Initio Creaturae* (*Catholic Homilies* I.1), *De Fide Catholica* (*Catholic Homilies* I.20), *Nativitas Domini* (*In principio erat Verbum*) (ÆHom1; Pope I), *De Sancta Trinitate et de Festis Diebus per Annum* (ÆHom12; Pope XIa), *De Falsis Diis* (ÆHom22; Pope XXI), and the *Third Nativity Homily* (*Lives of Saints* I [Christmas]).[25] In the third of these he captures the essence of his trinitarian teaching:

> Her is nu belocen on þysum lytlan ferse
> eall seo halige Ðrynnys þe is þrymwealdend God:
> se Fæder 7 his Word, þæt is his agen Wisdom,

for ðan þe word is wisdomes geswutelung,
7 se Halga Gast, þe hylt ealle þing. (84–8)

[Here in this little verse is held
the Holy Trinity, Heaven-ruling God:
the Father and his Word – that is, his Wisdom
(since wisdom is revealed in words),
and the Holy Ghost who holds all things.]

From the evidence of these lines, and all his sermons, it is easy to see that Ælfric understood his own mentality in the trinitarian terms Augustine developed. In *De Fide Catholica*, for example, he says, 'Man's soul has in its nature a likeness of the Holy Trinity, since it has three things in it: memory, understanding and will' (þæs mannes sawul hæfð on hire gecynde þære halgan þrynnysse anlicnysse. for þan ðe heo hæfð on hire ðreo ðing. þæt is gemynd. 7 andgit. 7 willa). He accepts this model so intuitively, though, that he never wrestles with its philosophical subtleties, which so obsess Augustine. In the same sermon he says of words only that they are one product of the will.[26]

The above lines from *Nativitas Domini* may imply the ideas we have been examining, but they certainly do not state them. If we are searching for the theology of the Word, the most promising place to look would be a homily on the opening of John, but Ælfric barely touches on it here, saying only grudgingly of Christ that 'He is wisdomes spræc us unasecgendlic' [132: He is Wisdom's speech, to us ineffable], and of the creation that

ealle hi synd gesceapene þurh þone soðan Wisdom,
ðe is Word gehaten on þisum godspelle. (174–5)

[All these are shaped by the true Wisdom,
which in this Gospel is called Word.]

In all his discussions of the Trinity, Ælfric identifies Christ as wisdom or understanding rather than the Word; he links them only in this one instance, and here only because the text of John 1:1 compels him.

De trinitate (and later adaptations of it) is one of the sources for both *De Fide Catholica* and the *Third Nativity Homily*. The sermons are unphilosophical and simplified compared to their source. Could that be because they are sermons? For its genre, actually, *De Fide Catholica* is exceptionally learned; Malcolm Godden says, 'No other Anglo-Saxon homily provides any sort of parallel for this detailed discussion of trinitarian doctrine; indeed it is impossible to find any precedent, at least in homilies and sermons, without going back to the period of St. Augustine.'[27] Yet it contains no trace of Augustine's discussion of words and the Word. (Augustine's own sermons treat the theme frequently,[28] so genre is probably not a sufficient explanation.)

The *Third Nativity Homily* is more loosely constructed. It begins with Mary, the Incarnation, and the Trinity, then ranges through dozens of other topics, including the parts and powers of the soul, the senses, the virtues and vices, etc. Even when Ælfric labours to explain patristic psychology, however, and his source text is *De trinitate*, he refuses to confuse the listener with philosophical arguments about language. He mentions in passing, 'Whatever things the soul knows or does not know, it can create in the mind when it hears them spoken of'; but that is only half a theory, perhaps reflecting Ælfric's Benedictine life of silence: the monk listens, but does not speak.

Perhaps these references show that six centuries after *De trinitate*, the relation of words to the Word, which the Hebrew and Greek languages had presented so differently, and which Augustine had rethought so carefully in Latin, had come to be forgotten or ignored in England. It is more likely, however, that the concept had come simply to be taken for granted as received doctrine in monastic culture. What began as a speculative philosophical inquiry six centuries earlier had gradually become internalized as a *mentalité* inhabited all but unconsciously in Ælfric's world. It might inform the use of language itself, in texts now as well-known and little understood as *The Dream of the Rood*, but it did not need to be belaboured or explained.

NOTES

1 Margaret Schlauch, 'The *Dream of the Rood* as Prosopopoeia,' in *Essays and Studies in Honor of Carleton Brown*, ed. P.W. Long (New York: New York University Press, 1940), 23–34; repr. in *Essential Articles for the Study of Old English Poetry*, ed. Jess B. Bessinger, Jr, and Stanley J. Kahrl (Hamden, CT: Archon, 1968), 428–41.
2 James W. Earl, *Thinking about 'Beowulf'* (Stanford: Stanford University Press, 1994), 87–99.
3 (Revised Standard Version.) The Vulgate reads: (18:2) 'Caeli enarrant glo-

riam Dei, et opera manuum eius annuntiat firmamentum. (3) dies diei eructat verbum, et nox nocti indicat scientiam.'

4 In Psalm 114 (113):5–8, the question-and-answer format is probably a genuine case: 'Why is it, O sea, that you flee? / O Jordan, that you turn back? / O mountains, that you skip like rams? / O hills, like lambs? / Tremble, O earth, at the presence of the Lord, / at the presence of the God of Jacob, / who turns the rock into a pool of water, / the flint into a spring of water' [(113:5) quid est tibi, mare, quod fugisti? et tu, Iordanis, quia conversus es retrorsum? (6) montes, exsultastis sicut arietes? et colles sicut agni ovium? (7) a facie Domini mota est terra, a facie Dei Iacob; (8) qui convertit petram in stagna aquarum, et rupem in fontes aquarum.]

5 Psalm 95:12, 'tunc exsultabunt omnia ligna silvarum (13) a facie Domini, quia venit.'

6 Psalm 148:7, 'Laudate Dominum ... (9) montes, et omnes colles, ligna fructifera, et omnes cedri!'

7 Is. 14:8, 'Abietes quoque laetatae sunt super te, et cedri Libani: ex quo dormisti, non ascendit qui succidat nos.'

8 'Et quid est hoc? Interrogavi terram, et dixit: "non sum." et quaecumque in eadem sunt, idem confessa sunt. interrogavi mare et abyssos et reptilia animarum vivarum, et responderunt, "non sumus deus tuus; quaere super nos" ... interrogavi caelum, solem, lunam, stellas: "neque nos sumus deus, quem quaeris," inquiunt. et dixi omnibus his quae circumstant fores carnis meae, "dicite mihi de deo meo, quod vos non estis, dicite mihi de illo aliquid," et exclamaverunt voce magna, "ipse fecit nos." interrogatio mea intentio mea, et responsio eorum species eorum' (Augustine, *Confessiones*, ed. James J. O'Donnell, 3 vols [Oxford: Oxford University Press, 1992], 2:122).

9 Augustine, *On the Trinity, Books 8–15*, trans. Stephen McKenna, ed. Gareth B. Matthews (Cambridge: Cambridge University Press, 2002), 34–5. 'In illa igitur aeterna veritate, ex qua temporalia facta sunt omnia formam secundum quam sumus ... visu mentis aspicimus: atque inde conceptam rerum veracem notitiam, tanquam verbum apud nos habemus, et discendo intus gignimus; nec a nobis nascendo discedit ... Nemo enim volens aliquid facit, quod non in corde suo prius dixerit. Quod verbum amore concipitur, sive creaturae, sive Creatoris, id est, aut naturae mutabilis, aut incommutabilis veritatis ... Verbum ergo nostrum et mentem de qua gignitur, quasi medius amor conjungit, seque cum eis tertium complexu incorporeo, sine ulla confusione constringit' (*PL* 42:967–8).

10 'Verbum est igitur ... cum amore notitia. Cum itaque se mens novit et amat, jungitur ei amore verbum ejus. Et quoniam amat notitiam et novit amorem,

et verbum in amore est, et amor in verbo, et utrumque in amante atque dicente' (*PL* 42:969).
11 Vance, *Mervelous Signals: Poetics and Sign Theory in the Middle Ages* (Lincoln: University of Nebraska Press, 1986).
12 'Appetitus quo inhiatur rei cognoscendae, fit amor cognitae, dum tenet atque amplectitur placitam prolem, id est, notitiam, gignentique conjungit. Et est quaedam imago Trinitatis, ipsa mens, et notitia ejus, quod est proles ejus ac de se ipsa verbum ejus, et amor tertius, et haec tria unum atque una substantia' (*PL* 42:972).
13 Isaac Rabinowitz, 'Towards a Valid Theory of Biblical Hebrew Literature,' in *The Classical Tradition: Literary and Historical Studies in Honor of Harry Caplan*, ed. Luitpold Wallach (Ithaca, NY: Cornell University Press, 1966), 315–28.
14 'Quaedam ergo cogitationes locutiones sunt cordis, ubi et os esse Dominus ostendit ... Una sententia duo quaedam hominis ora complexus est, unum corporis, alterum cordis' (*PL* 42:1070).
15 'Nec tamen quia dicimus locutiones cordis esse cogitationes, ideo non sunt etiam visiones exortae de notitiae visionibus, quando verae sunt. Foris enim cum per corpus haec fiunt, aliud est locutio, aliud visio: intus autem cum cogitamus, utrumque unum est' (*PL* 42:1070–1).
16 'Quisquis igitur potest intelligere verbum, non solum antequam sonet, verum etiam antequam sonorum eius imagines cogitatione volvantur ... iam potest videre per hoc speculum atque in hoc aenigmate aliquam Verbi illius similitudinem, de quo dictum est, "In principio erat Verbum"' (*PL* 42:1071).
17 '[Verbum hominis] quod neque prolativum est in sano, neque cogitativum in similitudine soni, quod alicuius linguae esse necesse sit, sed quod omnia quibus significatur signa praecedit, et gignitur de scientia quae manet in animo, quando eadem scientia intus dicitur, sicuti est' (*PL* 42:1072).
18 'Verbum autem nostrum illud non quod habet sonum neque cogitationem soni sed, hujus rei quam videndo intus dicimus, et ideo nullius linguae est; atque inde utcumque simile est in hoc aenigmate illi Verbo Dei, quod etiam Deus est, quoniam sic et hoc de nostra nascitur, quemadmodum et illud de scientia Patris natum est: nostrum ergo tale verbum, quod invenimus esse utcumque illi simile, quantum sit etiam dissimile sicut a nobis dici potuerit, non pigeat intueri' (*PL* 42:1077).
19 Earl, *Thinking About 'Beowulf,'* 91–3.
20 John V. Fleming, '*The Dream of the Rood* and Anglo-Saxon Monasticism,' *Traditio* 22 (1966): 43–72.
21 Martin Heidegger, 'Language,' in *Poetry, Language, Thought*, trans. Albert Hofstadter (New York: Harper & Row, 1971), 189.

22 Robert E. Meagher, *Augustine: An Introduction* (New York: Harper and Row, 1978), 11–28, contains a Heideggerian reading of Augustine's theology of the Word.
23 Rosemary Woolf, 'Doctrinal Influences on *The Dream of the Rood*,' *MÆ* 27 (1958): 137–53; repr. in her *Art and Doctrine: Essays on Medieval Literature*, ed. Heather O'Donoghue (London: Hambledon, 1986), 29–48.
24 Thomas D. Hill, 'The Cross as Symbolic Body: An Anglo-Latin Liturgical Analogue to *The Dream of the Rood*,' *Neophilologus* 77 (1993): 297–301.
25 *Ælfric's Catholic Homilies: The First Series. Text*, ed. Peter Clemoes, EETS s.s.17 (Oxford: Oxford University Press, 1997); *Ælfric's Catholic Homilies: The Second Series. Text*, ed. Malcolm Godden, EETS s.s. 5 (London: Oxford University Press, 1979); *Homilies of Ælfric: A Supplementary Collection*, ed. John C. Pope, 2 vols, EETS o.s. 259–60 (London: Oxford University Press, 1967–8); *Ælfric's Lives of Saints*, ed. Walter W. Skeat, EETS o.s. 76, 82, 94, 114 (1881–1900; repr. in 2 vols, Oxford: Oxford University Press, 1966).
26 *De Fide Catholica*, lines 195–7, 199–200, ed. Clemoes, page 342: 'Of þam willan cumað geþohtas. and word. and weorc.' See note 28.
27 Godden, *Ælfric's Catholic Homilies: Introduction, Commentary and Glossary*, EETS s.s. 18 (Oxford: Oxford University Press, 2000), 159.
28 See, for example, sermons 117–20, on 'In principio erat Verbum,' and 187, *PL* 38:661–80, 1001–2.

The Leaps of Christ and *The Dream of the Rood*

JAMES W. MARCHAND

It is an indication that we have emerged from the phase during which we sneered at 'patristic exegesis' that so many studies in recent years have been devoted to situating *The Dream of the Rood* in its Christian tradition. In preparing ourselves to read the poem, we need to invoke the themes associated with the Cross in the early Middle Ages. Francis Lee Utley did much to recover these for us in a well-known article, 'The Tree Called Chy,'[1] but we must remember that our poet drew such knowledge in with his mother's milk, so to speak, be it ever so difficult for us.

Another commonplace theme associated with the Crucifixion in the Middle Ages, 'the Leaps of Christ,' is likewise accessible today only through research. I shall begin with two pieces of the liturgy which have been somewhat neglected in the search for Christian sources and parallels:

> Dum medium silentium teneret omnia, et nox in suo cursu medium iter perageret, omnipotens sermo tuus, Domine, a regalibus sedibus venit [*al.* prosilivit, Wisd. 18:14–15].[2] Alleluia! (Roman Breviary, 4th Sunday in Advent, antiphon for the Magnificat)

> [For while all things were in quiet silence, and that night was in the midst of her swift course, thy Almighty word came (leapt) down from heaven out of thy royal throne. Alleluia!]

> Ecce, iste venit saliens in montibus. Veniendo quippe ad redemptionem nostram, quosdam, ut ita dicam, saltus dedit. Vultis, fratres carissimi, ipsos ejus saltus agnoscere? De caelo venit in uterum, de utero venit in

praesepe, de praesepe venit in Crucem, de Cruce venit in sepulcrum, de sepulcro rediit in caelum. Ecce, ut nos post se currere faceret, quosdam pro nobis saltus manifestata per carnem Veritas dedit; qui exsultavit ut gigas ad currendam viam suam, ut nos ei diceremus ... (Roman Breviary, 4th Sunday in Advent, antiphon for the Magnificat)

[Behold, He comes, leaping upon the mountains (Cant. 2:8). When He came for our redemption, he made, as I say, some leaps. Do you want, dear brethren, to know about His leaps? From heaven He came into the womb, from the womb He came into the cradle, from the cradle He came onto the Cross, from the Cross He came into the tomb, from the tomb He returned to heaven. Behold, in order that He might cause us to run after Him, Manifest Truth made leaps for us in the flesh; He rejoiced as a giant to run his way (Ps. 18:6), if we may put it that way ...]

These reflect the following proof-texts:

vox dilecti mei: ecce iste venit, saliens in montibus, transiliens colles. (Cant. 2:8)

[The voice of my beloved. Behold he cometh leaping upon the mountains, skipping over the hills.]

in sole posuit tabernaculum suum; et ipse tamquam sponsus procedens de thalamo suo. Exultavit ut gigans ad currendam viam suam; (7) a summo caelo egressio eius. (Ps. 18:6–7)

[He hath set his tabernacle in the sun: and he, as a bridegroom coming out of his bride chamber, hath rejoiced as a giant to run the way. His going out is from the end of heaven.][3]

cum enim quietum silentium contineret omnia, et nox in suo cursu medium iter haberet, (15) omnipotens sermo tuus de caelo a regalibus sedibus, durus debellator in mediam exterminii terram prosilivit.[4] (Wis. 18:14–15)

[For while all things were in quiet silence, and that night was in the midst of her swift course, thy Almighty word leaped down from heaven out of thy royal throne as a fierce man of war into the midst of a land of destruction.]

There are two standard proof-texts for the last of the Leaps of Christ that we perhaps ought to mention. The angels, unaware of Christ's descent, are surprised at his Ascension:[5]

> quis est iste rex gloriae? ... [And others answer:] (10) Dominus virtutum, ipse est rex gloriae. (Ps. 23:8, 10)
>
> [Who is this King of Glory? ... The Lord of hosts, he is the King of Glory.]

The same scene is played out in Isaiah 63,[6] the Old Testament source for the medieval image of Christ in the wine-press:[7]

> quis est iste, qui venit de Edom, tinctis vestibus de Bosra? ... (2) quare ergo rubrum est indumentum tuum, et vestimenta tua sicut calcantium in torculari? (3) torcular calcavi solus ... et omnia indumenta mea inquinavi. (Is. 63:1-3)
>
> [Who is this that cometh from Edom, with dyed garments from Bosra? ... Why then is thy apparel red, and thy garments like theirs that tread in the winepress? I have trodden the winepress alone ... and I have stained all my apparel.]

The Leaps of Christ appear prominently in Cynewulf's *Ascension* (*Christ II*):[8]

> Bi þon Salomon song,   sunu Dauiþes,
> giedda gearosnottor   gæstgerynum,
> waldend werþeoda,   ond þæt word acwæð:
> Cuð þæt geweorðeð,   þætte cyning engla,
> meotud, meahtum swið,   munt gestylleð,
> gehleapeð hea dune,   hyllas ond cnollas
> bewrið mid his wuldre,   woruld alyseð,
> ealle eorðbuend,   þurh þone æþelan styll.
> Wæs se forma hlyp   þa he on fæmnan astag,
> mægeð unmæle,   ond þær mennisc hiw
> onfeng butan firenum   þæt to frofre gewearð
> eallum eorðwarum.   Wæs se oþer stiell
> bearnes gebyrda,   þa he in binne wæs,
> in cildes hiw   claþum bewunden,
> ealra þrymma þrym. *Wæs se þridda hlyp,*

rodorcyninges ræs,   þa he on rode astag,
fæder, frofre gæst. Wæs se feorða stiell
in byrgenne,   þa he þone beam ofgeaf,
foldærne fæst. Wæs se fifta hlyp
þa he hellwarena   heap forbygde in
cwicsusle,   cyning inne gebond,
feonda foresprecan,   fyrnum teagum,
gromhydigne,   þær he gen ligeð
in carcerne,   clommum gefæstnad,
synnum gesæled.   Wæs se siexta hlyp,
haliges hyhtplega,   þa he to heofonum astag
on his ealdcyððe.   Þa wæs engla þreat
on þa halgan tid   hleahtre bliðe
wynnum geworden. (712–42a; emphasis mine)

[Of that Solomon, the Son of David, the ruler of nations, skilled in measures, sang in his meditations [Cant. 2:8], and uttered these words: 'It shall be made known that the King of angels, the Lord great in might, shall go upon the mount, leap upon the lofty downs, shall garb with His glory the hills and the peaks, redeem the world, all dwellers upon earth, by the noble leap.' The first leap was when He passed into the Virgin, the spotless Maiden, and there took on man's form free from sin; that came to be a solace for all men on earth. The second leap was the Child's birth, when He, the Glory of all glories, was in a manger, swaddled in garments, in the form of a babe. *The third leap, the bound of the heavenly King, was when He, the Father, the Comforter, was raised on the cross.* The fourth leap was to the sepulchre, fast in the tomb, when he forsook the tree. The fifth leap was when He hurled down the host of hell to living torment, bound the king within, the fierce leader of the fiends, with fiery fetters, where yet he lies in prison, held fast in chains, shackled by sins. The sixth leap, the Holy One's joyful play, was when He ascended to heaven, to His former dwelling. Then the host of angels at that holy time grew blissfully joyous in their rapture.] [9]

A.S. Cook's excellent review of the theme identified the immediate source in Gregory the Great.[10] I will, in passing, correct Cook's mistaken belief that this idea originated with Ambrose; it is found earlier in Hippolytus (third century), as Roland Williams and Alois Haas, among others, point out.[11] I would also refer to R.E. Kaske's article on 'Gigas' in *Piers Plowman*, based on our second proof-text, Psalm 18:6.[12]

This notion of the Leaps of Christ may seem unusual, perhaps even grotesque, to us, but in the Middle Ages it is repeated innumerable times. In fact, it was the hook upon which the Theory of Salvation and the presentation of the *Pia fraus* were often hung. One could easily write a book on each of the leaps. I cannot treat them here; suffice it to say that when I call the Leaps of Christ a commonplace, I do mean *commonplace*.

Note that the third leap ('hlyp') in Cynewulf's enumeration, 'the bound of the heavenly King' ('rodorcyninges ræs'), was when Christ leapt ('astag') onto the Cross. Moving back to *The Dream of the Rood*, we read that Christ boldy hastens to the Cross and, in an action described with the same root verb -*stigan* (*gestigan/gestah*) used by Cynewulf, leaps upon it:

>   Geseah ic þa frean mancynnes
> efstan elne mycle   þæt he me wolde on gestigan.
> Þær ic þa ne dorste   ofer dryhtnes word
> bugan oððe berstan,   þa ic bifian geseah
> eorðan sceatas.   Ealle ic mihte
> feondas gefyllan,   hwæðre ic fæste stod.
> Ongyrede hine ða geong hæleð,   þæt wæs god ælmihtig,
> strang ond stiþmod.   Gestah he on gealgan heanne,
> modig on manigra gesyhðe,   þa he wolde mancyn lysan.
> Bifode ic þa me se beorn ymbclypte.   Ne dorste ic hwæðre bugan to eorðan,
> feallan to foldan sceatum,   ac ic sceolde fæste standan. (33b–43)

[Then I saw the Lord of mankind hasten with great zeal, that he wanted to climb upon me. Then and there I dared not against the word of the Lord bow nor break, when I saw tremble the womb of the earth. I might have felled all the enemies, but I stood firm. [He] undressed himself the young hero (that was God Almighty), strong and unflinching. He climbed upon the high cross brave in the sight of many, when he desired to redeem mankind I trembled when the Man embraced me; but I dared not bow to the earth, fall to the bosom of the earth, but I was supposed to stand firm.]

This Crucifixion scene differs so strongly from that usually drawn in the Middle Ages that it has been a great puzzle for scholars. In contrast to the obvious reluctance of the Cross to receive Him, Christ eagerly rushes to the Cross. The charged energy of this passage has been noticed by Rosemary Woolf: 'the heroic quality of Christ is suggested by the three actions ascribed to Him: He advances to the Cross with bold speed, strips Himself, and ascends it ...'[13] This is not the tired Christ so often depicted in medieval Crucifixion scenes, not the Man of Sorrows,[14] but the *Miles Christus*, the *durus debellator* of Wisdom 18:15, reflecting the theological point made over and over again that Christ was crucified because *he* wanted it, and at the time *he* desired:

Geseah ic þa Frean mancynnes
efstan elne mycle þæt he me wolde on gestigan. (33b–4)

Perhaps we could translate line 34a most simply as 'hasten with great force.' But even with the understanding that this is the *Miles Christus*, eager to 'reign from the tree' and to do battle with Leviathan on the Cross, this makes hard reading. The tree prepares itself to receive Christ, not daring to budge or bend. Now Christ is referred to as the hero, the *hæleð*, the athlete, the warrior of Wisdom 18, reflected in the antiphon for the Magnificat of the 4th Sunday in Advent, the *durus debellator* ['fierce man of war']. He undresses himself, to complete our picture of the athlete, the *gymnicus*, who, as we know, must fight naked.[15] In fact, he is preparing to do battle not against flesh and blood, but against the prince of this world (Eph. 6:12; Col. 2:15), to redeem mankind ('mancyn lysan,' 41b): he is our wrestler, anointed and naked.[16] Echoes of *nudus nudum Christum sequi* ring in our ears. We may remember that St Ambrose has him undress himself: 'pulchre ascensurus crucem regalia vestimenta deposuit' [about to ascend the Cross, he put off most elegantly his royal vestments].[17]

The expression *on gestigan*, which is used twice in our short selection, is almost universally translated as 'to climb onto,' but 'climb,' with its inherent iterative meaning, cannot be right if we believe our OE grammars.[18] All are opposed by John Lindemann, who bases his own theories on a quite limited corpus (the OE versions of Matthew).[19] The *ge*-prefix shows that this must be a perfective (or, if one prefers, 'complexive') verb.[20] Perhaps 'mount,' also used, will work, or 'ascend,' the *ascendere* of Latin hymnology; but I must insist on the aspectual force of the prefix, and the best translation, it seems to me, is 'leap.' Christ does not intend to climb the tree, he intends to leap upon it, to embrace it. The action of the tree supports this reading. It has to brace itself to receive the hero, stand firm, though it does tremble when the young hero embraces ('ymbclyppan') it, embracing, that is, in the view of medieval exegesis, the ends of the earth.[21] Note that Christ must be facing the Cross at this moment in our narrative. Still, even with the understanding that the *ge-* of *gestigan* is perfective, isn't this forcing the meaning somewhat, since *stigan* inherently means 'to climb'? Does it? A glance at *Christ II* shows that Cynewulf twice uses *astigan* to mean 'leap,' once for the leap into the womb (721), and once for the leap onto the Cross (739). Christ does not move onto the Cross in repetitive action, step-by-step, as 'climb' would indicate, but in one movement. Given the commonplace nature of the Leaps of Christ, 'leap' seems the best translation. Christ leapt upon the Cross and embraced it, for he wished to save mankind.

In this little essay I have tried to illustrate again, preaching to the converted as it were, the necessity for close attention to the intertextuality of the medieval poet, for steeping oneself in his ambience. *Se non e ben trovato, e vero.*

NOTES

1 Utley identifies the 'Tree called Chy' with the Chi-Rho cross: 'The Prose *Salomon and Saturn* and the Tree Called Chy,' *MS* 19 (1957): 55–78. See also Eleanor Simmons Greenhill on the cosmic Cross: 'The Child in the Tree: A Study of the Cosmological Tree in Christian Tradition,' *Traditio* 10 (1954): 323–71.
2 Most of the authors who cite this passage before the tenth century seem to prefer *prosilivit* 'leapt'; cf. *PL* 20:877 (Gaudentius of Brescia, *Sermo* VI); 85:328 (this is the Mozarabic 'Missale mixtum,' with our text for the Saturday of the second week in Lent); 91:553 (Bede, *Allegorica expositio in Samuelem*); 91:1059 (Bede, *Fragmenta in Proverbia Salomonis*): 'Quod autem dicit eum prosiluisse, inopinatum adventum ejus designavit'; 109:756 (Hrabanus, *Commentaria in librum Sapientiae*). The present Roman Missal has *venit* (*The Liber Usualis*, with introduction and rubrics in English, ed. by the Benedictines of Solesmes [Tournai: Desclee, 1962], 1255) as does the Roman Breviary (*Breviarium Romanum, ex decreto SS. Concilii Tridentini Restitutum, pars hiemalis* [Würzburg: Pustet, 1952], 432). The Douay translation has 'leapt.'
3 I have followed Douay in translating *exultavit* as 'rejoiced,' though 'leapt' might be a better translation, and it was often so understood in the Middle Ages.

4 It is important for our discussion to note the *durus debellator* [fierce man of war] of the Vulgate and most of the texts cited above, p. 81.
5 Wolfgang Babilas, 'Die Unterrichtung der Engel von Christi Inkarnation,' in his *Untersuchungen zu den Sermoni Subalpini mit einem Exkurs über die Zehn-Engelchor-Lehre*, Münchner Romanistische Arbeiten 24 (Munich: Max Hueber, 1968), 71–9.
6 See Paul B. d'Azy, 'Les Anges devant le mystère de l'Incarnation,' *Bulletin de littérature ecclésiastique* (Toulouse) 69 (1948): 87–106, 129–47, esp. 147ff.
7 See Alois Thomas, *Die Darstellung Christi in der Kelter*, Forschungen zur Volkskunde 20–1 (Düsseldorf: Schwann, 1935); and 'Christus in der Kelter,' *Reallexikon für deutsche Kunstgeschichte* 3 (1954): 673–87.
8 On the Leaps of Christ see R.E. Kaske, 'Eve's "Leaps" in the *Ancrene Riwle*,' *MÆ* 29 (1960): 22–4; Thomas D. Hill, '"Mary, the Rose Bush" and the Leaps of Christ,' *ES* 67 (1986): 478–82; Andrew Breeze, 'Varia VI: The "Leaps" That Christ Made,' *Ériu* 40 (1989): 190–3; Michael W. Twomey, 'Christ's Leap and Mary's Clean Catch in *Piers Plowman* B.12.136–44a and C.14.81–88a,' *YLS* 5 (1991): 165–74.
9 Trans. R.K. Gordon, *Anglo-Saxon Poetry* (New York: Dutton, 1954), 146 (emphasis mine).
10 A.S. Cook, *The 'Christ' of Cynewulf* (1900; repr. with a new preface by John C. Pope [Hamden, CT: Archon, 1964]), 143–4. The source is Gregory's *Homiliae in euangelia* XXIX.10, ed. R. Étaix, CCSL 141, 253–4. For an English translation of the homily, see M.J.B. Allen and Daniel G. Calder, *Sources and Analogues of Old English Poetry: The Major Latin Texts in Translation* (Cambridge: D.S. Brewer, 1976), 79–81.
11 Hippolytus of Rome, *Interpretatio Cantici Canticorum*, in *Traités d'Hippolyte sur David et Goliath, sur le Cantique des cantiques et sur l'Antéchrist*, ed. Gérard Garitte, CSCO 264, Scriptores Iberici 16 (Louvain: Secrétariat du CSCO, 1965), 41–2 (translation mine:): 'Oh, plan [*oeconomia*] of the New Grace! Oh, great mysteries: "Behold my brother came leaping." What was that leaping? The Word sprang from heaven into the body of the Virgin. It sprang from the tree into Hades, it sprang again onto the earth. Oh, the new arising: Again it sprang from the earth into heaven.' See Roland T. Williams, 'Cynewulf's "Ascension" (Christ II): A Critical Edition' (PhD diss., Bowling Green State University, 1974), 256–7; Alois M. Haas, 'Der Lichtsprung der Gottheit (Parz. 466),' in *Typologia Litterarum: Festschrift für Max Wehrli*, ed. Stefan Sonderegger, Alois M. Haas, and Harald Burger (Zurich: Atlantis, 1969), 205–32 at 227.
12 R.E. Kaske, '*Gigas* the Giant in *Piers Plowman*,' *JEGP* 56 (1957): 177–85.
13 Rosemary Woolf, 'Doctrinal Influences on *The Dream of the Rood*,' *MÆ* 27

(1958): 137–53 at 145–6. Peter Clemoes, too, has singled out this passage for comment; see his *Rhythm and Cosmic Order in Old English Christian Literature* (Cambridge: Cambridge University Press, 1970), 7–11.

14 Erwin Panofsky, 'Imago Pietatis,' in *Festschrift für Max J. Friedländer zum 60. Geburtstage* (Leipzig: E.A. Seemann, 1927), 261–308. See also *The Hours of Catherine of Cleves*, ed. John Plummer (New York: G. Braziller, n.d. [1966?], no. 25: 'Here Christ sits forlornly upon a hillock watching the preparation of the cross. His body is lacerated and, except for a loincloth, naked; His wrists are bound.'

15 Isidore of Seville, *Etymologiae* 18.18.1, ed. W.M. Lindsay, in *Isidori Hispalensis Etymologiarum sive Originum Libri XX*, 2 vols (1911; repr. Oxford: Clarendon, 1985): 'Genera gymnicorum quinque: id est *saltus*, cursus, iactus, uirtus atque luctatio.' Matthäus Bernards points out places in the Fathers where the Christian athlete must be nude; 'Nudus nudum Christum sequi,' *Wissenschaft und Weisheit* 14 (1951): 148–51. Gregory preserves the connection with the warrior: 'nudi ergo cum nudo luctari debemus' (*Homilia XXXII in euangelia*, ed. Étaix, CCSL 141:278).

16 A simple search for 'wrestle' in the *Ante and Post-Nicene Fathers* on the *Christian Classics Ethereal Library 2000* CD-ROM will show how frequent this metaphor is. Note also the Christmas sequence, *Eia recolamus*, where Christ 'certat ut miles armatura' [fights like a knight in armour]; ed. Wolfram von den Steinen, *Notker der Dichter und seine geistige Welt*, 2nd ed., 2 vols (Bern: A. Francke, 1978), 2:94, line 14.

17 Ambrose, *Expositio euangelii secundum Lucam*, PL 15:1830; cited by John V. Fleming, 'The Dream of the Rood and Anglo-Saxon Monasticism,' *Traditio* 22 (1966): 43–72 at 53.

18 Eduard Sievers and Karl Brunner, *Altenglische Grammatik*, 3rd rev. ed., Sammlung kurzer Grammatiken germanischer Dialekte, A. Hauptreihe 3 (Tübingen: Max Niemeyer, 1965), §366, n. 1; Randolf Quirk and C.L. Wrenn, *An Old English Grammar* (1957; repr. with a Supplemental Bibliography by Susan E. Deskis, DeKalb, IL: Northern Illinois University Press, 1994), §§129–30, 168, 170; Fernand Mossé, *Manuel de l'anglais du moyen âge*, vol. 1, *Vieil-anglais*, Bibliothèque de Philologie Germanique 8 (Paris: Aubier, 1965), 148-9; Martin Lehnert, *Altenglisches Elementarbuch: Einführung, Grammatik, Texte mit Übersetzung und Wörterbuch*, 8th ed., Sammlung Göschen 5125 (Berlin: de Gruyter, 1973), 104; Henry Sweet, *Sweet's Anglo-Saxon Primer*, rev. Norman Davis, 9th ed. (Oxford: Clarendon, 1952), 40.

19 J.W. Richard Lindemann, 'Old English Preverbal *ge-*: A Re-examination of Some Current Doctrines,' *JEGP* 64 (1965): 65–83. Note also Bruce Mitchell

and Fred C. Robinson, *A Guide to Old English*, 6th ed. (Oxford: Blackwell, 2001), 58.
20 See Alfred R. Wedel, 'Alliteration and the Prefix *ge-* in Cynewulf's *Elene*,' *JEGP* 100 (2001): 200–10. Wedel cites Albert L. Lloyd's definition of the 'complexive aspect' in Germanic *ga-/ge-/gi-* compounds as conveying a complete action or change, that is, 'an action which represents a complete change from one ... state of actional rest to another, different one' (*Anatomy of the Verb: The Gothic Verb as a Model for a Unified Theory of Aspect, Actional Types, and Verbal Velocity* (Amsterdam: John Benjamins, 1979), 28–9. Such a definition would equally accommodate the sense 'leap' for *gestigan*.
21 Cf. John 12:32-3: 'et ego si exaltatus fuero a terra, omnia traham ad me ipsum. (33) hoc autem dicebat, significans qua morte esset moriturus' ['And I, if I be lifted up from the earth, will draw all things to myself.' Now this he said, signifying what death he should die].

'Ðu eart se weallstan': Architectural Metaphor and Christological Imagery in the Old English *Christ I* and the Book of Kells

JOHANNA KRAMER

In the form it has been transmitted to us in the Exeter Book, the first complete sentence of the OE liturgical poem *Christ I* (*The Advent*) begins with a common metaphor for Christ: 'Ðu eart se weallstan' [You are the wall-stone]. In the poem's paraphrase of Psalm 117:21–3 on the rejected cornerstone, Christ is addressed as the stone that the workers cast aside, but which became the *caput anguli*, a slightly cryptic phrase that can be translated literally as 'head of the corner.' From this image of the cornerstone, the Anglo-Saxon poet develops in Lyric I (1–17) a series of mostly architectural metaphors, moving from the head of a glorious hall with sturdy walls to a ruined house and finally to a frail human body. This poetic trajectory results in a somewhat problematic assemblage of seemingly disjointed images. Since Albert S. Cook's edition of 1900,[1] various aspects of *Christ I*, including the imagery in Lyric I, have been under discussion. Despite the comparative wealth of scholarship on the poem overall, especially on particular lyrics, few commentators have discussed convincingly the dynamic interplay between the metaphors in Lyric I.[2] Some have, in fact, seen the contradictory images as evidence for poetic imperfection.[3] Since the publication of Robert Burlin's typological reading of *Christ I* in 1968, no recent study examines the lyric's use of architectural metaphor in a patristic context. More importantly for this essay, although the poem's prevalent spatial symbolism invites the comparison, only Robert Deshman, to the best of my knowledge, has suggested an artistic analogue to the poem.[4]

This lack of recent discussions justifies reconsidering the lyric's dense Christological imagery in light of biblical and patristic exegesis on the *caput anguli* and the *lapis angularis*, a phrase taken from Paul's letter to the Ephesians that is also commonly used to designate the stone at the corner, the angular stone. Moreover, it is important to contextualize the architectural imagery with reference to other insular works of literature and visual art. Thus, I will first elucidate the exegetical background of Lyric I. In reflection of the 'ruminative mode' of the text itself, I shall present in this first part an explication of the lyric's content that is also meant to serve as a layered and cumulative description of its richly multivalent character.[5] I will then compare the poem's allusive spatial and architectural imagery with the illuminated page from the Book of Kells known as 'The Temptation of Christ,' which provides a striking visual analogue to the poem that has not so far been discussed in any scholarship on *Christ I*. Scholars have previously argued that Lyric I, like *Christ I* as a whole, deserves attention as sophisticated, learned, and coherent poetry. A comparative and cross-disciplinary reading, as I undertake it here, considerably strengthens the view that the learned *Christ* poet's *Raummetaphorik* – that is, the symbolic use of space in literary and artistic expression – constructs a multi-faceted representation of Christological teachings in poetic form that, moreover, reverberates with imagery more broadly current in insular cultures at the time.

Christ I: Christ as the Cornerstone

Christ I consists of twelve subdivisions, nearly all of which derive from the liturgical antiphons of the Advent season and poetically expand the themes set out briefly by the Latin source texts.[6] The antiphon at the root of Lyric I belongs to the seven so-called Greater or O Antiphons and hails Christ as ruler: 'O Rex gentium, et desideratus earum, lapisque angularis, qui facis utraque unum: veni, et salva hominem, quem de limo formasti'[7] [O King of nations, and their desired one, and the cornerstone, you who make one out of two: come and save the human whom you have formed from clay].[8] The OE elaboration of this antiphon is as follows:

                          cyninge.[9]
  Ðu eart se weallstan   þe ða wyrhtan iu
  wiðwurpon to weorce.   Wel þe geriseð
  þæt þu heafod sie   healle mærre,
5 ond gesomnige   side weallas
  fæste gefoge,   flint unbræcne,

þæt geond eorðb[. .]g eall   eagna gesihþe
wundrien to worlde   wuldres ealdor.
Gesweotula nu þurh searocræft   þin sylfes weorc,
10 soðfæst, sigorbeorht,   ond sona forlæt
weall wið wealle.   Nu is þam weorce þearf
þæt se cræftga cume   ond se cyning sylfa,
ond þonne gebete,   nu gebrosnad is,
hus under hrofe.   He þæt hra gescop,
15 leomo læmena;   nu sceal liffrea
þone wergan heap   wraþum ahreddan,
earme from egsan,   swa he oft dyde. (1–17)

[... to the king.
You are the wall-stone, which the workers once
cast aside from the work. Well it befits you
that you be the head of the glorious hall
5 and join together the broad walls,
with firm bond, the unbroken stone,
so that throughout earth's dwellings all with the sight of their eyes
may marvel forever at the Lord of Glory.
Make bright now through your skilful craft your own work,
10 firm in truth, bright in victory, and at once leave (standing)
wall against wall. Now it is necessary for that work
that the craftsman come and the king himself
and restore what is now ruined,
the house beneath the roof. He formed that body,
15 the limbs of clay; now must the lord of life
free the wearied band from enemies,
the wretches from terror, as he has often done.]

Although the poet follows the content of the source antiphon quite closely, he (or she) has a different focus. While the antiphon contains the architectural image of the *lapis angularis*, it lacks a sustained and encompassing architectural theme. In contrast, with the help of the combined images of Christ as cornerstone of the church and as head of the mystical body, the OE poet assembles a complex but coherent metaphorical sequence of architectural images, into which he deftly incorporates all of the antiphonal elements (the exalted king, the cornerstone, Christ's unifying and salvific agency, the creation and fallen condition of mankind). Thus, the central theme of Lyric I, rather than depending narrowly on the antiphon, consists of a more broadly informed and richly expressive architectural metaphor for Christ.

The Latin phrase *lapis angularis* of the source antiphon is taken from a passage in Ephesians that, in turn, echoes Isaiah 28:16. The image of the rejected stone, however, stems from Psalm 117, in which the famous verses on the *caput anguli* occur:

> confitebor tibi quoniam exaudisti me et factus es mihi in salutem. (22) lapidem quem reprobaverunt aedificantes hic factus est in caput anguli. (23) a Domino factum est istud, hoc est mirabile in oculis nostris. (Ps. 117:21–3)

> [I will give glory to thee because thou hast heard me: and art become my salvation. The stone which the builders rejected; the same is become the head of the corner. This is the Lord's doing: and it is wonderful in our eyes.]

The *caput anguli*, along with the *lapis angularis* of Isaiah 28:16, was a recurrent motif of patristic and later medieval exegesis.[10] Even in early New Testament writings, the cornerstone, initially an isolated motif, is already integrated with another architectural metaphor, namely, that of the Christian church as a temple, as a House of God.[11] The cornerstone and the temple were among the most common types of Christ and the Church and, throughout the Middle Ages, acted as catalysts for fertile Christological imagery.[12] The cornerstone is read figuratively as Christ already in the New Testament, most influentially in Ephesians.[13] Weaving Old Testament imagery into his teachings on the incarnation and sacrifice of Christ, Paul emphasizes the dominant theme of 'joining':

> nunc autem in Christo Iesu vos qui aliquando eratis longe facti estis prope in sanguine Christi. (14) ipse est enim pax nostra *qui fecit utraque unum*, et medium parietem maceriae solvens inimicitiam in carne sua ... (19) ergo iam non estis hospites et advenae, sed estis cives sanctorum et domestici Dei (20) superaedificati super fundamentum apostolorum et prophetarum ipso summo *angulari lapide* Christo Iesu. (21) in quo omnis aedificatio constructa crescit in templum sanctum in Domino; (22) in quo et vos coaedificamini in habitaculum Dei in Spiritu. (Eph. 2:13–22, emphases added)

> [But now in Christ Jesus you, who were once afar off, have been brought near through the blood of Christ. For he himself is our peace, he it is *who*

has made both one, and has broken down the intervening wall of the enclosure, the enmity, in his flesh ... Therefore, you are now no longer strangers and foreigners, but you are citizens with the saints and members of God's household: you are built upon the foundation of the apostles and prophets with Christ Jesus himself as the chief *corner stone*. In him the whole structure is closely fitted together and grows into a temple holy in the Lord; in him you too are being built together into a dwelling place for God in the Spirit.]

Two of the epistle's phrases became part of the Advent antiphon that is the source for the first lyric of *Christ I*: the reference to Christ's joining ('fecit utraque unum') and the reference to him as the cornerstone ('angulari lapide'). Paul conceives of these two functions of Christ as separate statements. The *lapis angularis* is a stone in the foundation but is *not* a stone that joins two walls representing Jews and Gentiles, and it appears exclusively in connection with the growing temple of God. Paul nevertheless places the phrase that expressly communicates Christ's joining ability ('fecit utraque unum') into a spatial context by introducing the partitioning wall that separates Jews and Gentiles.[14] Rather than joining walls, as in later exegesis and in *Christ I*, Christ joins the two spaces on either side of a torn-down wall.

The conceptualization of the *lapis angularis* that prevails in most post-Pauline patristic exegesis is that of a stone connecting two walls, apparently in a conflation of the elements still distinct in Ephesians. The walls receive multiple interpretations: most commonly as Jews and Gentiles (following the Pauline letter), but also as representing the heavenly and earthly realms. Jerome adopts this twofold reading in his commentary on the Pauline letters,[15] and to Gregory the Great the walls signify 'the church on earth and the angels in heaven,' an interpretation he offers in *Moralia in Job*.[16] The Anglo-Saxon church also knew the two-fold interpretation of the joined walls; both Bede and Ælfric adopt the double reading of the walls as Jews/Gentiles and as angels/mankind in their homilies.[17] The reading of Christ as reconciling heavenly and earthly spheres, through whatever channels it may have been known to the *Christ* poet, seems to bear on *Christ I*. The Christ who joins walls as *caput anguli* corresponds to the artificer Christ in Lyric I. This interpretation, as we shall see, proves essential to the poet's endeavour to depict Christ's dual nature and the relationship of Christ the head to his mystical body, the *Ecclesia*. Even a cursory survey of early exegetical writings makes clear that in the metaphor of the *caput anguli* the *Christ* poet inherited a thoroughly conventional spatial image, but one with potential for richly symbolic expression of theological subtleties.

From the Old Testament use of the phrases *caput anguli* and *lapis angularis*, one cannot precisely determine where this 'head of the corner' may be located in relation to the wall or building to which it is imagined to belong. This inherent semantic ambiguity of both phrases has led to disparate exegetical readings of the cornerstone as well as much debate in current biblical, classical, and patristic scholarship.[18] Early exegetes – and their later medieval commentators – envision the *lapis angularis* either as set in the corner of the foundation of a building or, placed at an elevation, as a cornerstone just beneath the roof or a capstone of an arch or vault. Occasionally high and low placements of the stone are combined.[19] The *Christ* poet interprets the rejected 'weallstan' as an elevated stone: by calling his Christ the 'heafod healle mærre,' he shows preference for the phrase *caput anguli* over the *lapis angularis* of Psalm 117 and Ephesians 2. This metaphor employs as its vehicle the head which is typically located at an elevation as part of the human physique. The phrase thus immediately points to a higher placement of the *weallstan*. The OE poet indeed imagines Christ the head as raised aloft – he is the roof of the imagined building, almost soaring above it – to reinforce Christ's vantage point so that the world can marvel at him (7–8).

The lyric's development of the architectural metaphor of Christ as *caput anguli* is made complicated not least because it contains what appear to be, upon first reading, dissonant images: after invoking the glorified *caput anguli*, the poet suddenly speaks no longer of the glorious hall but of a ruined house (11a–14). This house, in turn, becomes the helpless human body, signifying both the individual (14b–15) and the collective body of all humanity (16–17), that is, the faithful who form Christ's body and whose moral corruption is reflected in the ruined state of the house. The glorious hall 'nu gebrosnad is,' and the 'hus under hrofe,' that is, the *Ecclesia*, requires renovation. By employing *Bildervermischung*, a blending of motifs or images, the poet then presents Christ not only as a building, but also as the creator of that same space.[20] Christ, as a craftsman ('cræftga') and as the original architect of the building, is called upon to come and restore the crumbling hall, which, paradoxically, is also his own body. The image of the decaying house – a negative image – appears somewhat unexpectedly following the hall's initial function as a referent to Christ and does not immediately accord with the images in the surrounding lines. The palette of contradictory images, however, aims at a cumulative effect with the ruined house of Lyric I fulfilling a distinct role in the complete cycle of images.

In his commentary, A.S. Cook asserts that the word *hra* (14) is 'not to be identified with *hūs*; we have now passed to the second half of the Antiphon.'[21] Cook's strict separation of the architectural from the bodily term (mirrored by his separation of the two parts of the antiphon) comes as a surprise, since he also points out that 'Ælfric recognizes *hūs*, as a metaphor, in two senses: (a) The one church universal; (b) the individual Christian.'[22] If *hus* can refer to the individual Christian, it is difficult to see why *hra* 'the human body, corpse' should not function as a poetic variant for *hus*. The two words appear, moreover, in the same line and they alliterate. Both function on literal and, more importantly, metaphorical levels, through which they are rendered equivalents of each other: *hus* = church = all Christians = Christ's body = the individual body = *hra*. Through these equivalencies, a larger poetic context is created that, in fact, urges a continuous reading from *hus* to *hra* and thus a semantic equation of the word complex *healle/hus/hra/heap* and their associated theological interpretations. Significantly, the semantic connection of *healle/hus/hra/heap* is also borne out by the word *gebete* (13). The verb *gebetan* can simply mean 'to make good, mend, repair, restore' (*DOE*, s.v. *ge·betan* A.1. and specifically A.1.a.),[23] as one does when repairing an object. Significantly, it is also commonly used in reference to 'spiritual or moral concerns,' in particular 'of a person or his sin' in the meaning of 'to correct, reform, amend' (A.2.e. and A.2.e.ii) as well as with the meaning of 'to atone for, repent of (something, usually sin)' (B.1.). In an interpretation well suited for Lyric I, the past participle form of *gebetan* is also attested in the specific meaning of 'fortified (by a wall)' (*DOE*, s.v. *ge·bett* A.2.b.).[24] The architectural imagery used for Christ consists of poetically rich and effective metaphors that help the poet to embody, and his audience to visualize, Christ's relationship to the church. The polysemy of *gebetan* invokes the polysemy of the metaphors themselves, inviting an active symbolic reading of the overarching *Raummetaphorik*. As the craftsman Christ restores the house of the faithful community and fortifies the protective but dilapidated walls, each penitent Christian soul becomes reformed. Conversely, when each individual does penance, then the condition of the house, that is, *Ecclesia*, Christ's body, improves. These processes are two sides of the same coin. Beyond the level of the individual, the hall's two stages symbolize Christ's dual nature as well as his complex relationship to the church and to all humanity. As *Deus*, Christ created and continuously restores, while as *Homo* he participates himself in the bodily church.

The shifting metaphors (wall-stone to glorious hall to ruined house to helpless human being) also reflect the cyclical and contradictory nature of liturgical time.[25] Through precise choices in verbal mood, the poet replicates the central temporal paradox inherent in Christian liturgy and theology. While addressing Christ as the 'wall-stone' (with the indicative *eart*, line 2), the poet only envisions the appropriateness of Christ as head of the glorious hall (with the subjunctive *sie*, line 4), implying that the structure nears its crowning completion but has not quite reached it yet. Equally, the ruined building requires repair now (with the indicative *is*, lines 11 and 13) – the poet heightens the sense of expectant urgency by repeatedly inserting *nu* – but the coming of the craftsman and the restoration are anticipated only, not yet fulfilled (with the subjunctives *cume* and *gebete*, lines 12 and 13). In liturgical terms, even though Christ has redeemed humanity through his First Coming, Christians re-await his coming annually during Advent.[26] This temporal paradox of simultaneous fulfillment and anticipation finds expression in the double image of the glorious hall/ruined house, especially since the source antiphon belongs to the liturgy of the Advent, when the arrival of the Lord is, from a liturgical point of view, truly imminent. The liturgical posture of waiting for Christ's return reminds the faithful that, as Christians in history, they continually live in a state of anticipation, and the double image of the glorious hall/ruined house represents this tentative state between the First and the Second Coming of the historical church. His sacrifice has already saved humanity and enclosed it with the protecting walls of Christ's universal church, yet all believers still travel on perilous paths that may endanger their salvation and thus still live in need of reform and saving.[27] The ruin stands for the fragile and vexed existence of this life and for the constant threat of losing the joys of eternity while, in an inversion of the famous simile of the sparrow in Bede's *Historia ecclesiastica*, the glorious hall promises a joyous and convivial hereafter.

As my reading of Lyric I shows, the initially contradictory images of the overarching architectural metaphor – each based on orthodox theology – merge into an integrated whole. At the same time, the poet preserves the paradoxical character of the Christian experience and solves the considerable artistic problem of depicting the confounding mystery of Christ's dual nature. The lyric's signification succeeds due to the poet's precisely controlled *Raummetaphorik*. He reflects on the implications of the architectural metaphor and carries it to its logical conclusion: if the glorious hall expresses Christ's true and the church's potential perfection in a positive image, then the negative or reverse image, the ruined house, signals human fallibility. By fashioning the iconography that had accumulated around the cornerstone into a dense poetic representation of Christ, the poet vividly and accessibly translates scriptural, exegetical, and liturgical traditions.

Ælfric and Bede: Living Stones and the Spiritual Church of Christ

Before moving to the visual parallel of the *caput anguli* in the Book of Kells, I want to briefly comment on the use of architectural metaphor in two Anglo-Saxon texts – one vernacular, one Latin. These parallels have been pointed out before,[28] but it is worth taking another look at them, for the complex representation of the metaphor in each of these texts has not been fully appreciated. In his Homily XL for the dedication of a church, Ælfric develops the image of Christ building the church from the living stones of the faithful and invokes both 1 Peter 2:5–7 and Psalm 117 (also cited by Peter).[29] Not only does Ælfric treat the same motif as the *Christ* poet, but Ælfric's vocabulary reflects a similar emphasis on the very materiality of the physical process – the building material, the fitting together of stones, foundation, and framework – and thus his pronounced interest in craftsmanship and architectural construction. A more complex use of *Raummetaphorik* can be found in Bede, who stands out among Anglo-Saxon authors in his intense concern with the symbolism of biblical architecture.[30] Book 1 of his exegetical treatise *De templo* proves relevant as a conceptual and topical analogue to Lyric I. Reading the physical temple and tabernacle as prefigurations of the spiritual church built in Christ, Bede offers a wide range of figurative meanings in a presentation as dense as that of the *Christ* poet.[31] Although Bede and the *Christ* poet share an interest in spatial symbolism, Bede is less fascinated by the material elements of the spiritual temple than he is by the exegetical opportunities afforded by the architectural metaphor. Besides symbolizing the incarnate Christ, the temple, with its changing significance throughout Jewish and Christian history, represents for him the past, present, and future states of the *Ecclesia*. Christ as temple is, of course, a central image in Lyric I, while the temporal paradox of the church's suspended state between earthly pilgrimage and heavenly reign, explicitly mentioned by Bede, is paralleled by the poem's cyclical liturgical function.[32] The examples from Bede and Ælfric serve to remind us of the motif's currency in Anglo-Saxon England and to affirm that the *Christ* poet could reasonably expect his audience to recognize the symbolically rich architectural metaphor of Christ as the *lapis angularis/caput anguli* and to be able to appreciate, and perhaps to visualize, at least some of its typological implications.

A Visual Analogue to *Christ I*: The 'Temptation of Christ' in the Book of Kells

An artistic analogue to the *Raummetaphorik* of *Christ I* in the Book of Kells affords some insight into how such Christological imagery might have been realized in visual form. The depiction of 'The Temptation of Christ' (fol. 202v) in Trinity College Dublin MS 58, more popularly known as the Book of Kells (see Figure 2),[33] faces the opening of Luke 4, the chapter that narrates Christ's temptations by the devil.[34] The full-page illustration depicts the third temptation in Luke, in which the devil places Jesus on the temple in Jerusalem and challenges him to plunge to the ground.[35] While the page's immediate subject matter is clear, its finely layered symbolism indicates that the artist (or artists) was interested in relaying more than just the temptation scene. I juxtapose this page from the Book of Kells with *Christ I* to suggest that the illustration is an iconographic attempt to express the same Christological paradoxes as Lyric I. Like the Christ poet, the Kells artist also employs the architectural imagery of Christ as *lapis angularis* and relies on the viewers' recognition of its associated spatial symbolism. This image from the Book of Kells and the OE lyric have not hitherto been read in conjunction with one another. While my comments on the image necessarily remain brief and limited in scope, even a brief analysis reveals striking similarities with the poem.

When viewing the image, one's eye is first drawn to the bust of a majestic Christ enveloped by a costly robe and placed on top of a rectangular building. Christ looks at the viewer but extends his arms towards the picture's right side. He is holding a scroll, perhaps to indicate that he is citing Deuteronomy 6:16 ('Thou shalt not tempt the Lord thy God') during this temptation.[36] Near the right frame of the illustration, an emaciated, black tempting devil floats in mid-air, also holding a scroll, presumably in reference to his mendacious echo of Psalm 90:11–

Figure 2. Dublin, Trinity College, MS 58, fol. 202v. The Temptation of Christ. Courtesy of The Board of Trinity College Dublin.

12 to Christ ('For he hath given his angels charge over thee; to keep thee in all thy ways. In their hands they shall bear thee up: lest thou dash thy foot against a stone').[37] To the left of Christ, a crowd of nine onlookers fills the space between the building and the left frame. Above Christ's head, two winged angels hover, partially covered by his ornamented halo. Underneath Christ's bust, a bulky and richly ornate building dominates the lower half of the image. This building, presumably the temple in Jerusalem, has the shape of a medieval insular hall, with heavy beams framing the house and carved animal heads crowning the ends of the roof, reminiscent of the gloriously decorated hall in *Christ I*.[38] In a doorway at the centre of the hall, a haloed half-figure appears, holding two flower sceptres in front of his chest. In the hall's foundation, two groups of heads (one with twelve, the other with thirteen heads) face each other, separated by a vertical, decorative strip placed just below the doorway. All of the defining elements of the image are enclosed in an architecturally styled framework with columns left and right and a rooflike structure suspended above. An angel surrounded by vegetative decoration and holding a book appears in each of the top corners of the page.

Certain aspects make this 'Temptation of Christ' stand out. No crowd appears in any of the scriptural versions of this scene, and attendant angels are mentioned only by Matthew and Mark, but not as part of the actual temptations.[39] Luke, in whose Gospel the illustration appears in the Book of Kells, mentions no angels at all. These added figures can be interpreted in their own right, based on common biblical, exegetical, and liturgical sources. Carol Ann Farr has offered the most comprehensive art historical discussion of this image.[40] She suggests that Christ is depicted in his vocation as a preacher and that the group by his side represents a crowd listening to a sermon by Christ. This interpretation also dovetails with a Hiberno-Latin tradition that views the pinnacle of the temple as the *sedes doctorum*.[41] The two angels hovering above Christ's head, according to Farr, may allude to the angels of Psalm 90 or could be seen as the angels protecting the Ark of the Covenant.[42] Shirley Ann Brown, in turn, identifies all four depicted angels as the most widely known archangels Michael, Gabriel, Raphael, and Uriel.[43] She also suggests that the crowds in the image belong to the second temptation in Luke and 'represent the different nations of the world, over which Christ refused temporal sovereignty.'[44]

These interpretations, though certainly valid, tend to stay fairly close to the immediate motif or to compartmentalize the depicted elements, inhibiting either a broader symbolic or an integrated reading of this complex image. The unconventional representation of a conventional subject implicitly invites viewers to read beyond the limited narrative of Christ's temptation and to seek spiritual interpretations, such as that of Christ as reconciling founder and protector of God's church, or of the Christian master narrative of salvation history.[45] Such a process of interpretation, I argue, parallels Bede's figurative reading of the physical – the literal – temple and thus models common medieval practices of exegesis. Equally, then, we can draw a connection between the illustration and *Christ I*. The prompting for a spiritual interpretation of the literal image resembles the effects of *Christ I*: the text is a liturgical poem, setting antiphons to verse, but also far exceeds this immediate goal by insinuating complex theological issues. Therefore, the 'reading processes' that audiences undergo for the Kells illustration and for the poem, respectively, are similar. Both works represent one subject on the surface – a poeticized Advent antiphon and the biblical Temptation scene – but both also employ *Raummetaphorik* associated with the *caput anguli* and the church as Christ's mystical body in order to prompt meditation on broader theological and typological concerns.

The most unusual aspect of the Temptation scene in the Book of Kells is the artist's choice to draw Christ as part of the building that takes up the majority of the image. Rather than hovering in isolated space by himself or standing in full length above the temple, as in most Temptation depictions, Christ appears only as a bust. His lower body *is* – quite literally – the temple building. Thus, I would contend that Christ is depicted as the 'head of the hall.' The artist has not merely placed the bust approximately above the building but has drawn it carefully in a triangular shape that geometrically completes the angle formed by the two sides of the rising roof. Christ's figure complements the architectural structure so well because he *is* the *caput anguli*;[46] he fulfills his function as the joining stone, the *lapis angularis*, that unites walls and perfects the church.

Given the wide dissemination of exegesis on the *caput anguli*, one can reasonably assume that a portrayal of Christ as *caput anguli* was informed by the most commonly known biblical and patristic exegesis on Psalm 117 (and Isaiah 28:16). The various elements of the illustration, then, can be read against this background. The attendant crowd and the hovering angels belong to the metaphorical context of the temple and the cornerstone. The figures to the left of Christ embody the church that already reigns with Christ in heaven, since they are positioned on a level with Christ but are not actually part of the building that represents the church still on pilgrimage. They may include the patriarchs or members of the universal church, to be redeemed on Judgment Day but not participating in the historical Christian *Ecclesia*. Moreover, Bede and other exegetes emphasize the close connection between the house of God and the presence of chosen angels; the angels hovering above Christ may be explained by this connection.[47]

Reading the image in light of exegesis on the *caput anguli/lapis angularis* affords multiple interpretations of the figures at the bottom of the temple. The two groups of heads constitute the foundation of the hall that rises above them. In accordance with conventional Pauline typology from Ephesians 2:13–22, these figures can be seen as the prophets and the apostles, whom Paul identifies as the foundation of the church and Bede describes in Book 1 of *De templo*. Read as an element of the *Ecclesia*, the figures represent the members of the historical church, including the currently living ones. Faithful viewers of the illustration can identify with this multitude that enjoys the protection of the hall while still on pilgrimage through time. They wait to enter through the door of salvation (the doorway at the center of the hall) into the next life, represented by the building itself, which is Christ's protecting body. As we know, this multitude appears in *Christ I*: the hall is ruined due to the sinful nature of its human members, the 'wergan heap,' the 'wearied band' of sinners of the current church in need of spiritual renewal.

The *Christ* poet, Bede, and Ælfric, presumably at least in part under influence of Ephesians 2, envision the community of faithful as living stones, and the figures in the foundation also function as these *lapides vivi*, that is, the living souls, upon which the church is built but who are also in need of the stabilizing and restoring force of Christ, the craftsman. Indeed, the Kells artist might even be said to show the gradual transformation of these faithful stones into the blocks from which Christ constructs the church: the pattern of the human figures in the bottom panel is echoed by the pattern of rounded shapes in the panel with the doorway. In the top panel (the roof), the lines and shapes become yet less ornate and more angular, forming a geometric pattern. This upward movement, as if showing the human building blocks and simulating the process of renovating construction (also so fervently desired by the speaker of the OE poem), naturally leads back to the top of the now restored temple, where the most precious stone Christ, the head of the *Ecclesia*, rests in glory.

The choice of the Kells artist to depict the Temptation on the temple in such unusual terms may seem peculiar. However, Christ's proclamation of himself as the temple, the prevalent connection in exegesis of the temple and the cornerstone, and the polysemy of the Christological imagery surrounding the *lapis angularis* may have inspired the artist to fold these rich layers of signification into the immediate motif of the temptation. As a consequence, the devil tempts not merely an individual Christ after his stay in the desert. By approaching Christ in his role as head of the church, the devil tempts the entire church and all its members, and Christ's resistance to temptation is a resistance in lieu of all believers. At the same time, the image teaches that when Christians follow Christ's example and resist temptation individually, they, in turn, fortify the entire church. 'Reading' this image demands an openness to polysemy much like Bede's exegesis and the *Christ I* poet's elaboration of the Advent antiphon.

Conclusion

I propose in this essay that the insular 'texts' – *Christ I* and the Book of Kells illustration – can profitably be read in comparison with each other. My reading assumes that the OE poet allusively plays on a series of architectural figures to create an intricate poetic text that reflects theological complexity and exegetical learning and possesses much greater thematic coherence than has been granted in the past. Moreover, these architectural figures serve as disjointed but intricately meaningful temporal referents. The poet moves with ease from references to Creation and Judgment Day, to the impending Advent of Christ and the responsibilities of his fellow-Christians, in an attempt to integrate the historical, liturgical, and theological dimensions of *Ecclesia*. The poetic skill and complexity of Lyric I have been pointed out by other scholars, but one of the challenges of OE literary criticism is the paucity of comparanda in this language; for example, there are no other Advent poems to which one could compare *Christ I*. By extending our range of comparison to insular art, as I have done here, we can not only strengthen our understanding of one particular OE poem, but we can also appreciate more fully the aesthetic and intellectual richness of early medieval insular culture in general. *Raummetaphorik* facilitates the comparative process, allowing us to cross disciplinary boundaries and to situate the poetic text within a larger cultural context, and this, it seems to me, is precisely the goal that Tom Hill's work has consistently exemplified and encouraged.

NOTES

I am grateful to Celia Chazelle, Carol V. Kaske, and Thomas D. Hill for their helpful comments at various stages of this paper. The article was completed with support from an Andrew W. Mellon Foundation Graduate Fellowship at the Society for the Humanities at Cornell University in 2004–5. An earlier version was delivered at the 39th International Congress on Medieval Studies at Kalamazoo in May 2004.

1 Cook, *The 'Christ' of Cynewulf: A Poem in Three Parts* (1900; repr. with a new preface by John C. Pope, Hamden, CT: Archon, 1964).
2 The most recent book-length study of *Christ I* is Robert B. Burlin, *The Old English 'Advent': A Typological Commentary* (New Haven: Yale University Press, 1968). The most recent edition with commentary is Bernard J. Muir, *The Exeter Anthology of Old English Poetry: An Edition of Exeter Dean and Chapter MS 3501*, 2nd ed., 2 vols (Exeter: University of Exeter Press, 2000). For various readings of the imagery of Lyric I, all taking different approaches to the text, see Roger Lass, 'Poem as Sacrament: Transcendence of Time in the *Advent Sequence* from the Exeter Book,' *Annuale Mediaevale* 7 (1966): 3–15 at 7; Thomas D. Hill, 'Notes on the Imagery and Structure of the Old English "Christ I,"' *NQ* n.s. 19 (1972): 84–9 at 85; Sarah Larratt Keefer, 'The "Techne" of the *Christ I* Poet,' *Neophilologus* 62 (1978): 447–54 at 447–50; and Lara Farina, 'Before Affection: Christ I and the Social Erotic,' *Exemplaria* 13 (2001): 469–96 at 483–6.
3 Burlin, *Old English 'Advent*,' 64, n. 13, speculates that the 'house in disrepair may be a confused recollection of Paul's image [in Eph. 2:14] of the "broken middle wall of partition."' Cook, *The 'Christ*,' 76, expresses uncertainty about the poet's use of nouns and their interrelation when he comments on *heap* (16): 'Seems to mean *mankind* (cf. the Antiphon); but the transition from the sing. *hra* is abrupt.'
4 Robert Deshman, 'The Imagery of the Living Ecclesia and the English Monastic Reform,' in *Sources of Anglo-Saxon Culture*, ed. Paul E. Szarmach with the assistance of Virginia Darrow Oggins, Studies in Medieval Culture 20 (Kalamazoo: Medieval Institute Publications, 1986), 261–82 at 272, 277–8; in a discussion of artistic depictions of the living Ecclesia and of Christ as the cornerstone, he touches briefly on *Christ I* as an analogue to the image of the Nativity in the Benedictional of St Æthelwold and posits a shared influence of the Advent liturgy on image and poem. Deshman's essay, with its comparative reading of text and image, models an art historical approach complementary to my literary approach. Barbara Raw, 'Two Ver-

sions of Advent: The Benedictional of Æthelwold and *The Advent Lyrics*,' *Leeds Studies in English* n.s. 34 (2003): 1–28, reads *Christ I* in light of the Advent theme as it appears in the Benedictional of Æthelwold. She does not, however, present a reciprocal reading of the Benedictional and the OE text, instead discussing the two separately and emphasizing that the 'treatment of the theme of Advent in the Old English poem ... is ... very different from that in Æthelwold's Benedictional' (20).

5 On the poem's 'ruminative mode,' see Hill, 'Notes on the Imagery,' 87–9.
6 Cook, *The 'Christ*,' 72–108, gives the Latin antiphons. Only Lyrics VII and XI are not based on Advent antiphons. For the sources of Lyric VII (164–213), see Thomas D. Hill, 'A Liturgical Source for *Christ I* 164–213 (Advent Lyric VII),' *MÆ* 46 (1977): 12–15. For the sources of Lyric XII (378–415), see Cook, *The Christ*, 108; Edward Burgert, *The Dependence of Part I of Cynewulf's 'Christ' upon the Antiphonary* (Washington, DC: Catholic University Press, 1921), 44–5; Burlin, *Old English 'Advent*,' 63; and Muir, *The Exeter Anthology*, 2:400. For a more detailed evaluation of *Christ I*'s relationship to early medieval English liturgy, see Susan Rankin, 'The Liturgical Background of the Old English Advent Lyrics: A Reappraisal,' in *Learning and Literature in Anglo-Saxon England: Studies Presented to Peter Clemoes on the Occasion of His Sixty-Fifth Birthday*, ed. Michael Lapidge and Helmut Gneuss (Cambridge: Cambridge University Press, 1985), 317–40.
7 Cook, *The 'Christ*,' 73. Cook identifies the individual antiphonal phrases as the following biblical verses (in order of appearance): Jer. 10:7, Hag. 2:8, Eph. 2:20, Eph. 2:14, Gen. 2:7/Tob. 8:8.
8 All translations from OE and Latin are mine unless otherwise noted.
9 The poem begins on a fragmented line due to at least one missing folio at the beginning of the manuscript. The lyric's lost lines presumably versified the antiphon's first two phrases, 'O Rex gentium, et desideratus earum,' and further sections might have preceded Lyric I. Krapp and Dobbie, *The Exeter Book*, ASPR 3:247, would restore 'eorðb[yr]g' in line 7, but Muir reads 'eorðb[old]' (cf. his note, *The Exeter Anthology*, 2:385).
10 See Gerhart B. Ladner, 'The Symbolism of the Biblical Corner Stone in the Mediaeval West,' *MS* 4 (1942): 43–60, who lists numerous examples from patristic and medieval exegesis on the *caput anguli/lapis angularis*. The influential passage from Isaiah is as follows: 'idcirco haec dicit Dominus Deus: ecce ego mittam in fundamentis Sion lapidem, lapidem probatum angularem pretiosum in fundamento fundatum. qui crediderit non festinet' [Therefore thus saith the Lord God: Behold I will lay a stone in the foundations of Sion, a tried stone, a cornerstone, a precious stone, founded in the foundation. He that believeth, let him not hasten].

11 See Ursula Maiburg, 'Christus der Eckstein: Ps. 118,22 und Jes. 28,16 im Neuen Testament und bei den lateinischen Vätern,' in *Vivarium: Festschrift Theodor Klauser zum 90. Geburtstag*, ed. Ernst Dassmann and Klaus Thraede, Jahrbuch für Antike und Christentum, Ergänzungsband 11 (Münster: Aschendorffsche Verlagsbuchhandlung, 1984), 247–56 at 249. Maiburg usefully details the history of the cornerstone image and its subsequent disappearance as an isolated motif.

12 See Jennifer O'Reilly, Introduction, in *Bede: On the Temple*, trans. Seán Connolly, Translated Texts for Historians 21 (Liverpool: Liverpool University Press, 1995), xvii–lv at xxiii–xxviii, for a brief overview of the theme of the temple in patristic exegesis. See also Ladner, 'Symbolism,' for medieval occurrences of the *caput anguli/lapis angularis*.

13 For New Testament uses of Psalm 117:22–3, see Matt. 21:42, Mark 12:10–11, Luke 20:17, Acts 4:11, Eph. 2:19–22, 1 Pet. 2:5–7.

14 Paul refers to Jews and Gentiles in Eph. 2:11–12, the lines immediately preceding the passage under discussion here.

15 Jerome, *Commentarii in iv epistulas Paulinas, Ad Ephesios* 1.508, PL 26:476C: '[S]ummus autem angularis lapis, qui populum utrumque contineat (sive iuxta secundam interpretationem coelestia iungat atque terrena), christus est dominus noster' [But the highest stone of the corner, which holds together both peoples (or, according to a second interpretation, joins the heavenly and the earthly) is our Lord Christ].

16 For this comment on Job 38:6, see Cook, *The 'Christ,'* 75, note on the phrase *weall wið wealle* (11). Sedulius Scottus also gives the twofold reading in *Collectaneum in Apostolum*, In epistolam ad Ephesios 2.20 (*Sedulii Scotti Collectaneum in Apostolum*, ed. Hermann Josef Frede and Herbert Stanjek, 2 vols, Aus der Geschichte der lateinischen Bibel 31–2 [Freiburg: Herder, 1996], 572); so does Hrabanus Maurus, *In honorem Sanctae Crucis* 1.C1, CCCM 100:32, and in *De universo* [*De rerum naturis*], PL 111:20D.

17 For Bede, see *Homeliarum euangelii libri ii* 2.3, CCSL 122:104–5. For Ælfric's reading of the walls as Jews and Gentiles, see *Catholic Homilies* I.7, ed. Peter Clemoes, *Ælfric's Catholic Homilies: The First Series. Text*, EETS s.s.17 (Oxford: Oxford University Press, 1997), 232–40, esp. 233–4; for that of angels and mankind, see *Catholic Homilies* II.45, ed. Malcolm Godden, *Ælfric's Catholic Homilies: The Second Series. Text*, EETS s.s. 5 (London: Oxford University Press, 1979), 335–45, esp. 336–8.

18 For representative views in this debate, see Joachim Jeremias, 'Der Eckstein,' *Angelos: Archiv für Neutestamentliche Zeitgeschichte und Kulturkunde* 1 (1925): 65–70; Jeremias, 'Eckstein – Schlußstein,' *Zeitschrift für die Neutestamentliche Wissenschaft* 36.1/2 (1937): 154–7; and Jeremias, 'Κεφαλὴ γωνίας –

-'Ἀκρογωνιαῖος,' *Zeitschrift für die Neutestamentliche Wissenschaft* 29 (1930): 264–80. Jeremias argues for an exclusively high placement of the cornerstone in the New Testament. Karl Th. Schäfer, 'Lapis Summus Angularis,' in *Der Mensch und die Künste: Festschrift für Heinrich Lützeler zum 60. Geburtstage*, ed. Günter Bandmann et al. (Dusseldorf: Schwann, 1962), 9–23, strictly opposes Jeremias, though he acknowledges that in medieval interpretations the high placement of the stone occurs regularly (22). See Maiburg, 'Christus der Eckstein,' 247–56, for additional bibliography on the debate.

19 For such a combination, see, for example, the commentary by Pelagius on Ephesians *Pelagius's Expositions of Thirteen Epistles of St. Paul*, ed. Alexander Souter, 2 vols (Cambridge: Cambridge University Press, 1926), 2:356: 'Prophetarum noui testamenti ... Christus est fundamentum, qui etiam lapis dicitur [lapis] angularis, duos coniungens et continens parietes. ideo autem et fundamentum et summus est, quia in ipso et fundatur et consummatur ecclesia' [Christ is the foundation of the prophets of the New Testament, which stone is also called the stone of the corner that joins and holds together the walls. Therefore, he is indeed the foundation and the highest because in him the church is both founded and brought to perfect completion]. Sedulius Scottus, in his commentary on Eph. 2:20, presents an almost identical passage (*Collectaneum in Apostolum*, ed. Frede and Stanjek, 572). See Ladner, 'Symbolism,' 48–54, for grouped listings of the stone's different locations as interpreted by patristic and medieval authors in exegesis and liturgy. He mentions that Augustine reads *summus* as metaphorically referring to Christ's divine nature rather than to a literal elevated placement (50).

20 On the motif of 'artifex et conditor Deus,' see also Heb. 11:10 and Bede, *In Cantica canticorum libri vi* 4.7, CCSL 119B:317. On *Bildervermischung*, specifically of Christ as building, divine architect, and inhabitant of the temple, see Maiburg, 'Christus der Eckstein,' 251–2, n. 41.

21 Cook, *The 'Christ,'* 76

22 Cook, *The 'Christ,'* 75, note on line 14. When the poet expresses his hope for restoration through Christ, he invokes both Ælfrician senses of *hus*: he specifically mentions both the 'wergan heap' (16), the 'wearied band' that may be read as the collective universal church, and the individual human created by God (14–15). The transition from *hra* to the collective noun *heap* is therefore not as abrupt as it appeared to Cook (see n. 3). See Burlin, *Old English 'Advent,'* 64–6, and Keefer, '"Techne,"' 449–50, for coherent readings of the *hra-hus-heap* sequence.

23 Cook, *The 'Christ,'* 248, gives 'restore, repair' for *gebetan*.

24 It is important to point out that *gebetan* commonly appears in law texts with the meaning 'to make compensation, compensate, pay' (*DOE*, s.v. ge•betan

C.). For the full range of the verb's uses in OE, see *DOE* under *ge•betan*, *betan*, and *ge•bett*. Significantly, *gebrosnian*, the alliterating counterpart to *gebetan* in the same line, can equally be read literally as well as figuratively and can thus apply to buildings, bodies, and souls (*DOE*, s.v. *brosnian*, *ge•brosnian*, and *ge•brosnod*).

25 Cf. Lass, 'Poem as Sacrament,' 7, for a reading of the temporal paradox of Lyric I, though not in architectural terms.
26 Cf. Lass, 'Poem as Sacrament,' 3–7, and Hill, 'Notes on the Imagery,' 85.
27 For a lucid discussion of this dual existence of Christians, see Hugo Rahner, *Griechische Mythen in Christlicher Deutung* (Zurich: Rhein-Verlag, 1957), 118–19.
28 Cook, *The 'Christ*,' 75–6, simply quotes the relevant passage from Ælfric's *Catholic Homilies* II.40, but does not comment on it at all; Burlin, *Old English 'Advent*,' 60–2, discusses Ælfric's passage largely in conjunction with the building of Solomon's temple.
29 *Catholic Homilies* II.40 ('In Dedicatione Ecclesiae'), ed. Godden, 337–8.
30 Bede devoted two entire treatises, portions of one other treatise, and three homilies to the exegesis of the temple and the tabernacle of the Old Testament; see O'Reilly, Introduction, xvii.
31 Bede, *De Templo Libri II* 1, lines 1–44, CCSL 119A:147. For a translation, see Bede, *On the Temple*, 5–6.
32 One might add that Bede, through a compressed presentation of his material, which O'Reilly (Introduction, xxix) calls a tour de force, achieves an effect similar to the densely packed, shifting images of Lyric I.
33 The image is reproduced with permission of The Board of Trinity College Dublin.
34 The page is in its original binding location, but the illustration's choice of subject matter and placement within Luke are not easily explained (Carol Farr, *The Book of Kells: Its Function and Audience* [London: British Library, 1997], 52). Although the Western liturgy of the Mass prescribes the Temptation as the reading for the first Sunday in Lent (Quadragesima Sunday), the version used is almost always Matthew's not Luke's. Cf. also Ursula Lenker, *Die Westsächsische Evangelienversion und die Perikopenordnungen im Angelsächsischen England*, Texte und Untersuchungen zur Englischen Philologie 20 (Munich: Wilhelm Fink Verlag, 1997), 309, 348, for evidence of lections used in Anglo-Saxon England.
35 The Temptation on the temple is the third in Luke and the second in Matthew. In using the word 'illustration' to refer to the image, I follow Farr, *Book of Kells*, 43.
36 See Farr, *Book of Kells*, 51.

37 Cf. Charles D. Wright, 'Blickling Homily III on the Temptations in the Desert,' *Anglia* 106 (1988): 130–7 at 130–1, for the exegetical tradition of the devil's misappropriation of Scripture. The figure of the devil is of some interest. Art historians do not agree on what conditioned the depiction of the devil as a skinny, black figure. For discussion of the Kells devil, see Françoise Henry, 'The Book and Its Decoration,' in *The Book of Kells: Reproductions from the Manuscript in Trinity College, Dublin* (New York: Alfred A. Knopf, 1974), 147–230 at 189–90, and Carl Nordenfalk, 'Another Look at the Book of Kells,' in *Festschrift Wolfgang Braunfels*, ed. Friedrich Piel and Jörg Traeger (Tubingen: Ernst Wasmuth, 1977), 275–9 at 277. For images and further notes on the colour, shape, and attributes of early medieval devils, see Otto Pächt, *The St. Albans Psalter* (London: Warburg Institute, 1960), 86, plates 23 and 107.

38 The depicted building closely resembles the reconstruction, based on archaeological evidence, of one of the halls at Yeavering; see Brian Hope-Taylor, *Yeavering: An Anglo-British Centre of Early Northumbria*, Department of the Environment Archaeological Reports 7 (London: Her Majesty's Stationery Office, 1977), plate 105. Shirley Ann Brown, in Michael W. Herren and Shirley Ann Brown, *Christ in Celtic Christianity: Britain and Ireland from the Fifth to the Tenth Century*, Studies in Celtic History 20 (Woodbridge: Boydell, 2002), 246, identifies the building as 'a small Irish-type church or houseshrine.' It is interesting to note in this context that carpentry (along with other crafts) was considered a worthy royal and noble pastime and even a mark of aristocratic distinction in Germanic societies; see Geoffrey R. Russom, 'A Germanic Concept of Nobility in *The Gifts of Men* and *Beowulf*,' *Speculum* 53 (1978): 1–15, esp. 5, 7–9. Appropriately, therefore, the majestic Kells Christ is the head of an exquisitely constructed timbered hall. Equally appropriately, the *Christ* poet fuses the antiphon that addresses Christ as *rex gentium* ('king of nations') with images of masonry and craftsmanship.

39 Matt. 4:11 and Mark 1:13.

40 Farr, *Book of Kells*, 51–103. But see also Herren and Brown, *Christ in Celtic Christianity*, 246–50; Brown offers a reading of the image as directed specifically at a monastic audience.

41 Farr, *Book of Kells*, 66, bases her view on scriptural and exegetical writings that mention instances of preaching from the pinnacle of the temple; see also Carol Farr, 'Lection and Interpretation: The Liturgical and Exegetical Background of the Illustrations in the Book of Kells' (PhD dissertation, University of Texas at Austin, 1989), 74. On the motif of the *sedes doctorum* in Hiberno-Latin writings, see Herren and Brown, *Christ in Celtic Christian-*

ity, 248–9, and Charles D. Wright, *The Irish Tradition in Old English Literature*, CSASE 6 (Cambridge: Cambridge University Press, 1993), 227 and n. 60.

42 Farr, *Book of Kells*, 53–4, speculates that the page as a whole alludes to the Ark, with the angels belonging to this allusion. I would add that the angels might be intended to draw attention to Christ's haloed head to emphasize his divinity, as opposed to his humanity, which is represented by his house-body. Angels occur in this function in other early medieval images of Christ in Majesty; see Adolph Katzenellenbogen, 'The Image of Christ in the Early Middle Ages,' in *Life and Thought in the Early Middle Ages*, ed. Richard S. Hoyt (Minneapolis: University of Minnesota Press, 1967), 66–84, esp. 72–3; see also figures 14–18, between 70 and 71, for examples of early medieval Christ in Majesty depictions.

43 Herren and Brown, *Christ in Celtic Christianity*, 246.

44 Herren and Brown, *Christ in Celtic Christianity*, 247.

45 This invitation to a spiritual reading of the Temptation scene has also been recognized by Jennifer O'Reilly, 'Exegesis and the Book of Kells: The Lucan Genealogy,' in *The Book of Kells: Proceedings of a Conference at Trinity College Dublin, 6–9 September 1992*, ed. Felicity O'Mahony (Aldershot: Scolar Press for Trinity College Library Dublin, 1994), 344–97 at 358–61, who connects the page with patristic teachings on baptism and on Christ's body as the temple as well as to the Lucan genealogy in the Book of Kells, which immediately precedes the Temptation illustration. 'The Temptation of Christ' is not the only image in the Book of Kells in which such metaphoric, theological, and exegetical density can be found. Art historians have suggested a similar richness for the image called 'The Arrest of Christ' (fol. 114r in the Gospel of Matthew), the only other full-page 'illustration' in the manuscript. For a discussion on the exegetical density of 'The Arrest of Christ,' see Farr, *Book of Kells*, 104–39. On the liturgical character of full-page illuminations in the Book of Kells, see Suzanne Lewis, 'Sacred Calligraphy: The Chi Rho Page in the Book of Kells,' *Traditio* 36 (1980): 139–59. Martin Werner, 'Crucifixi, Sepulti, Suscitati: Remarks on the Decoration of the Book of Kells,' in *The Book of Kells*, ed. O'Mahony, 450–88, offers an interpretation of a comprehensive iconographic program in the manuscript.

46 Carl Nordenfalk, 'Another Look,' 277, in passing suggests a similar possibility by pointing to the passage in Prudentius's 'Dittochaeum' entitled 'Pinna templi,' but he does not put the image in a biblical, exegetical, patristic, or further literary context. O'Reilly 'Exegesis,' 359–60, also briefly refers to Jesus' depiction as the cornerstone in the Temptation scene, but her main interest lies in the image of the temple; she reads this page in its manuscript

context and against a patristic background, but makes no reference to any vernacular literary analogues.

47 Bede, *De templo* 1, CCSL 119A:147. Among the numerous exegetes that mention angels in connection with the temple are, for example, Jerome, *Commentarius in Ecclesiasten* 12:1, line 33, ed. M. Adriaen, CCSL 72:350, and Alcuin, *Commentaria super Ecclesiasten*, PL 100:715A.

Remembering in Circles: *The Wife's Lament*, *Conversatio*, and the Community of Memory

SACHI SHIMOMURA

As a meditation on temporality in narrative, I would like to draw attention to temporal disjunctions that characterize *The Wife's Lament*. The poem, I will argue, manipulates time, memory, and repetition. Its temporal disjunctions govern a movement from individual to social memory, which sheds light on a central critical controversy: whether *The Wife's Lament* refers to a specific figure whose story we have misplaced in the murk of the literary past, or instead, evokes a representative situation as a 'mood piece' whose lyric speaker is either a generic or composite figure of exile and grief. The poem itself addresses that issue as it moves from personal to communal and gnomic; its result is necessarily generalized, regardless of the specificity of its originating situation. To frame these temporal disjunctions in relation to the concept of social time in Anglo-Saxon England, I will first discuss the use of the term *conversatio* and its OE equivalents *drohtoþ/droht(n)ung* in Bede's *Historia Ecclesiastica*, its OE translation, and *Beowulf*.

Social Time and the Anglo-Saxon Contexts of *Conversatio*

Temporality in *The Wife's Lament* is best understood in the context of an Anglo-Saxon view of time as social process. This concept underlies the Latin term *conversatio* and its OE equivalents, *drohtoþ* or *droht(n)ung*. In Bede's *HE*, *conversatio* regularly indicates 'way of life' as in 'monachicae conuersationis': 'of monastic life' (in the OE Bede, 'drohtunge munuclifes').[1] Yet this term comprises a broader nexus of meanings in contexts that impel an awareness of repetition, memory, or progression beyond an earlier state. In Book 3, for instance, Fursa, motivated by heavenly and infernal visions in which he is burned on his shoulder because he possesses a sinner's property, eventually moves beyond monastic life 'et ipse ab omnibus mundi rebus liber in anchoretica conuersatione uitam finire disposuit' [and, being free from all worldly cares, he resolved to end his life as a hermit] ('ond he from eallum middangeardes þingum freo in ancorlifes drohtunge gestihhade his life geendian').[2] This context lends *conversatio* the temporal dimension of a process, both religious and social, that takes him beyond worldly society and its cares.

The term's temporal scope is reflected in the manuscript tradition and publication history of the *Rule* of St Benedict by frequent scribal and editorial replacement of *conversatio* with *conversio*. This more limited term denotes a turn from old to new, especially religious conversion (to Christianity or inclusion under a monastic rule).[3] The idea of social 'conversion' echoes the linguistic registers of *conversatio*, literally 'turning (from),' whose common metaphorized sense, 'way of life,' focuses on human interaction, often the social interactions of religious life.[4] The social focus remains in the modern term 'conversation' and its emphasis on speech. Continuing intersection of the concepts of *conversio*/conversion and *conversatio*/conversation is most clearly visible in Dante's progress through hell, which necessitates his conversations with those sinners who are not yet so excluded from the human community as to be bereft of speech. Yet the damned are trapped in repetitive punishment, so that sterile redundancy breeds its own hellish temporality. Their willful retention of faults underlies the impossibility of repentance or change, and with it their fundamental exclusion from society. Such socially constructed time has a curious modern analogy in the movie *Groundhog Day*, whose main character is trapped in an endlessly repeated day. Unlike the residents of Dante's *Inferno*, he escapes temporal isolation as he begins to see and remember the benefits of repeating time, and improves his own life and then his community's.[5] Like the pilgrim Dante, he undergoes a *conversio*, a turning point in his life, measured in conversations, that reintegrates him into his desired society. If medieval authors show conversion through inclusion in religious communities, this modern movie shows redemption through productive membership in secular society, demonstrated in part by the repeated use of polite, empathic linguistic forms and socially appropriate conversational gambits. The *Rule* of St Benedict, as a guide to monastic life, analogously structures medieval monastic *conversatio* by repetitions that assign social value to time (and measure the development of the monastic community), by its directive to read the rules to novices three separate times before they finally commit to abide by them, and by its emphasis upon the gradual development of monastic habit in the twelve steps of humility: on achieving the final step, his very bearing will constantly communicate his humility, or as Æthelwold of Winchester's OE version puts it, 'he gehylt þa gewunlican god haligre drohtnunge' [he then holds the accustomed good of holy living].[6] Such forms of social interaction, which serve in lieu of idle conversations banned by the *Rule*, emphasize repetition, memory, and progression.

One pair of examples in *HE* is worth examining in detail because it suggests an even fuller temporal context for *conversatio*. The term occurs twice in Book 5 at the transition from chapter 12 to 13: Dryhthelm 'multisque et uerbo et conuersatione saluti fuit' [and led many to salvation by his words and life] ('& he monegum mannum ge in wordum ge on his lifes bisene on hælo wæs'). The following chapter begins, 'At contra fuit quidam in prouincia Merciorum, cuius uisiones ac uerba, non autem et conuersatio, plurimis, sed non sibimet ipsi, profuit' [On the other hand, there was a man in the Mercian kingdom whose visions and words, but not his way of life, profited many but not himself] ('Ongeæng þissum spelle wæs sum mon in Mercna londe, þæs gesihðe & word, nales his drohtung & his lif, monegum monna ne eac him seolfum brycsade').[7] These passages render a rhetorical contrast. Dryhthelm, like Fursa, received visions of heaven and hell that motivate his religious ardour. To conclude his story, Bede yokes together *verbo* and *conversatione* as complementary aspects of Dryhthelm's moral influence. The text describes his way of life, by which he influences his immediate society, through repeated experience or condition. For instance, Dryhthelm inhabits a 'locum mansionis secretiorem' [a more secret retreat] to engage 'continuis in orationibus' [in constant prayer]. The repetition of prayers delineates his inclusion in a society that is divine and salvific, not earthly. His withdrawn ('secretiorem') space within society reinforces, as in monastic rules, his religious progress.[8] The text further stresses, through terms like *solebat* and *saepius*, how Dryhthelm repeatedly castigates his flesh with cold water and fasts constantly ('quotidiana ieiunia'). These repetitions define his *conversatio*.

Bede highlights the meaningful repetition of both the story, the *verbum*, of Dryhthelm's experience, and Dryhthelm's own asceticisms. In social context, the repetitions are no longer merely either *quotidiana* [daily] or quotidian in the more modern sense, but define a way of life (*conversatio*) that enables spiritual benefit. His repeated asceticisms also have social force as a model for others; they yield a spiritual kernel for a community ranging into the future. Such socially effectual repetition reflects Bede's own tactic in this section of *HE*, where constant miraculous tales (Dryhthelm's vision in chapter 12, Cynred's thane's vision in chapter 13, a monk's vision in chapter 14) reinforce each other to reach out to a broader spiritual society. Bede concludes at the end of chapter 14 that the tale induced many to penance, 'Quod utinam exhinc nostrarum lectione literarum fiat' [And may the reading of this account of ours have the same effect!].[9]

The second passage, about Cynred's thane, contrasts the role of *visiones* and *verba* with the role of *conversatio*. The text reveals a jarring disjunction between them, made all the more jarring by how smoothly word and *conversatio* aligned in the previous narrative. Cynred's thane, however, neglects his spiritual well-being, and when, in a vision, he sees a big book of his sins and a tiny book of his good deeds, he despairs and suffers damnation rather than amending his life. The narrative emphasizes that this man repeatedly ('frequenter') disregards his king's admonitions to amend himself spiritually even before his final denial. Repetition is key to his *conversatio*; he excludes himself from the society of the saved by his constant refusals, even though his story, repeated, leads others to salvation.

The OE Bede translates the first *conversatio* as 'lifes bisene' [life's example] and expands the second into the form 'his drohtung & his lif' [his conduct and life]. It thus shifts the rhetorical emphasis of the contrast from the repetitions of *verbum* and *conversatio* to the repetitions of *word* and *lif*, and as a result simplifies the narrative. The shift counters the breadth of *droht(n)ung* so as to heighten the difference of 'life' versus 'words,' whereas *droht(n)ung*, like *conversatio*, elides that difference. Both *droht(n)ung* and *drohtoþ* relate to the verb *droht(n)ian*, which BT defines first as 'to converse, dwell, or keep company with.' These definitions emphasize social context. The *DOE* reduces the scope of the terms by looking at only their most immediate contexts; however, definition 1.b. 'to live an indefinite length of time' and 1.c. 'to live a stated length of time' of *droht(n)ian* imply its temporal dimension. The terms *drohtoþ* and *droht(n)ung*, defined variously as 'conversation,' 'way of life,' or 'condition, conduct, society' (BT), suggest that words – conversation – define a way of life, one's social condition, or the company one keeps. Like *conversatio*, these terms in the OE Bede connote duration, repetition, or change – temporal dimensions that impact the attainment and society of a religious life.

In this culturally significant tradition, then, time is socially defined. The contrast of socially productive versus unproductive repetition also occurs in Anglo-Saxon texts, such as in *Beowulf*, when Grendel, encountering Beowulf, 'wolde on heolster fleon, / secan deofla gedræg; ne wæs his drohtoð þær / swylce he on ealderdagum ær gemette' [755b–7: wished to flee into darkness, seek the company of devils; nor was his condition there like any he encountered before in his life-days]. Grendel's association with the company of devils merely reinforces the unproductiveness of his *drohtoð*, his way of life, now seemingly predicated on repetition through the generations of Cain's descendants, as well as his own reiterated attacks that lead nowhere, except to define his exclusion from human society. Beowulf, on the contrary, 'Gemunde þa ... æfenspræce' [758a–9a: then remembered his evening-speech]. His memory of the past is socially inclusive, defined through his speech and vows before the company of warriors; thus, his use of time and repetition moves him into society, rather than trapping him outside it.

Secular Memory and Social Time in *The Wife's Lament*

Similar ideas shape *The Wife's Lament*. In this poem, a moment of lyric consciousness expands and reiterates itself until it is resolved by social intervention: a generalized, gnomic consciousness and the broader perspective that it enables.[10] The moment when the lyric speaker steps back from her memories and grief and into gnomic wisdom is also the moment when she accepts her inclusion in a society whose established customs and traditions reorder repetition into something more meaningful than her individual experience alone.[11] The way memory works to present a choice between stagnation and progress hinges in this poem upon emotional perspectives, but also upon fiction's capacity to reinvent and restructure remembered reality within a social framework; society, as well as time, reorders memory.[12]

The Wife's Lament relates the story of a woman in exile; her lament first reveals details of her present exile and the inertial force of her memories, and then traces the process whereby she achieves peace or resignation for herself. The poem thus maps her *conversatio*. As a 'turn' between ways of life and as a communication of memory restructured through society, her narrative is also a 'conversation' in the most medieval sense. In speaking, even as she begins in the present, 'Ic þis giedd wrece' [1a: I utter this song/tale], she entangles past with present. Her narrative does not clearly demarcate her prior exile from her own people, upon joining her husband's people, from her current exile from him. Thus, she expresses nearly simultaneously the loneliness caused by both exiles:

> Ærest min hlaford gewat   heonan of leodum
> ofer yþa gelac;   hæfde ic uhtceare
> hwær min leodfruma   londes wære.
> Ða ic me feran gewat   folgað secan,
> wineleas wræcca,   for minre weaþearfe.
> Ongunnon þæt þæs monnes   magas hycgan
> þurh dyrne geþoht   þæt hy todælden unc,
> þæt wit gewidost   in woruldrice
> lifdon laðlicost,   ond mec longade.
> Het mec hlaford min   her eard niman,
> ahte ic leofra lyt   on þissum londstede,
> holdra freonda.   Forþon is min hyge geomor (6–17)[13]

[First my lord went hence from the people over the sea; I have had care at dawn about where my lord might be on land. Then I set off to seek service/protection, a friendless exile, for my woeful plight; my lord's kinsmen plotted secretly how they might separate us from each other that we two might live most wretchedly, apart most widely in the world; and I languished. My lord had ordered me to take up my abode here, though I had few dear loyal friends in this place. Therefore my mind is sad.]

The lyric speaker's shift, in the last line, from past-tense verbs (*longade, ahte*) to the present-tense declaration, 'Forþon is min hyge geomor,' decisively mingles her emotions of past and present. Indeed, she also phrases the beginning of her lament in such a temporal mingling, as she declares that she will tell 'hwæt ic yrmþa gebad, siþþan ic up weox, / niwes oþþe ealdes, no ma þonne nu. / A ic wite wonn minra wræcsiþa' [4–5: what miseries I endured since I grew up, past or present, no more than now. Ever (or always), I had suffering from my exile]. The conflation of past and present into 'always' (*a*) points at the expansion and reiteration of her thoughts as narrative echoing a time now past or passing. The speaker reveals a hint of this process and how it recasts her present and past when she mourns, 'eft is þæt onhworfen, / is nu ... swa hit no wære, / freondscipe uncer' [23b–5a: That is changed back again; it is now ... as though it never had been, the friendship of us two]. Her near erasure of memory denies the past an identity separate from the present and reenacts her estrangement from society.[14] The poem ends only when she stops recreating and recasting this entrapping process within the emotional structure of the lyric.

The middle of the poem, when she is still caught up in grief, stresses that sense of emotional enclosure. Her surroundings reflect her awareness of being hedged around and cut off from others. She dwells in an *eorðscræf* or *eorðsele*, a cave or abode in the earth, under an oak tree, in a gloomy valley beset with hedges and briars (27–37). She explains, 'Ful oft mec her wraþe begeat / fromsiþ frean' [32b–3a: Very often here the departure of my lord assailed me sharply], as if her emotional pain has transmuted into the sharp thorny vegetation that imprisons her like a Sleeping Beauty. The exact geographical contours of her dwelling are a matter of much critical debate, but its psychological contours shape a prison of grief, isolation, and the solitary gloom of her own thoughts.[15] In this environment, she defines herself against society, singular – *ana* – against plural: 'Frynd sind on eorþan, / leofe lifgende, leger weardiað, / þonne ic on uhtan ana gonge / under actreo geond þas eorþscrafu' [33b–6: Friends are on earth, living dear ones occupy a bed, when I at dawn go alone under an oak tree around (or throughout) the earth-caves]. The imagery in her lament contrasts the social intimacy of the shared bed with her solitude at innumerably repeated dawns.[16] The implied pressure of time merely enforces her perceived isolation. Even the tension in the phrase 'geond þas eorþscrafu' between motion [*geond*] and the limits of her dwelling suggests the constant frustration of outward motion.

Towards the end of the poem, she escapes that encompassing solitude, insofar as she lets go of her solipsistic contemplation to achieve a more generalized view of her situation. Her voice then transcends private emotional responses to reach a more gnomic and universal understanding. The lyric depicts this turn outward in lines 42–5b, as she declares,

A scyle geong mon   wesan geomormod,
heard heortan geþoht,   swylce habban sceal
bliþe gebæro,   eac þon breostceare,
sinsorgna gedreag ...

[Ever must a youth be sober in mind, his heart's thought resolute; he must also have a cheerful bearing, likewise care in the breast, a multitude of continual sorrows.][17]

Here, the sense of the adverb *a* contrasts with her earlier use of the term; instead of locking her within a personal and recursive grief, it frees her. This 'ever' or 'always' sustains the universality of repeated experience, in lieu of individual and ultimately prosaic repetitions of narratives of adversity. The gnomic voice, itself an act of repetition – since the force of a gnomic statement arises from its general social acceptance and preexistence within a community – redefines her act of lyric repetition. It suggests that her voice, the speaking voice of the poem, exists as a conversation with society, or at least with its gnomes and its lyric conventions of time.

The poem has by then equally redefined the *ic* of its opening lines as the persona whose transformations are expressed within the poem. This redefinition situates the speaker more clearly within her social context, much as Anglo-Saxon riddles commonly map the transformations of a first-person speaker (often a cultural artefact like a book, sword, or drinking horn) that comes into being in the course of the riddle. In *The Wife's Lament*, however, these transformations are more social than physical, as the individual voice of the speaker converts into a communal voice that allows her to reenter human conversation: to become a speaker no longer defined only by exclusion. Even if, as some scholars have suggested, she speaks these words as a curse upon the man who has left her to her loneliness, rather than solely as a gnomic consolation, she reenters society through her participation in the social constructions of a life worth living.[18] This focus on social transformation helps to explain why the gender of the speaker is marked only by grammatical endings in the first two lines.[19] The dearth of gender markings in the remainder of the poem emphasizes the speaker's conversion away from individual grappling with grief, and towards a communal (and hence unmarked) lyric voice that modulates memory into gnomic expression.

The broadened perspective of gnomic resolution allows the Wife to escape the emotional enclosure implied by her confining abode. In turn, at the end of the poem, she gains the ability to visualize her lord's grief, as though in reflection of her own.[20] She concludes that 'he gemon to oft / wynlicran wic' [51b–2a: he remembers too often a more pleasant dwelling]. His memory, as she imagines it, echoes hers. Here, however, the repetition of memory (*oft*) recuperates rather than rejects a socially integrated past. The image of the *wynlicran wic* suggests that she too remembers that joint dwelling, set in a more pleasant past, so that she no longer flattens her griefs of present and past into an endless recursive 'always.' Memory no longer enforces stasis (as her memory of lovers at dawn did), but offers a more productive conversation between past and present. The lyric speaker also sees her lord 'under stanhliþe storme behrimed' in a dwelling 'wætre beflowen' [48–9: under a cliff made icy with storms ... bounded by the sea]. The sea literally separates husband and wife, isolates them from each other; yet it also joins them in a mutual isolation reminiscent of *Wulf and Eadwacer*, whose even more cryptic lament bemoans lovers immured on separate islands. Significantly, sea and storm alone comprise the geographical containment and isolation at the end of *The Wife's Lament*. The sea more often functions as a metaphor for freedom in OE and other earlier Germanic texts – an appropriate association, in view of the ocean's role in facilitating travel both physical and metaphysical.[21] Its sundering capacity, more contingent and less final than the Wife's own absorption in grief and despair, offers her membership in a community of isolation and worldly suffering, within which she takes her place. Such membership, her acceptance of the universality of exile, transcends physical isolation and thereby frees her. Her lyric voice joins that of other lonely exiles. Indeed, voice alone – the voices of all exiles in Anglo-Saxon literature – constructs that community, as a joint *conversatio* upon the physical margins of society.

That liminal ocean also evokes a temporal geography for the isolated Wife. It sets her in the eye of the storm: a still moment in time and space and emotion, necessarily fleeting. It defines her situation much as a corresponding liminal geography delineates Grendel's place in the created world of *Beowulf*; Grendel too exists in social isolation, indeed seems to define himself by such estrangement. Their comparison illuminates the metaphysics of an Anglo-Saxon view of space and time that sets memory, social conventions, and human bonds (including poetry, narrative, and speech) against encroaching temporal and spatial isolation. The estranged speaker of *The Wife's Lament* first embraces and then transcends the space and time of her grief, so that her lyric exists, finally, both inside and outside her state of isolation. Grendel similarly exists inside and outside the realm of humanity, by slipping, as it were, into its psychological borderlands, where there be monsters. I refer here to the mysterious way in which Grendel emerges into the narrative, as much mindset as physical entity. His social exclusion isolates him more radically and less recuperably from humanity than the physical and emotional exile portrayed in *The Wife's Lament*. His entrance at once threatens to annihilate the human world upon which he encroaches, and lends it certain definition: light limned against shadow, creation against destruction.

The sense of unrelenting repetition highlights that contrast. Grendel 'þrage geþolode ... / þæt he dogora gehwam dream gehyrde / hludne in healle; þær wæs hearpan sweg, / swutol sang scopes' [87a–90a: miserably endured a period of distress ... in that each day he heard joy loud in the hall; there was the sound of the harp, the poet's clear song]; his entry reflects the consciousness of repetitive time, of each day – a constant microcosm of the creation of light out of darkness – that excludes him. The song's celebration of creation enhances human community; for Grendel, however, it only reiterates estrangement. Grendel's subsequent repeated incursions delineate his way of life. It is not the action, but its repetition, that most strongly characterizes Grendel's possession of the hall.

Full consideration of the social roles of memory in *Beowulf* would exceed the scope of this paper; it suffices here to suggest that the poem's relationship with the past shapes its present through the social inclusions and exclusions entailed by its memories. The poem emphasizes the 'singale sæcce' [154a: continual strife] generated by Grendel, and with it, Hrothgar's continual grief ('Swa ða mælceare maga Healfdenes / singala seað' [189–90a: So that time's trouble continually seethed for Healfdene's kinsman]). When Hrothgar talks about how 'ful oft' his warriors vowed to fight Grendel (480–3), he invokes a picture of the gradual, repeated attrition of his men in a way that suggests the force of repetition and reinforced failure. Grendel, then, is a monster of memory antithetical to proper social order and practices, such as the heroic responsibilities of lords and retainers. Beowulf appears to fear neither Grendel nor the social dissolution that he seemingly represents. A different, more socially proactive memory impels him: the memory by which his greatness might be remembered, or, perhaps, the memory of the social bonds, debts, and obligations, linking his father and Hrothgar. His socially productive use of the past affirms human connections.

Grendel's past produces no such communal memories. He remains outcast, outside society, 'ana wið eallum' (145), defined precisely as one against many. Unlike Grendel, the Wife reintegrates herself figurally into human society, as she uses the very words and images of her isolation to attain a generalized, gnomic appreciation of her place in the temporal expanse of humanity and its remembered wisdom and traditions.

The broadened perspective of a gnomic turn – a move away from individuality and towards generality, similar to the central impetus of *The Wife's Lament* – drives both *The Wanderer* and *The Seafarer*. In each, it connotes a metaphysical *conversio*: isolation or exile on earthly travels and sea journeys becomes a metaphor for the journey to the heavenly kingdom, or the pilgrimage of life itself. The Seafarer explicitly declares why he travels: 'Forþon me hatran sind / dryhtnes dreamas þonne þis deade lif, / læne on londe' [64b–6a: Therefore the Lord's joys are sweeter to me / than this dead transitory life on land]. Yet one goal of such pilgrimage is to gain access to a perfect society in heaven in the company of angels. The turn towards religion goes in tandem with a turn towards inclusion in a wider or more enduring society: the perfect social order of paradise, in which memory need not substitute for loss.[22]

In the context of these peregrinations, the gnomic resignation of the latter portion of *The Wife's Lament* expresses a 'third-person omniscient' view similar to God's and explicitly reaching beyond the transitory repetitions of past and present that engross the earlier portions of the lyric. If the Wife does not embrace a fully Christian and metaphysical perspective, she nevertheless transcends the temporal bounds of her lament. This process shows how narrative structures can echo the divine: even without the ordering of God or of a religious rule, the Wife's narrative evolution provides a framework for extracting a substrate of meaning from the everyday. The temporality of her lyric, conflating past and present, imprisons her in a state that cannot change or progress. She escapes that repetitive circularity not by any evolution of actual events, but by an evolution of her reception of them: she modulates her lament into a more general mode – a mode that orders and measures, rather than merely reiterates, her grief. Ultimately, the modulation of her lament frees her from her own specificity of language and from an internal circularity that subsumes chronology.

As Alice Sheppard's article in this volume suggests, *The Wanderer* dramatizes an analogous process of moving beyond fixation on memory and its emotionally binding details. *The Wanderer* reveals the entanglements of memory and words and time:

Þinceð him on mode þæt he his mondryhten
clyppe and cysse, ond on cneo lecge
honda ond heafod, swa he hwilum ær
in geardagum giefstolas breac.
Ðonne onwæcneð eft wineleas guma,

>   gesihð him biforan   fealwe wegas,
>   baþian brimfuglas,   brædan feþra,
>   hreosan hrim and snaw,   hagle gemenged.
>   Þonne beoð þy hefigran   heortan benne,
>   sare æfter swæsne.   Sorg bið geniwad,
>   þonne maga gemynd   mod geondhweorfeð;
>   greteð gliwstafum,   georne geondsceawað
>   secga geseldan.   Swimmað oft on weg!
>   Fleotendra ferð   no þær fela bringeð
>   cuðra cwidegiedda. (41–55a)

[It seems to him in his mind/memory that he embraces and kisses his lord, and on his knee lays head and hand as at times before in former days, when he received his lord's gifts; then, joyless man, he awakens again, sees before him fallow waves, seabirds bathing, stretching their wings, rime and snow falling mingled with hail. Then the heart's wounds seem the heavier, grief for the dear one. Sorrow is renewed when memory of kinsmen moves around his mind; he greets them with glad notes, scans the companions of men eagerly; they swim away often/always; the spirit of the floating ones brings there but few of the well-known sayings.]

These lines picture his immersion in memory. The strength and specificity of physical imagery – 'clyppe and cysse, ond on cneo lecge / honda ond heafod' – reinforce the social yearning of the Wanderer that repeatedly renews his memory. Such specificity ties him to the unrecoverable past. Here, the poem associates the circularity and involution of this memory with the flight of birds: 'þonne maga gemynd mod geondhweorfeð; / greteð gliwstafum, georne geondsceawað.' The birds and their present voices tangle in the recesses of his mind or memory to recall to him the words and songs and companionship of his kinsmen: 'Sorg bið geniwad, / þonne maga gemynd mod geondhweorfeð.'[23] The repetition of *geond-* in the compounds *geondhweorfeð* and *geondsceawað* reinforces the spatial circularity of the flying birds and the temporal circularity of his *gemynd*. His entanglement in memory and grief thus resembles that of the Wife.[24] Just as the seabirds flock around the shores of the sea, so his thoughts flock around the borders of his grief, blurring past and present, memory and reality, remembered speech and the real repeating cries of the seabirds. Even as the birds emphasize his literal exile, they – and the poignance of his memories – also imply his figural inclusion in human bonds.

Thus the birds' cries, echoing in the Wanderer's mind like well-known songs and the greetings of absent friends, establish a metaphor of unwilled solitude similar to that implicit in the spatial imagery of *The Wife's Lament*. Yet the birds and their unfettered songs evoke the potential for freedom, as does *The Wife's Lament* itself. Like the wife's engrossment in isolation, the birds represent thoughts that can either be free, or repetitive, cyclical, and trapped in the present moment. These birds of memory, like poetic imagination itself, underline the ability of words and song and memory either to reiterate or to transcend physical presence. Poetry then engages with the past more actively than merely by reflecting past events; it provides a model for moving beyond such a recursive response. The flights of poetry and memory coincide even in the gnomic lore about Óðinn, the Norse god who is a source of wisdom and poetry, and who knows all that occurs because two ravens, named Huginn and Muninn, 'Thought' and 'Memory,' report all things to him.[25] These raven messengers free his wisdom and knowledge from the necessity of physical presence. In addition, they portray the twinned natures of thought and memory: each, perhaps, containing the past of the other.

In conclusion, I wish to suggest that this meditation on temporality in *The Wife's Lament* – its manipulation of time, memory, and the social space of the past – helps to define the social framework of time in OE texts. Time, treated as social process, enables repetitions to define inclusion in or exclusion from society. Progress here is, paradoxically, circular; it entails a return to society, just as at the beginning of the *Rule* of St Benedict it is a return to God: a circular route where the past converses with the present.[26] As a commonplace in religious *conversatio*, the social productiveness of time through memory and repetition orders monastic lives; for Christians, exhortations to remember regulate everyday life within salvation history; even the circular calendar of saints' days brings to daily life a constant echo of the past. The uses of time in Anglo-Saxon poetry recall this communal memory of the past into a more secular realm. Finally, the temporal context of *The Wife's Lament* displays how the meaning of the past must be processed as a conversation with the present in a way that generates understanding and social consciousness, precisely because of the unrecoverability of the specific past.[27]

NOTES

1 Bede, *HE* 4.4 (346–7); *The Old English Version of Bede's Ecclesiastical History of the English People*, ed. and trans. Thomas Miller, EETS o.s. 95, 96, 110, 111 (1890–8; repr. in two vols, Millwood, NY: Kraus Reprints, 1988), 4.4 [272].
2 Bede, *HE* 3.19 (276–7); *The Old English Version* 3.14, ed. and trans. Miller (218).
3 For a study of these words, see *The Rule of Saint Benedict: In Latin and English*, ed. and trans. Justin McCann (London: Burns, Oates, 1952), 168 (n. 12) and 202–8 (n. 107).
4 R.W. Southern, *Saint Anselm and His Biographer* (1963; repr. London: Cambridge University Press, 1966), 332: 'In the Benedictine Rule, and generally in Benedictine writers, this word comprised the whole discipline of regular religious life. Traditionally therefore it referred to something essentially corporate and public.' Also see *RB 1980: The Rule of St. Benedict in Latin and English with Notes*, ed. and trans. Timothy Fry (Collegeville, MN: Liturgical Press, 1981), 460–5, and *Thesaurus Linguae Latinae* (Leipzig: B.G. Teubner, 1900–), s.v. 'conversatio.'
5 *Groundhog Day*, produced by Trevor Albert and Harold Ramis, directed by Harold Ramis, 101 min. videocassette (Columbia Pictures, 1993). Janet H. Murray, *Hamlet on the Holodeck: The Future of Narrative in Cyberspace* (1997; repr. Cambridge, MA: MIT Press, 1999), sees in the movie 'an updating of the familiar marriage plot, like the ones in Jane Austen's novels, in which courtship is depicted as a process of moral education' (36). The explicitly social outcome of such 'moral education' is relevant to my argument.
6 Æthelwold, *The Old English Rule*, in *Die angelsächsischen Prosabearbeitungen der Benedictinerregel*, ed. Arnold Schröer, BaP 2 (Kassel: Wigand, 1885), ch. 7b.12 (page 32); ch. 58 (pages 96–9).
7 Bede, *HE* 5.12–13 (498–9); *The Old English Version* 5.13–14, ed. and trans. Miller (436).
8 The continuing life of this idea is evident in Chaucer's *Canterbury Tales*; Chaucer reverses this imagery in his depiction of the Monk, an outrider who clearly neglects monastic *conversatio* and departs its society for more worldly pursuits, like hunting.
9 Bede, *HE* 5.14 (504–5).
10 See Anne L. Klinck, ed., *The Old English Elegies: A Critical Edition and Genre Study* (Montreal: McGill-Queen's University Press, 1992), 226: 'The speaker anticipates no end to her pain, but she comes to terms with it by externalizing it as the focus of speech moves away from the self towards a final gnomic generalization.'

11 It is, perhaps, somewhat oxymoronic that traditional gnomic wisdom is, in this case, progressive, even as it connects the speaker to the past, albeit in a different way. Cf. Clare A. Lees, *Tradition and Belief: Religious Writing in Late Anglo-Saxon England*, Medieval Cultures 19 (Minneapolis: University of Minnesota Press, 1999), 28: 'Tradition does not mean that everything stays the same; traditions selectively reproduce the past in order to evoke an impression of sameness.'

12 See Shari Horner, 'En/closed Subjects: *The Wife's Lament* and the Culture of Early Medieval Female Monasticism,' in *Old English Literature: Critical Essays*, ed. R.M. Liuzza (New Haven: Yale University Press, 2002), 381–91. She invokes Judith Butler's formulations of gender to suggest that the speaker's identity is likewise shaped by repetition, 'a repeated set of culturally and socially established acts' (383). Horner sees these repetitions as constitutive of a discourse of female monastic enclosure; while I disagree with Horner's view of the centrality of that discourse to the poem, I agree that repetition and enclosure establish the Wife's social identity and place.

13 Texts of shorter poetry are from *The Exeter Book*, ed. Krapp and Dobbie, ASPR 3, by line number; exceptions are noted. I draw on notes or glossaries in Klinck, *Old English Elegies*; R.F. Leslie, ed., *Three Old English Elegies: The Wife's Lament, The Husband's Message, The Ruin* (1961; repr. Manchester: University of Manchester Press, 1966); and Bernard J. Muir, ed., *The Exeter Anthology of Old English Poetry: An Edition of Exeter Dean and Chapter MS 3501*, 2nd ed., 2 vols (Exeter: University of Exeter Press, 2000). For the problematic line 15 *her eard*, I use Leslie's reading. In line 9a, *Ða* could be 'when,' with no full stop at the end of line 10, a reading which would reinforce the explicit temporal dimensions here; see Klinck, *Old English Elegies*, 179.

14 Helen T. Bennett, 'Exile and the Semiosis of Gender in Old English Elegies,' in *Class and Gender in Early English Literature: Intersections*, ed. Britton J. Harwood and Gillian R. Overing (Bloomington: Indiana University Press, 1994), 43–58 at 45, also emphasizes such a pattern of social estrangement: 'The female exiles in *The Wife's Lament* and *Wulf and Eadwacer* present no clearcut contrast between a past inclusion in society and a present exile, between past joy and present sorrow. Instead, the speakers portray a history of ambivalent relations with their societies and their mates, expressed in personal, emotional terms, transcending social ritual.' Bennett argues further that the 'men's elegies' contrast 'timelessness' to 'earthly transience,' but 'the boundaries between time and timelessness ... are blurred in the women's poems' (52); her argument, while it privileges gender, supports my claim about the social nature of time – and hence, of remembered pasts.

15 Klinck, *Old English Elegies*, summarizes critical views of the environment (notes to lines 27–9, pages 183–4). See also Paul Battles, 'Of Graves, Caves, and Subterranean Dwellings: *Eorðscræf* and *Eorðsele* in the *Wife's Lament*,' *PQ* 73 (1994): 267–86; Martin Green, 'Time, Memory, and Elegy in *The Wife's Lament*,' in *The Old English Elegies: New Essays in Criticism and Research*, ed. Martin Green (Rutherford, NJ: Fairleigh Dickinson University Press, 1983), 123–32 at 125–9.

16 Alain Renoir, 'A Reading of *The Wife's Lament*,' *ES* 58 (1977): 4–19 at 15, n. 45. See also Green, 'Time, Memory, and Elegy,' 125–6: 'The image of the summer-long day combined with the image of the cave and the tree creates a sense of temporal suspension. Her time is all present – a present without end.'

17 See Thomas D. Hill, 'The Unchanging Hero: A Stoic Maxim in *The Wanderer* and Its Contexts,' *SP* 101 (2004): 233–49 at 240, for a useful context for *geomormod*.

18 For this counterreading of these lines, see especially John D. Niles, 'The Problem of the Ending of *The Wife's Lament*,' *Speculum* 78 (2003): 1107–50. While Niles argues that the poem constructs 'one specific individual suffering one unique fate' (1149), he classes her among those who can fight only with words; thus, she is, if not precisely representative, yet reminiscent of a segment of society. This type of generality is what I would most strongly argue for her, and it does not necessarily preclude the type of narrative-historical specificity that Niles and other scholars have seen in her.

19 Leslie, *Three Old English Elegies*, 3: 'That the speaker is a woman is clear from the feminine forms in the opening lines, a fact ignored or disregarded by the earliest editors.' Klinck, *The Old English Elegies*, summarizes critics' responses (177–8, notes to lines 1–2).

20 Klinck, *The Old English Elegies*, 187, notes to lines 47b–52a: 'Also, the place is described in terms which recall the wife's own dwelling – a gloomy chamber enclosed or dominated by rock, as she imagines for her husband an unhappiness like her own.'

21 See, for instance, *The Seafarer*, esp. lines 36–66; cf. the role of the ocean in Icelandic sagas, especially during the Age of Settlement, when sea travel enables those who wish to escape royal authority to do so. Even ocean imagery in *Beowulf* – vessels that are *utfus* (33) to roam the *swan-rad* (200) – emphasize how the sea facilitates travel. For the relationship of sea journeys to more metaphorical journeys, see Malcolm R. Godden, 'Anglo-Saxons on the Mind,' in *Learning and Literature in Anglo-Saxon England: Studies Presented to Peter Clemoes on the Occasion of His Sixty-Fifth Birthday*, ed. Michael Lapidge and Helmut Gneuss (Cambridge: Cambridge University

Press, 1985), 271–98; repr. in *Old English Literature*, ed. Liuzza, 284–314 at 306.

22 The idea of being alone and bereft of friends might have had particular echoes in a religious context, since friendship alone maintains its character from this life to the afterlife. As Southern writes about Anselm, 'The "conversation" he desired was the community of monastic discipline; and the "full joys of the life to come" referred at least as much to the joys of Heaven as to the pleasures of companionship on earth. The dignity of friendship lay in this: of all things belonging to the natural world it alone continues essentially unaltered in Heaven' (*Saint Anselm*, 73). Cf. Klinck, *The Old English Elegies*, 225: 'In *The Wanderer*, *The Seafarer*, *The Riming Poem*, and *Resignation*, the ordered human society is juxtaposed with an eternal order, the desire for which transcends all feelings of human loneliness.'

23 Klinck, *The Old English Elegies*, 116–17, note on *The Wanderer*, lines 53–4: 'On one level the "companions of men" [secga geseldan] are seabirds, but on another they are a reminder of the illusory vision which vanishes, just as the birds swim away.'

24 See Andy Orchard, 'Re-Reading *The Wanderer*: The Value of Cross-References,' in *Via Crucis: Essays on Early Medieval Sources and Ideas in Memory of J.E. Cross*, ed. Thomas N. Hall with assistance from Thomas D. Hill and Charles D. Wright, Medieval European Studies 1 (Morgantown, WV: West Virginia University Press, 2002), 1–26. Orchard describes in *The Wanderer* a similar 'development from an exclusive self-obsession to an inclusive selflessness' that he sees 'achieved through the creative use of unique or rare compounds, of psychological confinement and restraint in the early stages of the poem, giving way to the language of psychological movement and freedom' (10). See Alice Sheppard's article in this volume for further consideration of the use of *geond-* compounds.

25 Snorri Sturluson, *Edda: Prologue and Gylfaginning*, ed. Anthony Faulkes (Oxford: Clarendon, 1982), 32–3.

26 Æthelwold, *The Old English Rule*, ed. Schröer, 1: '... þæt ðu mid þinre hyrsumnesse geswince to Gode gecyrre, þe þu ær fram buge mid asolcennysse ðinre unhyrsumnesse.'

27 I would like to thank Tom Hill, who listened to or read and commented on at least four early versions of this paper with great patience, generosity, and good humour.

A Word to the Wise: Thinking, Knowledge, and Wisdom in *The Wanderer*

ALICE SHEPPARD

Critics of *The Wanderer* have made much of the poem's lexicographical difficulty, the blurred boundaries between its speakers, and its vivid imagery. The narrative action centres on the speaker's apparent transformation from an *anhaga* [solitary person] in distress to a reconciled *snottor on mode* [one wise in mind].[1] Using a blend of formal proverbs and axiomatic sayings, the *Wanderer* poet dramatizes this journey as a search for knowledge that will offer solace for the speaker's painful existence. Yet at the end of the poem, although the speaker appears to have achieved some degree of reconciliation or transcendence, the lessons he learns from the proverbs seem to have intensified rather than alleviated his pain. This tension between the knowledge the proverbs provide and the wisdom the speaker seeks enables a reading of *The Wanderer* as a wisdom text that I will call a narrative *gyd*.[2]

The problems of using 'wisdom text' and *gyd* as genre terms are many and well known. Discussions of these problems have often emphasized similarity of content or literary form as the primary criterion for inclusion. If, however, we focus not on the specifics of the plot or genre, but on the *Wanderer* poet's narrative techniques, then the advantage of reading the poem as a wisdom text becomes clear. Like a proverb itself, *The Wanderer* as a narrative poem generates meaning both at the immediate literal level of its story and in a broader conceptual manner. At the literal level, the story recounts and interprets the journey of a sorrowing *anhaga* whose quest for reconciliation and wisdom draws upon the conventions of the warrior ethos and the tenets of his own personal faith. As a *gyd*, however, *The Wanderer* exemplifies an interpretive approach to reading wisdom poetry. The poet undergirds the literal story of the speaker with a poetics of interpretive process using the rare verb *geondþencan*, 'to reflect upon, consider,' or, more literally, 'to think through or beyond.'[3]

In *The Wanderer*, *geondþencan* is to look beyond the surface details of the proverbs and of the speaker's own situation and to peer through to the deeper processes of reading, thinking, and interpreting. At the end of the poem, the speaker's apparently pain-free existence is not so much a function of what he has learned from the individual proverbs as it is a marker of his ability to acknowledge the importance of thinking through and beyond proverbs, without necessarily applying their specific teachings. This distinction is mirrored in the text's extension of meaning beyond the details of the surface narrative to the way in which the reader constructs meaning.

Many poems have multiple meanings, but the OE poems that identify themselves as *gyd* – namely *The Seafarer*, *The Wife's Lament*, and *Wulf and Eadwacer* – are different. In the extant OE corpus, these are the only poems narrated from a subject position with which the reader might conceivably personally identify. They seem to be poems about possible experience. Designating these texts as *gyd* expands this personal aspect by invoking the riddling, enigmatic difficulty associated with the more formally recognizable texts of this kind. Just as the reader expects the riddles to have 'obvious' and less obvious solutions, so the designation of *gyd* prepares the reader to find that the ultimate significance of the narrative detail is less obvious than the motivating situation might suggest. The subsequent layering of meaning allows these emotional narratives to signify beyond their immediate narrative context. For the narrative *gyd* of the Exeter Book, the personal is not only individual; it has a communal significance. This generalized dimension allows these poems to function as part of the diverse OE tradition of poetic wisdom literature.

The Wanderer as *gyd*

Defining what is (and what is not) a wisdom text is still one of the central open questions of the field. The scope of the issue – which goes beyond the parameters of this essay – ranges from matters of proverbial syntax (the distinction between *sceal* and *bið* proverbs is particularly important for OE literary scholarship)[4] to problems of genre (how can riddle, catalogue, proverb, and instructional texts be interpreted as similar kinds of literary production?).

The Wanderer defines its relationship to wisdom and wisdom poetry explicitly. The search for wisdom is at the core of its motivating story; the poem's speaker seeks knowledge from two kinds of proverbial sayings. He misses his lord's 'larcwidum' [38a: teachings], and he relates how a sorrowing mind may seek relief in well-known 'cwidegiedda' [55a: sayings]. Semantically, these are relatively unproblematic words, but as genre terms, they are less familiar and less straightforward.

OE *lar* ('precept,' 'exhortation,' or 'advice' [BT]), *cwide* ('speech,' 'saying,' 'word,' or 'proverb' [*DOE* C.1226–35]), and *gyd* ('song,' 'poem,' 'saying,' 'proverb,' and 'riddle' [BT]) designate a wide variety of wisdom texts.[5] OE *cwide* is relatively neutral. It has a wide range of meanings that include a simple 'utterance' to 'wise utterance,' 'saying,' and 'proverb'; more narrowly, *cwide* can refer to a 'prophecy' or 'prediction' or a Latin *sententia*.[6] The *lar*- element in *larcwide* formalizes the meaning of *cwide* by adding to its less specific meaning the more moralistic and prescriptive ideas of 'doctrines,' 'precepts,' 'ordinances,' and 'advice' and 'counsel' (BT). Specifically, a *lar* is a 'speech intended to instruct or inform,' synonymous with Latin *paradigma*.[7] Although its definitions will soon be superseded by the new *DOE* entry, BT gives 'song, lay, poem' and 'speech, tale, sermon, riddle.' This is revised in BTS to 'a metrical composition, poem, song' and, as subcategories of formal speech, 'maxim, sentence, proverb, didactic speech, eloquent oratical speech, figurative speech, and prophecy.'

In addition to connoting a short axiomatic utterance or proverb, OE *gyd* frequently has been used as a name for longer narrative texts whose content seems similar. As such, it has been the subject of a number of studies that attempt to align the term with a specific literary form. Lois Bragg, citing Roscoe Parker, calls a *gyd* a 'brief work of verbal art,'[8] while Richard North sees a *gyd* as an 'inherently sad genre of composition.'[9] The most recent (and most encyclopedic) study of the term, by Karl Reichl, distinguishes four general categories of *gyd*: 'proverbs and memorable sayings,' 'utterances of the Prophets,' 'New Testament parables,' and 'poetry and song including the Psalms.'[10]

In my reading of *The Wanderer* as a narrative *gyd*, I adopt Reichl's third category – 'New Testament parables' – to justify placing less critical attention on the specific, literal advice offered by the proverbs and to support my focus on process and general wisdom. In Reichl's grouping, forms of OE *gyd* gloss Latin *proverbium* [proverb], *similitudo* [metaphor/simile], *parabola* [parable/comparison], and *elogium* [maxim, inscription]. For Reichl, these terms are linked primarily by their relevance to the New Testament. While accepting, as Reichl notes, that forms of *gyd* do not appear as a gloss for parable in OE poetry,[11] I would like to suggest that, despite differing form and content, OE *gyd* can be connected by the interpretive demands they levy upon their readers.

To understand such texts – and to this list I would add an *enigma*[12] – one must read beyond the literal meaning to arrive at their veiled significance.[13] Proverbial knowledge and wisdom texts are often characterized by their enigmatic quality. Under *gidding* (as a gloss on *enigmata*), BTS offers 'dark saying, riddle, enigma.' 'Dark saying' appears to be a BTS interpretive gloss as opposed to a direct correlation of something in either OE or Latin, but the claim that wisdom texts are 'difficult' might productively be seen as a characteristic of the genre.

As Thomas D. Hill has argued, 'The notion that proverbs are not straightforward, that they can be defined as "aenigmata sapientium," "riddles of the wise" (Prov. 1:6), is part of the biblical definition of the genre. The obscurity of wisdom literature is based in part on the compressed, enigmatic, and often figurative language characteristic of proverbial texts.'[14] Hill's description certainly helps readers approach such obvious and yet confusing proverbial statements from *Maxims I (B)* as, 'Forst sceal freosan, fyr wudu meltan' [1: frost must freeze, fire consume wood]. My focus is on how *gyd* as a genre term asks the reader to think *through* the obscurity evoked by such obvious facts and *beyond* the literal details of the individual speaker's situation as a way of developing an interpretive strategy that suits both *The Wanderer* and the other *gyd* of the Exeter Book.

Reading the *gyd* in this way changes how we understand the wisdom and genre of *The Wanderer*. Both at the level of its individual proverbs and at the level of a narrative poem, *The Wanderer* is, in keeping with the words *larcwide* and *cwidegyd*, a self-consciously doubly defined wisdom poem. In the story of the lordless speaker's journey, the poet conveys a body of secular and Christian situation-specific knowledge. This assembly of 'facts' is sufficient both to inform the reader of some of the central tenets of the faith and to instruct him or her in the principles of being a warrior. Nonetheless, in that they leave the reader with as many questions as answers, the facts of the poem are also startlingly insufficient.

For example, in the concluding lines – lines that we, as readers, might be tempted to see as determinative – the speaker learns that 'Her bið feoh læne' [108: Here riches are transitory] and 'Wel bið þam þe him are seceð, / frofre to fæder on heofonum' [114b–15a: It is well for him who seeks grace, comfort from the father in the heavens]. The knowledge communicated here is reassuring, but it is not directly responsible for the speaker's self-positioning as a man, *snottor on mode*. As a *gyd*, *The Wanderer* first focuses on process, that is, the means by which the speaker learns to distinguish situation-specific factual knowledge from the process of recognizing generalized wisdom. At the heart of this process is the convention of verbal exchange.

Getting to *Gyd*

The literary wisdom tradition of Anglo-Saxon England emphasizes the importance of trading wise sayings. As the opening lines of *Maxims I (A)* suggest, exchanging wisdom is an essential part of what separates a wise man from any other learned man. The speaker declares:

> Frige mec frodum wordum.   Ne læt þinne ferð onhælne
> degol þæt þu deopost cunne.   Nelle ic þe min dyrne gesecgan,
> gif þu me þinne hygecræft hylest   ond þine heortan geþohtas.
> Gleawe men sceolon   gieddum wrixlan. (1–4a)

> [Ask me questions with wise words. Do not let your spirit be hidden nor that which you know most deeply be kept secret. I do not want to reveal my secrets if you hide from me the wisdom of your mind and the thoughts of your heart. Wise men must exchange wise words.]

The poem continues with relatively quotidian proverbs; these are the *gyd* wise men exchange. Neither *Maxims I (A)* nor the other similar proverb poems reveal why exchange is important. As a result, the poems' readers have tended to focus first on what the wise men say and then on what they see as a corresponding lack of importance in such informational statements as: 'Forst sceal freosan, fyr wudu meltan, / eorþe growan, is brycgian, / wæter helm wegan, wundrum lucan / eorþan ciþas' [Frost must freeze, fire consume wood, / soil grow, ice make a bridge, / water sustain a covering, and wondrously lock / the seeds of the earth] (*Maxims I (B)*, 1–4a). Indeed, the paradox posed by the mundane and obvious quality of these sayings as vehicles for 'wisdom' is well documented in the criticism. T.A. Shippey once stated that the 'dark, secret, and hidden' was what the Anglo-Saxons wanted in a wisdom text, and that 'the very nature of Anglo-Saxon wisdom must also seem uncongenial, baffling, even downright irritating'[15] to today's readers.[16]

I would suggest that this critical difficulty is of our own making; we have misread the significance, if not the literal meaning, of the poem's opening lines. The poet of *Maxims I (A)* states, 'Gleawe men sceolon gieddum wrixlan' [4a: Wise men must exchange wise words]. He does not specify what those words are or why the exchange should be undertaken; he focuses only on the process of the exchange. This defines the wisdom of the wise men, not the quality of the insight they share.

Given this literary tradition, I would argue that, in the context of *The Wanderer* as a *gyd*, the act of reciting proverbs may be a stronger indicator of wisdom than the knowledge the sayings transmit. My focus on the process of exchanging proverbs and not on the content of their wisdom makes sense of the fact that, although they purport to teach the speaker how to overcome his pain, the poem does not conclude with the *snottor on mode* celebrating his hard-won solace. Rather, the isolation of the speaker and the lack of specificity about his situation suggest that a journey to wisdom may both define wisdom itself and be more important than the poem's specific knowledge.

Talk Therapy: From Content to Process via Exchange

The story of the speaker and his search for wisdom in the proverbs he utters are now a familiar part of the poem's interpretive tradition. We are, for example, accustomed to finding that the speaker, 'earfeþa gemyndig, / wraþra wælsleahta, winemæga hryre' [6b–7: mindful of hardships, of terrible slaughterings, and of the destruction of his dear kinsmen], recites his cares using a sequence of proverblike statements. And we know that, although the speaker is able to remember the ideals of his warrior ethos, the specific teachings, that is, the facts, of the proverbs are not efficacious: they remind him of the isolation of his situation and of the reason he was out alone at dawn in the first place. In his discussion of stoicism and *apatheia*, Thomas D. Hill has shown how suppression and denial of emotion is a defining requirement of the warrior ethos, but the *Wanderer* poet, moving away from the facts of heroic life, does not see silence as a means to his end.[17] Thus, when the poet depicts the speaker turning uselessly to the warrior ethos as a resource, he draws upon the conventions that are familiar to Anglo-Saxon readers only in order to further his point about reading through and beyond.

In this context, I wish to reconsider the importance of the literary poetic tradition in *The Wanderer*. Playing with genre terms, the *Wanderer* poet permits the reader alert to the riddling nature of a *gyd* a deeper perspective. When the speaker is caught by the contradictions of his situation, he formulates a second strategy: if reciting proverbs does not help, he will recall the familiar wisdom of his lord. The speaker explains that a man who for a long time has had to do without his dear lord's 'larcwidum' [teachings] imagines embracing and kissing his lord and placing his head upon his lord's knees:

> Forþon wat se þe sceal his winedryhtenes
> leofes larcwidum longe forþolian –
> ðonne sorg ond slæp somod ætgædre
> earmne anhogan oft gebindað,
> þinceð him on mode þæt he his mondryhten
> clyppe ond cysse, ond on cneo lecge
> honda ond heafod, swa he hwilum ær
> in geardagum giefstolas breac. (37–44)

[Therefore, he who must forgo the teachings of his dear lord and friend for a long time knows – when sorrow and sleep together often bind the unhappy solitary one, it seems to him in his mind that he embraces and kisses his lord, and lays his hand and head upon his knee, as he at times in former days had received treasure from the throne.]

For the reader focused on the circumstantial details, this is certainly an emotionally compelling image. The speaker desires the lord's teachings, but the lord's absence seems to obscure the fact that he already has access to the lord's wisdom: he has just recited some proverbs. For the reader who is alive to the poem's language, this scene also demonstrates the necessity of the double reading implied by 'thinking through and beyond.'

The poet's use of *larcwide*, a redundant formulation attested only once elsewhere,[18] is significant. In defining his terms, the poet calls to mind the modes and conventions of wisdom poetry: the *lar*, the *cwide*, the *gyd*, and *sententiae* of the Anglo-Saxon literary tradition. In this world, it is neither surprising nor particularly helpful to know that frost must freeze; it is, rather, the exchange of this wisdom that is important. The meaning and significance of the saying itself is supposed to be obscure. Thus to expect his lord's proverbial sayings to have a material effect upon the speaker's situation is a misapprehension, the consequences of which are clearly marked in the dream sequence.

When the speaker awakes from a vision of his lord, he sees only a desolate seascape populated by birds. Sorrowing over this scene, the lordless man's *mod* ('mind') leaves its body.[19] The speaker observes that, as sorrowful as it is, the mind cannot linger over its specific memories – the *mod* must proceed to search for wisdom:

> Sorg bið geniwad
> þonne maga gemynd   mod geondhweorfeð;
> greteð gliwstafum,   georne geondsceawað
> secga geseldan;   swimmað oft on weg –
> fleotendra ferð   no þær fela bringeð
> cuðra cwidegiedda. (50b–5a)

[Sorrow is renewed when the mind passes through the memory of kinsmen; greets them with joy, and eagerly looks its warrior friends up and down; they often swim away – the spirit of floating ones does not bring back many of the well-known sayings.]

In the image of the mind scanning the figures from his memory – a response to the detail of what he remembers – the *Wanderer* poet suggests that the speaker once more seeks situation-specific content. Simultaneously, however, he both explains to the reader how the speaker might alleviate his pain and suggests how the poem as a whole can be read. In the story, the mind may seek *cwidegiedda* as a remedy, but the reader should not miss the fact that *cwidegyd* is a critically significant word. In the word *cwidegyd* the poet introduces another doubly defined genre term, a *hapax legomenon* and possible neologism that underscores both the importance of the wisdom tradition and the process of thinking through to the general significance of its knowledge. The conventions of the *cwidegyd* are more important to an understanding of the poem than the factual advice of any single *gyd* with which the mind could return. And it is this notion of process upon which a nonpersonalized understanding of *The Wanderer* and the other wisdom texts of the Exeter Book rest.

Thinking It Through

As the speaker develops from an *anhaga* to a *snottor on mode*, the language of the poem changes according to his skill at separating factual advice or content from process. Lines 1–57 contain a number of axiomatic sayings, but the wisdom they communicate is often not expressed in either of the two dominant syntactical forms that most readily identify declarative sentences as formal proverbs. Thus, the speaker often mulls over such passively and indirectly articulated wisdom as: 'Wat se þe cunnað / hu sliþen bið sorg to geferan, / þam þe him lyt hafað leofra geholena' [29–31: He who has experienced it knows how cruel sorrow is as a companion to him who has few dear close friends].

Nonetheless, three expressions of proverbial wisdom differentiate the positioning of the speaker of the second section (58–115) from that of the first. At each moment, the speaker's metacomment about his ability to think through demonstrates his newly found knowledge, whereas previously, in the first half of the poem, he might have been drawn to the content:

Forþon ic geþencan ne mæg   geond þas woruld
for hwan modsefa   min ne gesweorce
þonne ic eorla lif   eal geondþence ... (58–60)

[Therefore I can think of no reason in this world why my mind does not become dark when I think through all the life of men ...][20]

Ongietan sceal glæw hæle   hu gæstlic bið
þonne ealre þisse worulde wela   weste stondeð ... (73–4)

[The wise man must perceive (with the sense of understanding) how awesomely spiritual[21] it will be when the riches of all this world stand deserted ...]

Se þonne þisne wealsteal   wise geþohte
ond þis deorce lif   deope geondþenceð,
frod in ferðe,   feor oft gemon ... (88–90)

[He who deeply thinks through in wise thought this walled place and this dark life, a man prudent in spirit, often remembers far back in time ...]

Here, the importance of process as opposed to content is marked in the poet's vocabulary, and it is particularly noticeable in his use of *geond* as a prefix. In OE, forms of *geond* are acceptable prefixes for a wide variety of verbs. In *The Wanderer*, the poet uses *geond* customarily (3 and 75), but the first two verbs to which he attaches it are significant. They are *geondsceawian* ('to look upon') and *geondhweorfan* ('to pass over or pass through'), verbs that trace the actions of a frantic *mod* (50–2, quoted above, page 137). *Geondsceawian* and *geondhweorfan* are also the last actions the *mod* completes as it sets out on its search for the *cwidegiedda*, the sayings that the speaker desires.

Given this immediate and visible connection between verbs prefixed by *geond* and the speaker's search for wisdom, it is doubly significant that to describe the thinking process that will free the speaker, the poet uses *geondþencan*, a word that appears twice in *The Wanderer* (69b and 80b) and only once more in the corpus of OE poetry. In *The Wanderer*, *geondþencan* appears, significantly, at the moments when the speaker handles wisdom correctly: that is, when he looks through and beyond the facts of the proverbial sayings. For the speaker, the repeated use of *geond-* compounds links the outcome of the search (a new way of thinking) to its beginning. For the reader, the repetition emphasizes the importance of this new approach to thought and interpretation.

To highlight the connection between OE *geondþencan* and the speaker's new thought pattern, the poet includes sequences of proverbial wisdom, suggesting that the act of repeating the wisdom and not the facts of the knowledge transforms the *anhaga* into the *snottor on mode*. When the speaker questions why his mind does not grow dark, he answers himself with an image of a bleak landscape and the claim that 'ne mæg wearþan wis wer, ær he age / wintra dæl in woruldrice' [64–5a: a man cannot become wise, before he possesses a certain number of winters in the earthly kingdom]. He follows this claim with a sequence of *sceal* proverbs. This particular style of proverbial expression with (and perhaps because of) its concomitant sense of obligation defines what it means to be a wise man. In effect, the proverbs simultaneously teach the speaker how to behave as if he has recovered the world he once lost while holding out the possibility of again living in this world. But in this third moment, the speaker makes no effort to resume his previous life or to apply the facts to his situation; he merely recites:

Ongietan sceal gleaw hæle   hu gæstlic bið
þonne ealre þisse worulde wela   weste stondeð ... (73–4)

[The wise man must perceive (with the sense of understanding) how awesomely spiritual it will be when the riches of all this world stand deserted ...]

So forceful are the proverbs in form that their prescriptions seem self-evident. The speaker has adopted the wise man's perspective and his thinking habits: there is no necessity, proverbial or factual, that compels the *gleaw hæle* to comprehend how the world will be transformed. Yet the speaker insists with full proverbial force (if not form): 'Ongietan sceal gleaw hæle hu gæstlic bið ...' (73). In the first half of the poem, such a statement would have brought back painful memories and anguished attempts to apply this insight to the speaker's situation. Now, however, the speaker controls the images of the *ubi sunt* sequence. The fleeting glimpses of devastation are only images, not personal memories; he who can think through (*geondþencan*) the 'wealsteal' [88a: wall-place] and remembers the 'wælsleahta worn' [91a: large number of slaughters] can comprehend his own experience. The speaker begins with a series of questions, using the *ubi sunt* formula to establish desperation and pain; he follows that with a description of a devastated landscape, but he controls that description with a series of axioms that define and circumscribe the picture he paints. He can see past the agonizing details and beyond the individual; the process of being able to recall is more important than the details of the vision itself. This is how *larcwide* and *cwidegyd* function. This is the privileged knowledge granted the reader of wisdom poetry.

A Word to the Would-Be Wise

By the end of the poem, the speaker appears to be at ease. Both the individual *gyd* and the process of 'thinking through' prevent personal memory from distracting him with literal factual detail. The poem concludes with an unprompted demonstration of his art:

> Til biþ se þe his treowe gehealdeþ,   ne sceal næfre his torn to rycene
> beorn of his breostum acyþan,   nemþe he ær þa bote cunne,
> eorl mid elne gefremman.   Wel bið þam þe him are seceð,
> frofre to fæder on heofonum,   þær us eal seo fæstnung stondeð. (112–15)

> [He who holds to his pledge is good, nor must a man ever announce the anger from his breast too quickly, unless he knows beforehand how to bring about the remedy for it with courage. It is well for him who seeks grace, comfort from the father in the heavens where all our stability is.]

Because these hypermetric lines stand out in the context of the poem and because their content is so suited to the facts of the narrative, the reader is tempted to give them extra interpretive weight. Yet to see these as the most important part of the poem, the recommendations that finally enable the speaker to transcend his secular world with the knowledge of Christianity, would be to prioritize content over process and to misunderstand the wisdom of the poem as a whole.

In representing the speaker's transformation from *anhaga* to *snottor on mode*, the poem consistently uses its language and syntax to define the gap between the individual and the general and between process and content. Even at the microlevel, these factors delineate the speaker's journey. At its beginning, as critics such as William Alfred and Carolyne Larrington have noted, the poem dramatizes the speaker's struggle by alternating between the first person (for the speaker's experience) and the third person (for the recommendations of proverbial wisdom).[22] But when we understand the poem's own analytical language, we can see how these examples of the poem's form and content work together to argue for the importance of 'thinking through and beyond.' To place this latter program at the centre of the poem is to alter the genre and thus the interpretive parameters of the poem, thereby changing the meaning of its speaker's journey. While the constituent narrative elements remain the same, the Christian wisdom of the end need not be the final interpretive word.

Reading the poem as a *gyd* does more than meaningfully include both the Christian and secular proverbs and preserve the poem's strong emotional dynamic; it also explains the poem's place as a fulcrum for the Exeter Book. The manuscript begins with the *Advent Lyrics*, the *Ascension*, and *Christ in Judgement*, two versions of the *Life of Saint Guthlac*, *The Canticles of the Three Youths*, the *Phoenix*, and *Juliana*. It concludes with the so-called elegies – *The Wanderer, The Seafarer, The Wife's Lament, Wulf and Eadwacer*, and *The Husband's Message*, the instructional texts, bestiary poems, and the riddles. With its search for wisdom and its study of interpretive practice, *The Wanderer* bridges the gap between the poems that celebrate the mysteries of Christianity and those that ponder the mundanities of human existence. In teaching its readers how to handle wisdom, it asks them to interpret generalities in even the most personalized of narratives, and in so doing, it takes its place literally and conceptually at the centre of the Exeter Book.

NOTES

1 *The Wanderer*, ed. Bernard J. Muir, in *The Exeter Anthology of Old English Poetry: An Edition of Exeter Dean and Chapter MS 3501*, 2nd ed., 2 vols (Exeter: University of Exeter Press, 2000), lines 1 and 111. Quotations from

the Exeter Book poems throughout are from Muir's edition; I adopt Muir's titles. What the poem's readers have made of this transformation has depended, for the most part, on what they see as the text's genre or primary mode. The problem of genre in *The Wanderer* has been complicated by the existence of its companion piece, *The Seafarer*, and the other Exeter Book poems with haunting dramatic voices; the question dominates early to mid-twentieth century scholarship. Stanley B. Greenfield, *The Interpretation of Old English Poems* (London: Routledge and Kegan Paul, 1972), 135, writes: 'If the elegies are a genre in Old English, they are so by force of our present, rather than determinate historical, perspective; that is, by our "feel" for them as a group possessing certain features in common.' Greenfield's comments anticipate the more theoretical work of Hans Robert Jauss. Ranging over questions of aesthetics, genre, and medieval literature, Jauss points out that genre is as much prescriptive as descriptive. See Jauss, *Toward an Aesthetic of Reception*, trans. Timothy Bahti (Minneapolis: University of Minnesota Press, 1982), 3–45 (on genres and reading) and 76–109 (on medieval literary genre).

2 I am, of course, not the first to see *The Wanderer* as part of the wisdom tradition; see, most compellingly, T.A. Shippey, '*The Wanderer* and *The Seafarer* as Wisdom Poetry,' in *Companion to Old English Poetry*, ed. Henk Aertsen and Rolf H. Bremmer, Jr (Amsterdam: VU University Press, 1994), 145–58. The most recent discussion of the poem's genre and its critical history is Andy Orchard, 'Re-Reading *The Wanderer*: The Value of Cross-References,' in *Via Crucis: Essays on Early Medieval Sources and Ideas in Memory of J.E. Cross*, ed. Thomas N. Hall with assistance from Thomas D. Hill and Charles D. Wright, Medieval European Studies 1 (Morgantown: West Virginia University Press, 2002), 1–26, esp. 1-5. My approach to wisdom poetry as a genre is informed by this nuanced discussion of the ambiguities of the poetic language and its careful positioning vis à vis the heroic and homiletic traditions and careful analysis of the ways in which it engages its reader in the making of literary meaning.

3 In the extant OE corpus, the only other instance of *geondþencan* (in the form 'ieondðence') is in Charter 1622 (Somner), B15.7.2, a charter of Archbishop Wulfred (cited from the *DOE Corpus*, accessed April 12, 2006). Paired with *asmeaie* (from *asmeagan*, 'to look closely into, examine,' BTS), *geondþencan* here has a more literal, but similar sense of analysing to the deepest extent possible.

4 Carolyne Larrington, *A Store of Common Sense: Gnomic Theme and Style in Old Icelandic and Old English Wisdom Poetry* (Oxford: Clarendon, 1993), 6–9, provides a brief summary of the problem. Paul Cavill, *Maxims in Old*

Thinking, Knowledge, and Wisdom in *The Wanderer* 143

English Poetry (Woodbridge, Suffolk: D.S. Brewer, 1999), 45–50, modifies Larrington's discussion, pointing out that the translations (and thus genre distinctions) are less consistent than the scholarly community would like to think.

5 Unless quoting, I use the form *gyd* because of the cross-reference of *DOE*, C.1235.
6 *DOE*, C.1226–35.
7 *DOE*, C.1226–35. Where I use BT's Latin equivalents, I have confirmed their attestation in the online *DOE Corpus* (accessed 12 April 2004).
8 Roscoe E. Parker, '*Gyd, leoð, sang* in Old English Poetry,' *Tennessee Studies in English Literature* 1 (1956): 59–63; cited by Lois Bragg, *The Lyric Speakers of Old English Poetry* (Rutherford, NJ: Fairleigh Dickinson University Press, 1991), 19.
9 Richard North, *Pagan Words and Christian Meanings* (Amsterdam: Rodopi, 1991), 39–41; quotation at 40.
10 Karl Reichl, 'Old English *giedd*, Middle English *yedding* as Genre Terms,' in *Words, Texts, and Manuscripts: Studies in Anglo-Saxon Culture Presented to Helmut Gneuss on the Occasion of His Sixty-Fifth Birthday*, ed. Michael Korhammer, Karl Reichl, and Hans Sauer (Cambridge: D.S. Brewer, 1992), 349–70 at 358. This is by no means a complete summary of possible uses for *gyd*.
11 Reichl, 'Old English *giedd*,' 359.
12 Technically, *(a)enigma* is glossed by *geddung*: examples are the *Cleopatra Glossary*: 'Enigmata: geddunga' (cited from the *DOE Corpus*), and BT, 462.
13 BTS, 462, also acknowledges this kind of double layering under its second definition: 'of figurative speech.' If they were later medieval texts, they might be described as exploiting their *integumentum* ('covering' or perhaps 'veil').
14 Thomas D. Hill, 'Wisdom (Sapiential) Literature,' in *Medieval England: An Encyclopedia*, ed. Paul E. Szarmach, M. Teresa Tavormina, and Joel T. Rosenthal (New York: Garland, 1998), 805–7 at 806.
15 T.A. Shippey, *Poems of Wisdom and Learning in Old English* (Cambridge: D.S. Brewer, 1976), 3.
16 Shippey, *Poems of Wisdom*, 4. Shippey's work has, of course, shed much light on the OE wisdom texts. See his essays 'Maxims in Old English Narrative: Literary Art or Traditional Wisdom,' in *Oral Tradition, Literary Tradition: A Symposium*, ed. Hans Bekker-Nielsen (Odense: Odense University Press, 1977), 28–46; 'Miscomprehension and Re-interpretation in Old and Early Middle English Proverb Collections,' in *Text und Zeittiefe*, ed. Hildegard L.C. Tristram (Tubingen: Gunter Narr Verlag, 1994), 293–311; and '*The Wanderer* and *The Seafarer* as Wisdom Poetry.'

17 Thomas D. Hill, 'The Unchanging Hero: A Stoic Maxim in *The Wanderer* and Its Contexts,' *SP* 101 (2004): 233–49.
18 *Andreas*, line 672.
19 See Peter Clemoes, '*Mens absentia cogitans* in *The Seafarer* and *The Wanderer*,' in *Medieval Literature and Civilization: Studies in Memory of G.N. Garmonsway*, ed. D.A. Pearsall and R.A. Waldron (London: Athlone, 1969), 62–77; Andrew Galloway, 'Dream-Theory in *The Dream of the Rood* and *The Wanderer*,' *RES* n.s. 45 (1994): 475–85; M.R. Godden, 'Anglo-Saxons on the Mind,' in *Learning and Literature in Anglo-Saxon England: Studies Presented to Peter Clemoes on the Occasion of His Sixty-Fifth Birthday*, ed. Michael Lapidge and Helmut Gneuss (Cambridge: Cambridge University Press, 1985), 271–98, repr. in *Old English Literature: Critical Essays*, ed. R.M. Liuzza (New Haven: Yale University Press, 2002), 284–314; and Antonina Harbus, 'Deceptive Dreams in *The Wanderer*,' *SP* 93 (1996): 164–79.
20 On this translation, see Muir, *Exeter Anthology of Old English Poetry*, 2:510. The central issue here is the state of the speaker's mind: is it dark, will it become dark, and what is the relationship of darkness to wisdom?
21 On the translation of *gæstlic* and the relevance of its spiritual dimension, see Muir, *Exeter Anthology of Old English Poetry*, 2:511.
22 See William Alfred, 'The Drama of *The Wanderer*,' in *The Wisdom of Poetry: Essays in Early English Literature in Honor of Morton W. Bloomfield*, ed. Larry D. Benson and Siegfried Wenzel (Kalamazoo: Medieval Institute Publications, 1982), 31–44 and 268–70 at 36; and Larrington, *A Store of Common Sense*, 192.

PART III
Old English Prose

Alfred's Nero

PAUL E. SZARMACH

By the late ninth century the emperor Nero had so terrible a reputation that no early medieval spin doctor – had there been such a person at the time – would have been able to restore it. Many texts and traditions transmitted this negative judgment, but perhaps none was so influential and effective as Boethius's *De Consolatione Philosophiae*. In that 'golden volume not unworthy of the leisure of Plato or Tully' that dominated the intellectual horizon of the Middle Ages,[1] Nero appears as an exemplum of the wicked tyrant and as the image of a moral agent out of control.

This paper is a study of King Alfred's reception of Nero, how he reworked the myth of Nero, and what he in turn contributed to the complex of themes launched in the *Consolatio*. When Alfred set out to translate the *Consolatio*, he had no choice but to receive the Boethian view and the weight of tradition. For his authoritative study of rulership Alfred likely inherited the commentary tradition, but he nevertheless contributed his own shape and sense of the Neronian myth. One distinctive feature in Alfred's work is the 'double rendering,' that is, when Alfred translates Boethius's metres into prose, then into verse, and thus relates the same material, allowing for two perspectives.[2] Alfred does not particularly follow his own prescriptions on translation practice, as he describes them in the Preface to the *Pastoral Care*. The differences in the renderings reveal various aspects of Alfred's take on royal power, its limits, and its problematics. Alfred demonstrates a complex response, all in all, which is a witness to his considered views of royal power and which demonstrates his capacity for what one might call a form of speculative political thought.

The complexity begins in the histories of the Roman Empire and later antiquity. It is well beyond the scope of this paper to offer anything other than a sketch of the pre-Anglo-Saxon Nero.[3] Two histories are of special interest to the Anglo-Saxon literary tradition: Paulus Orosius, *Historiarum adversus paganos libri VII* and Bede, *Historia ecclesiastica*.[4] The OE versions of these two works, once considered to be translated by Alfred, are no longer part of the Alfredian canon, but they are important examples of the revival of learning in late ninth-century England.[5] Now they are deemed 'Alfredian' in a secondary sense, meaning that Alfred may have authorized them directly or indirectly or inspired the zeitgeist that made them possible. Orosius, who, it must be remembered, wrote ideological history without apology, offers a portrait of Nero in Book VII.7 [= OE *Orosius* VI.5] describing virtually every sort of depravity. The topic sentence in the account says it all: 'Omnia uitia ac scelera sectator immo transgressor, petulantiam libidinem luxuriam auaritiam crudelitatem nullo non scelere exercuit' [There was no form of vice that he did not practice – wantonness, lust, extravagances, avarice and cruelty].[6] Specifications of these broad charges include incest, transsexuality, indecorous theatricality, persecution of Christians to include the martyrdom of Peter and Paul, and military-political disasters. There are specific details about the burning of Rome, namely, how Nero brought it off, from where he viewed the fire (the tower of Maecenas), and how he dressed as an actor and recited the *Iliad* as the fire burned, and how he died a suicide after having heard that Galba was made emperor in Spain by the army. The OE version is a précis of this account, reducing the narrative to about a quarter of the Latin. Murder, incest, perceived sexual deviation, politics, and war all disappear. Nero's relationship to his line, specifically his connection to Claudius and his suicide as the end of the Julio-Claudian line, frame the account. The sharp and comparatively laconic focus is on the fire and the Christian persecutions, including the martyrdom of Peter and Paul, which, compared to the Latin, is rather abbreviated.

Bede mentions Nero briefly (*HE* 1.3) in his rapid survey of the Roman Empire and its relation to Britain:

Succedens autem Claudio in imperium Nero, nihil omnino in re militari ausus est. Unde inter alia Romani regni detrimenta innumera Brittaniam pene amisit: nam duo sub eo nobilissima oppida illic capta atque subuersa sunt. (24–5)

[Nero, who succeeded Claudius as emperor, undertook no military campaigns of any kind. Consequently he brought countless other disasters upon the Roman Empire, and nearly lost Britain as well. For two very noble cities were captured and destroyed there during his reign.]

Bede's less than pacific view of Nero's military policy failures would seem to strike a discordant note, especially in the provocative 'nihil ... ausus est.' Bede is actually following Eutropius here, almost word for word, even in the error of naming two cities, when there were actually three that fell to the rebellious Britons under Boadicea.[7] L.D. Reynolds points to a Northumbrian tradition that, perhaps reflected in Bede, predates the earliest extant manuscripts.[8] It is at the same time the consensus of contemporary historians of Roman history that Nero was indeed no warrior-emperor, lavishing his attentions on, as one might say, other things.[9] It is noteworthy that Bede does not mention Nero's remarkable personal failures, such as matricide and fratricide, the burning of Rome, the martyrdom of Peter and Paul, and the sensational beginning of the persecution of the Christians. The translator of the OE Bede seems to make it worse by virtue of his bald directness: 'Ða feng Neron to rice æfter Claudie þam casere. Se naht ongan on þære cynewisan, ac betwuh oðera unrim æwyrdeleana Romwara rices, þæt he Breotone rice forlet'[10] [Nero succeeded to Claudius. He did no service in the state, but among countless other disasters to the Roman empire, he also lost the dominion of Britain].

There are three *metra* in the *Consolatio* that concern Nero: II.m.6 [= OE *Metre* 9, OE Prose 16], III.m.4 [= OE *Metre* 15, OE prose 28], and IV.m.2 [= OE *Metre* 25, OE Prose 37].[11] The first two poems mention Nero explicitly, while the last, to follow Gerard O'Daly, places the theme of Nero 'in broader ethical context.'[12] Here I will concentrate on II.m.6 and III.m.4, and III.pr.5 [= OE Prose 29], which offers the third direct mention of Nero.

In its seventeen lines the first metre to discuss Nero presents the mainline myth succinctly.[13] While hardly a sonnet, the poem has a kind of tightness and clarity of design one could associate with a Shakespearean 8-4-2 or a Petrarchan 8-6 with an added trailing couplet. Here the structural pattern is 7-8-2: the first section treats Nero's personal failings, the second section his global power, and the two-line conclusion is a moral exclamation that summarizes the moral and ethical situation almost to an aphorism. In the first section the poet recalls Nero's personal crimes as part of a shared tradition, for both poet and audience know: 'Novimus ...' The burning of Rome is the first crime, the killing of senators the second, and these more public instances yield to the familial crimes, namely, the killing of brother and mother. At line 5 the poet gives Nero's appalling reaction to the familial crimes by the description of Nero's gaze on his mother's body. The body is 'gelidum,' but the eye of Nero must be equally cold, for Nero sheds no tears as he evidently runs his eye over his mother's body, described as 'extincti ... decoris.' Incest is implicit in this surface description. The context of the poem shifts with the key word *tamen*, which here signals an entirely new discussion, juxtaposed to the first seven lines. The poet now gives an expansive global view of Nero's power. The personification of the sun through the mention of Phoebus maintains a human or humanizing view over the sweep of Nero's power across the four corners of the earth. The rhetorical question which occupies lines 14–15 invites the negative answer through the particle *num*, a subtlety lost in any translation to English. Insanity (*rabies*) and power (*potestas*) exist together in disjoined moral spheres, rendering power ineffectual as a moral force to control the uncontrollable. The exclamation contemplates the awful situation (*sortem*) when power does join bitter rage. Power, as *iniquus gladius*, embodies a transferred epithet where Nero is *iniquus* in his killing. *Consolatio* II.m.6 offers a chilling portrait of the powerful and uncontrollable tyrant and an aesthetic tour de force in the portrayal of evil.

How does Boethius's Latin brilliance carry over into the OE in its double translation? The general scholarly consensus, as suggested above, holds that Alfred offers a prose translation, which he then fashions into a poetic version based on that prose translation, not directly on the Latin. The OE prose goes forward to an interpretive translation that is neither word-for-word nor sense-for-sense, the dual Alfredian standard cited in the Preface to the *Pastoral Care*.[14] Indeed, the poetic marker *Hwæt* opens the prose translation as if in a double cross-over from the Latin and the poetic OE. *We witon* translates *Novimus*, introducing the facts, which then flow as a listing of five categories of crimes. The third category, *unryhthæmedu*, brings sexual crimes into the open, and the first mention of Nero brings with his name the epithet *unrihtwisa* (*iniquus*). Alfred now injects information not found in the Latin that Nero ordered Rome set afire after the precedent of Troy and that he wanted to see how it burned, how long, and with how much flame. He also amplifies the killing. The *patres*, mother, and brother are cited, but Alfred goes on to say that Nero killed his wife with his own sword and that Nero's reaction was not only remorseless, but he was positively the happier and more joyful. Like the Latin, Alfred employs *þeah* as the signpost to new content, adding a summary prepositional phrase 'betwuh þyllicum unrihtum' as if his audience would have missed the acts of injustice just related. Alfred continues into the description of Nero's global power, giving the four directions of the world to underline its extent. The allusion to Phoebus disappears, as does the extended metaphor associated with his moving across the earth. Presumably the reference to Phoebus would have been one more thing to explain within the text. Alfred now takes the rendition in a totally different direction, away from the abstract discussion of personal probity and power. First, Alfred asks rhetorically whether divine power could not have dispatched Nero's, had it wished. The obvious answer, which comes from the traditional discussion about the problem of evil, is given by 'ic' who says, 'I know that he/it could if he/it wanted.' One may well ask who 'ic' is – certainly not Lady Philosophy, the supposed singer of II.m.6, and not likely the 'OE Boethius figure.' Alfred the prose writer breaks voice and intrudes to bring the translation closer to its moral home. For the exclamation that finishes the Latin poem Alfred offers a reflection on the *geoc* that 'he' – here Nero – laid on his people and how bloody his sword was at the expense of the innocent. These thoughts seem clear enough, but the concluding sentence seems convoluted: 'Hu ne was þær genog sweotol þæt se anweald his agenes ðonces god næs, þa se god næs þe he to com.'[15] Sedgefield offers this translation: 'Is it not now clear enough that his power was not good of itself, since he to whom it was given was no good man.'[16] Essentially, Alfred the prose writer has changed his source into a straightforward meditation on royal power and its dangers for king and subjects alike. The pursuit of power is no true good when it is unbridled.

The special complications of the OE poetic rendition of II.m.6 give evidence of an aesthetic of amplification, as it does in *Metre* 20, for example. That amplification necessarily moves the text into different directions.[17] The demands of metre will necessarily invoke the inventory of poetry, namely formulas, formulaic patterns, alliteration and, if the OE poetry stands out as a second remove from the Latin, only a strong poetic hand could steer away from mere 'drift' in sense and meaning. Seventeen Latin lines become 63 OE lines and a new verbal creation. The first section of the Latin poem has its mirror in the OE poem. While the *gefrignan*-formula could have been a natural opener for Alfred the poet, he retains the prosaic *we witon*. His first noticeable change occurs in the opening presentation of Nero who, we learn, has a kingdom (4) that is 'hehst under heofenum, hryre to monegum' [highest under the heavens, a terror to many]. Nero as global and terrible power is the subject of the second section in both the Latin and OE prose, but it would appear that Alfred the poet has decided to open with at least some of the rhetorical emphasis that one might find in poems of history that rely upon an opening *gefrignan*-formula in similar moves to indicate the importance of the subject. The catalogue of Nero's crimes follows, *morðor* being added and linked by alliteration to *man*. Lines 9–22 amplify the burning of Rome. The significant departure from the prose version (and indeed the Latin) is the amplification of a new theme: Nero's sporting folly. Whereas the Latin merely mentions the fire and the prose gives a relatively factual account, Alfred the poet offers information going to motive – of a sort. Nero ordered the fire 'to gamene' [9: as a sport]. The phrase, used two more times in *Metre* 9 (19 and 46), occurs nowhere else in the *Metres*. The lack of seriousness becomes almost a folly of scientific experiment, which we might call 'comparative urban pyrotechnics.' Nero, for 'unsnyttrum' [11: silliness; stupidity, folly] wanted to 'fandian' if Rome would burn as Troy was reputed to have. Behind the apparent folly, however, is *libido dominandi*; Alfred the poet, observing in understatement that the action was not a 'herlic dæd' [a praiseworthy deed], suggests that Nero sought nothing else except to manifest his power. With these suggestions regarding Nero's state of mind and intentions Alfred the poet moves the level of discussion from Boethius's phrasal allusion to the burning of Rome through an amplification of the action to a psychological analysis of a ruler out of control.

The focus shifts to Nero's murderous crimes. The Senate, personalized in Boethius as *patres* and called the 'wisestan witan' in the OE prose, lose their wisdom in the *Metre*, so to speak, becoming 'ricestan Romana witan' and 'æþelestan eorlgebyrdum.' The killings of mother, brother, and wife receive the same negative-positive formulation: Nero did not sorrow, but rather was the happier. At this point Alfred the poet injects a moralizing reflection, present neither in Boethius nor in the prose version, about how Nero did not worry over whether 'mihtig Drihten' would mete out retribution, but on the contrary he took joy in these crimes. Another negative-positive rhetorical formulation makes the insertion quite emphatic.

Alfred the poet follows the Latin and the OE prose in the use of an equivalent for the axial word *tamen*, here *emne swa þeah*. The global view of his dominion and power, however, acquires new details that more or less humanize the reckless world power. Every warrior had to obey Nero because of need or desire and Nero made miserable, or killed, earthly kings. The humiliation of kings was 'to gamene' [as a sport] for Nero as he rose 'in gylp' [in glory]. The word *gylp* seems to have a negative range only, connected as *idel gylp* to *vana gloria*; BT also give *gloria* and *ostentatio* as equivalents. Significantly, *Orosius* uses the word in a similar geopolitical context: 'Hu Orosius spræc ymb Romana gylp, hu hi manega folc oferwinnan' [How Orosius spoke of the glory of the Romans, how they overcame many peoples]. Alfred the poet follows the prose in the somewhat rhetorical question begun 'Wenst ðu' (48), which asks about God's power to overthrow Nero's cruel reign. The answer is generally as in the prose, that is, 'of course God could,' but the poetry gives a little more scope. Alfred the poet can call Nero *gelpscaðan*, 'boastful foe' according to BT, the only occurrence in the entire corpus; in addition the alliterative need gives the opportunity to use harsh *r*-alliteration to describe God's potential overthrow of Nero: 'rice berædan and bereafian' (50). Alfred the poet, however, moves forward a little more into the problem of evil. Whereas in the prose the answer is straightforward, the poetry offers:

Eala, gif he wolde,   ðæt he wel meahte,
þæt unriht him   eaðe forbiodan. (53–4)

[Oh that He would only,   as He easily might,
All such felony   fain forbid him!][18]

Line 53 is the prose answer, effectively, but the elaboration of line 54 injects an emphasis on injustice. There now comes an unsettling ambiguity in the poetry. In the prose the one who imposes the yoke of oppression seems pretty clearly to be Nero; in the poetry the effective agent and subject of the sentence is *se Hlaford*.[19] Is this lord Nero or God? Sedgefield renders the demonstrative with full force: 'that lord,' making it clear that he sees Nero here. If we take the reference to be to God (i.e., 'the Lord') then it is God who imposes suffering on the thegns and warriors mentioned, not Nero. If this reading can be sustained, then Alfred the poet is alluding to a central moral-theological dilemma: if God is all-powerful (and all-good), then how and why does he allow evil in the world? When in line 60 the reference is to the bloody sword, the 'he' who holds it is surely Nero. This brief passage has its fuzzy possibilities deriving from 'floating subjects and pronouns.' But the final three poetic lines are rather clearer than the prose in its differentiation of power and the good:

> þær wæs swiðe sweotol   þæt we sædon oft,
> þæt se anwald ne deð   awiht godes
> gif ac se wel nele   þe his geweald hafað. (61–3)

> [Thus we see clearly,   as we have oft said,
> That dominion   can do no good
> If he that hath gained it   have no good will.][20]

Nero's power does not make him a good man.

Did Alfred amplify his *Boethius* with the aid of commentaries when he went beyond the 'mere' translation of the Latin? Before answering this question in the general, if partial, affirmative, I must point out that the question is an old one with major positions already staked out. Joseph Wittig, whose excellent study of the Orpheus metre is the ultimate model for those pursuing the question of the commentaries, observes that in the Orpheus metre '[s]hared traditions, coincidence, and a full consideration of context seem to me to account for practically all of the parallels between Alfred and the Latin glosses.'[21] For the Alfredian rendition of the Boethian Odysseus and Circe, Klaus Grinda, carefully weighing and correcting Kurt Otten's work, suggests that Alfred did have a source, described as 'a collection of exegetical notes on Boethius of remarkably high quality ... lost some time after Alfred' – and 'precisely what one would expect from a commentary.'[22] Susan Irvine takes another view of Odysseus-Circe literary relations in her essay, stressing rather Alfred's original response to Boethius.[23] But the matter is actually worse than contending interpretations. Simply put, scholars interpreting the vernacular go too confidently to the commentary tradition for support of one position or another, when, given the state of current knowledge, they ought not to rely comfortably on the Latin scholarship on the commentaries. Jacqueline Beaumont scores major points when she discusses the question of Remigius of Auxerre, whose name is synonymous with the phrase 'Boethian commentary.' Now Remigius died in 908, and according to Pierre Courcelle probably wrote his commentary in 902.[24] Alfred died in 899. More important than vital statistics, however, is Beaumont's overall assessment about the Remigian commentary, only excerpts of which have been published: 'No agreement has been reached as to what represents the work of Remigius.'[25] At least now we have a *Clavis* to the works of Remigius and may begin more focused study, thanks to the work of Colette Jeudy.[26] In this fraught business let me turn to the Anglo-Saxon commentary tradition, which Diane K. Bolton numbers as some fourteen glossed Anglo-Saxon copies of the *Consolatio*.[27] The focus here is Cambridge, University Library (CUL) Kk.3.21, an Abingdon manuscript of ca. 1000, and only for general comparison Paris, Bibliothèque nationale MS lat. 6401A, Christ Church Canterbury, ca. 1000.[28] I would also like to consider Cambridge, Trinity College O.3.7, a St Augustine's Canterbury manuscript of the tenth century. Gibson and Smith describe CUL Kk.3.21 as 'virtually a facsimile of MS. Cambridge Trinity College O.3.7,' but with the authority of Diane Bolton and based on my own selective research I would not be so bold.[29] In broad terms there are two main axes of investigation on a commented page: interlinear glosses that often serve as word or grammatical glosses, but also verge on interpretations; and marginal glosses, often keyed in CUL Kk.3.21 by Latin or Greek letters to points of the text, that often draw out explanations of the text or take the explanations to a new register. The reader learns that Nero killed his teacher Seneca, which does not come forth at this point of the OE [cf. Prose 29]. The particular point of correspondence between this manuscript and Alfred's translation lies in the connection between Alfred's addition of reflections on power and the good. However rough the OE appears to be, it does appear to derive from the gloss to line 14, 'ualuit potestas.' The cue is between *ualuit* and *potestas*, and the gloss is at the top of the page (fol. 30r, line 5). The gloss reads: 'Potestas regni non ualuit mutare ferocitatem animi illius ac per hoc non fuit uera potestas. Ergo non est potestas summum bonum quia non potest facere bonos de malis' [The power to rule cannot change the ferocity of that soul and as a result of this it is not true power. Therefore, power is not the highest good because it cannot effect good things from bad]. The emphasis in *Metre* 9.63 on the will of the one holding power offers secondary proof of a connection with this page of Latin interpretation. For lines 16–17, 'Iniquus / Additur saeuo gladius ueneno ...' the gloss appears in line 3 at the top of fol. 30r and also between the lines as 'Uenenum appellat malam uoluntatem' and 'male uoluntati' over 'ueneno' respectively. The intersection of themes here in the Latin glosses corresponds to the Alfredian themes in the translation, which are not apparent in the original Boethius. The wording, the context, and the placement here seem close enough to argue that Alfred took his translator's cue from a similarly glossed passage. CUL Kk.3.21 is about a century later than Alfred, of course, and cannot be the specific manuscript he saw. BN lat. 6401A, fols. 27v–8r, offers a useful counterpoint to the full CUL manuscript, offering 'Nero lite' so to speak. It has some of the glosses found in CUL, but not all of them, omitting the discussion of power and the highest good, yet retaining the gloss on *iniquus gladius*. At least this system of Latin glosses suggests that there was nothing forced or uniform in the tradition.

Some might prefer to argue that OE Prose 16, which considers the *summum bonum* and power at some length, might naturally lead to the ending of *Metre* 9. To be sure, Prose 16 is an excellent example, as the Nero texts are, of Alfred's obsession with right and just power. Indeed, the whole of Gregory's *Pastoralis*, which concerns *ars artium regimen animarum*, is an exercise in scruples over how to rule. It is even easy to see that Alfred reacts to Nero as a negative self-projection, a reflection of his personal fears about his own *libido dominandi* and how it could go bad. One may observe that Hrothgar's fears for Beowulf in the Heremod 'digression,' which concern the bad use of power, are similarly Alfredian fears, but here these Alfredian fears wear classical dress, not Germanic. But for this interpreter the connection to the commentary tradition represented by CUL Kk.3.21 is close enough in wording and location to suggest that Alfred followed an antecedent commentary when he developed the point. The correspondence between the Alfredian passage and the commentary shows more than shared tradition and shared themes. This view does not require that Alfred follow the commentary in some slavish, point-for-point way, just as the commentaries themselves did not. Rather, as all sides in the issue of Alfred and the commentaries would seem to affirm, Alfred, Boethius, and the commentaries form an intertextual system, and Alfred shows himself to be able to produce his text as an active part of it.

Consolatio III.m.4, the second Nero poem, concerns the relations of power and glory and their display:

Quamuis se Tyrio superbus ostro
   comeret et niueis lapillis,
inuisus tamen omnibus uigebat
   luxuriae Nero saeuientis;
sed quondam dabat improbus uerendis   5
   patribus indecores curules.
Quis illos igitur putet beatos
   quos miseri tribuunt honores?

[Much as he might deck himself proudly in Tyrian purple and snow white pearls, Nero was still hated by everybody, rank in his raging excess. Yet the monster used to confer on revered (5) senators curule offices – but ones that brought no glory. Who, then, would consider those men blessed to whom the wretched grant honours?][30]

As he so often does with themes that link various parts of the *Consolatio* and reflect the argument of the whole, O'Daly suggests that the subtle textures in this short eight-line poem allude to family biography associating Boethius and his sons with power and office in the tyrannical state.[31] The first four lines paint a hollow picture of Nero, who wears deep royal purple and snow-white pearls, which is a visually stunning fashion statement immediately undercut by two lines flatly stating that Nero was hated by all. There is an emphasis on Nero's *luxuria*, crafted in part by the masterful line 4 where the name *Nero* falls between *luxuria* and *saeuientis*.[32] But the moral censure falls not solely on the raging emperor. Nero gave honours to the revered senators who hated him. And, likely without choice, they took those honours. A direct question provides closure to the poem, 'Who, then, would consider those men blessed to whom the wretched grant honours?' Certainly Nero the luxurious, as the exemplar of the tribe of tyrants, is the 'wretched,' but just as wretched must be those who receive the tainted, honours without honour.

Alfred the prose writer takes the Boethian poem, which could be construed as two sentences, one complicated declarative sentence and one moral question, and turns it into three rhetorical questions. The change in structure gives a direct dynamism to the short poem, brushing by the subtle touch of irony in the Latin lines that contrast Nero's imperial finery with the hate directed towards him. Any perceivable Boethian biography disappears for good. The opening concessive clause offers only a generalized picture of good clothes and jewellry. Presumably a literal rendering of the Latin would not have the same resonance with an Anglo-Saxon audience. The equivalent of Latin lines 5–6 is shortened to achieve the OE version of the Boethian question somewhat more abruptly. The next OE question hammers home a similar point about the worthlessness of a tyrant's honour with an Alfredian theme: 'What wise man could say that he were the more worthy for it, though he [Nero] honoured him.' The pronoun chase in these lines regarding its referent(s) does not obscure the change from Latin *beatos* to OE *gesceadwis*, which signals the Alfredian theme of wisdom (or discretion).

Alfred the poet returns the poem to the Latin structure where about the first half of the poem focuses on Nero and the rest more on honours from the tyrant. The prose residue from the composition process remains as in lines 5–6a: '... lað 7 unweorð, / firen[lustes] full ...' but the alliterative resources of the poetry assist line formation when the filler-formula 'on his lifdagum' seeks to build line 5. So too does the filler 'wundorlice' in line 3b, joining the alliterative pair 'wlitegum wædum' in 3a. Line 3, 'golde geglengde 7 gimcynnum' raises the level of composition somewhat with the poetic development of 'gimmum geglengde' found in the prose. The poem, nevertheless, amplifies and extends the theme of wisdom in large measure at the expense of Nero whom the poet cites as 'cyninga dysegast' (11b) and' se dysega' (13a). The emphasis at the end on 'gesceadwis mon,' and even the nearly pedestrian reference to 'wise men' (5b) now function with Nero as the counterpoint. Though Alfred never *shows* why Nero is foolish here – he only *tells* – the audience can perceive some antithetical balancing that gives the poem thematic shape. Three charged words animate Metre 15: *scealc*, *duguðum*, and *feond*. *Scealc* has always had a pejorative connotation, thanks to *The Battle of Maldon*, but there is a positive range, found often in biblical translations where it translates *servus* (cf. BT, BTS, s.v.). If *duguðum* functions as a 'comitatus' word here and *feond* can be rendered as 'devil,' then the 'darlings' are really part of the devil's tribe, which would describe a remarkable metamorphosis, a demonization of the emperor either directly or, from another perspective, by means of a prior Christianizing tendency of the classical record. Except for the unelaborated mention of 'lust' (6b), Nero the luxurious plays a slight role in the OE poem and not much more in the prose version.

In the treatment of the second Nero poem Alfred takes relatively independent control of the text. The commentaries, as represented by Trinity and CUL, do not give him anywhere near the material that the first Nero poem did: eight lines are only eight lines, after all. Still, there are three themes, which these two commentaries share, that reflect on Alfredian composition in this instance. The first is the imperial colour purple. The gloss explains that the purple comes from a certain fish, *sarra*, which is abundant in the Tyre region. As is manifest from the foregoing, Alfred avoids any such particularizing of finery and accordingly needs to explain nothing. Both glosses stress the major theme of worthless honours in an opening marginal comment that summarizes virtually the whole poem. It is, of course, the same thematic line that Alfred takes in his treatment. And here lies the dilemma of textual relations:

except for the matter of the purple the Boethius poem is generally straightforward. Did Alfred have to consult a prose summary to understand what lies on the poetic surface? Ockham's razor suggests that 'no' should be the answer to this rhetorical question. One might speculate that, freed of textual complexity, Alfred was able to shape the text into an embedded discussion of wisdom, quite independently of Boethius or (as far as presently can be determined) the Latin glosses. Alfred does deemphasize the major theme of *luxuria,* which is drawn out in the margins of CUL and Trinity. There the glosses sketch Nero's incest with sister and mother, among other depravities, and both cite Suetonius as the source for their information. Alfred thus perhaps misses his chance to be the first to cite Suetonius in the vernacular anywhere and (perhaps) the first in Anglo-Saxon literature in either of its two linguistic expressions. All of this means to say that there is no solid proof that Alfred worked with commentaries in rendering III.m.4. There are no particular word-for-word correspondences, and there is no pattern here where absence of treatment is meaningful. The themes that are common would easily fall in with Wittig's general characterizations of the Orpheus metre.

Consolatio III.pr.5 extends the themes of III.m.4 to a consideration of the wealth and power that a 'king' might give his courtiers. Philosophy cites two pairs of examples from Roman history, Nero and Seneca, and Antoninus and Paphianus. The point of departure is a description of the psychology of power wherein Philosophy shows how great rulers are poor and impoverished creatures, dependent on servants, and, as we might say, insecure in inverse proportion to their apparent power. Philosophy offers Nero-Seneca as her first example in straightforward prose:

> Nero Senecam familiarem praeceptorem suum ad eligendae mortis coegit arbitrium, Papianum diu inter aulicos potentem militum gladiis Antoninus obiecit. Atqui uterque potentiae suae renuntiare uoluerunt, quorum Seneca opes etiam suas tradere Neroni seque in otium conferre conatus est; sed dum ruituros moles ipsa trahit, neuter quod uoluit effecit. Quae est igitur ista potentia, quam pertimescunt habentes, quam nec cum habere uelis tutus sis si cum deponere cupias uitare non possis?

> [Nero forced his friend and teacher, Seneca, to choose his own manner of execution; Antoninus had Papianus cut down by the swords of the soldiers, even though he had long been a power among the courtiers. Both of

160   Paul E. Szarmach

these unfortunate men wanted to give up their power; indeed, Seneca tried to give his wealth to Nero and retire. But both were destroyed by their very greatness and neither could have what he wanted. What, then, is the value of power which frightens those who have it, endangers those who want it, and irrevocably traps those who have it?][33]

The OE equivalent easily moves off into amplification and elaboration. Thus:

Hwæt, we witon ðæt se unrihtwisa [cyning] Neron wolde hatan his agenne magister 7 his fosterfæder acwellan, þæs nama wæs Seneca; se wæs uþwita. Þa he þa onfunde þæt he dead bion [scolde], þa bead he ealle his æhta [wið his feore; þa nolde se cyning þæs on]fon, ne him his feores geunnan. Þa [he þa] þæt ongeat, þa geceas he (him) þone deað ðæt hine mon oflete blodes on ðæm earme; 7 ða dyde swa mon.

[Do we not know that the wicked king Nero was willing to order his own teacher and foster-father, whose name was Seneca, a philosopher, to be put to death? And when this man found that he must die he offered his possessions for his life. But the king would none of them, nor grant him his life. Perceiving this he chose to die by being let blood in the arm; and so it was done.][34]

Alfred volunteers that Seneca was a philosopher and that he died by his own hand by opening his veins, which additions suggest an incorporated gloss, and, further, in a passage without parallel in the Latin:

Hwæt, ealle men witan þæt se Seneca wæ[s N]erone 7 Papianus þa weorð[est]an 7 þa leofestan 7 [mæstne] anwald hæfdon ge on hiora hirede ge buton, 7 þe abuton ælcre scylde wurdon fordo[ne].

[Now all men know that Seneca was held in most honour and most love by Nero, as was Papianus by Antoninus, and they were most powerful both within the court and without; and yet though void of offence, they were done to death.][35]

Philosophy then concludes most of these themes in III.m.5 with a Stoic message that power begins when an individual first has power over his own thoughts and control over his own vices.

CUL Kk.3.21, fol. 43v and Trinity O.3.7, fol. 21v give similar but not identical glosses on Seneca and Paphianus. Both manuscripts, for example, mention Seneca's opening of his veins, which link them to Alfred, and a poison ring, which Alfred does not mention. CUL goes on to indicate that 'antiqui enim potentes et nobiles' had poison under their rings. These glosses elaborate the manner of Seneca's death, which is not likely to be inferred from Boethius directly, and suggest Alfred's knowledge of a gloss tradition. But clearly Alfred is choosing the details he wants to incorporate, if it is an earlier tradition of CUL that he is following.

In summary, then, the commentary tradition provides a framework of understanding necessary to identify Alfred's translation. 'Word for word' and 'sense for sense' are insufficient mantras for Alfredian composition. When the evidence is clear enough to establish close verbal correspondences in particular locations, places where 'unforced' translations are clear, Alfred's translation can only be what it is: a translation as understood within the tradition and in some sense proceeding from it. When the evidence is not cogent for the use of the commentary tradition in a certain textual location, the commentary tradition nevertheless provides some context and contrast for Alfred's message and method, reflecting as in the prior case his choices. Alfred is not the Lone Translator, 'silent upon a peak in Darien.'

NOTES

I presented earlier versions of this paper at the annual meeting of the Medieval Association of the Pacific, Portland State University, 29 March 2003, and at a symposium sponsored by the Alfredian Boethius Project, Oxford University, 24 July 2003. I am grateful to Joseph Wittig for reading this essay and offering helpful suggestions.

1 The phrase is Gibbon's and the generality is the consensus opinion. See Edward Gibbon, *The History of the Decline and Fall of the Roman Empire*, ed. David Womersley (London: Penguin, 1994), 2:553 (ch. 39).
2 See Stanley B. Greenfield and Daniel G. Calder, *A New Critical History of Old English Literature*, with a Survey of the Anglo-Latin Background by Michael Lapidge (New York: New York University Press, 1986), 46–51, esp. 47. R.D. Fulk and Christopher M. Cain, *A History of Old English Literature*, with a Chapter on Saints' Legends by Rachel S. Anderson (Malden, MA: Blackwell, 2003), 34–9, share a similar but updated point of view.

3 Tacitus, Suetonius, and Dio Cassio are the major figures at the foundation of the portrait of Nero, but there are over a dozen 'major minors' who contribute to the Neronian myth and its perpetuation. The historiography of Nero begins with Tacitus, who in *Annales* 13–14 offers the first extant account. Working from antecedent sources mentioned by name in 13.20 (Pliny the Elder, Cluvius Rufus, and Fabius Rusticus) and succinctly evaluated, Tacitus follows Nero from accession through 66 CE, two years before his death. The wearisome tale of intrigue and betrayal, murder and wantonness, gossip-laced fact and all kinds of sensationalism more than makes up for the incomplete record. There is no evidence for the direct presence of Tacitus in Anglo-Saxon England. R.J. Tarrant discusses Tacitus's *Annales* 11–16 in 'Tacitus,' in *Texts and Transmission: A Survey of the Latin Classics* (Oxford: Clarendon, 1983), 407–9. Tarrant's discussion of the *Annales* concerns mainly the later Middle Ages. Suetonius, who served as a model for Einhard and his *Life of Charlemagne* and whose fingerprint is on Sulpicius Severus's *Life of Martin*, devotes book 6 of his *The Lives of the Caesars* to Nero. S.J. Tibbetts, noting that there are over 200 extant manuscripts of *De vita Caesarum*, cites Paris, Bibliothèque nationale lat. 6115, a Tours manuscript of about 820, as the earliest witness, and Durham, Cathedral Library C.III.18, late eleventh century, as the apparently earliest manuscript with Anglo-Saxon connections. See Tibbets, 'Suetonius,' in *Texts and Transmission*, ed. Reynolds, 399–404. Dio Cassius, a third-century consul, wrote a *History of Rome* in Greek, whose books on Nero survive in Byzantine excerpts. To these three major sources Christoph Schubert adds many contemporary and subsequent sources in his admirable overview, *Studien zum Nerobild in der lateinischen Dichtung der Antike*, Beiträge zur Altertumskunde 116 (Stuttgart: B.G. Teubner, 1998). Anonymous works aside, the list includes Seneca, Persius, Lucan, Petronius, Martial, Juvenal, and, in late antiquity Arator, Ausonius, Dracontius, Ennodius, Prudentius, Sidonius, among others (Boethius included). Waltraud Jacob-Sonnabend, *Untersuchungen zum Nero-Bild der Spätantike*, Altertumswissenschaftliche Texte und Studien 18 (Hildesheim: Olms-Weidmann, 1990), gives further information on later antiquity, which amplifies Schubert's work. Jacob-Sonnabend focuses on various late antique themes, such as Nero the arsonist and Nero the persecutor of Christians, as well as the Nero tradition in works by Sextus Aurelius Victor, Eutropius, Sulpicius Severus, and Orosius. An online search for 'Nero' will yield, in addition to notices of Rex Stout's Nero Wolfe, 'Suetonius: Electronic Texts and Resources,' produced by Stoa and the Perseus Project, at http://www.stoa.org/suetonius. For notices of Nero in OE consult the *DOE Corpus*. Maria Wyke discusses Hollywood, the late Peter

Ustinov, and Nero in 'Make Like Nero! The Appeal of a Cinematic Emperor,' in *Reflections of Nero: Culture, History and Representation*, ed. Jas Elsner and Jamie Masters (Chapel Hill: University of North Carolina Press, 1994), 11–28. See also Jean-Michel Croisille, René Martin, and Yves Perrin, eds, *Neronia V: Néron, Histoire et légende. Actes du Ve Colloque international de la SIEN (Clermont-Ferrand et Saint-Etienne, 2–6 novembre 1994)*, Collection Latomus 247 (Brussels: Latomus, 1999) for a wide-ranging set of articles treating the image of Nero through the present time.

4 The relevant editions and translations are Paulus Orosius, *Historiarum adversus paganos libri VII*, ed. Karl Zangemeister, CSEL 5 (1882; repr. Hildesheim: G. Olms, 1967); *Paulus Orosius: The Seven Books of History against the Pagans*, trans. Roy J. Deferrari, Fathers of the Church 50 (Washington, DC: Catholic University of America Press, 1964); *The Old English Orosius*, ed. Janet M. Bately, EETS s.s. 6 (London: Oxford University Press, 1980); Bede, *HE*, ed. Colgrave and Mynors; *The Old English Version of Bede's Ecclesiastical History of the English People*, ed. and trans. Thomas Miller, EETS o.s. 95, 96, 110, 111 (1890–8; repr. in two vols, Millwood, NY: Kraus Reprints, 1988).

5 For a review of the contents of the Alfredian canon see Janet M. Bately, 'Lexical Evidence for the Authorship of the Prose Psalms in the Paris Psalter,' *ASE* 10 (1982): 69–95, and her 'Old English Prose before and during the Reign of Alfred,' *ASE* 17 (1988): 93–138.

6 Ed. Zangemeister, 452; trans. Deferrari, 297.

7 Eutropius, *Breviarium ab Urbe Condita* 7.14, ed. H. Droysen, MGH, AA 2 (1879; repr. Munich: MGH, 1978), 124, writing a scathing assessment of Nero, observes: '[Nero] bonis omnibus hostis fuit. In re militari nihil omnino ausus Brittaniam paene amisit. Nam duo sub eo nobilissima oppida capta illic atque euersa sunt' [Nero was an enemy to all good things. In the military sphere he, having dared nothing, almost utterly lost Britain. For under him two most noble cities were captured there and destroyed]. The three cities were Camoludunum (Colchester), Verulamium (St Albans), and London. Orosius also mentions only two cities unnamed, ed. Zangemeister, 455.

8 L.D. Reynolds, 'Eutropius,' in *Texts and Transmission*, ed. Reynolds, 159–62 at 161–2.

9 David Shotter, *Nero* (London: Routledge, 1997), 25: 'Nero is (and was) regarded as one of the most unmilitary of emperors.' Shotter develops 'Nero's peace' in his chapter 'Empire and Provinces,' 25–39.

10 *The Old English Version*, ed. and trans. Miller, 30–1.

11 The Latin text of the *Consolatio* here followed is *Anicii Manlii Severini Boethii*

164   Paul E. Szarmach

Philosophiae Consolatio, ed. Ludwig Bieler, CCSL 94 (Turnhout: Brepols, 1957). The OE text here followed is *King Alfred's Version of Boethius De Consolatione Philosophiae*, ed. Walter Sedgefield (1899; repr. Darmstadt: Wissenschaftliche Buchgesellschaft, 1968); Sedgefield offers a translation in *King Alfred's Version of the 'Consolations' of Boethius Done into Modern English, with an Introduction* (Oxford: Clarendon, 1900). See Malcolm Godden, 'Editing Old English and the Problem of Alfred's *Boethius*,' in *The Editing of Old English: Papers from the 1990 Manchester Conference*, ed. D.G. Scragg and Paul E. Szarmach with the assistance of Helene Scheck and Holly Holbrook (Cambridge: D.S. Brewer, 1994), 163–76. The Alfred Boethius Project, directed by Godden and funded by the Arts and Humanities Research Board (UK), has begun a welcome new edition of this work. See now Godden, 'The Alfredian Boethius Project,' *OEN* 37.1 (fall 2003): 26–34. Its first publication is Rohini Jayatilaka, 'A Select Bibliography,' *The Alfredian Boethius Project*, http://www.english.ox.ac.uk/boethius/BoethiusBibliography.html. This Project works in concert with Kevin Kiernan, who is digitizing the badly burned London, BL Cotton Otho A.vi. under a three-year grant from the National Endowment for the Humanities ('Electronic Boethius: Alfred the Great's Old English Translation of Boethius's Consolation of Philosophy,' http://www.rch.uky.edu). See also *Alfred's Metres of Boethius*, ed. Bill Griffiths (Pinner, Middlesex: Anglo-Saxon Books, 1991), with helpful notes and applied bibliography. For a more general bibliography on Alfred see Nicole Guenther Discenza, 'Alfred the Great: A Bibliography with Special Reference to Literature,' in *Old English Prose: Basic Readings*, ed. Paul E. Szarmach with the assistance of Deborah Oosterhouse (New York: Garland, 2000), 463–502.

12 Gerard O'Daly, *The Poetry of Boethius* (Chapel Hill: University of North Carolina Press, 1991), 95. Because Nero is not named, I have excluded the third poem from discussion here. It should be manifest that O'Daly's work has been a major source for my discussion of the content of these poems.

13 *Consolatio* II.m.6, ed. Bieler, 31–2, presented here for convenience:

> Nouimus quantas dederit ruinas
> urbe flammata patribus caesis
> fratre qui quondam ferus interempto
> matris effusio maduit cruore
> corpus et uisu gelidum pererrans   5
> ora non tinxit lacrimis, sed esse
> censor exstincti potuit decoris.
> Hic tamen sceptro populos regebat

> quos uidet condens radios sub undas
> Phoebus, extremo ueniens ab ortu,   10
> quos premunt septem gelidi triones,
> quos Notus sicco uiolentus aestu
> torret ardentes recoquens harenas.
> Celsa num tandem ualuit potestas
> uertere praui rabiem Neronis?   15
> Heu grauem sortem, quotiens iniquus
> additur saeuo gladius ueneno!

O'Daly, *The Poetry of Boethius*, 82–3, translates: 'We know how much destruction he once caused, with the city ablaze and its senators slaughtered, that savage man who murdered his brother and was drenched with his mother's gushing blood, who ran his eye over the cold body (5), and did not wet his face with tears, but could evaluate her destroyed beauty. Yet this man ruled with kingly sceptre the people that Phoebus sees as he hides his rays under the waves, or comes from the farthest east (10), those overpowered by the icy grip of the north, and those burnt by the dry heat of the fierce sirocco as it scorches the hot sands once again. Was lofty power ineffectual to alter evil Nero's madness? (15) O harsh destiny, when the sword of injustice is joined to the poison of rage!'

14 The Preface to the *Pastoral Care* is oft-anthologized, as in Bruce Mitchell and Fred C. Robinson, *A Guide to Old English*, 6th ed. (Oxford: Blackwell, 2001), 207 (line 69).
15 *King Alfred's Version*, ed. Sedgefield, 40.
16 *King Alfred's Version*, 40. Sedgefield duly flags this sentence as an Alfredian addition with his standard practice of italicizing passages not near the Boethian text. This sentence seems to mean in sum that Nero did not see clearly that the good he may have seen in his own power was not good when he came to attain that power.
17 See my study, 'The *Timaeus* in Old English,' in *Lexis and Texts in Early English: Studies Presented to Jane Roberts*, ed. Christian J. Kay and Louise M. Sylvester, Costerus n.s. 133 (Amsterdam: Rodopi, 2001), 255–67.
18 *King Alfred's Version of the 'Consolations,'* trans. Sedgefield, 192.
19 I am, of course, aware that my capitalization is loaded with meaning and interpretation.
20 *King Alfred's Version of the 'Consolations,'* trans. Sedgefield, 192.
21 Wittig, 'King Alfred's *Boethius* and Its Latin Sources: A Reconsideration,' *ASE* 11 (1983): 157–98 at 183.
22 Glaus Grinda, 'The Myth of Circe in King Alfred's *Boethius*,' trans. Paul Bat-

tles, in *Old English Prose: Basic Readings*, ed. Szarmach, 237–65 at 252 and 253; originally published in *Motive und Themen in englischsprachiger Literatur als Indikatoren literaturgeschichtlicher Prozesse: Festschrift zum 65. Geburtstag von Theodor Wolpers*, ed. Heinz-Joachim Müllenbrock and Alfons Klein (Tubingen: Max Niemeyer, 1990), 1–23. See also *König Alfreds Boethius*, ed. Kurt Otten, Studien zur englischen Philologie N.F. 3 (Tubingen: Max Niemeyer, 1964).

23 Susan Irvine, 'Ulysses and Circe in King Alfred's *Boethius*: A Classical Myth Transformed,' in *Studies in English Language and Literature: Doubt Wisely; Papers in Honour of E.G. Stanley*, ed. M.J. Toswell and E.M. Tyler (London: Routledge, 1996), 387–401.

24 For issues of dating see Wittig, 'King Alfred's *Boethius*,' 159, and especially Pierre Courcelle, *La Consolation de Philosophie dans la tradition littéraire: Antécédents et postérité de Boèce* (Paris: Études Augustiniennes, 1967), 241–96.

25 Jacqueline Beaumont, 'The Latin Tradition of the *De Consolatione Philosophiae*,' in *Boethius: His Life, Thought, and Influence*, ed. Margaret Gibson (Oxford: Blackwell, 1981), 278–305 at 285.

26 Colette Jeudy, 'Remigii autissiodorensis opera (*Clavis*),' in *L'École carolingienne d'Auxerre de Murethach à Remi 830–908: Entretiens d'Auxerre 1989*, ed. Dominique Iogna-Prat, Colette Jeudy, and Guy Lobrichon (Paris: Beauchesne, 1991), 457–500. Central now to the study of the commentary background is Joseph Wittig's essay in the present volume (below, pp. 168–200).

27 Diane K. Bolton, 'The Study of the *Consolation of Philosophy* in Anglo-Saxon England,' *Archives d'histoire doctrinale et littéraire du Moyen Age* 44 (1977): 33–78.

28 For CUL Kk.3.21, see N.R. Ker, *Catalogue of Manuscripts Containing Anglo-Saxon* (1957; repr. with a Supplement, Oxford: Oxford University Press, 1990), no. 24, and Helmut Gneuss, *Handlist of Anglo-Saxon Manuscripts: A List of Manuscripts and Manuscript Fragments Written or Owned in England up to 1100*, MRTS 241 (Tempe: Arizona Center for Medieval and Renaissance Studies, 2001), no. 23; for Paris lat. 6401A, see *Codices Boethiani: A Conspectus of Manuscripts of the Works of Boethius*, vol. 1, *Great Britain and the Republic of Ireland*, ed. M.T. Gibson and Lesley Smith with the assistance of Joseph Ziegler, Warburg Institute Surveys and Texts 25 (London: Warburg Institute, 1995), 81–2.

29 *Codices Boethiani*, ed. Gibson and Smith, 44. Bolton identifies the content of the respective commentaries as from two different traditions, 40–1. In the matter of layout and design CUL Kk.3.21 can hardly be a facsimile.

30 Ed. Bieler, 44; trans. O'Daly, *The Poetry of Boethius*, 91.
31 O'Daly, *The Poetry of Boethius*, 91–4.
32 O'Daly, *The Poetry of Boethius*, 93, points out this placement.
33 *Consolatio*, ed. Bieler, 45; trans. Richard Green, *Boethius: The Consolation of Philosophy* (Indianapolis: Bobbs-Merrill, 1962), 51–2.
34 *King Alfred's Version*, ed. Sedgefield, 66; *King Alfred's Version of the 'Consolations,'* trans. Sedgefield, 71–2.
35 *King Alfred's Version*, ed. Sedgefield, 67; *King Alfred's Version of the 'Consolations,'* trans. Sedgefield, 72.

The 'Remigian' Glosses on Boethius's *Consolatio Philosophiae* in Context

JOSEPH WITTIG

My topic for this essay arises from Malcolm Godden's invitation to participate in the Annual Symposiums for the Alfredian Boethius Project (Oxford, July 2003, 2004, and August 2006) and so to reprise a project begun long ago and set aside. In 1973 my colleague Petrus Tax was working on his edition of *Notker der Deutsche: Boethius, 'De consolatione Philosophiae'* and hence interested in the Latin 'St Gall' commentary on the *Consolatio*. He pointed out to me that only limited selections of the nearly contemporary commentary ascribed to Remigius of Auxerre had been edited and he suggested that I undertake a full edition. Pierre Courcelle's magisterial *La Consolation de Philosophie dans la tradition littéraire*, which discussed the commentary and conveniently listed the manuscripts containing it, had appeared in 1967[1] and would presumably make the project straightforward. Anyone experienced in this sort of enterprise will wonder at the naivety that led me to take it on. After some dozen years of concentrated work on the project, entangled in detail, no end in sight, and with eyes bleared from reading microfilm, I put the project aside. The invitation to address the subject for the Boethius Symposium gave me a chance to return to it with fresh perspective, and I offer here an overview of what I will call, for reasons to emerge, 'Remigian glosses' on Boethius's *Consolatio*.[2]

As I began to use Courcelle's list of manuscripts in earnest, problems and inconsistencies appeared, and Diane Bolton's 1977 article confirmed that Courcelle had overlooked manuscripts. It therefore became necessary not only to examine those Courcelle (and subsequently Bolton) had identified, but also to search more thoroughly for manuscripts of the *Consolatio* and commentaries on it in such sources as the lists provided by editions of Boethius, descriptions of libraries, and manuscript catalogues. (Bolton had looked only for Anglo-Saxon copies; so far as I am aware, no complete list of *Consolatio* manuscripts has yet been published.) This search included two extended trips to manuscript collections.[3]

Since this volume focuses on the Anglo-Saxon period, and since the commentaries' possible influence on the Alfredian translation of Boethius constitutes a major reason for Anglo-Saxonists' interest in them, I begin with an overview of the early manuscript tradition of the *Consolatio*. Boethius's text appears to have resurfaced at the beginning of the ninth century.[4] From that time until the early eleventh century it survives, in whole or in part, in some forty-seven manuscripts. Six of these contain only selected metres.[5] Forty-one contain the entire text.[6] Of these forty-one, the overwhelming majority, thirty-seven, contain interlinear and at least some marginal glosses: six of the St Gall type, twenty of the Remigian type, and eleven with glosses not clearly identifiable as either.[7] There survive from this period, in addition to glossed copies of the text, 'glossa continua' (glosses accompanied by only lemmata from the text): three of the St Gall and one of the Remigian. In addition, glosses on *Consolatio* III.m.9 circulated separately: three copies of the 'Remigian' glosses on this metre, two copies of a commentary ascribed to Bovo of Corvey, and two of glosses ascribed to an 'anonymous of Einsiedeln.'[8] One can generalize that 'Remigian' glosses predominate: of the manuscripts with glosses of some kind, twenty-four have the Remigian type (including the continua),[9] and nine the St Gall (including the continua), as compared to eleven texts with glosses of other origin.[10] These 'other' glosses are typically much less full, with more interlinear than marginal comments, and they predominate up to about 900 (five out of eight glossed manuscripts).[11] The Remigian glosses do not circulate until the tenth century, and what seems to be the earliest manuscript with clearly 'Remigian' glosses, B (text s. ix/x), has very few of them. If King Alfred's manuscript(s) of the *Consolatio* had glosses, it seems very likely that they were of this 'other' type; one further suspects that the early manuscripts that Courcelle characterized as mixed Remigius-St Gall actually contained early comments which were subsequently incorporated into the St Gall or Remigian sets of glosses (e.g., B M2 M3 On V1, and the lost Bonn 175).

In order to understand the development of these glosses, it is instructive to consider for a moment what Courcelle characterized as 'the St Gall commentary.'[12] He posited one commentary, composed in the late ninth century, at St Gall. I have not collated these manuscripts as extensively as I have those containing the Remigian glosses, but there are clearly at least two versions of them, one 'shorter' (generally containing fewer glosses), one 'longer' (generally containing more). Two early manuscripts (N and G) have the shorter version: the text of the *Consolatio* in these manuscripts was apparently written in France, possibly in the Loire region, in the second half of the ninth century; the glosses, interlinear and marginal, are thought to have been written at St Gall, probably in the tenth century. Another tenth-century manuscript of unknown provenance (P14) contains a continuous copy of many glosses of this version. The longer version is preserved in four manuscripts: two are continuous commentaries without text (E1 G1) and contain also a copy of a Remigian continua on III.m.9. They are dated to the tenth century and are supposed to have been written at St Gall; G1 is a direct copy of E1. The other two manuscripts are also closely related. L4, whose text is early tenth century, was written in the vicinity of Cologne.[13] It contains interlinear and marginal glosses that generally correspond to those in the two continuous copies of St Gall, but in this manuscript the 'longer' version of St Gall has been written by two different hands – or at least in two different passes, one clearly after the other – and Remigian glosses have also been added. Another manuscript, Ma, copied by Fromund of Tegernsee at Cologne ca. 1000, is closely related to L4, though not, I think, a direct copy of it; it contains the same longer version of St Gall, interlinear and marginal.[14] Thus one finds 'St Gall' in at least two forms. But other early manuscripts share some of these glosses. One is mid-ninth century, from Western Germany (M2); Courcelle classified it as a 'fragment' of Remigius plus St Gall. I would classify it as 'other' and think it has some glosses that were later incorporated into 'St Gall.'[15] A number of tenth-century manuscripts have many of the same glosses (E E2); and another late-tenth-century manuscript shares some of them (W1). These manuscripts seem inevitably to raise the question of whether one is dealing with 'creation' or 'branching evolution' and how one answers is significant. Creation implies one active scholar or centre producing a commentary that could then be copied, perhaps rather passively, or incompletely, or incompetently, perhaps even for addition to a 'collection' of texts rather than for active use. It implies that the longer version is the original (as Courcelle thought), and that the shorter is simply pruned from it. It implies further that those manuscripts that share a few of its glosses simply borrowed selectively from the original stock. Evolution, on the contrary, implies a more active encounter with the text, by numerous readers, in numerous places. I think the manuscript evidence, in the case of St Gall, strongly suggests the latter kind of evolution.[16]

As for the Remigian glosses, as one discovers and studies them one must both qualify Courcelle's characterization and correct his list of the manuscripts in which they can be found.[17] Given the scope of his book, one must first admire how much Courcelle seems to have got right. But as he himself states, he knew 'Remigius' from extracts published by Schepss, Naumann, and Stewart, and directly from a single actual manuscript copy: Paris, BN lat. 15090 (my P7).[18] Courcelle argued that we indeed had the work of Remigius of Auxerre, teaching in Paris, at St Germain-des-Prés, in the first years of the tenth century. Courcelle identified thirty-three manuscripts that preserved all or part of the commentary (that number includes copies written through the fourteenth century); he allowed that there was one active reviser of it, whose work affected chiefly the commentary on III.m.9. The situation with 'Remigius' is much more complex than that of St Gall, but Courcelle's picture is fundamentally misleading; his list of manuscripts containing the 'Remigian' glosses must be corrected and expanded and his ideas about this 'commentary' reexamined.

As for the manuscript witnesses, a corrected list of those containing all or some 'Remigian' glosses is given in Appendix I. This list is presented as a revision of Courcelle's, giving his general characterization of the manuscripts with comments, corrections, and deletions indicated. Manuscripts added (either by Diane Bolton or by me) appear in bold. A summary of these corrections and additions appears at the end of the list. In short, whereas Courcelle actually listed twenty-eight extant manuscripts of these glosses, there are at least fifty (from the beginning through the fourteenth century).

Turning to the question of authorship and origin, we must ask how secure is their ascription to Remigius of Auxerre? In 1906, E.K. Rand pointed out that in one copy of these glosses, Trier, Stadtbibliothek 1093 (T), there was an attribution at the beginning of the *Consolatio* that says: 'Incipit Expositio in Libro Boetii De Consolatione Philosophiae Remigii Autissiodorensis Magistri.'[19] A few years later Hans Naumann noted that a gloss on the Greek verse at III.p.12, line 91 reads: 'secundum commentum Remigii explanatio greci versus deest quia penitus corruptus est.'[20] But there are problems with these attributions. Neither the one at the beginning of the *Consolatio* nor the one at III.p.12 is found in any other manuscript. The Trier manuscript itself dates from the later tenth century[21] and was apparently written at Echternach. The first attribution prefaces not the commentary itself but accessus material: several lives of Boethius and Lupus of Ferrières' tract on the metres, which have never been thought part of the 'Remigian' commentary.[22] The Trier gloss on the Greek near the end of III.p.12 simply adds the 'secundum commentum Remigii' to a gloss already in circulation.[23] Since collation of Trier shows that this manuscript adds numerous glosses to what is apparently an earlier 'Remigian' collection, one has reason to be sceptical of these attributions; and given the plausibility that the scribe writing the glosses on III.p.12 was acting under the inducement of the opening attribution when he prefixed 'secundum commentum Remigii' to the gloss on the Greek, the attribution at the beginning of the *Consolatio* in T remains the sole independent one and its reliability totally uncertain.

Courcelle certainly found it questionable and therefore attempted to support it with arguments based on the contents of the 'Remigian' glosses: their content, he argued, resembled the information found in other commentaries attributed to Remigius.[24] But his argument from similar content is problematical: Courcelle offers only eight instances; even some of these eight propose extremely loose 'parallels'; and none of them shows more than similar information in two different glosses. As a demonstration of authorship they seem very inadequate. In the cases both of the Trier scribe and of modern scholars one senses an understandable desire to associate an imposing body of information with the name of a famous teacher. Possibly the scribe of Trier did not himself invent the attribution; possibly he saw it in a manuscript now lost to us or heard it as academic gossip. It is possible that Remigius, who taught at the famous school of Auxerre and who was remembered in later years as a famous teacher, might legitimately have had his name associated with some glosses, and that the scribe who wrote the *accessus* material in the Trier manuscript generalized such an association into a more sweeping claim. But Trier's attribution is, I think, too oddly placed and too solitary to carry very much weight.

One turns next to ponder the difference between creation and branching evolution. When I was working in the Bodleian in 1975, Richard Hunt asked if I did not find editing such glosses the equivalent of trying to capture the penumbral glow around a star. He could not have put it better. As soon as one begins to transcribe and collate them one discovers the difference between a 'commentary' and glosses. The continuous commentary by Bovo of Corvey on III.m.9 is indeed a commentary: a coherent and unified exposition, marked by a distinctive point of view and a distinctive style. If the word 'commentary' implies such a coherent and unified explanation of a text, it is a bad one to use for the St Gall or the Remigian glosses, for these are simply discrete notes, in workaday Latin. They remain such, even when written as a continuous gloss. And the evidence of the manuscripts leads one to doubt that they are even a single set of glosses by a single author. Sometimes many manuscripts will repeat a long paragraph verbatim, with only minor variants; obviously someone, somewhere, drafted that paragraph and it was widely copied. Sometimes a group of manuscripts will have alternative paragraphs, or several alternatives, for a single long gloss. Manuscripts sometimes present the same information in marginal and interlinear glosses. Even short glosses – words, phrases, clauses – will sometimes recur with great consistency; at other times similar information will be recast in half a dozen different forms, and occasionally there will be a bewildering variety of them.

As these facts gradually became apparent, it seemed that before one could 'edit' rationally it was necessary to discover the relationship between manuscripts and versions and that the only way to manage this would be to transcribe and collate completely several sections of the glosses, on the analogy of core samples. Two of the sections I chose were III.p.9, line 86 through m.9 and III.p.12, line 59 through III.m.12. (There are reasons for not choosing the glosses at the beginning of the text: first folios are often rubbed and stained to the point of illegibility, glossing projects often begin enthusiastically and fall off early, and *accessus* material of various kinds accumulates there and complicates analysis.)

The manuscripts preserving Remigian glosses present an overwhelming variety of evidence by which one might seek to group them: presence or absence of glosses, shared variants, arrangement and sequence of the glosses, even the signs used to key marginal glosses to Boethius's text. On the basis of fifty-six shared longer glosses (ranging from a sentence to a paragraph), those I have collated for III.m.9 sort themselves into four large groups. I will give some specific examples illustrating these but begin with an overview. I designate these groups by the metasigles **W, X, Y,** and **Z**. The order implies working hypotheses about the general direction of development. (Appendix III gives a summary list of manuscript groups by metasigle and of manuscripts by date and origin.)

W comprises L4b E1 T Ma P9 V5 V4 M An M1 L P4 V7. At its core is a stable group of tenth-century copies: L4b E1 T Ma P9 V5 M An. One of the earliest manuscripts, B, has one of these glosses and shorter versions of three others, a piece of evidence supporting the conclusion that these glosses accumulated over time rather than issuing at once from an individual author.

Z comprises a set of Anglo-Saxon manuscripts of the later tenth and eleventh centuries: C2 O Es P9 (hand b) P V3 A C4 Ge P6.[25] Shared variants subdivide this group into **z1** (C2 O Es) and **z2** (P9b P V3 A C4 Ge P6); **z2** has half a dozen glosses found in no other manuscripts.

Shared glosses and variants in seven other manuscripts suggest two other much less stable groups. **X** comprises V2 P7 P10 L1,[26] **Y** the three closely related manuscripts P8 P5 P1. **X** shares with **W** thirteen glosses not found in **Z**; **Y** has one of these. **Y** shares eleven glosses with **Z** which are not found in **W**; one or two **X** manuscripts share seven of these. Without wishing to imply a simple stemma, I suggest that **X** is a set of glosses that developed from **W** with no influence on **Z**, while **Y** seems intermediate between **W** and **Z** with occasional agreements with **X**. A number of other manuscripts are 'outliers' which do not, on the evidence of these longer glosses, fit clearly into any of the groups.[27]

Seven of the 'core' **W** glosses occur widely across **XYZ** manuscripts. Part of one **W** gloss is found in the early manuscript B. L4 (dated s. x¹), An E1 V5 T (all s. x), and Ma (ca. 1000 and closely related to L4) are early and continental (France, Rhineland [Cologne?], St Gall, Echternach, Tegernsee). One of the earliest Anglo-Saxon manuscripts, P9, has the **W** glosses as its first layer. Influenced by these considerations more than by the homeland of Remigius, I hypothesize that **W** was early and the direction of the shared glosses is reflected by the alphabetical order of the metasigles.

One cannot assume that what holds for glosses on one section of the text must be true for all. The notoriously difficult subject matter of III.m.9 generated an exceptional amount of glossing. Nevertheless the patterns that arise here match those thus far found in the glosses of III.m.12.

Let us come, finally, to some actual glosses. In doing so, one should recall Richard Hunt's phrase 'penumbral glow.' The glosses on III.m.9 often offer alternative ideas for interpretation, and their character is exploratory and additive, frequently rearranging or restating very similar material. In fact, 'editing' them at all, with base text and variants, sometimes amounts to creating a Platonic entity ('the text' of 'the gloss'). Consider one set of examples. III.m.9, lines 13–14 say: 'Tu triplicis mediam naturae cuncta moventem / conectens animam ...' [You bind the middle soul of threefold nature (that is) moving all things ...]. In context (especially to readers not intimately familiar with the *Timaeus*, which Boethius is tightly compressing in these verses), what (or whose) soul might *anima* refer to, what might be its threefold nature, and how is it *media*? In the glosses presented below, the sigles of manuscripts containing the gloss follow each gloss in parentheses; *par[tim]* means that those following manuscripts have only part of the gloss, as detailed in the variants. Curly brackets enclose notes on position, order, and the like. In the variants '~' means the following MSS invert word order, '//' that the gloss in the following manuscripts stop at this point.

The glosses in the early manuscript On show two lines of thought: this soul is the sun, or the human soul; if the sun, its triple nature can be suggested (key words emphasized here):

A[28] quod nec in celo nec in terra semper sit *sol.* vel *anima* hominis (On)

B connectens animam. id est *solem* qui cuncta fovet suo calore ac splendore qui per consona membra currit id est lunae et stellarum (On)

Both these ideas appear in short St Gall glosses, and the human soul appears as *media*; for example:

C *solis* qui lucet, fovet, incendit, vel caeli, terrae marisque (N E1 *par* L4)
    L4: qui lucet, nutrit, incidit {inl at TRIPLICIS; **marisque**: et maris E1[1], ac maris E1[2].
    {L4: inl erased on [MED]IAM NAT. C. M[OVENTEM], legible over [M]OVENTEM and line end: ...res condu- i. solis quia lucet, fovet, incendit.}

D medium dicit quia similitudinem ac *anima* traxit quae in corde, quid medium est, maxime iugit (L4)

A longer gloss in St Gall manuscripts combines and elaborates both lines of thought:

E :-mediam animam dicit solem qui inter caelum et terram videtur

176 Joseph Wittig

> spatium trahere, quod totum corpus unum esse asserunt, i. caelum et terram mareque, in modum ovi. quod tribus consistit partibus. extremum pro caelo, quod inferius est pro aqua, quod infimum pro terra accipiunt. unde vocabulum trahit. quod anima sit media quia philosophi affirmant quod anima cor maxime complectat, quod per medietatem corporis infixum esse liquet, et illo quoque cogitationes inhaerent. non minus vero sol pro anima accipitur quia medietatem videtur possidere (L4 P14² Ma1 E1)
>> *qui*: quia P14. *corpus unum*: ~ P14. *esse asserunt*: ~ Ma, asserit E1. *caelum ... mareque*: celum terram mare P14. *ovi: ad.* figurari Ma, dicunt figurari E1. *tribus*: in tribus E1. *extremum*: extremam P14 Ma, extrema E1², externa E1¹. *quod inferius est*: *om* est Ma, inferior E1. *quod infimum*: infima E1. *vero*: *om* P14. *accipiunt*: accipitur Ma, *om* E1. *unde*: inde P14. *quod anima ... cor*: quod anima sit anima quod anima cor*us* [sic] P14. *complectat*: circumplectat P14, complectetur Ma E1. *illo*: illi P14, ipsi quoque E1. *vero: om* P14 Ma. *videtur possidere*: ~ P14.

And new ways of understanding a triple nature for the human soul emerge:

> **F** AUGustinus in vii° libro de civitate dei. Varro tres affirmat esse gradus animae in omni natura sub caelo. unum quod omnes partes corporis transit quae vivunt et non habet sensum sed tantum valitudinem ad vivendum. hanc vim in nostro corpore permanere dicit, in ossa, ungues, capillos sicut et arbores sine sensu crescunt et modo quodam suo vivunt. secundum gradum animae in quo sensus est hanc vim pervenire in oculos, nares, aures, os, tactum. tertium gradum esse animae summum quod vocatur animus, in quo intellegentia praeminet. hoc praeter hominem omnes carere mortales. hanc partem animae mundi dicit deum. Sed haec opinatio tantum philosophorum non veritas (N)
>> {N: keyed to line 13. The attribution 'AUG ... dei' and the comment 'Sed haec ... veritas' appear by position to have been added after the gloss was written, but by the glossing hand. See Augustine, *De ciuitate Dei* 2.23, ed. B. Dombart and A. Kalb, 2 vols., CCSL 47–48 [Turnhout: Brepols, 1955].}

> **G** maxima mundi anima quae omnem mundum movet triplicis naturae est, i. *rationabilis, concupiscibilis, irascibilis*. hinc virgilius: principio caelum ac terras. hinc alio in loco: his equidem signis atque sideribus. et psalmista: qui dat aescam omni carni (E1)

{E1[1] from 'solis qui lucet ... et maris.' E1[2] from 'mediam animam dicit solem ... videtur possidere.'}

These few selections cannot adequately illustrate how the glosses present both briefer and more elaborate expositions, and repeat ideas, often both marginally and interlinearly; but they illustrate how ideas emerged and became elaborated; and they seem to have provided bases which Remigian glosses further developed.

The Remigian manuscripts by and large contain the same repetitions and combinations of interlinear and marginal comments as do the St Gall,[29] and presenting only a few longer glosses out of this context runs the risk of obscuring that fact. But space permits just three illustrations on 'mediam animam triplicis naturae.' The first represents the **W** group and what I take to be its underlying complexity. The second illustrates the same for the **X Y Z** groups. First I give the glosses, then an analysis of them.[30] The third contains parts of both. Each should really be regarded as a gloss set, a selection of originally separate comments gathered into a longer construct.

H 1 media dicitur anima non quod a meditullio corporis, i. ab umbilico, sit porrecta sed quia in corde sedes illius proprie est ubi est pontificium vitae. **2** aut certe media dicitur quod sit anima rationabilis media inter animam pecudum et spiritum angelorum. omnis autem spiritus aut carne tegitur et cum carne moritur, aut carne quidem tegitur sed cum carne non moritur, aut nec carne tegitur nec moritur. anima pecudum carne tegitur et cum carne moritur, anima hominis carne quidem tegitur sed cum carne non moritur, spiritus angelorum nec carne tegitur nec moritur. **3** prudentioribus autem videtur hoc loco potius animam rationabilem debere intellegi quae magnam concordiam habet cum mundo, unde et homo graece microcosmos dicitur, i. minor mundus. sicut enim mundus quattuor elementis et quattuor temporibus constat ita et homo quattuor humoribus et quattuor temporibus. videamus ergo mundi et hominis concordiam. quattuor sunt elementa, aer ignis aqua terra. **4** aer calidus et humidus est, ver calidum et humidum similiter, et humidus sanguis qui est in puero aeque calidus et humidus, pueritia calida et humida. **5** ignis calidus est et siccus, aestas calida et sicca, colera rubea quae abundat in adolescente calida et sicca, adolescentia etiam calida et sicca. **6** terra frigida et sicca, autumnus frigidus et siccus, melancolia i. colera nigra quae est in iuvenibus frigida et sicca, iuventus frigida et sicca. **7** aqua frigida et humida est, hiems frigida et humida, flegma quae abundat in senibus frigida et humida, senectus frigida et humida. **8** iste ergo minor mundus habet animam triplicis naturae, est enim irascibilis concupiscibilis rationabilis. irascibilis ut vitiis irascatur et corporis voluptatibus, concupiscibilis est ut deum diligat et virtutes appetat, rationabilis est ut inter creatorem et creaturam, inter bonum et malum discernere possit. **9** quae tria si rationabiliter fuerint custodita coniungunt creaturam creatori. si vero fuerint permutata mentem debilem reddunt. **10** si illa pars fuerit corrupta quae irascibilis dicitur fit homo tristis, rancidus, felle amaritudinis plenus. **11** si autem illa pars vitiata fuerit quae concupiscibilis dicitur fit homo ebriosus, libidinosus et voluptatum servus. **12** si vero illa pars animae corrumpatur quae vocatur rationabilis fit homo superbus, hereticus, omnibus subiectus vitiis (Ma T L4b V5 Ab E1 M P3 P4 V7 B1 *par* B P9 V6 V2)

{P9 writes 1–4 in one block, 5–6 in another, where 6 diverges and P9 gloss ends: see variants at 6 'terra frigida.' V6 has 1–2, to 'tegitur nec moritur,' in one block and adds 8 to end ('iste' ff.) after the gloss 'quidem philosophorum.' V2 has 1–2, to ' tegitur nec moritur,' plus 8 to end ('iste' ff.). B has 1–2 to 'tegitur nec moritur.'}

1 *ad.* corporis B1. *in ... proprie est*: sedes illius in corde est proprie B1. **2** *autem*: namque T L4b E1 V6. *tegitur*: 3 dots P9. *aut carne tegitur ... aut carne quidem tegitur*: aut cum carne tegitur quidem B. *aut carne quidem ...*: {V6 rephrases rest of 2} ut anima pecudum aut carne tegitur et non cum carne moritur ut hominis anima aut nec carne tegitur nec moritur ut spiritus angelicus V6. *aut nec*: aut non B1. *aut nec ... cum carne moritur*: *om* P3. *aut nec ... non moritur*: *om* V7. *anima pecudum ... non moritur*: *om* Ma. *moritur.*: // B. (3–7: *om* V6 V2.) **3** *temporibus(1) ... concordiam*: *om* V7. *temporibus(2)*: aetatibus P9 V5 Ab. *mundi*: *om* V5 Ab M P3 P4 B1, mundi et *om* P9. **4** *qui*: *om* B1. **5** *colera rubea ... sicca(1)*: *om* P3, *... sicca(2)*: *om* E1, *ad.* by corr. M. *adolescente*: adolescentibus P4 V7 B1. **6–10**: {P9 diverges} terra frigida triplicis naturae est videlicet propter substantiam calorem splendorem, habet enim tria officia in se inluminati [sic] aduret fovet {cf. 'vis animae'}. ALITER anima triplicis naturae irascibilis concupiscibilis rationabilis. // P9 {see 8 ('iste' ff.) below}. **6** *terra frigida et sicca*: *om* P4. *melancholia*: melanconia V5 M, melancholica Ma Ab P3 B1. *nigra*: rubea B1. **7** *flegma ... et humida*: *om* Ab. **8** *iste*: *ad.* est B1. *vitiis*: vinculis V5. *deum*: *om* B1, *ad.* et proximum V6. *et virtutes appetat*: *om* V6 V2. **9** *quae tria ... creatori*: *om* T L4b E1 V6 V2. *si vero... reddunt*: *om* V6 V2. **10** *si*: nam si T L4b E1, si autem Ab. **11** *si illa pars ... ebriosus*: {V2 recasts} si homo fuerit irascibilis fit tristis felle amaritudinis plenus. si fuerit concupiscibilis fit ebriosus V2. *vitiata fuerit*: ~ A **12** *si illa pars fuerit ... rationabilis*: {V6 recasts} si irascibilis pars corrupta fuerit tristis fit homo felle amaritudinis plenus. si concupiscibilis vitiatur fit ebriosus libidinosus. si illa pars animae quae rationabilis dicitur corrumpatur V6. *si autem ... servus*: om P4. *autem illa*: autem ea Ma Ab M P3 V7 B1. *vitiata fuerit*: fuerit corrupta viciata B1. *vero ... rationabilis*: om M. *animae corrumpatur*: fuerit animae corrupta T, animae corrupta fuerit A. *omnibus*: ad. –que P3 V7 B1, qui P4.

I 1 quidam philosophorum animam mundi solem dixerunt quod, sicut anima corpus humanum, ita calore illius vivificantur omnia nascentia eiusque calor diffusus per creaturas facit eas gignere, et re vera calore illius omnia et gignunt et gignuntur pariter cum humore deo ita disponente. **2** quem solem triplicis naturae esse dixerunt videlicet quia est eius substantia, calor quoque et splendor. sed non satis praesenti loco congruit hanc animam accipi quoniam non potest prosequi ratio. **3** dixerunt et de hoc loco diversi diversa, quorum opiniones omittentes quod prudentioribus visum est succincte dicamus. homo graeco vocabulo microsmus appelatur i. minor mundus, habet siquidem concordiam cum mundo huiusmodi. **4** mundus constat ex quattuor elementis et quattuor temporibus et homo similiter, habet enim corpus ex terra, sanguinem ex igne, humorem ab aqua, flatum ab aere. **5** potest et aliter dici. concordiam habet cum aere et vernali tempore, quae habent humorem et calorem, in pueritia et sanguine; **6** cum aestate et igne, quae habent calorem et siccitatem, in adolescentia vel iuventute et in colera rubea; cum autumno et terra et melancholia, quae habent ariditatem et frigus, in senectute; **7** concordat cum aqua et hieme et flegmate, quae habent frigus et humorem, in decrepita aetate – proprium est enim senibus frigidos esse. **8** iste minor mundus i. homo habet animam triplicis naturae quoniam secundum quod augustinus et cassianus in collationibus claudianus quoque atque cassiodorus dicunt est rationabilis, irascibilis, concupiscibilis, quae tria dum rationabiliter disponuntur coniungunt creaturam creatori. **9** si vero permutata fuerint removent eum longe a creatoris contemplatione, quoniam si ratio pervertatur excrescit in superbiam et vanam gloriam, si ira in tristitiam et accediam, si concupiscentia in libidinem et gastrimargiam. **10** debet enim ratione uti discernendo creatorem a creatura, bonum a malo; debet sibi irasci ne consentiat corpori; et debet summum bonum rationabiliter concupiscere (P5 P1 P10 A P V3 P6 Ge C4 *par* Es L P8 V6 V2)

{L has this gloss to 3, then continues with the gloss 'sed quod beatus gregorius,' and then with the gloss 'nam et homo' – with the former cf. 'media dicitur anima' 2, with the latter 3–4 here. P8 begins at 8 'naturae quoniam.' V6 has the gloss through 7, then continues with the W version, 8 ('iste' ff.) – see 'media dicitur anima.' V2 has the gloss to 8 'triplicis naturae,' and in a separate gloss has the W version, 8 ('iste' ff.). Es has much of this gloss (sections 1–2, 3 & 8, 9, 10) in five separate blocks scattered over three pages, with substantial omissions and variants.}

{Es A P V3 P6 Ge C4 cont. immed. with 15 'quae anima ... quae foris vidit.' In P8 'quae anima' is the next gloss, in P5 it follows mid-line after a separating stroke, in P1 it continues with just a new capital.}

1 (V2 cropped until *sicut.*) *philosophorum*: philosophi Es A P V3 P6 Ge C4. *dixerunt*: esse dixerunt L A P V3 P6 Ge C4. *quod*: quia: A Ge [A badly faded]. *humanum*: *ad.* vivificat A P V3 Ge. *ita*: data C4. *omnia*: cuncta Es A P V3 P6 Ge C4. *eiusque*: eius A P V3 P6 Ge C4. *eiusque ... disponente*: *om* Es. *facit*: faciat P5 [ex. corr.] P1. *pariter ... disponente*: tamen pariter omnia deo cum honore ita disponente L. *cum: & V2.* **2** *quem*: *ad.* i. V2, idem P10, id est P5. *naturae esse*: ~ A P V3 P6 Ge C4, est naturae Es. *videlicet ... splendor*: lucet enim fovet et [incendit] (occidit corr. to incidit) Es. *est ... splendor*: *om* V3. *est eius substantia*: eius substantia est L V6 V2 A P P6 Ge C4, eius substantia V3. *quoque*: eius P10, *om* P1 A P V3 P6 Ge C4. *splendor*: *ad.* sol praeterea medius est inter planetas L P10. *hanc animam*: in hanc animam A P V3 P6 Ge, hunc animam Es, hunc solem animam P10, ut solem animam L. *accipi ... ratio*: esse dicamus // L, accipi quoniam ratio oppugnavit Es {the end of 1st block in Es}. **3** *succincte dicamus*: succincte. Dicamus A P P6 Ge C4. {P1 begins new para w. new key.} *homo*: *om* P1 *homo ... appelatur*: Homo quia grecis macrocosmos i. est minor mundus appellatur Es. *habet om from here to* 8 habet Es. *huiusmodi*: huiuscemodi A P V3 P6 Ge C4. **4** *ex ... similiter*: ex quattuor temporibus V6. *sanguinem*: calorem A P V3 P6 Ge C4. *ex igne*: ab igne V2 P5 P1. **5** *quae habent*: qui habent A P V3 P6 Ge, qui habet C4. *et sanguine*: id est in sanguine P10, et sanguinem A P V3 P6 Ge C4. **6** *cum: et V2. quae habent*: qui habent A P V3 P6 Ge, qui habet C4. *in colera rubea*: colera rubea P10 A P V3 P6 Ge C4. *habent ariditatem et frigus*: ariditatem frigusque habet A P V3 P6 Ge C4. **6** *cum autumno ... 7 aetate*: cum terra et autumno quae habent ariditatem in senectute et melancolia vel colera nigra; cum aqua et hieme quae habent frigus et humorem concordat in decrepita aetate et flegma V6 {V6 uses pattern of first two sets}. **7** *concordat*: concordant P5 P1. *esse*: // V6. **8** *iste minor mundus ... rationabilis*: (Es *resuming here*) habet triplicis naturae animam est enim rationabilis Es. *mundus i.: mundus s. V2. naturae*: naturae // V2; *inc* Naturae P8. **9** *accediam*: *ad* i. taedium, anxietatem mentis P10. *gastrimargiam*: *ad.* i. in voracitatem gulae P10. **10** {P1 begins 3rd block.} *ratione*:

rationem Es. *ne*: nec A P Ge. *et*: *om* Es A P V3 P6 C4. *concupiscere*: concupisci Es A P V3 P6 Ge C4.

J 1 sed quod beatus gregorius in dialogorum libro dicit melius hoc loco congruit. nam ut ipse testatur tres utiles spiritus creavit omnipotens deus: unum qui nec carne tegitur nec cum carne moritur, i. angelorum; alium qui carne tegitur sed non cum carne moritur, hominum; tertium qui et carne tegitur et cum carne moritur, brutorum animalium. homo vero, sicut in medio est conditus, ita habet aliquid commune cum infimo, immortalitatem quippe spiritus cum angelo. mortalitatem vero carnis habet cum iumento, et ideo recte anima media dicitur. **2** nam et homo graeca appellatione microcosmus, i. minor mundus, appellatur. habet siquidem huiusmodi concordiam cum mundo. mundus enim constat quattuor elementis, quattuor temporibus, et homo similiter. habet enim corpus ex terra, sanguinem ab igne, humorem ab aqua ...(L)
{L: expl. With 1 cf. 'media dicitur anima' 2, with 2 'quidem philosophorum' 3–4. See Gregory, *Dialogorum libri iv* 4.3, ed. Adalbert de Vogüé, *Sources Chrétiennes* 256, 260, 265 [Paris, 1978–80].}

Note, first, that reading **H** and **I** without attention to the sigle list and apparatus would yield a very false impression of the existence of 'a text.' Some of the manuscripts have the entire construct pretty much as edited; others have only part, and the variants show many omissions, rephrasings, and additions. Secondly, an examination reveals the individual units that have gradually accreted in these longer constructs.

Example **H** combines, I suggest, four originally separate glosses: section **1**, section **2**, sections **3–7**, and sections **8–10**. Section **1**, asserting that the soul is *media* not because it extends from the middle of the body but because its seat is in the heart, rejects an idea not clearly expressed in any gloss I have seen but repeats and affirms one found in examples **D** and **E**. Section **2** adds an alternative: the human soul is *media* between the souls of beasts and angels. Further evidence that **2** began as a separate gloss is its appearance as such in two other manuscripts,[31] and its occurrence in example **J**, with attribution, conceivably represents its original form; in **H** the attribution has been dropped and the language itself (the permutations on *caro, moritur, tegitur*) becomes the focus of interest.[32] A third unit of thought appears in sections **3–7**. Its beginning, saying 'the more prudent' reject some other interpretations, seems not to react to **1** and **2**, which also see *anima* as the human soul; more likely this cautionary reaction arose in response to a gloss like example F[33] or even to glosses proposing *anima* as sun.[34] In any case, the new unit is additive, a result of glossarial accretion. This new idea[35] elaborates the rational soul as microcosm, *minor mundus*;[36] the scheme involves the four elements, the four qualities (and their four possible combinations), the four seasons, the four humours, and the four ages of man. Typical of glosses in larger constructs, it is concerned with a neat set of parallel correspondences. The last unit, sections **8–10**, follows from the third (picking up 'iste minor mundus') and returns to the idea of the triple nature of the human soul, now based on its three appetites (cf. example **G**), elaborating on the purpose and the possible corruption of each.

Example **H** appears, with variations, in the core **W** manuscripts: L4b E1 T Ma V5 M P3 P4 V7. The first two units (sections **1, 2**) appear in the early B and in V6 V2. V6 V2 have unit four (**8–10**) as a separate gloss. Two English manuscripts which have **Z**-type glosses but which contain those of the **W** type as well have much of it: P9 has the first two units and most of the third (**3–5**); A's hand c adds nearly all of it (omitting only part of the third unit, section **7**). The variant in B, presenting less parallel structure, may show an earlier, less polished version of unit 2; V6 rephrases and abbreviates the same unit. If these variants reflect incipient stages of the underlying glosses, others suggest eye-skip in copying an original (see Ma P3 V7 at section **2**, V7 at section **3**, and note that these manuscripts are continuous glosses).

Example **I** also seems to combine originally separate glosses: section **1**, section **2**, sections **3–7**, and sections **8–10**. As in **H**, the first two of **I** are closely related, and glosses three and four of **I** are somewhat different versions of glosses three and four in **H**. That the whole shows glossing by accretion appears from **1** 'quidam philosophorum,' **2** 'quem solem' (the syntax suggests addition of an idea), **3** 'dixerunt et de hoc loco diversi diversa, quorum opiniones omittentes quod prudentioribus visum est ...,' **5** 'potest et aliter dici.'

Whereas **H** had ignored the idea of *anima* as sun, that explanation appears in the first two units here. **1** says that the soul animates the body as the sun vivifies all creatures with its heat (cf. example **B**); **2** finds a triple nature in the sun's substance, heat, and splendour (cf. **C**), but then rejects this line of thought: 'but it does not adequately suit the present passage that this soul [the sun] be understood, because the explanation just does not work out [*non potest prosequi ratio*].' The explanation thus seems to be presented as passé, to be dismissed before moving on to what can be taken seriously.[37] Next (**3–7**) comes the gloss on man as microcosm, aligning the elements, seasons, qualities, humours, and ages; 4, aligning the elements with human body, blood, 'humour,' and breath, is not in H and seems actually to reflect an originally separate gloss found in example J,[38] which has led to the 'potest et aliter dici' of section 5. 5–7 slightly rephrase the ideas in H and align the ages in a slightly different fashion. The last part of I, 8–10, has the same material as H but in slightly different order: in H the proper function of the appetites comes first, in I last; besides some minor variations, the most significant addition is the named authorities at 8.

The total construct I occurs in manuscripts I designate as the X Y Z groups: V2 P10 (X), P5 P1 (Y), and Es A P V3 C4 Ge P6 (Z). A P V3 C4 Ge P6 (z2) represent a distinct recasting: they share many variants, seem to have been copied from nearly identical exemplars, and show both common errors (e.g., the misdivision at 3) and 'corrections' (e.g., tinkering with pronouns and verb agreement in 5–6). Es (the only member of z1 to have this gloss) has Z variants but repeatedly separates itself from z2; despite its palaeographically later date, its omissions, arrangement, and one striking carry-over from St Gall (compare it at 2 with example C) might reflect an earlier state of the Z revisions. My edition of I reflects my hypothesis that X Y represent prior versions. For example, the very compressed syntax at the end of 2 ('hanc animam accipi' for '[that the sun] be understood as this soul' – the reading of V6 V2 P5 P1) seems the *difficilior lectio* with which subsequent writers have variously tinkered.

These examples can serve, I hope, to illustrate what examination of the Remigian glosses indicates about their nature and likely development. If one had begun with a 'master commentary,' it seems unlikely that even the long glosses would so obviously be constructs of earlier and originally separate explanations. On the contrary, the presence in all the manuscripts of many short glosses (inadequately illustrated here) and the way chunks of the longer constructs appear in various combinations suggest a kind of branching evolution in which ideas accumulated and were variously recast and recombined. Some of them may well reflect lecture notes. Some were likely copied selectively from a borrowed *Consolatio*. Obviously at some point individuals drafted constructs that were later widely copied and actively revised. Some of this revision probably was in the direction of 'dumbing down' and 'prettying up': simplifying complex ideas and rewriting glosses to emphasize neatly parallel syntax. But rather than testifying to the gradual decay of an individual, original achievement the glosses as we have them indicate, I think, much active involvement with Boethius's text, by many individuals, and in many centres of learning.

APPENDIX A: Additions and Corrections to Courcelle's 1967 List of Manuscripts Containing All or Some of the 'Remigian' Commentary.[39]

(Those in this typeface in Courcelle pp. 405–6, with his characterization. For him 'comp[let]' meant the manuscript contained the full commentary, 'fragment' meant the manuscript contained some of the glosses, and 'revised' acknowledged a second version of the complete R with revised glosses on III.m.9.)
Those in bold added to his list by Bolton or Wittig.
Those in italics should be recharacterized or removed from Courcelle's list of R mss.
CPh = Consolatio Philosophiae; R = 'Remigian' commentary; G = St Gall commentary.)

MSS	GENERAL CHARACTERIZATION
Alençon 12	comp *[but x, not xii]*
Antwerp MusPM M.16.8	**comp (Bolton)**
Bern 179	fragment *[comparatively few glosses]*
Bern 181	**III.m.9, inserted in text of CPh (Wittig)**
Bern 413	**fragment (Wittig) [some R type glosses]**
<<Bonn 175	fragment, with G; LOST during WWII >>
Cambridge CCC 214	**fragment (Bolton) [incompletely glossed]**
Cambridge G&CC 309/707	**fragment (Wittig) [some R type glosses]**
Cambridge Trin.Coll. O.3.7	comp
Cambridge UL Gg.5.35	**fragment (Bolton) [some R type glosses]**
Cambridge UL Kk.3.21	**comp (Bolton)**
<<Chartres 59	comp but lacks end 405; LOST during WWII >>
Cockerell	comp *[now Geneva Bodmer 175]*
Einsiedeln 179	III.m.9 inserted in G
Erfurt 35	III.m.9
El Escorial e.II.1	**comp (Bolton)**
Gotha 103	fragment *[some glosses]*
Heiligenkreuz 130	comp *[actually fragment, and on fols 84v–91r]*
London BL Add 15601	**fragment (Wittig) [continua on I.m.1 – III.m.9]**
London BL Add 19726	**fragment (text with some R type glosses)**
London BL Egerton 267	**fragment (Bolton) [one leaf of a fully glossed text]**
London BL Egerton 628	**III.m.9 (Wittig)**
London BL Harley 3095	*fragment [actually G with R]*

'Remigian' Glosses on Boethius's *Consolatio Philosophiae* 185

Maihingen, fols 60–112	comp [*now Krakow Lat. Quarto 939*]
Maihingen, fols 4–57	*fragment [now Krakow, G, with some R glosses]*
Munich clm 14836	comp [*actually III.m.9 continua*]
Munich clm 15825	**fragment (Wittig) [continua on V.p.1, 1 – V.m.4, 19]**
Munich clm 18765	fragment, with G [*some brief glosses of R type*]
Munich clm 19452	comp
Oxford Bodl Auct F.1.15	**fragment (Bolton) [incompletely glossed text]**
Oxford CCC E. 59	fragment (Wittig) [*some R type glosses*]
Oxford CCC E. 74	comp (Bolton)
Oxford Merton Coll. 3.12	**fragment (Bolton) [two leaves of a fully glossed text]**
Paris BN lat 6401A	revised
Paris BN lat 6402	revised
Paris BN lat 6769	**fragment (Wittig) [some shorter R type glosses]**
Paris BN lat 8039	III.m.9, inserted in text of CPh
Paris BN lat 8308	III.m.9, inserted in text of CPh
Paris BN lat 12961	revised
Paris BN lat 14380	revised
Paris BN lat 15090	comp, as rarely lacking R, rarely including G
Paris BN lat 16093	revised
Paris BN lat 17814	comp [*as lacking beg. and end*]
Paris BN n.a. lat 1478	comp, as some of revised on III.m.9
St Gall 845	III.m.9, inserted in G
Trier Stadtbibl 1093	comp
Vat lat 1592	*comp, 'scattered' [very few glosses, unidentifiable as R]*
Vat lat 3865	comp, lacks end
Vat lat 4254	revised
Vat lat 5956	**fragment (Wittig) [some R type glosses]**
Vat Pal lat 1581	comp, 'very complete' [*not nearly as full as many*]
Vat Reg lat 1433	comp, 'scattered' [*but clearly R type*]
Vat Reg lat 1727	III.m.9
Vienna 242	*fragment, very incompl and not III.m.9 [not R glosses]*

186   Joseph Wittig

SUMMARY OF CORRECTIONS TO COURCELLE'S LIST

[Two MSS were listed twice under complete:
   Vat lat 3865, Vat Pal lat 1581.]
Two MSS were lost in WWII: Bonn 175, Chartres 59
Listed as complete, actually a fragment:
   Heiligenkreuz 130
Listed as complete, actually III.m.9 only:
   Munich clm 14836
Listed as fragment, actually R, including III.m.9
   London, BL Harley 3095
Listed as fragment, actually not identifiable as R
   Maihingen, fols 4–57 (St Gall)
   Vat lat 1592
   Vienna 242

Add to list:
4 'complete' copies: Antwerp, CUL Kk.3.21, El Escorial, Oxf. CCC E.74.
15 'fragments':

   2 bits of what look to have been completely glossed texts: London BL Egerton
      267, Oxford Merton Coll. 3.12
   2 copies of III.m.9 alone: Bern 181, London BL Egerton 628
   1 copy of a continua on bks I–III: London BL Add 15601
   1 copy of a continua on bk V.p.1–V.m.4,19: Munich clm 15825
   2 complete texts to which part of the R glosses were added: Cambridge CCC
      214, Oxford Bodl Auct F.1.15
   7 mss which contain some R type glosses: Bern 413, Cambridge G&CC 309/
      707, CUL Gg.5.35, London BL Add 19726, Oxford CCC E. 59, Paris BN lat
      6769, Vat lat 5956

COUNT
23 'Complete': 17 + 6 'Revised'
17 'Fragments': 10 full texts with at least some R glosses, 3 full but incomplete
      continua, 2 incompletely glossed texts, and 2 fragments of what seem to
      have been fully glossed texts
10 with R on III.m.9 only

50

APPENDIX B: List of MSS and Sigles

This list includes all manuscripts I have collated for any part of the glosses. **Those with sigles in boldface have been edited for III.p.9 line 85 through m.9 (which has been abbreviated below as III.p.9,85–m.9).**
Mss are listed in alphabetical order by sigle.
Abbreviations in this list:
  Gloss type: R (version of 'Remi'), G (version of anon. Sancti Galli), O (other early glosses)
  Other abbrev: CPh = Consolatio Philosophiae, inl (interlinear), mg (marginal), f (fragmentary or incomplete copy of version); Gneuss, *Handlist*: Helmut Gneuss, *Handlist of Anglo-Saxon Manuscripts: A List of Manuscripts and Manuscript Fragments Written or Owned in England up to 1100*, MRTS 241 (Tempe, AZ: Arizona Center for Medieval and Renaissance Studies, 2001).
  W, X, Y and **Z** refer to versions of 'R' reflected by mss groupings.
Accessus material (including the *Vitae* of Boethius and Lupus on the metres) is not described here.
Information about date and origin/provenance is derived from published descriptions of the mss unless otherwise stated.

A   Antwerp, Museum Plantin-Moretus, M. 16. 8 (olim lat. 190). s. x^{ex}/xi^{in}, Abingdon. Gneuss, *Handlist*, no. 776. Gloss: R. (CPh with inl and mg glosses on fols 1–116. At least 2 glossing hands, approx. contemporary with text: [a] wrote first, keys and mg glosses = MS P – see below; b wrote second and perhaps in several stages and seems to have written the inl glosses; c looks exactly like a, but wrote after a, adding **W** glosses in inner mg and on an added half sheet, fol. 55.) III.9.85–m.9 on: fols 53v–6r.

An   Alençon, Bibliothèque municipale 12. s. x, France (at St-Évroul from c. 1100). Gloss: R. (CPh with inl and mg glosses on fols 1–57v. A hand contemporary with text writes the R glosses, but none after III.m.9,12; another hand, transcribed separately and not reported here, looks s. xii and writes most of the inl glosses on III.m.9.) III.p.9,85–m.9 on: fols 25v–6v.

B   Bern, Bürgerbibliothek, Cod. 179. s. ix^2, Brittany? (at Fleury by s. xi). Gloss: R,f. (CPh with inl and mg glosses on fols 1r–63v. Glossing heavy until I.p.4, fol. 5, then nothing until fol. 8; heavy on II.p.1 to III.p.2, and again on III.p.3–III.p.10. Thereafter both inl and mg rare and some in later hands. The few on III.m.9 are R type.) III.p.9,85–m.9 on: fols 31r–v.

B1   Bern, Bürgerbibliothek, Cod. 181. s. xi. Gloss: R III.m.9; O. (CPh on fols 1–83v, R continua on III.m.9 inserted after the metre in text hand; some inl and mg glosses through fol. 19, thereafter very few.) III.m.9 on: fols 43r–5r.

B2 Bern, Bürgerbibliothek, Cod. 413. s. xii². Gloss: R,f. (CPh with inl and mg glosses, text incomplete, expl. V.p.6. Glosses in contemporary hand through IV.p.2; on III.m.9 only a few inl.) III.p.9,85–m.9 on: fols 23r–v.

C Cambridge, Corpus Christi College 214. s. xi¹, S-E England. Gneuss, *Handlist*, no. 68. Gloss: R,f. (CPh with inl and mg glosses on fols 1r–122r. Glossing heavy on fols 1–25r, I.m.1 to II.m.5; thereafter scanty. Also OE glosses and paving letters, e.g. on III.m.12. The MS has suffered serious damage to outside margins.) III.p.9,85–m.9 on: 54r–5r.

C1 Cambridge, Gonville and Caius College 309/707. s. xii¹, Gloucester. Gloss: R. (CPh with inl and mg glosses on fols 28v–86v. A hand contemporary with text writes a few R glosses; a later, which M.R. James called 'xiv cursive,' writes 2 mg, on III.m.9,4 and 6, and some inl similar to R (transcribed separately and not reported here.) III.p.9,85–m.9 on: fols 55r–6r.

C2 Cambridge, Trinity College O. 3. 7. s. x², St Augustine's, Canterbury. Gneuss, *Handlist*, no. 193. Gloss: R. (CPh with inl and mg glosses on fols 1r–51v.) III.p.9,85–m.9 on: fols 24v–5r.

C3 Cambridge, University Library Gg. 5. 35. s. xi², England (St Augustine's, Canterbury?). Gneuss, *Handlist*, no. 12. Gloss: R? (CPh with inl and mg glosses on fols 170r–209v. On III.m.9 there are a few inl similar to R, not much mg.) III.p.9,85–m.9 on: fols 188v–9r.

C4 Cambridge, University Library Kk. 3. 21. s. x^{ex}/xi^{in}, Abingdon. Gneuss, *Handlist*, no. 23. Gloss: R. (CPh with inl and mg glosses on fols 1r–103r.) III.p.9,85–m.9 on: fols 49r–50r.

E Einsiedeln, Stiftsbibliothek 149. s. x (at Einsiedeln s. xiii). Gloss: G. (CPh with inl and mg glosses on pp. 52–178.) III.p.9,85–m.9 on: pp. 105–6.

E1 Einsiedeln, Stiftsbibliothek 179. s. x, St Gall. Gloss: G, R III.m.9. (Continuous commentaries on pp. 96a–185b. There is a second copy of the G continua on III.m.9, 'ITEM ANNOTATIONES TERTII LIBRI,' at the end of the complete G version; the R continua is inserted in the full G version immediately after the first glosses on III.m.9.) III.p.9,85–m.9 on: pp. 143b–5b (E1¹, first copy of G), pp. 145b–9a (E1,R), pp. 185b–7b (E1², second copy of G).

E2 Einsiedeln, Stiftsbibliothek 302. s. x, St Gall. Gloss: G. (CPh with inl and mg glosses on pp. 65a–110b. Also the 'anon. of Einsiedeln 302' continua on III.m.9, p. 27. Leaves of the CPh have been lost at four places, including this passage.) III.p.9,85–m.9 wanting.

E3 Einsiedeln, Stiftsbibliothek 322. s. x, St Gall? Gloss: G,f (*ex inf.* Petrus Tax).

Er Erfurt, Wissenschaftliche Bibliothek, Amplona F. 35. s. xiv^{ex}. Gloss: R III.m.9. (CPh on fols 99r–113v, expl. '... totus liber a.D. 1394° pro festo invencionis sance crucis Erphordie per Henricum de Berka ...') III.m.9 on: fols 114v–15r.

Es   El Escorial, Real Biblioteca, e.II.1. s. xi[1], England (at Horton). Gloss: R. (CPh with inl and mg glosses on fols 8v–117r.) III.p.9,85–m.9 on: fols 63r–4r.

G   St Gallen, Stiftsbibliothek 844. Text s. ix; glosses s. x, St Gall. Gloss: G. (CPh with inl and mg glosses on pp. 13–186. The glosses closely match those in N.) III.p.9,85–m.9 on: pp. 93–5.

G1   St Gallen, Stiftsbibliothek 845. s. x, St Gall. Gloss: G, R III.m.9. (A copy of E1 by several different hands, some very unskilled. G continua on pp. 13–240; as in E1, R on III.m.9 inserted after G on III.m.9. A direct copy of E1, incomplete at end, expl. IV.m.7, 17 'poma.') III.p.9,85–m.9 on: pp. 152–8 (G), pp. 158–68 (R).

Ge   *Olim* Geneva, Bibliotheca Bodmeriana, Cod. 175. s. x^{ex}/xi^{in}, England (St Augustine's, Canterbury?). Gneuss, *Handlist*, no. 829. Gloss: R. (CPh with inl and mg glosses on 1v–111v.) III.p.9,85–m.9 on: fols 54r–5r. Sold through Sotheby's 7 July 2005 to an anonymous buyer.

Go   Gotha, Forschungsbibliothek, M. II. 103. s. xi/xii, Germany. Gloss: R/G,f. (CPh on fols 42v–123v with inl and a few mg glosses on I.m.1–I.p.5, at 51v; thereafter some inl and scant mg except for III.m.9.) III.p.9,85–m.9 on: fol. 82r–v.

H   Heiligenkreuz, Stiftsbibliothek 130. s. xii, Heiligenkreuz. Glosses: R,f. (See N. Haring, *MS* 31 [1969]: 287–316). CPh with inl and mg glosses on fols 4v–75r; glosses on III.m.9 are a compilation of R,G, and anon. of Erf. Q.53; glosses on III.m.12 include some RG type. On fols 76r–84v a continua on I.m.1–III.p.2,60, according to Haring the anon. of Erf. Q.5. On fols 84v–91r a copy of R continua on I.m.1–II.p.7,28. On fols 92r–120r another continua, identified by Haring as Guillaume de Conches.) III.p.9.86–m.9 on: fols 36r–8v.

L   London, BL, Add. 15601. s. x^{ex}/xi^{in}, S. Germany? (at Avignon). Gloss R,f; O. (R continua on I.m.1–III.m.9, fols 1–16v, followed by CPh fols 17–59r with frequent inl and, except on III.m.9, rare mg not = R and transcribed separately.) III.p.9,86–m.9 on: fols 15v–16v.

L1   London, BL, Add. 19726. s. x^{ex}/xi^{in}, Germany (at Tegernsee s. xi^{med}). Gloss: R. (CPh with inl and mg glosses on fols 2–57.) III.p.9,85–m.9 on: 28v–29r.

L2   London, BL, Egerton 267. s. xi^{in}, England. Gneuss, *Handlist*, no. 408. Gloss: R,f. (Item xi, 37r–v, is a single leaf containing CPh I.p.4,104 'pro' – 139 'adversae,' with inl and mg glosses of R type).

L3   London, BL, Egerton 628. s. xiii[2] (at S. Maria de Camberone, Cambrai). Gloss: R III.m.9. (CPh interspersed with continua on fols 5r–161v: Courcelle identifies continua as Guillaume de Conches. R continua on III.m.9 on fols 162r–4v; not collated here but R is the **W** version to which several later, long glosses have been added.) III.p.9,85–m.9 on: fols 162r–4v.

L4 London, BL, Harley 3095. s. x^1, Rhineland (Cologne?). Gloss: G,R. (CPh with inl and mg glosses on fols 1v–112v. Both R and G glosses written inl and mg throughout, but only G inl and mg at the text of III.m.9, after which the continua of Bovo of Corvey is inserted and, ironically, on the lemmata of this the R glosses are written. The continua of the anon. of Einsiedeln 302 follows on fols 59r–61v. Closely related to Ma though not its direct exemplar. Glossing hand [a] writes G inl and mg with the text, in several passes; R is written, for III.m.9, 'inl' and mg, keyed to the lemmata in the Bovo continua by a hand not always clearly distinguishable from [a], but which I identify as 'L4b.') III.p.9,85–m.9 on: fols 46r–7r (G), 47r–59r (R).

M Munich, Bayerische Staatsbibliothek, clm 14836. s. xi, Germany. Gloss: R III.m.9. (Continua in a miscellany of 'mathematical' works.) III.m.9 on: fols 10v–15v.

M1 Munich, Bayerische Staatsbibliothek, clm 19452. s. xi, S. Germany. Gloss: R. (CPh with inl and mg glosses on fols 2r–76v, incomplete, expl. at V.p.4,97 'nullus.') III.p.9,85–m.9 on: fols 39r–40r.

M2 Munich, Bayerische Staatsbibliothek, clm 18765. s. ix/x, W. Germany. Gloss: O. (CPh with inl and mg glosses on fols 15r–74v. Two hands write brief lexical glosses, some similar to R/G; transcribed separately.) III.p.9,85–m.9 on: fols 42v–3v.

M3 Munich, Bayerische Staatsbibliothek, clm 14324. s. ix^{med} (at St Emmeram). Gloss: O/G. (CPh with inl and mg glosses on fols 37r–70v. Transcribed separately; mostly inl glosses, some similar to the G glosses in N E1 L4.) III.p.9,85–m.9 on: fols 54v–5r.

M4 Munich, Bayerische Staatsbibliothek, clm 15825. s. xi, Salzburg. Gloss: R,f; O. (CPh with inl and mg glosses on fols 2v–67r; some inl simply rearrange word order, others are lexical glosses similar to R/G. Transcribed separately. R continua on V.p.1,5–V.m.4,19 on fols 66, 67v–75r – 66 belongs between 74/75.) III.p.9,85–m.9 on: fols 33r–4v.

Ma Kraków, Biblioteka Jaglellónska, Lat. Quarto 939 (*olim* Berlin, Staatsbibliothek der Stiftung Preussischer Kulturbesitz, lat.4o, 939, *olim* Maihingen, Bibliotheca Wallersteiniana, I, 2, Lat. 4o 3). s. x^{ex}, Tegernsee. Gloss: G, R. (CPh with inl and mg glosses on fols 4r–57v; continua on CPh on fols 60r–112r. Fromund copied the text and the G glosses at Cologne; his students wrote the R continua at Tegernsee. Derived from a MS much like L4 though not directly.) III.p.9,85–m.9 on: fols 28r–9r (G), 85v–7v (R).

N   Naples, Biblioteca Nazionale, IV G. 68. Text s. ix, France (Tours?), glosses s. x, St Gall. Gloss: G. (CPh with inl and mg glosses on fols 4v–92r.) III.p.9,85–m.9 on: fols 46v–7v.

O   Oxford, Bodleian Library, Auct. F. 1. 15. x^2, St Augustine's, Canterbury. Gneuss, *Handlist*, no. 533. Gloss: R,f. (CPh with inl and some mg glosses on fols 5r–77r. Several glossing hands: one contemporary with text if not identical glossed I.m.1–I.p.3,26, on 5r–8r, fully and III.m.9, on 39v–40r; another wrote glosses for V.p.2–V.m.4, on 66v–72v; a third supplied inl glosses and keys – only – for mg glosses for I.m.5,44–II.p.1,35, on 13r–17r.) III.p.9,85–m.9 on: fols 39v–40r.

O1 Oxford, Corpus Christi College 59. s. xiii (at Lanthony Priory, Gloucestershire). Gloss: R. (CPh with inl and mg glosses on fols 72r–112r.) III.p.9,85–m.9 on: fol. 90r.

O2 Oxford, Corpus Christi College 74. s. xi[1]. Gneuss, *Handlist*, no. 74. Gloss: R. (CPh with inl and mg glosses on fols 1r–61v.) III.p.9,85–m.9 on: fols 30r–1r.

O3 Oxford, Merton College E.3.12. s. x^{ex}/xi^{in}, England. Gneuss, *Handlist*, no. 678. Gloss: R,f. (2 fols, text of CPh V.p.4,80 '– ra mentis' – V.m.4.35 'excitus' with inl and mg gl, reported by Bolton to = C4.)

On Orléans, Bibliothèque municipale, 270. s. ix^{in}, glosses ix[1], Fleury. Gloss: O. (CPh with inl and some mg glosses on pp. 3–229. Glosses in three or four hands, two nearly contemporary with text; I have transcribed the glosses on III.m.9 with G.) III.p.9,85–m.9 on: pp. 108–10.

P   Paris, BN, lat. 6401A. s. x^{ex}, Christ Church, Canterbury. Gneuss, *Handlist*, no. 887. Gloss: R. (CPh with inl and mg glosses on fols 1r–94v.) III.p.9,85–m.9 on: fols 45r–6r.

P1 Paris, BN, lat. 6402. s. xi^{ex}–xii[1], W. or S-W. France (Poitiers-Toulouse?). Gloss: R. (CPh with inl and mg glosses on fols 1r–71r.) III.p.9,85–m.9 on: fols 35v–6r.

P2 Paris, BN, lat. 6769. s. xiii. Gloss: abbreviated R? (CPh with mostly inl glosses on fols 1v–54r; on III.m.9 only short inl, reduced or incipient R; transcribed separately.) III.p.9,85–m.9 on: fols 26v–7r.

P3 Paris, BN, lat. 8039. s. x^2? Gloss: R III.m.9. (CPh with inl and mg glosses on fols 51r–77v, with R continua on III.m.9 inserted after the metre. The text hand writes the R continua, which begins with the glosses to line 13. Another, apparently contemporary, hand b writes R type inl and mg on the text, at fols 63rb–3va. Other, probably later, hands add some brief glosses not reported here.) III.m.9 on: fols 63rb–3va (text), 63vb–4va (continua).

P4 Paris, BN, lat. 8308. s. xii. Gloss: R III.m.9. (CPh with inl and mg glosses on 16r–71v with R continua inserted after the metre by the text hand. Like P3 the continua begins with line 13. There are no glosses on the text, at 40v.) III.m.9 on: fols 41v–3r.

P5 Paris, BN, lat. 12961. s. xi², E. France (Lorraine, Metz? at Corbie). Gloss: R. (CPh with inl and mg glosses on fols 2r–90v.) III.p.9,85–m.9 on: fols 44v–5v.

P6 Paris, BN, lat. 14380. s. xi¹, Christ Church, Canterbury. Gneuss, *Handlist*, no. 899. Gloss: R. (CPh with inl and mg glosses on fols 2r–64v.) III.p.9,85–m.9 on: fols 31v–2r.

P7 Paris, BN, lat. 15090. s. x, St Evre, Toul. Gloss: R. (CPh with inl and mg glosses on fols 2v–88v.) III.p.9,85–m.9 on: fols 42v–4r.

P8 Paris, BN, lat. 16093. s. xi^{med}, Loire (Fleury?). Gloss: R. (CPh with inl and mg glosses on fols 1r–68r. Also continua on III.m.9, fol. 69v, which Courcelle identified as s. xiii Anon. of Erfurt Q 5.) III.p.9,85–m.9 on: fols 35v–6r.

P9 Paris, BN, lat. 17814. s. x^{ex}/xi^{in}, Canterbury. Gneuss, *Handlist*, no. 901. Gloss: R. (CPh with inl and mg glosses on fols 9r–122v; incomplete at end, expl. V.p.5,114 'quoque' – end supplied s. xviii. Probably several glossing hands contemporary with text and writing in several passes; [a] is much like text and writes version W; b, very similar, adds Z glosses, corresponding to MS P. Trevet's commentary has been added in a later cursive, and some of the original glosses have been erased to make room for it.) III.p.9,85–m.9 on: fols 63r–4r.

P10 Paris, BN, nouv. acq. lat. 1478. s. xi¹, France (at Cluny). Gloss: R. (CPh with inl and mg glosses on fols 1r–55v.) III.p.9,85–m.9 on: fols 29v–30r.

P11 Paris, BN, lat. 6639. s. x, France (Puy?). Gloss: O. (CPh with inl glosses on fols 3r–72v. Lexical and short phrasal glosses only, sometimes similar to an abbreviated or incipient R; transcribed separately.) III.p.9,85–m.9 on: fol. 36r–v.

P12 Paris, BN, lat. 7183. s. x/xi. Gloss: O. (CPh with some inl glosses and a few mg on fols 24r–66r. Incomplete at beginning, inc. I.p.5,21 'meorum.' Side notes giving Greek rhetorical terms. Transcribed separately.) III.p.9,85–m.9 on: fols 40v–1r.

P14 Paris, BN, lat. 13953. s. x, Germany. Gloss: G. (Continua on CPh on fols 25va–41va. The same hand writes glosses on III.m.9 in two sections: on 35vb line 6 he writes 'ALITER' and begins the second. I have identified the second run as P14².) III.p.9,85–m.9 on: 35va–6rb.

T   Trier, Stadtbibliothek, 1093. s. xi^{med} (*recte* x/xi?), Echternach. Gloss: R. (CPh with inl and mg glosses on fols 118r–68r. On the evidence of shared variants, T is closely related to L4b.) III.p.9,85–m.9 on: fols 139v–41r.

V   Vatican City, Biblioteca Apostolica Vaticana, lat. 1592. s. xi/xii, Central Italy? Gloss: O. (CPh with brief inl glosses on fols 33r–83v. Glosses in at least 2 hands roughly contemporary with text. On III.m.9 the only mg glosses are by later cursive hands. Earlier inl glosses transcribed separately.) III.p.9,85–m.9 on: fol. 58r–v.

V1   Vatican City, Biblioteca Apostolica Vaticana, lat. 3363. Gneuss, *Handlist*, no. 908. Text s. ix^1, Loire region, glosses later – see Parkes in *Boethius*, ed. Gibson, 425–7 and Wittig, 'King Alfred's Boethius,' 161 n. 20 [see note 2, below]. Gloss: O. (CPh with inl and mg glosses on fols 1r–60r. Glosses often illegible. Transcribed separately.) III.p.9,85–m.9 on: fol. 29r–v.

V2   Vatican City, Biblioteca Apostolica Vaticana, lat. 3865. s. ix^{ex}, France. Gloss: R. (CPh with inl and mg glosses on fols 1r–57v.) III.p.9,85–m.9 on: fols 28v–9r.

V3   Vatican City, Biblioteca Apostolica Vaticana, lat. 4254. s. xiii^2, France. Gloss: R. (CPh with inl and mg glosses on fols 4v–80r. This manuscript stands out as a late, and continental?, copy of the English Z version.) III.p.9,85–m.9 on: fols 40v–1r.

V4   Vatican City, Biblioteca Apostolica Vaticana, lat. 5956. s. ix/x. Gloss: R,f; O. (CPh with inl and mg glosses on fols 2v–65v. The Bovo continua follows on 66r–73v in text hand. The mg glosses on fol. 33v have apparently been erased to make room for Bovo. At least 2 glossing hands contemporary with text; another, later by perhaps a century, writes many inl and mg, not always legible; these transcribed separately. Other glosses in still later hands.) III.p.9,85–m.9 on: fol. 33r–v.

V5   Vatican City, Biblioteca Apostolica Vaticana, Pal. lat 1581. s. x/xi, Germany. Gloss: R. (CPh with inl and mg glosses on fols 2r–69v.) III.p.9,85–m.9 on: fols 34v–5v.

V6   Vatican City, Biblioteca Apostolica Vaticana, Reg. lat. 1433. s. xii. Gloss: R. (CPh with inl and mg glosses on fols 1r–60r.) III.p.9,85–m.9 on: fols 29v–30r.

V7   Vatican City, Biblioteca Apostolica Vaticana, Reg. lat. 1727. s. xii. Gloss: R III.m.9. (CPh with many inl and a few mg glosses on fols 1r–23v, R continua inserted after metre in text hand. Mg esp. on I.m.1 and III.m.9; those on III.m.9, closest to Adalbold of Utrecht, transcribed separately.) III.p.9,85–m.9 on: fols 10v–11v.

W   Vienna, Österreichische Nationalbibliothek, 242. s. xii^{in}, S-W. Germany (Reichenau?). Gloss: O. (CPh with inl and some mg glosses on fols 2r–84r. Transcribed separately.) III.p.9,85–m.9 on: fols 39r–40r.

W1   Vienna, Österreichische Nationalbibliothek, 271. s. x^{ex}, S-W. Germany

(Reichenau?). Gloss: G/O. (CPh with inl and brief mg glosses on fols 2r–76r. Transcribed separately, though III.m.9 very badly faded and often illegible even with uv light.) III.p.9,85–m.9 on: fol. 37v.

Summary of 'continua' copies of R:
R on III.m.9 alone: B1, E1, Er, G1, L3, L4b, M, P3, P4, V7 (all but L4b written as continua).
R continua on more than or other than III.m.9: H, L, M4, Ma.

APPENDIX C: 'R' MSS: Sigles Grouped by Gloss Type, Date, and Provenance

Manuscripts Grouped by Longer Gloss Type for III.m.9 (and III.m.12)

W	(B) L4b E1 T Ma P9 V5 V4 (Ac) M P3 An M1 L
X	*x1* V2 P7
	x2 L1 P10
Y	P8 P5 P1
Z	*z1* C2 O Es
	z2 P9b P V3 A C4 Ge P6

Manuscripts Grouped by Date and (very crudely) Provenance

	'FRANCE'	'GERMANY'	ENGLAND	UNCERTAIN
s. x^1:	B	L4		V4
s. x:	An P7	E1 G1		P3
s. x^2:		T	C2 O	
s. x/xi:		Ma L L1 V5	P9 A P Ge C4 L2 O3	
s. xi^1:	P10		C Es O2 P6	
s. xi:	P8	M M1 M4	B1	
s. xi^2:	P5		C3	
s. xi/xii:	P1 V2	Go		V
s. xii^1:				
s. xii:		H	C1	P4 V6 V7
s. xii^2:				B2
s. xii/xiii:				
s. xiii^1:				
s. xiii:			O1	P2
s. xiii^2:	V3			
s. xiii/xiv:				L3
s. xiv^1:				
s. xiv:				
s. xiv^2:		Er		

Further details on origin / provenance:

B: Loire reg.	L4: Rhineland (Cologne?)	C2: St Aug. Cant.
An: (at St Evroul)	E1 G1: St Gall	O: St Aug. Cant.
P7: St Evre, Toul	T: Echternach	P9: Canterbury

P10: (at Cluny)	Ma: Cologne/Tegernsee	A: Abingdon
P5: (at Corbie)	L: So. Germany?	P: Christ Ch. Cant.
P8: Loire (Fleury?)	M1: So. Germany	Ge: Canterbury?
P1: W./S.W. (Poitiers? Toulouse?)	M4: Salzburg	C4: Abingdon
		Es: (at Horton)
		C3: St Aug. Cant
		O1: (at Lanthony Priory)

Uncertain. V: Central Italy?

NOTES

1 Pierre Courcelle, *La Consolation de Philosophie dans la tradition littéraire: Antécédents et postérité de Boèce* (Paris: Études Augustiniennes, 1967). The St Gall commentary is dated, on the evidence of the manuscripts, s. ix^{ex}; Remigius lived ca. 841–ca. 908 and Courcelle put the commentary on the *Consolatio* near the end of his career (but on his authorship see further below). Courcelle lists on page 406 the partial editions from Remigius published by Stewart, Silk, and Silvestre. For a list of published extracts by Stewart, Silk, Courcelle, Bolton, and Wittig see Colette Jeudy, 'Remigii autissiodorensis opera (*Clavis*),' in *L'École carolingienne d'Auxerre de Murethach à Remi 830–908: Entretiens d'Auxerre 1989*, ed. Dominique Iogna-Prat, Colette Jeudy, and Guy Lobrichon (Paris: Beauchesne, 1991), 457–500 at 485.

2 On the commentaries subsequent to Courcelle, see the following: Fabio Troncarelli, *Boethiana Aetas: Modelli grafici e fortuna manoscritta della 'Consolatio Philosophiae' tra IX e XII secolo* (Alessandria: Edizioni dell'Orso, 1987); Diane K. Bolton, 'The Study of the Consolation of Philosophy in Anglo-Saxon England,' *Archives d'histoire doctrinale et littéraire du Moyen Age* 44 (1977): 33–78; Troncarelli, *Tradizioni perdute: La 'Consolatio philosophiae' nell'alto medioevo* (Padua: Antenore, 1981); Jacqueline Beaumont, 'The Latin Tradition of the *De Consolatione Philosophiae*,' in *Boethius: His Life, Thought and Influence*, ed. Margaret Gibson (Oxford: Blackwell, 1981), 278–305; Joseph S. Wittig, 'King Alfred's Boethius and Its Latin Sources: A Reconsideration,' *ASE* 11 (1983): 157–98 [please note two errors in the list of manuscripts on page 188: P2 is BN lat. 6769; P6 is BN lat. 14380]; and Colette Jeudy, 'L'œuvre de Remi d'Auxerre: État de la question,' in *L'École carolingienne d'Auxerre*, ed. Iogna-Prat et al., 373–7 at 388. For a recent, succinct overview of the commentaries, see John Marenbon, *Boethius* (Oxford: Oxford University Press, 2003), 175–6. My edition of St Gall, Remigian, and other

early glosses on III.m.9 and m.12, will be published in conjunction with the Alfredian Boethius Project.

3 The first in 1975 was made possible by an ACLS grant, the second in 1981 by one from the Reynolds Foundation at the University of North Carolina at Chapel Hill supplemented by a grant from the American Philosophical Society. Troncarelli's survey of the early manuscript tradition of the *Consolatio* would not appear until 1987. *Codices Boethiani* will eventually offer a comprehensive census of manuscripts containing Boethius's works; the first three volumes of this series have now been published: *Codices Boethiani: A Conspectus of Manuscripts of the Works of Boethius*, vol. 1, *Great Britain and the Republic of Ireland*, ed. M.T. Gibson and Lesley Smith; vol. 2, *Austria, Belgium, Denmark, Luxembourg, The Netherlands, Sweden, Switerzland*, ed. Lesley Smith; vol. 3, *Italy and the Vatican City*, ed. Marina Passalacqua and Lesley Smith, Warburg Institute Surveys and Texts 25, 27, 28 (London: Warburg Institute, 1995–2001).

4 The earliest known manuscript is On (Orléans, Bibliothèque municipale, MS 270: for economy all MSS listed in Appendix II are referenced by sigles, which are resolved there). On's text is s. ix^{in}, apparently written at Fleury. Troncarelli, *Tradizioni perdute*, mounted a learned and elaborate argument that later copies of the text depend upon an exemplar originally prepared by Cassiodorus at Vivarium; Marenbon, *Boethius*, seems to accept Troncarelli's conclusions, but though the argument is informative I do not find it persuasive.

5 Five are late ninth- or early tenth-century manuscripts, one is tenth-century. The two fullest are both in Bern, Burgerbibliothek: MS 455, s. ix–x, is an anthology of poems containing eleven metres from CPh along with the designation of their metrical types but no other glosses (fols 26–32); MS A92.7, s. x, is a collection of twenty-two metres, or extracts therefrom, with a selection from Lupus of Ferrières' metrical tract; there is one lexical gloss.

6 I included here manuscripts dated s. ix, ix–x, x, and x–xi (not those dated s. xi or later). Three of these forty-one manuscripts, though once apparently complete copies, now survive only as fragments of two or three leaves. A forty-second full copy, Bonn MS 175 (36), reported by Courcelle as s. ix–x, was apparently lost during the Second World War.

7 Courcelle reported that the now lost Bonn 175 contained glosses of a mixed Remigius and St Gall type.

8 Bovo II, abbot of Corvey, 910–16. For these, and for the edition of them by R.B. Huygens, see Courcelle, *La Consolation*, 407–8.

9 For a complete list of Remigian manuscripts known to me see Appendix I;

since this list includes manuscripts dating from after the early eleventh century, it contains more than twenty-four entries. Manuscript 'counts' are complicated by the fact that some contain a combination of glosses, for example L4 and Ma, discussed below.
10 G, a St Gall gloss, also contains on the first recto an unidentified continuous gloss on CPh I.m.1 – I.p.1, 22.
11 V1 M2 M3 On, and Tours Bibl. mun. MS 803.
12 See Courcelle, *La Consolation*, esp. 275–8 and 403–4. Cf. Beaumont, 'The Latin Tradition,' 283–4.
13 On the date of the manuscript, see Hubert Silvestre, 'A propos de nouvelles éditions de commentaires à la Consolation de Boèce,' *Scriptorium* 9 (1955): 278–81 at 279.
14 'Remigian' glosses have been added to both manuscripts. L4 was obviously an elaborate enterprise: see David Ganz, 'A Tenth-Century Drawing of Philosophy Visiting Boethius,' in *Boethius: His Life, Thought and Influence*, ed. Gibson, 275–7. At III.m.9 the Bovo continuous commentary has been inserted immediately after the text of the metre and Remigian glosses subsequently written, marginally, on the lemmata of the Bovo continua; the 'Anonymous of Einsiedeln' continua on III.m.9 follows, then the text of the *Consolatio* resumes. Elsewhere in L4, where the text is less heavily glossed than 3M9, Remigian glosses have been added interlinearly and marginally. In Ma, a continuous copy of the Remigian glosses on the whole *Consolatio* follows the text.
15 My classification is based chiefly on the glosses of III.m.12.
16 Troncarelli, 'Per una ricerca sui commenti altomedievali al *de Consolatione* di Boezio,' in *Miscellanea in Memoria di Giorgio Cencetti*, Università degli studi di Roma, Sevola speciale per archivisti e bibliotecari (Turin: Bottega d'Erasmo, 1973), 363–80, arrived at similar conclusions concerning some of these early manuscripts; and see Marenbon on 'school' glossing (*From the Circle of Alcuin to the School of Auxerre* [Cambridge: Cambridge University Press, 1981], 116).
17 On Remigius, see Courcelle, *La Consolation*, esp. 278–90 and 405–6.
18 Courcelle, *La Consolation*, 241.
19 E.K. Rand, *Johannes Scottus* (Munich: Beck, 1906), 96. (The attribution is written in orange rustic capitals at the top of fol. 115v.)
20 Hans Naumann, *Notkers Boethius: Untersuchung über Quellen und Stil* (Strassburg: K.J. Trübner, 1913), 2. (The gloss occurs on fol. 146r.)
21 It is usually dated to the 'first half' of the eleventh century on the basis of the date 1048 in an Easter table on fol. 115r. Whatever cogency this argument might have, the hand that writes this table is not identical with the

one that writes the Boethian material, and the inks used to colour it are the same as those used to colour a diagram on fol. 140v which, though drawn before the glosses there (which are written around it), was never completed (it would have schematized the 'microcosm' discussed in the long glosses printed below) and it seems to have been rather crudely and inconsequentially 'decorated' later. It seems possible that both table and the colouring of the diagram were added independently of the Boethius (as material was added elsewhere in the manuscript) and that the date in the table has no direct bearing on the date of the Boethian material.

22 The attribution at the top of fol. 115v is followed by *Vitae* 3, 4, 2.4 – end. In the middle of the folio appears an incipit to the *Consolatio* (with the *cursus honorum* of Boethius's titles), followed by *Vita* 5.10–end and other introductory matter. Fol. 116r was originally blank; fols 116v–17 have a composite *Vita* (not edited with the others) and Lupus's metrical tract. There is another decorative incipit to the *Consolatio* on fol. 117v. The text itself begins on fol. 118r, the first leaf of a new quire. For the published *Vitae* see Rudolf Peiper, ed., *Anicii Manlii Severini Boetii Philosophiae Consolationis libri quinque* (Leipzig: Teubner, 1871), xxx–xxxv, and xiv–xxix for the metrical tract.

23 The gloss reads: 'explanatio greci versus deest quia penitus corruptus est' (L4, a relatively early copy of these glosses); cf. a gloss on the immediately following Latin that points out that the Latin supplies the sense of corrupted Greek: 'explanatio greci versus qui penitus corruptus est' (M1 Ma An).

24 Courcelle, *La Consolation*, 241–4.

25 V3 is neither Anglo-Saxon nor early, but apparently French and s. xiii^2; nevertheless its exemplar was clearly P or an exact copy of P. In P9 a second hand has added Z to W.

26 X seems to fall into two distinguishable subsets, *x1* (V2 P7) and *x2* (P10 L1).

27 For example, the longer glosses in V6 are found in either P10 or V2, those in O2 and C1 are found in P10. (This seems to confirm the X subgroups.)

28 The capital letters at the head of each gloss have been added here as a means of referencing the glosses.

29 I say 'by and large' because some of them are continuous commentaries; but even these contain glosses of every sort: lexical, brief phrases or clauses, and developed paragraphs. Since the Remigian glosses on III.m.9 circulated separately, continua played a particularly important part in preserving the W group on III.m.9: E1 Ma M P3 P4 V7. L4b, written as it is on the lemmata of the Bovo commentary, in effect resembles a continuous gloss on this metre.

30 In these longer glosses I have introduced boldfaced Arabic numerals to reference the gloss's sections.

31 P10 and L1 have it as a short, separate gloss, in nearly the same form as **H**.
32 Gloss **J**, the last one in MS L (a continua, S. Germany, s. xi^1), would then evidence the 'survival' of an earlier state of this gloss. It seems possible that an original gloss might be a comparatively full and learned one that subsequently got 'digested' and simplified as it was incorporated into a 'standard' set.
33 Rohini Jayatilaka reminds me that example **F**, an excerpt from Varro via Augustine, also occurs in M3 where it appears on fol. 36v, before CPh among *accesus* material. M3 is apparently earlier than N (ix^{med}) but lacks the attribution to Augustine and has textual variants which argue against N being copied directly from M3, so this gloss seems to have been in circulation. M3 shares the concluding tag 'opinatio tantum philosophorum non veritas,' which reflects in a generalized way Augustine's rejection of Varro's idea in *De ciuitate Dei*, and this explanation never became incorporated into a standard gloss set.
34 Compare the beginning of example **I**, where this notion is what the 'more prudent' set aside.
35 I have not yet found a suggestion of it in any earlier gloss.
36 'Mundus' probably harks back, at least in part, to lines 8–9 of the metre: 'Ducis ab exemplo ... mundum mente gerens similique in imagine formans.'
37 One might at first think that, since gloss **I** retains explanations found in earlier manuscripts, **I** is earlier than **H**. I would argue for seeing **I** as a teacher's 'sophistication' of **H**. **I** discards the more pallid comments on human *anima*, replaces them with an old chestnut to reject before offering a safer explanation. The phrasing of **I** at 3, alluding to a wide array of opinions some to be omitted, others compressed, suggests elaboration of the language in **H**; so does the addition of named authorities in section **8**.
38 See **J** 2. The continua in MS L stops at this point, apparently in mid gloss.
39 Jeudy, 'Remigii autissiodorensis opera,' 485–8, adds two items to this list: one, London BL Harley 2684 (s. ix$^{4/4}$) has glosses that I thought too few and brief to classify as Remi; the other, Florence, Biblioteca Medicea Laurenziana, San Marco 170 (s. x), which she says contains some glosses 'extraites en partie de Remi,' I have not seen.

Why Ditch the *Dialogues*? Reclaiming an Invisible Text

DAVID F. JOHNSON

Bishop Wærferth's OE translation of Pope Gregory the Great's *Dialogues* has, to date, inspired few scholars to pursue the text critically, or indeed to notice it at all. Recently Kees Dekker made the following observation: 'Apart from Hecht's 1900 edition, and several publications on language translation and manuscript provenance ... Anglo-Saxonists have not paid a great deal of attention to the Old English *Dialogi*.'[1] Reviewing the lack of scholarly attention received by the OE *Dialogues* over the past 100 years, one is forced to wonder why we bother to include them in the canon of Alfredian prose at all. True, they have not been literally exiled from that canon: no one has questioned, really, that Alfred commissioned their translation, though Alfred Smyth does doubt Bishop Wærferth's authorship.[2] But in fact, with some very few exceptions, the OE *Dialogues* have been almost completely rejected as a legitimate subject of critical research in our field.

This is a sorry state of affairs for the foundational text of the canon of Alfredian writings, and, as used to be thought, the very beginnings of English literary prose.[3] The cursory treatment of the *Dialogues* in the anthologies and introductions to Anglo-Saxon prose associated with Alfred's court is an indication of how the *Dialogues* are regarded generally in our field. In George K. Anderson's and Michael Alexander's surveys they are merely mentioned in a listing of Alfredian works without further comment.[4] Stanley B. Greenfield and Allen Calder note their status as the earliest of the translations, and echo Dorothy Whitelock's conclusion that they were intended for Alfred's own personal use, but there is nothing here that would recommend the work for further study, except for the importance of the two recensions for our understanding of the development of the language.[5] A.S. Cook and Chauncey Tinker's *Select Translations from Old English Prose*, reprinted in 1968, includes an extensive section of prose passages under the heading, 'The Works of King Alfred, and the Matter relating to Alfred.'[6] There the reader finds selections from Asser's *Life*, the *Pastoral Care*, *Orosius*, *Boethius*, and the *Soliloquies*. Apparently the *Dialogues* did not even qualify as 'Matter relating to Alfred.' Similar examples from other introductory surveys of Old English literature could be multiplied.[7]

Alfred's most recent biographers, Frantzen, Abels, and Smyth, are understandably preoccupied with the king, and restrict their discussion to the texts Alfred is thought to have written himself.[8] The *Dialogues* are noted, but little more than that. Smyth alone pays some attention to the subject, though his main concern is with the so-called pseudo-Asser, and, again, in the end he casts serious doubt on the likelihood of the text having been translated at Alfred's behest by Bishop Wærferth, as is generally believed.

In her discussion of the nature of OE prose in *The Cambridge Companion to Old English Literature*, Janet Bately does actually include a pair of passages from the *Dialogues*, but no further mention of the work is to be found in that volume.[9] The *Dialogues* are conspicuously absent as well from Bately's 1980 inaugural lecture 'The Literary Prose of King Alfred's Reign: Translation or Transformation?,' most recently anthologized in *Old English Prose: Basic Readings* (2000) edited by Paul Szarmach.[10]

Students of OE prose will have to turn elsewhere, then, for basic readings on the *Dialogues*, and it is not readily apparent where they should go. Szarmach's earlier collection of essays on OE prose *did* include one article devoted to the *Dialogues*, a brief piece by David Yerkes on their textual transmission, but in the other sixteen original essays any reference to the *Dialogues* is limited either to their position in the Alfredian canon – i.e., an item on the list – or to the Latin version. A glance at the select bibliography devoted to the *Dialogues* in that volume is equally telling: three scholars produced thirteen articles on the text worthy of mention prior to 1986.[11] No fewer than eleven of these were the work of one man, David Yerkes, whom Malcom Godden describes as the 'heroic exception' to the general critical marginalization of Wærferth's work, and 'whose two books and numerous articles on the Old English *Dialogues* have kept Wærferth visible almost single-handedly in the last two decades.'[12] Occasioning this remark is Godden's observation that 'it has always been hard to see where the work fitted into the king's scheme or his interests, and Wærferth remains a

Why Ditch the *Dialogues*? Reclaiming an Invisible Text   203

rather marginal figure in the story of Alfredian prose.'[13] I shall return to this problem in a moment.

But first let us explore the bibliographies just a bit further. In the new *Basic Readings* collection on OE prose mentioned above, Nicole Guenther Discenza provides an extensive bibliography on the works of Alfred, entitled 'Alfred the Great: A Bibliography with Special Reference to Literature.' It is divided into two parts, the first dealing with the primary texts: editions, facsimiles, and translations, followed by a much lengthier section on the secondary literature. The total number of primary works in the first section comes to ninety-one. Of these, thirty-one are devoted to the *Anglo-Saxon Chronicle*, thirteen to the *Boethius*, twelve to the *Laws*, seven each to the *Pastoral Care*, the *Soliloquies*, and the *Orosius*, and six to Asser and the Paris Psalter.[14] A further five items fall under the miscellaneous category, which includes material from several of the Alfredian texts, though notably not the *Dialogues*. Only one work in this rather long list pertains to our text: Hans Hecht's edition in Grein's *Bibliothek der angelsächsischen Prosa*. That is, less than 1 per cent of all the primary texts produced between 1568 and 2000 were devoted to the *Dialogues*.[15]

The bibliography of secondary literature reveals the same general picture. Of the 431 items in this section, 158 deal with the historical and cultural context of Alfred's day and age, including numismatics and the language and the chronology of Alfred's writings. Of the remainder, the works by Alfred himself have received the lion's share of critical attention: seventy-nine items pertain directly to the *Boethius*, forty-six to the *Pastoral Care*, and twenty, eighteen, and twenty-three to the *Psalms*, *Soliloquies*, and *Laws* respectively. Yet the *Orosius* – which like the *Dialogues* was not translated by Alfred himself – has attracted no fewer than forty-six studies. In this list, with its special reference to literature, there appear just three items dealing specifically with the *Dialogues*.

Now, the relative dearth of primary sources may be cited as one reason why the *Dialogues* have effectively been ditched, but this bibliography reveals a further, presumably unconscious bias. Its title and scope was no doubt chosen both to conserve space and keep it in line with the contributions appearing in the volume, most of which are concerned with the cultural contexts and literary contents of the Alfredian works they discuss, and not their language or manuscript transmission. This seems a reasonable explanation for the exclusion of Yerkes's considerable body of scholarship on the *Dialogues*. But why, then, does it include studies such as Kazumi Manabe 'Alfredian Finite and Non-Finite Clauses,' or John Tinkler, *Vocabulary and Syntax of the Old English Version of the Paris*

Psalter: A Critical Commentary?[16] There are numerous others here whose connection to literature and culture seems equally tenuous.[17]

Why, then, have the *Dialogues* suffered such neglect at the hands of Anglo-Saxonists? It seems to me that there are at least three main reasons for the short shrift given this text in the modern age, namely: 1) issues of canonicity and orthodoxy; 2) notions of correctness and literary worth; and 3) the lack of an accessible, reliable 'full service' edition.

Issues of Canonicity and Orthodoxy

As the foregoing survey in part demonstrates, not all critics would agree with Alfred Smyth's notion of which works belong in the Alfredian canon. Smyth's canon consists of Alfred's own productions and the works definitely commissioned by him: the *Dialogues*, *Psalms*, *Pastoral Care*, *Boethius* and *Soliloquies*. 'It may be,' he says, 'that we ought to view the works definitely associated with the king as an anthology inspired by his personal devotional and intellectual preferences, while other works less firmly associated with Alfred, bear the hallmarks of a more coherent scheme.'[18] Alfred's literary achievement, seriousness of purpose, piety, and devotion to learning are all esteemed by scholars, to some extent because of the strength of his legend and his status as a king whose own interests were so well aligned with those of the church. It would seem that the less Alfred has to do with a text, the less interested we are, revealing, perhaps, a disturbing tendency to construct hierarchies of texts based on other-than-literary reasons. Malcolm Godden contributes to this trend, perhaps unwittingly, when he writes, 'Given the brevity of the preface, and the uncertainty of its true authorship, it is hard to say what drove the king to commission a translation, if he really did.'[19] Because we cannot grasp the king's motives, or because those motives do not fit our preconceptions of a monarch's interests, we question even his tangential role in the production of the *Dialogues*. This kind of dissociation is perhaps the truest sign that the *Dialogues* have been all but ditched. Similarly, the *Dialogues* have been eclipsed by the later OE prose writings, presumably also because Wærferth (if indeed we accept Wærferth's authorship) was no Ælfric.

Notions of Correctness and Literary Worth

To a certain extent the degree to which we appreciate an adaptive translation is based on our perception of its relation to the original. How accurate a translation is it? Does its author misread that original at all? If so, how frequently and how seriously? Moreover, how skilfull an adaptation is it? That is, what does it add to the text, in terms of language, imagery, topical references, or alterations of material to make it more relevant or comprehensible to its new audience, and how well does it do this?

As textual scholars and philologists we are conditioned to ask these questions, to compare the translation to the original, put them side by side and closely scrutinize them to assess the relative skill of the translator. Inevitably, then, the level of success of such texts is determined by their relation to the original. This is all part of the business of textual scholarship and source study, and there is nothing inherently wrong with it. Unless it reduces the chances that a text will be read at all.

The *Dialogues* are for the most part a fairly close literal translation, although they are not entirely lacking in the kind of adaptive interventions found elsewhere in the canon that expose the voice of the adapter and his concerns for the value and purpose of the literary work for his own age. The work is neglected perhaps partly because of the perception that Wærferth did not translate with the same degree of imagination that Alfred did. Moreover, there is the added belief that Wærferth's command of Latin was so poor that it hardly warrants attention.[20] The consequences of this kind of attitude for the derogation of the *Dialogues* within the canon are far-reaching. For example, C.D. Jeffery's 1980 study of the underlying Latin texts of the *Dialogues* concludes with a statement that could hardly be more denigrating of its own subject:

> Taken together, the evidence presented here [i.e., on a postulated family of Latin manuscripts in England] suggests that interesting results might come from thorough study of these manuscripts. It also indicates that Gregory's *Dialogues* need the rigorous treatment given to the *Benedictine Rule* by Dr. Gretsch, though this would be no light undertaking, for the *Dialogues* are longer, and their pious credulity and primitive narrative make them irksome reading, whether in Latin or Old English.[21]

Something of the same attitude is reflected in the words of C.L. Wrenn, who, while he has some complimentary things to say about Wærferth's style, describes the contents as 'extremely naive' and 'often of a somewhat trivial character' and remarks that they have 'inevitably lost their appeal since the Middle Ages.'[22] A final statement by Wrenn essentially counters its own praise with gentle condemnation:

But with their emphasis on the greatness of St. Benedict in the second book, they would have a special attraction to the Anglo-Saxon religious public, and their simple and even credulous piety would accord well with what Asser tells us of King Alfred's own spiritual development.[23]

'Primitive,' 'naive,' 'trivial,' and 'credulous' are hardly the sorts of words to inspire a commitment to the *Dialogues* as a legitimate object of study. Charles Plummer's statement on this aspect of the *Dialogues* encapsulates a still lingering attitude towards them:

> If any evidence were needed to show that Alfred, with all his true and earnest piety, was yet in his religious thought the child of his century, it would be found in the fact that he should have chosen the *Dialogues* of Gregory as the first of all books to be translated. The work was enormously popular in the Middle Ages; but to our thought it is the least edifying of all Gregory's writings. In it the principle of St. James, that 'the effectual fervent prayer of a righteous man availeth much,' is materialised, until the prayers of the saints become a mere sort of lucky bag or wishing cap for the obtaining of anything that is wanted, from the raising of the dead, or the punishment of an enemy, to the supply of the most ordinary articles of domestic economy, such as oil, and wine, or the mending of a broken sieve ...[24]

The implication here is that the *Dialogues* reflect the uncritical faith of Alfred's day, and by extension his own early steps in that faith, which he was destined to outgrow.[25] Consequently they are not worthy of our attention, either.

Lack of an Accessible, Reliable, 'Full-service' Edition

The history of the edition we have is itself to some degree indicative of the problem with the *Dialogues*: the project was handed from scholar to scholar like some unwanted foster-child. Many of the biggest names in philology of the nineteenth century accepted, then passed on it until it finally landed on the desk of Hans Hecht – it passed first through the hands of Cockayne, Krebs, Skeat, Zupitza, Henry Johnson (at Wülker's suggestion), and Napier. Even then, when it was finally published, it was not in the series that at the time had the greatest influence on canon formation; it was not published by the Early English Text Society, but in Grein's *Bibliothek der angelsächsischen Prosa*. Not an insignificant venue by any means, the series essentially filled in gaps in coverage but it certainly did not have the staying power of EETS, a fact that would prove to be significant, I think, by the latter half of the twentieth century. Szarmach sums up the problem nicely in his recently published lament on the deplorable state of editions of the Alfredian corpus: 'Just as a good edition can direct study and the development of knowledge, the absence of good editions can have a chilling effect on a text or a system of texts.'[26] Szarmach's study considers

> the lamentable state of the texts that comprise the Alfredian corpus. Why the output of Alfred (*and his circle* [emphasis mine]) is not a major industry within Anglo-Saxon studies, given its strong start about one hundred years ago, may reflect several likely contributing causes, but the central contention here is that the failure of literary scholars to rise to the primary task has seriously blunted any movement towards an understanding of the literary and cultural record of Alfred and his circle ... What we read and what we study both leads and follows what we read and study in a reciprocal relationship that, in Alfredian studies, could and should be more fruitful.

Szarmach's analysis is accurate, but it also illustrates how the bias noted earlier has taken hold in what he reads and studies, for he makes no mention whatsoever of the *Dialogues*, a work which by anyone's reckoning must belong to Alfred's circle. Hecht's edition is not widely available, then, and this may have contributed to the fact that excerpts from the work have never been widely anthologized in our textbooks. They are not generally read and studied and their significance has fallen so low that they do not even merit inclusion in a general lament of the sorry state of Alfredian editions.[27]

In the article mentioned at the outset of this essay, Dekker counters one of the most important biases underlying the neglect of the *Dialogues*. He shows how Wærferth emphasized – through additions and adaptations in his translation, both at the lexical level and that of imagery – the use of miracle stories as a means of teaching, as examples to be followed by those who would lead the virtuous Christian life.[28] Furthermore, he argues that the audience for the book was not Alfred alone, but the secular clergy.[29] In fact, Dekker argues, a solid link can be forged between the purpose of the *Pastoral Care* and the *Dialogues*, in that we know that the former was translated for the benefit of those 'whose Latin was not yet sufficient for reading the work in its original form, and was meant to serve as a didactic instrument to educate the sons of the nobility for high offices in the Church.'[30] Like Dekker, I can see no reason why the *Dialogues* would not have served the same purpose: 'Whereas the *Regula pastoralis* taught the cognitive aspects of church governance, the *Dialogi* provided instruction into attitudinal aspects of governance, in that they were an inspiration for Christian virtuous conduct.'

The Latin *Dialogi*, too, have come under fire by critics who feel that such basic fare, such fabulous tales of miracles, could not have been written by the same mind who gave us the *Moralia in Job*, or the *Cura Pastoralis*. Dekker reminds us of how until recently the *Dialogi* were regarded as (in J.M. Petersen's characterization of previous scholarship) 'an aberration of an otherwise noble mind,' and how even the editor of what for a long time was the standard edition, Umberto Moricca, objected to (in Petersen's words) 'its superstition, credulity and historical inaccuracy.'[31] This attitude seems to have spilled over into the realm of the OE *Dialogues*, as well. William D. McCready's study of the *Dialogi* provides the single most significant corrective to this view.[32] For Gregory these miracles functioned as examples of virtuous living, and were meant to inspire the reader to strive for the same level of virtue.[33] Gregory's attitude towards the miracles sprang from his 'inclination to view the world allegorically.'[34] What indications are there that the Anglo-Saxons did not understand Gregory's purpose? Why should we suppose that the *Dialogues* were not read profitably by Alfred and later generations of Anglo-Saxons? We may not know exactly how widely disseminated the text was, but the existence of four manuscripts and possibly four redactions points irrefutably to serious interest in it.[35] Bede recommended it, as did Asser and Ælfric, the former for the eloquence of the translation, and the latter implicitly as an aid to the audience he was addressing in one of his homilies. The following passage appears in a brief hortatory address on the efficacy of the Mass in Ælfric's sermon on Tuesday of Rogationtide:

> Eac se halga papa Gregorius awrat on ðære bec dialogorum. hu micclum seo halige mæsse manegum fremode. Seo boc is on englisc awend. on ðære mæg gehwa be ðison genihtsumlice gehyran. se ðe hi oferrædan wile.[36]

[And the saintly Pope Gregory wrote in the book of the Dialogues about how Holy Mass had performed great things for so many. This work has been translated into English, in which whoever wishes to read through it may find much concerning this.]

The immediate context in Ælfric's homily is the story of the man taken captive by his enemies, whose bonds periodically burst because his brother, assuming him dead, has Masses said in his memory. On the face of it there is little difference between this anecdote and dozens of similar ones included in the *Dialogues*. The importance of Ælfric for the development of OE prose notwithstanding, this suggests how a charge of naivety against the narratives in the *Dialogues* is perhaps somewhat difficult to sustain.

Ælfric says that the OE translation is there to be read by 'whoever wishes to know more,' the underlying assumption being that some translation of the *Dialogi* is readily available and moreover appropriate for the audience he is addressing with this particular homily. That same audience, we may suppose, would have been included in the intended one for the original production of the *Dialogues*. If we acknowledge that Gregory's Latin *Dialogi* were actually written by him and worthy of consideration, and not just a collection of naive tales, we should also be prepared to recognize that they would have been read in OE in ways similar to their Latin counterparts. The uses to which they might be put are varied: as a missionary text and aid in conversion; as initial instruction for the unlearned who would never learn Latin; as a teaching text for someone who was learning the language (Alfred himself? OE and Latin could be laid side-by-side); or as an English language text to be read in a more sophisticated manner.

The *Dialogues* have virtually disappeared from Anglo-Saxon studies, then, because of their uncertain position within the Alfredian canon and some persistent misconceptions about their intended purpose, as well as the lack of an accessible, full-service edition. But finally, in this instance, as in a few others, perhaps we are not willing to grant vernacularity the respect it is due.

Let me conclude with two examples from our text, the first a story in book I of a nun who, while strolling in the garden of her convent spots a delicious-looking head of lettuce and is so overcome with desire for it that she does not wait to bless it with the sign of the cross before biting into it. In doing so, she unwittingly swallows a demon and falls to the ground, possessed. When Abbot Equitious is summoned to exorcize the devil, the latter complains that he was just minding his own business there on the lettuce when she came up and ate him. In the OE:

> þa ongan se deofol, þe þa nunnan swencte, of hire muþe clypian swylce he dædbote don wolde 7 þus cwæð, 'Hwaet dyde ic hire? Hwæt dyde ic hire? Ic me sæt on anum leahtrice, þa com heo 7 bat me.'[37]

> [Then the devil who had tricked the nun began to speak through her mouth as if he had come to confession, saying thus: 'What did I do to her? What did I do to her? I was just sitting on a lettuce when she came up and ate me.']

The devil is driven out, the nun restored, and a valuable lesson learned about the importance of blessing one's food before eating it.[38]

The second example is the story of the gardener (*wyrtweard*), the snake, and the thief (book I, ch. 3).[39] Here Gregory repeats a story told him by the monastery's newly elected provost Felix, who had previously been the gardener. He had noticed how the plants in the garden were being stolen and trampled, and so he sought out a snake and commanded it to stand watch at the place in the garden wall where the thief was wont to enter. This the snake did without protest, and the thief was caught, admonished, and reformed.

What would a member of the secular clergy, one being tutored, perhaps, because he had no Latin and could not (yet) appreciate it in the original, make of these stories? Does the first teach that there is a devil set aside for all our vegetables? Would he have been encouraged to view the second as a mere illustration of 'the effectual fervent prayer of a righteous man,' as Plummer would have it, or a more practical recommendation to use snakes as garden watchdogs? Both, in my view, are equally absurd. Rather, we would do well to remember Gregory's inclination to view the world allegorically mentioned above. Thomas D. Hill has shown how the Anglo-Saxons would have learned to read saints' lives figurally, whether in Latin or the vernacular:

> The point is that hagiographers and their audience believed simultaneously in the reality of the miraculous and yet were aware that a given miracle in a specific saint's life might bear symbolic meaning as well. And if it was only a symbol, if the miracle never existed as an event within history, this did not affect the larger truth of the narrative as a whole.[40]

The significance of a snake standing guard over a garden, then, would not have escaped a reader (or teacher) schooled in the interpretive methods promoted by Gregory, and the implications for the use of the

the work seem clear. While it contains only one saint's life proper (book II, the *Life of St. Benedict*) I would argue that the *Dialogues* may be most profitably read in the realm of hagiography: they constitute a storehouse of some of the earliest surviving vernacular hagiographical anecdotes and exempla we have, and as such should be read, perhaps, alongside the *Lives* written by Ælfric, rather than against the other translations in King Alfred's program.[41] To the Anglo-Saxons, the cultural importance of the *Dialogues* was their function within what Michael Lapidge calls the 'cumbersome apparatus for knowing [the saints] and appealing to them ... in an age when other kinds of spiritual comfort were few.'[42]

While I would not argue that the *Dialogues* are a masterpiece, callously and inexplicably overlooked by most of our predecessors and many of our colleagues, there does seem to be a considerable discrepancy in the critical principles applied in our post-enlightenment age and those wielded by the literate Anglo-Saxons who constituted their audience, and this has had detrimental consequences for our reception of the OE text. Those principles define the aesthetic by which these works are judged, and upon some reflection one may agree that this is hardly fair from a cultural-historical point of view. Finally, then, we need a new edition of this text,[43] but we also need to take the *Dialogues* out from under the shadow of Alfred the King, and at the same time put them back where they belong, in his canon of books 'most fit for men to know.'

NOTES

Earlier versions of this paper were delivered at the International Medieval Conference at Leeds in 2002, and the conference 'Making the Text: Medieval and Beyond' at Cornell University in 2004. I wish to thank all those who provided feedback on those occasions, especially Elaine Treharne, Jonathan Wilcox, Andrew Galloway, Anne Middleton, and Thomas D. Hill.

1 Kees Dekker, 'King Alfred's Translation of Gregory's *Dialogi*: Tales for the Unlearned?' in *Rome and the North: The Early Reception of Gregory the Great in Germanic Europe*, ed. Rolf H. Bremmer, Jr, Kees Dekker, and David F. Johnson, Mediaevalia Groningana n.s. 4 (Paris: Peeters, 2001), 27–50 at 27.
2 Alfred Smyth, *King Alfred the Great* (Oxford: Oxford University Press, 1995), 543–8.

3 But see Janet Bately, 'Old English Prose before and during the Reign of Alfred,' *ASE* 17 (1988): 93–138, who makes a good case for an Old English prose tradition and style predating the Alfredian texts, including the *Dialogues*.
4 George K. Anderson, *The Literature of the Anglo-Saxons* (New York: Russell & Russell, 1962), 291; Michael Alexander, *Old English Literature* (New York: Schocken Books, 1983), 144–5.
5 Stanley B. Greenfield and Allen Calder, *A New Critical History of Old English Literature*, with a Survey of the Anglo-Latin Background by Michael Lapidge (New York: New York University Press, 1986), 42–3; Dorothy Whitelock, 'The Prose of Alfred's Reign,' in *Continuations and Beginnings: Studies in Old English Literature*, ed. Eric Gerald Stanley (London: Nelson, 1966), 67–103 at 68.
6 A.S. Cook and Chauncey Tinker, eds and trans., *Select Translations from Old English Prose* (New York: Gordian, 1968), 3–146.
7 Similarly, M.W. Grose and Deirdre McKenna's volume *Old English Literature*, Literature in Perspective (Totowa, NJ: Rowman and Littlefield, 1973), includes a section on Alfredian prose but fails even to mention Wærferth's translation (see pages 30–40).
8 Allen J. Frantzen (*King Alfred* [Boston: Twayne, 1986], 8) includes the following disclaimer: 'Anyone wishing to appreciate the literary context of Alfred's England must study these texts. But because we know that Alfred did not translate them, and because we cannot be sure if most of them bear any certain relationship to his own literary program, they fall outside the limits of the present study.' See also Richard Abels, *Alfred the Great: War, Kingship and Culture in Anglo-Saxon England*, The Medieval World (London: Longman, 1998), for a similar view.
9 Bately, 'The Nature of Old English Prose,' in *The Cambridge Companion to Old English Literature*, ed. Malcolm Godden and Michael Lapidge (Cambridge: Cambridge University Press, 1991), 71–87.
10 Janet Bately, 'The Literary Prose of King Alfred's Reign: Translation or Transformation?' in *Old English Prose: Basic Readings*, ed. Paul E. Szarmach with the assistance of Deborah Oosterhouse (New York: Garland, 2000), 3–27.
11 Yerkes, 'The Translation of Gregory's *Dialogues* and Its Revision: Textual History, Provenance, Authorship,' in *Studies in Earlier Old English Prose*, ed. Paul E. Szarmach (Albany, NY: SUNY Press, 1986), 335–43; Carl T. Berkhout, 'Appendix: Research on Early Old English Literary Prose, 1973–82,' ibid., 401–9 at 406–7.
12 Malcolm Godden, 'Wærferth and King Alfred: The Fate of the Old English *Dialogues*,' in *Alfred the Wise: Studies in Honour of Janet Bately on the Occasion*

of Her Sixty-Fifth Birthday, ed. Jane Roberts, Janet L. Nelson, and Malcolm Godden (Cambridge and Rochester, NY: D.S. Brewer, 1997), 35–51 at 35, n.2.

13 Godden, 'Wærferth and King Alfred,' 35.

14 We may now add Patrick O'Neill's new edition of the Paris Psalter, thus increasing the number of primary works devoted to the psalms to seven: *King Alfred's Old English Prose Translation of the First Fifty Psalms,* ed. O'Neill, Medieval Academy Books 104 (Cambridge, MA: Medieval Academy of America, 2001).

15 The first primary text published was Lambarde, *APXAIONOMIA, sive de priscis Anglorum legibus libri, sermone Anglico, vetustate antiquissimo* ... (1568), rev. by Abraham Wheloc (Cambridge: R. Daniel, 1644). Among the others I do not include the translation of Asser and other Alfredian sources in Simon Keynes and Michael Lapidge, trans., *Alfred the Great: Asser's 'Life of King Alfred' and Other Contemporary Sources* (Harmondsworth: Penguin, 1983), or in J.A. Giles, ed., *The Whole Works of King Alfred the Great, with Preliminary Essays Illustrative of the History, Arts, and Manners of the Ninth Century,* Jubilee ed., 2 vols (Oxford: J.F. Smith, 1852), because both include only Alfred's Preface to Wærferth's translation. Keynes and Lapidge also print a translation of the metrical preface to MS O (British Library MS Cotton Otho C.i), long assumed to be by Bishop Wulfsige, though this has been recently questioned by Smyth.

16 Kazumi Manabe, 'Alfredian Finite and Non-Finite Clauses,' *Studies in English Language and Literature* 38 (1988): 87–107; John Tinkler, *Vocabulary and Syntax of the Old English Version of the Paris Psalter: A Critical Commentary* (The Hague: Mouton, 1971).

17 To name just two, Otto Exter, '*Beon* und *wesan* in Alfreds Übersetzungen des Boethius "De Consolatione Philosophiae"' (PhD dissertation, Königl. Christian-Albrechts-Universität, 1911), and Max Förster, 'Die altenglischen Texte der Pariser Nationalbibliothek,' *Englische Studien* 62 (1927): 113–31.

18 Smyth, *King Alfred,* 530.

19 Godden, 'Wærferth and King Alfred,' 48.

20 Alfred's biographer, Asser, had a higher regard for Wærferth's Latinity than some modern readers: 'Werferth, the bishop of Worcester, a man thoroughly learned in holy writings who at the king's command translated for the first time the *Dialogues* between Pope Gregory and his disciple Peter from Latin into the English language, sometimes rendering sense for sense, translating intelligently and in a very polished style ...'; *Vita Alfredi,* in *King Alfred,* trans. Keynes and Lapidge, 92.

21 C.D. Jeffery, 'The Latin Texts Underlying the Old English *Gregory's Dialogues* and *Pastoral Care,*' *NQ* n.s. 27 (1980): 483–8 at 487.

22 C.L. Wrenn, *A Study of Old English Literature* (London: George G. Harrap, 1967), 213.
23 Wrenn, *A Study of Old English Literature*, 214.
24 Charles Plummer, *The Life and Times of Alfred the Great*, Ford Lectures, 1901 (1902; repr. New York: Haskell House, 1970), 142–3.
25 In 'Wærferth and King Alfred,' Godden makes much the same argument, though based on a different aspect of the OE *Dialogues*, namely Wærferth's less than competent rendering of them from Latin. His Latin was so bad as to lead Godden to 'ponder whether the king had by this stage surpassed the bishop, and what is more, whether he knew that he had. But the gap between them was perhaps not only a question of Latinity and style but also a matter of content and ideology. Given the brevity of the preface, and the uncertainty of its true authorship, it is hard to say what drove the king to commission a translation, if he really did' (48). Godden goes on to wonder about the imperfect historical parallels to Alfred's situation offered by the *Dialogues*, as compared to the *Orosius* and the introduction to the *Boethius*. Here, in my view, he rather misses the mark. Why should the *Dialogues* have 'to provide the sustained account of history he got' from those other texts? That does not seem to me to be the right question to ask in relation to the *Dialogues*. Godden's conclusion was as follows: 'Alfred probably learnt to be less than impressed with the learning of Wærferth; but he grew also more concerned with a learning which related to the problems of government' (51). This may have been the case, but the *Dialogues* does not strike me as the kind of text upon which one could impose such demands.
26 Paul E. Szarmach, 'Editions of Alfred: The Wages of Un-influence,' in *Early Medieval English Texts and Interpretations: Studies Presented to Donald G. Scragg*, ed. Elaine Treharne and Susan Rosser, MRTS 252 (Tempe: Arizona Center for Medieval and Renaissance Studies, 2002), 135–49 at 135; the quotation following is from page 1. Emphasis is mine.
27 I know of only one exception to this 'rule,' namely Peter S. Baker's online 'Old English Aerobics,' which includes a passage from book II on the Life of St Benedict. See http://www.engl.virginia.edu/OE/OEA/.
28 Dekker, 'King Alfred's Translation,' 46, makes an extremely compelling case for the claim that Alfred, like Gregory, 'considered miracles to be signs of sanctity, and regarded the stories as examples containing implicit instruction on the nature of Christian life for the edification of the readers.'
29 Dekker, 'King Alfred's Translation': 'King Alfred's interest in Gregory's *Dialogues* teaches us, if anything, that he must have been sympathetic towards monastic communities, and aware of their importance for the Church and religion' (48). Gregory's interest in monasticism (reflected in

the *Dialogi* by the abundance of stories dealing with monks, nuns, abbots, monasteries and the like) is not, Dekker remarks, reflected in Alfred's own policies, as he is likely to have given 'the organization and reconstruction of the secular church precedence over the founding of monasteries' (ibid.). His conclusion states: 'It is likely, therefore, that the Old English translation of the *Dialogues* was intended primarily for an audience of secular clergy, to be educated in the Minster Schools attached to a bishop's see' (ibid.).

30 Dekker, 'King Alfred's Translation,' 48 (the quotation following is from the same page).
31 Dekker, 'King Alfred's Translation,' 31 and n. 26, citing Joan M. Petersen, *The 'Dialogues' of Gregory the Great in Their Late Antique Cultural Background*, Studies and Texts 69 (Toronto: Pontifical Institute of Mediaeval Studies, 1984), xv–xvi.
32 William D. McCready, *Signs of Sanctity: Miracles in the Thought of Gregory the Great*, Studies and Texts 91 (Toronto: Pontifical Institute of Mediaeval Studies, 1989).
33 Dekker, 'King Alfred's Translation,' 32.
34 McCready, *Signs of Sanctity*, 5.
35 See Paul E. Szarmach, 'Another Old English Translation of Gregory the Great's *Dialogues*?' *ES* 62 (1981): 97–109, on the underlying OE translation of the *Dialogues* in Vercelli Homily XIV, as well as Godden, 'Wærferth and King Alfred,' 44, who notes that Wulfstan used someone else's translation of book IV, ch. 1. Together with the two redactions represented in the manuscripts C, H, O and A, then, we have evidence of the existence of two further redactions.
36 *Ælfric's Catholic Homilies: The Second Series. Text*, ed. Malcolm Godden, EETS s.s. 5 (London: Oxford University Press, 1979), 205 (translation mine). MS G adds: 'gyf he þæt angit understandan cann.'
37 *Bischofs Wærferth von Worcester Übersetzung der Dialoge Gregors des Grossen*, ed. Hans Hecht, 2 vols, BaP 5 (1900; repr. in one vol., Darmstadt: Wissenschaftliche Buchgesellschaft, 1965), bk 1, ch. 4, pp. 30–1.
38 See Paul Schaffner, 'The Errant Morsel in *Solomon and Saturn II*: Liturgy, Lore, and Lexicon,' *MS* 57 (1995): 223–57, for further associations of signing one's food, but especially the Eucharist, in a wide range of early Christian and medieval texts.
39 *Bischofs Wærferth*, ed. Hecht, bk. I, ch. 3, pp. 23–5.
40 Thomas D. Hill, '*Imago Dei*: Genre, Symbolism, and Anglo-Saxon Hagiography,' in *Holy Men and Holy Women: Old English Prose Saints' Lives and Their Contexts*, ed. Paul E. Szarmach (Albany, NY: SUNY Press, 1996), 35–50 at 46.
41 I am indebted to Jonathan Wilcox for this helpful insight.

42 Michael Lapidge, 'The Saintly Life in Anglo-Saxon England,' in *The Cambridge Companion*, ed. Godden and Lapidge, 243–63 at 261.
43 At this juncture in the argument it may not surprise the reader to learn that I am engaged in preparing just such a new edition, together with Rolf H. Bremmer, Jr, of Leiden University.

Hagiography and Violence: Military Men in Ælfric's *Lives of Saints*

E. GORDON WHATLEY

This paper examines the intersection of Christian sanctity and violence in Ælfric's *Lives of Saints*, where legends of military martyrs such as King Edmund are juxtaposed with those of warrior saints such as King Oswald. While the military martyr stories celebrate soldiers who, like Edmund, give up their lives passively, without resisting their heathen persecutors, a small group of legends glorifies saints like Oswald who fight and kill their heathen foes. The collection in this way prompts us to think about war and peace in a Christian context, and more specifically about the place of sanctioned violence within a religion ostensibly grounded in love and non-violence.[1]

It is well known that Ælfric compiled his *Lives of Saints* late in the closing decade of the tenth century at a time of developing military and social crisis in England, when large Viking fleets were raiding English ports, venturing inland to encounter only occasionally tough resistance from the local militias, and extorting huge amounts of tribute money from the English leadership. Ælfric's *Lives*, commissioned by and for two of these leaders – Æthelweard *ealdorman* and his son Æthelmær – is an intriguing work to fit into this historical context.[2] Since the dedicatees of the collection were members of the West-Saxon military aristocracy, it is understandable that the largest group of legends in the strictly hagiographic portion of the collection should concern laymen, and especially royal saints and military types (ten out of twenty-six by my count, and there are more if one includes additional figures like Gallicanus in *Lives* VII [Agnes]). This secular male group is twice as large as any other in the *Lives*.[3] Most of them are martyrs, however, including most notably King Edmund (*Lives* XXXII [Edmund]). In a memorable passage, Edmund confronts his Viking enemies by renouncing violence and 'throwing away his weapons' [103: awearp his wæpna], in explicit imitation of Jesus in Gethsamene when he forbade his disciple Peter to 'fight with weapons' [105: mid wæpnum to winnenne]. After this Edmund patiently submits to torture and, ultimately, execution without resisting his Viking foe, Hingwar (106–26).

This striking vignette of a Germanic warrior king repudiating combat has seemed puzzling or at least awkward to modern readers,[4] and it is not surprising that some later medieval English writers revised the story to show Edmund fighting and defeating the Danish army prior to his capture.[5] Edmund's martyrdom has been explained by some historians (commenting not so much on Ælfric as on his Latin source, Abbo of Fleury's *Passio Eadmundi*),[6] as a representation of the ideal of sacralized kingship, and Edmund's priestlike renunciation of violence as a reflection of his 'sacerdotal' status.[7] A recent, more radically historicist reading argues that Ælfric in his simplified rendering of the Latin *passio* is advocating a policy of non-violence and Christian pacifism towards the Danes, who were once again ravaging England a century or more after Edmund's martyrdom.[8]

In a parallel vignette, in Ælfric's life of Saint Martin of Tours (*Lives* XXXI [Martin]), Martin decides to quit his military service the day before an impending battle against invading barbarians, and when the emperor Julian therefore accuses him of cowardice, Martin declares himself willing to be placed unarmed in the Roman front lines when battle is joined. God, however, prompts the invaders to sue for peace, not merely to save Martin's life but also so that, as Ælfric explains (following the Latin life by Sulpicius), other men's deaths should not sully Martin's sight, 'þæt furðon næron ge-wemmede / martines gesihþa on oðra manna deaðe' (126–7).[9]

In Ælfric's legend of the Theban Legion (*Lives* XXVIII [Maurice]), Christ's refusal to allow Peter to use his sword to fight off the guards in Gethsemane is again invoked, this time by the Roman Christian officers, Maurice and Exuperius, who order the entire Theban legion, all Christians, to 'throw down their weapons' [awurpan heora wæpna him fram] and submit to execution by pagan troops of the emperor Maximian, for refusing to sacrifice to the emperor's gods (59–65). Ælfric tells how the executioners go to work, 'as if chopping wood' [69: swa swa mann wudu hywð], while the Theban legionaries happily stretch out their necks 'to be slaughtered for Christ and would not fight with weapons against them' [70–2: mid glædnysse efston / astræhton heora swuran to slæge for criste / and noldon mid wæpnum winnan him togeanes].

Earlier in the collection, Ælfric's patrons would have encountered the legend of the Sebasteni (*Lives* XI [Forty Soldiers]), another group of Christian legionaries who passively submit to various tortures before their execution, offering only prayers to God as a defence against pain and humiliation. Stripped naked by their pagan persecutors, they are shamefully taunted, 'mid bysmorfullum edwite,' and, in the middle of a severe winter, forced to stand for a whole night in the icy waters of a mountain lake (141–55). Ælfric's *Lives* collection as a whole, with its many other martyrs, male and female, is of course full of images of patient suffering in the name of Christ. But the images of military men such as Edmund, the Thebans, and the Sebasteni, giving up their weapons and lives without a struggle, must have been especially striking and, one would suppose, disturbing to warrior aristocrats like Ælfric's patrons.

Readings of a different kind, however, are available in the *Lives*, in the group of legends that the Cotton manuscript scribe numbers XXV–XXVII, and that provides a more positive image of conventional warfare and military activity. Not only is *Lives* XXV (The Maccabees) the second longest item in Ælfric's collection (862 lines), it was also apparently among the most popular, surviving today in eight copies.[10] Although beginning with the martyr stories of the scribe Eleazar and the mother and her seven sons (1–204), most of this lengthy work is devoted to the armed resistance mounted by Judas Machabeus and his brothers against the Seleucid kings who claimed hegemony over Israel in the second century B.C. Recent studies have pointed out various ways in which Ælfric has rewritten the Vulgate Maccabees so as to frame its Old Testament heroes in a Christian perspective, in the process toning down some of the violence in the original.[11] But it seems to me misleading to suggest that Ælfric's version 'fully reverse[s] the glorification of physical battle' displayed in the Latin original.[12] On the contrary, Ælfric seems happy to indulge occasionally in the poetry of war, even while simplifying and abbreviating this copious source in his habitual manner.

In the initial description of Judas Machabeus, for example, Ælfric renders the prosaic Latin, 'Et surrexit Iudas, qui vocabatur Machabeus,' into a heroic verse rich in sound effects, introduced by the untranslatable *hwæt* with its native poetic associations: 'Hwæt ða iudas machabeus mihtiglice aras / in his fæder stede' [274–5: *Hwæt*! then Judas Machabeus mightily rose up / in his father's stead]. The rest of the passage follows the Vulgate closely (1 Macc. 3:1–3) but Ælfric adds touches of glamour here and there: for example, Judas's breastplate (Vulgate *lorica*) becomes 'his scynendan byrnan' [279: shining corslet] and wearing it he resembles not just a giant (Vulgate *gigas*) but an 'ormæte ent' [280: huge giant].

After this spirited ode to Judas's warfare and fame, Ælfric devotes the next 400 lines to a sort of military celebration, replete with purple passages,[13] of a series of Maccabean victories over the Seleucid armies, giving frequent prominence to the courage and ferocity of the Jewish warriors, their determination never to resort to flight merely to save their lives, the justice of their cause, and their piety and reliance on prayer to God before each battle: all of which enables them to defeat much larger forces than their own. Finally, Ælfric recounts the death of Judas Machabeus in battle (672) and pauses to sum up and offer interpretations that reveal his ambivalence about the warfare that was endemic in Old Testament times and urgently necessary in his own (*Lives* XXV, 676–714). Here he uses language apparently calculated to invoke the idea of the just war (discussed below). He explains that Judas's battles and 'ealle ða mihte þe he mærlice gefremode' [678: all the mighty deeds that he gloriously performed] were 'for his freonda ware ... his folce to gebeorge' [677, 679: to protect his kinsmen ... and defend his people]. Ælfric's choice of words here implies the morality of Judas's warfare, undertaken to defend his supporters and his people against an unrighteous, heathen enemy, and to do the will of the Almighty, 'for willan þæs ælmihtigan' (683).[14] Notice the rhetorical linkage between the divine epithet 'ælmihtigan' and 'ealle ða mihte' [678: all the mighty deeds] which made Judas famous. For such reasons, Ælfric concludes, Judas Machabeus, 'godes ðegen' [686: God's thane] who defended his people against the 'onwinnendan' [687: invaders], is just as 'holy' in the Old Testament as 'God's chosen,' the apostles, in the New Testament (681–2). But at this point, having seemingly endorsed the concept of the holy warrior and invoked the notion of just war, Ælfric appears to do an about-face. Suddenly he reminds us of the barrier between the Old and New Testaments. Christ, he says, taught us differently, that is, 'to preserve peace and righteousness' [689: healdan sibbe and soðfæstnysse], by doing battle with spiritual weapons, not against physical foes but spiritual, invisible ones 'who wish to slay our souls with vices' (692). We must gain protection [693: 'gescyldnysse'] from sin through prayer and be God's champions [697: 'godes cempan'] in a spiritual conflict. The physical conflicts depicted in the Old Testament are apparently to be read for their spiritual signification, 'getacnunge' (702), as moral contests waged by Christian holy men with spiritual weapons against invisible ('ungesewenlican') enemies (688–93). So after hundreds of lines of carefully detailed military heroism and holy war, we are told it is all meant to be read typologically and allegorically, as a sort of *Psychomachia*.

Another about-face follows quickly, however, as Ælfric cites the teachings of the doctors of the church, 'lareowas,' concerning the four types of war, the first of which is *justum*, 'rihtlic,' which Ælfric, embellishing Isidore of Seville,[15] pointedly exemplifies as the kind being fought against the 'reðan flot-menn' [the cruel Vikings] and others who wish to destroy the land (705–9). The parallel between this and the Maccabean struggles is plain enough.[16]

Thus Ælfric in quick succession seems to endorse, then reject, then endorse the appropriateness of physical warfare for Christians. He goes some way to resolving this apparent contradiction in the well-known coda to the Maccabees chapter of the *Lives*, where he invokes the theory of the three orders of society: '*laboratores, oratores, bellatores*' (814–15).[17] Here he again affirms the validity of warfare aimed at an invading army, 'onwinnendne here' (818), a phrase that he has used twice before to characterize the enemies of the Hebrew insurgents (589, 719), and that he would use some years later in the letter to the nobleman Sigeweard, urging him to take inspiration from such biblical histories as Judith and Holofernes and the Maccabees, and defend his country 'mid wæ(p)num' against the Danish invaders.[18] Here in the Maccabees coda (812–26) Ælfric also seems to clarify what he meant earlier about the New Testament successors of the Old Testament warriors doing battle with spiritual rather than physical weapons. He explains that the *oratores*, the order of clergy, who must 'feohtan gastlice wið þa ungesewenlican fynd' [822: fight in a spiritual way against the invisible enemies], are physically protected as they do so by the *bellatores*, or 'woruld-cempa(n)' [secular warriors]. The rest of the coda reveals Ælfric's unequivocal concern to discredit what some of the English clergy were doing at this time: namely, going to war.[19] It would appear from this that Ælfric's figurative interpretation of Old Testament warfare applies to his own *ordo* of monks and priests, whom he vehemently forbids to do military service, but not to laymen, who are free to take Judas Machabeus as a literal model when they 'wið þa gesewenlican gesewenlice feohtað' [826: fight visibly against the visible (enemies)].

Comparisons of ostensibly just Christian fighters to the Maccabees were not uncommon before Ælfric's time. As J.E. Cross has pointed out,

Stephen of Ripon in his life of Bishop Wilfrid tells how, in response to a revolt of the 'bestial' Picts, King Ecgfrith of Northumbria 'trusting in God like Judas Machabeus ... attacked [them] with his little band of God's people' and slew so many of them that he filled two rivers with their corpses.[20] Such improvised typologies were also cultivated by Carolingian and Ottonian writers.[21] Ælfric's topos of invisible and visible enemies was likewise something of a commonplace. It figures prominently in pseudo-Basil, *Admonitio ad filium spiritualem*, reputedly translated by Ælfric himself,[22] and had also been invoked by Augustine of Hippo in an important letter to Count Boniface, the embattled and controversial military governor of North Africa during the closing years of Roman rule (ca. 423–30), in which the bishop assures the count (who after his first wife's death had been contemplating monastic withdrawal) that his military calling is acceptable to God, although less exalted than that of the celibate clergy:

> Do not imagine that no one can please God while he is engaged in military service ... Those who serve God with the highest self-discipline of chastity, by renouncing all ... worldly activities, have a more prominent place before Him: 'But everyone hath his proper gift from God, one after this manner and another after that' [1 Cor. 7:7]. Thus, some fight for you against invisible enemies by prayer, while you strive for them against visible barbarians by fighting.[23]

Less complicated than Ælfric's *Maccabees* in their portrayal of Christian warfare are the two legends immediately following in the *Lives*: *King Oswald* (XXVI) and *The Exaltation of the Holy Cross* (XXVII), both of which associate the Christian cross with violence. Ælfric's story of Oswald of Northumbria, taken from Bede's *Historia Ecclesiastica*, is too well known to need detailed rehearsal here: most pertinent are the lines summarizing Oswald's early battle against Cædwalla, king of the Britons: 'Oswold him com to and him cenlice wiðfeaht / mid lytlum werode ac his geleafa hine getrymde, / and crist him gefylste to his feonda slege' [14–16: Oswald came at him and fought against him bravely with a small force, but his faith strengthened him, and Christ helped him kill his enemies]. The phrase 'mid lytlum werode' recalls Judas Machabeus's first battle (*Lives* XXV [Maccabees], 352, 'mid lytlum werode'), but one is somewhat taken aback by the bald statement that 'crist' helped Oswald to kill his enemies. Bede is more evasive, using an anonymous passive verb, *interemtus est*, for the killing of Cædwalla, and a participial construction explaining that 'faith in Christ' made up for the Northumbrians' small numbers: 'cum paruo exercitu, sed fide Christi munito.'[24] Ælfric follows Bede closely, however, in relating a few lines later how Oswald evokes the formulas of just warfare during his call to prayer at the foot of the famous cross erected near the site of the coming battle: 'god sylf wat geare þæt we winnað rihtlice / wið þysne reðan cyning to ahredenne ure leode' [22–4: God himself knows well that it is right for us to fight against this cruel king, to save our people].[25] A few lines earlier (11–12), Ælfric has followed Bede in emphasizing the wickedness of Cædwalla's conduct among the Northumbrians, implying that Oswald's war is just not only because he is defending his people, but also because he is inflicting due punishment for a neighbouring ruler's unredressed wrongs. This, and not simply defence of homeland, was the justification for war according to Augustine of Hippo.[26]

Righteous warfare, both defensive and punitive, figures prominently also in the Holy Cross legend (*Lives* XXVII [Exaltation of the Cross])[27] immediately following *King Oswald* in Ælfric's collection, which for reasons of space I can only glance at. Here we find another surprising one-liner crediting Christ himself with killing a human being. The pious emperor Heraclius first dispatches the Persian commander in single combat and later beheads his father, the mad emperor, Cosdrue, who has stolen the Holy Cross from Jerusalem and, thinking himself a god, keeps it as his consort ('geferan') next to his throne (42–3). It is for this act of sacrilege, according to Ælfric, that 'crist hine fordyde' [45: Christ destroyed him], which has no equivalent in the surviving texts of the source.[28] It should be pointed out that, of the three military legends we have been considering, this one involves the least loss of life, as Heraclius single-handedly dispatches only the two Persian leaders, one of whom he tries to spare.[29]

In his consecutive summer-season legends of Judas Machabeus (1 August), King Oswald (5 August), and Heraclius and the Exaltation of the Holy Cross (14 September), Ælfric offers his high-ranking patrons lively images of pious warrior kings full of prayer, but also full of fight, waging wars presented by Ælfric as indisputably just in the sight of God. Moreover, as we have seen, Ælfric twice departs from his Latin sources to credit Christ with the deliberate destruction of human life. How did Ælfric and his Anglo-Saxon readers reconcile this triptych of Judaeo-Christian military violence with the parade of soldier martyrs preceding and following it, and especially the legend of King Edmund, where Christ is invoked as the avatar of peace and non-violence?

The apparent contradiction between martyrdom and militarism is, of course, inherent in the history and culture of early Christianity. The religion began as an extremist, apocalyptic sect, for the most part pacifist because its crucified founder preached a gospel of love, peace, and forgiveness, and sanctified in his own life the patient suffering of abuse and even death. Evidence from the earliest centuries suggests that most Christian thinkers abhorred warfare and violence. Tertullian states flatly that every soldier of later times was 'ungirded' by Jesus, when he disarmed Peter.[30] But in the course of the fourth century, through the policies of Constantine the Great and his successors, Christianity became increasingly involved in the most powerful military system in ancient history. Whereas most early Christians had avoided or refused military service, because bearing arms violated New Testament precepts of peace and patience, by the fifth century no one could serve in the Roman army who was *not* a Christian,[31] so as not to offend the Almighty God to whom the Empire now looked for support in its struggle against the barbarism outside, and sedition inside, its borders.

Around the same time, Augustine of Hippo, in the footsteps of Ambrose of Milan, had threaded his way through a complex of arguments and texts to effect a reconciliation between New Testament pacifism and the Old Testament militarism roundly condemned by his former coreligionists, the Manichees.[32] In effect he bequeathed to later generations the doctrinal flexibility to celebrate both the non-violent posture of individual Christian martyrs and the collective violence of Christian states and their leaders. The fundamental distinction Augustine and Ambrose seem to have made, when dealing with issues of violence and non-violence, was between state and individual. They took it for granted, of course, that involvement in war and violence was 'alien' to the priestly and monastic vocation,[33] but they went further and insisted that every individual Christian must be a pacifist, avoiding violence at all costs, even to protect his or her own life and property, because such ephemera were unimportant, and even inimical, to spiritual health and the practice of Christian peace and love. To fight to save one's own life was, in Augustine's view, to give in to the *libido*. In the treatise *De libero arbitrio*, while admitting that secular law permits individuals to kill in self-defence when wrongly attacked, Augustine argues that 'the law does not *compel* them to kill, but leaves the decision to do so in their discretion. They are free *not* to kill anyone for the sake of things which they can lose against their will, and therefore ought not to love ... If [the soul] cannot be destroyed, there is no occasion for fear [of the death of the body].'[34]

This uncompromising position had already been presented more bluntly and concisely by Ambrose in his *De officiis*, a treatise on the duties of the clergy but ranging widely over the human condition in general:

> [N]evertheless, a Christian man, a just and a wise man, ought never to try to save his own life at the cost of death to someone else. Indeed, even if he encounters an armed robber, he is not at liberty to hit back when his assailant hits him, lest in his anxiety to defend his own life he mar the sense of obligation he ought to feel towards the man. The principle given to us about this in the gospel records is crystal clear: 'Put away your sword: for everyone who strikes with the sword shall perish by the sword.'[35]

In the same treatise, however, Ambrose, himself a former provincial governor and son of the prefect of Gaul, takes it for granted that war is a part of public life and a natural arena for the exercise of human courage provided this is combined with other virtues, including justice. Thus he eulogizes King David for combining martial courage with restraint, prudence, and piety: 'he never undertook a war without consulting the Lord first. And so it was that he emerged victorious in every battle he fought.' Ambrose also celebrates Moses' defence of a fellow Hebrew by killing the Egyptian overseer (Exod. 2:11–12), thereby taking 'his earliest steps towards proving his courage in war.'[36] Violence and the taking of human life are, for Ambrose, permissible provided there is just cause.

Augustine, with his characteristic thoroughness, elaborated on these basic tenets, and explored their implications for contemporary conditions, with much greater subtlety (and, one senses, with more anxiety and reluctance) than Ambrose in a variety of contexts too numerous to discuss here, but his basic underlying belief was that killing is not wrong when God wills it: when a soldier killed an enemy of the state in battle, in the course of a just war ordered by God or his earthly deputy, he was innocent of wrong-doing; the same was true for a public official responsible for the execution of a convicted criminal.[37] The Roman-Christian ideals of public order, justice, and peace rendered war and a system of judicial punishments inevitable and just.[38] Augustine endorsed military service to the state by Christians along with payment of taxes and other public obligations of private citizens, and assured his correspondents among the Roman governing class that their military activity was sanctioned by God and scripture. The Old Testament, of course, abounded in examples of divinely sanctioned warfare and slaughter, so much so that Augustine hardly mentions it, but grapples instead with apparently pacifist commandments such as 'turn the other cheek,' 'resist not evil' (Mt. 5:39), and other unpromising New Testament contexts.[39] His basic argument is that such injunctions, particularly in the public contexts of warfare, law, and government, apply to inner feelings rather than to external actions. As the just magistrate punishes or the obedient soldier kills, he must do so without feelings of pleasure, cruelty, anger, or vengefulness, but rather with feelings of patience and benevolence, to promote peace and prevent further wrong.[40] As he writes to Count Boniface, 'Be, then, a peacemaker even while you make war ... let it be necessity not choice that kills your warring enemy.'[41]

I cannot prove that Ælfric and his fellow monks were personally familiar with these arguments and contexts in the works of Ambrose and Augustine, although it is not impossible.[42] But it seems clear that Ælfric's strenuous insistence on clerical exemption from military service, his glorification of martyrs in general and of military martyrs in particular, and his simultaneous celebration of the warfare of Old Testament and Christian warriors conform to patristic teachings on violence and non-violence and are not mutually contradictory in an early medieval Christian context. Albeit with varying emphases, such ideas underlay the partnership of clergy and warrior laity who together ruled the post-Roman kingdoms of Europe. That Augustine in particular was regarded, at least by the higher Carolingian clergy a century or more before Ælfric, as a rich source of Christian perspectives on warfare and violence is evident in the treatise on the duties of kingship, *De regis persona*, by the prominent ecclesiast and statesman, Archbishop Hincmar of Rheims, composed in 870 for Charles the Bald. The treatise is virtually an anthology of quotations from Augustine's *De ciuitate Dei* and also makes detailed use of his letter to Count Boniface.[43] But I have so far found no traces of Anglo-Saxon knowledge of Hincmar's treatise, or of its currency outside the court of Charles, although likely enough it was known to Abbo of Fleury, author of the *Passio Sancti Eadmundi*.

In any event, the distinctions made by Ambrose and Augustine between private and public violence provide us with a way to resolve the apparent contradictions in the most problematic legend in Ælfric's

Lives, that of King Edmund (XXXII). Rereading Ælfric's *Edmund* against the patristic background allows one to see clearly how it conforms with orthodox Christian thought and does nothing to discredit the idea of Christian warfare. When Edmund receives the Danes' offer to become their underking, in return for dividing with them his treasure and inheritance, his first preference, as he tells his spineless bishop, is to die fighting, 'on feohte feolle wið þam þe min folc / moste heora eardes brucan' [66–7: in order that my people might possess their own land], reflecting the criteria for just warfare and kingly duty that, as indicated above, were commonplace at this time. Ælfric appropriately characterizes this speech of Edmund's as 'cynelice' [63: kingly]. But the speed and secrecy of the Danish invasion are such that most of Edmund's soldiers have already been killed in their homes and armed resistance is out of the question. The issue before them, the bishop insists, is simply one of the king's own individual safety. Ælfric has the bishop highlight this through repetition of the key word 'save' ('gebeorge'): either the king should save his life through fleeing or save himself by agreeing to the enemy's terms: 'mid fleame þinum feore gebeorge . / oððe þu þe swa gebeorge þæt þu buge to him' (71–2). Edmund's immediate response, that he has no desire to survive his slaughtered thanes and he has never been one to run away, voices the warrior's code of honour and Ælfric introduces this speech, appropriately, with 'þa cwæþ eadmund cyning swa swa he ful cene wæs' [73: Then said Edmund the king, full brave as he was]. It is not until his third speech in this scene, by which point it has been made abundantly clear that *only his own individual life is at stake*, that Edmund invokes the Christian formula of non-violence and Christ's rebuke of Peter in Gethsemane, expressing his willingness to suffer death at the hands of the Danes, rather than submit to their terms, unless they agree to convert to Christianity.

From here on the emphasis in the story is all on Edmund's enactment of the classic martyr role: patience in suffering, faith in Christ, in the face of the Danes' hatred of Christianity. But it is neither a pacifist argument for turning the other cheek to the Danes harrying Ælfric's Wessex, nor can it be termed 'a ... shocking or subversive model for national policy.'[44] Ælfric has taken good care, as did Abbo, to show that a Christian warrior only throws down his weapons and refuses to fight and kill after his public role as defender of his country is no longer possible or relevant, and further fighting would be merely to save his own life or to avenge his slaughtered followers before he himself is killed. Either would be sinful, not to mention unsaintly, according to the standards of

Ælfric's patristic authorities. From the practical, political point of view, moreover, the story as originally crafted by Abbo, and retold by Ælfric, implicitly rejects and discredits any policy of appeasement or collaboration, such as is suggested by the nameless bishop whose advice to the king, that he should accede ('gebuge') to the Danes' terms of surrender, is prompted by fear and concern for preserving life (59–61). The king's willing embrace of death is an exemplum of faith and constancy: 'se æþela cyning nolde criste wið-sacan / ac mid anrædum geleafan hine æfre clypode' [120–1: the noble king would not deny Christ, but with resolute faith continually invoked him], and one that angers and thwarts the Danes. When read against the backdrop of the Danish incursions of the 990s and later, Edmund's willingness to stand and die, violently, rather than flee or negotiate, looks more like an image of defiance and resistance than an attempt to undermine a national military policy. Such willingness was something the Danes encountered in Æthelræd's English all too rarely.

Edmund's legend is an extreme case, and its transmitters took special care to avoid giving the wrong impression as to its meaning. In the legends of the other military martyrs in Ælfric's collection, the saints' predicament from the outset is never anything more than a choice between dying for their Christian faith or saving their individual lives by compromising their beliefs. Yet even here, the original legends, and their Anglo-Saxon interpreter, carefully preserve the legitimacy of the martyrs' military identities and duties. It is not warfare they reject, but paganism, sacrilege, apostasy, and fear of death. In the stories of the Theban Legion and the Sebastani, the exemplary warlike credentials of the martyrs prior to their religious persecution are strongly emphasized, as they refer proudly to their battlefield exploits and give no hint that there is any contradiction between being Christians and warriors, even under a pagan emperor. Three times in the Sebastani legend (*Lives* XI [Forty Soldiers] 27–9, 68–77, 84–8) Ælfric preserves and elaborates this motif from his Latin source, while considerably abridging other portions. And even as the soldiers' tortures begin, divine power inflicts rough retribution on their assailants, as stones rebound on their throwers and an 'ormetne flint' [huge flint] breaks open the head of the pagan 'heah-gerefa' (98–104). In the midst of the Christian soldiers' ordeal of weaponless, passive suffering, the legend endorses warfare and punitive violence in Christian culture.

Similarly in the legend of the Theban Legion (*Lives* XXVIII [Maurice]), nothing suggests that the legionaries' military service per se, even to an idolatrous emperor, compromises their Christian faith. Although he greatly abbreviates and simplifies the opening of the narrative in some respects, Ælfric adds various comments, unprompted by the Latin *passio*, that bring Christianity and warfare into normal association. Whereas in the Latin account of Maximian's army only the Theban legion itself is said to be Christian, Ælfric remarks, 'þa wæron on þære fyrde fela cristene men' [8: There were in the army many Christian men], before he singles out the Theban legion as comprising 'swiþe cristene menn þam casere folgiende . / for-þan þe hi sceoldon fyrdrian swa swa eall folc dyde' [10–11: very Christian men, following the emperor, because they had to do military service just as everyone did]. The Latin *passio* has nothing resembling this explanation, but Ælfric's use of words like *fyrd* (8) and *fyrdrian* (11) would doubtless remind his readers of the late Anglo-Saxon local militias and levies conscripted to oppose the Viking *here*, further normalizing the idea of Christian warfare. At the same time, he omits the Latin author's comment that the Thebans preferred their religion to their military vocation.[45] Out of all Ælfric's military saints, only Martin of Tours, whose destiny is clearly to fight with spiritual weapons as monk and bishop, appears firmly against involvement in warfare under any circumstances, when he refuses to accept his soldier's pay and abandons his weapons of war.

In a recent article that surveys much of the same military ground as this paper, Hugh Magennis argues that overall Ælfric 'presents a softly focused picture of army life' and distances the military saints from the real violence of war and any of the unpleasant associations of their profession, as part of his larger effort, as hagiographer, to create 'a world that he clearly intends to be seen as different from the real world.' With some reservations (e.g., the elevated style of portions of the Maccabees narrative), I agree that Ælfric's actual depiction of war is idealized rather than realistic and rarely heroic in the traditional sense, and that without doubt one of his aims was to provide his lay audience with 'suitable heroes (unlike those of secular literature)'[46] such as, presumably, Hengest, Waldhere, Beowulf and even Byrhtnoth himself. It occurs to me, however, that Ælfric's 'softly focused' presentation of war and violence, whether he intended it as such, embodies an Augustinian ideal of dispassionate warfare and rulership, whereby armies are defeated, enemies killed, criminals executed or flogged, only in obedience to higher commands and the principles of justice and love of the good, with the aim of securing peace and order (such as Ælfric shows Heraclius achieving in Persia, and Oswald in England). His holy warriors mirror the Augustinian ideal in lacking any personal lust for blood, power, or glory, or any feelings of hatred, cruelty, or uncontrolled anger towards the victims or perpetrators of violence. Such 'libidinous' emotions are attributed, however, to Cædwalla, the 'modigan ... reðan' [*Lives* XXVI (King Oswald), 21, 23: proud ... savage] enemy of Oswald, and are also routinely displayed by the pagan persecutors in the martyrs' passions,[47] contributing markedly to the typically hagiographic effect of stylized, 'unrealistic' portrayal of character.[48]

Ælfric's sanitized violence, however, as I hope this paper has helped make clear, is neither pacifist propaganda nor monastic detachment from the crises of his time, but rather a symptom of the Church's incorporation of violence into Christian thought and practice. Nothing illustrates this more vividly to my mind than a bizarre Eastern legend about the death of Julian the Apostate, a legend of which Ælfric himself seems to have been particularly fond, since he retells it twice in some detail and alludes to it briefly on a third occasion. According to this legend, of which Ælfric's fullest version is in *Lives* III (Basil), 205–91, Saint Basil of Caesarea learned in a vision how Julian was assassinated in Persia by order of the Virgin Mary herself after a celestial council of war with the Apostles. The killing was carried out by the military martyr, Saint Mercurius, 'asend / fram cristes meder to þæs caseres slæge' [251–2: sent by Christ's mother to slay the emperor], using the lance that was reputedly among the relics at the saint's shrine in Caesarea. Missing on the night of Basil's vision, the lance was found the next morning 'fula be-gleddod / mid Iulianes blode' [266–7: foully stained with Julian's blood].[49] This violent tale, in which the Blessed Virgin's role can at best be said to be shockingly out of character, nicely illustrates the patristic distinction between holy martyr and holy warrior, between private pacifism and public violence, on which I have tried to throw some light in the foregoing pages. Mercurius, a military martyr like those discussed earlier, had in his mortal life submitted patiently, without violent resistance, to torture and execution as an individual whose bodily life was less precious than his Christian faith and desire to avoid committing sacrilege. But in his capacity as a soldier of the heavenly court, in obedience to his sovereign's command, he is portrayed as legitimately executing an apostate emperor condemned as an enemy of the church. For Ælfric, apparently, as for the seminal Christian thinkers of the late Roman age, there was no irony or contradiction in such a reversal of roles. The somewhat paradoxical process by which a fabled group of passive, weaponless victims – the soldier martyrs of late antiquity – became the violent patron saints of crusading knights and medieval kings is thus seen to be well underway in Ælfric's *Lives of Saints*.[50]

NOTES

1 Tom Hill, in his numerous, wide-ranging studies in medieval literature, has rarely focused on the writings of Ælfric, and so I cannot claim to be building on his work in any specific sense here, but I gratefully acknowledge being among the *rimtalu* of medievalists who have benefited not only from his selfless encouragement and support early in their professional careers, but also from the stimulating example of his use of early Christian and medieval Latin sources for solving problems in vernacular texts.

2 *Ælfric's Lives of Saints*, ed. Walter W. Skeat, EETS o.s. 76, 82, 94, 114 (1881–1900; repr. in 2 vols, Oxford: Oxford University Press, 1966), Praefatio, lines 35–8. The edition quoted and cited (as simply *Lives*) by chapter and line numbers here is Skeat's (omitting his accent marks and manuscript punctuation), whose translations are sometimes used verbatim, but more often freely adapted or disagreed with. On Æthelweard and Æthelmær, see *Ælfric's Prefaces*, ed. Jonathan Wilcox, Durham Medieval Texts 9 (1994; repr. Durham: Durham Medieval Texts, 1996), 9–13.

3 The secular male saints are Sebastian (V); Gallicanus, John, and Paul in Agnes (VII); Forty Soldiers (XI); George (XIV); Alban (XIX); Abdon and Sennes, King Abgar (XXIV); Maccabees (XXV); King Oswald (XXVI); Heraclius, Longinus in Exaltation of the Cross (XXVII); Maurice (XXVIII); King Edmund (XXXII). Of these only Alban is neither royal nor military.

4 See, for example, Theodor Wolpers, *Die englische Heiligenlegende des Mittelalters: Eine Formengeschichte des Legendenerzählens von der spätantiken lateinischen Tradition bis zur Mitte des 16. Jahrhunderts*, Buchreihe der Anglia 10 (Tübingen: Max Niemeyer, 1964), 143; Antonia Gransden, 'Abbo of Fleury's "Passio Sancti Eadmundi,"' *Revue Bénédictine* 105 (1995): 20–78 at 53–4; Michael Benskin, 'The Literary Structure of Ælfric's *Life of King Edmund*,' in *Loyal Letters: Studies on Mediaeval Alliterative Poetry & Prose*, ed. L.A.J.R. Houwen and A.A. MacDonald (Groningen: Egbert Forsten, 1994), 1–27 at 16–17.

5 Grant Loomis, 'The Growth of the Saint Edmund Legend,' *Harvard Studies and Notes in Philology and Literature* 14 (1932): 83–113 at 97–103.

6 *Three Lives of English Saints*, ed. Michael Winterbottom, Toronto Medieval Latin Texts (Toronto: Pontifical Institute of Mediaeval Studies, 1972), 65–87, 91–2; for a facing translation, see Francis Hervey, *Corolla Sancti Eadmundi:*

The Garland of Saint Edmund, King and Martyr (London: J. Murray, 1907), 7–59. For a persuasive challenge to the historicity of the legend, see Paul Cavill, 'Analogy and Genre in the Legend of St Edmund,' *Nottingham Medieval Studies* 47 (2003): 21–45.

7 Gransden, 'Abbo,' 50. For alternative interpretations of the role of kingship, see Susan J. Ridyard, *The Royal Saints of Anglo-Saxon England: A Study of West Saxon and East Anglian Cults* (Cambridge: Cambridge University Press, 1988), 61–9, 92–5; and Thomas Head, *Hagiography and the Cult of the Saints: The Diocese of Orléans, 800–1200* (Cambridge: Cambridge University Press, 1990), 240–4. On clergy who did not renounce warfare, see Janet L. Nelson, 'The Church's Military Service in the Ninth Century: A Contemporary Comparative View?' *Studies in Church History* 20 (1983): 15–30.

8 James W. Earl, 'Violence and Non-Violence in Anglo-Saxon England: Ælfric's "Passion of St. Edmund,"' *PQ* 78 (1999): 125–49. See also John Edward Damon, *Soldier Saints and Holy Warriors: Warfare and Sanctity in the Literature of Early England* (Aldershot; Ashgate, 2003), 167–91 and 215–18 (I became aware of Damon's book only after my paper had been submitted for publication in 2004 and have only been able to add this brief citation. See my review of Damon in *Speculum* 81 [2006]: 497–9). See also his 'Advisors for Peace in the Reign of Æthelræd Unræd,' in *Peace and Negotiation: Strategies for Coexistence in the Middle Ages and the Renaissance*, ed. Diane Wolfthal, Arizona Studies in the Middle Ages and the Renaissance 4 (Turnhout: Brepols, 2000), 57–78.

9 Ælfric's wording closely follows that of Sulpicius Severus, *Vita Martini* 4.1.8; *Sulpice Sévère. Vie de saint Martin*, ed. and trans. Jacques Fontaine, 3 vols, Sources chrétiennes 133–5 (Paris: Cerf, 1967–9), 1:260. See T.D. Barnes, 'The Military Career of Martin of Tours,' *Analecta Bollandiana* 114 (1996): 25–32. Ælfric's presentation of Martin's military career is explored with particular care by Hugh Magennis, 'Warrior Saints, Warfare, and the Hagiography of Ælfric of Eynsham,' *Traditio* 56 (2001): 27–51 at 30–40 and 43.

10 Joyce Hill, 'The Dissemination of Ælfric's *Lives of Saints*: A Preliminary Survey,' in *Holy Men and Holy Women: Old English Prose Saints' Lives and Their Contexts*, ed. Paul E. Szarmach (Albany: State University of New York Press), 235–59 at 245 and 250–1. In addition to Skeat's edition, see also that of Stuart D. Lee, based like Skeat's on London, British Library, MS Cotton Julius E. vii; 'Ælfric's Homilies on *Judith*, *Esther* and *The Maccabees*,' (1999), http://users.ox.ac.uk/~stuart/kings/.

11 For a detailed sourcing of Ælfric's Maccabees, see Lee, 'Ælfric's Homilies,' and *Fontes Anglo-Saxonici* (http://fontes.english.ox.ac.uk/data/); for analysis, see Jonathan Wilcox, 'A Reluctant Translator in Late Anglo-Saxon

England: Ælfric and Maccabees,' *Proceedings of the Medieval Association of the Midwest* 2 (1993): 1–18; and Stuart D. Lee, 'Ælfric's Treatment of Source Material in His Homily on the Books of the Maccabees,' *Bulletin of the John Rylands University Library of Manchester* 77.3 (autumn 1995): 165–76. I am grateful to Dr Lee for supplying additional notes on the Maccabees.

12 Wilcox, 'Reluctant Translator,' 9.
13 See, for example, 'Hi bleowon þa heora byman and bealdlice fuhton . / oð þæt þa hæðenan flugon to fyrlenum landum / and iudas hi to-ðræfde swa swa deor to wuda' [354–6: They blew their horns and boldly fought until the heathen fled to their far-off lands, and Judas drove them away like wild beasts to the woods]. Notice the triple alliteration in line 354, a rarity in Ælfric's rhythmic prose, and the forceful simile in line 356, Ælfric's addition. Cf. 1 Macc. 4:13–15.
14 One of Augustine of Hippo's criteria for a just war is that God wills it. See below and n. 37.
15 Isidore of Seville, *Etymologiae* 18.1.2–4, ed. W. M. Lindsay, in *Isidori Hispalensis Etymologiarum sive Originum Libri XX*, 2 vols (1911; repr. Oxford: Clarendon, 1985). See Grant Loomis, 'Further Sources of Ælfric's Saints' Lives,' *Harvard Studies and Notes in Philology and Literature* 13 (1931): 1–8 at 3, n. 1; and J.E. Cross, 'The Ethic of War in Old English,' in *England Before the Conquest: Studies in Primary Sources Presented to Dorothy Whitelock*, ed. Peter Clemoes and Kathleen Hughes (Cambridge: Cambridge University Press, 1971), 269–82 at 272, n. 3.
16 This parallelism has been frequently remarked by Malcolm Godden, most recently in 'Apocalypse and Invasion in Late Anglo-Saxon England,' in *From Anglo-Saxon to Early Middle English: Studies Presented to E.G. Stanley*, ed. Malcolm Godden, Douglas Gray, and Terry Hoad (Oxford: Clarendon, 1994), 130–62 at 140.
17 Cross, 'Ethic of War,' 272–3, and Timothy E. Powell, 'The "Three Orders" of Society in Anglo-Saxon England,' *ASE* 23 (1994): 103–32. See also Lee, 'Ælfric's Homilies,' Part VIII (Themes), section 5d (Defence of War II), and Part XIII (Notes), on lines 722–73.
18 *Letter to Sigeweard*, lines 772–838; see *The Old English Version of the Heptateuch, Ælfric's Treatise on the Old and New Testament, and His Preface to Genesis*, ed. S.J. Crawford, EETS o.s. 160 (London: Oxford University Press, 1922), 48–50. See also Godden, 'Apocalypse and Invasion,' 141–2.
19 See Powell, "Three Orders," 125–8, and Nelson, 'Church's Military Service.' The complementary roles of clergy and warriors are similarly propounded by Ælfric to Archbishop Wulfstan in his Pastoral Letter 2a.14 (*De bellico aparatu*); *Councils & Synods with Other Documents Relating to the English*

Church. I: A.D. 871–1204. Part I: 871–1066, ed. Dorothy Whitelock (Oxford: Clarendon, 1981), 252; see also Whitelock's discussion, 244–5.

20 Stephen of Ripon, *Vita S. Wilfridi* 19, ed. and trans. Bertram Colgrave, in *The Life of Bishop Wilfrid by Eddius Stephanus* (1927; repr. Cambridge: Cambridge University Press, 1985), 40–3; and Cross, 'Ethic of War,' 276.

21 On Carolingian and Ottonian appropriations of Judas Machabeus as prototypical 'holy warrior,' see Klaus Schreiner, *Märtyrer, Schlachtenhelfer, Friedenstifter: Krieg und Frieden im Spiegel mittelalterlicher und frühneuzeitlicher Heiligenverehrung*, Otto-von-Freising-Vorlesungen der Katholischen Universität Eichstätt 18 (Opladen: Leske & Budrich, 2000), 30–1; and Jean Dunbabin, 'The Maccabees as Exemplars in the Tenth and Eleventh Centuries,' in *The Bible in the Medieval World: Essays in Memory of Beryl Smalley*, ed. Katherine Walsh and Diana Wood (Oxford: Blackwell for the Ecclesiastical History Society, 1985), 31–41.

22 See the first chapter (*De Militia Spirituali*), in *The Anglo-Saxon Version of the Hexameron of St. Basil, or, Be Godes six daga weorcum. And the Anglo-Saxon Remains of St. Basil's Admonitio ad filium spiritualem*, ed. Henry W. Norman, 2nd ed. (London: J.R. Smith, 1849), 34–9. For the Latin original, see *Die Admonitio S. Basilii ad filium spiritualem*, ed. Paul Lehmann, Sitzungsberichte der Bayerischen Akademie der Wissenschaften, Philosophisch-historische Klasse, Jahrgang 1955, Heft 7 (Munich: Bayerischen Akademie der Wissenschaften, 1955), 30–2. On the Old English version, see M.A. Locherbie-Cameron, 'From Caesarea to Eynsham: A Consideration of the Proposed Route(s) of the *Admonition to a Spiritual Son* to Anglo-Saxon England,' *Heroic Age: A Journal of Early Medieval Northwestern Europe* 3 (summer 2000): http://www.mun.ca/mst/heroicage.org/issues/3/cameron.html.

23 Letter no. 189, *PL* 33:855a; trans. Sister Wilfrid Parsons, *Saint Augustine: Letters*, vol. 4 (165–203), Fathers of the Church 30 (New York: Fathers of the Church, 1955), 269. For the same topos in an Augustinian sermon (*PL* 39:1905), see Lee, 'Ælfric's Treatment,' 171.

24 *HE* 3.1, pages 214–15; see also J.M. Wallace-Hadrill, *Bede's 'Ecclesiastical History of the English People': A Historical Commentary*, Oxford Medieval Texts (Oxford: Clarendon, 1988), 88–9; and Victoria A. Gunn, 'Bede and the Martyrdom of St Oswald,' in *Martyrs and Martyrologies: Papers Read at the 1992 Summer Meeting and the 1993 Winter Meeting of the Ecclesiastical History Society*, ed. Diana Wood (Oxford: Blackwell, 1993), 57–66.

25 Cf. Bede, *HE* 3.2, pages 214–15. The righteousness of defensive warfare was widely assumed, as in Ælfric's version of pseudo-Cyprian, *De duodecim abusiuis huius seculi*, where the good king by definition must 'festlice winnan wið onsiʒendne here, and haldan his eþel' [relentlessly battle against (the)

invading army and protect his country]; *Old English Homilies and Homiletic Treatises ... of the Twelfth and Thirteenth Centuries*, ed. Richard Morris, EETS o.s. 29, 34 (1867–68; repr. New York: Greenwood, 1969), 114–15.

26 See below and n. 37.

27 Mombritius's edition is cited below for convenience, but I am grateful to Dr Stephan Borgehammar for allowing me to consult a draft of his edition and translation of the *Exaltatio* or *Reversio Sanctae Crucis* (BHL 4178), Ælfric's probable source. See also 'Iesus Christus, Exaltatio Sanctae Crucis,' in *Sources of Anglo-Saxon Literary Culture*, vol. 1, *Abbo of Fleury, Abbo of Saint-Germain-des-Prés, and Acta Sanctorum*, ed. Frederick M. Biggs, Thomas D. Hill, Paul E. Szarmach, and E. Gordon Whatley (Kalamazoo: Medieval Institute Publications, 2001), 259–63.

28 Cf. 'atque iuxta se quasi collegam dei Crucem dominicam posuerat'; *Sanctuarium seu Vitae Sanctorum*, ed. Boninus Mombritius, 2 vols (1910; repr. Hildesheim: Georg Olms, 1978), 1:380, lines 7–8.

29 On the emperor Theodosius's lack of vindictiveness towards defeated enemies, see Augustine, *De ciuitate Dei contra paganos*, 5.26, ed. B. Dombart and A. Kalb, 2 vols, CCSL 47–8 (Turnhout: Brepols, 1955), 1:161–3; and Richard Shelly Hartigan, 'Saint Augustine on War and Killing: The Problem of the Innocent,' *Journal of the History of Ideas* 27 (1966): 195–204 at 201.

30 Tertullian, *De idololatria* 19.3: 'omnem postea militem dominus in Petro exarmando discinxit'; ed. J.H. Waszink and J.C.M. Van Winden (Leiden: Brill, 1987), 62, lines 11–12. See also Roland H. Bainton, *Christian Attitudes towards War and Peace: A Historical Survey and Critical Re-evaluation* (Nashville, TN: Abingdon, 1960), 73.

31 Bainton, *Christian Attitudes*, 88 and n. 10.

32 David A. Lenihan, 'The Just War Theory in the Work of Saint Augustine,' *Augustinian Studies* 19 (1988): 37–70 at 44–6.

33 See, for example, Ambrose, *De officiis* 1.35.175, ed. Ivor J. Davidson, 2 vols (Oxford: Oxford University Press, 2001), 1: 218–19; and Augustine's letter to Count Boniface, quoted above (page 222).

34 *De libero arbitrio* 1.5.12.37, ed. W.M. Green, CCSL 29 (Turnhout: Brepols, 1970), 218; trans. John H.S. Burleigh, *Augustine: Earlier Writings* (Philadelphia: Westminster, 1953), 119 (italics mine). This context is widely cited: see, for example, Louis J. Swift, *The Early Fathers on War and Military Service* (Wilmington, DE: Glazier, 1983), 128–34.

35 Ambrose, *De officiis* 3.4.27, ed. Davidson, 1:370–1. For Ambrose's views on war, as regards the individual and the state, see Bainton, *Christian Attitudes*, 89–91; and Swift, *Early Fathers*, 96–110. On *De officiis* in Anglo-Saxon England, see Dabney Anderson Bankert, Jessica Wegmann, and Charles D. Wright,

Ambrose in Anglo-Saxon England with Pseudo-Ambrose and Ambrosiaster, OEN Subsidia 25 (Kalamazoo: Medieval Institute Publications, 1997), 35.
36 Ambrose *De officiis* 1.35.177, 1.36.179; ed. Davidson, 1:220–1.
37 Augustine, *De ciuitate Dei* 1.21, ed. Dombart and Kalb, 1:23; trans. Henry Bettenson, *St Augustine: Concerning the City of God against the Pagans* (1972; repr. with a new introduction by G.R. Evans, Harmondsworth: Penguin, 2003), 32: 'the commandment forbidding killing was not broken by those who have waged wars on the authority of God, or those who have imposed the death-penalty on criminals when representing the authority of the State in accordance with the laws of the State, the justest and most reasonable source of power.'
38 In addition to linking just warfare to God's will or command (see previous note), Augustine also defined it as war undertaken 'to avenge injuries, when the nation or city against which warlike action is to be directed has neglected either to punish wrong committed by its own citizens or to restore what has been unjustly taken by it'; *Quaestiones in Heptateuchum* 6.10, *PL* 34:781; trans. Hartigan, 'Saint Augustine,' 199. For overviews of Augustine on war, see Herbert A. Deane, *The Political and Social Ideas of St. Augustine* (New York: Columbia University Press, 1963), 154–71; and Swift, *Early Fathers*, 110–39.
39 See, for example, Letter 189.4, to Boniface, *PL* 33:855 (trans. Parsons, *Saint Augustine: Letters*, 268), regarding Matt. 8:8–10, Luke 3:12–14, and Acts 10:1–8, 30–3. See Swift, *Early Fathers*, 126–7.
40 See Deane, *Political and Social Ideas*, 164–5. Important is Augustine's *De sermone Domini in monte libri duo* 1.19.56 – 1.20.66, ed. Almut Mutzenbecher, CCSL 35 (Turnhout: Brepols, 1967), 63–7; trans. Denis J. Kavanagh, *Saint Augustine: Commentary on the Lord's Sermon on the Mount with Seventeen Related Sermons*, Fathers of the Church 11 (1951; repr. Washington, D.C.: Catholic University of America, 1977), 80–94. For Ælfric's knowledge of this work, see M.R. Godden, *Ælfric's Catholic Homilies: Introduction, Commentary and Glossary*, EETS s.s. 18 (Oxford: Oxford University Press, 2000), 634.
41 Letter 189.6, to Boniface, *PL* 33:856; trans. Parsons, *Saint Augustine: Letters*, 269.
42 The two extant Anglo-Saxon copies of Augustine's *De libero arbitrio* are dated late-eleventh century by Helmut Gneuss (nos. 689 and 717), as is the oldest English copy of the letter to Boniface (no. 235); *Handlist of Anglo-Saxon Manuscripts: A List of Manuscripts and Manuscript Fragments Written or Owned in England up to 1100*, MRTS 241 (Tempe: Arizona Center for Medieval and Renaissance Studies, 2001).

43 Hincmar, *De regis persona* 6–14; *PL* 125:840–4. The treatise was adapted from a set of synodal canons from the reign of Louis the Pious, ca. 830; see Gerhard Laehr and Carl Erdmann, 'Ein karolingischer Konzilsbrief und der Fürstenspiegel Hincmars von Reims,' *Neues Archiv der Gesellschaft für ältere deutsche Geschichtskunde* 50 (1935): 106–34. For Hincmar's views on war, see Jean Devisse, *Hincmar, archevêque de Reims, 845–882*, 3 vols (Geneva: Droz, 1975–6), 1:528–34.

44 Earl, 'Violence and Non-violence,' 132.

45 '... fidemque sacram virtute et armis omnibus praeponebant': *Passio sancti Mauricii et sociorum eius*, in *AASS*, 6 Sept.: 345C.

46 Magennis, 'Warrior Saints,' 46, 48, 49.

47 For example, among the epithets for Maximian and his henchmen in *Lives* XXVIII (Maurice) are 'cene and reðe' [5: bold and cruel], 'wodlice' [16, 69: insanely], and 'se wælhreowa' [84: the bloodthirsty one].

48 In a parallel observation, Clare Lees, if I understand her correctly, argues that in the virgin martyr legends in Ælfric's *Lives* opportunities for the reader's illicit enjoyment of the 'sexed body' in the text are 'highly defended against'; *Tradition and Belief: Religious Writing in Late Anglo-Saxon England*, Medieval Cultures 19 (Minneapolis: University of Minnesota Press, 1999), 147–50.

49 The second lengthy account is in a homily for Mary's Assumption, *Catholic Homilies* I.30, ed. Peter Clemoes, *Ælfric's Catholic Homilies: The First Series. Text*, EETS s.s. 17 (Oxford: Oxford University Press, 1997), 436–8, lines 199–264; and see Godden, *Ælfric's Catholic Homilies: Introduction*, 254–6. See also *Lives* VII (Agnes), lines 419–20. On the assassination legend, see Robert Browning, *The Emperor Julian* (Berkeley and Los Angeles: University of California Press, 1976), 226–7. On the pseudo-Amphilochian life of Basil (*BHL* 1023), see *Sources*, ed. Biggs et al., 104–6 (Basilius); and Gabriella Corona, *Ælfric's Life of Saint Basil the Great: Background and Context*, Anglo-Saxon Texts 5 (Cambridge: Brewer, 2006), 6–28 and 223–47 (first edition of the Latin text).

50 Among the military martyrs credited with battlefield exploits on behalf of medieval Christian armies are Theodore, George, Demetrius, Mercurius, and Maurice. On the early role of military martyrs as patrons of Christian militarism and the migration of this idea from East to West, see Carl Erdmann, *The Origin of the Idea of Crusade*, trans. Marshall W. Baldwin and Walter Goffart (Princeton: Princeton University Press, 1977), 273–81. On the military martyrs see Hippolyte Delehaye, *Les Légendes grecques des saints militaires* (1909; repr. New York: Arno, 1975); and the valuable internet site of David Woods, 'The Military Martyrs,' http://www.ucc.ie/milmart/.

Addendum. Earlier versions of this paper were presented to a session honouring Professor Hill at the 38th International Congress on Medieval Studies, Kalamazoo, Michigan (May 2003); The Friends of the Saints, at the Graduate Center, City University of New York (March 2004); and the Anglo-Saxon Studies Colloquium, at New York University (March 2005). My thanks to members of these audiences for their suggestions and support.

A New Latin Source for Two Old English Homilies (Fadda I and Blickling I): Pseudo-Augustine, *Sermo* App. 125, and the Ideology of Chastity in the Anglo-Saxon Benedictine Reform

CHARLES D. WRIGHT

A pseudo-Augustinian Nativity sermon (App. 125)[1] is the hitherto unrecognized source for an extended passage in an OE sermon for Lent edited by A.M. Luiselli Fadda from Oxford, Bodleian Library Junius 85/86, fols 25r–40r (Fadda I),[2] as well as for a brief passage in Blickling Homily I (unrubricated, but probably for the Annunciation rather than the Nativity).[3] The author of Fadda I directly invokes the authority of this source by quoting a tag in Latin, yet at several points he covertly alters its meaning when he wishes to say something different – whether about the inevitability of sin, or about the culpability of women. Such alterations become visible, of course, only when the discovery of a Latin source enables a one-to-one comparison; in this case, the discovery also enables a triangulation, throwing into relief the divergent responses of the two vernacular homilists to the Latin sermon's invocation of the exemplary virginity of Christ, the *auctor castitatis*. The divergence, I will argue, exposes an ideological debate centering on the OE word *clænness* during the Benedictine Reform period – a debate in which Ælfric, a Benedictine partisan, may also have used *Sermo* App. 125 in staking out his position on clerical celibacy.

According to Henri Barré and Hermann J. Frede, the Latin sermon originated in Gaul in the sixth or seventh century.[4] It was included in several early homiliaries: St Peter's in the Vatican (sixth-century),[5] Alanus of Farfa (744x757), Egino of Verona (796x799),[6] Montpellier (tenth-century),[7] and (in a variant recension of §§2–4) Casinensis (eleventh-century).[8] The only manuscript evidence for the circulation of these homiliaries in Anglo-Saxon England is a single fragment of the homiliary of Alanus, written probably in northern France in the middle of the ninth century, whose provenance is Canterbury, St Augustine's.[9] There is some circumstantial evidence for the circulation of Alanus's homiliary in Anglo-Saxon England, but the main source of Blickling I (Pseudo-Augustine, *Sermo* App. 120) does not occur in Alanus or in any of these homiliaries that transmit *Sermo* App. 125,[10] and neither do the other two known Latin sources of Fadda I, rare variant texts of the so-called Three Utterances sermon and a pseudo-Augustinian Doomsday sermon (App. 251).[11] While it is possible that one or both Anglo-Saxon homilists encountered *Sermo* App. 125 in Alanus's homiliary, it is more likely that they used some less widely circulated compilations.

The correspondences between the two OE homilies and the Latin sermon are set forth in parallel columns in table 1 (the first column translates the Latin; substantive differences between the Latin and the OE will be detailed below).

Sermo App. 125 and Fadda Homily I

Although the author of Fadda Homily I was clearly translating some version of this pseudo-Augustinian sermon, the Latin tag he includes near the beginning of the passage (§13b) suggests that his copy differed substantively from the text reprinted by Migne, and was probably also corrupt. Indeed, the opening question and answer as quoted by the homilist say something rather different. In Migne's text the question and answer mean, 'But why did our God wish to refashion us to (eternal) life in this way, by being born of a virgin? So that, because death entered this world through a woman, salvation should be restored through the Virgin.'[18] As quoted by the homilist, the Latin tag is corrupt, but presumably means, 'But why did our God wish to be refashioned into (human) life in this way? So that, because he had entered this world through a woman ...' The remainder of the answer is not quoted in Latin, but it is translated by the homilist (§13d), whose vernacular rendering of the question corresponds more closely in sense to the text in Migne than to the text he actually quotes, but is recast as a rhetorical question incorporating part of the answer as a negative condition: 'But why was the Lord born through the womb of a virgin, if not [*butan*] that he wished to fashion us to eternal life? Because it happened formerly through Eve, Adam's wife, that death was entering

Table 1: Correspondences between the Old English Homilies and the Latin Sermon.

Pseudo-Augustine, App. 125 (translation)	Pseudo-Augustine, App. 125, PL 39:1993–4	Fadda I, ed Luiselli Fadda 11.60–15.111	Blickling I, ed. Morris 13.19–27
The evangelist thus most clearly demonstrated the nativity of our Lord Jesus Christ according to the flesh, in order to show that he was born from the Holy Spirit and the Virgin Mary, on account of the slyness of heretics, who deny that God assumed man. But for that reason our Lord sought a virginal abode for himself, in order to show us that God should be carried in a chaste body. For God assumed man in himself	**1.** Nativitatem Domini nostri Jesu Christi secundum carnem ita Evangelista apertissime demonstravit, ut ostenderet eum ex Spiritu sancto et Maria virgine natum, propter haereticorum astutiam, qui negant Deum hominem suscepisse. Sed ideo Dominus noster virgineum sibi requisivit hospitium, ut nobis ostenderet in casto corpore Deum portari debere. Ad hoc enim Deus hominem suscepit in se,		
in order that we might also receive God in ourselves, just as he himself said, 'Abide in me, and I in you.'	ut et nos Deum suscipiamus in nobis, sicut ipse dicit, *Manete in me, et ego in vobis* [Jn. 15:4] ...[12]	**12.** Ond forþan Drihten him sohte fæmnan innoð onto eardianne, þæt he us þurh þæt ætewde þæt we sculan beforan Godes gesihðe Drihtnes onfænege on him seluum geseon þæt he wæs man gewordan.	
But why did our God wish to refashion us to (eternal) life in this way, by being born of a virgin? So that, because death entered this world through a woman,	**3.** Sed quare Deus noster nascendo per Virginem, nos sic voluit reformare ad vitam? Ut quia per mulierem in hunc mundum mors intravit,	**13. (a)** Forþan we þanne nu sculan Gode onfon mid us swa he selfa cwæð: '*In me manet<e> et ego in uobis*'; **(b)** *sed quare Deus noster nascendo per uirgine<m> sic uoluit reformari ad uita? Vt quia per mulierem in hunc mundum intrauerat* ... **(c)** He cwæð Drihten be þissum manniscum kynne: 'Wuniaþ on me ond ic on eow. **(d)** Ac forhwan wæs Drihten acænned þurh fæmnan innoð butan þæt he wolde us gescyppan to þam ecean life?'	

Table 1: (*Continued*)

Pseudo-Augustine, App. 125 (translation)	Pseudo-Augustine, App. 125, PL 39:1993–4	Fadda I, ed Luiselli Fadda 11.60–15.111	Blickling I, ed. Morris 13.19–27
salvation should be restored through the Virgin.	salus per Virginem redderetur.	**14. (a)** Forþan þæt geara gelamp þurh Euan, Adames wif, þæt deaþ wæs gangende on middangeard, ond þa wæs þissum middangearde eft hiera hæle agyfen þurh Marian þa fæmnan.	
And thereafter when Christ arose from hell on the third day, women first came worshipping to meet him through the angel: therefore they were bidden to proclaim the Resurrection to the Apostles, in order to show to men, See, the resurrection of the dead is proclaimed to you by the one through whom you fell into death.	Denique et quando Christus tertia die ab inferis resurrexit, primum mulieres per angelum adorantes occurrunt: quibus ideo jubetur resurrectionem Apostolis nuntiare, ut hominibus ostenderetur, Ecce per quam cecidistis in mortem, per ipsam vobis resurrectio mortuorum nuntiatur.	**(b)** Ond cuðlice þa Drihten by briddan dæge of deaþe aras fram helwarum; ond þa[14] gebædan him ærest wif ond heom wæs beboden þæt hie urnon[15] ond bodedan his apostolum his ærist; ond he wæs ærest fram þam wimmannum ætywed, forþan us ærest deað þurh wifman on gefeoll; ond þa eft forþan wifmæn ærest bodadan ond cyþdan mannum his ærist.	
For because a woman had first tasted (death), a woman is likewise shown to have witnessed the Resurrection first, so that she should not bear the reproach of perpetual guilt among men; and she who had dispensed guilt to us also dispensed grace.	Mulier enim quia [mortem][13] prior gustaverat, prior etiam resurrectionem vidisse monstratur, ut non perpetui reatus apud viros opprobrium sustineret; et quae culpam nobis transfuderat, transfudit et gratiam.	**(c)** Ond þæt wif þæt ærest deaðes byrigde, **15.** þa wæs heo eft forþan edwit þrowigende from hire were ond þa scylde þe heo þær dyde seo hire wærp on ecnesse ongewrecen ond hira synna weron miclum begoten ofer us.	

Table 1: (Continued)

Pseudo-Augustine, App. 125 (translation)	Pseudo-Augustine, App. 125, PL 39:1993–4	Fadda I, ed Luiselli Fadda 11.60–15.111	Blickling I, ed. Morris 13.19–27
Lastly, our Lord came to the earth through the members of a chaste virgin for this reason, to show that God is the founder of chastity.	4. Denique Dominus noster ideo per castae virginis membra venit ad terras, ut ostenderet Deum castitatis esse auctorem.	16. Ond þa us wutodlice becom ure Drihten þurh Marian leoma, þære halchan fæmnan, þæt wæs þæt Drihten com to eorþan þurh hie ond God ætewde on ðam þæt he is ealra clænnessa fruma.	Wel þæt eac gedafenaþ þæt he to eorpan astige þurh þa clænan leomu þære halgan fæmnan þæt we þe gearor wiston

þæt he is ordfruma |
| Therefore just as our God received us in himself, let us also receive God in ourselves. | Ergo sicuti Deus noster nos suscepit in se, et nos suscipiamus Deum in nobis. | 17. (a) Ond þus us onfeng ure Drihten þurh hine selfne þæt he wolde þæt we hine onfengon on us.

(b) þis word þanne tacnaþ þæt se man onfehþ Godes se ðe rihtlice geherеþ swa swa hine wise gelæraδ. | |
| Let us therefore in a chaste body bear God, whom the chaste members of the Virgin had borne. | Portemus ergo et nos Deum in casto corpore, quem virginis casta membra portaverunt. | (c) God us hafað beboden þæt we him beowigen on clænan lichaman, forþan he wæs geboren þurh þære clænan fæmnan leoma; | |
| For Christ is the master of chastity, and that is why whoever is unchaste cannot bear Christ. | Christus enim magister est castitatis: et ideo qui castitatem non habet, portare Christum non potest. | forþan he is lareow ælcere clænnesse ond ne mæg se næfre wesan clæne se ðe nyle his synna geswican, ær his ændedæge. | ond lareow ealre clænnesse; ond we þæs gelefað ond geare witon þæt swa hwylc man swa mildheortnesse nafað, ne biþ þær Cristes eardung ne his wunung on þære heortan. |

Table 1: (*Continued*)

Pseudo-Augustine, App. 125 (translation)	Pseudo-Augustine, App. 125, PL 39:1993–4	Fadda I, ed Luiselli Fadda 11.60–15.111	Blickling I, ed. Morris 13.19–27
Yet we, beloved, who believe in God, so that we may always be able to bear Christ in our heart, let us keep ourselves chaste and pure from all sin, so that Christ may be able to dwell in us.	Sed et nos, charissimi, qui Deo credimus, ut semper Christum in corde nostro portare possimus, castos ac puros nos exhibeamus ab omni peccato; ut Christus habitare possit in nobis.	18. (a) Ond nu mænnisc*lice*[16] we þe Crist witen, lufian we hine forþan simle mid clæne lichaman ond mid hluttre geþance. (b) Þanne adligað he us Crist fram eallum urum synnum ond we magon geearnian, gif we selfe willaþ, þæt Crist eardað an us. 19. (a) Þis word þanne tacnað þæt Crist selfa behealdeð þa þe tela doð, ond deofol tihtað þam þe on þweorh þænceað.	Nu þonne, men þa leofestan, gelyfan we on urne Drihten,
For whoever does not have Christ within him, cannot be called a Christian.	Qui enim Christum non habet in se, christianus non potest dici.	(b) Ond soþlice þa þe Crist ne lufiað, hu magan þa cweðan þæt hie sien cristene?	
Nor ought anyone be proud merely to the extent that he calls himself a Christian in name, yet shows himself an adversary in deeds.	Nec enim ita se extollere debet unusquisque, ut christianum se nomine dicat tantum, et factis inimicum ostendat.	20. (a) Ac us gedafnaþ anra gehwilcum þæt he us ahebbe on þa soþan cristennesse ond forlæte þa weorc þe se earma feond mæn læraþ.	
For how is one a Christian who strives to live in opposition to the commandments of Christ?	Quomodo christianus est, qui contra Christi praecepta vivere contendit?	(b) Hu mæg se man beon cristen gif he fliteð wið Cristes bebodu?	

Table 1: (Concluded)

Pseudo-Augustine, App. 125 (translation)	Pseudo-Augustine, App. 125, PL 39:1993–4	Fadda I, ed Luiselli Fadda 11.60–15.111	Blickling I, ed. Morris 13.19–27
But you who serve God and keep his commandments, he has power to grant you eternal life, who lives and reigns forever with the Father and the Holy Spirit, amen.	Sed vos qui Deo servitis, et ejus praecepta custoditis, potens est vobis concedere vitam aeternam, qui cum Patre et Spiritu sancto vivit et regnat in saecula saeculorum. Amen.	(c) Ac þa ðe siendan þurh God gewordene, 21. healdeð ge nu þanne Godes bebodu forþan he is swiðe mihtig þæt he eow forgyfe eces lifes reste	ond hine lufian, ond his bebodu healdan,
		swa he selfa wæs sprecende ond he cwæð: '*Diliges Dominum Deum tuum ex toto corde tuo et ex tota anima tua et ex totis uiribus tuis; deinde dlligis proximum tuum quam te ipsum; qui enim dlligit proximum tuum totam legem impleuit.*'[17] He cwæð ure Drihten be þissum mænniscean cynne: "Lufiaþ ge eowerne Drihten God mid ealre eowre hearten ond mid ealre eowre saule ond mid ealle mægne. Ond þanne æfter þissum, lufiaþ eowre þa nihstan swa eow selfe; ond þanne wutodlice se þe lufaþ his þane nihstan þanne gefylllað se ælce Godes æ'...	þonne bið on ús gefylled þæt he sylfa cwæþ,

'Eadige beoþ þa clænan heortan, forþon þe hie God geseoð'... |

into the world, and then this world was given salvation again through the Virgin Mary.' Perhaps the Latin tag, already corrupt in the manuscript consulted by homilist, has been further corrupted in the transmission of Fadda I, since it seems unlikely that the homilist would have quoted a Latin tag whose meaning differed so substantially from his own translation of it.

The inclusion of Latin tags or incipits in OE homilies is by no means unprecedented, but the method of the author of Fadda I seems to have been to quote in Latin the opening words of a new source-text (or in this case, a sentence that occurs early in a passage he translates, though it is not actually the first one). He also quotes the incipits of the Doomsday and Three Utterances sermons, introducing both the Latin quotations and the accompanying translations with vernacular attributions of the words to Christ ('he cwæð'), which suggests that the Latin tags were to be read aloud. His purpose, then, seems to have been to authorize his vernacular discourse by directly invoking its Latin sources, as well as to signal the beginning of each passage based on a different Latin source.

The tags from the Nativity and Three Utterances sermons both begin with biblical verses, and it is not immediately clear to what extent the homilist distinguishes scripture as a separate and uniquely authoritative discourse. Nancy Thompson has recently drawn attention to the 'conflation of canon and commentary' in the anonymous homilies,[19] and Fadda I provides a particularly instructive example of this phenomenon. Luiselli Fadda punctuates the translation of the Latin tag from the Nativity sermon as if the homilist were attributing to Christ not merely Jn. 15:4, but the following question and answer as well. This is possible, indeed likely, since the biblical quotation is introduced by a vernacular attribution to Christ ('swa he selfa cwæð'), as is its translation ('He cwæð Drihten ...'), and in both cases the homiletic tag follows immediately without any explicit distinction from the biblical quotation. Still, the adversative conjunctions (*sed/ac*) immediately following the scriptural verse, as well as the third-person references to God (*Deus/Drihten ... he*), might have been regarded as sufficient to denote a transition from Christ's own words to those of an (anonymous) Christian-Latin authority. In the case of the Three Utterances, Luiselli Fadda assumes that the Latin tag immediately following the Latin quotation of Mt. 13:33 is an intrusive gloss back-translating the corresponding OE sentence; but as Mary Wack and I have shown, the words 'anima homines peccatores [*sic for* hominis peccatoris] cum exierat de corpore' are in fact the incipit of his Latin source.[20] Here again there is room for doubt as to whether the homilist distinguishes the biblical verse he correctly attributes to Christ from the non-scriptural tag that follows without a break both in the Latin and the OE translation; the impersonal construction (*Hit gelimpeð þanne*) that he uses to render *cum* in the Latin incipit might imply a shift from Christ's voice to the homilist's own narrative voice. Yet the homilist goes on to characterize the Three Utterances narrative as *godspel* ('hit is cweden on þissum godspelle'; [it is said in this 'gospel']).[21]

That the boundary between Christ's *ipsissima verba* from canonical scripture and material drawn from non-scriptural Christian-Latin sources is indeed fluid is strikingly confirmed by the Latin quotation from the Doomsday sermon.[22] This time there is no scriptural verse, yet despite the fact that the sermon incipit addresses 'fratres dilectissimi' and includes third-person reference to 'Dominus,' the homilist explicitly attributes it to 'the Lord himself':

> Swa Drihten selfa wæs sprecende ond he cwæð: '*O fratres dilectissimi, quam timendus est dies ille in quo Dominus proposuit uenire cum flammam ignis quod inflammabit in aduersarios.*' He cwæð: 'Eala, men ða leofestan, hu eow is to ondrædanne se dæg se ðe Drihten oncymeð to eow mid fyres ligum, ond he ðonne forbærneð ealle his þa wiðerweardan!'

> [Just as the Lord himself was saying, and he said: 'O dearest brethren, how that day is to be feared in which the Lord intends to come with a blaze of fire that will consume his adversaries.' He said: 'Alas, dearest men, how you are to fear the day on which the Lord will come to you with flames of fire, and then he will consume all his adversaries!']

Apparently for our homilist any Christian-Latin text that he regards as authoritative and orthodox can be attributed to Christ, either because he has a very loose notion of what constitutes scripture, or because he views all such discourse as divinely inspired and therefore sanctioned by Christ, who may thus be said to have spoken it himself.

The homilist's self-consciousness about the relation between his own authority and that of his Latin sources is evident not only from the way he signals his major sources by quoting a bit of the Latin from each, but also by the way he twice flags his own explanatory additions to the Nativity sermon with the phrase 'Þis word þanne tacnaþ þæt ...' [§§17b, 19a: This statement moreover signifies that ...] (the significance of these elaborations in their immediate contexts will be discussed below). Identification of the source helps to identify these as additions, and clarifies the function of the homilist's repeated phrase as a marker of his elaborations. The phrase subordinates his own authority to that of his sources, yet at the same time asserts his authority to mediate and interpret them for his audience.

This does not mean, however, that the homilist is unwilling to alter his Latin source significantly and without acknowledgment.[23] Aside from recasting the syntactical form of some sentences, as he does with the opening question and answer, the homilist sometimes also makes substantive changes of emphasis and even of literal meaning that cannot readily be explained by assuming he was translating a variant Latin text. In the vernacular answer to the question he gives in both Latin and English, he conflates two separate 'ut (nobis) ostenderet' clauses in the Latin that stipulate different reasons why Christ was born of a Virgin: to show that he was truly born of the Holy Spirit by Mary (thus refuting heretics who denied that God assumed man); and to show that God should be carried in a chaste body. The homilist reduces this to a single 'þæt he us þurh þæt ætewde' clause whose main correspondence is with the first reason in the Latin (though the homilist omits the Latin sermon's reference to heretics): 'so that he might show us thereby that we are to see in himself that he became man' (§12). In effect, the homilist conflates the words 'Sed ideo Dominus noster virgineum sibi requisivit hospitium, ut nobis ostenderet' with 'eum ... hominem suscepisse' from the preceding sentence.[24]

The homilist's alterations go well beyond mere compression and simplification, for he also revises subtly the theological implications of certain passages in the source. A recurring metaphor in the Latin sermon is that it is possible for those with pure hearts and chaste bodies not only to receive (*suscipere*) but also to bear (*portare*) God within them, just as Christ was carried in the chaste womb of the Virgin. The homilist was not troubled by verbs denoting the reception or indwelling of Christ within human beings. He renders *suscipere* with forms of *onfon* 'receive,' *habitare* with *eardian* 'inhabit,' and the scriptural *manere (in)* with *wunian (on)* 'dwell in':

§13a: we þanne nu *sculan* Gode *onfon* mid us
    nos Deum *suscipiamus* in nobis
§17a: we hine *onfengon* on us[25]
    et nos *suscipiamus* Deum in nobis

§18b: Crist *eardað* an us
    Christus *habitare* possit in nobis
§13a: In me *manet<e>* et ego in uobis
§13c: *Wuniaþ* on me ond ic on eow

Yet he was clearly uncomfortable with the idea that human beings might 'bear' God, for not only does he leave untranslated the phrases 'Deum portari debere' (at §12) and 'portare Christum non potest' (at §17c), but whenever he does translate phrases in which God or Christ is the object of *portare* (or *habere in se*) he does not use *beran* 'bear' but such non-metaphorical verbs as *þeowigan* 'serve' or *lufian* 'love':[26]

§17c: God us hafað beboden þæt we him *þeowigen* on clænan lichaman
    Portemus ergo et nos Deum in casto corpore
§18a: *lufian* we hine forþan simle mid clæne lichaman
    semper Christum in corde nostro *portare* possimus
§19b: Ond soþlice þa þe Crist *ne lufiað*
    Qui enim Christum *non habet in se*

It is difficult to say why the homilist was troubled by this metaphor, since it is sanctioned by Paul, who bids Christians, 'Glorificate et portate Deum in corpore uestro' [1 Cor. 6:20: Glorify God and bear him in your body]. Perhaps because 'bearing' God implies not just receptivity, but agency, the homilist wished to clarify that while human beings whose sins have been remitted may 'receive' God, they do not 'bear' God through their own merit. When the Latin preacher exhorts his audience to 'bear' God in a chaste body, warning that the unchaste cannot bear God, the homilist not only changes the exhortation to 'loving' God, but also adds a clause (§17c) insisting that no one can be *clæne* who does not cease from his sins before death. And when the Latin preacher exhorts his audience, 'Let us keep ourselves chaste and pure from all sin,' the homilist makes it clear that it is impossible for human beings to keep themselves free of sin by rephrasing (in §18a) to say that 'if we love Christ with pure bodies and clean thoughts, Christ will eradicate [*adilgað*] all sins from us, so that we may deserve (if we desire it ourselves) to have Christ dwell within us' (but not, again, to 'bear' Christ). Finally, when the Latin text addresses 'those who serve God and keep his commands,' the homilist in §§20c–21 refers somewhat obscurely to those who are created by God (if that is the sense of 'þa ðe siendan þurh God gewordene') and bids them to keep his commandments, substituting an imperative *healdaþ* for the Latin indicative *custoditis*. He then explains that 'Christ himself watches over those who do well, and the devil incites those who think perversely' (§19a, one of the two additions signalled with 'This word moreover signifies that ...'). The homilist's gloss stresses that good deeds or evil thoughts are not wholly independent movements of the human will, but are superintended by divine or demonic agency. Nor, as the homilist asserts in his other elaboration, do we 'receive' God without the good offices of human teachers (§17b: 'This statement moreover signifies that the man receives God who rightly obeys as wise men teach him').

The homilist has also recast §20a in order to emphasize the agency of Christ and the devil in inspiring good or evil. What is remarkable here is how so many of the main Latin words have a direct correspondence in the OE (*debet/gedafnaþ; unusquisque/anra gehwylcum; extollere/ ahebbe; christianum/cristenesse; factis/weorc; inimicum/feond; ostendat/ tæcþ*), and yet with so many changes in their grammatical form and syntactic relation that the result is a completely different statement:

Latin: Nor ought anyone be proud merely to the extent that he calls himself a Christian in name, yet shows himself an adversary [*inimicum*] in deeds.

OE: But it behooves each of us that He [the antecedent is presumably 'Christ' from the preceding sentence] should raise us into the true Christian faith, and that each person should abandon the deed that the wretched demon [*feond*] teaches men.

It seems unlikely that scribal variation in the Latin sermon would have resulted in a close equivalent to what the homilist says. Assuming that he was translating something identical or very similar to the Latin text that survives, it is as if the homilist felt bound to match the majority of the Latin words with some lexical equivalent, but equally free to say something different with them. Yet he translates a good deal of the sermon reasonably accurately and rather closely, so it is not that he merely understood the words without understanding how to construe them. Rather, he revises his source freely, but only as necessary to modify or clarify its doctrinal implications. In most cases this involves nudging passages that smack of semi-Pelagianism in the direction of an Augustinian theology of sin and grace.

Another possible motive for the homilist's deletion of the image of 'bearing' Christ is that the analogy with the Virgin Mary's bearing of Christ ('Portemus ergo et nos Deum in casto corpore, quem virginis casta membra portaverunt') metaphorically feminizes the Christian subject, which is usually gendered masculine. Indeed, his most striking alteration of the Latin source pertains to the guilt of Eve and the role of Mary and the women who bore witness to Christ's Resurrection in reversing Eve's condemnation and the reproach ('opprobrium') that women have endured as a result. The Latin sermon includes a classic expression of the Eve-Mary antithesis,[27] but it complicates this binary opposition by also invoking the women at the tomb, who can potentially stand in for all women, and for 'Woman,' more readily than can Mary.[28] The preacher explains that after Christ's Resurrection on the third day, women came to him first and were bidden to inform the Apostles; the reason was to show to men, 'Behold, the resurrection of the dead is proclaimed to you by the one through whom you fell into death.' Up to this point (§14a–b) the homilist translates fairly straightforwardly, apart from replacing the second-person plural address of the Latin (*cecidistis/vobis nuntiatur*) with a mixed first-person plural and third-person plural construction (*us ... on gefeoll/cyðdon mannum*). But in the next sentence the homilist actually reverses the import of the Latin text. Borrowing a phrase from Ambrose, Pseudo-Augustine had drawn explicitly the social implications of the risen Christ's appearance to women:[29] 'because a woman first tasted (death), a woman is likewise shown to have witnessed the Resurrection first, so that she [that is, 'Woman'] should not bear the reproach of perpetual guilt among men [non perpetui reatus apud viros opprobrium sustineret]; and she who had dispensed guilt to us also dispensed grace.' Evidently this concession to women was uncongenial to the Anglo-Saxon preacher. He does retain the example of the women at the tomb, but only as part of a typological symmetry that complements the Eve-Mary antithesis; and whereas the Latin sermon derives positive consequences for wives from the appearance of the risen Christ to women, the OE homily derives only negative consequences from the curse of Eve, both for her and for all humanity. The homilist fails to translate the phrase 'prior etiam resurrectionem vidisse monstratur,' focusing instead solely on Eve's priority in 'tasting' death: 'And the woman that first tasted death, she was henceforth suffering scorn from her husband, and the guilt which she committed there is perpetually avenged upon her, and their sins have been greatly poured out over us' (§§14c–15). At first glance it looks as if the word *non* had accidentally been omitted in the phrase 'non perpetui reatus apud viros opprobrium sustineret'; but there is also nothing in the OE corresponding to the clause 'transfudit et gratiam,' whereas 'hira synna weron miclum begoten ofer us' [their sins were greatly poured out over us] corresponds loosely to 'quae culpam nobis transfuderat.' The homilist picks up on the allusion to the *poculum mortis* motif in the Latin verb *transfundo*, 'decant' or 'pour out,'[30] but declines to say that a woman dispensed grace as well as guilt. The scorn ('edwit') that Eve suffers from her husband Adam, no longer cancelled by the witnessing of women to Christ's resurrection,[31] apparently now constitutes the 'perpetual vengeance' that women must endure for Eve's guilt.[32] I suspect, therefore, that deliberate tampering by the homilist has robbed 'woman' of her role as a conduit for grace and, instead delimiting or balancing the guilt of Eve, subjects her perpetually to its vengeance, and humankind to its consequences.

Sermo App. 125 and the Ideology of Chastity in the Benedictine Reform

The homilist's willingness to modify the theological and social implications of his source suggests that what he retained essentially unchanged was consistent with his own views. Following the Latin sermon's repeated injunctions to observe chastity, the homilist's emphasis on *clænness* and on the necessity for a pure body (*clæne lichaman*) with which to receive, serve, and love God suggests that he was an advocate of clerical celibacy, and hence was either a monk or a member of the regular clergy. The most likely context for a homily that exalts *clænness* in the sense of 'chastity' is the restoration of regular monasticism and the renewed emphasis on clerical celibacy during the Benedictine Reform era of the second half of the tenth century.[33] As Pauline Stafford has noted, the reformers expressed their commitment to monasticism 'in a language of purity,' emphasizing *clænness* in its more restricted sense of 'chastity' as a preeminent (and preeminently clerical) virtue.[34] The author of Fadda I seems to have chosen this Latin sermon precisely for its insistence on the relation between chastity and holiness. His alteration of the sermon's mitigation of the guilt of Eve is likewise consistent with the reformer's view that, in Stafford's words, '"Woman" symbolized all that the male cleric was to reject ...' This clerical ideology, Stafford argues, 'readily aligned "woman" with all the notions of impurity and, specifically, with those which were coming to be seen as markers of the laity.'[35]

Even if the homilist was a monk or celibate priest, his audience must have included married persons, whom he admonishes towards the beginning of the homily to observe the forty days of Lent 'on clænnessa ond on forhæfednesse unrihtlices lichaman lustes' [§6 lines 24–5: in purity and in renunciation of unlawful bodily desire]. Here *clænness* refers not to perpetual virginity but to the temporary abstinence of married persons during the holy season. While the homilist acknowledges that there were different forms of *clænness* appropriate to different estates,[36] in the passage drawn from the Nativity sermon he accepts without qualification its equation of *castitas* with the virginity exemplified and founded by Christ, the *castitatis auctor* and *magister castitatis*, translating these epithets closely as 'ealra clænnessa fruma' (§16) and 'lareow ælcere clænnesse' (§17c) and linking the expression to the obligation to serve Christ in a pure body ('on clænan lichaman,' §17c).

The Nativity sermon's definition of Christ as model and master of *castitas* may also have influenced Ælfric, who uses closely similar designations for Christ in *Catholic Homilies* I.21 ('ord 7 angin ealra clænnyssa' [origin and beginning of all chastity]) and in the Latin and OE versions of his First Pastoral Letter to Wulfstan ('origo castitatis/ordfruma ealre clænnesse').[37] In several other works Ælfric alludes to the idea that Christ 'instituted' (*instituit/astealde*) chastity through his Incarnation.[38] The phrase *magister castitatis* was applied to the Holy Spirit by Ambrose, but to Christ by Leo the Great,[39] and Christ is termed *auctor castitatis* in a number of other early Latin sources, including Aldhelm.[40] I have found no other example of Ælfric's term *origo castitatis*, but it is likely to be a mere variation of Pseudo-Augustine's *auctor castitatis*, especially since Ælfric's vernacular equivalent is closely similar to the phrasing of Fadda I and Blickling I, both of which are demonstrably dependent upon Pseudo-Augustine, who, like Ælfric, links the expression to Christ's choice to be born of a Virgin.

The 'discourse of chastity' in Ælfric's writings has recently been explored in valuable studies by Clare Lees and Robert Upchurch,[41] though neither focuses specifically on these formulations of Christ's foundational chastity that Ælfric so persistently used to stake out a rigorist position on clerical celibacy. In his pastoral letter to Wulfstan, Ælfric explicitly links Christ's foundational chastity to the celibacy of his followers, including monks, nuns, and mass-priests, and in *Catholic Homilies* I.21 he explains the epithet with reference to Luke 14:26, which he cites in the reduced form, 'He who comes to me may not be my disciple unless he hates his wife' – translating only *uxorem* in the sequence '(et non odit) patrem suum, et matrem, et uxorem.'[42] Ælfric links Christ's establishment of *clænness* explicitly to the chastity of his followers again in his Letter to Sigefyrth,[43] which Wulfstan paraphrased in Napier Homily L, asserting that a mass-priest should not live like a *ceorl* because 'Crist sylf astealde þa clænnysse and his halgan apostolas, þe him her on life folgedon, þe we godes þeowas healdan scilan' [Christ himself instituted chastity – and his holy apostles, who followed him here in life – which we as servants of God ought to observe].[44] Like the author of Fadda I, Ælfric allows for a less perfect form of *clænness* attainable by married persons, though he also suggests that they should abstain not only during holy seasons but also permanently after the wife's menopause. In his Second Series homily for Sexagesima Sunday, Ælfric links his discussion of marital celibacy to a denunciation of married priests, and Upchurch has suggested that Ælfric's 'disdain' for married secular clergy informs his exhortations to married lay persons, effectively creating an affinity between the obedient laity and the reformed priesthood.[45] For Ælfric and the author of Fadda I, then, Christ's designation as the 'origin of all chastity' implied an obligation to celibacy in the priesthood as well as an obligation for the laity to remain chaste during holy seasons. For these homilists 'chastity' is the predominant sense of the word *clænness*, and *clænness* is the predominant Christian virtue for both clergy and laypersons.

It was not so for the author of Blickling Homily I, who makes Christ's exemplary chastity applicable to a broader audience by exploiting the ambiguity of OE *clænness*, the primary senses of which are 'moral purity, freedom from sin' and 'specifically: chastity' (*DOE*, s.v. *clænness* 1.a.–1.b). The bulk of the homily, as Fiedler demonstrated,[46] is based upon another Pseudo-Augustinian sermon (App. 121), though there are briefer passages drawn from other sources, including Bede.[47] The two sentences drawn from *Sermo* App. 125 (corresponding loosely to Fadda I §16 and the last clause of §17c) come near the end of the homily.[48] The Blickling homilist translates the first sentence of *Sermo* App. 125 §4, then skips two sentences in order to conflate the closely similar but separate terms *castitatis ... auctorem* and *magister ... castitatis* into a single phrase, 'ordfruma ond lareow ealre clænnesse' [origin and teacher of all chastity/moral purity]. He alters significantly the following statement in the Latin, however ('et ideo qui castitatem non habet, portare Christum non potest') by substituting 'mercy' (*mildheortnes*) for Latin *castitas*, revealing that he does not wish to restrict to the chaste alone the capacity to have Christ dwell in the heart: 'and we believe this and know it well, that whoever has not mercy, Christ's dwelling will not be there, nor his abiding in that heart.' The Blickling homilist is obviously not translating *castitas* directly; instead, through a suppressed intermediate equation with *clænness* he arrives at an alternative virtue not tied to sexual renunciation: *castitas* [= *clænness* 'chastity' = *clænness* 'moral purity'] = *mildheortnes*. After this semantic sleight of hand he passes over the Latin admonitions to 'bear God in a chaste body [*casto corpore*]' and to be 'chaste [*castos*] and pure from all sin,' retaining only the subsequent allusion to following God's commandments (recast as an imperative, as in Fadda I), to which he adds admonitions to believe in and love God, capped off with a quotation of the beatitude from Mt. 5:8: 'Now then, beloved men, let us believe in our Lord, and love him and obey his commandments, and then will be fulfilled in us what he himself said, "Blessed are the clean [*clæne*] in heart, for they shall see God."' The Blickling homilist, in short, interprets *clænness* more broadly than the author of Fadda I, or Ælfric and Wulfstan, for all of whom it means 'chastity.'[49] For the Blickling homilist, although the virginity of Christ and Mary constitutes the purest form of *clænness*, the virtue can also be fulfilled by Christians who have mercy, faith, love, and obedience. The homilist apparently wished to make *clænness* relevant to an audience consisting of laypersons or of secular clergy who might marry, but in any case probably not one made up exclusively of monks or unmarried regular clergy. It is not necessary to assume that the homilist himself was a secular priest, much less a married one; but whatever his own estate, he has adapted the Nativity sermon in order to expand its privileging of chastity to a more inclusive set of Christian virtues. His motive may have been to distance himself from the connotation of clerical celibacy that had been attached to the word *clænness* by the reformers.

I have argued elsewhere that the proper definition of the virtue *timor Domini* was similarly contested during the Benedictine Reform.[50] The reformers wished to define the virtue *timor Domini* in relation to monastic ascesis, specifically obedience to a rule and renunciation of personal property, thereby implying that the secular clergy were not, and could not be, God-fearing. The author of Vercelli Homilies XI–XIII, on the other hand, who may have been a secular cleric, attempted to reconcile fear of God with a spiritual life that permitted wealth. Just as 'fear of God' was open to alternative constructions, so too was 'cleanness.' An ambiguous term, *clænness* might be restricted to 'chastity' through equation with Latin *castitas,* and thus appropriated by monks, nuns, and reformed clergy, but it was also open to a broader interpretation as 'moral purity,' a conveniently fungible virtue not confined to sexual renunciation, and therefore accessible to the laity and to married clergy as a range of moral virtues including mercy, love of God, and obedience to his commandments (but not necessarily to a 'rule'). These constructions of *clænness* were not in strict complementary distribution, for the broader construction could equally apply to monks and regular clergy, while the narrower one could apply to widows, to unmarried secular clergy, and to laypersons who chose to remain chaste. Yet for Ælfric, Wulfstan, and the author of Fadda I, Christ's exemplary *clænness* was specifically a model of sexual purity, which suggests that the term had been polarized by the reformers' insistence on celibacy as a distinguishing virtue of monks and regular clergy. It is no accident that the reformers focused on the virtues of fear of God and *clænness,* for the one directly engaged the monastic vows of poverty and obedience, the other the vow of chastity, and both could be invoked to validate the reformers' claim to a distinctive holiness and their concomitant claim to ecclesiastical supremacy.

That a common Latin source (allowing for possible variant readings) should have been made to support divergent views of the relation between *clænness* and holiness – in some cases in contradiction of the source itself – is a salutary reminder that Anglo-Saxon vernacular authors might betray what they translated to make it accord with their own presuppositions or with the needs and conditions of their intended audience. Source analysis does not, as sometimes alleged, inevitably privilege Latin 'originals' over vernacular 'derivatives,' or blind us to the purposes or agendas that OE texts that happen to have Latin sources may have served in their own time.[51] On the contrary, the discovery of Latin sources opens a window upon their interested manipulation by vernacular authors, making us privy to deletions, additions, and alterations that were concealed in the very act of translation, and enabling us to make connections not only with the antecedent Latin texts, but also with the OE texts' historical moment.

NOTES

1 *PL* 39:1993–4 (in quoting the *PL* I have omitted the editorial headings summarizing the content of each section of the homily). See Jan Machielsen,

A New Latin Source for Two Old English Homilies 257

Clavis Patristica Pseudepigraphorum Medii Aevi IA–B: Opera Homiletica, 2 vols. CCSL (Turnhout: Brepols, 1990): IA, 166 (no. 910 = no. 5552), and Hermann Josef Frede, Kirchenschriftsteller: Verzeichnis und Sigel, 4th ed., Vetus Latina: Die Reste der altlateinischen Bibel 1.1 (Freiburg im Breisgau: Herder, 1995), 267. The *In Principio* database lists two additional copies in Rome, Biblioteca Vallicelliana III, fol. 40, and XXVI, fols 55v–6, for which see Anna Maria Vichi Giorgetti and Sergio Mottironi, *Catalogo dei manoscritti della Biblioteca Vallicelliana*, vol. 1, Ministero della pubblica istruzione, indici e cataloghi n.s. 7 (Rome: Istituto poligrafico dello Stato, Libreria dello Stato, 1961), 1:42 and 379.

2 *Nuove omelie anglosassoni della rinascenza benedettina*, ed. A.M. Luiselli Fadda, Filologia germanica, Testi e studi 1 (Florence: Felice Le Monnier, 1977), 11–15; I have occasionally altered Luiselli Fadda's punctuation where the Latin source suggests a different clause- or sentence-division. Where her numbered sections include more than one sentence, I have distinguished them by letter (a, b, etc.) in order to facilitate cross-reference in the discussion below. On the manuscript, see N.R. Ker, *Catalogue of Manuscripts Containing Anglo-Saxon* (1957; repr. with a Supplement, Oxford: Oxford University Press, 1990), item 336 art. 6. For bibliography on the homily, see Janet M. Bately, *Anonymous Old English Homilies: A Preliminary Bibliography of Source Studies* (Binghamton, NY: Center for Medieval and Early Renaissance Studies, 1993), 52–3 (Hom M 5 [B.3.5.5]).

3 *The Blickling Homilies*, ed. and trans. R. Morris, EETS o.s. 58, 63, 73 (1874–80; repr. in one vol., London: Oxford University Press, 1967), 13, lines 19–27; *The Blickling Homilies: Edition and Translation*, ed. and trans. Richard J. Kelly (London: Continuum, 2003), 8, lines 145–52. Kelly argues that the homily is for the Nativity; earlier scholars, including Rudolf Willard, regarded it as an Annunciation homily (see Kelly's discussion, 164). Mary Clayton, however, points to evidence in favour of the Annunciation that seems decisive (*The Cult of the Virgin Mary in Anglo-Saxon England*, CSASE 2 [Cambridge: Cambridge University Press, 1990], 223). For further references, see Bately, *Anonymous Old English Homilies*: HomU 18 (B.3.4.18).

4 Henri Barré, 'Le "mystère" d'Ève à la fin de l'époque patristique en Occident,' *Bulletin de la société française d'Études Mariales* 13 (1955): 61–97 at 92 (no. 64); Frede, *Kirchenschriftsteller*, 162.

5 Réginald Grégoire, *Homéliaires liturgiques médiévaux: analyse de manuscrits*, Biblioteca degli 'Studi medievali' 12 (Spoleto: Centro italiano di studi sull'Alto Medioevo, 1980), 229.

6 Grégoire, *Homéliaires liturgiques*, 141 (Alanus) and 195 (Egino). For the homiliary of Alanus, see also Edoardo Hosp, 'Il sermonario di Alano di

Farfa,' *Ephemerides Liturgicae* 50 (1936): 375–83; 51 (1937): 210–41.
7 See Henri Barré, 'Sermons mariales inédits "in Natale Domini,"' *Marianum* 25 (1963): 39–93 at 85. On the authority of Heinrich Schenkl, *Bibliotheca Patrum Latinorum Britannica* (1891–1908; repr. Hildesheim: G. Olms, 1969), Barré ('Le "mystère" d'Ève,' 92), states that the sermon also occurs in 'Cheltenham 1326' (now Chicago, Newberry Library, MS 1); but Schenkl was incorrect in identifying this sermon as *Sermo* App. 125. See Maurice P. Cunningham, 'Contents of the Newberry Library Homiliarium,' *Sacris Erudiri* 7 (1955): 267–301 at 279.
8 Antoine Chavasse, 'Le Sermonnaire d'Agimond: Ses sources immédiates,' in *Kyriakon: Festschrift Johannes Quasten*, ed. Patrick Granfield and Josef A. Jungmann, 2 vols (Münster: Aschendorff, 1970), 2:800–10 at 804; and *Biblioteca Casinensis seu codicum manuscriptorum qui in tabulario Casinensi asservantur series*, 5 vols ([Monte Cassino]: ex Typographia Casinensi, 1873–94), 1:262–3.
9 London, BL Harley 652, fols 1*–4*; Helmut Gneuss, *Handlist of Anglo-Saxon Manuscripts: A List of Manuscripts and Manuscript Fragments Written or Owned in England up to 1100*, MRTS 241 (Tempe: Arizona Center for Medieval and Renaissance Studies, 2001), no. 423.9. See J.E. Cross and Thomas N. Hall, 'Fragments of Alanus of Farfa's Roman Homiliary and Abridgments of Saints' Lives by Goscelin in London, British Library, Harley 652,' in *Bright is the Ring of Words: Festschrift für Horst Weinstock zum 65. Geburtstag*, ed. Clausdirk Pollner, Helmut Rohlfing, and Frank-Rutger Hausmann, Abhandlungen zur Sprache und Literatur 85 (Bonn: Romanistischer Verlag, 1996), 49–61 (the fragment does not include *Sermo* App. 125). Another pseudo-Augustinian sermon for the feast of the Virgin included in the homiliary of Alanus was used by OE poets and homilists, but it is not certain that it was transmitted to them via Alanus. See Clayton, *The Cult of the Virgin Mary*, 188–9; cf. also 211–12. J.E. Cross, 'Blickling Homily XIV and the Old English Martyrology on John the Baptist,' *Anglia* 93 (1975): 145–60, has argued that one OE homilist 'had available a homiliary largely based on Alanus' (147). Cf. also Cross, *Cambridge Pembroke College MS. 25: A Carolingian Sermonary Used by Anglo-Saxon Preachers*, King's College London Medieval Studies 1 (London: King's College, 1987), 61–3.
10 I am aware of only one homiliary that transmits both these sermons, that preserved in Melk, Benediktinerstift MS 432 [218] (s. xv), fols 28r–30r (App. 120) and 42v–3v (App. 125). See the online index of Melk manuscripts, Kommission für Schrift- und Buchwesen des Mittelalters der Österreichischen Akademie der Wissenschaften, Stiftsbibliothek Melk (OSB), Autorenregister, http://www.oeaw.ac.at/ksbm/melk/aut.htm, under 'Pseudo-

Augustine.' On Melk 432, a late copy of 'un receuil de sermons anciens,' see Raymond Étaix, 'Trois nouveaux sermons à restituer à la collection de pseudo-Maxime,' *Revue Bénédictine* 97 (1987): 28–41 at 28–9.
11 For these sermons, see below, nn. 20 and 22.
12 At this point a substantial section of the Latin homily (from 'O sacrum et coeleste mysterium' to 'ipse etiam liberator esset, qui fuerat et creator') has been passed over by the homilist. The omitted passage includes an excellent example of the motif of Adam's creation from the 'virginal' earth, which has been discussed in connection with *Guthlac B* by Thomas D. Hill, 'The First Beginning and the Purest Earth: *Guthlac B*, Lines 1–14,' *NQ* n.s. 28 (1981): 387–9.
13 The obvious omission of *mortem* is confirmed by the Ambrosian source for this sentence, 'quae mortem prior gustauerat ...' (on the sermon's use of Ambrose see below, p. 251). Ambrose's 'quae ... prior' and Fadda I's 'þæt ærest' also suggest that that the homilist's text of App. 125 read *quae* instead of *quia*.
14 It is tempting to omit *ond* here, yielding a correlative *þa ... þa* construction with the previous clause.
15 This clearly renders *occurrunt*, though in the Latin the verb belongs to the previous clause.
16 Fadda's reading (she translates the clause 'noi che conosciamo Cristo nella sua natura umana') is an emendation of MS *mænnisilce* corrected from *mænniscile*; but in view of the Latin *charissimi* (there is no reference to Christ's humanity) one suspects that this is a corruption of an abbreviation for 'men þa leofestan.'
17 Fadda cites Deut. 6:5, Matt. 22:37–40, Mark 12:30–1, Luke 10:27; the quotation (through 'quam te ipsum') is closest to Matthew, but the last clause ('qui enim diligit ... impleuit') is not from Matthew, but from Romans 13:8.
18 The ambiguity of the Latin *per Virginem* ('through the Virgin' or 'through a virgin') cannot be captured in English.
19 Nancy M. Thompson, '*Hit Segð on Halgum Bocum*: The Logic of Composite Old English Homilies,' *PQ* 81 (2002): 383–419; see also her dissertation, 'The Milk of Doctrine: Translation and Homiletic Method in Early England' (PhD diss., Stanford University, 1994).
20 Mary F. Wack and Charles D. Wright, 'A New Latin Source for the Old English "Three Utterances" Exemplum,' *ASE* 20 (1990): 187–202; Charles D. Wright, *The Irish Tradition in Old English Literature*, CSASE 6 (Cambridge: Cambridge University Press, 1993), 215–16, 264–5. A Latin parallel, though perhaps not a direct source, for another passage (§§25, 28–9) was noted by Fadda (*Nuove omelie*, 2–3); for additional parallels see Charles D. Wright,

'*Docet Deus, Docet Diabolus*: A Hiberno-Latin Theme in an Old English Body-and-Soul Homily,' *NQ* n.s. 34 (1987): 451–3 at 453, n. 14.

21 That *euangelium/godspel* might refer not simply to one of the four Gospels but more generally to 'the body of doctrine taught by Christ and his apostles' (BTS, s.v. 'god-spell' I) is suggested by Matt. 24:14 (cited by BTS).

22 Pseudo-Augustine, *Sermo* App. 251 (*PL* 39:2210); another version, falsely attributed to Ambrose, is printed in *PL* 17:673. See J.E. Cross, 'A Doomsday Passage in an Old English Sermon for Lent,' *Anglia* 100 (1982): 103–8; Wright, *The Irish Tradition*, 218. In a paper in preparation I identify another version of the Doomsday sermon whose text is significantly closer to Fadda I. As Wack and Wright note, the Three Utterances and Doomsday sermons often circulated together. They are also conflated in a sermon in the homiliary of the bishop of Prague (*Das Homiliar des Bischofs von Prag. Saec. XII*, ed. Ferd. Hecht, Beiträge zur Geschichte Böhmens 1.1 [Prague: H. Mercy, 1863], 66–7). See Charles D. Wright and Roger Wright, 'Additions to the Bobbio Missal: *De dies malus* and *Joca monachorum* (fols. 6r–8v),' in *The Bobbio Missal: Liturgy and Religious Culture in Merovingian Gaul*, ed. Yitzhak Hen and Rob Meens, Cambridge Studies in Palaeography and Codicology (Cambridge: Cambridge University Press, 2004), 79–139 at 85, n. 11.

23 If the homilist was prepared to alter his source for doctrinal or ideological reasons, he does not seem to have been interested in rhetorical heightening for its own sake. In the passages translated from known Latin sources there is little in the way of alliteration, homoeoteleuton, anaphora, doublets, or other figures of repetition that we find in many OE anonymous homilies (and indeed in some of the unsourced parts of Fadda I), and such as do occur here seem incidental, or inevitably carried over in translation (e.g., §17a: *onfeng ... onfengon*; cf. *suscepit ... suscipiamus*). In §14b, however, the sequence *gebædan ... wæs beboden ... ond bodedan* is generated from the non-alliterating verbs *jubetur ... nuntiare* in the Latin, and there is one possible doublet (§14b: *bodedan ond cyðdon*), but these verbs are not really synonymous. The paronomasia in §14b-c on *ærest* 'first' and *ærist* 'resurrection,' however, is not echoed in the Latin (cf. *primum ... resurrectionem*) and is effective whether it was deliberate or accidental. On the stylistic features of rhythmical prose in OE anonymous homilies, see Otto Funke, 'Studien zur alliterierenden und rhythmisierenden Prosa in der älteren altenglischen Homiletik,' *Anglia* 80 (1962): 9–36.

24 This conflation of the two Latin clauses was not the result of homoeoteleuton induced by the repetition of 'ut nobis ostenderet,' because the homilist

omits the second explanation rather than the first. The curious phrase 'Drihtnes onfæncge' may also bear some relation to 'Deum ... suscepisse,' but does not accurately translate it, and there is no plausible equivalent in the Latin for 'beforan Godes gesihðe.'

25 Cf. the phrase 'se man onfehþ Godes ...' (§17b, the homilist's addition).
26 He is willing to use *beran* when *portare* refers to Mary carrying Christ in her womb (§17c: 'he wæs geboren þurh þære clænan fæmnan leoma,' cf. 'Deum ... quem virginis casta membra portaverunt'); but even here *wæs geboren* is ambiguous, and the primary sense seems to be 'was born through' rather 'was borne/carried by.'
27 See Barré, 'Le "mystère" d'Eve.' A concise (and more accessible) discussion of the Eve-Mary antithesis, with reference to patristic sources, is J.N.D. Kelly, *Early Christian Doctrines*, 5th ed. (San Francisco: Harper & Row, 1976), 493–7.
28 Pseudo-Augustine does not specifically name Mary Magdalene, but she is clearly the 'mulier' to whom the Resurrection was first declared.
29 Part of this sentence (from 'non perpetui reatus' to 'transfudit et gratiam') is taken almost verbatim from Ambrose's *Expositio euangelii secundum Lucam* X.156, CSEL 32:514), as Barré noted ('Le "mystère" d'Ève,' 74). The same sentence from Ambrose was cited by Bede in his commentaries on Mark and Luke (ed. D. Hurst, CCSL 120:643 and 412–13).
30 As Thomas N. Hall has shown, the contrast between Eve and Mary Magdalene, a well developed variant of the Eve–Virgin Mary antithesis in patristic and medieval tradition, was often linked to the image of the *poculum mortis* or 'drink of death' dispensed to Adam by Eve. See Hall, 'A Gregorian Model for Eve's *biter drync* in *Guthlac B*,' *RES* n.s. 44 (1993): 157–75 at 167–73.
31 The homilist's reluctance to apply to the female sex generally the honour accorded to the women who first saw the risen Christ was not shared by Odo of Cluny, who correlated the Eve-Mary antithesis with Mary Magdalene, through whom 'the shame of the female sex has been undone, and the splendor of our resurrection, which arose in the Lord's resurrection, has been granted to us by her': *Occupatio* 6.367–8, a passage translated in Jaroslav Pelikan, *The Growth of Medieval Theology (600–1300)*, vol. 3 of *The Christian Tradition: A History of the Development of Doctrine* (Chicago: University of Chicago Press, 1978), 167. The unique manuscript of this work, Paris, Bibliothèque Sainte-Geneviève 2410 (s. x^{ex} – xi^{in}), was probably written at Canterbury (see Gneuss, *Handlist*, no. 903). This passage is closely similar to one from Odo's sermon on the veneration of the Magdalene quoted by Hall, 'A Gregorian Model,' 171. That the female sex was exalted through

Christ's appearance to the women at the tomb was a patristic commonplace. See generally Rosemarie Nürnberg, 'Apostolae Apostolorum: Die Frauen am Grab als erste Zeuginnen der Auferstehung in der Väterexegese,' in *Stimuli: Exegese und ihre Hermeneutik in Antike und Christentum. Festschrift für Ernst Dassmann*, ed. Georg Schöllgen and Clemens Scholten, Jahrbuch für Antike und Christentum, Ergänzungsband 23 (Münster: Aschendorffsche Verlagsbuchhandlung, 1996), 228–42.

32 In context (and supported by comparison with the Latin, despite the other changes made by the homilist) this seems to be the most likely meaning of 'hire wærþ on ecnesse ongewrecen,' since the 'vengeance' that Eve herself suffered came to an end with the Harrowing of Hell. The perverse logic is reminiscent of the claim in the *Collectio Canonum Hibernensis* that women have no legal standing as witnesses because the apostles did not believe the women who told them Christ had risen: 'Testimonium feminae non accipitur, sicut apostoli testimonium feminarum non acceperunt de resurrectione Christi' (*Hib.* XVI.iii.g, ed. F.H.W. Wasserschleben, in *Die irische Kanonensammlung*, 2nd ed. [1885; repr. Aalen: Scientia, 1966], 46).

33 Although the homily cannot be dated narrowly on linguistic grounds alone, according to Luiselli Fadda's analysis its language is compatible (as the title of her edition implies) with a Benedictine Reform context.

34 Pauline Stafford, 'Queens, Nunneries and Reforming Churchmen: Gender, Religious Status and Reform in Tenth- and Eleventh-Century England,' *Past and Present* 163 (1999): 3–35 at 7; the two following quotations are from pages 8–9.

35 The reformers' veneration of the Virgin Mary was no paradox, for Mary was superior to and distinct from all other women, and was praised as much for her obedience to God's will as for her perpetual virginity.

36 Ælfric makes the same distinction in his exegesis of the Parable of the Sower in *Catholic Homilies* II.6, ed. Malcolm Godden, *Ælfric's Catholic Homilies: The Second Series. Text*, EETS s.s. 5 (London: Oxford University Press, 1979), 57, lines 136–42 and 145–6. On Ælfric's typically more restrictive definition of *clænness* as 'chastity,' see below, pp. 253–4.

37 See *Catholic Homilies* I.21, ed. Peter Clemoes, in *Ælfric's Catholic Homilies: The First Series. Text*. EETS s.s.17 (Oxford: Oxford University Press, 1997), 352, lines 218–23. In his commentary (*Ælfric's Catholic Homilies: Introduction, Commentary and Glossary*, EETS s.s. 18 [Oxford: Oxford University Press, 2000], 174), Malcolm Godden does not identify a source for this passage apart from the biblical quotation, but notes that Ælfric is here developing a reference to Christ's chastity in his Gregorian source for the preceding passage. For the pastoral letter, see *Die Hirtenbriefe Ælfrics in altenglischer und*

lateinischer Fassung, ed. Bernhard Fehr, BaP 9 (1914; repr. with a supplement by Peter Clemoes, Darmstadt: Wissenschaftliche Buchgesellschaft, 1966), Brief 2 [Latin], page 36 (§§7–9), and Brief 2 [Old English: ÆLet 2 (Wulfstan 1)], pages 75–6 (§11–13). The OE letter is also edited by Dorothy Whitelock, in *Councils & Synods with Other Documents Relating to the English Church. I: A.D. 871–1204. Part I: 871–1066*, ed. Whitelock, M. Brett, and C.N.L. Brooke (Oxford: Clarendon, 1981), 260–302.

38 ÆLet 1 (Wulfsige), in *Die Hirtenbriefe*, ed. Fehr, Brief I, page 2 (§2), and page 5 (§17), also ed. Whitelock, *Councils & Synods*, 196 and 200; ÆLet 5 (Sigefyrth), in *Angelsächsische Homilien und Heiligenleben*, ed. Bruno Assmann, BaP 3 (Kassel: Wigand, 1889), Homily II, page 16, lines 61–3 (this section is reused in Ælfric's homily *De sancta uirginitate*, collated by Assmann; cf. Aaron J Kleist, 'Ælfric's Corpus: A Conspectus,' *Florilegium* 18.2 [2001]: 113–64 at 120–1 and 137). See also *Catholic Homilies* II.1, ed. Godden, page 11, lines 283–5; ÆHomM 8, in *Angelsächsische Homilien*, ed. Assmann, Homily III, page 47, line 564; ÆHom 20, in *Homilies of Ælfric: A Supplementary Collection*, Homily XIX, ed. John C. Pope, 2 vols, EETS o.s. 259–60 (London: Oxford University Press, 1967–8), 2:624; *Lives of Saints* (Æthelthryth), ed. Walter W. Skeat, *Ælfric's Lives of Saints*, EETS o.s. 76, 82, 94, 114 (1881–1900; repr. in 2 vols, Oxford: Oxford University Press, 1966), line 131, and *Lives of Saints* (Peter's Chair), ed. Skeat, line 202. None of these passages has a known patristic source.

39 Ambrose, *Expositio in evangelii secundum Lucam*, PL 15:1803; Leo, *Sermones*, PL 57:749.

40 Cassiodorus, *Variae* X.III.5, PL 69:797; *Vita S. Mariae Aegyptiacae*, PL 73:684 (the source of the phrase 'ealdor æghwilcre clænnysse' in *Lives of Saints* 23 (Mary of Egypt), ed. Hugh Magennis, *The Old English Life of St Mary of Egypt: An Edition of the Old English Text with Modern English Parallel-Text Translation*, Exeter Medieval Texts and Studies [Exeter: University of Exeter Press, 2002], 100, lines 654–5); Aldhelm, *De virginitate* XXIII, ed. Scott Gwara, CCSL 124:269; Pseudo-Alcuin, *Homilia*, PL 101:1300; Sedulius Scottus, *Sedulii Scotti Collectaneum in Apostolum*, ed. Hermann Josef Frede and Herbert Stanjek, 2 vols, Aus der Geschichte der lateinischen Bibel 31–2 (Freiburg: Herder, 1996), 2:628, line 8; Ado of Vienne, *Martyrology*, PL 123:311; *Vita Amalbergae virginis*, in *AASS*, 3 Jul.: 90, line 62.

41 Clare A. Lees, *Tradition and Belief: Religious Writing in Late Anglo-Saxon England*, Medieval Cultures 19 (Minneapolis: University of Minnesota Press, 1999), 133–53; Robert Upchurch, 'For Pastoral Care and Political Gain: Ælfric of Eynsham's Preaching on Marital Celibacy,' *Traditio* 59 (2004): 39–78.

42 Ælfric cites the verse in similarly reduced form in his Letter for Wulfsige (ed. Whitelock, *Councils & Synods*, 197).
43 'ge þurh hine sylfne, ge þurh his halgan þegenas, / ge wæpmenn, ge wimmenn, þe wunedon on clænnysse' (*Angelsächsische Homilien*, ed. Assmann, page 16, lines 62–3).
44 *Wulfstan: Sammlung der ihm zugeschriebenen Homilien nebst Untersuchungen über ihre Echtheit*, ed. Arthur Napier (1883; repr. with a bibliographical supplement by Klaus Ostheeren, Dublin: Weidmann, 1967), 269, lines 29–31. On Wulfstan's authorship of this work, see Dorothy Bethurum, ed., *The Homilies of Wulfstan* (Oxford: Clarendon, 1957), 39–41, who characterizes it as notes for an address rather than a sermon, and Joyce Tally Lionarons, 'Napier Homily L: Wulfstan's Eschatology at the Close of His Career,' in *Wulfstan, Archbishop of York: The Proceedings of the Second Alcuin Conference*, ed. Matthew Townend, Studies in the Early Middle Ages 10 (Turnhout: Brepols, 2004), 413–28. Fehr, *Die Hirtenbriefe*, page lxxvii (who suggests inserting the words '[heoldon þa clænnysse]' between 'folgedon' and 'þe we') considered the passage an echo of Ælfric's First Pastoral Letter II.17, but the phrasing is much closer to the Letter to Sigefyrth. Malcolm Godden, 'The Relations of Wulfstan and Ælfric: A Reassessment,' in *Wulfstan, Archbishop of York*, ed. Townend, 353–74 at 373, has stated that Wulfstan 'had more relaxed views on clerical chastity' than Ælfric, citing a revision of Letter 1 that removes deacons from the requirement.
45 Upchurch, 'For Pastoral Care,' 71–5, with reference to *Catholic Homilies* II.6, ed. Godden, pages 57–8, lines 136–66.
46 H.G. Fiedler, 'The Source of the First Blickling Homily,' *Modern Language Quarterly* 6 (1904): 122–4.
47 For these, see Mary Clayton, 'The Sources of Blickling Homily 1' (1996), in *Fontes Anglo-Saxonici: World Wide Web Register*, http://fontes.english.ox.ac.uk/, accessed 27 November 2004.
48 Clayton, who has closely compared the Blickling homily with its previously discovered sources (*The Cult of the Virgin Mary*, 222–30), had tentatively suggested (229) that the conclusion may have been the homilist's own addition.
49 The majority of the citations in *DOE* for the sense 'chastity' are from Ælfric.
50 See Charles D. Wright, 'Vercelli Homilies XI–XIII and the Anglo-Saxon Benedictine Reform: Tailored Sources and Implied Audiences,' in *Preacher, Sermon and Audience in the Middle Ages*, ed. Carolyn Muessig, New History of the Sermon 2 (Leiden: Brill, 2002), 203–27.
51 Source analysis does, however, privilege the immediate contexts of the composition of an OE text by an author, who is assumed to have chosen the

Latin source and translated it for specific purposes. In the case of a vernacular homily, the main purpose would normally have been to indoctrinate an audience (whether a congregation or a readership) who did not share the preacher's access to the Latin source, and who would not be privy to the changes he made. The homilist's translation is thus itself an instance of 'reception' of the Latin text, which he in turn mediates for his audience. For a fuller discussion, see my 'Anonymous Homilies and Latin Sources,' forthcoming in *Precedent, Practice, and Appropriation: The Old English Homily*, ed. Aaron J Kleist (Turnhout: Brepols).

Christ's Birth through Mary's Right Breast: An Echo of Carolingian Heresy in the Old English *Adrian and Ritheus*

THOMAS N. HALL

It would be difficult to single out the most arcane publication ever issued under the name of Thomas D. Hill, but a leading contender is surely the edition and translation of the two OE question-and-answer dialogues known as *Solomon and Saturn* and *Adrian and Ritheus*, which he published together with J.E. Cross in 1982.[1] The labyrinthine commentary that accompanies Cross and Hill's edition of these texts is a magical mystery tour through some of the most extravagant and recondite learning of the early Middle Ages, an overflowing cornucopia of curiosities. What makes this edition such a fascinating work of scholarship is that Cross and Hill are completely at home in this remote and unfamiliar world, finding no difficulty at all situating these texts within the scattered framework of medieval proverbial and sapiential literature in Latin, Greek, and over half a dozen medieval vernaculars. This is a world of biblical mysteries and marvels of nature bound up in questions about where lightning comes from, who planted the first vineyard, what man first spoke to a dog, why the raven is black and the sea is salty, how many wings the soul flies on when it ascends to heaven, where the grave of Moses is to be found, and what son first avenged his father in his mother's womb (the answer to that one is the son of the serpent). For each of these questions Cross and Hill generate a bibliographical farrago of sources, analogues, near-analogues, and suspected potential quasi-analogues to map out the territory that these questions inhabit, but in one solitary instance they find themselves at a loss for an explanation, and this is in their commentary on *Adrian and Ritheus* question number 41, which reads in its entirety: 'Saga me hu wæs crist acenned of maria his meder. Ic þe secge, ðurc þæt swiðre breost' [Tell me how Christ was born from his mother Mary. I tell you, through the right breast].[2]

To the first-time reader this answer is so unexpected that one's initial response is probably to wonder whether the text is corrupt at this point or whether there is a play on words that is lost to a modern audience. But the language is unequivocal and allows little room for another translation. The only word in the sentence 'Ic þe secge, ðurc þæt swiðre breost' that has enough of a semantic range in OE to permit a variety of interpretations is the word *breost*, which depending on context can sometimes mean 'chest' or 'stomach,' and in the poetry frequently has the sense of 'mind,' 'thought,' or 'consciousness' as one of the intellectual faculties or cognitive activities that Anglo-Saxon poets typically locate within the breast.[3] But this does not alter the fact that the primary sense of the word *breost* in OE prose is physiological, and that in just as many cases as not it simply means 'breast.'[4] Even if through some unusual extended metaphorical application of this word the compiler of *Adrian and Ritheus* intended *breost* to denote Mary's womb,[5] we would still have to contend with the idea that she had two of them, one on the left and one on the right, and that the one on the right is the one from which Christ was born. So far as I can make out, a native Anglo-Saxon's reading of this line would have been essentially the same as ours: that Christ was born, literally and physically, through Mary's right breast.

In the characteristically learned commentary that Cross and Hill append to this question, they start out by suggesting a possible connection to one or more mythological or folkloristic traditions involving divine miraculous birth, and here is what they say:

> We have no exact parallels for this question in the dialogue literature or elsewhere. There are, however, two kinds of traditional speculation which probably influenced its formulation. One is the folkloristic motif that a hero is born in some extraordinary way. The theme of the hero 'born through the mother's side' (Caesarean birth) is widely attested (see Stith Thompson T 540.1 and A 511.1) in English balladry and elsewhere. Also Jerome records a god-figure Buddha being born from a virgin's side on the authority of the Gymnosophists: 'apud Gymnosophistas Indiae, quasi per manus huius opinionis auctoritas traditur, quod Buddam (*al* Buldam) principem dogmatis eorum, a latera suo virgo generavit' (*Adversus Jovinianum* I.42, PL 23 [1845], col 275). The Irish author of the *Saltair na Rann* (I:i above) was influenced, possibly at some remove, by the classical story of Minerva's birth from the head of Jove, although this could have been an acceptable adaptation of Christian mythography since Minerva was god-

dess of wisdom and Christ is the 'Wisdom' of God. Certain authors, taking a curiously literalistic approach to the description of the Virgin's conception in scripture when Gabriel came and spoke, had Christ conceived and born through the ear as in I:ii above (for other examples see Hirn, *The Sacred Shrine*, 211).

But there may be another influence pertaining to theological discussion and heretical belief. A number of heresies remain in OE literature merely by the transmission of 'authoritative' texts. The sober M.R. James (*Latin Infancy Gospels* [Cambridge: Cambridge University Press 1927], xxv) sees a docetic belief about the birth of Christ in the infancy gospels, preserved in English manuscripts of the tenth and eleventh centuries, which are extensions on the *Protevangelium*. He notes that, in these, 'the birth is not a real birth at all,' and that 'here that which is born is a Light which gradually takes the form of a child. It has no weight, it needs no cleansing, it does not cry, it has intelligence from the moment of birth ... it is in short not a human child at all.'[6]

In the end, however, Cross and Hill throw up their hands and admit defeat, conceding that 'if there is not some obtuse, and, to us, undetectable, error, the OE answer could be a crude attempt to emphasize the "virginitas in partu" of Mary or be an echo of an heretical belief. But our writing around the topic above is a confession of our mystification.'[7] And with this they proceed to the next question in the dialogue.

These remarks by Cross and Hill constitute the sum of critical commentary on *Adrian and Ritheus* question 41. Their attempt to uncover the 'traditional speculation' that could have given rise to this claim about the manner of Christ's birth may not quite dispel all of the mystery surrounding this item in the dialogue, but it does, I believe, open up several relevant areas for exploration that will bear further scrutiny, and in the discussion that follows I propose to pick up where Cross and Hill left off, pursue some of the threads in their commentary, and attempt to place this question and its answer within the context of a particular theological debate that would certainly have been known to a late Anglo-Saxon religious community. In the end my argument will remain tentative, something on the order of an educated guess, but it will try to make the point that Cross and Hill were on the right track to begin with, even if they were not aware of it.

A reasonable place to begin is with the most promising clues in Cross and Hill's commentary, building on their analysis by offering some additional supporting examples. From a literary perspective one of the most intriguing sets of analogues adduced by Cross and Hill is the group of folkloric narratives about a hero born from his mother's side. For witnesses to stories of this kind, Cross and Hill defer to Stith Thompson's *Motif-Index of Folk-Literature*, which catalogues instances from numerous literary traditions in several languages but which for this particular tale-type unfortunately looks to a much later period.[8] The English ballads that they cite, for instance, are nearly all from the sixteenth century and later.[9] One can, however, look beyond Stith Thompson to find examples that are arguably from a period and literary tradition a little closer to *Adrian and Ritheus*, including several tales from early Irish legend that chronicle the adventures of characters who are all born from their mother's side or who are cut from their mother's womb. Several Irish kings and heroes are either born this way or are prophesied to be born this way, including Goll mac Morna, the one-eyed rival of Finn Mac Cumaill;[10] Furbaide Fer Bend, the prince of Ulster who is so beautiful that his enemies are rendered powerless in his presence;[11] and Furbaide's better-known father, Conchobar mac Nessa, who according to one recension of his birth-tale *Compert Conchobuir* leapt from his mother's side on the night Christ was born and plunged head over heels into the river.[12] The Yellow Book of Lecan preserves a tale about Fiacha Muillethan, the legendary king of Munster whose druidical father announced to his mother when she was about to give birth that if their son were born that very day he would never be more than a wizard's child, whereas if she could forestall his birth so that he were born the following day he would grow up to be king. To this prophecy the mother replies: 'Unless he shall come through my side, he shall not go the proper way till the morrow.' She then seats herself firmly on a flat stone to prevent the child's delivery, and the next day Fiacha is born at sunrise destined to be king.[13] Still another example from Irish literature appears in a tenth-century anecdote about the poet Athirne, who is credited with composing a spell while in his mother's womb that a poet can use to curse his host if denied a drink of ale. The anecdote begins by explaining why Athirne was known as 'Athirne the unmannerly':

> Why was he so called? Not hard to answer: from the chanting of a spell in his mother's womb. His mother came to fetch fire from a house where preparation for a feast was at hand. At the smell of the ale he leapt in her womb, and pitched her headlong as she was leaving the house. Then the woman thrice demanded a drink of the ale. Thrice the brewer refused,

saying that though she should die of it, and though her child should come forth through her side, the ale should not be broached for her, however long she might wait for the delivery.[14]

At these words Athirne unleashes a curse on the brewer's ale from within the womb. The ale explodes from its casks and floods the house, and as his mother is carried off in the deluge she gulps down three great draughts on her way out the door. The anecdote concludes before Athirne's birth actually takes place, but the brewer's refusal to give any ale to Athirne's mother even if Athirne should emerge from her side seems to indicate that this was the expected means of delivery in a moment of crisis.[15] In cataloguing later examples of stories about heroes born from their mothers' side, Stith Thompson designates these stories etiological accounts of the origin of Caesarean birth, a practice that may have been more common in the Middle Ages than it is today. In her 1990 monograph on Caesarean birth in the Middle Ages and the Renaissance, Renate Blumenfeld-Kosinski draws attention to a number of medieval manuscripts with illuminations depicting children being born through their mother's side or stomach.[16] To such visual representations of Caesarean birth one can add at least two narrative examples from twelfth-century English historiography: in the first, the *Liber Eliensis* informs us that Archbishop Wulfstan of York (d. 1023), the great homilist and statesman, was delivered by Caesarean section;[17] and in the second, the *Chronicle of the Archbishops of York* reports that according to local gossip one of Wulfstan's successors, Archbishop Cynesige of York (1051–60), was likewise cut from his mother's belly.[18] From the twelfth century onwards, ecclesiastical support for this method of delivery was encouraged by authorities such as Moses Maimonides and Odon de Sully, who advised women to deliver their children through an incision cut along one side.[19] There is, in other words, an established historical and iconographic record that makes it possible to link these narratives involving Caesarean birth to actual medieval practice. Cross and Hill see an important corollary to these heroic narratives in the myth of the Buddha figure born from the side of a virgin that Jerome documents in his treatise against Jovinian.[20] Since Jerome's account was known and repeated by Carolingian authors, it may conceivably have served, like the folktales, as an influential model for an Insular account of miraculous birth.[21]

From a different tradition entirely comes the interpretation of Christ's birth in the twelfth-century Irish Latin Infancy Gospel, which

M.R. James believed indebted to the docetic *Gospel of Peter*. Although it manifests itself in different ways, the fundamental tenet of docetism is the denial of the material reality of Christ's body, the belief that while on earth Christ was a purely spiritual being who nevertheless possessed a non-physical bodily appearance.[22] Beliefs of a docetic character are attested from as early as the second century, and their influence can be traced through a wide range of Gnostic and patristic writings, but the docetic interpretation of the Nativity was best known in the Middle Ages through translations of the Greek Infancy Gospel known as the *Protevangelium of James*, which dates to the late second century.[23] In the *Protevangelium*, Christ is born not in a manger as the canonical Gospel of Luke would have it but in a cave just outside Bethlehem where the Virgin Mary stops to rest on her journey. As she waits for Joseph to return with a midwife, a bright cloud suddenly envelops Mary, then dissipates as a blinding light fills the cave. When the light withdraws, Mary sees that the Christ child has miraculously appeared as a fully formed infant.[24] This account in the *Protevangelium* is virtually identical to the one in the Irish Infancy Gospel written a millennium later edited by James; docetic accounts of the Nativity were unquestionably available to Anglo-Saxon authors, but for reasons I will soon discuss, it is probably in opposition to such an idea rather than in support of it that the statement about Mary's right breast appears in *Adrian and Ritheus*.

Although they do not pursue it, an explanation that Cross and Hill at least gesture towards at the end of their commentary is that the answer to question 41 attempts in some crude if not heretical way to affirm the perpetual virginity of Mary, and here, I think, is where they were really on to something. As it turns out, several statements resembling the one in *Adrian and Ritheus* occur in Carolingian debates over the nature of the Virgin birth. At the heart of these debates is the ancient and traditional and widespread view that Christ's birth must have been a miraculous birth *ex utero clauso:* when Jesus was born, the womb remained closed, and Mary's virginity was preserved intact. In patristic and medieval commentary this miracle is often explained metaphorically by comparing Christ's emergence from the closed womb to his emergence from the closed sepulchre after the Resurrection or to his entry into the upper room through a closed door. Medieval writers often enforce these analogies by describing Mary's womb in terms of the biblical images of the sealed fountain and enclosed garden from the Song of Songs 4:12 or the closed portal of Ezek. 44:1–2.[25] Yet the precise manner of this miraculous birth – the way in which Christ physically came into the world as other children yet somehow avoided emerging from the womb – was never determined by anything approaching an infallible doctrinal authority. In 649, a Lateran council under Pope St Martin I proclaimed that Mary's virginity had been both perfect and perpetual, a claim that eventually gave rise to the formulaic creed that Mary maintained her virginity before, during, and after the Nativity. But not until the First Lateran Council of 1123 was the Nativity declared to have occurred 'without corruption.' Up until that point there was little guidance on the matter, and the actual details remained a mystery to the faithful.[26] One can imagine, then, that before the twelfth century the imprecise formulation of these teachings about the Virgin birth invited considerable speculation about how Christ was born.

One important witness to such speculation is Ratramnus of Corbie's tract *On the Parturition of Mary*, composed about 853, which relates a belief current in ninth-century Frankish territories to the effect that Christ was born not as other children but in a mysterious and unnatural way:

> There is a report, and we know of no one who doubts its authenticity, that throughout parts of Germany the ancient serpent is spreading the poison of a new perfidy and is attempting to subvert the catholic belief about the Saviour's Nativity with I know not what kind of devious fraud, insisting that Christ's birth took place not through the portal of the virginal womb as a true human birth, but unnaturally from some unknown and hidden recess as a beam of light shining forth into the air, so that he was not born but explosively discharged. For in that he did not follow the ways of the womb in being born, but came out by some other route just as if he were bursting through the wall of a house, he was not in a true sense born but was violently expelled.[27]

For all its apparent eccentricity, the account Ratramnus describes here bears the distinct imprint of docetism, the belief that because Christ was a fundamentally spiritual being who transcended human nature, his birth must have occurred in a divine and mysterious manner beyond the scope of physical human experience. Like the author of the *Protevangelium*, these anonymous Frankish heretics to whom Ratramnus refers evidently held that Christ came into the world as an immaterial presence, an unlocalizable emanation of brilliant light that then took human form.

That traces of docetism were present in northern Francia during the mid-ninth century when Ratramnus was writing is confirmed by another source. Just a year or two after Ratramnus composed his tract on the parturition, his abbot and mentor Paschasius Radbertus (d. ca. 860), living and working alongside Ratramnus at Corbie, wrote a treatise on the same subject (in part to refute Ratramnus) that alludes incidentally to a related form of the same idea.[28] In responding to a letter from a nun at Soissons who had asked him to explain the manner of Christ's birth since she had heard so many conflicting accounts, Radbertus reminds his correspondent that there are those who would argue that Christ was born just as any normal human child:

> They say that the blessed Virgin Mary could not have given birth and ought not have done so in any manner other than according to the common law of nature and in the same manner as all other women, so that it might be possible to speak of a real birth of Christ. They say, moreover, that if he was not born as other children, then his birth was not a true one. And for this reason they do not hold to the fantasy that Christ came forth like water through a pipe, nor do they believe that he passed through the Virgin's womb without conforming to the procedure of ordinary birth, but they believe instead that it is proper to suppose that he was born according to the law of nature in the manner of other children, and that Mary gave birth just like all other women.[29]

In the ensuing discussion, Radbertus opposes this position by arguing that Christ's birth was a miracle and could not have occurred naturally. But in defining his opponents' views, he sketches out a total of three possibilities: first, his own belief, that Christ's birth was a miraculous physical birth that transcended natural law and preserved Mary's virginity; second, the opposing view, that the Nativity was a normal human birth that adhered to the laws of nature and consequently put an end to Mary's virginity; and a third view, that before Christ became incarnate he emerged as an immaterial presence and passed through the Virgin 'like water through a pipe.' This last comment may not actually reflect a belief current among Radbertus's contemporaries since it sounds suspiciously like a quote attributed to the Gnostic Valentinian in Irenaeus's *Against Heresies*, where this idea is explicitly denounced and derided as a manifestation of docetism.[30] So it may be that Radbertus introduces this third idea merely as an example of the kind of heresy he would urge his correspondent to avoid. Yet the larger context of this remark is a discussion of popular beliefs current in his own time, so the possibility remains that Radbertus's tract may be taken as a corroboration of Ratramnus's report about the incursion of docetism into northern Francia.

Although Ratramnus fits squarely into the camp of Radbertus's opponents because of his belief in a natural and normal rather than a miraculous birth, his arguments are equally useful for understanding popular interpretations of the Nativity. In his defence of Christ's essential humanity in his tract *On the Parturition of Mary*, which is written in the form of an unaddressed letter, Ratramnus speaks further about the outlandish theories of Christ's birth that were circulating in the vicinity of Corbie at the time:

> But I ask you, why do you refuse to attribute to Christ a natural delivery from the virginal portal? You claim that it is for this reason, that if he exited through the portal of the womb, then the Virgin's integrity was defiled. But in fact according to your own reasoning, her integrity would have been violated no matter which orifice he emerged from. For if the Saviour's birth was necessarily corrupt according to the law of nature, it was necessarily so no matter how he emerged, whether through the side, or from the stomach, or from the kidneys, or through the upper or lower parts of the body. He simply did not come forth without damaging her integrity.[31]

After arguing further, Ratramnus criticizes his opponents' beliefs by caricaturing several even more bizarre explanations of Christ's birth:

> He did not come out a-locally, for that would be characteristic of an incorporeal nature to be separated at some length from the physical body. So you have to decide for certain which part of the body you want to designate. If you dismiss the womb, then consider the navel, or if you prefer, some more respectable bodily orifice. But if the entrances provided by nature are unsatisfactory, then rip open the stomach, expose the ribs, split open the spine – or who knows how these raving lunatics imagine it – open up the armpit! And in this way from your shady and thickly covered mountain you make your case for the Saviour's Nativity.[32]

Just who among his contemporaries may have been propounding these beliefs is difficult to say since Ratramnus never identifies them or says where he encountered them. The tone of his remarks is so heated that it is also difficult to tell where he is alluding to the actual beliefs of some of his contemporaries and where he is exaggerating or lampooning them. But can it be that in addition to the adherents of docetism whose ravings had reached Ratramnus and Radbertus, there had also arisen by the mid-ninth century proponents of a different kind of belief which held that Christ had been born through Mary's side or navel, or through another part of her body, so that it might be argued that her virginity was preserved intact?

Three additional reports suggest that there had. Two centuries after Ratramnus and Radbertus were writing, Berengar of Tours (d. 1088) composed a tract on the Eucharist entitled *On the Holy Feast* as a challenge to the teachings of his contemporary Lanfranc, who had begun formulating an early theory of the transubstantiation. Towards the close of his treatise, in confronting the argument that Christ had been born as other children through an open womb, Berengar takes the opportunity to repudiate a certain *fabula* that he had encountered alleging that Christ had been born in an unnatural manner. Quoting from the infancy narratives in Luke, he writes: '"The time was fulfilled," says the evangelist, "that Elizabeth should deliver, and she brought forth a son" [Luke 1:57], and subsequently "the days of Mary became fulfilled that she should deliver, and she brought forth a son" [Luke 2:6]. Can it be beyond reason to understand what the evangelist says, "she brought forth a son," according to the old wives' tale that says Christ was born from beneath his mother's armpit or through her ribs?'[33] One would dearly love to know more about this old wives' tale – and especially where Berengar had encountered it – but at this point in the text the only surviving manuscript of Berengar's tract breaks off, and we learn nothing else about it.

The second report is both much earlier and more circumspect. In October of 745 a synod convened in Rome under Pope Zacharias to hear the case against a heretical Frankish priest named Aldebert, whose eccentricities are known chiefly through the writings of St Boniface, the Anglo-Saxon apostle to the Germans.[34] A portion of a biography of Aldebert, which was read to the Roman synod and which survives in part in one of Boniface's letters, declares that Aldebert was filled with the grace of God while still in his mother's womb and was born a saint *ex electione Dei*. This biography, which in fact seems to have been an *auto*biography authored by Aldebert himself as an act of self-promotion, asserts that before Aldebert's birth his mother dreamed that a calf emerged from her right side and informed her that an angel had bestowed grace upon him while he was yet unborn.[35] After the full dossier of materials on Aldebert, including this biography, was read before the Roman synod, Pope Zacharias pronounced Aldebert mad and ordered that he be relieved of his priestly duties and be forced to undergo penance. Although Boniface's record of the synod's proceedings says nothing specific about the synod's response to the story about Aldebert's mother's dream, Jeffrey Burton Russell has suggested that its account of Aldebert's birth, prefigured by a dream about a calf born from its mother's right side, would have been found 'peculiarly blasphemous in view of the popular belief that Christ had been born through the right side of the Virgin.'[36] Whether the members of the Roman synod were aware of such a belief, there is no way to know for sure, but the symbolism of the dream does appear to be predicated on the familiarity of the concept of divine or miraculous birth through the mother's right side, and the synod's response would make most sense if they viewed this dream as a blasphemous caricature of Christ's Nativity as it would have been known in both Rome and Francia at the time.

The third report takes us out of the realm of Frankish heresy and straight into the heart of the twelfth-century mystical theology of Hildegard of Bingen, who in one of her minor writings enters into a discussion of the virgin birth, which she understands to have been typologically determined by the painless and incorrupt birth of Eve from Adam:

> When the blessed virgin was a little weakened, as if drowsy with sleep, the infant came forth from her side – not from the opening of the womb – without her knowledge and without pain, corruption, or filth, just as Eve emerged from the side of Adam. He did not enter through the vagina, for if he had come out that way there would have been corruption; but since the mother was intact in that place, the infant did not emerge there. And no placenta covered the infant in the Virgin Mother's womb, in the manner of other infants, because he was not conceived from virile seed.[37]

Hildegard doesn't tell us whether the infant Christ emerged from Mary's left side or her right, but she does make it clear that the consequence if not the purpose of this method of delivery was that it left the Virgin physically incorrupt and 'intact,' as if the birth had never happened at all.

Although none of these passages by Ratramnus, Radbertus, Berengar, the Roman council condemning Aldebert, or Hildegard of Bingen specifically claims that Christ was born through Mary's right *breast*, it is tempting to speculate that the answer to question 41 in *Adrian and Ritheus* reflects an ingenious variant of the beliefs recorded by these writers, born out of debates over the nature of the Nativity and passed on orally or through the censure of a prominent ecclesiastic such as Boniface. Like Cross and Hill, I find no exact parallel for the OE answer, but within the curiously literal mentality of medieval Christological debate, it may be possible to reconstruct the reasoning behind such an idea. For anyone troubled by the question of how Christ could have been born to the Virgin Mary as a real human child without passing through her closed womb, the claim that he emerged from her right breast achieves the desired goals of affirming Mary's perpetual virginity, underscoring the miraculous nature of the Nativity, and conveniently avoiding the much graver heresy of docetism, which was repeatedly targeted in patristic and medieval debate as a dangerous theological error. At the same time, the assertion that Christ was born through Mary's *breast* recalls the apparently well attested claims that he was born from her side or stomach, a belief that is difficult to situate historically or geographically but that may have grown out of a popular mythology about Caesarian birth, reinforced by heroic narratives about superhuman figures who are born this way. One could speculate further that to the thinking of some medieval heretics Mary's breast was a more suitable organ of divine procreation than her ribs or kidneys since a mother's breasts provide vital nourishment for her infant, and since Mary's breast might be deemed more worthy of veneration than the base of her spine or armpit. From recent work in this area by Caroline Bynum and others we are well aware that Mary's body was the subject of considerable commentary and devotion throughout the Middle Ages and that Mary's breasts figure repeatedly as symbols of motherhood and of nurturing and affective preaching and instruction.[38] To claim that Christ was born from Mary's *right* as opposed to her left breast – or even from her right *side*, as some of Aldebert's contemporaries evidently believed – likewise invokes a fertile tradition in Western thought in which right and left are opposed as fundamental orientations of good and evil.[39] The elect will sit at the *right* hand of God at Judgment (Matt. 22:44, 25:33; Mark 16:19), Christ was pierced on the *right* side at the Crucifixion,[40] and it was from his *right* side that the church was symbolically born, as was foreseen by the prophet Ezechiel in his vision of the Temple in Ezek. 47:1–2, where a river of water issues from the *right* side of the Temple, itself a type of Christ and a type of the church.[41] Augustine even argued that the wound in Christ's side must have been on the same side as the door to Noah's ark, since the ark, another type of the church, could only be entered through its side door, an entrance into salvation for Noah and his family.[42] It was this same complex of symbolic thought that also gave rise to the familiar notion that Eve was born from the *left* side of Adam – the sinister side – although this is not always intended negatively. Avitus of Vienne, for instance, writing in the early sixth century, argued that God removed Eve from the left side of Adam not because it was the weaker or inferior or wicked side but because it was the side closest to his heart and therefore the one more receptive to his vital energies.[43] This is the tradition that lies behind Milton, who has the rib taken from Adam's left side, whence his 'cordial spirits warme' and 'Life-blood' stream.[44] Other instances of this directional symbolism could easily be cited, but for our purposes it is most important to be aware that one of the earliest expressions in English of Eve's emergence from Adam's left side occurs, of all places, in the OE *Adrian and Ritheus*, where the question is posed: 'Saga me on hwæðere Adames sidan nam ure drihten þæt ribb þe he þæt wif of geworhte. Ic þe secge, on ðære winstran' [Tell me from which side of Adam did our Lord take the rib from which he made woman. I tell you, from the left].[45]

I conclude, therefore, in my efforts to vindicate Cross and Hill for their intuitive brilliance as expositors of the dialogue literature by asserting boldly (if a little vaguely) that I am convinced there is a basis for their speculative claims about the conceptual background of *Adrian and Ritheus* 41. I think Cross and Hill were aiming in exactly the right direction on this question, and in the spirit of their commentary, which finds startling points of contact between the most amazing stray bits of esoteric lore on the outermost fringes of medieval learning, I want to close by throwing one further detail into the mix. This new potential quasi-analogue comes not from a literary text and certainly not from Anglo-Saxon England but from a full-page illumination in a fifteenth-century manuscript of the Ethiopic *History of Hannâ* or *Life of St Anne*, a manuscript that was once in the private collection of Ethiopic antiquities owned by Lady Valerie Meux (1847–1910) and consequently known as Lady Meux MS 4 [fig. 3].[46] The Ethiopic *History of Hannâ* is a long and rollicking narrative of the life of St Anne divided for a week's worth of liturgical readings and accompanied in the manuscript by several illustrations that were published along with an English transla-

Christ's Birth through Mary's Right Breast 279

ሐና ፡ ወኢያቂም ፡ ዘከመ ፡ ወለድዋ ፡
ለማርያም ፡ በፀሎሙ ፡

Figure 3 Lady Meux MS 4. Current location unknown. After Budge, *Legends of Our Lady Mary*, pl. V. Legend reads: 'The birth of Mary from Hanna's right side.'

tion of the *History of Hannâ* by Sir Wallis Budge in 1933.[47] St Anne is of course the mother of the Virgin Mary and consequently a sort of proto-Virgin whose life can be expected to mirror Mary's in various ways, and as the Ethiopic illumination in figure 3 clearly reveals, her parturition of Mary both reenacts and anticipates Mary's parturition of Jesus since Mary is shown to emerge from Anne's right side, as the Ethiopic inscription even informs us. If I were the compiler of the OE *Adrian and Ritheus*, this illustration would make perfect sense to me. It enacts an entirely plausible logical extension of the typological patterning that informs Hildegard of Bingen's argument about the birth of Christ from Mary's side as a symbolic event modelled on Eve's birth from Adam's side. In the sprawling imaginative world that embraces Frankish heresy, OE sapiential literature, Ethiopic apocrypha, and Hildegard's theology, the notion that Christ was born from Mary's right side inevitably provokes the possibility that Mary was in turn born from Anne's right side, and figure 3 shows its artistic realization. So I close with this image as a vivid testimony to the persistence and tenacity and resilience of precisely the kind of typological thought and directional symbolism that I think underlies the answer to *Adrian and Ritheus* question 41. In medieval literary studies the principle of analogy can occasionally be illuminating as a tool for understanding a text or image that is difficult to make sense of by itself, and in this instance the structural parallel between the Ethiopic illumination and the OE dialogue entry serves as an unforgettable reminder that even the most aberrant strains of early medieval religious thought tend to operate according to a sound and internally consistent logical economy.

NOTES

1 *The 'Prose Solomon and Saturn' and 'Adrian and Ritheus,'* ed. James E. Cross and Thomas D. Hill, McMaster Old English Studies and Texts 1 (Toronto: University of Toronto Press, 1982).
2 Cross and Hill, *'Prose Solomon and Saturn,'* 39 (text) and 155 (translation).
3 See BT, and *DOE*, s.v. *breost*. On the various metaphorical senses of the word *breost* in OE, see Michael Joseph Phillips, 'Heart, Mind, and Soul in Old English: A Semantic Study' (PhD dissertation, University of Illinois at Urbana-Champaign, 1985), 99–121; and Eric Jager, 'The Word in the "Breost": Interiority and the Fall in *Genesis B*,' *Neophilologus* 75 (1991): 279–90.

Christ's Birth through Mary's Right Breast   281

4 As Phillips observes, *'Breost* never strays far from its literal, physical meaning' ('Heart, Mind, and Soul,' 101).
5 Such a usage is not impossible. Of the roughly 400 instances of this word in the *DOE Corpus* (excluding compounds), there are two in which *breost* is used to refer specifically to Mary's womb. One occurs in a homily that speaks of the Holy Ghost dwelling and abiding in Mary's womb: '7 se halega gæst wunode in þam æðelan innoðe 7 in þam betstan bosme 7 in þam gecorenan hordfate, 7 in þam halegan breostum he eardode nigon monoð' [and the Holy Spirit dwelled in the noble womb and in the best bosom and in the choicest treasure chest; and in the holy breast he abode nine months]: Vercelli Homily X, lines 16–18, ed. D.G. Scragg, *The Vercelli Homilies and Related Texts*, EETS o.s. 300 (Oxford: Oxford University Press, 1992), 197. The second is an interlinear gloss to a Marian hymn in the eleventh-century Durham Hymnal that includes the line 'Fit domus pudici pectoris templum dei repente' [The dwelling of a modest breast suddenly becomes the temple of God], glossed in OE as 'gewearð hus sydefulles breostes tempel godes færlice': *The Hymns of the Anglo-Saxon Church: A Study and Edition of the 'Durham Hymnal,'* ed. Inge B. Milfull, CSASE 17 (Cambridge: Cambridge University Press, 1996), 214–15.
6 Cross and Hill, *'Prose Solomon and Saturn,'* 155–6.
7 Cross and Hill, *'Prose Solomon and Saturn,'* 156.
8 The most pertinent entries in Stith Thompson's *Motif-Index of Folk-Literature*, revised and enlarged ed., 6 vols (Copenhagen: Rosenkilde and Bagger, 1955–8) are nos A511.1.1 ('Culture hero snatched from mother's side'), T517.2 ('Conception through the mother's side'), T540.1 ('Supernatural birth of saints'), T541 ('Birth from unusual part of person's body'), and T584.1 ('Birth through the mother's side').
9 Two such ballads are noteworthy because they specify the side from which the child emerges. In a sixteenth-century ballad entitled 'The Death of Queen Jane,' Jane Seymour, the third wife of King Henry VIII, is said to deliver the future Prince Edward through Caesarean section ('Then her right side was opened / And the babe was set free'): *The English and Scottish Popular Ballads*, ed. Francis James Child, 5 vols (1882; repr. New York: Dover, 1965), 3:372–6 (no. 170), at 375 (text D, stanza 3). Another version of the same ballad (page 375, text E, stanzas 7–8) holds that the doctor opened her left side; see also the two additional versions of this ballad printed at 5:245–6, one specifying the left side, the other the right. In a later ballad known as 'Fair Mary of Wallington,' the fair Mary of the title, believing that she is destined to die in childbirth, takes a razor and delivers her child through her left side: Child, *Ballads* 2:312 (stanza 32) and 5:229.

10 Alwyn Rees and Brinley Rees, *Celtic Heritage: Ancient Tradition in Ireland and Wales* (London: Thames and Hudson, 1961), 237. In a later allusion to this story from the turn of the sixteenth century, a poem attributed to William Dunbar entitled 'The Manere of the Crying of Ane Playe' asserts that Goll mac Morna 'Out of that wyfis wame was schorne': *The Poems of William Dunbar*, ed. W. Mackay Mackenzie (1932; repr. London: Faber and Faber, 1966), 172, line 82.

11 The varying accounts of Furbaide's birth in the *Cóir Anmann, Cath Boinde, Aided Meidbe*, and the *Metrical, Rennes*, and *Bodleian Dindshenchas* are discussed by Donna Wong, 'Water-Births: Murder, Mystery and Medb Lethderg,' *Études celtiques* 32 (1996): 233–41, who interprets the core narrative behind these texts as a reminiscence of an ancient environmental myth concerning the origin of a lake as an outburst from the side of a river. Note that in both the *Cóir Anmann* and *Cath Boinde*, Furbaide's name is etymologized as deriving from the verbal noun *furbadh* (or *urbad*), an 'excision' or 'cutting out.'

12 Kuno Meyer, 'Anecdota from the Stowe MS. N° 992,' *Revue celtique* 6 (1884): 173–92 at 176, 180. The varying accounts of Conchobar's birth are printed, translated, and discussed by Kuno Meyer, *Hibernica Minora, being a Fragment of an Old-Irish Treatise on the Psalter*, Anecdota Oxoniensia, Mediaeval and Modern Series 8 (Oxford: Oxford University Press, 1894), 50; Whitley Stokes, 'Tidings of Conchobar mac Nessa,' *Ériu* 4 (1910): 18–38; Rudolf Thurneysen, *Die irische Helden- und Königsage bis zum siebzehnten Jahrhundert* (Halle: Max Niemeyer, 1921), 273–6; Vernam Hull, 'The Conception of Conchobor,' in *Irish Texts*, vol. 4, ed. J. Fraser, P. Grosjean, and J.G. O'Keeffe (London: Sheed and Ward, 1934), 4–12; and Tom Peete Cross and Clark Harris Slover, *Ancient Irish Tales* (1936; repr. New York: Barnes & Noble, 1996), 131–3.

13 Whitley Stokes, 'A Note about Fiacha Muillethan,' *Revue celtique* 11 (1894): 41–5 at 43. The consequent flattening of Fiacha's head against the stone his mother was sitting on is reflected in his epithet *muillethan*, which means 'broad-crowned.'

14 E.J. Gwynn, 'Athirne's Mother,' *Zeitschrift für celtische Philologie* 17 (1928): 153–6 at 154: 'Cidh dia raibhe dhó-somh? Ni hansa: dícheadal na laoidhe i mbru a mháthar. Doluidh a mhathair do breith teneadh i ttigh i mbaoi fuireg in fhogus. Coonclecht-somh ina brú la túth na corma, con-docorastar tara cenn ag taidhecht asan tigh. Tiomghart an bhen iaram go fa thrí digh don chormaimn. Alcuitig an sgoaire go fa thri 7 asbert cidh marbh dhe 7 gé thíosadh a gein tréna taobh, ní gluaisfidhthea dhi an chuirm modh rohanadh dia hindbhertadh.' For other tales involving Athirne, see Kuno

Meyer, 'The Guesting of Athirne,' *Ériu* 7 (1914): 1–9; Rudolf Thurneysen, 'A Third Copy of the Guesting of Athirne,' *Ériu* 7 (1914): 196–9; and Thurneysen, 'Zu irischen Texten: I, Athirne von seiner Ungastlichkeit geheilt,' *Zeitschrift für celtische Philologie* 12 (1918): 398–9.

15 This also seems to be the point of several Irish witnesses to an international folktale in which a woman declares, 'Gheóinn fear is ga'h ao' bhall agus mac as mo thaobh dheas' [I could get a husband anywhere and a son from my right side]: see Michael Tierney, 'An Ancient Motif in the Lament for Seán do Búrc,' *Éigse* 1 (1939): 236–8; and *Seán Ó Conaill's Book: Stories and Traditions from Iveragh*, ed. Séamus Ó Duilearga, trans. Máire MacNeill (Baile Átha Cliath: Comhairle Bhéaloideas Éireann, An Coláiste Ollscoile, 1981), 415.

16 Blumenfeld-Kosinski, *Not of Woman Born: Representations of Caesarean Birth in Medieval and Renaissance Culture* (Ithaca, NY: Cornell University Press, 1990), 49–90.

17 *Liber Eliensis* 2.87, ed. E.O. Blake, Camden Society 3rd ser. 92 (London: Royal Historical Society, 1962), 156; cf. Dorothy Bethurum, *The Homilies of Wulfstan* (Oxford: Clarendon, 1957), 55.

18 *The Chronicle of Battle Abbey*, ed. and trans. Eleanor Searle (Oxford: Clarendon, 1980), 344.

19 Blumenfeld-Kosinski, *Not of Woman Born*, 23 (Maimonides), 26 (Odon).

20 Jerome, *Adversus Jovinianum* 1.42 (*PL* 23:285). See the discussion by Albrecht Dihle, 'Buddha und Hieronymus,' *Mittellateinisches Jahrbuch* 2 (1965): 38–41.

21 The story is repeated by Ratramnus of Corbie, *De partu sanctae Mariae* 9, ed. J.M. Canal, 'La virginidad de María según Ratramno y Radberto, monjes de Corbie: Nueva edición de los textos,' *Marianum* 30 (1968): 53–160 at 90–1, lines 193–203 (also ed. *PL* 121:83AB).

22 On the rise of docetic beliefs and their impact on early Christological thought, see J.G. Davies, 'The Origins of Docetism,' in *Studia Patristica*, vol. 6, ed. F.L. Cross, Texte und Untersuchungen 81 (Berlin: Akademie-Verlag, 1962), 13–35; and Michael Slusser, 'Docetism: A Historical Definition,' *Second Century: A Journal of Early Christian Studies* 1 (1981): 163–72. A docetic interpretation of the Crucifixion is refuted by the author of the second Canterbury commentary on the Gospels (EvII 84): *Biblical Commentaries from the Canterbury School of Theodore and Hadrian*, ed. Bernhard Bischoff and Michael Lapidge, CSASE 10 (Cambridge: Cambridge University Press, 1994), 412–13, 524.

23 For general orientation on the *Protevangelium*, see J.K. Elliott, *The Apocryphal New Testament: A Collection of Apocryphal Christian Literature in an English Translation* (Oxford: Oxford University Press, 1993), 48–67. On the knowl-

edge of this apocryphon in Anglo-Saxon England, see Mary Clayton, *The Apocryphal Gospels of Mary in Anglo-Saxon England*, CSASE 26 (Cambridge: Cambridge University Press, 1998), 113–16, 315–22; and Frederick M. Biggs, ed., *Sources of Anglo-Saxon Literary Culture: The Apocrypha*, Instrumenta Anglistica Mediaevalia 1 (Kalamazoo: Medieval Institute Publications, 2007), 23–5.

24 Elliott, *Apocryphal New Testament*, 64.

25 Copious examples of these images from the writings of patristic and medieval authors are gathered and discussed by Thomas Livius, *The Blessed Virgin in the Fathers of the First Six Centuries* (London: Burns and Oates, 1893), 97–8, 114–16 (see also under 'The Eastern Gate always shut,' 'The inclosed garden,' and 'The sealed fountain' in the Index); Anselm Salzer, *Die Sinnbilder und Beiworte Mariens in der deutschen Literatur und lateinischen Hymnenpoesie des Mittelalters* (1893; repr. Darmstadt: Wissenschaftliche Buchgesellschaft, 1967), 9–10, 15–16, 281–4; Yrjö Hirn, *The Sacred Shrine: A Study of the Poetry and Art of the Catholic Church* (Boston: Beacon Press, 1957), 335, 446–9; Douglas Gray, *Themes and Images in the Medieval English Religious Lyric* (London: Routledge and Kegan Paul, 1972), 85, 89; Luigi Gambero, *Mary and the Fathers of the Church: The Blessed Virgin Mary in Patristic Thought*, trans. Thomas Buffer (San Francisco: Ignatius Press, 1999), 211, 287, 297; Gambero, *Mary in the Middle Ages: The Blessed Virgin Mary in the Thought of Medieval Latin Theologians*, trans. Thomas Buffer (San Francisco: Ignatius Press, 2005), 30, 49.

26 On patristic teachings on the nature of the virgin birth, see Philip J. Donnelly, 'The Perpetual Virginity of the Mother of God,' in *Mariology*, ed. Juniper B. Carol, 3 vols (Milwaukee, WI: Bruce, 1957), 2:228–96; J. Galot, 'La virginité de Marie et la naissance de Jésus,' *Nouvelle revue théologique* 82 (1960): 449–69; and Georg Söll, *Handbuch der Dogmengeschichte*, vol. 3, part 4: *Mariologie* (Freiburg: Herder, 1978), 41–7.

27 Ratramnus, *De partu sanctae Mariae*: 'Fama est, et quorumdam non contemnanda cognouimus relatione, quod per Germaniae partes serpens antiquus perfidiae nouae uenena diffundat, et catholicam super natiuitate Saluatoris fidem, nescio qua fraudis subtilitate subuertere molitur: dogmatizans Christi infantiam per uirginalis ianuam uuluae, humanae natiuitatis uerum non habuisse ortum, sed monstruose de secreto uentris, incerto tramite, luminis in auras exisse, quod non est nasci sed erumpi. Quod enim uias uteri nascendo non est secutum, sed quacumque uersum tamquam per parietem domus erupit, non iure natum esse sed uiolenter egressum' (ed. Canal, 'La virginidad de María,' 84, lines 17–25; *PL* 121:83AB). The debate between Ratramnus and Radbertus over the manner of the virgin birth is

examined in detail by Jean-Paul Bouhot, *Ratramne de Corbie: Histoire littéraire et controverses doctrinales* (Paris: Études Augustiniennes, 1976), 53–6; and Leo Scheffczyk, *Das Mariengeheimnis in Frömmigkeit und Lehre der Karolingerzeit*, Erfurter theologische Studien 5 (Leipzig: St Benno-Verlag, 1959), 137–65, 206–37. Bouhot suggests (at 53) that the *De partu sanctae Mariae* was written by Ratramnus for his abbot Odo of Corbie (d. 881) and was intended to be directed to Warin, the abbot of nearby Corvey, shortly before Warin's death in 856.

28 Bouhot, *Ratramne de Corbie*, 54, n. 54, dates Radbertus's tract to 854x856.

29 *Paschasii Radberti, De partu Virginis*, ed. E. Ann Matter, CCCM 56C (Turnhout: Brepols, 1985), 48: 'Dicunt enim non aliter beatam uirginem Mariam parere potuisse neque aliter debuisse quam communi lege naturae et sicut mos est omnium feminarum, ut uera natiuitas Christi dici possit. Alias autem, inquiunt, si non ita natus est ut caeteri nascuntur infantes, uera natiuitas non est. Et ideo ne phantasia putetur, aut ne sicut aqua per alueum transisse, ita per uterum uirginis absque nascentis ordine natus credatur, pium est sentire sic eum lege naturae natum fuisse, quomodo caeteri nascuntur infantes, et eam sic peperisse sicut reliquae pariunt mulieres.'

30 Irenaeus, *Adversus haereses* 1.7.2 (*PG* 7:515).

31 Ratramnus, *De partu sanctae Mariae*: 'Sed, quaeso, cur refugis ascribere Christo naturalem uirginalis portae progressum? Propterea, inquis, quoniam si uteri portam exiuit, non est uirginis integritas intemerata. Equidem per quemcumque fuerit locum egressus, consequenter secundum tuam sententiam integritas est uiolata. Si enim Saluatoris ortus uiam naturae necessario fuerat corrupturus, necessario quoque quacumque exiuit, siue per latus, siue per uentrem, siue per renes, siue per superiores inferioresue corporis partes, non absque integritatis damno processit' (ed. Canal, 'La virginidad de María,' 86, lines 66–73; *PL* 121:84B).

32 Ratramnus, *De partu sanctae Mariae*: 'Non inlocaliter est egressus; hoc est enim incorporeae proprium naturae, longe uero a corporea remotum. Constitue certe quam delegeris partem. Vuluam renuis, umbilicum attribue, uel, si malueris, honestius quodcumque corporis ostium. Ac si ostia quae dedit natura displicent, disice uentrem, nuda costas, spinam rumpe, uel quemadmodum nescio qui stultissimi delirant, aperi ascellam, et ita de monte umbroso et condenso natiuitatem contestare Saluatoris' (ed. Canal, 'La virginidad de María,' 90, lines 185–92; *PL* 121:86D–87A).

33 Berengar, *De sacra coena* 47, ed. W.H. Beekenkamp, *Berengarii Turonensis De sacra coena adversus Lanfrancum*, Kerkhistorische Studiën 2 (The Hague: M. Nijhoff, 1941), 166: '"Impletum est," inquit euuangelista, "tempus Elisabeth ut pareret et peperit filium," et consequenter "impleti sunt," inquit, "dies

286   Thomas N. Hall

Mariae ut pareret et peperit filium." Numquid interpretari potest insanus, quod dicit euangelista: peperit filium, secundum quod anilis ... fabula Christum de matre sub ascella uel per costas natum fuisse?' For discussion, see A.J. MacDonald, 'Berengar and the Virgin-Birth,' *Journal of Theological Studies* 30 (1928–9): 291–4.

34 The proceedings of this Roman synod include the text of a letter from Boniface to Pope Zacharias recounting Aldebert's heretical practices, as well as an excerpt from a Life of Aldebert, both preserved among Boniface's correspondence: see *Die Briefe des heiligen Bonifatius und Lullus*, ed. Michael Tangl, 2nd ed., MGH Epistolae Selectae 1 (Berlin: Weidmann, 1955), 108–20 (*Ep.* 59), and *The Letters of Saint Boniface*, trans. Ephraim Emerton (1940; repr. with a new introduction and bibliography by Thomas F.X. Noble, New York: Columbia University Press, 2000), 76–85.

35 *Die Briefe des heiligen Bonifatius*, ed. Tangl, 114; *The Letters of Saint Boniface*, trans. Emerton, 81.

36 Jeffrey B. Russell, 'Saint Boniface and the Eccentrics,' *Church History* 33 (1964): 235–47 at 236.

37 English translation by Barbara Newman, *Sister of Wisdom: St. Hildegard's Theology of the Feminine* (Berkeley and Los Angeles: University of California Press, 1987), 176, based on the text edited by Heinrich Schipperges, 'Ein unveröffentlichtes Hildegard-Fragment,' *Sudhoffs Archiv für Geschichte der Medizin und der Naturwissenschaften* 40 (1956): 41–77 at 68: 'Quo instante beata virgine viribus aliquantum debilitata et quasi in somno sopita infans ipsa nesciente de latere eius sine dolore, sine corruptione et sine sorde velut eva de latere ade exivit et non in ore vulve; quia ibi non intravit, quoniam si ibi exisset, corruptio ibi fuisset, sed quia mater ibi integra fuit, infans ibi non exivit. Et pellicula eundem infantem in utero matris virginis natura aliorum infancium non circumdedit, quoniam de virili semine conceptus non est.' My thanks to Mary Dzon for bringing this passage to my attention.

38 Caroline Walker Bynum, *Jesus as Mother: Studies in the Spirituality of the High Middle Ages* (Berkeley and Los Angeles: University of California Press, 1982), 115–24; Klaus Schreiner, *Maria: Jungfrau, Mutter, Herrscherin* (Munich: C. Hanser, 1994), 178–204; Beth Williamson, 'The Virgin *Lactans* as Second Eve: Image of the *Salvatrix*,' *Studies in Iconography* 19 (1998): 105–38; Salvador Ryan, 'The Persuasive Power of a Mother's Breast: The Most Desperate Act of the Virgin Mary's Advocacy,' *Studia Hibernica* 32 (2002–3): 59–74. For a remarkable infiltration of this image into early Irish hagiography, in the story of the seventh-century Irish saint Findchú, who suckles an infant with milk from his right breast, see Dorothy Bray, 'Suckling at the Breast of

Christ: A Spiritual Lesson in an Irish Hagiographical Motif,' *Peritia* 14 (2000): 282–96.

39 A seminal investigation into this directional symbolism across multiple cultures is Robert Hertz's essay, 'The Pre-eminence of the Right Hand: A Study in Religious Polarity,' in his *Death and The Right Hand*, trans. Rodney and Claudia Needham (Glencoe, IL: Free Press, 1960), 89–113, 155–60. See further Anthony P. Wagener, *Popular Associations of Right and Left in Roman Literature* (Baltimore, MD: J.H. Furst, 1912); Alois Gornatowski, *Rechts und Links im antiken Aberglauben* (Breslau: R. Nischkowski, 1936); Joseph Cuillandre, *La droite et la gauche dans les poèmes homériques en concordance avec la doctrine pythagoricienne et la tradition celtique* (Paris: Société d'edition 'Les belles lettres,' 1944); G.E.R. Lloyd, 'Right and Left in Greek Philosophy,' *Journal of Hellenic Studies* 82 (1962): 56–66; Otto Nussbaum, 'Die Bewertung von Rechts und Links in der römischen Liturgie,' *Jahrbuch für Antike und Christentum* 5 (1962): 158–71; Ursula Deitmaring, 'Die Bedeutung von Rechts und Links in theologischen und literarischen Texten bis um 1200,' *Zeitschrift für deutsches Altertum und deutsche Literatur* 98 (1969): 265–92; J. Gonda, 'The Significance of the Right Hand and the Right Side in Vedic Ritual,' *Religion* 2 (1972): 1–23, repr. in his *Selected Studies*, 6 vols in 7 (Leiden: E.J. Brill, 1975–91), 6.1:41–63; Manfred Lurker, 'Die Symbolbedeutung von Rechts und Links und ihr Niederschlag in der abendländisch-christlichen Kunst,' *Symbolon* N.F. 5 (1980): 95–128; François Guillaumont, 'Laeva prospera: Remarques sur la droite et la gauche dans la divination romaine,' in *D'Héraklès à Poséidon: Mythologie et protohistoire*, ed. Raymond Bloch, Hautes études du monde gréco-romain 14 (Geneva: Droz, 1985), 159–77; Pierre-Michel Bertrand, 'La Fortune mi-partie: Un exemple de la symbolique de la droite et de la gauche au moyen âge,' *Cahiers de civilisation médiévale* 40 (1997): 373–9; and Joel W. Palka, 'Left/Right Symbolism and the Body in Ancient Maya Iconography and Culture,' *Latin American Antiquity* 13 (2002): 419–43.

40 The extrabiblical tradition concerning this detail is discussed by A.A. Barb, 'The Wound in Christ's Side,' *Journal of the Warburg and Courtauld Institutes* 34 (1971): 320–1; Vladimir Gurewich, 'Observations on the Iconography of the Wound in Christ's Side, with Special Reference to Its Position,' *Journal of the Warburg and Courtauld Institutes* 20 (1957): 358–62; Rudolf Hofmann, *Das Leben Jesu nach den Apokryphen im Zusammenhänge aus den Quellen erzählt und wissenschaftlich untersucht* (Leipzig: F. Voigt, 1851), 381–2; and Éamonn Ó Carragáin, '*Vidi aquam*: The Liturgical Background to *The Dream of the Rood* 20a: "swætan on þa swiðran healfe,"' *NQ* n.s. 30 (1983): 8–15.

41 See S. Tromp, 'De Nativitate Ecclesiae ex Corde Iesu in Cruce,' *Gregorianum*

13 (1932): 489–527; Guy de Broglie, 'L'Église, nouvelle Ève, née du Sacré-Cœur,' *Nouvelle revue théologique* 1 (1946): 3–25; and Hugo Rahner, 'Geburt aus dem Herzen,' *Gloria Dei* 4 (1949–50): 89–99.

42 Augustine, *De civitate Dei* 15.26, ed. Bernard Dombart and Alfonse Kalb, *Sancti Aurelii Augustini Episcopi De Civitate Dei Libri XXII*, 5th ed., 2 vols, Bibliotheca Scriptorum Graecorum et Romanorum Teubneriana (Stuttgart: Teubner, 1981), 2:115, lines 10–12. Other passages in the works of Augustine that rely on this directional symbolism are noted by Maurice Pontet, *L'Exégèse de s. Augustin prédicateur* (Paris: Aubier, n.d. [1946?]), 356, n. 152. For later connections between the door to Noah's Ark and the wound in Christ's side, see the anonymous thirteenth-century French biblical paraphrase *La Bible anonyme*, ed. Julia C. Szirmai, *La Bible anonyme du Ms. Paris B.N.f.fr. 763: édition critique*, Faux Titre 22 (Amsterdam: Rodopi, 1985), 239, lines 8626–7, and the note to these lines at 270.

43 Avitus, *De spiritalis historiae gestis* 1.155, ed. and trans. Nicole Hecquet-Noti, *Avit de Vienne: Histoire spirituelle*, Sources chrétiennes 444 (Paris: Cerf, 1999), 148.

44 John Milton, *Paradise Lost* 8.465–6, in *The Riverside Milton*, ed. Roy Flanagan (Boston: Houghton Mifflin, 1998), 575.

45 '*Prose Solomon and Saturn*,' ed. Cross and Hill, 35, 129–30. Additional examples of Eve born from Adam's left side in Insular and Insular-influenced texts are noted by Joyce Bazire and James E. Cross, eds, *Eleven Old English Rogationtide Homilies*, Toronto Old English Series 7 (Toronto: University of Toronto Press, 1982), 7 and 17 (Homily I, lines 29–30); and by J.E. Cross, 'Towards the Identification of Old English Literary Ideas – Old Workings and New Seams,' in *Sources of Anglo-Saxon Culture*, ed. Paul E. Szarmach with the assistance of Virginia Darrow Oggins, Studies in Medieval Culture 20 (Kalamazoo: Medieval Institute Publications, 1986), 77–101, at 80 and n. 16 (citing the Irish *Reference Bible*, since edited by Gerard McGinty, *The Reference Bible / Das Bibelwerk*, CCCM 173 [Turnhout: Brepols, 2000], where the relevant passage appears at page 82, line 15). The contrary notion, that Eve emerged from Adam's right side, was the historically dominant position in the Christian Latin West (Deitmaring, 'Bedeutung von Rechts und Links,' 283–4, n. 12; Hans Martin von Erffa, *Ikonologie der Genesis: Die christlichen Bildthemen aus dem Alten Testament und ihre Quellen*, vol. 1 [Munich: Deutscher Kunstverlag, 1989], 153) and is attested at least once in early Irish literature, in the (?twelfth-century) *Leabhar Breac* creation story, which asserts that 'do'n octmad arna uactarac cleib a leti deir Adaim doronta Eua, indur co m-[b]ad cutruma do hi' [of the eighth upper rib of the breast of the right side of Adam was made Eve, so that she should be equal to him]: see *The*

Codex Palatino-Vaticanus, No. 830 (Texts, Translations and Indices.), ed. B. Mac Carthy, Todd Lecture Series 3 (Dublin: Hodges, Figgis, 1892), 48–9; and *Irish Biblical Apocrypha: Selected Texts in Translation*, ed. Máire Herbert and Martin McNamara (Edinburgh: T & T Clark, 1989), 3.

46 Lady Meux acquired this manuscript in 1897 from Bernard Quaritch, who had purchased it from a British officer who had participated in the 1868 raid on Mäqdäla, the Ethiopian citadel of Emperor Tewodros II. On the history, contents, and eventual dispersal of Lady Meux's manuscripts following her death in 1910, see Rita Pankhurst, 'The Library of Emperor Tewodros II at Mäqdäla (Magdala),' *Bulletin of the School of Oriental and African Studies, University of London* 36.1 (1973): 15–42 at 26–9. I have been unable to trace the present whereabouts of Lady Meux MS 4.

47 *Legends of Our Lady Mary the Perpetual Virgin and Her Mother Hannâ Translated from the Ethiopic Manuscripts Collected by King Theodore at Makdalâ and Now in the British Museum*, trans. E.A. Wallis Budge (Oxford: Oxford University Press, 1933). The illumination in question is here reproduced from Budge's plate V. There is nothing within the text of the *History of Hannâ* that corresponds to this illustration of Mary's nativity.

PART IV
Old English beyond the Conquest

The Peterborough Chronicle and the Invention of 'Holding Court' in Twelfth-Century England

ANDREW GALLOWAY

'In the court I exist and of the court I speak, and what the court is, God knows, not I.' So declares Walter Map in *De nugis curialium*, his Latin collection of ghost stories, satires, and misogamy from the 1180s. Map manages only snatches of time for such writing, he claims elsewhere, so burdened is he by the administrative demands and machinations of his own service at court; but in fact he is verbose, and perhaps in his complaints about distraction he is merely justifying an anecdotal style and distractable mind. Yet Map claims to long for liberation from the demands and pressures of the court that allowed his literary 'trifles,' even while he suggests that the 'court' in some conceptual sense is eternal and, it seems, nearly inescapable. It is like time itself, as Augustine defines that: the parts all changeable yet the existence permanent. 'When I leave it, I know it perfectly,' Map says, but 'when I come back to it I find nothing or but little of what I left there.' Yet 'the court is not changed; it remains always the same.' And it is like Porphyry's concept of a *genus*: a collection of objects bearing a certain relation to one principle. Or, he adds – with the satiric edge that eventually invades most of his writing – it is like Boethius's definition of fortune, constant only in its inconstancy.[1]

Some four decades later, by 1227, the definition of a court in these terms was a standard feature in legal discussion, with important significance for medieval political thought. As the *Glossa ordinaria* on a passage in the *Corpus iuris civilis* shows, Map's views had by the early thirteenth century become a regular exercise in defining the permanent nature of many kinds of abstract social and political entities, all generated by analogy to the conception of a court:

For just as the [present] people of Bologna is the same that was a hundred years ago, even though all be dead now who then were quick, so must also the tribunal be the same if three or two judges have died and been replaced by substitutes. Likewise, [with regard to a legion], even though all soldiers may be dead and replaced by others it is still the same legion. Also, with regard to a ship, even if the ship has been partly rebuilt, and even if every single plank may have been replaced, it is nonetheless always the same ship.[2]

That the *Glossa* is concerned with a court of law and Map with a ruler's court simply shows how intermeshed were the legal and political functions and categories of the idea of a court, and how significant both were to legal and political thought. As Ernst Kantorowicz showed in his seminal study on medieval political theology, these notions stand at the beginning of a major set of ideas of juridical and political 'bodies,' whose elements change but whose conceptual existence persists: the sovereign; the People; the state.

Such invocations of a timeless Real of the court thus suggest, paradoxically, a particular if large and important history, and their earliest visible developments deserve close scrutiny on those grounds alone. Indeed, Map's observations on the court of the king and the court of law present an earlier instance of this conception than any of those that Kantorowicz observed. Yet the bases of this intellectual and legal tradition have deeper roots still, ones bound up in social and literary as well as intellectual history. These reach into the complex boundary between Anglo-Saxon culture and Anglo-Norman England. That historical moment is constituted not only by a newly broadened array of ancient and contemporary intellectual authorities and tools (and Map's Porphyry and Boethius would soon be supplemented by Aristotle and Accursius), but also, in England, by the suddenly increasing central political power of the royal court after the Norman Conquest, to which, however, Anglo-Saxon ideas, writings, and personnel made important contributions.

Linguistic and narrative changes, especially in chronicle writings, reflect these developments better, and earlier, than professional legal thought. Throughout twelfth-century England, in Latin and French writings, from chronicles to accounts of antiquity to sacred drama, 'the court' appears as a widespread and abstract concept, keyed to particular formulaic expressions. Especially common in the twelfth century is the phrase 'to hold court,' unattested before this so far as I can tell, yet rapidly replacing mere mention of the particulars when such and such king invited to a feast-day such and such lord or king or followers to give gifts, exchange vows, and pass judgments.[3] This essay pursues the origins of that phrase and something of its properties in narratives and chronicles that bridge Anglo-Saxon and Anglo-Norman England, including what Erich Auerbach, in a different sense than Walter Map, would have called 'the representation of reality' with which that phrase is associated.[4]

The English phrase *healdan curt* is first attested in the final entry of the Final Continuation of the Peterborough Chronicle, at Henry II's accession in 1154: that is, in what looks like the last vestige, almost a century after the Norman Conquest, of self-consciously continuous OE prose. At London, the Peterborough Chronicle entry tells us, Henry was received magnificently and consecrated king, in Carolingian and Anglo-Norman tradition, on the Sunday before Christmas, and on that occasion he held there a great court: 'þa was he underfangen mid micel wurtscipe, 7 to king bletcæd in Lundene on þe Sunnendæ beforen Midwintre Dæ, 7 held þære micel curt' (1154/6–7).[5] That is all we hear from that particular Peterborough chronicler about holding court, a point to which I will return at the end of this essay. Since the phrase is so emphatically used in Anglo-Norman culture, we might assume that its appearance first in English is merely an accident of preservation. Yet the phrase and indeed the abstract idea of 'holding court' are not exclusively due to Norman writers or simply the result of French and Latin influences on the final Continuator at Peterborough. Both are part of an important lexical and cultural amalgamation.

Curt is of course an Anglo-Norman word, first attested in English here, and *healdan curt* is clearly a calque on the French *tenir curt* and the Latin *curiam tenere*, both prevalent and frequently elaborated by this date of the mid-twelfth century. (The French word *curt* was in fact based not on Latin *curia* but on *cohor(tem)*, 'a crowd of attendants, a retinue,' but French *curt* had assimilated from an early date the senses of Latin *curia*, which did not itself survive in Romanic.) But looking for the earliest attestations of the phrase in any of these languages of Anglo-Norman England yields a curious pattern. The earliest datable antecedent formulation to this is found not in French or Latin but in earlier English. The phrase *hired healdan*, also referring to holding the royal court, appears out of the blue in 1085, also in the Peterborough Chronicle. That portion we know to be part of the materials inherited by the writer whom we call the First Continuator, who used a previous lost chronicle up to 1121 and wrote his own annals between 1121 and 1131, whereupon he is followed by the Second Continuator to 1154.

On the other side, these phrases are only tenuously or liminally part of OE literature. No previous OE phrases or formulae seem entirely to account for the coinage *hired healdan*. *Hird* (or *hired*) usually means 'family, company, followers' (translating and translated by Latin *familia*, which has all these meanings); but not until 1074 in the Peterborough Chronicle does *hird* appear indisputably as 'court.' English charters from the tenth century use *hird* as something like 'court,' but only in ecclesiastical senses, and none has the combined phrase *healdan hired*. A rare phrase, appearing apparently only in the OE translation of the *Dialogues* of Gregory the Great, refers to managing and directing a nunnery as 'wifhired to healdanne 7 to rihtanne.'[6] This is an important example, but it is not a direct precedent of our phrase. It is notable, however, that something like the later phrase for 'holding court' is present in English well before anything comparable is attested in Latin. The Latin behind the passage just quoted, for instance, does not directly correspond to this abstraction: 'in monasterio virginum, in quo ejusdem Patris cura vigilabat' [in a nunnery, which the father abbot's care watched over].[7] Moreover, OE *healdan* can mean 'to rule' (as in *Beowulf* 2732; see BT, s.v., sense III), and in the tenth century at least is attested the notion of 'holding' the hundred, presumably the hundred *gemot*, as in the opening of Edgar's Laws: 'þis is seo gerædnyss, hu mon þæt hundred haldan sceal' (this is the ordinance as to how the hundred [court] shall be held).[8]

But even with such hints of OE precedents, one would still assume that *hired healdan* is simply adopted wholesale from the French and Latin Norman world, since Latin *curiam tenere* and French *tenir curt* are very widespread in the mid-twelfth century and later. Yet the dissemination is directly traceable only in the other direction. It passes *from* the OE source text that the Peterborough Chronicle used for the years 1070–1121, *to* several of the chief twelfth-century Anglo-Latin historians, such as William of Malmesbury and others. In the early twelfth century, Henry of Huntingdon under the entry for 1086 draws directly on the English source for the Peterborough Chronicle: 'William the strong held his court at Christmas at Gloucester, at Easter at Winchester, at Whitsun at London.'[9] Beyond Anglo-Norman writers' demonstrable reliance on the late version of the Anglo-Saxon Chronicle used for the Peterborough Chronicle, only one additional Latin source can be noted. Possibly, but not certainly earlier than Henry of Huntingdon's use of the Anglo-Saxon Chronicle, and in any case independent from him and his OE source, appears a memorable passage in the anonymous *Life of Lanfranc* that also describes William's thrice-yearly holding of court:

> It was one of those three great festivals on which the king, wearing his crown, is accustomed to hold his court [*quibus rex coronatus solebat tenere curiam*]. On the day of the festival, when the king was seated at a table adorned in a crown and the royal robes, and with Lanfranc beside him, a certain jester, seeing the king resplendent in gold and jewels, cried out in the hall in great tones of adulation: 'Behold, I see God! Behold, I see God!'[10]

'Great tones of adulation' are of course elements of satiric theatre: accordingly, Archbishop Lanfranc advised the king to have the jester whipped.[11] We will bear in mind this satiric response to the Anglo-Norman splendour of holding court. But for the present, it is important only to note that the *Life of Lanfranc* is the only arguably early Latin invocation of the expression 'holding court' apparently independent of the Latin adaptations of the Peterborough Chronicle; and the composition of the *Life* is no earlier than 1130, and possibly as late as 1156 – thus conceivably late enough to be influenced by the Anglo-Saxon Chronicle or its source that most influentially offered the phrase to Anglo-Norman culture.[12] We can probably conclude that the Latin tradition did not begin using the formula widely until the English writers had given them the model.

So where did it come from? William the Conqueror's decision in 1085 to wear his crown at those three great feasts in order to 'hold court' seems the general occasion for the invention of the phrase, and also for its power and dramatic eventfulness. William Stubbs considered it 'probable' that the Anglo-Saxon *witenagemot*, the meetings of England's nobility to offer counsel to the king, established the timing that the Conqueror chose for his crown-wearings; but Sir Frank Stenton and others have denied that the Conqueror directly followed Anglo-Saxon tradition in his crown-wearings.[13] In what is still the most recent major study of the *witenagemot*, from which these historians' comments are collected, Tryggvi Oleson in 1955 showed that it is very doubtful that the Anglo-Saxon nobles and kings had established with any regularity the timing and nature of such pre-Conquest royal gatherings.[14]

Indeed, if anything can be said with certainty on the basis of the evidence that Oleson presents, it is that the Anglo-Saxon *witenagemot* was far more elusive in name, timing, political powers, and identity than the later parliamentary events to which it has sometimes been compared, much less to William the Conqueror's emphatic festivals of crown-wearing. Instead, the Conqueror's notion seems to draw directly on Carolingian ideas of holding court thrice yearly. Yet Einhard, Charlemagne's biographer, does not have a concrete term for those events, referring to them instead with such periphrases as 'ubi regis comitatus erat' [where the king's band of followers were].[15] Whatever antiquity the event possessed or claimed lies enfolded in a formula that is itself a novelty. It emerged in William's reign, yet it is not clear just when it appeared or exactly whence it was derived. The Conqueror's documents include a charter founding Salisbury Abbey granting the abbey 'possession' of rights to court (*curiam ... possidere*), in a phrase immediately next to one granting the abbey the rights to 'hold' the king's endowment.[16]

Perhaps the real novelty of the term in fact is in 'holding,' *tenir* or *tenere*, a newly loaded verb in twelfth-century French, English, and Latin, with the changes of laws and rule at the Conquest, and probably generated in some early collaboration between English clerics and Anglo-Norman potentates and lawyers. Holding court in the twelfth century is typically the locus for the vows and gifts and judgments that are the basis for 'holding' something 'of' someone. Possibly the phrase affords us a glimpse into the murky conceptual origins of Anglo-Norman lordship, military tenure, and land-holding traditionally called feudalism.

However close we may be to that complex nexus of legal thought and reality, we are certainly here contacting a key element of the cultural aura and prestige of lordship associated with holding power, authority, and position. For holding court is a persistent focus of literary and historical vision in the twelfth century. It is sensible to survey French and Latin literature, as the example of Walter Map shows; yet against those we may also consider the originality and precociousness of the First Continuation of the Peterborough Chronicle. The Latin and French narratives concerned with displaying what is involved in 'holding court' are more famous, if also slightly later, and they deserve a look first. The best known and most influential is Geoffrey of Monmouth's *Historia Regum Britanniae*, written about 1140, which includes King Arthur's decision to 'hold' a 'plenary court' at Caerleon where he will wear his crown at Whitsuntide: this then becomes an Arthurian antecedent for William the Conqueror's decision in 1085 to wear his crown at Westminster each Whitsuntide.[17] The narrative realization of Arthur's decision to hold court, with its elaborate pageantry and its climax of Arthur's 'code of courtliness' of generosity and bravery that (Geoffrey says) inspired nobles from far and wide to join him, exemplifies both a king's enactment of legal power and his celebration of the social order. The scene is reflected in all later romance elaborations of Arthuriana, from Chrétien de Troyes on (e.g., the occasion for the beauty contest at the opening of *Erec et Enide*). As Geoffrey recounts, Arthur 'decided ... to summon to this feast the leaders who owed him homage, so that he could celebrate Whitsun with greater reverence and renew the closest possible pacts of peace with his chieftains.'[18]

The sense of 'holding court' here is a kind of defined theatrical and legal event, celebrating a ruler's power and renewing the vows of loyalty and justice to his followers. Often too it is an occasion for intrigue and dramatic legal challenge. At this moment in Geoffrey's Arthurian chronicle, for instance, envoys from Caesar arrive amid the festivities to challenge Arthur's rule – and thus begin Arthur's wars with Rome.

By the mid-twelfth century, the shimmering, metaphysical, theatrical but somehow unmistakable entity of a 'court' is easily assimilated to other abstract closed spheres: the code of courtliness; the court of conscience; even the entire world of God's or the devil's order and justice. All these are evident in the mid- or late-twelfth-century French drama, the *Service for Representing Adam*, the best example of the timeless status of the court in twelfth-century representations. God is Adam's 'Sire' and Adam his 'serf,' and they interact in a clearly contemporary sense of a lord repaying a follower with bounty or exile and punishment (405).[19] When the first humans sin, God grimly and ironically declares that he will now give them their reward: 'Or te rendrai tel guerdon ... Jo toi rendrai ta deserte, / Jo t'en donrai por ton servise: / Mal te vendra en tute guise' [425, 450–2: Now I will give back to you such a reward ... I will render to you your just deserts, I will give them to you for your service: evil will come to you in every manner]. The same ironic phrasing appears in a court scene in the mid-twelfth-century romance elaboration of Statius, the *Roman de Thèbes*, where Etheocles, in one of the many medieval insertions of scenes of holding court (*tenir curt*) lacking in the Latin original, curses a soldier who, against orders, has not killed a messenger bringing a challenge from his rival for the throne of Thebes: 'Tu as basti tiel traïson / don tu auras tiel gueredon / que tu serras desherité / et de ton regne fors jetté' [Such treason have you committed, and thus you will have such a reward: that you will be disinherited and thrown out of your kingdom].[20]

The irony in speaking of such a 'reward' depends on the primary function of a king at court, indeed the basic rationale for a king to hold court: to give rewards, gifts, and judgments. A chain of gifts ties together the *Service for Representing Adam*, and these establish the scene as the court of a supreme lord's dispensations and judgments: 'La femme que tu me donas, / Ele fist prime icest trepas: / Donat le moi, e jo mangai' [The woman you gave me committed first this trespass: she gave it to me, and I ate], Adam tells God (417–19). But the court that the *Ordo* constructs also becomes the setting for the birth of historical consciousness, by becoming the court of conscience: 'De notre mal veiste le comencement' [547: I see the origins of our evil], Adam can lament after succumbing; 'Si jo mesfis, jo en suffre la haschee ... Le mien mesfait mult iert longe retraite' [561, 564: If I did wrong, I suffer torment for it ... My misdeed will long be reproached], Eve adds. They realize their sins will be written 'en estoire' [534: in the historical record].

The burden of the *longue durée* of human history that settles on the minds of Adam and Eve complexly transects the play's continuous emphasis on the topicality of their styles and language. With these two axes of temporality, God's holding court there at the beginning of history is shown to be a transhistorical event; its referencing of twelfth-century features of homage and holding court, in ways that Adam and Eve are just beginning to recognize, encompasses all history in its sphere of gifts, power, intrigue, and punishment. Their laments are not so different from Walter Map's.

More contemporary versions of holding court often appear in Anglo-Norman historical writings. Detailed portrayals of holding court appear in the chronicle of Battle Abbey, ca. 1155–80, which might be thought of as the direct 'Norman' antitype to the 'Anglo-Saxon' chronicle at Peterborough.[21] The Battle chronicle is wonderfully full of the drama of holding court, in the various struggles the abbey wages at court against its ecclesiastical and lay challengers – including the king himself. At one point the monks send representatives to where the king is holding court to gain his endorsement of their new candidate for abbot. They are nerve-wrackingly called before other petitioners, then lengthily delayed by the king's councillors, who make clear that the king does not want their candidate. Finally the king appears, and both he and the Battle monks wearily agree to take a compromise candidate, Odo the prior of Canterbury, who has come to court simply to have the king confirm copies of charters for Canterbury that had burned in the abbey's fire. Old Odo, taken by surprise, balks at the sudden demand that he take rule of another religious house: on one side he resists the king's demands that on the spot he yield his current position, and on the other he repels the monks of Battle Abbey, whom he refuses to let touch him ('et ne se contingerent interposita appellatione inhibebat').[22] 'The day was drawing to a close with no settlement made ... the king was unwilling to give up what he had undertaken, and was as indefatigable in pressing as the prior was stubborn in not yielding.'

Finally Odo recalls the story of Theophilus, who 'stubbornly spurned the church that called him,' so that in despair Theophilus made a written contract to serve the devil and deny Christ. Theophilus's dramatic struggle, made into an actual play in the thirteenth century by Rutebeuf, is perhaps pertinent in other ways to the scene of courtly theatre that Odo faces: an eleventh-century poetic version of the Theophilus story attributed to Marbod of Rennes has Satan as a king (*rex*) who demands a charter of fealty, surrounded by a procession of demons in a spectacular courtly display.[23] That image is followed in Gautier de Coinci's later twelfth-century poetic version, where Satan and the demons appear in what is explicitly called a *cort*.[24] As Walter Map coyly notes, court is not precisely the same as hell, but bears a likeness to it, as a stallion's hoof resembles a mare's.[25] Yet Odo considers that he might have met the worse fate of spiritual pride, and the monks of Battle return gratefully with their new abbot, the reward of their unexpected struggle in the court that the king has held.

Such examples of the power and theatre of holding court in Anglo-Norman England could be greatly multiplied. Their chief pertinence here, however, is to help make us attentive to the emphases on and complexities in holding court presented in the first part of the Peterborough Chronicle, at a date considerably earlier than any of these Anglo-Norman narrative moments. Unlike any other Anglo-Saxon chronicler, the First Continuator and his source-text frame most of the narratives in terms of the king holding court. The first example, with the Conqueror's decision in 1086 to hold court thrice a year wearing a crown, happens to include the first reference in England to knighthood (as Cecily Clark notes): 'Her se cyng bær his corona 7 heold his hired on Winceastre to þam Eastran. 7 Swa he ferde þet he wæs to þam Pentecosten æt Wæstmyunstre, 7 dubbade his sunu Henric to ridere þær' [108(6)/1–4: Here the king wore his crown and held his court in Winchester at Easter; and thus travelled so that for Pentecost he was at Westminster, and dubbed his son Henry as a knight there]. The next entry, on William's death in 1087, including an elaborate consideration of William's character in prose and verse, identifies the writer as a member of William's court: 'ðone will we be him awritan swa swa we hine ageaton ðe him on locodan 7 oðre hwile on his hirede wunedon' [108(7)/60–2: Thus we will write about him as we perceived him, we who looked upon him and sometimes dwelled in his court].

And from 1086 until 1124, so common is an initial statement about the king holding court somewhere that omissions of it as a narrative gesture are more notable than its presence. Nearly all entries from 1085 through 1121 – that is, the portion representing the Anglo-Saxon source-text used by the First Continuator and several Latin chroniclers – open with an assertion that particular Anglo-Norman and Angevin kings *hired healdan* in particular locations. When the phrase itself does not appear, the narrative often implies it in its opening sentence (e.g., 1113/1–2). Even the king's thwarted intention to hold court at such and such a place is 'news' in this stretch of narrative (as at the opening of the 1097 entry).

From 1121 on, where the First Continuator evidently writes in his own time, the formula appears less regularly, but attention to what the king does when he holds court, and how it matters, is if anything increased and complicated. The 1127 entry is an excellent example. In order to assess the full narrative and cultural importance of the phrase it is necessary to quote almost two-thirds of this dense entry:

Ðis gear heald se kyng Heanri his hird æt Cristesmæsse on Windlesoure. þær wæs se Scotte kyng Dauid 7 eall ða heaued, læred 7 læuued, þet wæs on Engleland. 7 þær he let sweren ercebiscopes 7 biscopes 7 abbotes 7 eorles 7 ealle þa ðeines ða þær wæron his dohter Æðelic Englaland 7 Normandi to hande æfter his dæi, þe ær wæs ðes Caseres wif of Sexlande; 7 sende hire siððen to Normandi, 7 mid hire ferde hire broðer Rotbert eorl of Gleucestre 7 Brian þes eorles sunu Alein Fergan, 7 lett hire beweddan þes eorles sunu of Angeow, Gosfreið Martæl wæs gehaten: hit ofþuhte naþema ealle frencisc 7 englisc, oc se kyng hit dide for to hauene sibbe of se eorl of Angeow 7 for helpe to hauene togænes his neue Willelm. Ðes ilces gæres on þone lententide wæs se eorl Karle of Flandres ofslagen on ane circe þær he læi 7 bæd hine to Gode tofor þone weofede amang þane mese fram his agene manne. 7 Se kyng of France brohte þone eorles sunu Willelm of Normandi, 7 iæf hine þone eorldom, 7 þet landfolc him wið toc. Þes ilce Willelm hæfde æror numen ðes eorles dohter of Angeow to wife, oc hi wæron siððen totweamde for sibreden: þet wes eall ðurh ðone kyng Heanri of Engleland. Siððen þa nam he þes kynges wifes swuster of France to wife; 7 forþi iæf se kyng him þone eorldom of Flandres. Ðes ilce gæres he gæf þone abbotrice of Burch an abbot, Heanri wæs gehaten, of Peitowe, se hæfde his abbotrice Sancte Iohannis of Angeli on hande. 7 Ealle þa ærcebiscopes 7 biscopes seidon þet hit wæs togeanes riht, 7 þet he ne mihte hafen twa abbotrices on hande. Oc se ilce Heanri dide þone king to understandne þet he hæfde læten his abbotrice for þet micele unsibbe þet wæs on þet land, 7 þet he dide ðurh þes Papes ræd 7 leue of Rome 7 ðurh þes abbotes of Clunni 7 þurh þæt he wæs legat of ðone romescott: oc hit ne wæs naðema eallswa, oc he wolde hauen baðe on hande, 7 swa hafde swa lange swa Godes wille wæs. He wæs on his clærchade biscop on Scesscuns; siððan warð he munec on Clunni, 7 siððon prior on þone seolue minstre; 7 siððon he wærð prior on Sauenni. Þaræftor, þurh þet he wæs ðes kynges mæi of Engleland 7 þes eorles of Peitowe, þa geaf se eorl him þone abbotrice of Sancte Iohannis ministre of Angeli. Siððon, þurh his micele wrences, ða beiæt he þone ærcebiscoprice of Besencun, 7 hæfde hit þa on hande þre dagas; þa forlæs he þet mid rihte, forþi þet he hit hæfde æror beieten mid unrihte. Siððon þa beiet he þone biscoprice of Seintes, þet wæs fif mile fram his abbotrice; þet he hæfde fulneah seoueniht on hande; þenon brohte se abbot him of Clunni, swa swa he æror dide of Besencun. þa beþohte he him þet gif he mihte ben rotfest on Engleland þet he mihte habben eal his wille. Besohte þa ðone kyng 7 sæide him þet he wæs eald man 7 forbroken man, 7 þet he ne mihte ðolen þa micele unrihte 7 þa micele unsibbe ða wæron on here land, 7 iærnde þa þurh him 7 ðurh ealle his freond namcuðlice þone abbotrice of Burhc. 7 Se kyng hit him iætte, forði þet he wæs his mæi 7 forþi þet he wæs an hæfod ða að to swerene 7 witnesse to berene þær ða eorles sunu of Normandi 7 þes eorles dohter of Angeow wæron totwemde for sibreden. Þus earmlice wæs þone abbotrice gifen betwix Cristesmesse 7 Candelmesse at Lundene.

[This year the king Henry held his court at Christmas in Windsor. David the king of Scots was there, and all the chiefmen, clerical and lay, who were in England. And there he had archbishops, and bishops, and abbots, and earls, and all those thegns who were there, swear (to grant) England and Normandy after his day into the hand of his daughter Ethelic, who was earlier wife of the emperor of Saxony; and afterwards sent her to

Normandy – and with her travelled her brother Robert, earl of Gloucester, and Brian, son of the earl Alan Fergant – and had her wedded to the son of the earl of Anjou, who was called Geoffrey Martel. It offended all the French and English, but the king did it to have peace from the earl of Anjou and to have help against his nephew William (the Clito). In the same year in spring the earl Charles of Flanders was killed by his own men in a certain church where he lay before the altar and prayed to God during the mass. And the king of France brought William the son of the earl of Normandy, and gave him the earldom, and the local people accepted him. This same William had earlier taken to wife the daughter of the earl of Anjou, but they were afterwards divorced for consanguinity. That was all through the king Henry of England; afterward (William Clito) took as a wife the sister of the wife of the king of France, and therefore the king (of France) gave him the earldom of Flanders. This same year he gave the abbacy of Peterborough to an abbot who was called Henri of Poitou. He had his abbacy of St Jean d'Angély in hand, and all the archbishops and bishops said it was against the law, and that he could not have two abbacies in hand; but the same Henri gave the king to understand that he had left his abbacy because of the great hostility that was in that land, and he did that through the advice and leave of the pope of Rome and of the abbot of Cluny, and because he was legate about the Rome-tax. But despite that it was just not so; but he wanted to have both in hand – and had so, for as long as it was God's will. While in his clerk's orders he was bishop in Soissons; afterwards he became a monk in Cluny, and later became prior in the same minster; and later he became prior in Savigny. After that, because he was a relative of the king of England and of the earl of Poitou, the earl gave him the abbacy of St Jean d'Angély. Afterwards through his great tricks he then got hold of the archbishopric of Besançon, and then had it in hand for three days; then he lost it, justly, because earlier he had got hold of it unjustly. Then afterwards he got hold of the bishopric of Saintes, which was five miles from his abbacy; he had that in hand well-nigh a week; the abbot of Cluny got him out from there, just as he earlier did from Besançon. Then it occurred to him that, if he could get firmly rooted in England, he could get all his own way; then he besought the king, and said to him that he was an old man and a broken-down man, and that he could not endure the great injustices and the great hostilities there were in their land; and then, personally and by means of all his well-known friends, begged for the abbacy of Peterborough. And the king granted it to him because he was his relative, and because he had been a principal in swearing the oath and witnessing when the son of the earl of Normandy (William Clito) and the daughter of the earl of Anjou were divorced for consanguinity. Thus wretchedly the abbacy was given, between Christmas and Candlemas at London.][26]

Two examples of the king holding court, the first to gain an oath of loyalty for his daughter, the second to give away the abbacy of Peterborough, set in motion and bring to focus everything else. Holding court involves a king making and publicly displaying contracts of general social importance, and thus includes a courtly audience's reactions, which in turn confirm that a court has been held. Both when Henry gains his followers' loyalty to his daughter as heir, and later when he gives away the abbacy of Peterborough, an audience to the king is brought partly into view, chiefly by their dislike of what Henry has done. In the first court scene, everyone is assembled, and later it is said that French and English resented the marriage or the oath or both ('hit ofþuht naþema ealle frencisc 7 englisc'), since it imposed a woman as heir to the throne and the hated earl of Anjou in a position of great power. But the king had his reasons, as the chronicler begins expanding to declare: he needed peace with the earl of Anjou to gain help against his nephew William 'Clito,' whose claim on Normandy and marriage to the daughter of the earl of Anjou constituted threats. Further background follows, showing Henry's action in holding this court as part of a game against both William Clito and the king of France: the murder of Charles the Good of Flanders leads the French king to grant William Clito the earldom of Flanders; but for his part Henry had managed to get William Clito divorced from the earl of Anjou's daughter on the grounds of consanguinity. Having separated William Clito from Anjou's daughter, marrying his own daughter to the earl of Anjou himself positioned his progeny's claims to Anjou against both William Clito and the king of France, as indeed the subsequent 'Angevin' lineage shows – although the resentment Matilda and Geoffrey of Anjou fostered among Henry's own followers also led a few years beyond this writer's lifetime to the nobles rejecting this oath, and to the anarchy under Stephen.

The next scene of the king holding court, his preemptive gift of the abbacy at Peterborough, intervenes as if a non-sequitur in the narrative. It might be easy to dismiss such ruptures as signs of careless compilation of multiple sources. But in fact that scene gradually reveals its deep connections to the first scene. The king's gift of the abbacy is implicitly but unmistakably again before a kind of court, now with a clerical audience visible by their dissent ('7 Ealle þa ærcebiscopes 7 biscopes seidon þet hit wæs togeanes riht'). This time extensive background is spliced into the scene and then the scene is resumed, a resumption signalled by repetition of some phrases. We hear the arguments of Henri of Poitou begin, followed by caustic background on his career; then we return to his appeal before the king, which closes with Henri of Poitou's remark on his frail dotage. The repetition of Henri of Poitou's plea based on 'þet micele unsibbe þet wæs on þet land' [28: the great unrest that was in that land], repeated and concluded a dozen lines later, shows that the scene before this digression is being resumed: 'þa micele unsibbe ða wæron on here land' (47–8).

The presentation of the moment of an appeal to the king before a clerical audience at court opens outward and backward with a narrative 'envelope' structure, not unlike what we find in *Beowulf* but providing more politically pointed and satirical context than is typical for Anglo-Saxon poetry. The king's reply to this petition, granting the request in spite of the court audience's reaction, is revealed with a similar suspended structure: it hinges not on Henri's wheedling appeal, but on Henri of Poitou's utility to the king as a principal oath-taker to the charge of consanguinity used to divorce William Clito from the daughter of the earl of Anjou, crucial background to the first scene of holding court. The layers of courtly craft and of the chronicler's subtlety here reach deep: the repeated use of the word *unsibbe* [enmity] in the paraphrase of Henri of Poitou's request just might be a punning mimicry of his own ability to hint to the king about his usefulness in the earlier case of consanguinity (*sibreden*). If that is the effect implied, the subtlety of Henri of Poitou's hint would be necessary because of the court audience, of listening and disapproving bishops and archbishops.

This chronicle entry is an elaborate dissection of holding court. We might say that the narrative's repeated supply of background information encloses the royal demands and royal gifts at court within the historian's court of judgment, whose views are refracted into the resentful murmuring faintly heard in both scenes of holding court. Such uses of audience reactions to convey the historian's judgment become the staple of later monastic chroniclers describing royal courts.[27]

The First Continuator's focus on courtly performance and its background shows him exploiting the ironies and political complexities of this new central stage well before Anglo-Norman French and Latin writers. Although we lack access to his English source, we may assume that he comes very near to the founding of this cultural and narrative focus; certainly, as the evidence of his influence shows, if he did not actually invent it, he gave it cultural currency. In its cynicism and suspenseful detail, this concern is a kind of 'courtliness' constituting the theatrical and satirical side of the 'elegance of manners' that C. Stephen Jaeger has traced among eleventh-century courtier bishops.[28] Even the conclusion of the 1127 Peterborough annal, which presents a story of ghostly black hunters who haunt the landscape during Henri of Poitou's abbacy, is squarely in the style of Walter Map, who presents many similar stories of ghostly wanderers and openly connects these to the immoral intrigues and unquiet consciences of members of the contemporary court. Map directly remarks after one story of ghostly apparitions, 'I would have this publicity known about our court, for never yet has there been one like it heard of in the past, nor is such another to be feared in the future. I am anxious ... that the chivalry of posterity should remember its malice, and learn that what they suffer is tolerable, from us who have undergone intolerable things.' With abbots imposed by kings, and court the framework for so much of reality, the court world for the First Continuator is almost as consuming and his feelings almost as ambivalent as his more verbose later Anglo-Norman compatriot Walter Map. 'In this pitiable and care-ridden court I languish, renouncing my own pleasure to please others,' Map laments. 'While there are very few who can help one, it is in the power of anyone to injure; unless I singly have appeased the whole body, I am nowhere.'[29]

Another perspective altogether, however, emerges from the Second Continuator at Peterborough. From 1132, when the manuscript hand and the general narrative structure and language change, to the chronicle's end in 1154, the phrase and notion of holding court along with any interest in the courtly world disappear. Once noted, the omission is striking, and relevant to a broader shift of point of view in this second writer: his attention to 'national' history is certainly evident, but that is now seen from the outside of the centres of administrative power. The idea of holding court is still present, but as something from an unreachable and unappealing world. It is this writer who first uses the English phrase *heald curt*, at Henry II's accession, yet he offers no interest in or view into the actions of the court there or elsewhere. If the first phase in the Peterborough Chronicle is to invent the idea of holding court, the second phase is to renounce any share in it.

Partly this may be because in the Second Continuator's time, holding court presents an ideal of national governance that is not possible until Henry II, at whose accession he stops. Stephen, the vile effects of whose reign so vividly occupy the Second Continuator, does not 'hold court'; rather, at one point the writer notes that 'macod he his gadering' [he made his assembly – i.e., he held his council], a contemptuous variation (1137/6–7). This *gadering* is a repellent following of sycophants and ruffians, who torture 'the people' and extort money endlessly from them. In this period, the writer declares, 'Gif two men oþer iii coman ridend to an tun, al þe tunscipe flugæn for heom, wenden ðat hi wæron ræueres' [1137/50–2: if two or three men come riding into town, the whole township flee from them, thinking they are robbers]. No matter what courtly faction these 'riders' represent, they are no longer knights to be put in the same honorific as the king holding court, as in the 1086 entry, but feared assailants from a dangerous and loathsome world.

Thus although the Second Continuator is the first writer in English actually to say 'hold court,' his predecessor the First Continuator and the still earlier OE writer whom that Continuator uses are the more intriguingly 'courtly' English writers, bridging the Anglo-Saxon and the Anglo-Norman world. For those earlier writers precociously elaborate and even help create from unknown materials *hired healdan* as a phrase, and as a central literary and historical frame of thought – even, like Walter Map and other French and Latin writers, as an engulfing framework for reality. If English writers seem less courtly in any sense than French and Latin ones for a long time thereafter (and not even Chaucer or Gower in the late fourteenth century can present a connection to the royal court as securely as can John Lydgate in the early fifteenth century), we may put that against the evidence of a brief, mutually enriching, though far from Edenic intimacy of English writers with the early Anglo-Norman court, followed by a long cultural and literary exile.

NOTES

1 Walter Map, *De Nugis Curialium: Courtiers' Trifles*, ed. and trans. M.R. James, rev. C.N.L. Brooke and R.A.B. Mynors (Oxford: Clarendon, 1983), dist. i, pages 2–3. I use James's translation. Unless otherwise noted, all other translation are my own.
2 This thirteenth-century gloss on the *Corpus iuris civilis* is translated in Ernst

H. Kantorowicz, *The King's Two Bodies: A Study in Medieval Political Theology* (Princeton: Princeton University Press, 1957), 295; the range of issues such corporate thinking entails in medieval culture is the subject of Kantorowicz's foundational study. He does not mention the early instance of the idea in Walter Map, or the other notions of 'holding court' discussed in this essay.

3 See, for example, a remarkable passage in the chronicle of Heinrich of Reichenau, when describing Emperor Henry III's meeting with King Peter of Hungary at the feast of Pentecost in 1045, where amid magnificent proceedings of gift-exchanges and oath-taking rivalling any later spectacle of holding court – absent only the use of that phrase – the floor of the old hall they are meeting in collapsed, killing the scholar-bishop Bruno of Würzburg (*Chronicon*, ed. G.H. Pertz, MGH, Scriptores 5 [Hannover: Hahn, 1844], 125; the passage is noted for other purposes by Margaret Gibson, *Lanfranc of Bec* [Oxford: Clarendon, 1978], 52).

4 Erich Auerbach, *Mimesis: The Representation of Reality in Western Literature*, trans. Willard R. Trask (Princeton: Princeton University Press, 1953).

5 All citations of the Peterborough Chronicle are from *The Peterborough Chronicle, 1070–1154*, ed. Cecily Clark, 2nd ed. (Oxford: Clarendon, 1970), by year and line number. For the dates, see C.R. Cheney, *Handbook of Dates for Students of English History*, Royal Historical Society Guides and Handbooks 4 (1945; repr. with corrections, Cambridge: Cambridge University Press, 1997), table 14.

6 Book 1, ch. 4; ed. Hans Hecht, *Bischofs Wærferth von Worcester Übersetzung der Dialoge Gregors des Grossen*, 2 vols, BaP 5 (1900; repr. in one vol., Darmstadt: Wissenschaftliche Buchgesellschaft, 1965), 27.

7 Gregory, *Dialogues*, 1.4; *PL* 77:165.

8 *Die Gesetze der Angelsachsen*, ed. Felix Liebermann, 3 vols (1903–16; repr. Aalen: Scientia, 1960), 1:192. I owe this reference to Fred Biggs.

9 *Historia Anglorum: The History of the English People*, ed. and trans. Diana Greenway (Oxford: Clarendon, 1996), 402.

10 *Life of Lanfranc*; *PL* 150:53–4.

11 On the scene, and the importance of the rituals William I used, see Janet L. Nelson, 'The Rites of the Conqueror,' *Proceedings of the Battle Conference on Anglo-Norman Studies* 4 (1981): 117–33.

12 See Gibson, *Lanfranc of Bec*, 196.

13 William Stubbs, *The Constitutional History of England*, 3 vols (Oxford: Oxford University Press, 1874–78), 1:138; F.M. Stenton, *Anglo-Saxon England*, 3rd ed., The Oxford History of England 2 (Oxford: Clarendon, 1971), 641.

14 Tryggvi J. Oleson, *The Witenagemot in the Reign of Edward the Confessor: A*

Study in the Constitutional History of Eleventh-Century England (Toronto: University of Toronto Press, 1955), 71–2.
15 *Vita Caroli*, ch. 14; *PL* 97:1081.
16 See William Dugdale, *Monasticon Anglicanum*, 6 vols in 8 (1661–82; repr. London: Bohn, 1846), 1:371; also *PL* 149:1360–1.
17 Geoffrey of Monmouth, *Historia Regum Britanniae*, book 9, ch. 12; trans. Lewis Thorpe, *The History of the Kings of Britain* (London: Penguin, 1972), 225.
18 Geoffrey of Monmouth, *Historia Regum Britanniae*, book 9, ch. 12 (trans. Thorpe, page 226).
19 Citations of *The Service for Representing Adam* are from *Medieval Drama*, ed. David Bevington (Boston: Houghton Mifflin, 1975), 80–121 by line numbers; translations are, however, my own.
20 *Le Roman de Thèbes*, ed. Francine Mora-Lebrun, Lettres gothiques (Paris: Librairie Générale Française, 1995), lines 1971–4.
21 See my comments on both in 'Writing History in England,' in *The Cambridge History of Medieval English Literature*, ed. David Wallace (1999; repr. with corrections, Cambridge: Cambridge University Press, 2002), 255–83, at 257–60.
22 *The Chronicle of Battle Abbey*, ed. and trans. Eleanor Searle (Oxford: Clarendon, 1980), 290; the following quotations are all from page 293.
23 *Vita Theophili metrica*; *PL* 171:1595.
24 Gautier de Coinci, *Le Miracle de Théophile*, ed. and trans. Annette Garnier, Textes et traductions des classiques français du Moyen Âge 6 (Paris: Honoré Champion, 1998), lines 28ff.
25 Map, *De Nugis*, dist. i, c. 10, pages 15–17.
26 The translation here draws from that in Michael J. Swanton, trans. and ed., *The Anglo-Saxon Chronicle* (New York: Routledge, 1998), 256–8.
27 For Matthew Paris's use of this technique, see my 'Writing History in England,' 258.
28 See Jaeger, *The Origins of Courtliness: Civilizing Trends and the Formation of Courtly Ideals – 939–1210* (Philadelphia: University of Pennsylvania Press, 1985), for example, 127–8, 196.
29 Map, *De Nugis*, dist. iv, c. 13, page 373.

Echoes of Old English Alliterative Collocations in Middle English Alliterative Proverbs

SUSAN E. DESKIS

One of the hallmarks of Thomas D. Hill's copious scholarship over the years has been its eclecticism. Tom has followed literary questions wherever they lead him, remaining cheerfully oblivious to such artificial boundaries as language and genre and to such disciplinary divides as those between OE and ME and literary studies and folkloristics.[1] In honour of Tom's long interest in proverbs[2] (among many other things) I offer this study of the continuity of the alliterative proverb across the divide of the Norman Conquest of England. As I will show, the roots of certain alliterative proverbs may lie in the Anglo-Saxon period, but these proverbs continued to grow and thrive for centuries afterwards.

The Norman Conquest of England and its attendant cultural changes produced a significant and long-lasting change in the nature of English literature. I am speaking, of course, of the introduction of end-rhyme as an essential feature of English poetics. End-rhyme had been known in Anglo-Saxon England: it was common in Latin poetry and was even toyed with in the vernacular, as witness the much-maligned *Rhyming Poem*. Still, it has become a scholarly and pedagogical commonplace that French influence following the Conquest replaced the native alliterative tradition with one of rhyme.[3]

Of course, that commonplace comes with caveats. Some early ME works like the *Brut* and the Katherine Group make significant use of alliteration. Furthermore, the Alliterative Revival of the fourteenth century proves that the metrical principles we associate with OE poetry persisted, though in altered form, several centuries later in the ME period. Just how that alliterative tradition survived is still a bit of a mystery, with some scholars arguing for continuity of the alliterative tradition through the oral circulation of verse, others pointing to the influence of metrical prose, and still others favouring the idea that alliterative poetry was simply re-invented in the fourteenth century, with no continuity between OE and ME.[4] The study of alliterative proverbs cannot solve the enigma of the Alliterative Revival, but it can illuminate one area in which alliteration remained important in marked verbal forms.

The first observation I can offer is that alliterative proverbs far outnumber rhymed ones in the medieval English corpus.[5] This preponderance of alliteration appears despite the fact that ME proverbs survive at a much higher rate than their OE counterparts. The paroemiological prejudice for alliteration may result from the conciseness of the form or it may represent a carry-over from the origins of the proverbs themselves.

The small size of the preserved OE corpus, and the formality of that corpus relative to everyday speech, make it difficult to collect proverbs. Although proverbs enjoyed greater respect throughout the Middle Ages than they do now, they were, even then, primarily oral in their transmission and were very probably more common in spoken than written discourse.[6] The evidence becomes even sparser when we limit our inquiry to alliterative proverbs. Nevertheless, there are a number of instances where the alliterating word-pairs of a ME proverb are well attested in OE. These repetitions indicate either that the proverb already existed in OE (most often without attestation as such in the written record) or that the alliterating words were so commonly linked that they became fixed in proverbial form at some later date. Because alliterative collocations often occur in non-proverbial contexts, other conditions must be met before we can posit an OE collocation as an embryonic form of a ME alliterative proverb. Specifically, instances of the collocation must also share some other distinctive feature with the proverb, whether lexical (apart from the collocation itself), syntactic, or semantic.[7] The following examples range from an alliterative collocation attested in essentially identical (allowing for linguistic changes) proverbs in OE and ME, to ME proverbs that employ alliterative collocations attested in OE.

1. When the cup is fullest bear it fairest (Whiting, C633)[8]
   Swa <u>fulre fæt</u> swa hit mann sceal <u>fægror</u> beran (*Durham Proverbs*)[9]
   When the coppe is <u>follest</u>, thenne ber hire <u>feyrest</u> (*Proverbs of Hendyng*)

This is a rare example of a proverb that appears in nearly identical forms in both OE and ME. The version from the *Proverbs of Hendyng* maintains the alliteration on 'full' and 'fair,' but has lost one other alliterative element through its replacement of 'fæt' by 'coppe.' In general, the author of the *Proverbs of Hendyng* uses alliteration only as an ornament, and, as J.P. Oakden points out, alliteration in that work 'is almost entirely due to the presence of certain traditional expressions and phrases.'[10] In this case, the 'traditional expression' dates back to the Anglo-Saxon period.

2a. All hights [promises] should be held (Whiting, H378)
    All hechtis suld haldin be! (Henryson, *Fables*)
2b. What you hight see you hold (Whiting, H379)
    Quhar thow hechtys, se thow hald (*Go way, Fore that*)

Bartlett Jere Whiting records two variants of this proverb, both from fifteenth-century Middle Scots texts. Despite their grammatical differences, these are clearly two expressions of the same proverb. Because this sentence does not appear as a proverb per se in the OE corpus, we must locate its background by searching for instances of matching alliterative pairs.

The OE sentences that link *hatan* and *healdan* exhibit small variations in form, but perfect consistency in meaning:

> ðæt he meahte gehealdan ðæt ðæt he ær gehet [ond] swor[11] [... so that he might keep to what he had promised and sworn]
> And þonne bið þæt fulluht, swylce hit wedd sy ealra þæra worda and ealles ðæs behates, gehealde, se ðe wille[12] [And that is baptism, as it were a pledge of all the words and all the vow, hold to it who will]

Like *Go way, Fore that* but unlike Henryson, the two OE examples use both alliterating words as verbs. The first example bears the closest semantic and grammatical similarity to the ME proverbs. The second, from Wulfstan's *Institutes of Polity*, also includes the modifier 'all' found in Henryson. Though both derive from OE translations of Latin texts, the fact that two different Anglo-Saxon translators chose to employ the same alliterative language in their prose may itself imply that the *hatan/healdan* collocation was common and familiar.

3a. Much will have more (Whiting, M786)

Bot ay mekill wald have mare as many man spellis (*The Wars of Alexander*)
Have thai never so mekyl mok he wyl have more (Poems of John Audelay)
Have he nevere so mykyl, gyt he wold have more (*The Castell of Perseverance*)
Mykull wulle more (Middle English Proverbs, Douce MS 52)
Nedeles moche wolde have more (*Proverbs of Salamon*)

3b. Of much they made more (Whiting, M787)
And as the maner is, of mych thay mad more. *Fama de magnis semper majore, vulgante* [A common saying: from much always more.] (*English Conquest*)

The collocation 'much' and 'more' is very common and productive in the early English proverbial tradition.[13] All of Whiting's examples exhibit strong proverbial form, and some are marked as current proverbs ('as many man spellis'; 'Fama de magnis semper majore, vulgante'). *The Oxford Dictionary of English Proverbs* adds more examples, extending the currency of the proverb to at least 1900.[14]

The proverbial pairing is equally common in OE, occurring at least ten times. It is especially well attested in the OE gloss to Defensor's *Liber scintillarum*,[15] where we find the version closest to the ME proverb: '[ond] swa micele mare swa he begytt swa micele mare he secð' (quanto magis adquirit tanto amplius querit) (ch. 30.20) [and the more he receives, the more he seeks]. Other examples from Defensor, as well as from Ælfric, Alfred's translation of Gregory's *Pastoral Care*, and elsewhere adjust the proverb to specific conditions by specifying exactly what a person has or seeks 'much' and 'more' of:

swa micele maran eadmodnysse þu sy þurhbeorht swa micele swa maran wurþnysse foresett (tanto maiore humilitate sis perspicuus quanto maiore dignitate prelatus). (Defensor, ch. 4.46) [the more radiant you are in humility, the more advanced you are in honor]
swa micelem swa on stowe hegra ys swa micelum on frecenysse maran wunað (Quantum loco superior est tantum in periculo maiore uersatur). (Defensor, ch. 32.53) [the higher a place is, the more one stands in danger]
lar swa micele swa heo rumlicor geseald byþ swa micele mara heo

genihtsumað (Doctrina quanto amplius data fuerit tanto magis abundat). (Defensor, ch. 32.100) [the more generously teaching is given, the more it abounds]

swa <u>micele</u> <u>maran</u> susla hi syllaþ swa <u>micele</u> swa hi <u>maran</u> synd [tanto maiora supplicia dabunt quanto et ipsa maiora sunt] (Defensor, ch. 58.56) [the greater they are, the more trouble they give]

ðætte sua <u>micle</u> sua hira onwald bið <u>mara</u> gesewen[16] [as much as their power is seen to be greater]

swa <u>micele</u> witodlice swa <u>mara</u> wurðmynt swa <u>miccle</u> <u>maran</u> beoð fræcednissa[17] [verily, the greater the glory the more the dangers]

and <u>micele</u> yrmða becumað ... <u>maran</u> and <u>maran</u>[18] [and much misery becomes ... more and more]

swa <u>micela</u> swa se heofenlica cyning is ... swa <u>micele</u> <u>mara</u>[19] [as great as the heavenly king is ... so much greater ...]

Se ealda cwide is swiðe soð þe mon gefyrn cwæð, þætte þa <u>micles</u> bedurfon þe <u>micel</u> agan willað, [ond] þa þurfon swiþe lytles þe <u>maran</u> ne wilniað þonne genoges[20] [The old saying is very true: they need much who desire much, and those who wish for no more than enough need very little]

Based on its abundant attestations, I would argue that the OE collocation 'micel ... mara' was what we might call a proverbial template, a traditional phrasing with a stable core and variable particulars; in the first example from Defensor this template was fully realized as a proverb. The ME proverbs show the continuation of the proverbial template with but a stripping away of the particulars.

4. Lief child behoves lore (Whiting, C216)
   <u>Lef</u> child bihoveth <u>lore</u>,
   And evere the <u>levere</u> the more (*Proverbs of Hendyng*)

   <u>Lef</u> child <u>lore</u> bihoveth (*The Good Wife Taught her Daughter*)

   My syre sayde so to me, and so did my dame,
   That the <u>levere</u> childe the more <u>lore</u> bihoveth (*Piers Plowman*)

   <u>Lefe</u> chylde <u>lore</u> be-hoveth (Douce MS 52)

   Seyd hit ys full yore

That lothe chylde <u>lore</u> behowyyt,
and <u>leve</u> chylde moche more (*The Good Wyfe Wold a Pylgremage*)

For, as the wyse man sayth and prevyth,
A <u>leve</u> chyld, <u>lore</u> he be-hoveth (*Symon's Lesson of Wysedome*)

This proverb is common and fairly stable in English from the thirteenth century on. Its proverbial status is reinforced by its earliest ME manifestations among the *Proverbs of Hendyng* and by its tendency to appear in texts of a didactic nature. Half of these examples are labelled as traditional wisdom, and the only real variation is the occasional expansion of the proverb from one line to two.

The belief that a beloved person (not necessarily a child) should be taught is widespread in OE, but not, apparently, proverbial. The alliterative collocation takes one of two forms: *leof* may be paired with the noun *lar* (as in the ME proverb) or with the verb *læran*. Because the ME examples do not use *leren*, the ME reflex of *læran*, I will concentrate first on the OE sentences that link *leof* and *lar*.

Cornelius gelaðode his <u>leofstan</u> freond, wolde þæt hi gehyrdon þa halgan <u>lare</u> æt Petre[21] [Cornelius summoned his dearest friends; he wanted them to hear the holy teaching from Peter]

Nu <u>lære</u> ic ðe swa swa <u>leofne</u> sunu, þæt ðu þæra cristenra <u>lare</u> forlæte mid ealle[22] [Now I counsel you like a beloved son, that you should altogether abandon Christian doctrine]

<u>Leofen</u> men, beorgað eow georne wið deofles <u>lara</u>[23] [Beloved men, guard yourselves zealously against the devil's teaching]

Forþon wat se þe sceal   his winedryhtnes
<u>leofes larcwidum</u>   longe forþolian (*The Wanderer* 37–8)
[Therefore he who must long forgo the teaching of his beloved lord knows]

These examples show little more in common than the use of the same alliterative collocation. In the ME proverb, lore is very much a good thing; in these OE sentences, it may be good or bad. In the *læran* sentences, however, the teaching is always positive:

Nu <u>lære</u> ic þe   swa man <u>leofne</u> sceal (*Exhortation to Christian Living* 1)

[Now I will teach you as one should a dear one]
Ne meahton we gelæran   leofne þeoden (*Beowulf* 3079)
[We could not counsel our beloved lord]
Forþon ic leofra gehwone   læran wille (*Christ II* 815)
[Therefore I will teach every dear one]
Forþon ic, leof weorud,   læran wille (*Juliana* 647)
[Therefore, beloved people, I wish to counsel you]
Leofan men, nu bidde ic and lære ælcne cristene man[24] [Beloved people, now I bid and teach every Christian]
Men þa leofestan, ic eow bidde [and] eaðmodlice lære[25] [Beloved people, I bid you and humbly counsel]
Leofan men, doð swa ic lære[26] [Beloved people, do as I teach]
Leofa, swa ic þe lære (*Genesis A* 2306a)
[Dear one, as I instruct you]
Leofan man, on eornost ic lære[27] [Dear ones, earnestly I teach]

Besides being more common, the *læran* form is more consistent in both form and content. It is useful for homilists, but can be found in both religious and secular literature, and in both poetry and prose. The teaching is always directed towards the *leof* person or persons (again, like the ME proverb). This collocation is firmly enough established in OE to qualify as a proverbial template, or even as a rhetorical topos, but it is unlikely to be the source of the ME proverb for two reasons. First, the ME versions of the proverb all use the noun *lore* instead of the verb *leren*; and second, none of the OE examples realizes proverbial or even sentential structure. Finally, none of the OE clauses includes the non-alliterative pairing of *child* and *behoveth* that is shared by all of the ME proverbs. So in this case, despite the alliterative collocation of *leof* and *lar* in the first group of OE clauses, no probable connection can be drawn with the ME proverbs.

I have included this negative finding here as a methodological caution: the mere attestation in OE of the same (or etymologically related) alliterative collocation, even in large numbers, does not suggest proverbial continuity. In order to propose an OE origin for a ME proverb we need to see at least some syntactic regularity combined with a consistent semantic sense. Syntactic regularity may trump content, as in 'Much will have more,' but in an instance where semantic content fails to match – the ME positive and OE mixed valences of *lar* – and syntactic form clashes as well – the noun 'lore' versus the verb *læran* – shared collocations alone cannot tell us much about proverbial origins.

5. In the heart is the hoard of ilk man's word (Whiting, H283)
   And in the <u>hert</u> thare es the <u>horde</u>
   And knawing of ilk man's worde (*Ywain and Gawain*)

Although this proverb appears as a two-line passage in the fourteenth-century romance, the OE parallels show that the alliterative first line contains the proverb itself, with the second line representing an expansion to fill out a rhyming couplet.

> Eorl oðerne   mid æfþancum
> ond mid teonwordum   tæleð behindan,
> spreceð fægere beforan,   ond þæt facen swa þeah
> hafað in his <u>heortan</u>,   <u>hord</u> unclæne. (*Homiletic Fragment I* 3–6)[28]
> [One man slanders another behind his back with insults and abuse; he speaks fairly before him, but he holds that treachery in his heart, an unclean hoard.]

> Ne magun <u>hord</u> weras,   <u>heortan</u> geþohtas,
> fore waldende   wihte bemiþan. (*Christ III* 1047–8)
> [Men cannot at all conceal their hoard, the thoughts of their hearts, before the Lord.]

>   ac se mæra dæg
> hreþerlocena <u>hord</u>,   <u>heortan</u> geþohtas,
> ealle ætyweð. (*Christ III* 1054b–6a)
> [... but that great day will reveal all, the hoard of the breast and the thoughts of the heart.]

Numerous characteristics link these OE passages to the ME proverb. First is the simple proximity of *heort* and *hord* and the fact that the *hord* is consistently described as being contained within the *heort*. Second is the flexibility of the hoard: in both OE and ME it may be morally good or bad. Furthermore, all three of the OE examples state or imply a potential disjuncture between the heart's true hoard and one's outward mien, as does the ME proverb. Finally, we may note that all but the last OE text assume a generalized, sentential form. Based on this evidence, I believe that the OE texts present a common, perhaps proverbial, sentiment that, through the accidents of preservation, occurs only in ME in a concise, proverbial form.

My final example finds ample attestation in OE and ME, but must be treated cautiously because all of the OE collocations are found in poetic texts. Thus, we may be looking at the OE roots of a ME proverb, but the absence of the collocation in prose makes the connection a little less certain.

6a. After bale comes boot (Whiting, B18)
   Hu after bale hem com bote (*Floriz and Blauncheflur*)
   After bale cometh boote (*The Tale of Gamelyn*)
   So aftir bale comyth bote (*The Tale of Beryn*)
   After Bale Boot thou bringes (Chester Plays)
   But aftre bale ther may come bote (*Royal Historie of ... Generides*)
   Ffore after bale ther comyht bote (*Speculum Misericordie*)
   After bale comyth bote (Rawlinson Proverbs)
6b. When bale is highest boot is nighest (Whiting, B22)
      For Aluered seide of olde quide,
      ... Wone the bale is alre-hecst,
      Thonne is the bote alrenecst (*The Owl and the Nightingale*)
   Bote ther the bale was alre meast, swa was te bote nehest (*Wohunge of Ure Laverd*)
   There the bale is mest, there is the bote nest (Proverbs of Hendyng)
   Lo, an olde proverbe aleged by many wyse: – Whan bale is greetest, than is bote a nye-bore (Usk, *Testament of Love*)
   For whon the bale was most,
      Then was the bote next (*A Talkyng of the Love of God*)
   Whenne bale ys aldermest, bote ys ful hende (*Firumbras*)
   When bale is most, bote is nexte (*Proverbs of Wysdom*)

These two proverbs are ubiquitous in the ME corpus: both are very stable, both are very common, and both contain the alliterative collocation 'bale' and 'boot.'[29] That pairing is similarly common in OE:

   in uprodor   eadigra gehwam
   æfter bealusiðe   bote lifes,
   lifigendra gehwam   langsumne ræd (*Exodus* 4–6)
   [in heaven above, to each of the blessed the reward of life after the baleful journey, to each of the living, long-lasting gain]

   gyf him edwenden   æfre scolde

<u>bealuwa</u> bisigu <u>bot</u> eft cuman (*Beowulf* 280–1)
[if a reversal should ever come for him, relief from the afflictions of evil ...]

          gif we sona eft
þara <u>bealudæda</u> <u>bote</u> gefremmaþ (*Elene* 514b–15)
[if we immediately make restitution for those sinful deeds]

se þe him <u>bealwa</u> to <u>bote</u> gelyfde (*Beowulf* 909)
[who expected from him relief from ills]

Habbað wræcmæcgas wergan gæstas,
hetlen helsceaþa, hearde genyrwad,
gebunden <u>bealorapum</u>. Is seo <u>bot</u> gelong
eall æt þe anum, ece dryhten. (*Christ I* 363–6)
[Cursed spirits, hostile devils, have hard beset the exiles, bound them in oppressive fetters. The remedy can only come from you, eternal Lord.]

Forgif me to lisse, lifgende god,
bitre <u>bealodæde</u>. Ic þa <u>bote</u> gemon,
cyninga wuldor, cume to, gif ic mot. (*Resignation [A]* 19–21)
[Forgive me in your mercy, living God, for my bitter sins. I am mindful of that help, glory of kings – let me come to it if I may.]

ond eal þæt mancynn þe him mid wunige,
elþeodigra inwitwrasnum,
<u>bealuwe</u> gebundene. Him sceal <u>bot</u> hraðe
weorþan in worulde (*Andreas* 945–8a)
[and (free) all the people who dwell with him, bound in trouble, from the hostile fetters of their foes. They shall quickly have help in this world ...]

The germ of the ME proverbs is present in these OE collocations, as they all assume that 'bale' necessitates or is followed by 'boot.' However, the OE examples show significant variation in the ways that they deploy the two terms. In four of the examples (over half), *bealu* appears as part of a compound, which gives it a more specific meaning. For example, *bealodæde* (sinful deeds) is more specific than simple *bealu*, (trouble). In another three examples, the two words appear together in the same line, but in different sentences. Whiting's B18 regularly (though not exclusively) links 'bale' and 'boot' with the verb 'come,' which we also see in the first of the OE examples, while the regular use of the adverb 'after' is paralleled by the use of *æfter* in *Exodus* and of *eft* in the second and third OE examples. However, B22, which relies not only on the alliteration of 'bale' and 'boot' but also on the rhyme, or near-rhyme, of *mest* or *hest* with *nest*, is more lasting; I have merely cut off my examples in the early sixteenth century. Thus, I would conclude that the alliterative collocation of *bealu* and *bot* was not proverbial in OE, but that its frequent use led to the fixing of proverbial form sometime later on. Whether or not I am correct in this assessment, we can observe that the example of 'bale and boot' illustrates a continuity of thought and expression linking the OE and ME periods.

In conclusion, let me return to the problem with which I began: the question of continuity in medieval English verbal culture. I hope to have shown that such continuity is very much in evidence in the case of the alliterative proverb, which established its popularity in the OE period and continued in ME as well. In his essay 'On the Continuity of English Poetry,' C.L. Wrenn observes that what he calls 'gnomic moralising' has remained a constant theme in the English poetic tradition, at least up until his day.[30] Even in the trilingual world of high- and late-medieval England, where the English language ranked last in status behind French and Latin, there seems to have been a special place reserved for English proverbial forms. For example, R.W. Chambers cites the case of an English anchorite named Hugh, who, around the year 1200, requested a Rule from a priest named Robert. Robert responded with a collection of 'diversas sententias' he had translated from English books into Latin. Chambers concludes that 'English, then, not Latin, was, in early Angevin days, the obvious language in which might be found precepts useful to a recluse.'[31]

We also find English proverbs surviving the francophone world of the courts of law. Paul Brand has noted that court reports, which are generally French accounts of what he believes to have been French proceedings, leave English proverbs untranslated. 'English proverbs,' Brand writes, 'seem to have been left in the original precisely because this was indeed the language in which they were spoken, used by the justices from time to time for its very pithiness or its quaintness.'[32] It is true that English proverbs are pithy, quaint, and often untranslatable.

Sermons are another multilingual environment where the English proverb throve. Siegfried Wenzel and G.R. Owst have both discussed the presence of vernacular proverbs in sermons.[33] Owst describes their appearance in John Bromyard's *Summa Predicantium*:

> As in earlier macaronic homilies abroad, vernacular phrases and quotations occur frequently, untranslated, in the body of the Latin text. The sermon-compiler is recording some favourite *bon-mot* or proverb of the day, some carefully chosen word, that it may spring again to the preacher's lips at the critical moment.[34]

Owst points out that 'many' of such proverbs use 'the much-loved alliteration.'[35]

Because this essay presents some preliminary findings from a larger study, there are other potentially interesting connections between OE texts and ME proverbs that, for now, must remain unexplored. For example, I have collected about a dozen examples of alliterative parallelisms in OE and ME that may owe their continuity to reinforcement by biblical (or other Latin) texts. In other instances, the ME proverb loses alliteration over time or shows variation between alliterative and non-alliterative forms. There is also a corpus of ME proverbs that use alliteration that cannot be a carry-over from OE because at least one of the alliterating words is of Romance origin. These developments are, however, more significant for the study of ME linguistic culture than for the OE that is the focus of this volume.

It can be said that proverbs, more than any other form, represent 'the poetry of the people.' Certainly, proverbs are poetic in that they use structures and ornaments different from those of unmarked prose. As for being 'of the people': a proverb does not become a proverb unless it is, well, popular. That popularity is revealed to us only through the limited documentation surviving from the Middle Ages, but even so, it is possible to see the alliterative proverb in OE and ME as one locus of continuity in a time of great cultural change.

NOTES

1 To give just a few examples from Tom's extensive bibliography, see his 'When God Blew Satan out of Heaven: The Motif of Exsufflation in *Vercelli Homily XIX* and Later English Literature,' *Leeds Studies in English* n.s. 16 [*Sources and Relations: Studies in Honour of J.E. Cross*, ed. Marie Collins, Jocelyn Price, and Andrew Hamer] (1985): 132–41; 'Two Notes on Exegetical

Allusion in Langland: *Piers Plowman* [B,] XI, 161–167, and B, I, 115–124,' *NM* 75 (1974): 92–7; '"The Green Path to Paradise" in Nineteenth-Century Ballad Tradition,' *NM* 91 (1990): 483–6.

2 See, for example, his 'The Foreseen Wolf and the Path of Wisdom: Proverbial and Beast Lore in *Atlakviða*,' *Neophilologus* 77 (1993): 675–7, and '"When the Leader is Brave ...": An Old English Proverb and Its Vernacular Context,' *Anglia* 119 (2001): 232–6, as well as two articles that Tom and I published together: '"The Wolf Doesn't Care": The Proverbial and Traditional Context of Laȝamon's *Brut* Lines 10624–36,' *RES* n.s. 46 (1995): 41–8, and '"The longe man ys seld wys": Proverbial Characterization and Langland's Long Will,' *YLS* 18 (2004): 73–9.

3 For an interesting argument for the choice of rhyme or alliteration in the eleventh century serving as a political statement, see Seth Lerer, 'Old English and Its Afterlife,' in *The Cambridge History of Medieval English Literature*, ed. David Wallace (Cambridge: Cambridge University Press, 1999), 7–34.

4 For a recent survey article on this subject, see Harold C. Zimmerman, 'Continuity and Innovation: Scholarship on the Middle English Alliterative Revival,' *Jahrbuch für Internationale Germanistik* 35.1 (2003): 107–23.

5 This observation is based on my reading through the entire collection of medieval English proverbs in Bartlett Jere Whiting with Helen Wescott Whiting, *Proverbs, Sentences, and Proverbial Phrases from English Writings Mainly before 1500* (Cambridge, MA: Belknap, 1968).

6 On the written transmission of medieval proverbs, see Susan E. Deskis, *'Beowulf' and the Medieval Proverb Tradition*, MRTS 155 (Tempe, AZ: MRTS, 1996), ch. 6.

7 Here I use the term 'collocation' somewhat loosely to describe pairs of words that appear near each other with some regularity. I would not argue that they are the fixed formulas addressed, for example, by Ursula Schaefer, 'Twin Collocations in the Early Middle English Lives of the *Katherine Group*,' in *Orality and Literacy in Early Middle English*, ed. Herbert Pilch, ScriptOralia 83 (Tubingen: Gunter Narr Verlag, 1996), 179–98, or Mark R.V. Southern, 'Formulaic Binomials, Morphosymbolism, and Behaghel's Law: The Grammatical Status of Expressive Iconicity,' *American Journal of Germanic Linguistics and Literatures* 12 (2000): 251–79. Southern (260) does point out some similarities in function between binomials and proverbs. For a formal, linguistic definition and classification of collocations, see Göran Kjellmer, *A Dictionary of English Collocations Based on the Brown Corpus*, 3 vols (Oxford: Clarendon, 1994), 1:xii–xxxiii.

8 Whiting, *Proverbs*, cited by lemma number; all citations of ME proverbs are from Whiting, so I give only the titles of the texts.

9 The Latin is 'Vas quantum plenior tantum moderatius ambulandum' (ed. Olaf Arngart, 'The Durham Proverbs,' *Speculum* 56 [1981]: 288–300 at 295).

10 J.P. Oakden, *Alliterative Poetry in Middle English: The Dialectal and Metrical Survey*, 2 vols in 1 (1930, 1935; repr. Hamden, CT: Archon, 1968), 2:8.

11 *King Alfred's West-Saxon Version of Gregory's Pastoral Care*, ed. Henry Sweet, EETS o.s. 45 and 50 (London: N. Trübner, 1871–2), 465, lines 26–7.

12 *Die 'Institutes of Polity, Civil and Ecclesiastical': Ein Werk Erzbischof Wulfstans von York*, ed. Karl Jost, Schweizer anglistische Arbeiten 47 (Bern: Francke, 1959) §§122 and 241. Though the object of *gehealde* here is *fulluht* rather than *behates*, the phrase *wedd ... ealles ðæs behates* describes *fulluht*, and *behates* is closely linked to *gehealde* by position and alliteration.

13 See further G.L. Apperson, *The Wordsworth Dictionary of Proverbs* (Ware: Wordsworth Editions, 1993), 433; and Morris P. Tilley, *A Dictionary of the Proverbs in England in the Sixteenth and Seventeenth Centuries* (Ann Arbor: University of Michigan Press, 1950), M1287.

14 F.P. Wilson, *The Oxford Dictionary of English Proverbs*, 3rd ed. (Oxford: Clarendon, 1970), 550.

15 Defensor of Ligugé, *Liber scintillarum*, ed. Sarah Sovereign Getty, 'An Edition with Commentary of the Latin/Anglo-Saxon *Liber scintillarum*' (PhD dissertation, University of Pennsylvania, 1969); cited from the *DOE Corpus*.

16 *King Alfred's West-Saxon Version*, ed. Sweet, 119, line 14.

17 Friedrich Kluge, 'Zu altenglischen Dichtungen,' *Englische Studien* 8 (1885): 472–9 at 472, line 7.

18 *Catholic Homilies* I.21, ed. Malcolm Godden, *Ælfric's Catholic Homilies: The Second Series. Text*, EETS s.s. 5. (London: Oxford University Press, 1979), 188, line 266.

19 *The Anglo-Saxon Version of the Hexameron of St. Basil, or, Be Godes six daga weorcum. And the Anglo-Saxon Remains of St. Basil's Admonitio ad filium spiritualem*, ed. Henry W. Norman, 2nd ed. (London: J.R. Smith, 1849), ch. 2, line 53.

20 *King Alfred's Version of Boethius De Consolatione Philosophiae*, ed. Walter Sedgefield (1899; repr. Darmstadt: Wissenschaftliche Buchgesellschaft, 1968), 31, line 20.

21 *Lives of Saints* (Peter's Chair), ed. Walter W. Skeat, *Ælfric's Lives of Saints*, EETS o.s. 76, 82, 94, 114 (1881–1900; repr. in 2 vols, Oxford: Oxford University Press, 1966), 228.

22 *Lives of Saints* (Saint George), ed. Skeat, 314. Note that this hybrid form includes both *læran* and *lar*.

23 Wulfstan, Homily VIIIc, in *The Homilies of Wulfstan*, ed. Dorothy Bethurum (Oxford: Clarendon, 1957), 183, line 156.

24 *Eleven Old English Rogationtide Homilies*, ed. Joyce Bazire and James E. Cross, Toronto Old English Series 7 (Toronto: University of Toronto Press, 1982), Homily 8, page 109, line 18.
25 *The Vercelli Homilies and Related Texts*, ed. D.G. Scragg, EETS o.s. 300 (Oxford: Oxford University Press, 1992), Homily IV, page 90, line 1.
26 Wulfstan, Homily Xc, ed. Bethurum, *The Homilies of Wulfstan*, 203, lines 76–7; cf. also *Die 'Institutes of Polity,'* ed. Jost, 173, §10, and Napier LIX [HomU 48], in Arthur Napier, *Wulfstan: Sammlung der ihm zugeschriebenen Homilien nebst Untersuchungen über ihre Echtheit* (1883; repr. with a bibliographical supplement by Klaus Ostheeren, Dublin: Weidmann, 1967), 307, line 2.
27 Wulfstan, Homily Xc, ed. Bethurum, *The Homilies of Wulfstan*, 206, line 118.
28 On this passage, see Thomas D. Hill, 'The Hypocritical Bee in the Old English "Homiletic Fragment I," Lines 18–30,' *NQ* n.s. 15 (1968): 123.
29 The ubiquity of these proverbs is further evidenced by the number of proverb collections in which they appear; see, for example: *The Wordsworth Dictionary of Proverbs*, ed. Apperson, 60; *The Oxford Dictionary of English Proverbs*, ed. Wilson, 28; *A Dictionary of the Proverbs in England*, ed. Tilley, B59; *Early English Proverbs: Chiefly of the Thirteenth and Fourteenth Centuries*, ed. Walter W. Skeat (Oxford: Clarendon, 1910), 83; Bartlett Jere Whiting, *Proverbs in the Earlier English Drama with Illustrations from Contemporary French Plays*, Harvard Studies in Comparative Literature 14 (Cambridge, MA: Harvard University Press, 1938), 193.
30 C.L. Wrenn, 'On the Continuity of English Poetry,' in Wrenn, *Word and Symbol: Studies in English Language* (London: Longmans, 1967), 78–94 at 88.
31 R.W. Chambers, *On the Continuity of English Prose from Alfred to More and His School*, EETS o.s. 191A (1932; repr. London: Oxford University Press, 1957), xciii.
32 Paul Brand, 'The Languages of the Law in Later Medieval England,' in *Multilingualism in Later Medieval Britain*, ed. D.A. Trotter (Cambridge: D.S. Brewer, 2000), 63–76 at 67.
33 Wenzel, *Macaronic Sermons: Bilingualism and Preaching in Late-Medieval England*, Recentiores: Later Latin Texts & Contexts (Ann Arbor: University of Michigan Press, 1994), 91–6; G.R. Owst, *Literature and Pulpit in Medieval England* (Cambridge: Cambridge University Press, 1933), 41–6.
34 G.R. Owst, *Preaching in Medieval England: An Introduction to Sermon Manuscripts of the Period c.1350–1450* (Cambridge: Cambridge University Press, 1926), 231.
35 Owst, *Preaching in Medieval England*, 231, n. 1.

PART V
Early Medieval Latin

Bede's Style: A Neglected Historiographical Model for the Style of the *Historia Ecclesiastica*?

DANUTA SHANZER

While the Latin of Avitus, Jerome, and Gregory of Tours has been closely analysed,[1] that of Bede's *Historia ecclesiastica* has suffered neglect. But Jones's concordance to Bede's *HE* and now the *Patrologia Latina* database can expedite stylistic analysis, formerly work for the chalcentéric.[2] Change is coming. Richard Sharpe has recently enodated the knotty style of Bede's *exegetica*.[3] I propose to reconsider the *HE*, starting from a seemingly simple question: Why is it written the way it is? I will explore opinions about, and descriptions of, the style and manner of the *HE*, and will conclude with a new suggestion about the origins of Bede's Latin prose style.

Style must be analysed in many ways. Lexical study encompasses individual words, types of words, semantics, and accidence. Syntax must be closely observed. David Druhan made useful generalizations about the syntax of the *HE*, working from Jones's concordance, and compared his usage to classical and Late Latin norms.[4] But the procedure was strictly enumerative, and he did not cover problems or anomalies in context, nor seriously consider lexicography or stylistics. Rhetoric too: What are the author's tropes and tricks? How long and complex are his sentences? Quantification plays a role. Bede scholars such as Grocock, Sharpe (he calls it the 'measurable case'), Kendall,[5] and Howlett, *count:* sentences, clauses, hyperbata, words. Then come all the unclassifiable idiosyncrasies of authors (their 'little ways') that the literary historian must note – for example, Bede's tic of beginning sentences with apparently contentless *siquidems* (= 'for' if anything at all),[6] or his occasional use of *nescio quo ordine* for *nescio quo modo*.[7] And finally the elusive trio: manner, tone, and voice.

Standard qualitative terms recur in the scholarship on Bede's style:

'straightforward,' 'simple,'[8] 'clear,'[9] 'limpid,'[10] 'lucid and clear,' 'klar und schlicht.'[11] In other words, 'Readable without a dictionary or grammar.' Some judgments carry implications about Bede's models or sources: the language and style of the *HE* bear a 'proud biblical stamp,'[12] Bede's language and syntax and style are 'classical,' or (more sophisticatedly) Bede's syntax comes from schoolmasterly study of handbooks.[13] Also identifications are made with Latin styles, such as Alcuin's: 'sermo simplex, stylo ad purum purgato.'[14] The modern scholar characterizes Bede's style as 'early medieval *sermo humilis*.'[15] Then there are assessments by negation: 'void of all pompousness and bombast,'[16] 'no affectation of a false classicality,' and 'no touch of the puerile pomposity of his contemporary Aldhelm.'[17] Not Hisperic. Not hermeneutic.

It is hard to resist some pot-shots: while Bede was strongly influenced by the Bible and cites it,[18] he is not writing in a biblical style or with a biblical voice. We find nothing in the *HE* like Gregory of Tours' famous Old Testamentary judgment of Clovis in *Histories* 2.40: 'Prosternebat enim cotidiae Deus hostes eius sub manu ipsius et augebat regnum eius, eo quod ambularet recto corde coram eo et facerit quae placita erant in oculis eius' [Day in day out God submitted the enemies of Clovis to his dominion and increased his power, for he walked before Him with an upright heart and did what was pleasing in His sight].[19] Lacking likewise are biblicisms, such as the instrumental use of *in*.[20] As for the *sermo humilis* – do Bede's periods or otherwise elaborate sentences befit a writer of the humble style?

Literary historians examine authors in context: location, date, and the company (both books and people) they keep. It is from these comparisons that one judges 'fit,' 'usualness,' and 'unusualness.' Scholars of Later Roman Gaul stop their time-machines at Sulpicius Severus, Sidonius, Avitus, then at Gregory of Tours, and finally at Fredegar. Increasing barbarity is comfortingly confirmed: the Bishop of Tours falls into accusative absolutes, and the abominations in Fredegar are hair-raising: *ducebus* is an acceptable nominative plural.[21] In the British Isles, however, what are the mile-stones? Patrick? His highly personal style combines the biblical, the Vulgar Latin and (occasionally) a Celtic substrate. Gildas is a better choice, though some deny him the status of historiographer.[22] He is an orator and preacher, his voice that of a latter-day Jeremiah.[23] But he should not be discounted as a model, for Bede regarded him as a *historicus*,[24] could have imitated his style, and incorporated material from the *De Excidio* into *HE* 1.[25] But Bede did not adopt Gildas's most distinctive features: intrusive biblical language that is *not* flagged as deliberate allusion or quotation,[26] and alliteration, deliberately recondite, even Hisperic, vocabulary (e.g., *Tithica valles* for 'sea,' *Titan* for 'sun').[27] Nor did he adopt Gildas's metaphors, long words, non-functional diminutives, non-emphatic hyperbaton,[28] etc. At the end of the seventh and in the earlier eighth century comes Aldhelm, whose style has been splendidly described by Michael Winterbottom.[29] And here again is a road *knowingly* not taken, for Bede described Aldhelm as 'sermone nitidus.'[30]

Scholarship on Bede's style has been confused by his setting. These might constitute the historical choices available to him: a Gildasian or Aldhelmic style (rejected), a style like that of the anonymous *Vita Gregorii* (described as 'bad Latin'),[31] or of Stephen of Ripon.[32] Continental developments were out of the question, given Bede's linguistic substrate. To us the style of a Gildas or of an Aldhelm looks very flamboyant or distinctive (viz. 'hard to read'), so it appears deviant or marked vis à vis some 'normal' default or unmarked style. On the other hand, if we put these early medieval authors in their later-Roman and sub-Roman context, their writing seems a natural development of Later Roman *Prunkstil* – with the occasional dash of Irish spice.[33] Paradoxically, it is Bede's style, unusual for its place and time, that requires explanation.

While avoiding counting, I will measure. I will examine long sentences, a feature Bede shares with some of his predecessors. Since exact comparison, one author's use of another, is always the best methodology,[34] we will begin with Gildas. Both can and do write long sentences, but length is much more of a tic in Gildas's case than in Bede's. There is also the question of periodicity. Gildas tries and usually fails. *De Excidio* 18.1 provides an example:

> Igitur Romani, patriae denuntiantes nequaquam se tam laboriosis expeditionibus posse frequentius vexari, et ob imbelles erraticosque latrunculos, Romana stigmata, tantum talemque exercitum, terra ac mari fatigari, sed ut potius sola consuescendo armis ac viriliter dimicando terram, substantiolam, coniuges, liberos et, quod his maius est, libertatem vitamque totis viribus vindicaret, et gentibus nequaquam sibi fortioribus, nisi segnitia et torpore dissolveretur, inermes vinclis vinciendas nullo modo, sed instructas peltis, ensibus, hastis et ad caedem promptas protenderet manus, suadentes, quia et hoc putabant aliquid derelinquendo populo commodi accrescere, murum non ut alterum, sumptu publico privatoque adiunctis secum miserabilibus indigenis, solito structurae more, tramite a

mari usque ad mare inter urbes, quae ibidem forte ob metum hostium collocatae fuerant, directo librant; fortia formidoloso populo monita tradunt, exemplaria instituendorum armorum relinquunt, in litore quoque Oceani ad meridianam plagam, quo naves eorum habebantur, quia et inde barbaricae ferae bestiae timebantur, turres per intervalla ad prospectum maris collocant, et valedicunt tanquam ultra non reversuri.

[The Romans therefore informed our country that they could not go on being bothered with such troublesome expeditions; the Roman standards, that great and splendid army, could not be worn out by land and sea for the sake of wandering thieves who had no taste for war. (1) Rather the British should stand alone, get used to arms, fight bravely, and defend with all their powers their land, property, wives, children, and, more important, their life and liberty. (2) Their enemies were no stronger than they, unless Britain chose to relax in laziness and torpor; they should not hold out to them for the chaining hands that held no arms, but hands equipped with shields, swords, and lances, ready for the kill. (3) This was the Romans' advice; and, in the belief that this would be a further boon to the people whom they proposed to abandon, they built a wall quite different from the first. (4) This one ran straight from the sea, linking towns that happened to have been sited there out of fear of the enemy. (5) They employed the normal method of construction, drew on private and public funds, and made the wretched inhabitants help them in the work. (6) They gave the frightened people stirring advice, and left them manuals on weapon training. (7) They also placed towers overlooking the sea at intervals on the south coast, where they kept their ships, for they were afraid of the wild barbarian beasts attacking on that front too. (8) Then they said goodbye, meaning never to return. (9)]

This is one close-to-periodic sentence in Latin. Its subject is 'Romani,' the main verb 'librant'; the two are 116 words apart! Winterbottom's translation employs nine separate and substantial English sentences.[35] Gildas's whole effort is misguided, an example of how if one wanted to get there one would not have started from here.[36] Consider what Bede did with this monstrosity.[37] Gildas had got it wrong: 'denuntiavere' had to be the main verb, and it was distracting to subordinate the complicated substance of the 'oratio obliqua' to a participle.

Tum Romani denuntiavere Brettonibus, non se ultra ob eorum defensionem tam laboriosis expeditionibus posse fatigari; ipsos potius monent arma corripere et certandi cum hostibus studium subire, qui non aliam ob causam quam si ipsi inertia solverentur eis possent esse fortiores. Quin etiam, quia et hoc sociis quos derelinquere cogebantur aliquid commodi adlaturum putabant, murum a mari ad mare recto tramite inter urbes quae ibidem ob metum hostium factae fuerant, ubi et Severus quondam vallum fecerat, firmo de lapide conlocarunt: quem videlicet murum hactenus famosum atque conspicuum, sumtu publico privatoque, adjuncta secum Brittanorum manu construebant, VIII pedes latum, et XII altum, recta ab Oriente in Occasum linea, ut usque hodie intuentibus clarum est; quo mox condito dant fortia segni populo monita, praebent instituendorum exemplaria armorum. Sed et in litore Oceani ad meridiem, quo naves eorum habebantur, quia et inde barbarorum inruptio timebatur, turres per intervalla ad prospectum maris conlocant, et valedicunt sociis tanquam ultra non reversuri. (*HE* 1.12)

[Then the Romans informed the Britons that they could no longer be burdened with such troublesome expeditions for their defence; they advised them to take up arms themselves and make an effort to oppose their foes, who would prove too powerful for them only if they themselves were weakened by sloth. Moreover, thinking that it might be some help to the allies whom they were compelled to abandon, they built a strong wall of stone from sea to sea in a straight line between the fortresses which had been built there for fear of the enemy, on the site which Severus had once made his rampart. So, at public and private expense and with the help of the Britons, they made a famous wall which is still to be seen. It is eight feet wide and twelve feet high, running in a straight line from east to west, as is plain for all to see even to this day. When it was complete they gave some heartening advice to this sluggish people and showed them how to make themselves weapons. In addition they built look-out towers at intervals along the shores of the ocean to the south, where their ships plied and where there was fear of barbarian attacks. And so they took leave of their allies never to return.]

There were texts such as the *Vita Germani* that Bede was prepared to excerpt and cite unadapted, but Gildas's *De Excidio* was not among them.[38]

Let's examine perhaps the most famous sentence in Bede, the sparrow simile:

Cuius suasioni verbisque prudentibus alius optimatum regis tribuens

334 Danuta Shanzer

assensum, continuo subdidit: 'Talis, inquiens, mihi videtur, rex, vita hominum praesens in terris, ad comparationem eius quod nobis incertum est temporis, quale cum te residente ad coenam cum ducibus ac ministris tuis tempore brumali, accenso quidem foco in medio et calido effecto caenaculo, furentibus autem foris per omnia turbinibus hiemalium pluviarum vel nivium, adveniens unus passerum domum citissime pervolaverit; qui cum per unum ostium ingrediens, mox per aliud exierit. Ipso quidem tempore quo intus est, hiemis tempestate non tangitur, sed tamen parvissimo spatio serenitatis ad momentum excurso, mox de hieme in hiemem regrediens, tuis oculis elabitur. Ita haec vita hominum ad modicum apparet; quid autem sequatur, quidve praecesserit, prorsus ignoramus.' (*HE* 2.13)

[Another of the king's chief men agreed with this advice and with these wise words and then added, 'This is how the present life of man on earth, king, appears to me in comparison with that time which is unknown to us. You are sitting feasting with your ealdormen and thegns in winter time; the fire is burning on the hearth in the middle of the hall and all inside is warm, while outside the wintry storms of rain and snow are raging; and a sparrow flies swiftly through the hall. It enters in at one door and quickly flies out through the other. For the few moments it is inside, the storm and wintry tempest cannot touch it, but after the briefest moment of calm, it flits from your sight, out of the wintry storm and into it again. So this life of man appears but for a moment; what follows or indeed what went before, we know not at all.']

The basic (slightly asymmetrical) structure is 'Talis videtur vita ... quale cum ... unus passerum pervolaverit.' In the middle is a long but comprehensible series of differentiated ablatives used to paint the scene: 'te residente ad caenam ... furentibus autem foris per omnia turbinibus hiemalium pluviarum vel nivium.' In order we have ablative absolute, prepositional phrase, temporal ablative, ablative absolute, ablative absolute, and ablative absolute. 'Quidem' effectively anticipates the upcoming contrast between warmth and cold stated in 'autem.'[39] The sentence ends with a relative clause that contrasts entrance ('ingrediens') and exit ('exierit'). The next sentence, 'Ipso quidem tempore,' is not a full period,[40] but achieves an elegant and elegiac periodic effect with the verb 'elabitur.' The paragraph highlights the sad but theologically significant word 'ignoramus,' through preposition of the double indirect question: 'quid ... quidve.' A ring-composition rounds out the speech: 'Talis *vita hominum* praesens ... videtur' and 'Ita haec *vita hominum* apparet.' Bede repeated the significant words *vita hominum* and employed *variatio* on others. There is an oddity: a stray *cum* in 'qui cum per unum ostium egrediens.' A false start? A scribal error? And there is the question of 'unus passerum,' which here looks suspiciously like an indefinite article 'a sparrow.'[41] But it betrays the *actual* literary source of the simile: the Gospel of Matthew 10:26–31.[42]

> (26) ne ergo timueritis eos: nihil enim opertum quod non revelabitur et occultum quod non scietur. (27) quod dico vobis in tenebris, dicite in lumine et quod in aure auditis, praedicate super tecta. (28) et nolite timere eos qui occidunt corpus; animam autem non possunt occidere; sed potius eum timete qui potest et animam et corpus perdere in gehennam. (29) *nonne duo passeres asse veneunt et unus ex illis non cadet super terram sine Patre vestro?* (30) vestri autem et capilli capitis omnes numerati sunt. (31) nolite ergo timere *multis passeribus* meliores estis vos. (Matt. 10:26–31, emphasis added)

[Therefore do not be afraid of them. For there is nothing concealed that will not be disclosed, and nothing hidden that will not be made known. What I tell you in darknesss, speak it in the light; and what you hear whispered, preach it on the housetops. And do not be afraid of those who kill the body but cannot kill the soul. But rather be afraid of him who is able to destroy both soul and body in hell. *Are not two sparrows sold for a farthing? And yet not one of them will fall to the ground without your Father's leave.* But as for you, the very hairs of your head are all numbered. Therefore do not be afraid; you are of more value *than many sparrows*.]

The nexus of significant shared ideas is clear: the known/the hidden, light/darkness, life/death, but most significant is the imitation in a contrasting context. Jesus emphasized revelation and knowledge and the survival of the soul after the death of the body, making an *a minori* argument that even the cheapest of birds, the sparrow, does not fall to earth without God's knowledge, and that men are far more important than sparrows. The pessimistic pagan nobleman is depicted as voicing an implicitly self-refuting analogy: God controls not just the fall, but presumably also the *flight* of the sparrow![43] And *unus* (a non-functional, but significant vestigial word) betrays the source.[44] It is worth looking at Bede closely for stylistic oddities.

This is the most artistic Bede. Control is the keyword.[45] It is far from easy to follow. Clearly it was meant to be read, not heard, whatever its dramatic context.[46] But it is not a representative Bedan long sentence. Against all the customary tasteful Bedan beige other comparable moments stand out, and their significance should be explored. Here are a few examples. A striking passage in the hagiography of Chad (*HE* 4.3) shows *variatio*, alliteration,[47] and Isidoran play with synonyms: 'repente *flatus venti maior* adsurgeret ... Si autem *violenter aura* insisteret ... At si *procella fortior* aut *nimbus* perurgeret, vel etiam corusci ac tonitrua terras et aera terrerent' [(If) ... suddenly a high wind arose ... If the wind increased in violence ... But if there were a violent storm of wind and rain or if lightning and thunder brought terror to earth and sky]. Bede on occasion slips into pretentious words that reflect his sources: the biblical and Grecizing *cauma* in *HE* 3.19 (not in attested versions of the *Vita Fursei* and unlikely to come from oral tradition)[48] and the pretentious and poetic *rheuma* ('tide' rather than 'catarrh') in *HE* 3.3[49] and 5.5.[50] Triplets in anaphora mark an exceptional moment of heightened rhetoric at *HE* 3.2, the verbal consecration of Hefenfelth:[51]

> Vocatur locus ille lingua Anglorum Hefenfelth, quod dici potest latine *caelestis* campus, quod certo utique praesagio futurorum antiquitus nomen accepit: significans nimirum quod ibidem *caeleste* erigendum trophaeum, *caelestis* inchoanda victoria, *caelestia* usque hodie forent miracula celebranda.

> [This place is called in English Heavenfield, and in Latin *Caelestis campus*, a name which it certainly received in days of old as an omen of future happenings; it signified that a heavenly sign was to be erected there, a heavenly victory won, and that heavenly miracles were to take place there continuing to this day.]

Soon followed by:

> Nec immerito, quia nullum, ut comperimus, fidei Christianae signum, nulla ecclesia, nullum altare in tota Berniciorum gente erectum est, priusquam hoc sacrae crucis vexillum novus militiae ductor, dictante fidei devotione, contra hostem immanissimum pugnaturus statueret.

> [And rightly so, for, as far as we know, no symbol of the Christian faith, no church, and no altar had been erected in the whole of Bernicia before that new leader of the host, inspired by his devotion to the faith, set up

the standard of the holy cross when he was about to fight his most savage enemy.]

Or the triple highway-safety of Edwin's reign in *HE* 2.16:

Tanta autem eo tempore pax in Brittania, quaquaversum imperium regis Aeduini pervenerat, fuisse perhibetur, ut, sicut usque hodie in proverbio dicitur, etiam si mulier una cum recens nato parvulo vellet totam perambulare insulam a mari ad mare, nullo se laedente valeret. Tantum rex idem utilitati suae gentis consuluit, ut plerisque in locis ubi fontes lucidos juxta puplicos viarum transitus conspexit, ibi ob refrigerium viantium, erectis stipitibus aereos caucos suspendi iuberet, neque hos quisquam, nisi ad usum necessarium, contingere prae magnitudine vel timoris eius auderet, vel amoris vellet. Tantum vero in regno excellentiae habuit, ut non solum in pugna ante illum vexilla gestarentur, sed et tempore pacis equitantem inter civitates sive villas aut provincias suas cum ministris, semper antecedere signifer consuesset ...

[It is related that there was so great a peace in Britain, wherever the dominion of King Edwin reached, that, as the proverb still runs, a woman with a new-born child could walk throughout the island from sea to sea and take no harm. The king cared so much for the good of the people that, in various places where he had noticed clear springs near the highway, he caused stakes to be set up and bronze drinking cups to be hung on them for the refreshment of travellers. No one dared to lay hands on them except for their proper purpose because they feared the king greatly nor did they wish to, because they loved him dearly. So great was his majesty in his realm that not only were banners carried before him in battle, but even in times of peace, as he rode about among his cities, estates, and kingdoms with his thegns, he always used to be preceded by a standard bearer ...]

Bede could orate, and such passages need literary commentary.

We shall now to turn to some sentences that are unremarkable in content, but interesting in a different way. They exemplify our problem: how to hunt the distinctive that is camouflaged as non-distinctive because it looks like good Classical Latin, but is, so to speak, far better than it ought to be. I am interested in Bede's attempts at elegant, controlled, comprehensible full or close-to-full periodicity. Here is a biographical example (with a slight flaw):

Cum ergo praedicante verbum Dei Paulino rex credere differret, et per aliquod tempus, ut diximus, horis competentibus solitarius sederet, quid agendum sibi esset, quae religio sequenda, sedulus secum ipse scrutari consuesset, ingrediens ad eum quadam die vir Dei, imposuit dexteram capiti eius, et an hoc signum agnosceret, requisivit. (*HE* 2.12)

[King Edwin hesitated to accept the word of God which Paulinus preached but, as we have said, used to sit alone for hours at a time, earnestly debating within himself what he ought to do and what religion he should follow. One day Paulinus came to him and, placing his right hand on the king's head, asked him if he recognized this sign.]

Here an historical one:

Turbatis itaque rebus Nordanhymbrorum huius articulo cladis, cum nil alicubi praesidii nisi in fuga esse videretur, Paulinus adsumpta secum regina Aedilberge quam pridem adduxerat, rediit Cantiam navigio, atque ab Honorio archiepiscopo et rege Eadbaldo multum honorifice susceptus est. (*HE* 2.20)

[As the affairs of Northumbria had been thrown into confusion at the time of this disaster and as there seemed no safety except in flight, Paulinus took with him Queen Æthelburh, whom he had previously brought thither, and returned by boat to Kent, where he was most honourably received by Archbishop Honorius and King Eadbald.]

My question is a literary historian's-cum-historiographer's one. Where did Bede learn this? Surely not from Gildas, Aldhelm, from any later Roman Gallic writer, or from Jerome or Augustine. And it is doubtful whether one can develop that sort of feel for natural (as opposed to strained and awkward) periodic writing from grammars.[52] No grammar taught one how to generate the *circuitus verborum*.[53] Bede must have had a model.[54] And he practised. In various places in the *HE* Bede works consciously on manoeuvering his verbs – here to an excessive extent – into final position.[55] Take *HE praef.*:

Lectoremque suppliciter *obsecro*, ut si qua in his quae *scripsimus* aliter quam se veritas *habet posita reppererit*,[56] non hoc nobis *imputet* qui, quod vera lex historiae *est*, simpliciter ea quae fama vulgante *collegimus* ad instructionem posteritatis literis mandare *studuimus*.

[So I humbly beg the reader, if he finds anything other than the truth set down in what I have written, not to impute it to me. For, in accordance with the principles of true history, I have simply sought to commit to writing what I have collected from common report, for the instruction of posterity.]

So who was Bede's model? There are two likely suspects. First Orosius, who could have indirectly transmitted Livian (and other sorts of) historical periods.[57] Orosius often, indeed too often, wrote in short narrative periods.[58] Take the moral pointed in the death of Nero:

Cumque incredibilia perturbandae, immo subruendae reipublicae mala moliretur, hostis a senatu pronuntiatus, et ignominiosissime fugiens, ad quartum ab Urbe lapidem sese ipse interfecit, atque in eo omnis Caesarum familia consumpta est. (Orosius 7.7.13)

[Since he was planning unbelievable atrocities to disturb, or rather undermine, the state completely, after he had been pronounced a public enemy by the state and was fleeing most ignominiously, he killed himself at the fourth milestone outside Rome and in his person the entire line of the Caesars came to an end.]

Or:

Titus vero magna ac diuturna obsidione Iudaeos premens, machinis cunctisque bellicis molibus non sine multo suorum sanguine tandem muros civitatis irrupit. (Orosius 7.9.4)

[But Titus, pressing the Jews with a mighty and long-lasting siege, using all his siege-engines and all the masses of troops used in war, finally broke through the walls of the city, though not without considerable losses on his own side.]

But he is unlikely to be the primary model for the smooth and slower Bede. It is partly a question of tone. Orosius's is argumentative and polemic.[59] But it is also one of line or what one might call 'wind' or 'haleine.' Orosius is *bumpier* than Bede, no doubt because he has to compress more.[60] His periods often become mechanical.[61] He aims for greater brevity, generally avoids doublets in narrative passages, features less *variatio* in construction, and strings more short sentences in sequence.[62] There is more frequent use of asyndeton.[63] Skill too played a role, as in the following example:

> Igitur Galli Senones, duce Brenno, exercitu copioso et robusto nimis cum urbem Clusini, quae nunc Tuscia dicitur, obsiderent, legatos Romanorum, qui tunc componendae inter eos pacis gratia venerant, in acie adversum se *videre* pugnantes:[64] qua indignatione permoti, Clusini oppidi obsidione dimissa, totis viribus Romam contendunt.[65] (Orosius 2.19.5)[66]

> [Therefore the Senonian Gauls, when they were besieging the city of Clusium, which is now called Tuscia, under Brennus with a large and very powerful army saw the ambassadors of the Romans who had come at that time to arrange a peace between them fighting in the battle-line against them; moved by this indignation, after having raised the siege of Clusium, with all their forces, they hastened to Rome.]

The source (though not the model) is Livy 5.36. Orosius ran into trouble working from a difficult classical stylist. He digresses in *nunc* and has to jerk the reader back with *tunc*. The introductory relative is awkward, for no *indignatio* has been mentioned. Above all he bungled his choice of main verb for this would-be period: the indignation upon all the attendant circumstances and departure in a huff should have concluded an effective period, along the lines of 'The Senonian Gauls, who had besieged Clusium ... when they saw the Roman ambassadors fighting, became highly indignant and hastened to Rome.'[67] Bede at his worst does better.

Now for the second suspect. Ennius wrote a famous line: 'quod est ante pedes nemo spectat, caeli scrutantur plagas' [No one sees what is before his feet: they are gazing at the heavenly regions].[68] This may have happened with Bede. Scholars in focusing on his role as the Eusebius of the Anglo-Saxons have failed to note the *vehicle* of Eusebius's *Historia Ecclesiastica*, namely Rufinus of Aquileia, although acquaintance with Rufinus's matter is acknowledged,[69] or similarities to Eusebius detected.[70] Suprisingly, there is only one explicit reference to Eusebius in the *HE*, though many elsewhere.[71]

Rufinus, a man of 'elegans ingenium,'[72] wrote lucid, impeccable Late Latin even when translating and favoured long and also periodic sentences. For an example, long, to be sure, but simple in structure and quite under control, see his proem to his translation of Eusebius's *Historia Ecclesiastica*:

Successiones sanctorum apostolorum et tempora quae a salvatore nostro ad nos usque decursa sunt, *quaeque et qualia* in his erga ecclesiae statum gesta sint, *qui* etiam insignes viri in locis maxime celeberrimis ecclesiis praefuerunt vel *qui* singulis quibusque temporibus seu scribendo seu docendo verbum dei nobiliter adstruxere, *quique* etiam vel *quanti vel quando* nova contra religionem dogmata proferentes ad profundum erroris studio contentionis elapsi falsae scientiae auctores se praeceptoresque professi sunt, passim velut lupi graves gregem Christi lacerantes, *nec non et ea mala* quae Iudaeorum gentem pro insidiis quas adversum salvatorem moliti sunt, vastaverunt, *quibus* etiam *modis et quotiens quibusve* temporibus doctrina Christi et sermo divinus a gentilibus impugnatus est, *quanti*que his tempestatibus usque ad suppliciorum patientiam et profusionem sanguinis pro veritate verbi dei certarunt, *sed et martyria* nostris suscepta temporibus atque in his domini et salvatoris nostri erga singulos quosque *unicum clementissimumque subsidium scribere mihi volenti* non aliunde *sumendum* videtur *exordium* quam ab ipsa domini et salvatoris nostri Iesu Christi praesentia corporali.

[For one like myself who wishes to write of the successors of the sacred apostles, and the times that have passed from our Lord's down to our own time, what and what sort of things have happened to the status of the church, what outstanding men were in charge of churches in the most famous places, and who at any time nobly increased the word of the Lord either by writing or teaching, and who also or how many and at what time, by producing new dogmas that were contrary to true religion, falling into the depth of error through their zeal for controversy, professed themselves authors and teachers of false knowledge, everywhere, like dangerous wolves tearing apart the flock of Christ, not to mention those evils that have beset the Jewish people in return for the traps that they set for the Saviour, in what ways, and how often, and at what times the teaching of Christ and the divine Word was attacked by heathens, and how many people during these times fought and even suffered execution and shed their blood for the truth of the Word of the Lord, not to mention the martyrdoms that occurred in our times and the special and kind help accorded each and everyone of them by our Lord; there is no other place to begin other than from the time when our Lord and Saviour, Jesus Christ, was present in the flesh.]

'A start must be made by me who wish to write of ...' plus a long series of accusatives combined with indirect questions. But more normal are much shorter items such as this one on the apostolic age:

> Sermo autem veritatis et lucis, qui per Petrum praedicabatur, universorum mentes placido inlustravit auditu, ita ut cottidie audientibus eum nulla umquam satietas fieret. (*Historia* 2.15.1)

> [The word of truth and light that was being preached by Peter enlightened the minds of all; so calm was it to hear that even those who heard it daily never had enough of it.]

Or this almost full period with medial spin-doctoring parenthesis:

> Etenim cum religiosissimus imperator Constantinus, Constanti adaeque moderatissimi et egregii principis filius, adversum Maxentium urbis Romae tyrannum bellum pararet atque exercitum duceret (erat quidem iam tunc Christianae religionis fautor verique dei venerator, nondum tamen, ut est solemne nostris initiari, signum dominicae passionis acceperat), cum igitur anxius et multa secum de inminentis belli necessitate pervolvens iter ageret atque ad caelum saepius oculos elevaret et inde sibi divinum precaretur auxilium, videt per soporem ad orientis partem in caelo signum crucis igneo fulgore rutilare. (*Historia* 8.8.15)

> [For when the most pious emperor Constantine, son of that equally moderate and outstanding prince Constantius, was preparing war against Maxentius, the usurper in the city of Rome, and was leading his army (he was indeed even then favourable to the Christian religion and a worshiper of the true God, but had not yet, however, as is the custom for our people to be initiated, received the sign of the Lord's passion), when, therefore, he was marching, worried, turning over many thoughts in his mind about the necessity of the imminent war, and was frequently raising his eyes to heaven and praying for divine help for himself thence, he saw in his sleep, in the eastern part of the sky that the sign of the cross was shining with a fiery red glow.]

Here is an elegant, enthusiastic conversion sentence that mutatis mutandis Bede could have written:

> Sed et ad Romanos et ad Graecos ad Scythas et barbaros et ad ipsa paene in ultimis orbis partibus reconditas nationes *in tantum* suavis odor de ecclesiae gestis et divinum quiddam respirans sancta conversationis aura

pervenit, *in tantum* ad aures omnium ac mentes felix Christianorum fama pervecta est, ut omne hominum genus legibus et superstitionibus patriis derelictis ad fidem se converteret Christi omnisque barbaries genuina fertilitate deposita ad Iesum concurreret ab eo quia mitis et et humilis corde. (*Historia* 4.7.14)

[But to the Romans and the Greeks and the Scythians and the barbarians and to those tribes that are hidden almost at the very ends of the earth, to such an extent has the sweet scent gone out from the deeds of the church and the sacred breeze of the holy lifestyle that is redolent of something divine, to such an extent has the joyful reputation of Christians been carried to the ears and minds of all, that, all types of human beings, abandoning their ancestral laws and superstitions, have converted themselves to the faith of Christ, and every barbarian, laying aside his native savagery, has rushed to join Jesus, because he is meek and humble of heart.]

Eusebius (and hence Rufinus) had far more violent subject matter than Bede,[73] including sensational description of martyrdoms, but one cannot fault the balanced elegance of an example such as this:

Deterrere etenim volentes inspectantem populum, nunc flagris usque ad interiora viscerum martyres laniabant, ita ut abdita corporis et quae natura in arcanis locaverat nudarentur, nunc autem marinas cochleas, quae conchylia vocant, et acuta quaeque fragmenta in dorsum supinatis martyribus substernebant: in quibus omne tormenti genus et poenae speciem consumentes ad ultimum devorandos eos bestiis exponebant. (*Historia* 4.15.4)

[Wishing to inspire terror in the onlookers, they at one time tore open the martyrs with whips all the way down to their inner organs, so that the secret parts of the body and the parts that nature had located in hidden places were exposed; at another they spread sea-snails, which they called conch-shells, and each and every sort of sharp fragment beneath the martyrs, who had been laid on their backs; exhausting every type of torture and species of punishment, in the end they exposed them to beasts to be devoured.]

Bede avoided such material in the *HE* and (as Tom Hill taught us) spent more time on ascetic good deaths than on violent deaths or *interitus*.[74] He rarely registers disapproval in critical vocabulary.[75] There are none of Rufinus's rhetorical questions and interjections.[76] But subject matter should not be permitted to act as a screen.[77] Strong syntactic control of long, complicated, and ample balanced structures was something Bede could have seen in this master.[78]

This is intended as an exploratory study. Bede's style *is* unusual in its own temporal and historical context. It is not, however, an artificial grammar and copybook style. It evolved, I suggest, from reading Orosius, but above all from a deep and careful immersion in the style of Rufinus.[79] The latter has to be thought of not just as a source for plan, structure, or historical mode or idea, but as a stylistic model too. Bede seems classical because he absorbed many features of a (neglected) first-rate later Roman translator's style.[80] It was ample at times, but never recondite or long-winded: inevitably clear, eloquent, and elegant. We need to think about a *Rufinian* Renaissance in Northumbrian Latin Prose.

NOTES

This paper is dedicated to my friend and former colleague Tom Hill, master of the *annotatiuncula*. Hidden in the middle, however, is a *Lesefrucht*. Special thanks go to Jim Adams (for a conversation long ago that got me thinking [which is what conversations are meant to do!]), Michael Lapidge, Richard Sharpe, and David Townsend.

1 Henri Goelzer, *Le Latin de saint Avit, évêque de Vienne (450?–526?)* (Paris: F. Alcan, 1909); Henri Goelzer, *Étude lexicographique et grammaticale de la latinité de saint Jérôme* (Paris: Hachette, 1884); and Max Bonnet, *Le Latin de Grégoire de Tours* (1890; repr. Hildesheim: G. Olms, 1968).
2 Putnam Fennell Jones, *A Concordance to the Historia Ecclesiastica of Bede*, Mediaeval Academy of America Publications 2 (Cambridge, MA: Mediaeval Academy of America, 1929).
3 Richard Sharpe, 'The Varieties of Bede's Prose,' in *Aspects of the Language of Latin Prose*, ed. Tobias Reinhardt, Michael Lapidge, and J.N. Adams, Proceedings of the British Academy 129 (Oxford: Oxford University Press, 2005), 339–55.
4 David Ross Druhan, *The Syntax of Bede's Historia Ecclesiastica*, Studies in Medieval and Renaissance Latin Language and Literature 8 (Washington, DC: Catholic University of America Press, 1938).
5 Christopher Grocock, 'Bede and the Golden Age of Latin Prose in

Northumbia,' in *Northumbria's Golden Age*, ed. Jane Hawkes and Susan Mills (Stroud: Sutton, 1999), 371–81; Sharpe, 'The Varieties of Bede's Prose'; Calvin B. Kendall, 'Bede's *Historia ecclesiastica*: The Rhetoric of Faith,' in *Medieval Eloquence: Studies in the Theory and Practice of Medieval Rhetoric*, ed. James J. Murphy (Berkeley and Los Angeles: University of California Press, 1978), 145–72 at 156, counts hyperbata; D.R. Howlett, *British Books in Biblical Style* (Dublin: Four Courts Press, 1997).

6 The practice is not biblical. Druhan, 'The Syntax,' 178–9, notes that it occurs thirty-one times, and cites J.B. Hofmann and Anton Szantyr, *Lateinische Syntax und Stilistik*, Handbuch der Altertumswissenschaft 2. Abteilung, Teil 2, Band 2 (Munich: C. Beck, 1972), 782. I suspect it may be Orosian, but Orosius does not inevitably place *siquidem* = 'for' at the very beginning of a sentence. Michael Lapidge has suggested to me that Bede's *siquidem* (which he compares to similar usages in Aldhelm [of which there are twenty-four]) is an Anglo-Latinism for OE *eallswa*.

7 See *HE* 5.12, pages 307 and 309 (ed. Charles Plummer, *Venerabilis Baedae Historia Ecclesiastica*, 2 vols [Oxford: Clarendon, 1896]), but also thirty times in other works.

8 Bertram Colgrave and R.A.B. Mynors, *Bede's Ecclesiastical History of the English People* (Oxford: Clarendon, 1969), xxxvi.

9 M. Roger, *L'Enseignement des lettres classiques d'Ausone à Alcuin: Introduction à l'histoire des écoles carolingiennes* (Paris: A. Picard, 1905), 309.

10 Plummer, *Venerabilis Baedae Historia Ecclesiastica*, liii.

11 Franz Brunhölzl, *Geschichte der lateinischen Literatur des Mittelalters*, 2 vols to date (Munich: Fink, 1975–), 1:207.

12 Roger Ray, 'Bede, the Exegete, as Historian,' in *Famulus Christi: Essays in Commemoration of the Thirteenth Centenary of the Birth of the Venerable Bede*, ed. Gerald Bonner (London: SPCK, 1976), 125–40 at 134.

13 Druhan, 'The Syntax,' xxii–xxiii.

14 Alcuin, *Ep.* 216 in MGH, Epistolae 4 (Karolini Aevi 2) ed. E. Dümmler (Berlin: Weidmann, 1895), 360, lines 16–19.

15 Ray, 'Bede, the Exegete, as Historian,' 134. See, however, Roger Ray, 'Bede and Cicero,' *ASE* 16 (1986): 1–16 at 9, for a prudent *retractatio*: 'Bede wrote in all three ... style levels.' Ray cites the letter to Plegwine (ed. C. Jones, *CCSL* 123C, 617–26) as high style. However, the phrase 'quod me audires a lascivientibus rusticis inter hereticos per pocula decantari' may be Plegwine's. The tone of the letter is inexplicably described by Ray, *Bede, Rhetoric, and the Creation of Christian Latin Culture*, Jarrow Lecture 1997 (Jarrow: [St Paul's Church], 1997), 1, as 'Latin vituperation that would have made Jerome proud,' despite vocatives such as 'dilectissime, dulcissime, etc.' The

writing is that of a man setting the record straight in a factual manner. *Ep. Pleg.* 14 'tuam simplicitatem ... admoneo' is tame as is *Ep. Pleg.* 15 'ipse satis doleo ... et quantum licet vel amplius irasci soleo quotiens a rusticis interrogor.' *Ep. Pleg.* 16 'humanae divinaeque scientiae paenitus expertem' is huffy and *Ep. Pleg.* 17 'insipientium ... conviciis' refers to others. Ray, 'Bede and Cicero,' 10, re-expresses the same views at greater length.

16 Wilhelm Levison, 'Bede as Historian,' in *Bede: His Life, Times, and Writings: Essays in Commemoration of the Twelfth Centenary of His Death*, ed. A. Hamilton Thompson (1935; repr. New York: Russell & Russell, 1966), 111–51 at 145.
17 Plummer, *Venerabilis Baedae Historia Ecclesiastica*, liii.
18 For biblical patterns in the *HE*, see, for example, Claudio Leonardi, 'Il Venerabile Beda e la cultura del secolo VIII,' in *I problemi dell'Occidente nel secolo VIII. Spoleto 6–12 aprile 1972* (Spoleto: Centro Italiano di studi sull'alto medioevo, 1973), 603–58 at 636–7.
19 Gregory of Tours, *Decem libri historiarum*, ed. B. Krusch and W. Levison, MGH SRM 1/1, page 91, line 6; trans. Lewis Thorpe, *Gregory of Tours: The History of the Franks* (Harmondsworth: Penguin, 1974), 156.
20 The few examples cited at Druhan, 'The Syntax,' 119, are not instrumental uses of *in* of the biblical sort, translating Greek *en*.
21 *Frédégaire: Chronique des temps mérovingiens: Livre IV et continuations*, ed. J.M. Wallace-Hadrill (Turnhout: Brepols, 2001), 47–8.
22 L.W. Barnard, 'Bede and Eusebius as Church Historians,' in *Famulus Christi*, ed. Bonner, 106–24 at 106: 'The Celts had produced no historiography of any significance (Gildas can hardly be classed as an historiographer).'
23 Gildas, *De Excidio* 1.5, ed. Michael Winterbottom, *Gildas: The Ruin of Britain and Other Works* (Chichester: Phillimore, 1978).
24 *HE* 1.22: 'historicus eorum Gildas flebili sermone describit.' Gildas called it an *epistula:* see *De Excidio* 1.1.
25 See, for example, *HE* 1.12, 1.14, 1.22.
26 For example, he equates people with apocalyptic animals. See Gildas, *De excidio* 28, 'inmundae leaenae ... catulus Constantinus'; 30, 31, 'pardo similis'; 32, 'urse'; 33, 'draco.'
27 Gildas, *De Excidio* 19.1, 'trans Tithicam vallem evecti, quasi in alto Titane incalescenteque caumate.'
28 See Kendall, 'Bede's *Historia ecclesiastica*,' 153–8, for Bede on hyperbaton. Kendall mentions separation used for relief and emphasis, but does not distinguish artful Late Latin non-emphatic hyperbaton, e.g., hyperbaton of the interlaced type: abab. Furthermore some hyperbata of the 'ad aeternam regni caelestis sedem' may appear non-emphatic, but may be intended to

prevent ambiguity in construction of the sandwiched genitive. Hyperbaton can be used to pack and separate, and phrases have to be examined in their contexts. To take an example, *HE* 1.7 (page 20), 'undam suis cessisse ac viam dedisse vestigiis' seems ornamental and possibly euphonic rather than functional. Likewise we find examples where the emphasis gained by separating noun and modifier is not functional, such as *HE* 4.22, 'in huius monasterio abbatissae'; 'carmina religioni et pietati apta' creates a nice chiasm; 'caelestem ... concessam esse gratiam'; 'religiosam eius linguam.'

29 Michael Winterbottom, 'Aldhelm's Prose Style and Its Origins,' *ASE* 6 (1977), 39–76.
30 *HE* 5.18.
31 Bertram Colgrave, *The Earliest Life of Gregory the Great by an Anonymous Monk of Whitby* (1968; repr. Cambridge: Cambridge University Press, 1985), 55.
32 Bertram Colgrave, *The Life of Bishop Wilfrid by Eddius Stephanus* (1927; repr. Cambridge: Cambridge University Press, 1985), xiii, rates it higher than the anonymous *Vita Gregorii*.
33 Winterbottom, 'Aldhelm's Prose Style.'
34 Levison, 'Bede as Historian,' 125, pointed out how Bede began by rewriting hagiographical texts such as the Passion of Anastasius and episodes from the life of Felix of Nola. In the latter case Bede, like his predecessor Gregory of Tours (*Gloria Martyrum* 103, ed. B. Krusch, MGH, SRM 1/2), paraphrased Paulinus of Nola's verse as prose. See his *Vita Felicis* (PL 94:789–98). For Gregory's paraphrastic activities as the 'virtual' *opus geminatum*, eventually to be realized by Bede, see Danuta Shanzer, 'Gregory of Tours and Poetry: Prose into Verse and Verse into Prose,' in *Aspects of the Language of Latin Prose*, ed. Reinhardt, Lapidge, and Adams, 303–19.
35 Ed. Winterbottom, *Gildas*, 94 (trans. at 22).
36 R.G. Mayer, 'The Impracticability of Latin "Kunstprosa,"' in *Aspects of the Language of Latin Prose*, ed. Reinhardt, Lapidge, and Adams, 195–210, uses the helpful expression 'over-charged.' Note however that there are equally or indeed less unsuccessful attempted periods at *De Excidio* 4.2–4 and 17.1–3.
37 *HE* 1.12, 'Tum Romani denuntiavere ... ultra non reversuri.' All translations of *HE* are from Colgrave and Mynors, *Bede's Ecclesiastical History*.
38 See *HE* 1.17.
39 'Quidem' again is used at 'ipso quidem tempore' below.
40 I.e., a structure that achieves complete suspension through postponement of the main verb till the end.
41 See Druhan, 'The Syntax,' 76 and 202. Contrast its clear use as a numeral in

Jerome, *Vita Pauli* 16, 'Domine, sine cuius nutu nec folium arboris defluit, nec unus passerum ad terram cadit' (*PL* 23:27).

42 M.F. Schuster, 'Bede and the Sparrow Simile,' *American Benedictine Review* 8 (1957): 46–50, does not cite or argue the connection, but presumably intends it, by, 'Christ, who also spoke about sparrows.'

43 Bede commented on the parallel passage in Luke 12:6–7 (ed. D. Hurst, CCSL 120:247; *PL* 92:488). Donald K. Fry, 'The Art of Bede: Edwin's Council,' in *Saints, Scholars, and Heroes: Studies in Medieval Culture in Honor of Charles W. Jones*, ed. Margot H. King and Wesley M. Stevens (Collegeville, MN: Hill Monastic Manuscript Library, Saint John's Abbey and University, 1979), 191–207 at 194–6, cited only the sparrow from Psalm 83:4, 'siquidem avis invenit domum et passer nidum sibi ubi ponat pullos suos' [For the sparrow hath found herself a house, and the turtle a next for herself where she may lay her young ones], and saw Edwin's nobles as half-way to conversion. J.M. Wallace-Hadrill, *Bede's 'Ecclesiastical History of the English People': A Historical Commentary*, Oxford Medieval Texts (Oxford: Clarendon, 1988), 72, is rightly sceptical. For a psalmic equation of soul and bird not cited by Fry, see Ps.10:2, 101:8, and 123:7, for which the Itala clearly read 'sicut passer.'

44 Druhan, 'The Syntax,' 76, sees in *unus* an indefinite article, but it is probably a vestige of the biblical *unus*, which was a real numeral. At page 202 Druhan concedes that the passages he cited at page 76 involved partitive constructions.

45 Roger, *L'Enseignement*, 309. Winthrop Wetherbee, 'Some Implications of Bede's Latin Style,' in *Bede and Anglo-Saxon England: Papers in Honour of the 1300th Anniversary of the Birth of Bede, given at Cornell University in 1973 and 1974*, ed. R.T. Farrell, British Archaeological Reports 46 (Oxford: BAR, 1978), 23–31 at 26, rightly draws attention to his 'unobtrusive, but complete linguistic control.'

46 Bede distinguishes. See *HE praef.* page 5, 'auditor sive lector,' and page 6, 'auditoribus sive lectoribus'; *HE* 5.13 (hearers and readers) and 5.14 (readers).

47 See Kendall, 'Bede's *Historia ecclesiastica*,' 159, for alliteration as a characteristic of Bede's style, not just an occasional effect. But a number of the examples discussed are sense figures, not just sound figures.

48 *Vita Fursei* (ed. B. Krusch, MGH, SRM 4:434–45). First in Jerome, *In Isaiam* 3.23 (*PL* 24:70) and Philippus Presbyter, *In Job* 30.30 'et ossa mea aruerunt prae caumate' (*PL* 23:1448). But also Gildas, *De Excidio* 19 and Aldhelm, *Carmen de virginitate*, 1.1192 (ed. Ehwald, MGH AA 15). Bede failed to catch it from Gildas above, and may have used it here from his source.

49 'Qui videlicet locus accedente ac recedente reumate bis quotidie instar insulae maris circumluitur undis.' It is qualified in *Vita Cuthberti pros.* 17, 'Farne dicitur insula medio in mari posita, quae non sicut Lindisfarnensium incolarum regio, bis quotidie accedente aestu Oceani, *quem rheuma vocant Graeci*, fit insula, bis renudatis abeunte *rheumate* littoribus contigua terrae redditur (*PL* 34:756). For more on Bede's poeticisms, see Michael Lapidge, 'Poeticism in Pre-Conquest Anglo-Latin Prose,' in *Aspects of the Language of Latin Prose*, ed. Reinhardt, Lapidge, and Adams, 321–7.

50 Presumably induced by the quasi-medical context: 'Memini enim beatae memoriae Theodorum archiepiscopum dicere, quia periculosa sit satis illius temporis phlebotomia, quando et lumen lunae, et rheuma Oceani in cremento est.' Again *pace* Druhan, 'The Syntax,' xxii–xxiii.

51 Discussed as polyptoton by Kendall, 'Bede's *Historia ecclesiastica*,' 161. The triplet is probably intentional. See Kendall, 168–9, for significant numbers in Bede.

52 Writing periods could have been learned through careful study of periodic prose. Michael Lapidge suggested to me that Bede may have been taught by a Roman Latin-speaker, such as John the Archcantor of St Peter's (in Northumbria, but when Bede was too young to have studied with him [*HE* 4.18]).

53 For the development of the period, see Cicero, *De Oratore* 3.198. For its description, Aristotle, *Rhetoric* 3.9.3, 1409B, ed. W.D. Ross (Oxford: Clarendon, 1959).

54 For a stimulating discussion of some of the problems involved in finding a model Latin style and – particularly in handling the writing of the period, see Mayer, 'The Impracticability.' Mayer notes Cicero's ineffective transfer of the period to philosophical writing, and analyses failed periods from various Latin authors.

55 There are further examples of fine small periods in the elegantly autobiographical *HE* 5.24: 'Qui natus ... dedi ... atque habui ... suscepi ... curavi.'

56 Verb pile-up (a classic problem for writers of periods) could have been avoided by 'si qua posita reppererit aliter quam se veritas habet.'

57 Orosius worked (inter al.) from Livy, Caesar's *De Bello Gallico*, Justin's epitome of Trogus, Eutropius, Eusebius-Jerome, Suetonius, and Tacitus.

58 For a monotonous sequence, see Orosius 7.25.1, ed. Karl Zangemeister, *Historiarum adversus paganos libri VII*, CSEL 5 (1882; repr. Hildesheim: G. Olms, 1967).

59 See Orosius 7.1.7–8 for rhetorical questions that are much more like Augustine in the *De ciuitate Dei* than like Bede. See 7.26.2 ff. for diatribic pugnacity

that would be unthinkable in Bede. Gennadius, *De viris inlustribus* 39 (*PL* 58:1081) notes his polemic.
60 Take examples such as Orosius 7.6.13 ff. 'Anno ... anno ... anno.'
61 See note 58 above.
62 Bump bump bump: 7.22.11, 'oppressus est ... interfectus est ... occisus est.'
63 For example, Orosius 7.7.1, 'petulantiam libidinem luxuriam avaritiam crudelitatem'; 7.12.5, place names; 7.22.7 'Graecia Macedonia Pontus Asia.'
64 Livy 5.36.6, 'legati contra ius gentium arma capiunt ... tres nobilissimi ... pugnarent' (ed. R.S. Conway, C.F. Walters, et al., *Titi Livi Ab urbe condita*, 6 vols [Oxford: Clarendon, 1914–99]).
65 Livy 5.36.8, 'omissa in Clusinos ira, receptui canunt minantes Romanis. Erant qui extemplo Romam eundum censerent.'
66 A sentence that Bede used in his *Chronica maiora* 3588.182 (ed. Theodor Mommsen, MGH, AA 13/3 = CCSL 123B:487).
67 Or alternatively one could envisage a 'hard-wired' periodic structure in which *qua indignatione* became a causal (either clause or participial expression) and *contendunt* was the final main verb. For helpful prescriptive material on the period, see Alexander W. Potts, *Hints towards Latin Prose Composition* (1881; repr. London: Macmillan, 1925), 82–107. For a more modern and descriptive treatment, see D.A. Russell, *An Anthology of Latin Prose* (Oxford: Clarendon, 1990), xviii-xxi.
68 Ennius, *Iphig.* fr. 95a (ed. H.D. Jocelyn *The Tragedies of Ennius*, Cambridge Classical Texts and Commentaries 10 [Cambridge: Cambridge University Press, 1967], 108).
69 Plummer, *Venerabilis Baedae Historia Ecclesiastica*, li; M.L.W. Laistner, 'The Library of the Venerable Bede,' in *Bede: His Life, Times, and Writings*, ed. Thompson, 237–66; repr. in *The Intellectual Heritage of the Early Middle Ages: Selected Essays*, ed. Chester G. Starr (Ithaca, NY: Cornell University Press, 1957), 117–49 at 244; Levison, 'Bede as Historian,' 133; Bertram Colgrave, 'Bede's Miracle Stories,' in *Bede: His Life, Times, and Writings*, ed. Thompson, 201–29 at 229, n. 1.
70 Barnard, 'Bede and Eusebius,' 107.
71 *HE* 3.25 (page 186) in Wilfrid's speech: 'ut ecclesiastica docet historia.' There are eighty-four other (raw) hits for *ecclesiastica* and *historia* in close proximity in Bede's writings in the *PL* database. Some refer to Bede's own writings, but Eusebius is fairly frequently cited in the *De temporum ratione*, *In Samuel*, *In Marcum*, *In Lucam*, *Expositio Actuum Apostolorum*, *Homiliae*, and *Martyrologium*. See J.D.A. Ogilvy, *Books Known to the English, 597–1066*, Mediaeval Academy of America Publications 76 (Cambridge, MA: Mediaeval Academy of America, 1967), 236. Cf. also the seventh-century and

possibly Northumbrian fragment of Rufinus's translation of Eusebius in Helmut Gneuss, *Handlist of Anglo-Saxon Manuscripts: A List of Manuscripts and Manuscript Fragments Written or Owned in England up to 1100*, MRTS 241 (Tempe, AZ: Arizona Center for Medieval and Renaissance Studies, 2001), no. 773.5.

72 See Gennadius, *De viris inlustribus* 17 (PL 58:1069–71). The following quotations from the *Historia ecclesiastica* are from Theodore Mommsen, ed., *Die Kirchengeschichte: Die Lateinische Übersetzung des Rufinus*, 3 vols; vol. 2 of *Eusebius Werke*, ed. Eduard Schwartz, Die griechischen christlichen Schriftsteller der ersten drei Jahrhunderte 9.1–3 (Leipzig: J.C. Hinrichs, 1903–9).

73 Though note that in the passage cited immediately below Rufinus has changed Eusebius's more explicit veins and arteries to 'interiora viscerum.'

74 Contrast the many 'bad deaths' or *interitus* in Gregory of Tours. *Interitus* occurs in Bede *HE* 2.2; 4.13; 4.26; 4.32; 5.6; 5.13. See Thomas D. Hill, 'The "Variegated Obit" as an Historiographic Motif in Old English Poetry and Anglo-Latin Historical Literature,' *Traditio* 44 (1988): 101–24.

75 For some exceptions, see *HE* 4.12 (page 228) on the invasion of Ethelred of Mercia: 'adducto maligno exercitu, vastaret, sine respectu pietatis, communi clade.' Also *HE* 4.15 (page 236) on Cædwalla's invasion: 'saeva caede ac depopulatione attrivit.' Also *HE* 4.26 for Ecgfrith's invasion of Ireland: 'vastavit misere gentem innoxiam.'

76 For example, see Rufinus, *Historia ecclesiastica* 8.12.1 passim. For three exclamations, see *HE* 3.27, 'O frater Ecgbercte!' 5.6, 'O quam magnum vae!' and 5.14, 'O quam grandi distantia divisit Deus inter lucem et tenebras!'

77 There seems to be no direct evidence that Bede used Rufinus's *Historia Monachorum*, although Ogilvy, *Books Known*, 236, notes that it was available to Aldhelm and Ælfric. Hence it would be mere, but perhaps not idle, speculation to wonder whether the tales of Holy Ones that are scattered throughout the *HE* (e.g., 3.5, 3.15, 3.19, 4.7–10, 4.17, 4.21, 4.25–8, 4.30, 5.1–6, and 5.12) are related to the Rufinian tales of holy tourism designed to bring the desert fathers to those who had not met them in the flesh or enjoyed their *conversatio*. (An alternative might be that Bede had some acquaintance with items such as Gregory of Tours' *Miracula* and *Vita Patrum*.) Bede, however, rarely intrudes in his own narrative: for the exception, hagiographical material mediated by oral informant or autopsy, see the visions of Dryhthelm, the anonymous thane of Cenred, and the anonymous monk mediated by Haemgisl, Pehthelm, and Bede himself in *HE* 5.12, 5.13, and 5.14. See Colgrave, 'Bede's Miracle Stories,' 206, for Bede's hagiographical sources. Obviously the relationship between Bede's historiography and hagiography is well known. See Levison, 'Bede as Historian,' 123–9. For the

equal presence of Bede the hagiographer and Bede the historian in the *HE*, see Colgrave, 'Bede's Miracle Stories,' 228–9.

78 Rufinus, stylist that he was, took pains even with material that he was translating from rather more primitive Greek. One might profitably examine sentences such as *Historia Monachorum* prol. 2 (almost entirely periodic with verb postponed till *adgrediar*); prol. 11 (fine non-periodic sentences in anaphora; parallel triplet structures with asyndeton between the members: e.g., 'quieti lenes tranquilli' and 'clementior altero humilior benignior ac patientior'); 1.1.7 (seven lines of periodic build-up before the verb *inquit* in 1.1.8): *Tyrannius Rufinus: Historia monachorum sive De vita sanctorum patrum*, ed. Eva Schulz-Flügel (Berlin and New York: W. De Gruyter, 1990); on Rufinus's style see Schulz-Flügel, 39–46.

79 Christopher Grocock, 'Bede and the Golden Age of Latin Prose,' 381, has got the immersion right, but is too much of a 'lumper.' At page 376 he speaks of Jerome's sermons as a model and at page 378 emphasizes the influence of Augustine (hardly correct for the *HE* at any rate). Paul Meyvaert, 'Bede and Gregory the Great,' in *Bede and His World: The Jarrow Lectures 1958–1993*, ed. Michael Lapidge, 2 vols (Aldershot: Variorum, 1994), 1:107–32 at 120–1, fails to explain what he means by 'the Gregorian flavour of certain sections of Bede.' For the chronology of Bede's acquaintance with Eusebius, see Barnard, 'Bede and Eusebius,' note 3.

80 This paper was delivered in Platinum Latin V on 11 May 2003 at the International Medieval Studies Conference at Kalamazoo. My commentator, David Townsend, raised the interesting question of whether Bede was aware that in adopting a Rufinian model he could be seen as signalling a cultural affinity with *Romanitas*.

Crux-busting on the Danube: *uel Coniectanea in* Cosmographiam Aethici, *ut dicitur*, Istri

MICHAEL W. HERREN

The work called the *Cosmography of Aethicus Ister* is one of the last great challenges of Medieval Latin philology. It has been the subject of three full editions, two of which were produced in the mid-nineteenth century, one at the end of the twentieth.[1] Alas, none of these is satisfactory, although the latest, that by Otto Prinz, surely marks an advance in most respects over the previous efforts.[2] To his credit, Dr Prinz established the work on a firm manuscript base, and succeeded in reconstructing the eighth-century archetype of the text. While he admirably performed the task of *recensio codicum*, he shrank from the editor's last obligation: *emendatio*. Prinz very rarely intervened in the received text, and only occasionally printed any of the intelligent corrections made by his predecessors. In a number of places he printed vulgarisms proffered by a single manuscript in preference to syntactically or morphologically correct readings given by the majority of the codices. Perhaps most seriously, the punctuation of Prinz's text leaves a great deal to be desired. One is often uncertain where one sentence ends or another begins. Still, anyone interested in this strange and fascinating text will be grateful for Prinz's hard work. The most valuable part of the edition, in my view, is the series of excellent notes explaining difficult words and tracking sources.

If editors of Latin works were to take inspiration from Roman generals, I should think that Fabius Maximus Cunctator, Fabius 'the Delayer,' would be the guiding genius for the editor of the *Cosmography*. The traps in this text are as deceptive and cruel as those laid for the mythical beasts described in our work, and it is all too tempting to leap at enticing, but facile, solutions to cruces, or simply correct errors of syntax and morphology that strike one as rebarbative. The Latin of the

Cosmography as presented by the early manuscripts is at once stupendously learned and incredibly vulgar. The author had control of a deeply rich vocabulary comprising technical terms relating to many fields. He also exhibited a Greek lexicon that surely had no rival in the Latin literature of the early Middle Ages prior to Eriugena.[3] Moreover, he possessed the capability to distinguish among the registers of his speakers, using one style for Hieronymus, another for Aethicus, yet another for the narrator.[4]

Linguistic talent of this level in a seventh- or eighth-century writer would lead one to believe that one was working with a Virgilius Maro Grammaticus, who, for all his oddities, generally wrote correct Latin according to Late Latin standards. But one would be badly fooled. The early manuscripts display every conceivable type of 'error' in syntax and morphology as well as orthography characteristic of texts written on the Continent before the Carolingian reform. Sometimes one reads words that are strung together without any apparent concern for accidence. At other times one finds several consecutive sentences that are perfectly correct by classical norms. However, one also notes the influence of Romance in usages such as *habet* in the sense of *il y a* and the preposition *a* used to mean 'to' rather than 'from.' Moreover, working on the *Cosmography* would not pose such a great difficulty had the author consistently employed what one might call a 'Romance word-order.' But this happens only incidentally. Often the author uses classical word-order, resorting to such devices as hyperbaton and chiasmus. In many instances, classical word-order leads to serious misunderstandings of sense if correct morphology, particularly in the case system, is not scrupulously observed. Decisions about meaning can be difficult when, for example, the manuscripts transmit a series of words all in the ablative case, where some words are meant as accusatives, others as ablatives. What is going on? Was the work of a highly educated and imaginative Irishman hijacked by Merovingian blockheads?

I hope that I shall not disappoint the honoree[5] or any other reader when I assert that I do not believe (or rather, no longer believe) that the author of the *Cosmography* was Virgil of Salzburg,[6] or for that matter, any Irishman. I have set out some of my reasons for this statement in a recent article.[7] However, I do believe that the true author (not Aethicus and certainly not Hieronymus) really did travel, though hardly to the extent portrayed in the work. I would envision our man travelling from Gaul with other Frankish scholars to Ireland, where, like other foreigners in the seventh century, he studied scriptures. From Ireland he may have continued to England. Canterbury, in particular, may well explain his unusual command of Greek vocabulary. A number of the graecisms employed cannot be traced to extant glossaries. During his travels in the Insular world the cosmographer encountered and utilized a number of peculiarly Irish works, among them the *De mirabilibus sacrae scripturae* (pseudo-Augustine), the grammatical writings of Virgilius Maro Grammaticus, and the *Hisperica Famina*.[8] The result is a very mixed kind of style: a farrago of Greek and other learned elements superimposed on a Vulgar Latin substrate – not unlike 'refained' Oxbridge attempting to cover broad Antipodean. The *Cosmography* is thus a fusion of two cultures, not only stylistically, but also in terms of educational background. The author combines citations of works he almost certainly read or acquired in Gaul (Fredegar, the *Liber historiae Francorum*) with texts of Irish provenance. The archetype of the work, probably written in the early eighth century (not long after the author's lifetime, I think) was written on the Continent; indeed, all of the eighth- and ninth-century manuscripts of the work are continental, most of them from South German centres. As Prinz pointed out in a separate article, the archetype betrays no traces of the spellings that we commonly associate with Insular works.[9]

If one gets rid of the omnipresent notion that the cosmographer was an Irishman,[10] it is much easier to adjust to the Latinity of the transmitted text. The assumption that the writer was trained to write Latin on the Continent in the later seventh century facilitates how one deals with what is usually called 'bad grammar' and 'bad spelling.' One has to acclimate oneself to the idea that *philosophus* can serve for an accusative plural as well as a nominative singular, *portam* might stand for an ablative as well as accusative singular, *rumores* could represent a genitive singular as well as nominative and accusative plural, and *omnis* could be written for *omnibus*. In other words, the editor will feel less impelled to normalize in the belief that by making the work more correct, he is making it more 'Irish' or more 'Insular.' (It is now generally accepted that Irish writers from Columbanus to Adomnán wrote Latin to a considerably higher standard than their contemporaries on the Continent, excepting, of course, the Latin writers of Spain.)

In preparing a new edition of this work for Oxford Medieval Texts, I, like Fabius, have delayed for some time. But in the meantime I have developed some general working principles for dealing with this unusual work. First, as the *Cosmography* was almost certainly written in the very late seventh or early eighth century by someone educated on the Continent, it would be foolhardy to tamper much with the spellings of the *consensus codicum*, except in cases where they completely inhibit understanding of the text. I plan to follow the same general rule with regard to syntax and morphology. Where I do plan to intervene – and decisively – is in punctuating the text, in noting obvious lacunae (there are numerous small ones, usually consisting of just one or two words), and in supplying different variants where the choice should be obvious. I shall also not hesitate to emend against the manuscripts where their agreement makes no sense, using the better conjectures of the nineteenth-century editors as well as my own. Finally, while attempting to respect the spellings of the *consensus codicum*, I shall not privilege a Vulgar reading over a normal one when it is given by only one mansucript. Admittedly, not everyone will find these principles congenial, even if applied consistently. But as Bernhard Bischoff used to say, 'Man tut was man kann.'

In the final analysis, it is the editor's job to supply sense. Readers should not be expected to edit texts for themselves as they read. But editors must also be honest; they are not authorized to invent works out of whole cloth. The following series of snippets is intended to illustrate how I intend to apply the principles I have enunciated. Where I make more than one correction to a passage I print my entire reconstruction. I discuss the first snippet in detail by way of illustration. The sigla used are those of Prinz's edition.

1. Prinz 88.2–6:
... quur Aethicus iste chosmografus tam difficilia appetisse didiceret, quaeque et Moyses et vetus historia in enarrando distulit et hic secerpens protulit. Unde legentibus obsecro, ne me temerario aestiment, cum tanta ob aliorum audacia mea indagatione cucurisse quae conpererint.

Start a new sentence. For *quur* read *Quae*; delete *et* before *hic*; read *protuli* for *protulit* (with *V1*); for *cucurrisse* read *concurrisse* (with *V2*). The text now reads:

Quae Aethicus iste chosmografus tam difficilia appetisse didiceret, quaeque et Moyses et uetus historia in enarrando distulit hic secerpens protuli. Vnde legentibus obsecro, ne me temerario aestiment, cum tanta ob aliorum audacia mea indagatione concurrisse quae conpererint.

[The very difficult things which the cosmographer Aethicus learned to pursue and also the matters that both Moses and the Old Testament omitted in their narrative I have reproduced here in excerpts. Hence I implore my readers not to think me rash when they discover that such important things owed to the great daring of others are harmonized by my investigation.]

Discussion: As Prinz's rendering of the received text makes little sense, how do we fix the two sentences? In the first place, *Quur* (for the usual *cur*) was puzzling, and the following *quaeque* provided the clue to the solution: *Quae*. As for *protulit/protuli*, it is clear from context that Aethicus is not providing selections of his own work, but that the hypothetical editor (Hieronymus) is making them, and that the editor is speaking in the first person. The scribe known as *V1* obviously made a good emendation in this case by correcting *protulit* to *protuli*. The same applies to the case of *concurisse* for *cucurisse* (correction by *V2*): nobody seemed to be running about. I had greater difficulty (the classicist's dis-ease) deciding about *temerario* and *audacia*, both of which should be in accusative, and indeed, accusatives are given by some manuscripts. Sticking to what were probably archetypal readings, I printed the 'mistakes' and relied on the translation to make the author's intended syntax clear. In any case, if one emended these to their correct forms, one would also have to emend *legentibus* to *legentes*. (In Classical Latin *obsecro* governs the accusative; in Old Latin one finds it with *abs te*.)

2. Prinz 90.14–91.4:
   ... eiusque conditione fieri tormentis ac poenis perpetuis sub terra collocata catagine sub illaque nulla inferius ad examinationem malorum crudelium atque damnabilium, quae quadrifarie secernendo scribit divisum.

For unattested *catagine* read *sartagine*:

[... and from it a condition was established for torment and perpetual punishments, a frying pan located beneath the ground, and beneath it there is nothing deeper for the inquisition of the evil, cruel, and damnable, which condition he wrote was divided into four parts.]

Discussion: Cf. Prinz 157.13–14 for the cosmographer's use of *sartago* as a metaphor for the River Acheron, and note *V*'s reading *cartagine*.

3. Prinz 91.11–13:
   Quam aquam purgatam animam a peccatis per ignem abluenda vitia vel refrigeranda post laborem.

Insert *per* before *quam*, place a comma after *peccatis*, and posit a missing word after *vel*: perhaps *corda*? The text now reads:

   Per quam aquam purgatam animam a peccatis, per ignem abluenda uitia uel <...> refrigeranda post laborem.

   [Through this water the soul is purged from sins, through fire vices are washed clean and (hearts?) will be refreshed after labour.]

Discussion: The supposition of a lost *per* can be explained by eye-skip: note the opening letters of the previous word *peccatis*. One would not expect 'vices' to be refreshed after labour(!); thus it should be obvious that a word has fallen out before *refrigeranda*.

4. Prinz 93.3–6:
   Mare adserit similitudinem pelbhloicam molliorem ac crassiorem mirphoicum quasi bitumine parte maxima in ea forma tenere cum diversis generibus piscium beluisque et bestiis, sablo similitudinem habere.

Read *pelliculam* for *pelbhloicam*; place a comma after *crassiorem* and a semi-colon after *bitumine*; for *mirphoicum* read *myrphoricum*, 'containing myrrh,' 'resinous' (note that MSS G and W have *myrphoicum*):

   Mare adserit similitudinem pelliculam molliorem ac crassiorem, myrphoricum quasi bitumine; parte maxima in ea forma tenere cum diuersis generibus piscium beluisque et bestiis, sablo similitudinem habere.

   [He states that the sea is like a fine skin, rather soft and thick and resinous like bitumen; a very great part of it, together with diverse types of fish and sea-monsters and beasts, are contained in that form, and it bears a resemblance to sand.]

Discussion: Understand *parte maxima* as accusative, and assume a reflexive meaning for *tenere*.

5. Prinz 95.10–14:
   Sicut ei fuit in ipsa massa vel materia rude et infernum damnatorum,

mole livores corrui malos et paradisum iustorum et angelorum vel sanctorum beatitudinem inmensam recipere et sine fine aeterna gaudia possidere.

Supply *sic* before *et paradisum*; insert *bonos* after *recipere* and before *et*; delete comma after *damnatorum* and insert one after *malos*:

> Sicut ei fuit in ipsa massa uel materia rude et infernum damnatorum mole liuores corrui malos, sic et paradisum iustorum et angelorum uel sanctorum beatitudinem inmensam recipere bonos et sine fine aeterna gaudia possidere.

[And just as for Him it was the case that on account of the weight of their envy the evil fall into this mass or rude matter and inferno of the damned, so too the good receive the paradise of the just and the blessedness of the angels and saints and possess eternal joys without end.]

Discussion: For the use of *sum* to mean 'the case that' see *OLD* s.v. 7; the author has replaced the construction with *ut* by the accusative and infinitive. *Corrui* should be understood as *corruere*: confusion of active and passive forms is frequent in this work.

6. Prinz 98.8–11:
> Quia quique creaturae praefulsit in ordine primus et viarum dei claruit in rude miraculum idemque primus in novissimo iudice terribili venturo poenas damnaturos ...

Read *daturus* for *damnaturos*:

> Quia quique creaturae praefulsit in ordine primus et uiarum dei claruit in rude miraculum idemque primus in nouissimo, iudice terribili uenturo, poenas daturus.

[Because he who flashed first in the order of creation and shone in the new miracle of God's paths will be the same who will first pay the penalty when the terrible Judge will come on the last day.]

Discussion: Cf. Avitus, *carm.* 2.47–8: 'quique creaturae praefulsit in ordine primus, / primas venturo pendet sub iudice poenas' (cit. Prinz, *ad loc.*). The author has replaced Avitus's *primas ... pendet ... poenas* with the normal Latin expression for 'paying a penalty': *poenas dare (daturus)*; cf. *OLD* s.v. 1.

7. Prinz 101.2–6:
> Tantam enim vim et vigorem angelorum manus ignitas habent, ut petrae minuatim scindantur, arborum evulsio desecetur, si hominum ira peccaminum vel hostium rebellium furor ingruerit, ut unius angeli ictu innumerabilium milium populorum divino irae mucrone caesi corruant.

For *peccaminum* read *peccantium*; perhaps supply a word such as *cunei* before *innumerabilium*; delete *ut* before *unius*.

> Tantam enim uim et uigorem angelorum manus ignitas habent, ut petra minuatim scindantur, arborum euulsio desecetur; si hominum ira peccantium uel hostium rebellium furor ingruerit, unius angeli ictu <...> innumerabilium milium populorum diuino irae mucrone caesi corruant.

[The fiery hands of angels have so much power and force that rocks are split into bits, trees are uprooted and cut down; if the anger of sinful men or rebel hosts should come in their way, by the stroke of a single angel (hosts of) innumerable thousands of people would fall, slain by the divine sword of wrath.]

Discussion: One would expect *ignitae* for *ignitas*; however, *ignitas* should not be emended, as the classical Latin feminine accusative plural in *-as* was frequently employed as a nominative in Merovingian literary texts; see especially the summary tables in Sas.[11] In some writers the substitution is 100 per cent.

8. Prinz 108.1–2:
> Et meridies opima aurea concordeque fulgit metalla temna infusa ...

For *temna* read *tenua*: [And the South is rich in golden <metal> and flashes agreeably with fine metals that can be melted ...]

Discussion: The nonsensical *temna* in the archetype was doubtless occasioned by misreading of the minims.

9. Prinz 111.4–6:
> Insolas quae supra praedixit et montem incognitum et accessibilem et has bestias et flatum austri mira indagatione adgressus est.

For *accessibilem* read *inaccessibilem* (with MSS *WV* and Winterbottom's review of Prinz, 431): [By marvellous tracking he approached the islands that he spoke about above and the unknown and inaccessible mountain and these beasts and the blast of the south wind.]

10. Prinz 117.10–13:
Aliarum gentium originem obmissam, quae agiografia veteris testamenti concelebrat, idem philosophus non scribit, quia omnes scripturas et legum et liberalium fontem vivum et matrem historiarum appellat.

Read *litterarum* after *liberalium* (with Winterbottom's review of Prinz, 431): [The same philosopher omitted a description of other peoples which are noted in the Old Testament of the sacred scripture, because he calls all of the scriptures the living fount of liberal letters and the mother of history.]

Discussion: Cf. Isidore, *Etymologiae* 14.4.10 'mater liberalium litterarum.'[12]

11. Prinz 121.9–11:
... aedificantes pilas praegrandes mirae magnitudinis et cloacas subtus marmore constructas, phyrram fontem gluttinantem, et appellaverunt Morcholom lingua sua ...

For *phyrram* read *Pierriam*: [... building huge gates of marvellous magnitude and sewers beneath, constructed out of marble, joining to the Fountain of the Muses, and they called it 'Morcholom' in their language ...]

Discussion: I retain the erroneous accidence of the archetype (note that *fontem* is masculine). The author's 'joke' is that barbarians build their sewers out of marble, and then allow them to pollute the source of poetry and culture (*Piereus*: 'sacred to the Muses').

12. Prinz 133.6–9:
In hac insola silvarum magnitudo et lacedemones bistiolas venenatas ita, ut tacto suorum dentium vel anelitus alias bestias maiores et homines peremant.

For *lacedemones* read *latent demones*: [On this island there is a large number of forests, and (in them) lurk demons, little beasts that are so poisonous that by the touch of their teeth or their breath they kill larger beasts and men.]

Discussion: Elsewhere the author uses *Lacedemon* to mean 'Lacedemonian,' a vague designation of a people in Greece or the Balkans; see Prinz's index.

13. Prinz 135.18–136.1:
> Monimenta urbium nimio terrore ululate brutorum mucrone eradicata, catasta pulchra redigetur, roobitarum moenia urbium dissoluta arteficum lacerta ...

For *roobitarum* read *robustarum* (with early eds): [Wail for the monuments of cities destroyed by the sword with great terror; the lovely structure will be reduced; the walls of stout cities will be dissolved by the power of the engineers.]

Discussion: Prinz ignores the sensible emendation of the nineteenth-century editors: *robustarum* for *roobitarum*. Understand *lacerto* for the manuscripts' *lacerta*, here used in the abstract sense.

14. Prinz 136.5–8:
> Ait enim in illa regione omni tempore frigus, monstra ibidem vidisse, quae incredibile videtur, ne prava videatur tot labores industria, quia terror magnus potest esse lectori et audientibus intollerabilis pavor.

Posit a lacuna after *videtur* and understand a phrase such as *et alia praetermittam*.

> Ait enim in illa regione omni tempore frigus, monstra ibidem uidisse quae incredibile uidetur; <...> ne praua uideatur tot labores industria, quia terror magnus potest esse lectori et audientibus intollerabilis pauor.

[For he said that in that region it was cold all the time, that he saw monsters in the same place, which seems incredible ... (and I shall pass over other matters) lest the effort of his entire work should appear disgraceful, because it produces great terror in his readers or intolerable fear among his hearers.]

Discussion: Understand *labores* as genitive singular. *Tot* is a mistake for *totius*, but I hesitate to emend.

15. Prinz 138.14:
   Alexander enim vir magnus et in omnium adinventionem vel utilitatem famosissimus vel operibus insignis egregius tam pravas gentes et perfidas, ut supra diximus, ad aquilonem cum conperisset Gogetas et Magogetas et Honargias forma et omnia lineamenta transformata et truculentissima tam in vita quam et in membris omnibus ...

For *Honargias* read *onagrias*; for *uita* read *uultu*:

   Alexander enim uir magnus et in omnium adinuentionem uel utilitatem famosissimus uel operibus insignis egregius tam prauas gentes et perfidas, ut supra diximus, ad aquilonem cum conperisset Gogetas et Magogetas et onagrias forma et omnia lineamenta transformata et truculentissima tam in uultu quam et in membris omnibus ...

   [When Alexander, the great man and most celebrated for the discovery of everything useful and distinguished for his great deeds, came upon the indecent and treacherous peoples to the North, as we mentioned above, (namely) the sons of Gog and Magog in the shape of wild asses and with all their features transformed and savage-looking in their faces as well as all their members ...]

Discussion: *Onagrius, a, um*, though not attested in Latin, is a well-formed adjectival coinage based on *onager*, 'wild ass.' The emendation of *uita* with *uultu* seems obvious from context, and is palaeographically plausible.

16. Prinz 142.11–15:
   Grande enim scrupolo idem philosophus adplicuit, in pauca nimpe navale gubernaculo velox stilus innectens manu calabat, ad nibe ocianum sinum inreductam filarchosmus cura laborum secutarum gentium maris vel stagna investigans.

Omit comma after *adplicuit*; insert *ut* before *velox* and place a period after *calabat*. Start a new sentence; for *ad nibe* read *Adhibet*. Place a comma after *maris* to separate it from the preceding string of genitives:

Grande enim scrupolo idem philosophus adplicuit in pauca nimpe nauale gubernaculo, <ut uelox> stilus innectens manu calabat. Adhibet ocianum sinum inreductam filarchosmus cura laborum secutarum gentium, maris uel stagna inuestigans.

[For the same philosopher exercised great care about a few matters, certainly those concerning the navigation of ships, as the swift pen joining to his hand proclaimed. The lover of order applies (himself) to the gulf of Ocean with the care and pains of the people following him, investigating even the lagoons of the sea.]

Discussion: Understand *scrupolo* as accusative (the object of *adplicuit*). Take *calabat* in its attested sense 'proclaimed,' contrary to Prinz (142, n. 315). *Filarchosmus* is either a mistake for $\phi\iota\lambda\acute{o}\kappa o\sigma\mu o\varsigma$, 'lover of order,' or else the author's coinage combining $\phi\iota\lambda$-, $\alpha\rho\chi$-, and $\kappa\acute{o}\sigma\mu o\varsigma$.

17. Prinz 146.5–9:
Pagani namque ipsum magum eorum magistrum in similitudinem deorum suorum connumerati sunt, eo quod in similitudinem griphorum animalium vel altilium pinnatorum eis ex aere et auro fusile simulacrum fabricavit.

For the first *similitudinem* read *multitudinem*:

Pagani namque ipsum magum eorum magistrum in multitudinem deorum suorum connumerati sunt, eo quod in similitudinem, etc.

[For the pagans numbered this magus their teacher in the multitude of their gods, because he fashioned for them a molten image made of bronze and gold in the likeness of griffins, beasts, or feathered birds ...]

Discussion: *Homioteleuton* is obviously the cause of this textual corruption.

18. Prinz 153.2–8:
Unde quaeso sapientibus qui legerint, me quoque non reprehensurus nec illis totum observare, sed consideranter quae utilia sunt legere, inutilia refutare, ne qui veritatis discipuli esse potuerant ad docendum, magistri errorum existant ad seducendum, ut, dum valde alta mundi quaesierint, de summo ad ima corruant ut Eonomius et Priscillianus.

Insert *in* before *totum*; for *consideranter* read *considerentur*:

> Vnde quaeso sapientibus qui legerint me quoque non reprehensurus, nec illis <in> totum obseruare, sed considerentur quae utilia sunt legere, inutilia refutare, ne qui ueritatis discipuli esse potuerant ad docendum magistri errorum existant ad seducendum, ut, dum ualde alta mundi quaesierint, de summo ad ima corruant ut Eonomius et Priscillianus.

> [Whence I beseech the philosophers who read (my work) not to blame me as well or heed those ones completely, but to consider which things are useful to select, which things useless to reject, lest those who were able to be disciples of the truth for the sake of teaching become teachers of error for the sake of misleading, with the result that, while they look into the very deep matters of the universe, they fall from the heights into the depths like Eunomius and Priscillian.]

Discussion: In the case of transmitted *consideranter*, sense requires a verb, not an adverb. The author usually distinguishes correctly between the indicative and subjunctive moods, but frequently confuses the active and passive voices.

19. Prinz 156.15–157.2:
> Resiliit aquilo calabris bello gerendo, termofiles specus voraginem appetit et meditullia secerpit.

For *aquilo* read *aquila;* for *calabris* read *charadris*:

> Resiliit aquila charadris bello gerendo, termofiles specus uoraginem appetit et meditullia secerpit.

> [The eagle waging war with the kites retreats, seeks out its warm lair in the chasm, and selects the middle part.]

Discussion: For the formation *termofiles*, literally 'heat-loving,' here used to mean simply 'warm,' see Herren.[13] For the use of Late Latin *secerpere* in the sense of 'select,' see the first example.

20. Prinz 170.17–171.7:
> ... in fabulis horum gesta pro vanitate, non pro utilitate suis codicibus nectebantur de diis gentium et diis suos, de astra et deicola ad suam stul-

> tam mundi disputare idolatriam, eo quod militiam caelorum, quod deus in suam gloriam praeparavit, ille in fanaticis et adversis ac diabolicis nominibus in nonnullis disputationibus posuerunt iuxta illud priscam vesaniam malignum eologium: 'Eritis sicut dii, scientes bonum et malum,' id est quasi daemonia scientes.

Start a new sentence ending at *nectebantur*. Begin another sentence with *De diis*; read *sua stulta* for *suam stultam*; for *idolatriam* read *idolatram*; read *illi* (with *OV*) for *ille*; for *nominibus* read *numinibus* (with *O2*):

> In fabulis horum gesta pro uanitate, non pro utilitate, suis codicibus nectebantur. De diis gentium et diis suos, de astra et deicola ad sua stulta mundi disputare idolatram, eo quod militiam caelorum, quod deus in suam gloriam praeparauit, illi in fanaticis et aduersis ac diabolicis numinibus in nonnullis disputationibus posuerunt iuxta illud priscam uesaniam malignum eologium: 'Eritis sicut dii, scientes bonum et malum,' id est quasi daemonia scientes.

> [The actions in their myths are woven into their books not for their utility, but because of vanity. According to the foolishness of the world the idolater discourses about the pagan gods and his own gods, about the stars, and the cult of the gods, because in their disputations they placed the kingdom of heaven, which God prepared in his glory, in fanatical, inimical, and diabolical powers according to that malignant curse of ancient madness: 'You shall be like gods, knowing good and evil,' that is having knowledge like that of demons.]

21. Prinz 193.17–194.2:
> Ubi et urbs inclitissima eorum Athenas, quam philosophus umbelicum Greciae praedixit, pingua illi<cib>us et ornata munilibus, erudita litteris, legem et scientiam, decorata ludis, foro et vectigalibus ...

For Prinz's *illi<cib>us* (for archetypal *illius*) read the palaeographically more convincing *illiciis*: [There too is their most famous city Athens, which (our) philosopher called the 'navel of Greece,' rich in allurements, decked out in jewellery, learned in literature, law, and science, distinguished for its games, oratory, and its power to exact tribute ...]

22. Prinz 196.11–14:
> Ibidem Hercolis conthorrus maiorque phorensis cruentator proximorum venatorum turmachus, Amfibroniae nummator ortus est, etc.

Read *cothurnus* for *conthorrus*, insert commas after *phorensis* and *proximorum*; for *Amfibroniae nummator* read *Amfitronis aemulatore*; end sentence at *ortus est*:

> Ibidem Hercolis cothurnus maiorque phorensis, cruentator proximorum, uenatorum turmarchus, Amfitrionis aemulatore ortus est.

> [In the same place Hercules, tragedian and great orator, bloodier of kinfolk, leader of hunters, sprang from the impersonator of Amphitryon.]

Discussion: Perhaps understand *cothurnus* not as 'a tragic actor,' but as the subject of tragedy. On *turmachus* see Herren.[14] *Amfibrioniae nummator* transmitted by the manuscripts contains several corruptions, not least of which is false word-separation: the *ae* belongs with the following word. *Br* and *tr* are easily confused in pre-Carolingian manuscripts; *nummator* (unattested in antiquity) is clearly influenced by the familiar word *nummus*.

23. Prinz 233.18–22:

> Nunc summatim ad orientem certatim gressum posuimus a cacumine Caucasi montis calles artissimus usque magnum Gangen propter aedificium arcae parentes coavi et camaras ac artificia illius, si ultra inundatio aquarum chosmo vim intulissit, qua arte reliquiae fratrum remansissent.

Place a period after *illius*, and start a new sentence. Insert a colon after *orientem*; read *artissimos* with the archetype; read *parietes* for *parentes*[15] and place a period after *illius*; for *coavi* read *coartari*:

> Nunc summatim ad orientem: certatim gressum posuimus a cacumine Caucasi montis calles artissimos usque magnum Gangen propter aedificium arcae, parietes coartari et camaras ac artificia illius. Si ultra innundatio aquarum chosmo uim intullissit, qua arte reliquiae fratrum remansissent.

> [Now briefly to the East: eagerly we made our way along very narrow paths from the peak of Mount Caucasus to the great Ganges on account of the edifice of the Ark, so that its walls and chambers and artefacts could be reinforced. If an inundation of water should bring its force against the world again, by this skill remnants of it would survive for the brethren (i.e., for the use of the brethren).]

Discussion: Whereas *coartaui* would be a more obvious emendation for the meaningless *coavi*, context forbids this. In the next breath Aethicus complains that he did not find the Ark! Thus it is clear that the remainder of the sentence expresses an intention rather than a fact.

When all is said and done, it must be admitted that many problems remain, and that the solutions proposed here will not satisfy everyone. Classicizers will want to bulldoze their way through the text and clear away the rubbish of error; manuscript purists will want to retain every precious scrap of testimony, however nonsensical. As stated at the beginning of this contribution, I have attempted to maintain the *via media*, preserving as far as possible what is probably authorial orthography, morphology, and syntax, but supplying sense by punctuating clearly and by choosing the best variants. Nor have I shrunk from conjecture, when this is called for. In sum, I think that texts should be edited according to the norms of the period and locale in which they were written. Even Erasmus, try as he did, did not write pure Ciceronian Latin, and his 'medievalisms' should be left alone by future editors.[16] It is unsurprising that our pseudo-Jerome did not succeed in imitating the style of the real St Jerome. Indeed, his grasp of the rules of Classical Latin did not match that of Gregory of Tours – and that surely is shocking.

NOTES

1 [Armand] d'Avezac, 'Mémoire sur Éthicus et sur les ouvrages cosmographiques intitulés de ce nom,' *Mémoires présentés par divers savants à l'Académie des inscriptions et belles-lettres*, 1st ser. 2 (1852): 230–551; *Die Kosmographie des Istrier Aithikos im lateinischen Auszuge des Hieronymus*, ed. Heinrich Wuttke (Leipzig: Dyk, 1853); *Die Kosmographie des Aethicus*, ed. Otto Prinz, MGH, Quellen zur Geistesgeschichte des Mittelalters 14 (Munich: MGH, 1993).
2 For judicious comments on the two early editions, see Prinz, *Die Kosmographie des Aethicus*, 70–2. For Prinz's edition see my detailed review, *JML* 3 (1993): 236–45; also Michael Winterbottom's review, *Peritia* 9 (1995): 430–2.
3 For a study of the author's use of Greek, see Michael W. Herren, 'The "Greek Element" in the *Cosmographia* of Aethicus Ister,' *JML* 11 (2001): 184–200.
4 See Hildegard L.C. Tristram, 'Ohthere, Wulfstan und der Aethicus Ister,'

Zeitschrift für deutschen Altertum und deutsche Literatur 111 (1982): 153–68 at 158.
5 Tom Hill's penchant for 'crux-busting' was the inspiration for the title of the current article.
6 The thesis of the identity of the author of the *Cosmography* with Virgil of Salzburg was put forward in two much-admired articles by Heinz Löwe: 'Ein literarischer Widersacher des Bonifatius: Virgil von Salzburg und die Kosmographie des Aethicus Ister,' *Abhandlungen der Akademie der Wissenschaften und der Literatur*, Geistes- und sozialwissenschaftliche Klasse, Jahrgang 1951, Nr. 11 (1951): 899–988, and 'Salzburg als Zentrum literarischen Schaffens im 8. Jahrhundert,' *Mitteilungen der Gesellschaft für Salzburger Landeskunde* 115 (1975): 99–143.
7 Michael W. Herren, 'The *Cosmography* of Aethicus Ister: Speculations about Its Date, Provenance, and Audience,' in *Nova de Veteribus: Festschrift für Prof. Dr. Paul Gerhard Schmidt*, ed. Andreas Bihrer and Elisabeth Stein (Munich: K. Sauer Verlag, 2004), 79–102.
8 This was observed some time ago by Löwe, 'Ein literarischer Widersacher,' 920–5. See also Kurt Smolak, 'Notizen zu Aethicus Ister,' *Filologia Mediolatina* 3 (1996): 135–52 at 151, and in more detail for the *Hisperica Famina*, Herren, 'The "Greek Element,"' 199.
9 Otto Prinz, 'Untersuchungen zur Überlieferung und zur Orthographie der Kosmographie des Aethicus,' *DA* 37 (1981): 474–510.
10 Most recently maintained by Peter Dronke, *Verse with Prose from Petronius to Dante: The Art and Scope of the Mixed Form* (Cambridge, MA: Harvard University Press, 1994), 14–19.
11 Louis Furman Sas, *The Noun Declension System in Merovingian Latin* (Paris: Pierre André, 1937), 502.
12 *Isidori Hispalensis Etymologiarum sive Originum Libri XX*, ed. W.M. Lindsay, 2 vols (1911; repr. Oxford: Clarendon, 1985).
13 Herren, 'The "Greek Element,"' 193.
14 Herren, 'The "Greek Element,"' 192.
15 The inspired suggestion of Gregory Hays, 'The Date and Identity of the Mythographer Fulgentius,' *JML* 13 (2003): 163–252 at 146, n. 42.
16 See the instructive article by Terence Tunberg, 'The Latinity of Erasmus and Medieval Latin: Continuities and Discontinuities,' *JML* 14 (2004): 147–70.

The *Revelationes* of Pseudo-Methodius and Scriptural Study at Salisbury in the Eleventh Century

MICHAEL W. TWOMEY

The *Revelationes* of Pseudo-Methodius (henceforth simply Pseudo-Methodius) was written in Syriac in about 690 as a response to Muslim advances against Byzantine Christianity.[1] A work of lurid and sensationalist anti-Islamic propaganda, it attempts to terrify Christians into action by depicting Islam within an apocalyptic framework that represents the seventh century as the end-time. Pseudo-Methodius derived its authority partly from its attribution to Methodius, bishop of Patara, who was martyred in 311, and partly by grafting itself onto biblical history. It was translated into Greek in about 700x710 and into Latin in about 732.[2] We now know of over thirty Greek and two hundred Latin manuscripts from the eighth through fifteenth centuries and from throughout Western and Eastern Europe.[3]

By the end of the Middle Ages there were four Greek and two Latin recensions of Pseudo-Methodius (henceforth R1 and R2), plus numerous translations from the Latin into vernacular languages, including English.[4] The original Syriac version is represented in the Latin R1. With one exception to be discussed below, all copies of Pseudo-Methodius written in England, whether in Latin or in English, are R2. For some time I have been working on a reception history of Pseudo-Methodius in England, and what I have found is that unlike on the Continent, in England Pseudo-Methodius was apparently not read as an apocalypse. England was far enough away from Islam that Pseudo-Methodius never had the national, ethnic, political, or religious significance for England that it had for seventh-century Syria, where it originated, or for eighth-century Byzantium, where it was translated into Greek. Instead, in England Pseudo-Methodius seems to have been used as a patristic source for the study of Old Testament history.

The original Syriac version of Pseudo-Methodius narrates world history from Creation through the succession of empires (Alexander to Rome), then foretells the rise of Islam, the eventual triumph of the last Roman emperor, the coming of Antichrist, and the end of the world. R2 skips from the first mention of the Ishmaelites in Genesis to their return as the nations of Islam in the final world age, omitting the succession of empires. Various studies have shown the significance of Pseudo-Methodius on the Continent as an apocalypse that directly influenced Adso's *Libellus de Antichristo*, the *Visions of Daniel*, the *Cosmography of Aethicus Ister*, and possibly the Pseudo-Ephremian 'Sermo de fine mundi.'[5] The role Pseudo-Methodius accorded to Alexander the Great, who imprisons Gog, Magog, and the 'unclean nations' until the end of the world, connected it to the medieval Alexander legend.[6]

Pseudo-Methodius is well known to intellectual historians and to theologians, but little has been written about its English reception.[7] Charlotte D'Evelyn, Aaron Jenkins Perry, and Gerrit H.V. Bunt have studied the ME versions, and as part of her study, D'Evelyn briefly described the Latin versions. Comparing the Latin R2 text to ME uses of Pseudo-Methodius, which she found in direct translations as well as in texts that adapted Methodian material, D'Evelyn observed that later medieval texts in England limit themselves to Cain and Abel and their twin sisters Calmana and Delbora, Jonitus the fourth son of Noah, dating of events in the first millennium, and the return of the Ishmaelites in the last world age.[8] My question is why this is so: in other words, what explains the English preference for the biblical material in Pseudo-Methodius? Since it is not possible to survey the entire tradition in this brief essay, here I will focus only on how the earliest occurrences of Pseudo-Methodius in England may point the way to its later reception.

British libraries hold fifty-three of the Latin manuscripts of Pseudo-Methodius. Of these, twenty-four have their origin or provenance in England before the end of the Middle Ages.[9] Others could be added from British medieval library catalogues, but in the interest of space I will ignore them here. In the ME period three vernacular versions were made.[10] The two earliest Latin manuscripts from England, Salisbury Cathedral Library MS 165 and London, BL MS Royal 5.F.xviii, were copied at the Salisbury Cathedral scriptorium before 1100.[11] On the basis of incipits, only R2 is found in England, both in Latin and vernacular manuscripts, with only one exception to be discussed momentarily. This fact is apparently not widely known, since bibliographical surveys (e.g., the Corpus of British Medieval Library Catalogues) routinely cite the editions of Sackur or even de la Bigne, which contain R1 texts, rather than the editions of D'Evelyn and Prinz, which contain the correct R2 texts.[12]

As Salisbury was established only in 1075, Salisbury 165 and Royal 5.F.xviii were part of the earliest program of copying in the cathedral scriptorium. In her magisterial study of the Salisbury scriptorium in its first fifty years, Teresa Webber observes that the Salisbury scribes did occasionally obtain exemplars from two different textual traditions, using the second manuscript as an exemplar for further copying. The manuscripts at Salisbury were copied rapidly, many from foreign exemplars since the texts were not available in Anglo-Saxon England, and in some cases it is possible to show that all English copies of a text derive from a Salisbury exemplar.[13]

Although I cannot claim that the Royal manuscript is the exemplar for any other R2 copies, I can say that Salisbury 165 is the sole R1 text that I have found in or from England; and the Royal manuscript is the earliest R2 text that I have found in or from England.[14] In the period Webber studies, there were two phases of copying, which Webber identifies in terms of two teams of scribes, Group I and Group II.[15] The text of Pseudo-Methodius in Salisbury 165 belongs to Group I, while the text of Pseudo-Methodius in Royal 5.F.xviii belongs to both Group I and Group II, since it was copied by a Group I scribe into a booklet that otherwise belongs to Group II, suggesting the continued activity of that scribe in the second phase of copying.[16] Thus, Salisbury 165 would be slightly earlier than Royal. It is therefore tempting to speculate that Royal was procured as a replacement and then used as an exemplar for further copying.

If the text of Pseudo-Methodius in Salisbury 165 was judged to need replacing, why was it? The booklet itself (fols 11r–22r) was clearly considered important enough to correct, as there are interlinear and marginal corrections, perhaps by the scribe who copied it. After the booklet containing Pseudo-Methodius was bound with the other booklets that comprise the manuscript, someone annotated the manuscript with the *nota* 'D.M' (*dignum memoria*; literally, 'worthy with respect to memory'). It is one of about twenty-five Salisbury manuscripts that bear 'D.M' marks written by this hand. Most of the 'D.M.' notes are in patristic *originalia*, and according to Webber their general function is to identify *sententiae* for excerpting. Webber admits that she is not able 'to discover any one criterion which accounts for all his choices of *senten-*

tiae,' but the pastoral, moral, and therefore potentially sermonic nature of the material marked 'D.M.' suggests to her that the notator may have been Archdeacon Hubald (active ca. 1078–99), who in turn may have been Webber's Group I scribe i, both a scribe and a corrector of a number of eleventh-century Salisbury books.[17] This notator wrote the heading for the text of Pseudo-Methodius on fol. 11r. The text itself was written by Group I scribe xii.[18]

In Salisbury 165's Pseudo-Methodius, what was worthy of committing to memory? The 'D.M.' marks are symmetrically placed. The first is on fol. 14r, where Alexander encloses the unclean nations in the twin mountains known as the *ubera aquilonis,* or 'breasts of the north,' and the other is on 19v, where the unclean nations break forth at the end of the world.[19] Since the difference between R1 and R2 is that R2 skips from the first mention of the Ishmaelites to their return as the Arabs (i.e., Muslims in the seventh century), it is immediately clear that the 'D.M.' marks do not indicate the difference between R1 and R2, since the Ishmaelites and unclean nations appear at very different points, the unclean nations occurring later both in past history and in future history. The Ishmaelites appear historically in the time of Isaac and eschatologically (because Pseudo-Methodius pretends to be 300 years prior to the seventh century) after the Christianization of Rome, whereas the unclean nations appear historically in the time of Alexander and eschatologically in the days of the Last Roman Emperor.

In R1 of Pseudo-Methodius, the unclean nations are said to be descended from Noah's son Japheth ('Sunt autem ex filiis Iapeth nepotes,' Salisbury 165, fol. 13v), whose cohort includes the biblical figures Gog and Magog: 'In novissimis vero temporibus secundum iezechielis prophetiam quę dicit: In novissimo die in fine seculi exiet gog et magog in terra israhel' [fol. 14r: In the last times, according to the prophecy of Ezekiel, who says: on the last day in the final age, Gog and Magog will go forth into the land of Israel].[20] Magog is listed as a descendant of Japheth in Gen. 10:2. Gog and Magog are paired in Ezek. 38–9 as scourges through whom God will punish Israel. In Apoc. 20:7–9, Gog and Magog are the peoples of the four quarters of the earth who are gathered for battle by Satan when he is released from his prison in the last days, and who are immediately destroyed by a fire sent by God from heaven. Together these biblical chapters inform the section about the unclean nations in Pseudo-Methodius, providing not only Gog and Magog, but the place of their imprisonment in the mountains of the north (Ezek. 38:1–6), their assault on Israel in the last days (Ezek. 38:8,

16), and their return and destruction at the end of time (Apoc. 20:7–9). The unclean nations themselves are not biblical. According to Paul Alexander, they come rather from the Pseudo-Ephraem, and they are found in other apocalypses akin to Pseudo-Methodius.[21]

The 'D.M.' *nota* on fol. 14r is to the right of lines 17–18 on the page, where God instructs Alexander to imprison the unclean nations in the *ubera aquilonis:* 'Continuo igitur deprecatus [est] deum Alexander et exaudiuit eius obsecrationem et precepit dominus deus duobus montibus quibus est uocabulum ubera aquilonis' [Alexander implored God unremittingly, and he heard his entreaty; and the Lord God directed him to the two mountains which are called the breasts of the north]. Since the 'D.M.' *nota* is placed at a distance from the text and not connected to it with any kind of marking, it is unwise to assume that the 'D.M.' *nota* refers only to this one sentence. It may, for instance, refer generally to the entire passage about the unclean nations, which begins at the bottom of fol. 13v and continues through the top of 14v. The other 'D.M.' *nota*, on fol. 19v, could likewise refer generally to the entire passage about the unclean nations. The folio begins by characterizing the time of peace that Pseudo-Methodius predicts will occur after the defeat of the Ishmaelites. Then the gates of the north are opened and the nations enclosed by Alexander pour forth, wreaking havoc. At that point the Last Roman Emperor appears. The *nota* mark is in the far left margin across from lines 21–4: 'Emittet dominus unum principem militię sue et percutiet eos in momento temporis. Et post hec descendet rex romanorum et commorabitur in ierusalem ebdomada temporum et dimidia' [The Lord will send the one who is foremost in his army, and he will smite them in an instant. And after this the king of the Romans will descend, and he will dwell in Jerusalem for a week and a half of times]. Thus in both cases the 'D.M.' mark is placed opposite references to kings.

As this last quotation shows, despite the neat symmetry of the passages about the enclosed nations, in R1 of Pseudo-Methodius, the Last Roman Emperor does not engage Gog, Magog, and the unclean nations. Instead, God dispatches the 'one who is foremost in his army,' perhaps the archangel Michael, to dispose of them 'in an instant.' Any typological relationship between Alexander and the Last Roman Emperor fails because the Last Roman Emperor is in fact reserved for battle against the Antichrist, or 'son of perdition,' who arises immediately after the appearance of the Last Roman Emperor: 'Et post hęc descendet rex romanorum et commorabitur in ierusalem ebdomada temporum et dimidia, quod est decem annos et dimidium, id est mensibus sex temporum. Tunc apparebit filius perditionis' [fol. 19v: And after this the king of the Romans will descend, and he will dwell in Jerusalem for a week and a half of times, which is ten years and a half, which is six months of times. Then the son of perdition will appear].[22]

The 'D.M.' marks suggest an interest in eschatology that is in keeping with what we already know about the development of scriptural studies in England after the Conquest. In the late eleventh century, English cathedrals witnessed a trend towards building collections in patristics, a renewal that spread to monastic houses in the twelfth century.[23] Salisbury in particular led this trend in cathedral libraries. William of Malmesbury says in *De gestis pontificum Anglorum* that Salisbury scholars were the most renowned for learning in all of England, and the evidence of surviving manuscripts bears this out, since Salisbury leads by far, followed by Canterbury, Exeter, and Durham.[24] About half of the books at Salisbury were patristic texts, and the collection was both broad and deep, formed out of *originalia* rather than extracts.[25] In her study of Salisbury manuscripts, Webber emphasizes that 'many of the texts copied at Salisbury were either not present in England before the Conquest, or were not widely available.'[26] For the most part, Salisbury's exemplars came from Normandy rather than from other English houses. The library at Salisbury was developed according to the recommendations of Cassiodorus in Book I of his *Institutiones*, which emphasized biblical and patristic study. The Cassiodorian renewal seems to have been a cathedral phenomenon rather than a monastic one. Salisbury was the first English library to attempt the program, which was also carried out more or less simultaneously by cathedral communities in Normandy such as Mont-Saint-Michel.[27]

Nevertheless, despite the attention indicated by the 'D.M.' *notae*, the R1 text in Salisbury 165 was probably recognized as deficient for biblical study, and the 'D.M.' marks themselves may in fact provide a clue as to why the scriptorium supplied itself with the R2 in Royal 5.F.xviii. As mentioned earlier, R2 skips from the first occurrence of the Ishmaelites to their return in the last days. By ending its historical section at that point, R2 focuses only on biblical (and pseudo-biblical) history and eschatology, omitting secular history as represented in R1 by Alexander and the succession of empires. There are no enclosed nations in R2 until the last days. In both R1 and R2, the Last Roman Emperor, identified in R2 as a Christian king, arises in response to the Ishmaelites, identified in R2 as Saracens, defeats them, and ushers in a period of peace.[28] At that point, the enclosed nations break forth, led by Gog and Magog. Since Gog, Magog, and the unclean nations have not been mentioned previously in R2, it is necessary now to identify them as the progeny of Japheth. As in R1, in R2 they are destroyed in an instant by an angel, although as in Apoc. 20:9, the agent of destruction is fire.[29] Thus, R2's handling of the enclosed nations is more in keeping with scripture, where they appear only in Apoc. 20 – that is, in the last days. Indicating this is possibly part or all of the intention of the 'D.M.' *notae* in Salisbury 165's Pseudo-Methodius.

Admittedly, this argument about Salisbury 165 has moved out on a conjectural limb. But there is other evidence that R2 was preferred in Salisbury, and later in England as a whole, because unlike R1 it was specifically aimed at scriptural study. The role of the R2 of Pseudo-Methodius in patristic studies at Salisbury can be explained partly by the long version of its prologue found in many manuscripts, which authorizes itself with claims that Methodius himself translated the text from Hebrew and Greek into Latin and that Jerome praised the book:

> In Christi nomine incipit liber beati Methodii episcopi aeclesiae Pateren[s]is et martiris Christi quam [i.e., quem] de hebreo et greco in latinum transfere curavit, id est de principio seculi et interregna gentium et finem seculorum. Quem illustrissimus virorum beatus Hieronymus in suis opusculis collaudavit. (Royal 5.F.xviii, fol. 29b).[30]

> [In the name of Christ, here begins the book of the blessed Methodius, bishop of the church of Patara and martyr of Christ, which he took pains to translate from Hebrew and Greek into Latin; that is, regarding the beginning of the world, the intervening kingdoms of the peoples, and the end of the world. The blessed Jerome, most noble of men, praised this book in his minor works.]

This pious fraud (which also misleads the reader about the *interregna gentium*) surely enhanced the status of R2, not only for the Salisbury canons but for many medieval readers, because it associated Pseudo-Methodius with books by Jerome such as the *Liber interpretationis hebraicorum nominum* that were a regular part of biblical study. Some later R2 manuscripts from England even show a variant prologue in which Jerome himself is said to be the translator into Latin.[31] Significantly, the R2 prologue presents Methodius as the Latin translator of texts originally in the biblical languages Hebrew and Greek. In contrast, R1 begins with an address by an unidentified 'Petrus monachus,' whose self-presentation as a Latin translator of an originally Greek text puts the Latin R1 at a further remove from Methodius than the incipit of R2, where Methodius himself is the Latin translator:

> ... doctrina beati igitur Methodii martyris dicta de Greco in Latino transferre sermone curavi, et quoniam nostris sunt aptius prophetata temporibus, *in quos finis saeculorum*, sicut apostolus inquid, *pervenerunt* (1 Cor. 10:11) ut iam per ipsa que nostris cernimus oculis vera esset credamus ea quae praedicta sunt a patribus nostris. Propter quod magis arbitratus sum hunc libellum de Greco in Latinum vertere laboravi.[32]

> [... I have taken pains, therefore, to translate sayings from the teaching of the blessed martyr Methodius out of Greek into Latin; and (I have done this) because the prophecies are more relevant to our own times, *upon whom, as the apostle says, the end of the world has come*, so that perhaps through those truths which we witness with our own eyes we may believe those things which were foretold by our fathers. Because I have perceived more, I have laboured to turn this little book from Greek into Latin.]

The R1 in Salisbury 165 probably disqualified itself because it lacked any sort of prologue at all to explain its origin or purpose. Its title, 'Liber Methodii Incipit,' written in majuscules above the first line of text, appears to have been added as an afterthought after the folio was written, rather than incorporated into the lineation of the page. The hand is wobbly and the line of letters is crooked. Since there is no evidence that Salisbury 165 ever left Salisbury Cathedral library or that it was ever used as an exemplar for other copies at the library, it seems likely that it was deemed inadequate for scriptural study, and a proper R2, with a prologue that explained its origin and pedigree, was acquired within a short time.

Having considered Pseudo-Methodius's two oldest witnesses in England, it is necessary to caution against assuming that a text's presence can be demonstrated only by its earliest known manuscript. One way of supplementing blank spaces in the manuscript record is through citation, allusion, adaptation, and other forms of intertextuality. Tom Hill's essay on the possible influence of Pseudo-Methodius on the West Saxon royal genealogies asks if the fourth son of Noah, inserted to provide an ancestor for Heremod (the same king who figures in *Beowulf*) in the genealogies, may be at least inspired by Ionitus from the *Revelationes*.[33] According to Pseudo-Methodius, in the 300th year of the third millennium, Noah sent his son Ionitus to the land of Eoam, where he went as far as the region of the sun, and there Ionitus received wisdom directly from God. He is said to be the inventor of astronomy and the teacher of Nebroth (who perhaps represents the biblical Nimrod), a giant descended from the line of Seth, and together they ruled.[34]

The fourth son of Noah in the West-Saxon genealogies is at some remove from Pseudo-Methodius's Ionitus. Two manuscripts of the genealogies call him Hraþra and the third calls him Sceaf, and only two of the three identify this person as the son of Noah. The difference in names can be explained by genealogical manipulation.[35] All three use the same formula to identify him as being born on the ark – 'se wæs geboren on þære earce Noes' – but even though Pseudo-Methodius makes it clear that Ionitus was born after the Flood, the idea of a fourth son of Noah could hardly have come from another source.[36] The only other known possibility would be the Syriac *Book of the Cave of Treasures*, which was almost certainly unknown in England because it was never translated into Latin.[37] English monks could have seen manuscripts of Pseudo-Methodius either in their travels or by courtesy of loans. There might have been manuscripts in England before Salisbury 165 that are now lost. Whatever the case, the West-Saxon genealogies offer the tantalizing possibility that Pseudo-Methodius may have been known in England, at least indirectly, before the end of the ninth century, the date of the Parker Chronicle, even if it is not attested by manuscript evidence. If Pseudo-Methodius lies behind even a small part of the West-Saxon genealogies, then even at this early date it is being used as an aid to scriptural study rather than as an apocalypse. If it does not, at the very least the West-Saxon genealogies show an interest in the kind of information that was later satisfied by Pseudo-Methodius.

More concrete evidence of this interest, and support of the argument I have advanced about the Salisbury manuscripts of Pseudo-Methodius, may be found in the OE *Hexateuch* (or *Heptateuch*) in London, BL MS Cotton Claudius B.iv, from St Augustine's, Canterbury, a 'part-Bible' by several translators, including Ælfric, who was responsible for Genesis at least as far as chapter 22.[38] Unlike the other eight manuscripts of the *Hexateuch*, Cotton Claudius B.iv contains some thirty late OE notes and many more Latin notes, all of which were written by two hands. The general interest of these notes is historical, chronological, onomastic, and genealogical; and the notes show wide reading in Roman, Greek, Jewish, and patristic authorities. N.R. Ker dates the notes by the earlier of the two hands, which are both in OE and Latin, to the mid-twelfth century.[39] Some of the notes by this hand (but not those by the later hand) contain material from Pseudo-Methodius, use of which ceases after the rise of Ishmael (Gen. 25), since at that point the historical account in Pseudo-Methodius diverges from that of Genesis. Not coincidentally, this is also where R2 departs from R1. Again, here is Pseudo-Methodius serving not as an apocalypse but rather as a source of supplemental information about the earliest period in biblical history.

In this chapter I have offered suggestions as to how the two earliest manuscripts of Pseudo-Methodius in Salisbury during the eleventh century may explain the preference for R2 of Pseudo-Methodius in England. I have also argued that from its first appearance in the eleventh century, Pseudo-Methodius was important in England for understanding biblical history. Before the existence of the two Salisbury manuscripts that bear witness to Pseudo-Methodius in England, the West-Saxon genealogies studied by Tom Hill show interest specifically in the descendants of Noah, an interest found also in Pseudo-Methodius. Not long after R1 was replaced by R2 at Salisbury, someone at Canterbury annotated the *Hexateuch* in Cotton Claudius B.iv with Methodian material that enabled the manuscript to be used for the study of biblical history. Without a manuscript stemma it is impossible to demonstrate a direct relationship between Royal 5.F.xviii, the first known R2 in England, and later copies of Pseudo-Methodius of English origin. However, given the pre-eminence of Salisbury for scriptural study in the early Anglo-Norman period, it is at least possible that some of the extant English manuscripts of Pseudo-Methodius were copied from the Royal manuscript or from an intermediary made from it.[40]

NOTES

1 *Die syrische Apokalypse des Pseudo-Methodius*, ed. G.J. Reinink, 2 vols, CSCO 540–1, Scriptores Syri 220–1 (Leuven: Peeters, 1993), 1:xii–xxix.
2 *Die Apokalypse des Pseudo-Methodius: Die ältesten griechischen und lateinischen Übersetzungen*, ed. Willem J. Aerts and George A.A. Kórtekaas, 2 vols, CSCO 569–70, Subsidia 97–8 (Leuven: Peeters, 1998), 1:1–35.
3 Greek manuscripts are listed in W.J. Aerts, 'Zu einer neuen Ausgabe der

"Revelationes" des Pseudo-Methodius (Syrisch-Griechisch-Lateinisch),' in *XXIV. Deutscher Orientalistentag vom 26. bis 30. September 1988 in Köln ausgewählte Vorträge*, ed. Werner Diem and Abdoldjavad Falaturi (Stuttgart: F. Steiner, 1990), 123–30. Latin manuscripts are listed in Marc Laureys and Daniel Verhelst, 'Pseudo-Methodius, *Revelationes:* Textgeschichte und Kritische Edition; Ein Leuven-Groninger Forschungsprojekt,' in *The Use and Abuse of Eschatology in the Middle Ages*, ed. Werner Verbeke, Daniel Verhelst, and Andries Welkenhuysen, Mediaevalia Lovaniensia ser. 1, Studia 15 (Leuven: Leuven University Press, 1988), 112–36.

4 Anastasios Lolos, ed., *Die Apokalypse des Ps. Methodios*, Beiträge zur klassischen Philologie 83 (Meisenheim am Glan: Hain, 1976), 4, 26–40; Laureys and Verhelst, 'Pseudo-Methodius, *Revelationes*'; Otto Prinz, 'Eine frühe abendländische Aktualisierung der lateinischen Übersetzung des Pseudo-Methodios,' *DA* 41 (1985): 1–23 at 4–5.

5 On Pseudo-Methodius as an apocalypse, see Paul Alexander's last work, *The Byzantine Apocalyptic Tradition*, ed. Dorothy deF. Abrahamse (Berkeley and Los Angeles: University of California Press, 1985); and also Walter Emil Kaegi, Jr, 'Initial Byzantine Reactions to the Arab Conquest,' *Church History* 39 (1969): 139–49; Francisco Javier Martinez, 'The Apocalyptic Genre in Syriac: The World of Pseudo-Methodius,' in *IV Symposium Syriacum, 1984: Literary Genres in Syriac Literature, Groningen-Oosterhesselen, 10–12 September*, ed. H.J.W. Drijvers et al., Orientalia Christiana Analecta 229 (Rome: Pontifical Institute for Oriental Studies, 1987), 337–52; Hannes Möhring, *Der Weltkaiser der Endzeit: Enstehung, Wandel und Wirkung einer tausendjährigen Weissagung*, Mittelalter-Forschungen 3 (Stuttgart: Jan Thorbecke, 2000), 54–104, 136–43, 321–49; G.J. Reinink, 'Pseudo-Methodius und die Legende vom römischen Endkaiser,' in *The Use and Abuse of Eschatology*, ed. Verbeke et al., 82–111; G.J. Reinink, 'Die syrische Wurzeln der mittelalterlichen Legende vom römischen Endkaiser,' in *Non Nova sed Nove: Mélanges de civilisation médiévale dédiés à Willem Noomen*, ed. M. Gosman and J. van Os (Groningen: Bouma's Boekhuis, 1984), 195–209; David J.A. Ross, *Alexander Historiatus: A Guide to Medieval Illustrated Alexander Literature*, 2nd ed., Athenäums Monografien, Altertumswissenschaft; Beiträge zur klassischen Philologie 186 (Frankfurt am Main: Athenäum, 1988), 34–5. On Pseudo-Methodius's influence on other apocalypses, see Daniel Verhelst, 'La préhistoire des conceptions d'Adson concernant l'Antichrist,' *Recherches de théologie ancienne et médiévale* 40 (1973): 52–103 at 94–7; Hermann Josef Frede, *Kirchenschriftsteller: Verzeichnis und Sigel*, 4th ed., Vetus Latina: Die Reste der altlateinischen Bibel 1.1 (Freiburg im Breisgau: Herder, 1995), 576; and G.J. Reinink, 'Pseudo-Methodius and the Pseudo-Ephremian "Sermo

de fine mundi,'" in *Media Latinitas: A Collection of Essays to Mark the Occasion of the Retirement of L.J. Engels*, ed. R.I.A. Nip et al., Instrumenta Patristica 28 (Turnhout: Brepols, 1996), 317–21.

6 Alexander, *Byzantine Apocalyptic Tradition*, 188–9 (English translation of Syriac text, page 41); Ross, *Alexander Historiatus*, 34; Gerrit H.V. Bunt, *Alexander the Great in the Literature of Medieval Britain*, Mediaevalia Groningana 14 (Groningen: Egbert Forsten, 1994), 9. More broadly on the theme of Alexander's imprisonment of the unclean nations, see Andrew Runni Anderson, *Alexander's Gate, Gog and Magog, and the Inclosed Nations*, Medieval Academy of America Monographs 5 (Cambridge, MA: Medieval Academy of America, 1932).

7 Katharine Scarfe Beckett devotes a chapter to Pseudo-Methodius in her recent book, *Anglo-Saxon Perceptions of the Islamic World*, CSASE 33 (Cambridge: Cambridge University Press, 2003). Unfortunately, though, Beckett's argument about late Anglo-Saxon knowledge of Pseudo-Methodius is based on a mistake about the date of the text of Pseudo-Methodius in Oxford, Bodleian Library, MS Bodley 163, which she believes is eleventh-century rather than twelfth-century. The first part of Bodley 163 was known in Anglo-Saxon England (Helmut Gneuss, *Handlist of Anglo-Saxon Manuscripts: A List of Manuscripts and Manuscript Fragments Written or Owned in England up to 1100*, MRTS 241 [Tempe, AZ: Arizona Center for Medieval and Renaissance Studies, 2001], no. 555), but Pseudo-Methodius occurs in the second part of the manuscript (fols 245–8v). The false notion that Bodley 163 is entirely from the eleventh century comes from N.R. Ker, *Catalogue of Manuscripts Containing Anglo-Saxon* (1957; repr. with a Supplement, Oxford: Oxford University Press, 1990), 151, which does not distinguish parts of the manuscript. Part 2 of the manuscript has most recently been dated to the early twelfth century by Karsten Friis-Jensen and James M.W. Willoughby, *Peterborough Abbey* (London: British Library, 2001), 6 and item BP8b.

8 Charlotte D'Evelyn, 'The Middle English Metrical Version of the *Revelations* of Methodius: With a Study of the Influence of Methodius in Middle English Writings,' *PMLA* 33 (1918): 135–203 at 146; corrigenda in *PMLA* 34 (1919): 112–13.

9 To the forty-eight from England in Laureys and Verhelst, 'Pseudo-Methodius, *Revelationes*,' I can add five in English libraries: Cambridge, University Library MS Mm.V.29, item 5, fols 119v–22v (s. xii, England?); Exeter, Cathedral Library MS 3514, item 1a, pp. 1–6 (s. xiii^{med}–xiii$^{3-4}$, probably England); Salisbury, Cathedral Library MS 165, item 2, fols 11r–22r; Winchester, Cathedral Library MS 7, item 12, fols 112r–15v (s. xii/xiii–xiii^{med}, origin

undetermined); York, Cathedral Library MS XVI.Q.14 (42), item 9, fol. 58r (s. xiii, origin undetermined). Sources: C. Hardwick and H.R. Luard, *A Catalogue of the Manuscripts Preserved in the Library of the University of Cambridge*, 5 vols and an index vol. (Cambridge: Cambridge University Press, 1856–67), 4:357*; Gneuss, *Handlist*, no. 749; N.R. Ker and A.J. Piper, *Medieval Manuscripts in British Libraries*, 5 vols (Oxford: Oxford University Press, 1969–2002), 2:822, 4:585, 4:781.

10 There are one verse and two prose versions. The metrical version, in London, BL MS Stowe 953 (s. xv$^{1-2}$, Norfolk), is edited by D'Evelyn, 'The Middle English Metrical Version.' One of the prose versions, in London, BL MS Harley 1900 (s. xv) and San Marino, CA, Huntington Library MS HM 28561 (s. xv) (a manuscript unknown to Perry), is edited by Aaron Jenkins Perry, *Dialogus inter Militem et Clericum, Richard FitzRalph's Sermon 'Defensio Curatorum,' and Methodius 'Þe Bygynnyng of þe World and þe Ende of Worldes' by John Trevisa*, EETS o.s. 167 (London: Oxford University Press, 1925). Although both manuscripts contain John Trevisa's translation of Ranulf Higden's *Polychronichon*, Perry established that Trevisa was not the translator of Pseudo-Methodius. The other prose versions are in London, BL Additional MS 37049 (s. xv) and in the now-lost Burleigh House manuscript owned by the Marquises of Exeter. Further see Perry, *Dialogus*, xv–xxvii, and Gerrit H.V. Bunt, 'The Middle English Translations of the Revelations of Pseudo-Methodius,' in *Polyphonia Byzantina: Studies in Honour of Willem J. Aerts*, ed. Hero Hokwerda, Edmé R. Smits, and Marinus M. Wosthuis, with the assistance of Lia van Midden, Mediaevalia Groningana 13 (Groningen: Egbert Forsten, 1993), 131–43.

11 See my entry, 'Ps Methodius, Revelationes,' in *Sources of Anglo-Saxon Literary Culture: A Trial Version*, ed. Frederick M. Biggs, Thomas D. Hill, and Paul E. Szarmach, with the assistance of Karen Hammond, MRTS 74 (Binghamton, NY: Center for Medieval and Early Renaissance Studies, 1990), 33–4. Two other early manuscripts belong probably to the twelfth century: (1) Oxford, Bodleian Library Bodley MS 163 (Peterborough) is a composite manuscript whose text of Pseudo-Methodius is in a booklet (fols 228–49) that appears to be later than the rest of the manuscript (see above, note 7). (2) Oxford, St John's College MS 128, although dated to the beginning of the eleventh century in H.O. Coxe, *Catalogus codicum manuscriptorum qui in collegiis aulisque Oxoniensibus hodie adservantur*, 2 vols (Oxford: Oxford University Press, 1852), 38–9, is put to the second half of the twelfth century by Otto Prinz, 'Eine frühe abendländische Aktualisierung,' 4, n. 17, on the advice of Bernhard Bischoff.

12 D'Evelyn's text is a transcription of Oxford, St John's College 128 with vari-

ants from Oxford, Bodleian Library MS Bodley 163. Prinz's text is based on three continental manuscripts plus St John's 128 and London, BL MS Royal 5.F.xviii. R1 incipit: 'Sciendum namque quomodo exeuntes Adam quidem et Evam [sic] de paradiso virgines fuisse.' Oldest manuscript: Zürich, Zentralbibliothek MS C 65, fols 80v–8v (St Gall, s. viii). R2 incipit: 'Sciendum namque, fratres karissimi, quomodo in principio ...' Oldest manuscript: Trier, Stadtbibliothek MS 564/806, fols 35r–49v (s. viii[ex]).

13 Teresa Webber, *Scribes and Scholars at Salisbury Cathedral c. 1075–c. 1125*, Oxford Historical Monographs (Oxford: Clarendon, 1992), 55, 45.

14 Identification of Salisbury 165 as R1 is based on my examination of the manuscript. I am grateful to S.M. Eward, Librarian and Keeper of the Muniments, Salisbury Cathedral, for permission to see it in May 1993. The date of the Royal manuscript is from a consideration of Webber, *Scribes and Scholars*, ch. 1, and dates proposed for the other surviving manuscripts.

15 Webber, *Scribes and Scholars*, 8–30, esp. 29–30.

16 Webber, *Scribes and Scholars*, 153 (no. 48), 145–6 (no. 9), 159 (no. 5).

17 Webber, *Scribes and Scholars*, 135, 132–9, esp. 138–9.

18 Webber, *Scribes and Scholars*, 153.

19 These passages correspond to *Sibyllinische Texte und Forschungen*, ed. Ernst Sackur (Halle: Niemeyer, 1898), 72–4, 91–3.

20 These passages correspond to *Sibyllinische Texte*, ed. Sackur, 72, 74. Here and elsewhere, the text shows variants unknown to Sackur, who for the second passage reads 'In novissimis vero temporibus secundum Ezechielis prophetiam, que dicit: In novissimo die consummationes [*var.* consummacionis] mundi exiet Gog et Magog in terra Israhel' [74: Truly in the last times according to the prophecy of Ezekiel, which says: 'On the last day of the end of the world Gog and Magog will go forth into the land of Israel']. In quoting from Salisbury 165 I have normalized punctuation and capitalization, and I have silently expanded abbreviations.

21 Alexander, *Byzantine Apocalyptic Tradition*, 187.

22 The text here in Salisbury 165 at first appears incorrect, but rather it is hypercorrect where it describes the period of the Last Roman Emperor's rule. Sackur (92–3) reads: 'et domorabitur in Hierusalem septimana temporum et dimedia, quod est anni et dimedium, et cum suppleruntur decem et demedium anni, apparebit filius perditionis' [and he will make his dwelling in Jerusalem for a week and a half of times, which is of year and a half periods; and when ten and a half years are fulfilled, the son of perdition will appear]. In Sackur's text, each 'time' is a year and a half; seven of these make ten and a half years. In Salisbury 165, 'a week and a half of

times' is directly converted into ten and a half years, but then a half year is defined as six months, apparently so as to avoid confusion with the half-time period in the phrase 'week and a half of times.'

23 R.M. Thomson, 'The Norman Conquest and English Libraries,' in *The Role of the Book in Medieval Culture: Proceedings of the Oxford International Symposium 26 September–1 October 1982*, ed. Peter Ganz, 2 vols, Bibliologia 3–4 (Turnhout: Brepols, 1986), 2:27–40 at 37–9.

24 William of Malmesbury: 'Clerique undecunque litteris insignes venientes, non solum libenter retenti, sed etiam liberaliter coacti ut remanerent. Denique emicabat ibi magis quam alias canonicorum claritas, cantibus et litteratura juxta nobilium' [The monks who were most outstanding in letters, coming from all over, were not only gladly retained, but they were even freely constrained to remain. Ultimately, the renown of the celebrated canons there spread equally for singing and for literature]; quoted from *De gestis pontificum Anglorum*, ed. N.E.S.A. Hamilton, Rolls Series 52 (London: Longman, 1870), 184. On eleventh-century English copying, see N.R. Ker, *English Manuscripts in the Century after the Norman Conquest*, The Lyell Lectures 1952–3 (Oxford: Clarendon, 1960), 7–8, and Thomson, 'The Norman Conquest and English Libraries,' esp. 33. On the unusual breadth and depth of the Salisbury canons' interests, see Webber, *Scribes and Scholars*, 32–4, 42–3, 75–81. Richard Gameson compares Exeter specifically to Salisbury in 'The Origin of the Exeter Book of Old English Poetry,' *ASE* 25 (1996): 135–85 at 158–9.

25 Webber, *Scribes and Scholars*, 31–2, 35, and ch. 2.

26 Webber, *Scribes and Scholars*, 45.

27 Webber, *Scribes and Scholars*, 31–7. The renewed copying in eleventh-century England may not have been entirely due to the Norman Conquest. J.E. Cross, 'Hiberno-Latin Commentaries in Salisbury Manuscripts,' *Hiberno-Latin Newsletter* 3 (1990): 8–9, demonstrated that a number of Salisbury manuscripts contain hitherto undetected Irish exegetical material.

28 Texts are in Sackur, *Sibyllinische Texte*, 88–91 and D'Evelyn, 'Middle English Metrical Version,' 200.

29 This passage is in D'Evelyn, 'Middle English Metrical Version,' 201.

30 Quoted from George F. Warner and Julius P. Gilson, *Catalogue of Western Manuscripts in the Old Royal and King's Collections*, 4 vols (London: British Museum, 1921), 1:126. Despite its inaccuracy the phrase 'et interregna gentium' (literally, 'and the intervals between the reigns of the people') is found in other R2 prologues, such as Oxford, Bodleian Library MS Bodley 163 and Oxford, St John's College MS 128 (quoted in D'Evelyn, 'The Middle English Metrical Version,' 192). Some R2 prologues omit it – for example,

the text in Prinz, 'Eine frühe abendländische Aktualisierung,' 6. The ME prose versions use the R2 prologue, including 'et interregna gentium,' either translating the prologue entirely into English (London, BL Harley MS 1900, fol. 21b; San Marino, Calif., Huntington Library MS 28561, fol. 21a) or beginning in Latin and then switching into English (London, BL MS Additional 37049, fol. 11a). Texts are given in Perry, *Dialogus*, xv, xxv, and xxiv.

31 For example, Cambridge, University Library MS Mm.V.29, item 5 (s. xii), fol. 119v (given incorrectly as 118b in the CUL catalogue): 'Libellus Bemetoli quem beatus Jeronimus de greco in latinum transtulit vel composuit' [The little book of 'Bemetolus' that the blessed Jerome translated or put together out of Greek into Latin].

32 *Sibyllinische Texte*, ed. Sackur, 59–60. Emphases in Sackur. Vulgate (ed. Weber) 1 Cor. 10:11 reads 'in quos fines saeculorum devenerunt' [unto whom the end of the world has come].

33 Thomas D. Hill, 'The Myth of the Ark-Born Son of Noe and the West-Saxon Royal Genealogical Tables,' *Harvard Theological Review* 80 (1987): 379–83.

34 See the text of R1 in *Sibyllinische Texte*, ed. Sackur, 63–4. R2's account is essentially the same: see D'Evelyn, 'Middle English Metrical Version,' 194–5.

35 The fact that this son is born on the ark is strikingly similar to the story of the origin of Sceaf in the chronicles of Æthelweard and of William of Malmesbury. See the note to lines 4–52 in Klaeber, *Beowulf*, 123.

36 First, both recensions specify that Ionitus was born in the 612th year of Noah's life, whereas the Flood took place in Noah's 601st year. Second, both recensions are quite clear that only eight people left the ark: Noah and his wife, and their three sons and their wives. R1: 'Iam in trium milium annorum, postquam exivit Noe de arca, aedificaverunt filii Noe novam possessionem in exteriora terra et appellaverunt nomen regionis illius Thamnon secundum nuncupationem numeri, qui exierunt de archa, id est VIII. C autem anno de terciam chiliadam natus est Noe filius secundum ipsius similitudinem et vocavit nomen eius Ionitum' [Now in the 3000th year, after Noah left the ark, the sons of Noah built a new estate in a foreign land, and they named the region Thamnon after the number of those who left the ark, that is, eight. But in the 100th year of the third chiliad a son was born to Noah in his likeness, and he called him Ionitus]; *Sibyllinische Texte*, ed. Sackur, 63. R2: 'Sexcentisimo et duodecimo anno uite Noe in tercio miliario seculi reędificare cępit Noe et filii eius nouam possessionem in terram et apellauerunt regiones illas tamnon secundum nuncupationem numeri quo [sic = qui] exierunt de archa, id sunt octo. Tricentesimo autem anno in

tercio miliario seculi genuit Noe filium et uocavit nomen eius Ionitum' [In the 612th year of Noah's life, in the third millennium of the world, Noah and his sons began to build a new estate on the earth, and they called those regions Tamnon according to the number of those who left the ark, that is, eight. But in the 300th year in the third millennium Noah begat a son, and he called him Ionitus]; 'Middle English Metrical Version,' ed. D'Evelyn, 194 (repunctuation my own).

37 *The Cave of Treasures* exists only in Syriac, Arabic, and Ethiopian versions (Stephen Gero, 'The Legend of the Fourth Son of Noah,' *Harvard Theological Review* 73 [1980]: 321–30 at 323 n. 14); neither is there any evidence of indirect knowledge in Anglo-Saxon England.

38 Ker, *Catalogue*, 142, dates the OE text to s. xi[1]. Texts: *The Old English Illustrated Hexateuch*, ed. C.R. Dodwell and Peter Clemoes, EEMF 18 (Copenhagen: Rosenkilde and Bagger, 1974); Samuel J. Crawford, 'The Late Old English Notes of MS. (British Museum) Cotton Claudius B. iv,' *Anglia* 47 (1923): 124–35. See also Richard Marsden, *The Text of the Old Testament in Anglo-Saxon England*, CSASE 15 (Cambridge: Cambridge University Press, 1995), 402–16.

39 Ker, *Catalogue*, 142.

40 Earlier versions of the essay were presented at the Center for Oriental, Medieval, and Early Renaissance Studies, Rijksuniversiteit Groningen (May 1993); the First International Medieval Congress, University of Leeds (July 1994); and the 30th International Congress on Medieval Studies, Western Michigan University, Kalamazoo, Mich. (May 1995). Here I wish to thank Alasdair MacDonald, Gerrit H.V. Bunt, Gerrit Reinink, Frederick M. Biggs, and William Stoneman for information shared at various stages.

Appendix 1: Publications of Thomas D. Hill

1. 'A Note on *Flamenca*, Line 2294.' *Romance Notes* 7 (1965–6): 80–2.
2. 'La Vieille's Digression on Free Love: A Note on Rhetorical Structure in the *Romance of the Rose*.' *Romance Notes* 8 (1966–7): 113–15.
3. 'Two Notes on Patristic Allusion in *Andreas*.' *Anglia* 84 (1966): 156–62.
4. 'Dante's Palm: Purgatorio XXII: 130–135.' *MLN* 82 (1967): 103–5.
5. 'The Hypocritical Bee in the Old English "Homiletic Fragment I," Lines 18–30.' *NQ* n.s. 15 (1968): 123.
6. 'An Irish-Latin Analogue for the Blessing of the Sods in the Old English Æcer-Bot Charm.' *NQ* n.s. 15 (1968): 362–3.
7. 'Punishment According to the Joints of the Body in the Old English "Soul and Body II."' *NQ* n.s. 15 (1968): 409–10.
8. 'The Tropological Context of Heat and Cold Imagery in Anglo-Saxon Poetry.' *NM* 69 (1968): 522–32.
9. 'Angelic Movement in Bede's "Historia Ecclesiastica," IV, 3.' *NQ* n.s. 16 (1969): 44–5.
10. 'Apocryphal Cosmography and the "Stream uton Sæ": A Note on *Christ and Satan*, Lines 4–12.' *PQ* 48 (1969): 550–4.
11. 'Eve's Light Answer: *Lilja*, Stanzas 16–17.' *Mediaeval Scandinavia* 2 (1969): 129–31.
12. '"Fiat lux" and the Generation of the Son: "Christ I," 214–48.' *NQ* n.s. 16 (1969): 246–8.
13. 'Figural Narrative in *Andreas:* The Conversion of the Mermedonians.' *NM* 70 (1969): 261–73.
14. 'Notes on the Eschatology of the Old English *Christ III*.' *NM* 70 (1969): 672–9.
15. 'Punishment According to the Joints of the Body, Again.' *NQ* n.s. 16 (1969): 246.

16. 'The Seven Joys of Heaven in "Christ III" and Old English Homiletic Texts.' *NQ* n.s. 16 (1969): 165–6.
17. 'Some Remarks on "The Site of Lucifer's Throne."' *Anglia* 87 (1969): 303–11.
18. 'The Falling Leaf and Buried Treasure: Two Notes on the Imagery of *Solomon and Saturn*, 314–22.' *NM* 71 (1970): 571–6.
19. 'History and Heroic Ethic in *Maldon*.' *Neophilologus* 54 (1970): 291–6.
20. 'Notes on the Old English "Maxims" I and II.' *NQ* n.s. 17 (1970): 445–7.
21. 'Number and Pattern in *Lilja*.' *JEGP* 69 (1970): 561–7.
22. '"Byrht Word" and "Hælendes Heafod": Christological Allusion in the Old English *Christ and Satan*.' *ELN* 8 (1970–1): 6–9.
23. 'Further Notes on the Eschatology of the Old English *Christ III*.' *NM* 72 (1971): 691–8.
24. '"Hwyrftum Scriþað": *Beowulf*, Line 163.' *MS* 33 (1971): 379–81.
25. 'Sapiential Structure and Figural Narrative in the Old English "Elene."' *Traditio* 27 (1971): 159–78. Repr. in *Cynewulf: Basic Readings*, ed. Robert E. Bjork, 207–28. New York: Garland, 1996.
26. 'Two Notes on *Solomon and Saturn*.' *MÆ* 40 (1971): 217–21.
27. 'Cosmic Stasis and the Birth of Christ: The Old English *Descent into Hell*, Lines 99–106.' *JEGP* 71 (1972): 382–9.
28. 'The Old World, The Levelling of the Earth, and the Burning of the Sea: Three Eschatological Images in the Old English "Christ III."' *NQ* n.s. 19 (1972): 323–5.
29. 'Notes on the Imagery and Structure of the Old English "Christ I."' *NQ* n.s. 19 (1972): 84–9.
30. 'Satan's Fiery Speech: "Christ and Satan" 78–9.' *NQ* n.s. 19 (1972): 2–4.
31. 'The Light that Blew the Saints to Heaven: *Piers Plowman* B, V.495–503.' *RES* n.s. 24 (1973): 444–9.
32. 'Vision and Judgement in the Old English *Christ III*.' *SP* 70 (1973): 233–42.
33. Review of R.H. Bowers, *The Legend of Jonah* (The Hague: Martinus Nijhoff, 1971). *Speculum* 48 (1973): 736–7.
34. 'The "fyrst ferhðbana": Old English "Exodus," 399.' *NQ* n.s. 21 (1974): 204–5.
35. 'Narcissus, Pygmalion, and the Castration of Saturn: Two Mythographical Themes in the *Roman de la Rose*.' *SP* 71 (1974): 404–26.
36. 'Raguel and Ragnel: Notes on the Literary Genealogy of a Devil.' *Names* 22 (1974): 145–9.

37. 'Two Notes on Exegetical Allusion in Langland: *Piers Plowman* [B,] XI, 161–167, and B, I, 115–124.' *NM* 75 (1974): 92–7.
38. 'The Fall of Angels and Man in the Old English *Genesis B*.' In *Anglo-Saxon Poetry: Essays in Appreciation for John C. McGalliard*, ed. Lewis E. Nicholson and Dolores W. Frese, 279–90. Notre Dame: University of Notre Dame Press, 1975.
39. 'A Liturgical Allusion in "Piers Plowman" B.XVI: 88: Filius, bi the Fader wille and frenesse of Spiritus Sancti.' *NQ* n.s. 22 (1975): 531–2.
40. 'Parody and Theme in the Middle English "Land of Cokaygne."' *NQ* n.s. 22 (1975): 55–9.
41. 'The Typology of the Week and the Numerical Structure of the Old English *Guthlac B*.' *MS* 37 (1975): 531–6.
42. 'Davidic Typology and the Characterization of Christ: "Piers Plowman" B.XIX, 95–103.' *NQ* n.s. 23 (1976): 291–4.
43. 'Drawing the Demon's Sting: A Note on a Traditional Motif in Felix's "Vita Sancti Guthlaci."' *NQ* n.s. 23 (1976): 388–90.
44. 'Hebrews, Israelites, and Wicked Jews: An Onomastic Crux in "Andreas" 161–167.' *Traditio* 32 (1976): 358–60.
45. 'The "Syrwarena Lond" and the Itinerary of the Phoenix: A Note on Typological Allusion in the Old English "Phoenix."' *NQ* n.s. 23 (1976): 482–4.
46. 'The *æcerbot* Charm and Its Christian User.' *ASE* 6 (1977): 213–21.
47. 'The Fall of Satan in the Old English *Christ and Satan*.' *JEGP* 76 (1977): 315–25.
48. 'A Liturgical Source for *Christ I* 164–213 (Advent Lyric VII).' *MÆ* 46 (1977): 12–15.
49. Preface to William O. Stevens, *The Cross in the Life and Literature of the Anglo-Saxons*, Yale Studies in English 22 (1904), repr. in *The Anglo-Saxon Cross*, 3–6. Hamden, CT: Archon Books, 1977.
50. Review of John Gardner, *The Construction of Christian Poetry in Old English* (Carbondale: Southern Illinois University Press, 1975). *Anglia* 95 (1977): 498–500.
51. Review of Micheline M. Larès, *Bible et civilisation anglaise: naissance d'une tradition (Ancien Testament)* (Paris: Didier, 1974). *MÆ* 46 (1977): 292–3.
52. 'Christ's "Thre Clothes": "Piers Plowman" C.XI. 193.' *NQ* n.s. 25 (1978): 200–3.
53. 'Dunbar's Giant: "On the Resurrection of Christ," Lines 17–24.' *Anglia* 96 (1978): 451–6.
54. '"Half-Waking, Half-Sleeping": A Tropological Motif in a Middle English Lyric and Its European Context.' *RES* n.s. 29 (1978): 50–6.

55. 'The Theme of the Cosmological Cross in Two Old English Cattle Theft Charms.' *NQ* n.s. 25 (1978): 488–90.
56. Review of Stephen A. Barney, *Word-Hoard: An Introduction to Old English Vocabulary* (New Haven: Yale University Press, 1977). *Speculum* 53 (1978): 786.
57. Review of Daniel G. Calder and Michael J.B. Allen, *Sources and Analogues of Old English Poetry: The Major Latin Texts in Translation* (Cambridge: D.S. Brewer, 1976). *NQ* n.s. 25 (1978): 247–8.
58. Review of T.A. Shippey, *Poems of Wisdom and Learning in Old English* (Totowa, NJ: Rowman and Littlefield, 1976). *Speculum* 53 (1978): 630–1.
59. 'The Fool on the Bridge: "Can vei la lauzeta mover," Stanza 5.' *MÆ* 48 (1979): 198–200.
60. 'The Middle Way: *Idel-wuldor* and *Egesa* in the Old English *Guthlac A*.' *RES* n.s. 30 (1979): 182–7.
61. 'The Return of the Broken Butterfly: *Beowulf*, Line 163, Again.' *Mediaevalia* 5 (1979): 271–81.
62. Review of W.F. Bolton, *Alcuin and Beowulf: An Eighth-Century View* (New Brunswick, NJ: Rutgers University Press, 1978). *JEGP* 78 (1979): 408–9.
63. 'Bethania, the House of Obedience: The Old English *Christ II*, 456–67.' *NQ* n.s. 27 (1980): 290–2.
64. 'The Blood of Elias and the Fire of Doom: A New Analogue for *Muspilli*, vss. 52 ff.' *NM* 81 (1980): 439–42. [With Arthur Groos.]
65. 'Bread and Stone, Again: "Elene" 611–18.' *NM* 81 (1980): 252–7.
66. 'Gawain's Jesting Lie: Towards an Interpretation of the Confessional Scene in *Gawain and the Green Knight*.' *SN* 52 (1980): 279–86.
67. 'The *Virga* of Moses and the Old English *Exodus*.' In *Old English Literature in Context: Ten Essays*, ed. John D. Niles, 57–65, 165–7. Cambridge: D.S. Brewer, 1980.
68. 'The Age of Man and the World in the Old English *Guthlac A*.' *JEGP* 80 (1981): 13–21.
69. 'The Evisceration of Bróðir in "Brennu-Njáls Saga."' *Traditio* 37 (1981): 437–44.
70. 'The First Beginning and the Purest Earth: *Guthlac B*, Lines 1–14.' *NQ* n.s. 28 (1981): 387–9.
71. 'Invocation of the Trinity and the Tradition of the *Lorica* in Old English Poetry.' *Speculum* 56 (1981): 259–67.
72. 'The Measure of Hell: *Christ and Satan* 695–772.' *PQ* 60 (1981): 409–14.
73. Review of Graham D. Caie, *The Judgment Day Theme in Old*

English Poetry, Publications of the Department of English, University of Copenhagen 2 (Copenhagen: Nova, 1976). *Anglia* 99 (1981): 490–2.
74. 'Adam's Noon: Paradiso XXVI, 139–42.' *Dante Studies* 100 (1982): 93–7.
75. 'The Confession of Beowulf and the Structure of *Volsunga Saga*.' In *The Vikings*, ed. R.T. Farrell, 165–79. London and Chichester: Phillimore, 1982.
76. *The 'Prose Solomon and Saturn' and 'Adrian and Ritheus*.' McMaster Old English Studies and Texts 1. Toronto: University of Toronto Press, 1982. [With J.E. Cross.]
77. 'The Seraphim's Song: The "Sanctus" in the Old English "Christ I," Lines 403–415.' *NM* 83 (1982): 26–30.
78. Review of *Ælfric's Catholic Homilies: The Second Series. Text*, ed. Malcolm Godden, EETS s.s. 5 (London: Oxford University Press, 1979). *JEGP* 81 (1982): 404–5.
79. Review of *Ivens Saga*, ed. Foster W. Blaisdell. Editiones Arnamagnaeanae, B, 18 (Copenhagen: C.A. Reitzel, 1979). *JEGP* 81 (1982): 527–8.
80. Review of Priscilla Martin, *Piers Plowman: The Field and the Tower* (London: Macmillan, 1979). *NQ* n.s. 29 (1982): 240–1.
81. 'Longinus, Charlemagne, and Oðinn: William of Malmesbury, *De Gestis Regum Anglorum* II, 135.' *Saga-Book of the Viking Society* 21 (1982–3): 80–4.
82. 'The Middle English Lyric "How Christ Shall Come": An Interpretation.' *MÆ* 52 (1983): 239–46.
83. '*VIII Genitus Homo* as a Nomen Sacrum in a Twelfth-Century Anglo-Latin Fever Charm.' *NQ* n.s. 30 (1983): 487–8.
84. 'The *Sphragis* as Apotropaic Sign: *Andreas* 1334–44.' *Anglia* 101 (1983): 147–51.
85. 'Satan's Injured Innocence in *Genesis B*, 360–2; 390–2: A Gregorian Source.' *ES* 65 (1984): 289–90.
86. Review of D.W. Robertson, *Essays in Medieval Culture* (Princeton: Princeton University Press, 1980). *ELN* 21 (1984): 63–5.
87. 'The Kingdom of the Father, Son and Counsellor: *Judgement Day II*, 290–300.' *NQ* n.s. 32 (1985): 7–8.
88. 'When God Blew Satan out of Heaven: The Motif of Exsufflation in *Vercelli Homily XIX* and Later English Literature.' *Leeds Studies in English* n.s. 16 [*Sources and Relations: Studies in Honour of J.E. Cross*, ed. Marie Collins, Jocelyn Price, and Andrew Hamer] (1985): 132–41.

89. Review of John V. Fleming, *Reason and the Lover* (Princeton: Princeton University Press, 1984). *Speculum* 60 (1985): 973–7.
90. Review of John D. Niles, *Beowulf: The Poem and Its Tradition* (Cambridge, MA: Harvard University Press, 1983). *JEGP* 84 (1985): 540–3.
91. Review of Charles R. Sleeth, *Studies in 'Christ and Satan,'* McMaster Old English Studies and Texts 3 (Toronto: University of Toronto Press, 1982). *Speculum* 60 (1985): 230–1.
92. 'Androgyny and Conversion in the Middle English Lyric, "In the Vaile of Restles Mynd."' *ELH* 53 (1986): 459–70.
93. 'Literary History and Old English Poetry: The Case of *Christ I, II,* and *III.*' In *Sources of Anglo-Saxon Culture*, ed. Paul E. Szarmach with the assistance of Virginia D. Oggins, 3–22. Studies in Medieval Culture 20. Kalamazoo: Medieval Institute Publications, 1986.
94. *Magister Regis: Studies in Honor of Robert Earl Kaske*, ed. Arthur Groos with Emerson Brown, Jr, Giuseppe Mazzotta, Thomas D. Hill, and Joseph S. Wittig. New York: Fordham University Press, 1986.
95. '"Mary, the Rose Bush" and the Leaps of Christ.' *ES* 67 (1986): 478–82.
96. 'Odin, Rinda and Thaney, the Mother of St. Kentigern.' *MÆ* 55 (1986): 230–7.
97. '*Rígsþula:* Some Medieval Christian Analogues.' *Speculum* 61 (1986): 79–89. Repr. in *The Poetic Edda: Essays on Old Norse Mythology*, ed. Paul Acker and Carolyne Larrington, 229–43. New York: Routledge, 2002.
98. 'Scyld Scefing and the *stirps regia:* Pagan Myth and Christian Kingship in *Beowulf.*' In *Magister Regis: Studies in Honor of Robert Earl Kaske*, ed. Arthur Groos with Emerson Brown, Jr, Giuseppe Mazzotta, Thomas D. Hill, and Joseph S. Wittig, 37–47. New York: Fordham University Press, 1986.
99. 'Enide's Colored Horse and Salernitan Color Theory: *Erec et Enide*, lines 5268–81.' *Romania* 108 (1987): 523–7.
100. '"Hirundines Habent Quidem Prescium": Why Henryson's "Preaching of a Swallow" Is Preached by a Swallow.' *Scottish Literary Journal Supplement* 26 (1987): 30–1.
101. 'The Myth of the Ark-Born Son of Noe and the West-Saxon Royal Genealogical Tables.' *Harvard Theological Review* 80 (1987): 379–83.
102. 'Seth the "Seeder" in *Piers Plowman* C.10.249.' *YLS* 1 (1987): 105–8.

103. Review of J.A. Burrow, *The Ages of Man: A Study in Medieval Writing and Thought* (Oxford: Clarendon, 1988). *Studies in the Age of Chaucer* 9 (1987): 198–9.
104. Review of *Duggals Leiðsla*, ed. Peter Cahill (Reykjavík: Stofnun Arna Magnússonar, 1983). *JEGP* 86 (1987): 82–3.
105. 'The Devil's Forms and the Pater Noster's Powers: "The Prose Solomon and Saturn *Pater Noster* Dialogue" and the Motif of the Transformation Combat.' *SP* 85 (1988): 164–76.
106. 'Saturn's Time Riddle: An Insular Latin Analogue for *Solomon and Saturn II*, lines 282–291.' *RES* n.s. 39 (1988): 273–6.
107. 'The "Variegated Obit" as an Historiographic Motif in Old English Poetry and Anglo-Latin Historical Literature.' *Traditio* 44 (1988): 101–24.
108. 'Woden as "Ninth-Father": Numerical Patterning in Some Old English Royal Genealogies.' In *Germania: Comparative Studies in the Old Germanic Languagues and Literatures*, ed. Daniel G. Calder and T. Craig Christy, 161–74. Woodbridge, Suffolk: D.S. Brewer, 1988.
109. Review Essay, 'Old English Catalogue Poems' [Nicholas Howe, *The Old English Catalogue Poems*, Anglistica 23 (Copenhagen: Rosenkilde and Bagger, 1985)]. *Papers on Language & Literature* 24 (1988): 448–9.
110. Review of A.J. Minnis, *Medieval Theory of Authorship: Scholastic Literary Attitudes in the Later Middle Ages* (London: Scolar Press, 1984). *Anglia* 106 (1988): 496–7.
111. 'Gestr's "Prime Sign": Source and Signification in *Norna-Gests þáttr*.' *Arkiv för nordisk Filologi* 104 (1989): 103–22. [With Joseph Harris.]
112. 'In Memoriam: Robert E. Kaske (1921–89).' *OEN* 23.1 (1989): 14.
113. 'Beowulf as Seldguma: *Beowulf*, lines 247–51.' *Neophilologus* 74 (1990): 637–9.
114. '"The Green Path to Paradise" in Nineteenth-Century Ballad Tradition.' *NM* 91 (1990): 483–6.
115. Introduction to *Sources of Anglo-Saxon Literary Culture: A Trial Version*. Medieval and Renaissance Texts and Studies 74, ed. Frederick M. Biggs, Thomas D. Hill, and Paul E. Szarmach, xv–xxix. Binghamton, NY: CEMERS, SUNY Binghamton, 1990. [Reprinted in revised form in no. 151.]
116. *Sources of Anglo-Saxon Literary Culture: A Trial Version*. Medieval and Renaissance Texts and Studies 74, ed. Frederick M. Biggs,

Thomas D. Hill, and Paul E. Szarmach. Binghamton, NY: CEMERS, SUNY Binghamton, 1990.
117. '"Wealhtheow" as a Foreign Slave: Some Continental Analogues.' *PQ* 69 (1990): 106–12.
118. 'Jaufré, Pwyll and the Receding Lady: An Essay on Comparative Horsemanship.' *French Studies Bulletin: A Quarterly Supplement* 37.1 (1990–1): 1–3.
119. 'Universal Salvation and Its Literary Context in *Piers Plowman* B.18.' *YLS* 5 [R.E. Kaske memorial issue] (1991): 65–76.
120. Review of John A. Alford, *A Companion to Piers Plowman* (Berkeley and Los Angeles: University of California Press, 1988). *Anglia* 109 (1991): 490–4.
121. Review of C. William Marx and Jeanne F. Drennan, *The Middle English Prose Complaint of Our Lady and Gospel of Nichodemus, Ed. from Cambridge, Magdalene College, MS Pepys 2498*. Middle English Texts 19 (Heidelberg: Carl Winter 1987). *Speculum* 66 (1991): 666–7.
122. 'CETEDOC and the Transformation of Anglo-Saxon Studies.' *OEN* 26.1 (1992): 46–8.
123. 'Delivering the Damned in Old English Anonymous Homilies and Jón Arason's *Ljómur*.' *MÆ* 61 (1992): 75–82.
124. 'The Edified Christian: *Piers Plowman* B.1.90.' *YLS* 6 (1992): 137–40.
125. Review of Judith N. Garde, *Old English Poetry in Medieval Christian Perspective: A Doctrinal Approach* (Woodbridge, Suffolk: D.S. Brewer, 1991). *MÆ* 61(1992): 309–10.
126. 'The Cross as Symbolic Body: An Anglo-Latin Liturgical Analogue to *The Dream of the Rood*.' *Neophilologus* 77 (1993): 297–301.
127. 'The Foreseen Wolf and the Path of Wisdom: Proverbial and Beast Lore in *Atlakviða*.' *Neophilologus* 77 (1993): 675–7.
128. 'Tormenting the Devil with Boiling Drops: An Apotropaic Motif in the Old English *Solomon and Saturn I* and Old Norse-Icelandic Literature.' *JEGP* 92 (1993): 157–66.
129. 'The Anchor of Hope and the Sea of This World: *Christ II*, 850–66.' *ES* 75 (1994): 289–92.
130. 'The Christian Language and Theme of *Beowulf*.' In *Companion to Old English Poetry*, ed. Henk Aertsen and Rolf H. Bremmer, Jr, 63–77. Amsterdam: Vrije University Press, 1994. Repr. in *Beowulf: A Verse Translation*. Trans. Seamus Heaney, ed. Daniel Donoghue, 197–211. Norton Critical Editions. New York: Norton, 2002.

131. 'The Genealogy of Galahad and the New Age of the World in the Old French Prose *Queste del Saint Graal.*' *PQ* 73 (1994): 287–97.
132. Review of Robert Boenig, *Saint and Hero: 'Andreas' and Medieval Doctrine* (Lewisburg, PA: Bucknell University Press, 1991). *Speculum* 69 (1994): 1123–4.
133. 'Guðlaugr Snorrason: The Red Faced Saint and the Refusal of Violence.' *Scandinavian Studies* 67 (1995): 145–52.
134. 'The Red Faced Saint, Again.' *Scandinavian Studies* 67 (1995): 544–7.
135. '"The Wolf Doesn't Care": The Proverbial and Traditional Context of Laȝamon's *Brut* Lines 10624–36.' *RES* n.s. 46 (1995): 41–8. [With Susan E. Deskis.]
136. Review of Mary Clayton, *The Cult of the Virgin Mary in Anglo-Saxon England*, CSASE 2 (Cambridge: Cambridge University Press, 1990). *RES* n.s. 46 (1995): 385–7.
137. '*Imago Dei:* Genre, Symbolism and Anglo-Saxon Hagiography.' In *Holy Men and Holy Women: Old English Prose Saints' Lives and Their Contexts*, ed. Paul E. Szarmach, 35–50. Albany, NY: SUNY Press, 1996.
138. 'In Memoriam: James E. Cross." *OEN* 30.1 (1996): 13. [With Charles D. Wright.]
139. 'R.E. Kaske, *Medieval Christian Literary Imagery:* A Review of Reviews.' *Mediaevalia* 22 (1996): 261–72.
140. Review of Joseph D. Wine, *Figurative Language in Cynewulf: Defining Aspects of a Poetic Style* (Frankfurt am Main: Peter Lang, 1993). *Medievalia et Humanistica* 23 (1996): 189–91.
141. Review of *The Old English Version of the Gospels*, vol. 1, ed. R.M. Liuzza, EETS o.s. 304 (Oxford: Oxford University Press, 1994). *Bryn Mawr Medieval Review* 96.10.05 [on-line journal, current title *The Medieval Review,* http://name.umdl.umich.edu/baj9928.9610.005].
142. 'The *Liber Eliensis* "Historical Selections" and the Old English *Battle of Maldon.*' *JEGP* 96 (1997): 1–12.
143. Review of Sam Newton, *The Origins of 'Beowulf' and the Pre-Viking Kingdom of East Anglia* (Woodbridge, Suffolk: Boydell and Brewer, 1993). *Speculum* 72 (1997): 541–3.
144. 'James E. Cross' [Obituary]. *Speculum* 73 (1998): 958–9. [With Susan E. Deskis and Charles D. Wright.]
145. 'Two Notes on the Old Frisian "Fia-Eth."' *Amsterdamer Beiträge*

zur älteren Germanistik 49 [*Approaches to Old Frisian Philology*, ed. Rolf H. Bremmer Jr et al.] (1998): 169–78.
146. 'Wisdom (Sapiential) Literature.' In *Medieval England: An Encyclopedia*, ed. Paul E. Szarmach, M. Teresa Tavormina, and Joel T. Rosenthal, 805–7. New York: Garland, 1998.
147. 'Satan's Pratfall and the Foot of Love: Some Pedal Images in *Piers Plowman* A, B, and C.' *YLS* 14 (2000): 153–61.
148. Review of *Judith*, ed. Mark Griffith, Exeter Medieval Texts and Studies (Exeter: University of Exeter Press, 1997). *Speculum* 75 (2000): 932–3.
149. '"The Ballad of St Steven and Herod": Biblical History and Medieval Popular Religious Culture.' *MÆ* 70 (2001): 240–9.
150. '"Dumb David': Silence and Zeal in Lady Church's Speech, *Piers Plowman* C. 2.30–40.' *YLS* 15 (2001): 203–11.
151. Introduction to *Sources of Anglo-Saxon Literary Culture I: Abbo of Fleury, Abbo of Saint-Germain-des-Prés and Acta Sanctorum*, ed. Frederick M. Biggs, Thomas D. Hill, Paul E. Szarmach and E. Gordon Whatley, xv–xxxiii. Kalamazoo, MI: Western Michigan University, 2001. [Revised and expanded version of no. 115.]
152. 'The Problem of Synecdochic Flesh: *Piers Plowman* B. 9.49–50.' *YLS* 15 (2001): 213–18.
153. 'A Riddle on the Three Orders in the *Collectanea Pseudo-Bedae*?' *PQ* 80 (2001): 205–12.
154. *Sources of Anglo-Saxon Literary Culture I: Abbo of Fleury, Abbo of Saint-Germain-des-Prés, and Acta Sanctorum*, ed. Frederick M. Biggs, Thomas D. Hill, Paul E. Szarmach, and E. Gordon Whatley. Kalamazoo, MI: Medieval Institute Publications, 2001.
155. '"When the Leader is Brave ...": An Old English Proverb and Its Vernacular Context.' *Anglia* 119 (2001): 232–6.
156. '*Consilium et Auxilium* and the Lament for Æschere: A Lordship Formula in *Beowulf.*' *The Haskins Society Journal* 12 (2002): 71–82.
157. 'The Crowning of Alfred and the Topos of *Sapientia et Fortitudo* in Asser's *Life of King Alfred.*' *Neophilologus* 86 (2002): 471–6.
158. 'Green and Filial Love: Two Notes on the Russell-Kane C Text: C. 8.215 and C.17.48.' *YLS* 16 (2002): 67–83.
159. '"Leger weardiað": *The Wife's Lament* 34b.' *ANQ* 15.2 (2002): 34–7.
160. 'The Old English Dough Riddle and the Power of Women's Magic: The Traditional Context of Exeter Book Riddle No. 45.' In *Via Crucis: Essays in Early Medieval Sources and Ideas in Memory of J.E. Cross*, ed. Thomas N. Hall with assistance from Thomas D.

Hill and Charles D. Wright, 50–60. Medieval European Studies 1. Morgantown: West Virginia University Press, 2002 [2nd corrected impression, 2002].
161. 'Pilate's Visionary Wife and the Innocence of Eve: An Old Saxon Source for the Old English *Genesis B.*' *JEGP* 101 (2002): 170–84.
162. 'The Swift Samaritan's Journey: Piers Plowman C XVIII-XIX.' *Anglia* 120 (2002): 184–99.
163. *Via Crucis: Essays in Early Medieval Sources and Ideas in Memory of J. E. Cross*, ed. Thomas N. Hall with asssistance from Thomas D. Hill and Charles D. Wright. Medieval European Studies 1. Morgantown: West Virginia University Press, 2002. [2nd corrected impression, 2002.]
164. Review of *Beowulf: An Edition with Relevant Shorter Texts*, ed. Bruce Mitchell and Fred C. Robinson (Oxford: Blackwell, 1998). *JEGP* 101 (2002): 437–8.
165. Review of Elaine M. Treharne, ed., *The Old English Life of St. Nicholas with the Old English Life of St. Giles*, Leeds Texts and Monographs N.S. 15 (Leeds: Leeds Studies in English, 1997). *Speculum* 77 (2002): 258–9.
166. '"Quhen Sabot all jugis": Dunbar's "The Tretis of the Tua Mariit Wemen and the Wedo," Lines 501–502.' *NQ* n.s. 51 (2003): 19–20.
167. '"The longe man ys seld wys": Proverbial Characterization and Langland's Long Will.' *YLS* 18 (2004): 73–9. [With Susan E. Deskis.]
168. 'The Unchanging Hero: A Stoic Maxim in *The Wanderer* and Its Contexts.' *SP* 101 (2004): 233–49.
169. Review of *J.R.R. Tolkien, Beowulf and the Critics*, ed. Michael D.C. Drout, Medieval and Renaissance Texts and Studies 248 (Tempe, AZ: Arizona Center for Medieval and Renaissance Studies, 2002). *Speculum* 79 (2004): 342–4.
170. Review of Alfred P. Smyth, *The Medieval Life of King Alfred the Great: A Translation and Commentary on the Text Attributed to Asser* (Basingstoke, Eng.: Palgrave, 2002). *Speculum* 79 (2004): 1144–5.
171. 'Adam, "The Fyrste Stocke" and the Political Context of Chaucer's *Gentilesse.*' In *"Seyd in forme and reverence": Essays on Chaucer and Chaucerians in Memory of Emerson Brown, Jr*, ed. T.L. Burton and John F. Plummer, 145–50. Provo, UT: The Chaucer Studio Press, 2005.
172. 'Annunciation, Birth, and Stasis: An Interpretation of a Faroese Marian/Lorica Ballad.' *Scandinavian Studies* 77 (2005): 439–50.

173. 'The Failing Torch: The Old English *Elene*, 1256–1259.' *NQ* n.s. 52 (2005): 155–60.
174. 'The "palmtwigede" Pater Noster: Horticultural Semantics and the Old English *Solomon and Saturn I*.' *MÆ* 74 (2005): 1–9.
175. '*Stet Verbum Regis:* Why Henryson's Husbandman Is Not a King.' *ES* 86 (2005): 127–32.
176. 'Wise Words: Old English Sapiential Poetry.' In *Readings in Medieval Texts: Interpreting Old and Middle English Literature*, ed. David F. Johnson and Elaine Treharne, 166–82. Oxford: Oxford University Press, 2005.
177. '"When God Whistled for Chickens": Birds and Poverty in *Piers Plowman* B. 15.462–82.' *YLS* 19 (2005): 45–58.
178. '"Non nisi uirgam tantum ... in manu": Sigeberht's Mosaic Aspirations (Bede, Historia Ecclesiastica III, 18).' *NQ* n.s. 53 (2006): 391–5.
179. 'Beowulf's Roman Rites: Roman Ritual and Germanic Tradition.' *JEGP* 106 (2007): 325–35.
180. 'Perchta the Belly Slitter and *Án hrísmagi: Laxdœla saga* cap. 48–49.' *JEGP* 106 (2007): 516–23.

Appendix 2: Dissertations Directed by Thomas D. Hill (all at Cornell University; through 2006)

1. Golden, John Thomas. 'Societal Bonds in Old English Heroic Poetry: A Legal and Typological Study' (1970).
2. Silver, Barbara Ellen Levy. 'A Critical Review of Anglo-Saxon Metrical Theory' (1970).
3. Earl, James Whitby. 'Literary Problems in Early Medieval Hagiography' (1971).
4. Tate, George Sheldon. '"Líknarbraut": A Skaldic "Drápa" on the Cross' (1974).
5. Wright, Charles Darwin. 'Irish and Anglo-Saxon Literary Culture: Insular Christian Traditions in Vercelli Homily IX and the Theban Anchorite Legend' (1984).
6. Biggs, Frederick Massey. 'Studies in the Sources of the Old English "Christ III"' (1987).
7. Stillinger, Thomas Clifford. 'Authorized Song: Lyric Poetry and the Medieval Book' (1988).
8. Morey, James Henry. '"Coram laycis": Spreading the Word in Early Middle English' (1990). [Director of record, †R.E. Kaske.]
9. Schaffner, Paul Frederick. 'The Ethics of Body and Soul in "Sir Gawain and the Green Knight"' (1990).
10. Johnson, David Frame. 'Studies in the Literary Career of the Fallen Angels: The Devil and His Body in Old English Literature' (1993).
11. Wallace, Dorothy Patricia. 'Religious Women and Their Men: Images of the Feminine in Anglo-Saxon Literature' (1994).
12. Redinbo, Emily Cooney. 'Reception, Revision, and Sacred Authority: A Literary Analysis of the Old English Bede' (1995).
13. Sheppard, Alice Juanita. 'Chronicled Communities: Narratives of Kingdom-Making, 850–1250' (1997).

14. Mangina, Elisa Miller. 'Selfhood and the Psalms: The First-Person Voice in Old English Poetry' (2002).
15. Kramer, Johanna. 'The Poetics of Materiality in Anglo-Saxon England: Religion and Material Reality in the *Æcerbot* Charm, Ascension Homilies, and *Christ I*' (2006).

Contributors

Frederick M. Biggs is Professor of English at the University of Connecticut at Storrs.

Susan E. Deskis is Associate Professor of English at Northern Illinois University.

James W. Earl is Professor of English at the University of Oregon.

Andrew Galloway is Professor of English and Medieval Studies at Cornell University.

Thomas N. Hall is Associate Professor of English at the University of Notre Dame.

Joseph Harris is Francis Lee Higginson Professor of English Literature and Professor of Folklore at Harvard University.

Michael W. Herren is Distinguished Research Professor emeritus, Classical Studies, York University, and Graduate Programme in Medieval Studies, University of Toronto.

David F. Johnson is Professor of English and Chair of the Department of Interdisciplinary Humanities at Florida State University and Executive Director of the International Society of Anglo-Saxonists.

Johanna Kramer is Assistant Professor of English at the University of Missouri-Columbia.

James W. Marchand is Professor emeritus of Germanic Languages and Literatures at the University of Illinois at Urbana-Champaign.

James H. Morey is Associate Professor of English at Emory University.

Danuta Shanzer is Professor of Classics and Medieval Studies at the University of Illinois at Urbana-Champaign.

Alice Sheppard, formerly Associate Professor of English and Comparative Literature at Penn State University, is a member of Axis Dance Company.

Sachi Shimomura is Associate Professor of English at Virginia Commonwealth University.

Paul E. Szarmach is Professor emeritus of English and Medieval Studies at Western Michigan University and Executive Director of The Medieval Academy of America.

Michael W. Twomey is Charles A. Dana Professor of Humanities and Professor of English at Ithaca College.

E. Gordon Whatley is Professor of English at Queens College and The Graduate Center, CUNY.

Joseph Wittig is Professor of English at the University of North Carolina at Chapel Hill.

Charles D. Wright is Professor of English and Medieval Studies at the University of Illinois at Urbana-Champaign.

Index

Index of Manuscripts

[Excludes manuscripts of glosses on Boethius, *De consolatione Philosophiae*, cited only by sigla or in abbreviated form in Wittig, pages 168–83 and 196–200, or listed only in Wittig, Appendices A–C, pages 184–96]

Bern, Burgerbibliothek **A.92.7**, 197n5; **455**, 197n5
Burleigh House manuscript of Pseudo-Methodius, *Revelationes* (lost), 382n10
Cambridge, Trinity College **O.3.7**, 155, 158, 159, 160–1
Cambridge, University Library **Kk.3.21**, 155, 156, 158, 159, 160–1, 166n29; **Mm.V.29**, 381n9, 385n31
Chicago, Newberry Library **1**, 258n7
Dublin, Trinity College **58** (Book of Kells), 72, 98, 91, 99–104, 109n34, 110n37, 111n45;
Durham, Cathedral Library **C.III.18**, 162n3
Exeter, Cathedral Library **3501** (The Exeter Book), 58n15, 106n9; **3514**, 381n9
Florence, Biblioteca Medicea Laurenziana **San Marco 170**, 200n39
Lady Meux **4** manuscript of Ethiopian *History of Hannâ* (untraced), 278–80
London, British Library: **Add. 37049**, 382n10, 385n30; **Cotton Claudius B.iv**, 378–9; **Cotton Julius E.vii**, 219, 232n10; **Cotton Otho A.vi**, 164n11; **Cotton Vitellius A.xv** (*Beowulf* manuscript), 52–9; **Harley 652**, 258n9; **Harley 1900**, 382n10, 385n30; **Harley 2684**, 200n39; **Henry Davis Collection 59 (M 30)**, 58n15; **Royal 5.F.xviii**, 371, 372, 375, 376, 383n12; **Stowe 953**, 382n10
Melk, Benediktinerstift **432 [218]**, 258–9n10
Orléans, Bibliothèque municipale **270**, 197n4
Oxford, Bodleian Library **Bodley 163**, 381n7, 382n11, 383n12, 384n30; **Junius 85/86**, 239
Oxford, St John's College **128**, 382n11, 383n12, 384n30

Paris, Bibliothèque nationale **lat. 6115**, 162n3; **6401A**, 155, 156; **15090**, 171; Bibliothèque Sainte-Geneviève **2410**, 261n31
Rome, Biblioteca Vallicelliana **III**, 257n1; **XXVI**, 257n1
Salisbury, Cathedral Library **165**, 371–7, 381n9, 383nn14, 20, 22
San Marino, CA, Huntington Library **HM 28561**, 382n10, 385n30
Trier, Stadtbibliothek **564/806**, 383n12; **1093**, 171–2, 198–9n21
Winchester, Cathedral Library **7**, 381–2n9
York, Cathedral Library **XVI.Q.14 (42)**, 382n9
Zürich, Zentralbibliothek **C 65**, 383n12

General Index

Abbo of Fleury: *Passio Eadmundi*, 218, 226, 227, 228
Abel. *See* Cain and Abel
Accursius, 294
Acheron, River, 357
Adalbold of Utrecht: glosses on Boethius, *De consolatione Philosophiae*, 193
Adam, 240, 276, 278, 280, 299–300; created from 'virginal earth,' 259n12, 261n30
Adils (= Eadgils in *Beowulf*), 48n23
Adomnán, 355
Ado of Vienne: *Martyrologium*, 263n40
Adrian and Ritheus, 266–89. See also *Solomon and Saturn* (prose)
Adso of Moutier-en-Der: *Libellus de Antichristo*, 371

Advent, liturgy of, 80–1, 91, 97, 105–6n4; Greater or O antiphons, 91, 102, 104, 106n9
Advent Lyrics. See *Christ I*
Ælfric of Eynsham, 63–79, 94, 96, 103, 108n22, 208, 217–38, 239, 314, 351n77
– *Catholic Homilies:* **I.1** (*De initio creaturae*), 74; **I.7** (Epiphany), 107n17; **I.20** (*De fide catholica*), 74, 75, 79n26; **I.21** (Ascension), 253–4, 262n37, 315; **I.30** (Assumptio Mariae), 237n49; **II.1** (Christmas), 263n38; **II.6** (Sexagesima), 208–9, 254, 262n36, 264n45; **II.45** (*In dedicatione ecclesiae*), 98, 107n17, 109n28
– Letters: Letter to Sigeweard, 221; Letter 1 to Wulfsige, 263n38, 264n42; Letter 1 to Wulfstan, 253, 264n44; Letter 2 to Wulfstan, 233n19; Letter 5 to Sigefyrth, 254, 264n44
– *Lives of Saints*, 217, 237n48; **I** (*Third Nativity Homily*), 74, 75, 76; **III** (Basil), 230; **V** (Sebastian), 231n3; **VII** (Agnes), 217, 231n3, 237n49; **X** (Peter's Chair), 263n38, 316; **XI** (Forty Soldiers), 219, 228, 231n3; **XIV** (George), 231n3, 316; **XX** (Æthelthryth), 263n38; **XXIII** (Mary of Egypt), 263n40; **XXIV** (Abdon and Sennes; King Abgar), 231n3; **XXV** (The Maccabees), 219–22, 223, 229, 231n3, 232–3n11; **XXVI** (Oswald), 222–3, 231n3; **XXVII** (Exaltation of the Holy Cross), 222, 223, 231n3; **XXVIII** (Maurice), 218, 228–9, 231n3, 237n47; **XXXI** (Martin), 218, 229;

XXXII (Edmund), 217–18, 223, 226–31
– other writings: *Admonitio ad filium spiritualem* (pseudo-Basil), 222, 234n22, 315; Assmann Homily III (Nativity of the Virgin), 263n38; *De duodecim abusiuis huius seculi* (pseudo-Cyprian), 234–5n25; *Genesis* (OE Hexateuch), 378; Pope Homily I (*Nativitas Domini*), 74–5; Pope Homily XIa (*De sancta Trinitate et de festis diebus per annum*), 74; Pope Homily XIX (*De doctrina apostolica*), 263n38; Pope Homily XXI (*De falsis diis*), 74; Pope Homily XXX (*De sancta virginitate*), 263n38
Æthelmær (son of Æthelweard), 217, 231n2
Æthelræd 'The Unready,' King, 228
Æthelweard, *ealdorman*, 217, 231n2; Chronicle of, 385n35
Æthelwold of Winchester: Old English translation of Benedict's *Rule*, 115, 205. *See also* Benedictional of St Æthelwold
Æthicus Ister: *Cosmographia*, 353–69, 371
Aided Meidbe, 282n11
Alcuin, 112n47, 330
Aldebert (Frankish heretic), 275–6, 286n34
Aldhelm, 253, 330, 331, 338, 351n77; *Carmen de virginitate*, 348n48; *De virginitate*, 263n40
Alexander the Great, 363, 371, 373, 374, 375, 381n6
Alfred, King, 28, 169; canon of writings, 163n5, 201, 204; laws of, 58n15, 203; Life of, by Asser, 202, 203, 206, 208, 213n20
– writings: *De Consolatione Philosophiae* (Boethius) and *Metres of Boethius*, 147–67, 202, 203, 204, 315; *Pastoral Care* (Gregory), 202, 203, 204, 207, 313, 314, 315; Preface to *Pastoral Care*, 147, 150; prose Preface to Wærferth's translation of Gregory's *Dialogues*, 213n15; Psalms with prose introductions (Paris Psalter), 203, 204, 213n14; *Soliloquies* (Augustine), 202, 203, 204. *See also* Wærferth
Alfredian Boethius Project, 164n11, 197n2
alliteration, 41, 49–50n32, 233n13, 260n23, 348n47
alliterative collocations and proverbs, 311–25
Alliterative Revival, 311, 312
Ambrose of Milan, 83, 224, 226, 235n35, 259n13; *De officiis*, 225, 235n33, 235–6n35, 251; *Expositio evangelii secundum Lucam*, 85, 253, 261n29
Andreas, 4, 40, 49n28, 320
angels, 82–3, 94, 101, 102, 103, 107n17, 111n42, 112n47, 123, 181, 276, 376
Anglo-Norman England, 293–310
Anglo-Saxon Chronicle, 49–50n32, 203, 296–7. *See also* Parker Chronicle; Peterborough Chronicle
Anglo-Saxon royal genealogies, 48n22, 377–9
Anne, St (mother of Mary), 278–80
Annolied, 8
anonymous of Einsiedeln: glosses on

406   Index

Boethius, *De Consolatione Philosophiae*, 169–200
Antichrist, 371, 374
antiphons, 80–1, 85. *See also under* Advent
Antoninus, Emperor, 159–60
apatheia, 135
apocrypha. *See names of specific apocryphal texts*
Arator, 162n3
architectural imagery (in *Christ I*), 90–112
Ariosto: *Orlando furioso*, 18–19n24
Aristotle, 294
Ark of the Covenant, 101, 111n42
Arthur, King, 298–9
Ascension, The. See Cynewulf: *Christ II*
Asser: *Vita Alfredi*, 202, 203, 206, 208, 213n20
Athirne, 269–70, 282–3n14
Atlakviða. See under *Poetic Edda*
Audelay, John, 314
Augustine of Hippo, 63–79, 108n19, 250, 288n42, 338; on just war, 223–6, 229–30, 233n14, 236nn37, 38; on language, 66–71, 74, 75, 76, 79n22; Trinitarian theology, 63–79
– writings: *Confessiones*, 65, 72; *De civitate Dei*, 176, 200n33, 226, 235n29, 278, 349n59; *De doctrina christiana*, 68; *De libero arbitrio*, 224–5, 236n42; *De magistro*, 69; *De sermone Domini in monte*, 236n40; *De trinitate*, 66–71, 74, 75, 76; *Epistola* 189 to Count Boniface, 222, 226, 235n33, 236nn39, 41, 42; *Quaestiones in Heptateuchum*, 236n38; sermons, 76, 79n27, 234n23; *Soliloquia*,

King Alfred's Old English translation of, 202
Ausonius, 162n3
Auxerre, school of, 172. *See also* Remigius of Auxerre
Avitus of Vienne, 329, 330; *Carmina*, 359; *De spiritalis historiae gestis*, 278
Azarias (*Canticle of the Three Youths*), 141

Baldr, 31
ballads, 18–19n24, 267, 269, 281n9; 'Death of Queen Jane,' 281n9; 'Fair Mary of Wallington,' 281n9; 'Twa Corbies/Three Ravens,' 24n58
baptism, 111n45
Basil of Caeserea, 230
Battle Abbey, 300–1
Battle of Brunanburh, The, 4, 10, 14, 20n31, 21n32
Battle of Maldon, The, 4, 16n4, 20n31, 23n51, 158
beasts of battle (topos), 3–25; in *Beowulf*, 4, 5, 11–14. *See also* eagles; ravens; wolf
Bede, 94, 102, 104, 109n30, 223; biblical patterns in, 346n18; Latinity and prose style, 329–52; poeticisms, 349n49
– writings: *Allegorica expositio in Samuelem*, 86n2; *Chronica maiora*, 350n66; *De templo*, 98, 103; *Epistola ad Plegwinum*, 345–6n15; *Fragmenta in Proverbia Salomonis* 86n2; *Historia ecclesiastica*, 113, 115–16, 148, 222, 329–52 (sparrow-simile in, 97, 334–5, 348nn42, 43; Old English translation of, see *Old English Bede*); *Homeliarium evangelii libri ii*,

107n17; *In Cantica canticorum*, 108n20; *In Lucam*, 261n29, 348n43; *In Marcum*, 261n29, 348n43; *Vita Cuthberti* (prose), 349n49; *Vita Felicis*, 347n34

Benedict, St, of Nursia: *Rule* (*Regula Sancti Benedicti*), 114–15, 125, 126n4, 206; Old English translation of *Rule*, (see Æthelwold of Winchester); Life of, in Gregory the Great's *Dialogi*, 211. *See also* Benedictine Reform, Anglo-Saxon; monasticism

Benedictine Reform, Anglo-Saxon, 239, 252–6, 262n33

Benedictional of St Æthelwold, 105–6n4

Beowulf, 4, 5, 7, 12, 13, 14, 19–20n30, 20n31, 23n49, 23n51, 26–51, 117, 121, 128n21, 296, 306, 317, 319–20, 378; blithe-hearted raven, 12, 13, 23n50; Cain and Abel story, 35, 39, 43, 50n36, 117; Danes, Geats, and Swedes, 26–51; dragon, 30, 44; Finnsburg episode, 40, 42; Frisian raid, 33; genealogies, 26, 30; Heathobard feud, 13, 26; Heorot, 39, 42, 43; Hrunting, 39; interlace, 46n9; kingship, 26–51; manuscript (fol. 179 and Scribe B), 52–9; modes of death (*adl, yldo, ecghete*), 26–51; Ravenswood, 29, 32; song of creation, 122

– characters, 26–51 (not itemized): Beowulf, 12, 13, 24n53, 117, 156, 229; Dæghrefn, 22n47; Grendel, 117, 121–2; Heremod, 156, 377; Hrothgar, 122, 156

Berengar of Tours: *De sacra coena*, 275, 276–7

Bethlehem, 271

Bible, 18–19n24, 26, 63, 69, 110n37, 330. *See also names of biblical persons*

– Old Testament, 93, 95, 109n30, 219, 220, 221, 224, 226, 330, 361, 370; Genesis, 371; **2:7**, 106n7; **5:20**, 40; **9:29**, 40; **10:2**, 373; **25**, 379; Exodus, **2:11–12**, 225; Deuteronomy, **6:5**, 259n17; **6:16**, 99; Tobit, **8:8**, 106n7; **4:13–15**, 233n13; Job, **38:6**, 107n16; Psalms, 9, 132; **10:2**, 348n43; **18:2–3**, 63–4; **18:6–7**, 81, 83; **23:8**, 10, 82; **77:52**, 30; **83:4**, 348; **90:11–12**, 99–101; **95:12–13**, 64; **101:8**, 348n43; **114:5–8**, 77n4; **117:21–3**, 90, 93, 95, 98, 102, 107n13; **123:7**, 348n43; **148:7**, 9, 64; Proverbs, **1:6**, 133; Canticles (Song of Songs), **2:8**, 81, 83; **4:12**, 271; Wisdom, **18:14–15**, 80–1, 85; Isaiah, **14:8**, 64; **28:16**, 93, 102; **63:1–3**, 82; Jeremiah, **10:7**, 106n7; Ezechiel, **38:1–6**, 373; **38:8**, 16, 373–4; **38–9**, 373, 383n20; **44:1–2**, 271; **47:1–2**, 277; Haggai, **2:8**, 106n7; Maccabees, 219; 1 Maccabees **3:1–3**, 219

– New Testament, 18–19n24, 69, 93, 132, 220, 224, 226; Matthew, 101, 109nn34, 35, 111n45; **4:11**, 110n39; **5:8**, 255; **5:39**, 226; **8:8–10**, 236n39; **9:36**, 30; **10:26–31**, 335; **13:33**, 246; **21:42**, 107n13; **22:37–40**, 259n17; **22:44**, 277; **24:14**, 260; **25:33**, 277; Mark, 101; **1:13**, 110n39; **12:10–11**, 107n13; **12:30–1**, 259n17; **16:19**, 277; Luke, 101, 109nn34, 35, 111n45; **1:57**, 275; **2:6**, 275; **3:12–14**, 236n39; **4**, 99; **10:27**, 259n17; **12:6–7**, 348n43; **14:26**, 253; **20:17**, 107n13; John, **1:1**, 70, 72, 75, 79n27; **10:11ff.**, 30;

12:32–3, 89n22; **15:4**, 246; Acts, **4:11**, 107n13; **10:1–8**, 30–3, 236n39; Romans, **13:8**, 259n17; 1 Corinthians, **6:20**, 249; **7:7**, 222; **10:11**, 385n32; Ephesians, 91, 94; **2:11–12**, 107n14; **2:13–22**, 93–4, 95, 103, 105n3; **2:14**, 105n3, 106n7; **2:19–22**, 107n13; **2:20**, 106n7, 108n19; **6:12**, 85; Colossians, **2:15**, 85; Hebrews, **11:10**, 108n20; 1 Peter, **2:5–7**, 98, 107n13; Apocalypse, **20:7–9**, 373, 374, 375
Bible anonyme, La, 288n42
binomials, 323n7
birth stories, 267, 269–70, 275–6, 281n8, 282nn10, 12, 283n15. *See also* Caesarian births
Biterolf und Dietleib, 18–19n24
Bjarkamál, 24n55
Boadicea, 149
boar symbol, 6
Boethius: *De consolatione Philosophiae*, 147–200, 293, 294; *accessus* material (incl. *Vitae* and *cursus honorum* of Boethius), 172, 187, 199n22, 200n33; commentaries on: Bovo II of Corvey, 169, 172–3, 190, 193, 198n14, 199n29; Nicholas Trevet, 192; glosses on: Adalbold of Utrecht, 193; anonymous of Einsiedeln, 169, 198n14; Guillaume de Conches, 189; in Anglo-Saxon manuscripts, 154–61; Remigian, 154–5, 168–200; St Gall type: 168–200; tract on metres of, by Lupus of Ferrières, 172, 197n5, 199n22. *See also under* King Alfred
Boniface, St: *Epistola 59*, 275–6
book of deeds, 116
Book of Kells: Arrest of Christ page, 111n45; John the Evangelist portrait, 72; Temptation of Christ page, 91, 99–104, 109n34, 110n37, 111n45
Book of the Cave of Treasures (Syriac), 378
Bovo of Corvey. *See under* Boethius
Bromyard, John: *Summa Predicantium*, 322
Brot af Sigurðarkviðu. *See under Poetic Edda*
Bruno of Würzburg, 309n3
Buddha, 267, 270
Byrhtnoth, 229. *See also Battle of Maldon*

Cædwalla, 222–3, 230, 351n75
Caerleon, 298
Caesar: *De Bello Gallico*, 349n57
Caesarian births, 267, 270, 277, 281n9
Cain and Abel, 371. *See also under Beowulf*
Calmana and Delbora (apocryphal sisters of Cain), 371
Camoldunum (Colchester), 163n7
Canterbury, 355, 375, 378, 379
Canterbury Commentaries (Theodore of Canterbury), 283n22
caritas and *cupiditas*, 68
carpentry, as Germanic aristocratic craft, 110n38
Cath Boinde, 282n11
Cassiodorus, 197n4; *Institutiones*, 375; *Variae*, 263n40
Cassius Dio. *See* Dio Cassius
Castell of Perseverance, The, 314
celibacy, clerical, 239, 252, 253–5
Chad, St, 336
chansons de geste, 18–19n24
Charles the Bald, 226

Charles the Good, king of Flanders, 305
charters, 298, 301
chastity, 239, 248, 252–6
Chaucer, Geoffrey, 308; *Canterbury Tales*, 126n8
Chester Plays, 319
Chrétien de Troyes: *Erec et Enide*, 299
Christ, 73, 74, 218, 219, 220, 223, 224, 226, 228, 246, 247, 248–65, 301, 335, 341, 342, 343, 348n42; as architect/craftsman (*artifex/conditor*), 95, 96, 103, 108n20; Ascension, 82–3; as athlete (*gymnicus*), 85, 88n16; birth, docetic accounts of, 271, 272; birth, *ex utero clauso*, 271; birth, from Mary's right breast, 266–89; as cornerstone (*caput anguli, lapis angularis*), 90–112; Crucifixion, 64, 73, 80–6, 277, 283n22; divine nature, 108n19; dual nature, 73, 94, 97, 111n42; at Gethsemane, 218, 227; Harrowing of Hell, 262n32; as head of mystical body of church, 91, 94, 96, 97, 98, 103, 104; Incarnation, 70, 74, 76, 93, 253; in Judgment, 73–4, 277; as king, 84, 91, 110n38; Leaps of, 80–9; in Majesty, 111n42; as model of chastity (*auctor castitatis*), 239, 253; Nativity, 97, 104, 105–6n4, 239, 257n3, 271, 272, 277; as preacher, 101; Resurrection, 251–2, 261n31, 271; sacrifice, 97; Second Coming, 97; as soldier/warrior (*miles, durus debellator*), 85, 87n4, 88n17; as temple, 98, 102, 104, 111n45, 278; Temptation, 99–104, 109nn34, 35, 111n45; in winepress, 82; as Wisdom, 75, 268; as Word (*Logos/Verbum*), 66–76, 79n22; wound in right side, 277, 287n39, 288n42. *See also* Trinity
Christ I (*Advent Lyrics*), 90–112, 141, 320
Christ II (*Ascension*), 82–3, 86, 141, 317.
Christ III (*Christ in Judgement*), 141, 318
Chronicle of Æthelweard, 385n35
Chronicle of Battle Abbey, 300–1
Chronicle of Heinrich of Reichenau, 309n3
Chronicle of the Archbishops of York, 270
chronicles, 294. *See also titles of specific chronicles*
church (*Ecclesia*), 92, 97, 98, 103, 104, 105n4, 108n22; Christians as living stones in, 98, 103; as mystical body of Christ, 91, 94, 95, 96, 101, 277; as temple, 93–4
Cicero, 349n54; *De Oratore*, 349n53
clergy, Carolingian, 226
Clovis I, king of the Franks, 330
Cluvius Rufus, 162n3
Cóir Anmann, 282n11
Collectio canonum Hibernensis, 262n32
collocations, 323n7. *See also* alliterative collocations and proverbs
Columbanus, 355
Compert Conchobuir, 269
Conchobar mac Nessa, 269, 282n12
Constantine the Great, Emperor, 224
conversatio/conversio, 113–17, 123, 125, 126n8, 129n22
cornerstone. *See under* Christ
Corpus iuris civilis, 293
Cosdrue, Emperor, 223
Cotton Library fire (1731), 53, 58n15
courts, royal, 293–310

cross, of Christ, 63–89, 222, 223. *See also* Ælfric: *Lives of Saints* (Exaltation of the Cross); *Dream of the Rood*
Cynesige of York, 270
Cynewulf. See *Christ II* (*Ascension*)
Cynred's thane, vision of (in Bede), 116, 351n77

Danes. *See* Vikings
Dante: *Inferno*, 114
David, King, 225
death, violent (*interitus*), 343, 351n74. See also *Beowulf*, modes of death; *poculum mortis*; 'variegated obits'
Defensor of Ligugé: *Liber Scintillarum*, 314; Old English gloss on, 314–15
Demetrius (martyr), 237n50
devil, 99, 101, 104, 110n37, 117, 209, 250, 299, 301
Dietrichs Flucht, 8, 18–19n24
Dindshenchas, 282n10
Dio Cassius: *Historiae Romanae*, 162n3
directional symbolism. *See* right and left, symbolism of
D.M. (*dignum memoria*) *notae*, in Salisbury 165 manuscript of Pseudo-Methodius, 372–7
docetism, 268, 271, 272, 277, 283n22
Doomsday sermon. *See* pseudo-Augustine, *Sermo* App. **251**
Dracontius, 162n3
Dream of the Rood, The, 63–89
Dryhthelm, vision of (in Bede), 115, 116
Durham, 375
Durham Hymnal, 281n5

Durham Proverbs, 312

eagles, 7, 8, 11, 14, 25n60. *See also* beasts of battle
Ecclesia. *See* church (*Ecclesia*)
Ecgfrith, king of Northumbria, 222, 351n75
Echternach, 172, 174
eddic poetry, 5, 6, 11, 14, 17n15, 23n50; *Haraldskvæði*, 14, 23n51, 24n54; *Waking of Angantýr*, 24n52. See also *Poetic Edda*
Eddius Stephanus. *See* Stephen of Ripon
Edgar, King, laws of, 296
Edmund, St and king of East Anglia, 217, 218, 219, 228. *See also under* Ælfric, *Lives of Saints* (Edmund)
Edwin, king of Northumbria, 337, 338, 348n43
Eia recolamus (Christmas sequence), 88n17
Einhard: *Vita Caroli*, 162n3, 298
Eleazar, 219
elegies, Old English, 142n1
Elene, 4, 5, 15, 20n31, 320
end-rhyme, 311, 323n3
English Conquest, 314
Ennius, 340
Enoch, 40, 49n28; and Elijah, 36
Ennodius, 162n3
envelope structure, 306
Equitius, St (in Gregory the Great's *Dialogorum libri iv*), 209
Eriugena, 354
Etheocles (in *Roman de Thèbes*), 299
Eucharist, 215n38, 275
Eusebius of Caesarea: *Chronicon* (*see under* Jerome); *Historia Ecclesiastica* (*see under* Rufinus of Aquileia)

Eutropius, 349n57; *Breviarium ab Urbe Condita*, 149, 163n3
Eve, 240, 251–2, 276, 280, 300; created from Adam's left side, 278, 288n45. *See also* Eve-Mary antithesis
Eve-Mary antithesis, 251, 261nn27, 30, 31
Exaltatio (Reversio) Sancti Crucis, 235n27. *See also* Ælfric, *Lives of Saints* (Exaltation of the Cross)
Exeter, 375
Exeter Book, The, 29, 58n15, 131, 133, 141, 142n1. *See also* titles of individual poems
Exhortation to Christian Living, 316
exile theme, 118–25, 127n14
Exodus, 4, 5, 7, 9, 14, 18–19n24, 19n28, 19–20n30, 20n31, 23n51, 319, 321
Ezechiel, 277

Fabius Rusticus, 162n3
Felix (provost of Fondi), 210
Felix of Nola, 347n34
feudalism, 298
Fiacha Muillethan, 269, 282n13
Fight at Finnsburg, The, 4, 20n31
Figura. *See* typology
Findchú, St, 286–7n38
Finn mac Cumaill, 269
First Lateran Council of 1123, 272
Firumbras, 319
Floriz and Blaunchefleur, 319
flyting, 39, 41
Fredegar, 330, 355
Freud, Sigmund, 64
Frodi/Frothi (= Froda in *Beowulf*), 47n18, 47–8n21
Fromund of Tegernsee, 170, 190
funeral mounds, 12, 13, 24n52, 47n18
Furbaide Fer Bend, 269, 282n11

Fursa, vision of (in Bede), 113–14, 115. *See also Vita Fursei*

Gabriel (archangel), 101, 268
Galba, Emperor, 148
Gallicanus, St, 231n3
Gaudentius of Brescia: *Sermo* VI, 86n2
Gautier de Coinci: *Le Miracle de Théophile*, 301
Genesis A, 4, 16n4, 20n31, 23n51, 40, 49n28, 317
Gennadius: *De viris inlustribus*, 350n59, 351n72
Geoffrey Martel, earl of Anjou, 302, 304, 305
Geoffrey of Monmouth: *Historia Regum Britanniae*, 298–9
George, Saint, 231n3, 237n50
Gibbon, Edward, 161n1
Gildas, 338, 346nn22, 24, 26; *De excidio Britanniae*, 330–2, 348n48
Glossa ordinaria, 293
gnomes and gnomic wisdom, 117–25, 126n10. *See also* proverbs; wisdom (sapiential) literature
gnosticism, 271, 273
Gog and Magog, 371, 373, 374, 375, 383n20
Goll mac Morna, 269, 282n10
Good Wife Taught her Daughter, The, 315
Good Wyfe Wold a Pylgremage, The, 316
Gospel of Peter, 271
Go way, Fore that, 313
Gower, John, 308
Graecisms, 336, 346n20, 355
Gregory the Great, 83; *Dialogorum libri iv*, 181, 208–11 (Old English

translation of, by Wærferth, 201–16; Metrical Preface to, by Wulfsige, 213n15); *Homiliae in evangelia*, 87n10, 88n16; *Moralia in Job*, 94, 208; *Regula pastoralis*, 156, 208 (Old English translation of, by King Alfred, 202, 203, 204, 207, 313, 314, 315; Old English translation of, in Vercelli Homily XIV, 215n35)
Gregory of Tours, 329, 368; *Decem libri historiarum*, 330; *Gloria Martyrum*, 347n34; *Miracula*, 351n77; *Vita Patrum*, 351n77
Groundhog Day (movie), 114
Guillaume de Conches. *See under* Boethius
Guthlac A and B (Life of Saint Guthlac), 141
Gymnosophists, 267

h, initial, in Old English, 49–50n32
Hæmgisl (monk, in Bede), 351n77
Halfdán/Halfdan (= Healfdene in *Beowulf*), 47n18, 47–8n21, 48n23
Haraldr fairhair, 14
Haraldskvæði, 14, 23n51, 24n54
harp, 13, 122; and waking topos, 24n55
heafodweard (funeral custom), 40–1, 49nn30, 31
Heidegger, Martin, 67, 73, 79n22
Heinrich of Reichenau: Chronicle, 309n3
Helgaqviða Hundingsbana in fyrri. See under *Poetic Edda*
Helgaqviða Hundingsbana ǫnnor. See under *Poetic Edda*
Helgi/Helghi (= Halga in *Beowulf*), 37, 47–8n21, 48n23
Hengest, 229

Henry I, King, 302, 305
Henry II, King, 295, 307–8
Henry III, Emperor, 309n3
Henry VIII, King 281n9
Henry of Huntington: *Historia Anglorum*, 296–7
Henri of Poitou (abbot of Peterborough), 306, 307
Henryson, Robert: *Fables*, 313
Heraclius, Emperor, 223, 229, 231n3
heresies and heretics, 268, 272–7, 280. *See also* docetism; gnosticism; Manichees
hermeneutic Latin, 330
Hiarvarth/Hjorvard (= Heorweard in *Beowulf*), 48n23
Hiberno-Latin, 101, 110–11n41
Hildegard of Bingen, 276, 277, 280
Himlingøje II brooch, 8
Hincmar of Rheims: *De regis persona*, 226, 237n43
Hingwar (Viking foe of King Edmund), 218
Hippolytus of Rome, 83
Hisperica Famina, 355
Hisperic Latin, 330, 331
History of Hannâ (Ethiopic *Life of St Anne*), 278–80, 289n47
Hǫgni (in *Njáls saga*), 5
Höð (slayer of Baldr), 31
'holding court' (*hired healdan/healdan curt/tenir curt/curiam tenere*), 293–310
Holofernes, 221
Holy Spirit, 66, 75, 94, 248, 253, 281n5. *See also* Trinity
Homer, 18–19n24; *Iliad*, 148
Homiletic Fragment I, 318
homiliaries: Alanus of Farfa, 239–40, 257–8n6, 258n9; Bishop of Prague,

260n22; Casinensis, 239; Egino of Verona, 239; Montpellier, 239; St Peter's in the Vatican, 239
Hrabanus Maurus: *Commentaria in librum Sapientiae*, 86n2; *De Universo*, 107n16; *In honorem Sanctae Crucis*, 107n16
Hraþra (apocryphal son of Noah), 378
Hroar/Roe (= Hrothgar in *Beowulf*), 37, 47–8n21
Hrok (nephew of Hrolf Kraki), 47–8n21
Hrolf Kraki (= Hrothulf in *Beowulf*), 37, 47–8n21, 48n23. See also *Saga of King Hrolf Kraki*
Hrómundar þáttr halta, 23n50
Hubald (archdeacon of Salisbury), 373
Hugh (English anchorite), 321
Huginn ['Thought'] and Muninn ['Mind'] (Óðinn's ravens), 6, 125
Humbli (son of Dan), 46n6
hundred *gemot*, 296
Hunferd/Hunferð/Unferth (names in *Anglo-Saxon Chronicle*), 49–50n32
Hurston, Zora Neale: *Their Eyes Were Watching God*, 24n58
Husband's Message, The, 141
Húskarlahvǫt, 24n55
hyperbaton, 329, 331, 346–7n28, 354

Incerti Auctoris Genealogia Regum Danie, 47–8n21
Infancy Gospel, Irish Latin, 270–1
Ingialldus (= Ingeld), 47n18
Ionitus: *See* Jonitus
Irenaeus: *Adversus haereses*, 273
Ireland, 354

Irish exegesis, 384n27. *See also* Irish *Reference Bible*
Irish folktale, 283n15
Irish *Reference Bible*, 288n45
Isaac, 373
Ishmael, 379
Ishmaelites, 371, 373, 374, 375
Isidore of Seville: *Etymologiae*, 88n16, 221, 361
Islam, representation of, in *Revelationes* of Pseudo-Methodius, 370, 373, 375
Itala (Old Latin Bible), 348n43

Japheth, 40, 373, 376
Jared, 40
Jerome, 94, 112n47, 329, 338, 345n15, 368, 376; *Adversus Jovinianum*, 267, 270; continuation *Chronicon* of Eusebius of Caesarea, 349n57; *In Isaiam*, 348n48; *Liber interpretationis hebraicorum nominum*, 376; sermons, 352n79; *Vita Pauli*, 347–8n41
Jerusalem, 223, 374, 383n22; pinnacle of, as *sedes doctorum*, 101, 110–11n41; temple of, 99, 101, 277–8
Jews, 339, 341; and Gentiles, 94, 107nn14, 17
John the archchanter (precentor of St Peter's, Rome), 349n52
John and Paul, Sts, 231n3
Jonitus (apocryphal son of Noah), 371, 378, 386n36
Joseph (husband of Mary), 271
Judgment Day, 73–4, 103, 104
Judas Machabeus, 219–20, 222, 234n21
Judith, 221
Judith, 4, 20n31, 23n51, 57n9
Julian the Apostate, 218, 230

Juliana, 141, 317
Justin: epitome of Trogus, 349n57
just war, theory of, 220, 224–6, 234–5n25, 236nn37, 38
Juvenal, 162n3

Kaiserchronik, 18–19n24
Kant, Immanuel, 67
Katherine Group, 311
kennings, 6, 12, 23n50
kingship, 218, 226; in *Beowulf*, 26–51; Germanic, 28–9, 44; King Alfred's conception of, 147–67. *See also* 'holding court'; primogeniture
knighthood, 301
Kudrun, 18–19n24, 19n27

Laʒamon: *Brut*, 311
Lambarde, William, 213n15
Landnámabók, 23n50
Lanfranc (archbishop of Canterbury), 275, 297
Langfeðgatal, 47–8n21
Langland, William: *Piers Plowman*, 72, 83
Last Roman Emperor, 371, 373, 374, 375, 383n22
Lateran Council of 649 (Pope Martin I), 272. *See also* First Lateran Council of 1123
laws: Old English, 41, 49n31, 58n15, 296; Old Norse, 49n29. *See also* titles of specific legal texts
Leabhar Breac, 288–9n45
Leaps of Christ, 80–9
lectio divina, 63
Lent, 253
Leo the Great: *Sermones*, 253
Leviathan, 85
Liber Eliensis, 270

Liber Vitae Dunelmensis, 49–50n32
Life of Lanfranc. See *Vita Lanfranci*
liturgy, 63, 80–1, 111n45; liturgical time, 97; of Mass, 109n34. *See also* Advent, liturgy of; antiphons; Quadragesima Sunday, lections for
Livy, 339, 340, 349n57
logos, 67, 69–70. *See also under* Christ, as Word
London, 163n7, 295
Louis the Pious, 237n43
love, kinds of (*amor, appetitus, caritas*), 68–9
Lucan, 162n3
Lupus of Ferrières. *See under* Boethius
Lydgate, John, 308

Maccabees. *See under* Bible; Ælfric, *Lives of Saints*
Magnificat, antiphon for, 80–1, 85
Manichees, 224
Mäqdäla, Ethiopia, 289n46
Marbod of Rennes: *Vita Theophili metrica*, 301
Martial, 162n3
Martin I, Pope, 272
Martin of Tours, St, 218, 229, 232n9. *See also under* Ælfric, *Lives of Saints*
martyrs, military, 217–38
Mary Magdalene, 261nn28, 30, 31
Mary, Virgin, 76, 230, 240, 246, 248, 251, 255, 261n26, 262n35, 271, 281n5; as closed portal, enclosed garden, and sealed fountain, 271; conception through ear, 268; gives birth to Christ through right breast, 266–89; nativity, 278–80, 289n47; perpetual virginity, 268,

271, 277. *See also* Eve-Mary antithesis
Matilda, Empress (daughter of King Henry I and wife of Emperor Henry V and Geoffrey of Anjou), 305
Maurice, St, 237n50. See also Ælfric, *Lives of Saints* (Maurice); *Passio Sancti Mauricii et sociorum eius*
Maximian, Emperor, 229, 237n47
Maxims I, 133, 134, 135
Maxims II, 4
Memory: in *The Wanderer*, 124–5; in *The Wife's Lament*, 113, 117–29
Mercurius, St, 230, 237n50
Methodius, bishop of Patara, 370, 376. *See also* Pseudo-Methodius
Metres of Boethius. *See under* Alfred, King
Michael (archangel), 101, 374
microcosm, 182, 199n21
Middle English Proverbs (Douce MS 52), 314, 315
Migration Period, 7, 10
militias and levies, Anglo-Saxon, 229
Milton, John: *Paradise Lost*, 278
monasticism, 72–3, 76, 113–17, 126nn4, 8, 127n12, 129n22, 214–15n29, 224, 230. *See also* Benedict, St, of Nursia, *Rule*; Benedictine Reform, Anglo-Saxon
Mont-Saint-Michel, 375
Moses, 225, 266
Moses Maimonides, 270
Mozarabic 'Missale mixtum,' 86n2

names: noa-names, 8; theophoric personal names, 17n8
Nebroth, 378
Nero, Emperor, 147–67, 339

Nimrod, 378
Njáls saga, 5
Noah, 373, 377, 378, 379, 385–6n36; ark of, 278, 288n42, 367–8, 378, 385nn35, 36
Norman Conquest, 294, 295, 298, 311, 375, 384
Normandy, 302–3, 304, 305, 375
Northumbria, 47–8n21, 149, 349n52; Northumbrians, 223
Nowell, Laurence, 52, 54, 58n15
nudus nudum Christum sequi topos, 85, 88n16

Odo (abbot of Corbie), 285n27
Odo (prior of Canterbury and abbot of Battle), 301
Odo of Cluny: *Occupatio*, 261n31; sermon on Mary Magdalene, 261n31
Odon de Sully, 270
Odysseus and Circe (in King Alfred's *Boethius*), 154
Old English Bede, 113, 115–16, 149
Old English Gospels (Matthew), 85
Old English Hexateuch, 378; Old English notes in, 378–9
Old English Homilies: Bazire and Cross 1, 288n45; Bazire and Cross 8, 317; Blickling I, 240, 243–5, 253, 254–5, 264n48; Fadda I, 239–65; HomU 16 (Kluge), 324n17; Vercelli IV, 317; X, 281n5; XI–XIII, 255; XIV, 215n35. *See also under* Ælfric; Wulfstan
Old English Orosius, 148, 153, 202, 203, 214n25
Old English words, meanings discussed: *breost*, 267, 280n3, 281nn4,

5; *clænness*, 239, 252–6, 262n36, 264n49; *cwide(gyd)*, 132, 133, 136, 137, 140; *drohtnoþ/droht(n)ung*, 113, 116–17; *ge-* prefix, 85–7, 89n21; *gebetan*, 96, 108–9n24; *geond-* compounds, 119, 124, 137–9; *geondþencan*, 131, 139–40, 142n3; *godspel*, 260n21; *gyd*, 130–41; *gylp*, 153; *heafodmæg* (and *heafod-* compounds), 40–1, 49n29; *hir(e)d (healdan)*, 295, 296, 308; *lar(cwide)*, 132, 133, 136, 140; *reordberend*, 72–3, 74; *scealc*, 158; *-stigan*, 84–6; *þyle* (Old Norse *þulr*), 50n33
Old Norse/Icelandic literature. *See* eddic poetry; flyting; *Poetic Edda*; sagas, Icelandic; skaldic poetry; Snorri Sturluson; Volsungs; *and titles of individual texts*
omens: avian, 10, 21–2n38; cry of wolf, 21–2n38
Oral Theory, 4, 5, 6
Orosius: *Historiarum adversus Paganos libri vii*, 148, 162n3, 339–40, 344, 345n6, 349nn57, 58, 349–50n59, 350nn60, 62, 63. See also *Old English Orosius*
Orpheus (in Boethius), 154, 159
Oswald, king of Northumbria, 217, 222–3, 230, 231n3
Owl and the Nightingale, The, 319
Óðinn, 6, 10, 12, 125. *See also* ravens, Óðinn's ravins; Woden, cult of

Parker Chronicle, 378
Paschasius Radbertus: *De partu Virginis*, 273–4, 276
Passion of Anastasius, 347n34
Passio Sancti Mauricii et sociorum eius, 229

Patrick, St, 330
patristic *originalia*, 372, 375
Paul (apostle), 90–1, 94, 103, 105n3, 148, 249. *See also his* Epistles *under* Bible
Pehthelm (source of monk's vision in Bede), 351n77
Pelagius, 108n19. *See also* semi-Pelagianism
Persius, 162n3
Peter (apostle), 218, 224, 227
Peter, king of Hungary, 309n3
Peter and Paul, martrydom of, 148, 149
Peterborough Chronicle, 293–310
Petronius, 162n3
Petrus monachus (in Pseudo-Methodius, *Revelationes*), 377
Philippus Presbyter: *In Job*, 348n48
Phoebus (in Boethius), 150, 151
Phoenix, The, 141
pia fraus, 84
Plato, 67
Pliny the Elder, 162n3
poculum mortis, 251, 261n30
Poetic Edda, 6; *Atlakviða*, 19n30; *Brot af Sigurðarkviðu*, 14; *Helgaqviða Hundingsbana in fyrri*, 13, 14, 23n51, 39; *Helgaqviða Hundingsbana ǫnnor*, 12, 14, 19–20n30, 22n42, 23n51; *Reginsmál*, 10, 21n37. *See also* eddic poetry
Porphyry, 293, 294
primogeniture, 28, 29, 31, 32, 34, 37, 38, 45n3. *See also* kingship
prosopopoeia, 63, 64, 66, 70, 72
Protevangelium of James, 268, 271, 272
proverbs, 130–44; alliterative, 311–25. *See also* gnomes and gnomic wisdom; wisdom (sapiential) literature

Proverbs of Hendying, 312, 313, 315, 316, 319
Proverbs of Solomon, 314
Proverbs of Wysdom, 319
Prudentius, 162n3; 'Dittochaeum,' 111n46
pseudo-Alcuin: *Homilia*, 263n40
pseudo-Ambrose: *Sermo* 24 (Doomsday sermon), 260n22
pseudo-Augustine, *De mirabilibus sacrae scripturae*, 355
pseudo-Amphilochius, *Life of St Basil*, 237n49
pseudo-Augustine: *Sermo* App. **120**, 240; **121**, 254; **125**, 239–65; **251** (Doomsday sermon), 240, 246, 247, 260n22
pseudo-Basil: *Admonitio ad filium spiritualem*, 222, 234n22
pseudo-Ephrem: *Sermo de fine mundi*, 371, 374
Pseudo-Methodius: *Revelationes*, 370–86; Middle English versions, 371

Quadragesima Sunday, lections for, 109n34
Quadripartitus, 49n31

Rabenschlacht, 8
Radbertus. *See* Paschasius Radbertus
Ranulf Higden: *Polychronicon. See* Trevisa, John
Raphael (archangel), 101
Ratramnus of Corbie: *De partu sanctae Mariae*, 272–5, 276, 283n21, 285n27
ravens, 3, 5, 7, 8, 11, 12, 13, 14, 16n3, 24n54; blithe-hearted raven in *Beowulf*, 12, 13, 23n50; colour of, 23n49; morning raven, 12, 13, 23n50; as omen, 10–11, 21–2n38; Óðinn's ravens (Huginn and Muninn), 6, 21–2n38; raven banners, 10, 21–2n38; raven god, 6; and valkyries, 24n56. *See also* beasts of battle
Rawlinson Proverbs, 319
Rectitudines Singularum Personarum, 49n31
Reges Danorum, 47–8n21
Reginsmál. See under *Poetic Edda*
Regula Sancti Benedicti. See Benedict, St, of Nursia
Remigius of Auxerre, 196n1; commentary on Boethius attributed to, 154–5, 168–200; manuscripts of, 184–96
Resignation [A], 320
Rhyming Poem, The, 311
rhythmical prose, 260n23
Riddles (Old English): 4, 63, 72, 120, 141
right and left, symbolism of, 277–8
Robert (priest): English translation of 'diversas sententias,' 320
Rolf Kraki. *See* Hrolf Kraki
Roman de Thèbes, 299
Roman Empire, 147–8, 224. *See also* Rome, burning of, *and names of individual emperors*
Rome, burning of, 148, 150, 152
Royal Historie of ... Generides, 319
Rufinus of Aquileia: *Historia monachorum*, 351n77, 352n78; translation of *Historia Ecclesiastica* of Eusebius of Caesarea, 340–4, 350–1n71, 351n73, 352n79
ruminatio, 91, 106n5
runic inscriptions, 6

Rutebeuf, 301
Ruthwell Cross, 63

Saga of King Hrolf Kraki, The, 26, 37, 47n18, 48–8n21, 48n23
sagas, Icelandic, 128n21
St Gall, 170
St Gall type glosses on Boethius, *De Consolatione Philosophiae*, 169–200
St Germain-des-Prés, 171
St Jean d'Angély (abbey), 303–4
Salisbury Abbey, 298
Salisbury Cathedral (scriptorium), 370–86
Saltair na Rann, 267
sarra (fish, source of imperial purple dye), 158
Satan, 301, 373
Saxo Grammaticus: *History of the Danes*, 28, 46n6, 48n23
Sceaf (in West-Saxon genealogies), 378, 385n35
sea, as metaphor, 121, 123, 128–9n21
Seafarer, The, 29, 123, 131, 141, 142n1
Sebasteni (Forty Soldiers). See Ælfric, *Lives of Saints* (Forty Soldiers)
sedes doctorum. See Jerusalem, temple of
Sedulius Scottus: *Collectaneum in Apostolum*, 107n16, 108n19, 263n40
semi-Pelagianism, 250
Seneca, 155, 159–61, 162n3
Series ac Brevior Historia Regum Daniae, 47–8n21
sermo humilis, 330
sermons, 321–2. See also Old English homilies; Doomsday sermon; Three Utterances sermon; *and under* Augustine and pseudo-Augustine
Service for Representing Adam (*Ordo repraesentacionis Adae / Jeu d'Adam*), 299–300
Seth, 378
Sextus Aurelius Victor, 162n3
Sidonius, 162n3, 330
Sigrún (valkyrie), 12, 14
signing food, 209–10, 215n38
Simon's Lesson of Wysedome, 316
singing weapons, 19–20n30
sister's son (in Germanic kinship system), 45n6
skaldic poetry, 5, 6, 7, 8, 9, 10, 14, 18n21, 19–20n30, 21n32
Skarpheðin (character in *Njáls saga*), 5
Skjöldungasaga (Latin epitome of), 47n18
Snorri Sturluson: *Prose Edda*, 6, 31; *Ynglingasaga*, 28, 47n18, 47–8n21, 48n23
social time, in Anglo-Saxon England and *The Wife's Lament*, 113–29
Solomon, temple of, 109n28
Solomon and Saturn (prose), 266. See also *Adrian and Ritheus*
soul, 335; compared to bird, 348n43; definition of *anima*, in glosses on Boethius, 175–83
Soul and Body I and *II*, 16n3
spatial symbolism (*Raummetaphorik*), 90–104
Speculum Misericordie (Middle English), 319
Statius, 299
Stephen, King, 308
Stephen of Ripon, 331; *Life of Wilfrid*, 222
Suetonius, 349n57; *De vita Caesarum*, 159, 162n3
Sulpicius Severus: *Vita Martini*, 162n3, 218, 232n9, 330

Sven Aggesen: *Short History of the Kings of Denmark*, 47–8n21
synod of 745 (Pope Zacharias), 275

Tacitus, 349n57; *Annales*, 162n3; *Germania*, 10, 11, 21–2n38, 28
Tale of Beryn, The, 319
Tale of Gamelyn, The, 319
Talkyng of the Love of God, A, 319
Tertullian: *De idololatria*, 224
Tewodros II, emperor of Ethiopia, 289n46
Theban Legion, 218, 228–9. See also Maurice, St
Theodore (martyr), 237n50
Theodore of Canterbury. See Canterbury Commentaries
Theophilus legend, 301
Theodosius, Emperor, 235n29
'thought, word, deed' triad, 67
three orders (*laboratores, oratores, bellatores*), 221
Three Utterances sermon, 240, 246–7
timor Domini, 255
Titus, Emperor, 339
transubstantiation, 275
Trevet, Nicholas. See *under* Boethius
Trevisa, John: translation of *Polychronicon* of Ranulf Higden, 382n10
Trinity: in Ælfric, 73–6; in Augustine of Hippo, 66–71
typology (*figura*), 65–6, 90, 93, 98–9, 102, 103, 276, 277–8, 374

Uriel (archangel), 101
Usk, Thomas: *Testament of Love*, 319

Valentinian (gnostic), 273

valkyries, 12, 14; and ravens, 24n56
'variegated obits,' 29, 31, 32, 36
Varro, 176, 200n33
Vedas, 72
Vendel grave I helmet, 11, 21–2n38
Vidigoia (Gothic hero name), 8
Vikings, 4, 221, 227, 228, 229
Virgil of Salzburg, 354
Virgilius Maro Grammaticus, 354, 355
Virgin birth, Carolingian debates over, 271–6, 284–5n27; patristic teachings on, 284n26. See also Mary, Virgin
Visions of Daniel, 371
Vita Alfredi. See Asser
Vita Amalbergae virginis, 263n40
Vita Fursei, 336. See also Fursa, vision of
Vita Germani, 333
Vita Gregorii, 21–2n38, 331, 347n32
Vita Lanfranci (?Milo Crispin of Bec), 297
Vita S. Mariae Aegyptiacae, 263n40
Vivarium, 197n4
Volsungs, 44
Vulgar Latin, 330, 355

Wærferth, bishop of Worcester, 213n20; Old English translation of *Dialogues* of Gregory, 201–16, 296. See also *under* Wulfsige
Waking of Angantýr, 24n52
waking topos, 24n55
Waldhere, 229
Walter Map: *De nugis curialium*, 293, 294, 295, 298, 300, 301, 307, 308, 309n2
Wanderer, The, 4, 123–5, 129n24, 130–44, 316
Warin (abbot of Corvey), 285n27

Wars of Alexander, The, 314
Welsh poetry, 6, 16n8, 19n26; Heledd group, 25n60
Wessex, 28, 227
Westminster, 299, 302
West-Saxon royal genealogies, 377–9. *See also* Anglo-Saxon royal genealogies
Wiener Exodus, 8
Wife's Lament, The, 113–29, 131, 141
Willehalm (Wolfram von Eschenbach), 8
William Clito, 305, 306
William the Conqueror, 297, 298, 299, 301, 309n11
William Dunbar, 282n10
William of Malmesbury, 296; Chronicle, 385n35; *De gestis pontificum Anglorum*, 375
wisdom (sapiential) literature, 130–44. *See also* gnomes and gnomic wisdom; proverbs
witanagemot, 297–8
Woden, cult of, 24n60. *See also* Óðinn

Wohunge of Ure Laverd, 319
wolf, 5, 6, 7, 8, 16n4, 20n31; cry of, as bad luck, 21n37; noa-names for, 8. *See also* beasts of battle
Wolfram von Eschenbach: *Willehalm*, 8
Wulf and Eadwacer, 121, 127n14, 131, 141
Wulfsige, bishop of Sherborne: Metrical Preface to Wærferth's translation of *Dialogues* of Gregory the Great, 213n15
Wulfstan of York, 215n35, 255, 270; Homily VIIIc, 316; Xc, 317; *Institutes of Polity*, 313; Napier Homily L, 254, 264n44

Yeavering (Anglo-Saxon halls at), 110n38
Yellow Book of Lecan, 269
Ywain and Gawain, 318

Zacharias, Pope, 275, 286n34

Toronto Old English Series

General Editor
ANDY ORCHARD

Editorial Board
ROBERTA FRANK
THOMAS N. HALL
ANTONETTE DIPAOLO HEALEY
MICHAEL LAPIDGE

1 *Computers and Old English Concordances* edited by Angus Cameron, Roberta Frank, and John Leyerle
2 *A Plan for the Dictionary of Old English* edited by Roberta Frank and Angus Cameron
3 *The Stowe Psalter* edited by Andrew C. Kimmens
4 *The Two Versions of Wærferth's Translation of Gregory's Dialogues: An Old English Thesaurus* David Yerkes
5 *Vercelli Homilies IX–XXIII* edited by Paul E. Szarmach
6 *The Dating of Beowulf* edited by Colin Chase
7 *Eleven Old English Rogationtide Homilies* edited by Joyce Bazire and James E. Cross
8 *Old English Word Studies: A Preliminary Author and Word Index* Angus Cameron, Allison Kingsmill, and Ashley Crandell Amos
9 *The Old English Life of Machutus* edited by David Yerkes
10 *Words and Works: Studies in Medieval English Language and Literature in Honour of Fred C. Robinson* edited by Peter S. Baker and Nicholas Howe
11 *Old English Glossed Psalters: Psalms 1–50* edited by Phillip Pulsiano
12 *Families of the King: Writing Identity in the Anglo-Saxon Chronicle* Alice Sheppard
13 *Verbal Encounters: Anglo-Saxon and Old Norse Studies for Roberta Frank* edited by Antonina Harbus and Russell Poole
14 *Latin Learning and English Lore: Studies in Anglo-Sexon Literature for Michael Lapidge* edited by Katherine O'Brien O'Keeffe and Andy Orchard
15 *Early English Metre* by Thomas A. Bredehoft
16 *Source of Wisdom: Old English and Early Medieval Latin Studies in Honour of Thomas D. Hill* edited by Charles D. Wright, Frederick M. Biggs, and Thomas N. Hall